Walking the Same Sure Foundation

Salvation
Righteousness
Grace
Mercy
Truth

K. E. Jenkins

Walking the Same Sure Foundation

Published by
21st Century Press
Springfield, MO 65807

21st Century Press is a Christian publisher dedicated to publishing books that have a high standard of family values. We believe the vision for our companies is to provide families and individuals with user-friendly materials that will help them in their daily lives and experiences. It is our prayer that this book will help you discover biblical truth for your own life and help you meet the needs of others. May God richly bless you.

Cover Design: Lee Fredrickson
Book Design: Lee Fredrickson

ISBN: 978-1-951774-18-9

Visit our website at: www.21stcenturypress.com
Printed in the United States of America

Works Cited

Tanakh The Holy Scriptures. Jewish Publication Society, 1985.

The Hebrew-Greek Key Study Bible. Authorized King James Version. AMG Publishers, 1984.

Abingdon's Strong's Exhaustive Concordance of the Bible. Abingdon, 1980.

Stern, David H. Complete Jewish Bible. Jewish New Testament Publications, 1998,Jerusalem, Israel.

Bernhart, C.L., Editor in Chief, et al. The American College Dictionary. Random House, 1967, New York. iii

Table of Contents

Book One

Walking the Same Sure Foundation of Salvation

Introduction

This is the first of five books in a mini-series with a unique purpose. Each book provides a verse to verse comparison of *TANAKH THE HOLY SCRIPTURES (*hereafter referred to as *Tanakh)* and the *AUTHORIZED KING JAMES VERSION* (hereafter referred to as *KJV*, Old Testament only) on a particular subject. Book One, *SALVATION,* includes dictionary references to assist new Christians and/or non-Christians with secular definitions to understand spiritual concepts as well as references from *TANAKH* footnotes and *STRONG'S CONCORDANCE* . Readers will quickly discover that all spiritual concepts presented on the following pages have physical actions that can be observed and experienced. This series is about relationship, not religion. Readers will come to know the true source of security, authority, and power as never before.

Each of the five books are in the same order and format for ease of use. Format, as well as use of *STRONG'S CONCORDANCE*, will be discussed in the section *How This Book is Organized.* Yeshua (Jesus) spoke about each of these subjects often before the New Testament was written. Modern-day readers who grasp these truths will be able to understand the teachings of the New Testament in the same way as people of Yeshua's (Jesus's) generation.

How This Book is Organized

TANAKH verse followed by TANAKH reference (each letter capitalized) with corresponding KJV reference (also capitalized) in parenthesis. Sometimes numbers will not match exactly but will be close. TANAKH reference will be highlighted in gray.

Example:

As for me, may my prayer come to you, O LORD, at a favorable moment; O God, in Your abundant faithfulness, answer me with Your sure deliverance. TEHILLIM 69:14 (PSALMS 69:13)

Spelling of highlighted *TANAKH* references is the same as the *COMPLETE JEWISH BIBLE* throughout the book to maintain its sense of Jewishness. Refer to *Works Cited* for additional information.

KJV will include the word salvation followed by a highlighted number in parenthesis within the verse. The highlighted number will be a reference number to *STRONG'S CONCORDANCE* (original Hebrew or Chaldee). The verse will be followed by the highlighted KJV reference only. Words in italic in the original text will be in italics. Archaic spelling of words will also be presented as the original authors intended .

Example:

But as for me, my prayer *is* unto thee, O LORD, *in* an acceptable time: O God, in the multitude of thy mercy hear me, in the truth of thy salvation (3468). PSALMS 69:13

> Salvation (3468) pronounced yeh'shah; from 3467; liberty, deliverance, prosperity, safety, salvation, saving.

Pronunciation is provided with the complete definition by *STRONG'S CONCORDANCE*. Readers will notice a second highlighted number in the above example. This is the primitive root word. It will be shown with pronunciation and complete definition by *STRONG'S CONCORDANCE* also.

Other dictionary references are included to assist readers with a more familiar, relatable vocabulary. Definitions will be distinguished from *STRONG'S CONCORDANCE* in the following manner:

> Salvation (3468).....
>
> > liberty (Dictionary) freedom from arbitrary or despotic government or, often, from other rule or law than that of a self-governing community; freedom from external or foreign rule; freedom from control, interference, obligation, restriction, hampering conditions, etc.; power or right of doing, thinking, speaking, etc., according to choice.

All (Dictionary) references are from the *AMERICAN COLLEGE DICTIONARY*. Refer to *Works Cited* for more information.

The primitive root will usually be listed last unless it is the only reference or the first of several references. The number of the root will be indented, under the verse, lining up with the first reference.

Example:

> Salvation (3468)...
>
> > liberty (Dictionary)...
>
> (3467) pronounced yaw-shah'; a prim. root; prop. to be open, wide or free, i.e. (by impl.) to be safe; causat. to free or succor: -x at all, avenging, defend, deliver (-er), help, preserve, rescue, be safe, bring (having) salvation, save (-iour), get victory.
>
> > succor (Dictionary) help, relief, aid, assistance in difficulty, need, or distress.

Abbreviations such as impl. and causat. will be identified in *Abbreviations Employed*, the next section of the book.

Occasionally, footnotes will be provided in *TANAKH*. When this occurs, the footnote will be noted exactly as referenced. If scripture references are available, they will also be included in the same format as above so that readers may be able to have immediate access to as much information as possible without turning pages.

The first of two examples below supplies a literal explanation as to how the original context would have been understood by its listeners.

And Hannah prayed: My heart exults in the LORD; I have triumphed through the LORD. I gloat over my enemies; I rejoice in Your deliverance. SH'MU'EL ALEF 2:1 (I SAMUEL 2:1)

> triumphed: Lit. "My horn is high." (TANAKH footnote)
>
> gloat: Lit. "My mouth is wide." (TANAKH footnote)

The second example directs the reader's attention to additional scripture for more information.

O God, the rock wherein I take shelter: My shield, my mighty champion, my fortress and refuge! My savior, You who rescue me from violence. SH'MU'EL BET 22:3 (II SAMUEL 22:3)

> God, the rock: Lit. "the God of my rock", Ps. 18:3 "my God, my rock"
> (TANAKH footnote)
>
> mighty champion: Lit. "horn of rescue" (TANAKH footnote)
>
> > He said: I adore you, O LORD, my strength, O LORD, my crag, my fortress, my rescuer, my God, my rock in whom I seek refuge, my shield, my mighty champion, my haven. TEHILLIM 18:2-3 (PSALMS 18:2-3)
> >
> > The LORD is my rock, and my fortress, and my deliverer; my God, my strength, in whom I will trust: my buckler, and the horn of my salvation, *and* my high tower. I will call upon the LORD *who is worthy* to be praised: so shall I be saved from mine enemies. PSALMS 18:2-3

KJV reference will always be added for comparison and continuity of the TANAKH footnote before continuing on to the corresponding KJV. In this example, II SAMUEL 22:3 will be the next entry.

Abbreviations Employed

Abstr.: abstract, abstractly

Cap.: capital

Caus., causat.: causative, causatively

Cf.: confer, compare

Etc.: et cetera, and others, and so forth, and so on

Fem.: feminine

Fig.: figurative, figuratively

Heb.: Hebrew, Hebraism

i.e.: id est, that is

impl.: implication, implied

lit.: literal, literally

mss.: message, messages

part.: participle, particular

pass,: passenger, passive

pers.: person, personal

prim.: primitive, primary

prop.: proper, properly

refl., reflex.: reflexive, reflexively

spir.: spirit, spiritual

SALVATION

I wait for Your deliverance, O LORD! B'RESHEET 49:18 (GENESIS 49:18)

I have waited for thy salvation (3444), O LORD. GENESIS 49:18

Salvation (3444) pronounced yesh-oo'-aw; fem. pass. part. of 3467; something saved, i.e. (abstr.) deliverance; hence aid, victory, prosperity:- deliverance, health, help (-ing), salvation, save, saving (health), welfare.

deliverance (Dictionary) the act of giving up or surrendering; giving into another's possession or keeping; to give forth in words; utter or pronounce; to deliver a verdict; setting free; disburden (oneself) of thoughts, opinions, etc.; Obsolete: to make known, assert; Obsolete or Archaic: agile, active, quick.

prosperity (Dictionary) flourishing or thriving condition; good fortune; success.

fortune (Dictionary) position in life as determined by wealth.

success (Dictionary) favorable or prosperous termination of attempts or endeavors; gaining of wealth, position, or the like; Obsolete: outcome.

welfare (Dictionary) state of faring well; well-being; prosperity; success; happiness; weal.

happiness (2) (Dictionary) good fortune, pleasure, content or gladness.

weal (1) (Dictionary) Archaic: well-being, prosperity , or happiness.

(3467) pronounced yaw-shah'; a prim. root; prop. to be open, wide or free, i.e. (by impl.) to be safe; causat. to free or succor: - x at all, avenging, defend, deliver (-er), help, preserve, rescue, be safe, bring (having) salvation, save (-iour), get victory.

succor (Dictionary) help, relief, aid, assistance in difficulty, need, or distress.

salvation (Dictionary) act of saving or delivering; a source, cause, or means of deliverance; deliverance from the power of penalty and sin; redemption.

sin (Dictionary) transgression of divine law; an act regarded as such transgression, or any violation, especially a willful or deliberate one of some religious or moral principle; to offend against a principle, standard, etc.

transgression (Dictionary) violation of a law, command, etc.; sin.

redemption (Dictionary) deliverance; rescue; repurchase, as of something sold; recovery by payment, as of something pledged.

Savior (Dictionary) one who saves, rescues, or delivers: the savior of the country; (cap.) a title of God, especially of Christ (commonly spelled Saviour).

SALVATION

But Moses said to the people, "Have no fear! Stand by, and witness the deliverance which the LORD will work for you today; for the Egyptians whom you see today you will never see again. The LORD will battle for you; you hold your peace!" SH'MOT 14:13-14 (EXODUS 14:13-14)

And Moses said unto the people, Fear ye not, stand still, and see the salvation (3444) of the LORD, which He will show to you today; for the Egyptians whom you have seen today, ye shall see them again no more forever. The LORD shall fight for you, and ye shall hold your peace. EXODUS 14:13-14

Salvation (3444) pronounced yesh-oo'-aw; fem. pass. part. of 3467; something saved, i.e. (abstr.) deliverance; hence aid, victory, prosperity:- deliverance, health, help (-ing), salvation, save, saving (health), welfare.

deliverance (Dictionary) the act of giving up or surrendering; giving into another's possession or keeping; to give forth in words; utter or pronounce; to deliver a verdict; setting free; disburden (oneself) of thoughts, opinions, etc.; Obsolete: to make known, assert; Obsolete or Archaic: agile, active, quick.

prosperity (Dictionary) flourishing or thriving condition; good fortune; success.

fortune (Dictionary) position in life as determined by wealth.

success (Dictionary) favorable or prosperous termination of attempts or endeavors; gaining of wealth, position, or the like; Obsolete: outcome.

welfare (Dictionary) state of faring well; well-being; prosperity; success; happiness; weal.

happiness (2) (Dictionary) good fortune, pleasure, content or gladness.

weal (1) (Dictionary) Archaic: well-being, prosperity , or happiness.

(3467) pronounced yaw-shah'; a prim. root; prop. to be open, wide or free, i.e. (by impl.) to be safe; causat. to free or succor: - x at all, avenging, defend, deliver (-er), help, preserve, rescue, be safe, bring (having) salvation, save (-iour), get victory.

succor (Dictionary) help, relief, aid, assistance in difficulty, need, or distress.

salvation (Dictionary) act of saving or delivering; a source, cause, or means of deliverance; deliverance from the power of penalty and sin; redemption.

sin (Dictionary) transgression of divine law; an act regarded as such transgression, or any violation, especially a willful or deliberate one of some religious or moral principle; to offend against a principle, standard, etc.

transgression (Dictionary) violation of a law, command, etc.; sin.

redemption (Dictionary) deliverance; rescue; repurchase, as of something sold; recovery by payment, as of something pledged.

Savior (Dictionary) one who saves, rescues, or delivers: the savior of the country; (cap.) a title of God, especially of Christ (commonly spelled Saviour).

The LORD is my strength and might; He is become my deliverance. This is my God and I will enshrine Him; the God of my father, and I will exalt Him. SH'MOT 15:2 (EXODUS 15:2)

Enshrine: Others "glorify" (TANAKH footnote)

The LORD is my strength and song, and He is become my salvation (3444); He is my God and I will prepare Him a habitation; my father's God, and I will exalt Him. EXODUS 15:2

Salvation (3444) pronounced yesh-oo'-aw; fem. pass. part. of 3467; something saved, i.e. (abstr.) deliverance; hence aid, victory, prosperity:- deliverance, health, help (-ing), salvation, save, saving (health), welfare.

deliverance (Dictionary) the act of giving up or surrendering; giving into another's possession or keeping; to give forth in words; utter or pronounce; to deliver a verdict; setting free; disburden (oneself) of thoughts, opinions, etc.; Obsolete: to make known, assert; Obsolete or Archaic: agile, active, quick.

prosperity (Dictionary) flourishing or thriving condition; good fortune; success.

fortune (Dictionary) position in life as determined by wealth.

success (Dictionary) favorable or prosperous termination of attempts or endeavors; gaining of wealth, position, or the like; Obsolete: outcome.

welfare (Dictionary) state of faring well; well-being; prosperity; success; happiness; weal.

happiness (2) (Dictionary) good fortune, pleasure, content or gladness.

weal (1) (Dictionary) Archaic: well-being, prosperity , or happiness.

(3467) pronounced yaw-shah'; a prim. root; prop. to be open, wide or free, i.e. (by impl.) to be safe; causat. to free or succor: - x at all, avenging, defend, deliver (-er), help, preserve, rescue, be safe, bring (having) salvation, save (-iour), get victory.

succor (Dictionary) help, relief, aid, assistance in difficulty, need, or distress.

salvation (Dictionary) act of saving or delivering; a source, cause, or means of deliverance; deliverance from the power of penalty and sin; redemption.

sin (Dictionary) transgression of divine law; an act regarded as such transgression, or any violation, especially a willful or deliberate one of some religious or moral principle; to offend against a principle, standard, etc.

transgression (Dictionary) violation of a law, command, etc.; sin.

redemption (Dictionary) deliverance; rescue; repurchase, as of something sold; recovery by payment, as of something pledged.

Savior (Dictionary) one who saves, rescues, or delivers: the savior of the country; (cap.) a title of God, especially of Christ (commonly spelled Saviour).

So Jeshurun grew fat and kicked-You grew fat and gross and coarse-He forsook the God who made him and spurned the Rock of his support. D'VARIM 32:15 (DEUTERONOMY 32:15)

But Jeshurun waxed fat, and kicked: thou art waxen fat, thou art grown thick, thou art covered *with fatness;* then he forsook God *which* made him, and lightly esteemed the Rock of his salvation (3444). DEUTERONOMY 32:15

Salvation (3444) pronounced yesh-oo'-aw; fem. pass. part. of 3467; something saved, i.e. (abstr.) deliverance; hence aid, victory, prosperity:- deliverance, health, help (-ing), salvation, save, saving (health), welfare.

deliverance (Dictionary) the act of giving up or surrendering; giving into another's possession or keeping; to give forth in words; utter or pronounce; to deliver a verdict; setting free; disburden (oneself) of thoughts, opinions, etc.; Obsolete: to make known, assert; Obsolete or Archaic: agile, active, quick.

prosperity (Dictionary) flourishing or thriving condition; good fortune; success.

fortune (Dictionary) position in life as determined by wealth.

success (Dictionary) favorable or prosperous termination of attempts or endeavors; gaining of wealth, position, or the like; Obsolete: outcome.

welfare (Dictionary) state of faring well; well-being; prosperity; success; happiness; weal.

happiness (2) (Dictionary) good fortune, pleasure, content or gladness.

weal (1) (Dictionary) Archaic: well-being, prosperity , or happiness.

(3467) pronounced yaw-shah'; a prim. root; prop. to be open, wide or free, i.e. (by impl.) to be safe; causat. to free or succor: - x at all, avenging, defend, deliver (-er), help, preserve, rescue, be safe, bring (having) salvation, save (-iour), get victory.

succor (Dictionary) help, relief, aid, assistance in difficulty, need, or distress.

salvation (Dictionary) act of saving or delivering; a source, cause, or means of deliverance; deliverance from the power of penalty and sin; redemption.

sin (Dictionary) transgression of divine law; an act regarded as such transgression, or any violation, especially a willful or deliberate one of some religious or moral principle; to offend against a principle, standard, etc.

transgression (Dictionary) violation of a law, command, etc.; sin.

redemption (Dictionary) deliverance; rescue; repurchase, as of something sold; recovery by payment, as of something pledged.

Savior (Dictionary) one who saves, rescues, or delivers: the savior of the country; (cap.) a title of God, especially of Christ (commonly spelled Saviour).

And Hannah prayed: My heart exults in the LORD; I have triumphed through the LORD. I gloat over my enemies; I rejoice in Your deliverance. SH'MU'EL ALEF 2:1 (I SAMUEL 2:1)

triumphed: Lit. "My horn is high." (TANAKH footnote)

gloat: Lit. "My mouth is wide." (TANAKH footnote)

And Hannah prayed, and said, My heart rejoiceth in the LORD, mine horn is exalted in the LORD; my mouth is enlarged over mine enemies; because I rejoice in thy salvation (3444). I SAMUEL 2:1

horn (Dictionary) a symbol of power, as in the BIBLE: horn of salvation.

Salvation (3444) pronounced yesh-oo'-aw; fem. pass. part. of 3467; something saved, i.e. (abstr.) deliverance; hence aid, victory, prosperity:- deliverance, health, help (-ing), salvation, save, saving (health), welfare.

deliverance (Dictionary) the act of giving up or surrendering; giving into another's possession or keeping; to give forth in words; utter or pronounce; to deliver a verdict; setting free; disburden (oneself) of thoughts, opinions, etc.; Obsolete: to make known, assert; Obsolete or Archaic: agile, active, quick.

prosperity (Dictionary) flourishing or thriving condition; good fortune; success.

fortune (Dictionary) position in life as determined by wealth.

success (Dictionary) favorable or prosperous termination of attempts or endeavors; gaining of wealth, position, or the like; Obsolete: outcome.

welfare (Dictionary) state of faring well; well-being; prosperity; success; happiness; weal.

happiness (2) (Dictionary) good fortune, pleasure, content or gladness.

weal (1) (Dictionary) Archaic: well-being, prosperity , or happiness.

(3467) pronounced yaw-shah'; a prim. root; prop. to be open, wide or free, i.e. (by impl.) to be safe; causat. to free or succor: - x at all, avenging, defend, deliver (-er), help, preserve, rescue, be safe, bring (having) salvation, save (-iour), get victory.

succor (Dictionary) help, relief, aid, assistance in difficulty, need, or distress.

salvation (Dictionary) act of saving or delivering; a source, cause, or means of deliverance; deliverance from the power of penalty and sin; redemption.

sin (Dictionary) transgression of divine law; an act regarded as such transgression, or any violation, especially a willful or deliberate one of some religious or moral principle; to offend against a principle, standard, etc.

transgression (Dictionary) violation of a law, command, etc.; sin.

redemption (Dictionary) deliverance; rescue; repurchase, as of something sold; recovery by payment, as of something pledged.

Savior (Dictionary) one who saves, rescues, or delivers: the savior of the country; (cap.) a title of God, especially of Christ (commonly spelled Saviour).

But Saul replied, "No man shall be put to death this day! For this day the LORD has brought victory to Israel." SH'MU'EL ALEF 11:13 (I SAMUEL 11:13)

And Saul said, There shall not a man be put to death this day; for today the LORD hath wrought salvation (8668) in Israel. I SAMUEL 11:13

Salvation (8668) pronounced tesh-oo-aw'; from 7768 in the sense of 3467; rescue (lit. or fig., pers., national, or spir.):- deliverance, help, safety, salvation, victory.

deliverance (Dictionary) the act of giving up or surrendering; giving into another's possession or keeping; to give forth in words; utter or pronounce; to deliver a verdict; setting free; disburden (oneself) of thoughts, opinions, etc.; Obsolete: to make known, assert; Obsolete or Archaic: agile, active, quick.

salvation (Dictionary) act of saving or delivering; a source, cause, or means of deliverance; deliverance from the power of penalty and sin; redemption.

sin (Dictionary) transgression of divine law; an act regarded as such transgression, or any violation, especially a willful or deliberate one of some religious or moral principle; to offend against a principle, standard, etc.

transgression (Dictionary) violation of a law, command, etc.; sin.

redemption (Dictionary) deliverance; rescue; repurchase, as of something sold; recovery by payment, as of something pledged.

(7768) pronounced shaw-vah'; a prim. root; prop. to be free; but used only causat. and reflex. to halloo (for help, i.e. freedom from some trouble):- cry (aloud, out), shout.

halloo (Dictionary) an exclamation used to attract attention, to incite the dogs in hunting, etc.; to call with a loud voice: shout, cry, as after dogs; to incite or chase with shouts and cries of "halloo".

(3467) pronounced yaw-shah'; a prim. root; prop. to be open, wide or free, i.e. (by impl.) to be safe; causat. to free or succor: - x at all, avenging, defend, deliver (-er), help, preserve, rescue, be safe, bring (having) salvation, save (-iour), get victory.

succor (Dictionary) help, relief, aid, assistance in difficulty, need, or distress.

salvation (Dictionary) act of saving or delivering; a source, cause, or means of deliverance; deliverance from the power of penalty and sin; redemption.

sin (Dictionary) transgression of divine law; an act regarded as such transgression, or any violation, especially a willful or deliberate one of some religious or moral principle; to offend against a principle, standard, etc.

transgression (Dictionary) violation of a law, command, etc.; sin.

redemption (Dictionary) deliverance; rescue; repurchase, as of something sold; recovery by payment, as of something pledged.

Savior (Dictionary) one who saves, rescues, or delivers: the savior of the country; (cap.) a title of God, especially of Christ (commonly spelled Saviour).

But the troops said to Saul, "Shall Jonathan die, after bringing this great victory to Israel? Never! As the LORD lives, not a hair of his head shall fall to the ground! For he brought this day to pass with the help of God." Thus the troops saved Jonathan and he did not die. SH'MU'EL ALEF 14:45
(I SAMUEL 14:45)

And the people said unto Saul, Shall Jonathan die, who hath wrought this great salvation (3444) in Israel? God forbid; *as* the LORD liveth, there shall not one hair of his head fall to the ground; for he hath wrought with God this day. So the people rescued Jonathan, that he died not. I SAMUEL 14:45

Salvation (3444) pronounced yesh-oo'-aw; fem. pass. part. of 3467; something saved, i.e. (abstr.) deliverance; hence aid, victory, prosperity:- deliverance, health, help (-ing), salvation, save, saving (health), welfare.

deliverance (Dictionary) the act of giving up or surrendering; giving into another's possession or keeping; to give forth in words; utter or pronounce; to deliver a verdict;

setting free; disburden (oneself) of thoughts, opinions, etc.; Obsolete: to make known, assert; Obsolete or Archaic: agile, active, quick.

prosperity (Dictionary) flourishing or thriving condition; good fortune; success.

fortune (Dictionary) position in life as determined by wealth.

success (Dictionary) favorable or prosperous termination of attempts or endeavors; gaining of wealth, position, or the like; Obsolete: outcome.

welfare (Dictionary) state of faring well; well-being; prosperity; success; happiness; weal.

happiness (2) (Dictionary) good fortune, pleasure, content or gladness.

weal (1) (Dictionary) Archaic: well-being, prosperity , or happiness.

(3467) pronounced yaw-shah'; a prim. root; prop. to be open, wide or free, i.e. (by impl.) to be safe; causat. to free or succor: - x at all, avenging, defend, deliver (-er), help, preserve, rescue, be safe, bring (having) salvation, save (-iour), get victory.

succor (Dictionary) help, relief, aid, assistance in difficulty, need, or distress.

salvation (Dictionary) act of saving or delivering; a source, cause, or means of deliverance; deliverance from the power of penalty and sin; redemption.

sin (Dictionary) transgression of divine law; an act regarded as such transgression, or any violation, especially a willful or deliberate one of some religious or moral principle; to offend against a principle, standard, etc.

transgression (Dictionary) violation of a law, command, etc.; sin.

redemption (Dictionary) deliverance; rescue; repurchase, as of something sold; recovery by payment, as of something pledged.

Savior (Dictionary) one who saves, rescues, or delivers: the savior of the country; (cap.) a title of God, especially of Christ (commonly spelled Saviour).

So Jonathan spoke well of David to his father Saul. He said to him, "Let not Your Majesty wrong his servant David, for he has not wronged you; indeed, all his actions have been very much to your advantage. He took his life in his hands and killed the Philistine, and the LORD wrought a great victory for all Israel. You saw it and rejoiced. Why then should you incur the guilt of shedding the blood of an innocent man, killing David without cause?" SH'MU'EL ALEF 19:4-5 (I SAMUEL 19:4-5)

And Jonathan spake good of David unto Saul his father, and said unto him, Let not the king sin against his servant against David; because he hath not sinned against thee, and because his works *have been to thee-ward very good: For he did put his life in his hand, and slew the Philistine, and the LORD wrought a great salvation (8668) for all Israel; thou sawest it; and didst rejoice: wherefore then wilt thou sin against innocent blood, to slay David without a cause? I SAMUEL 19:4-5*

Salvation (8668) pronounced tesh-oo-aw'; from 7768 in the sense of 3467; rescue (lit. or fig., pers., national, or spir.):- deliverance, help, safety, salvation, victory.

deliverance (Dictionary) the act of giving up or surrendering; giving into another's possession or keeping; to give forth in words; utter or pronounce; to deliver a verdict; setting free; disburden (oneself) of thoughts, opinions, etc.; Obsolete: to make known, assert; Obsolete or Archaic: agile, active, quick.

salvation (Dictionary) act of saving or delivering; a source, cause, or means of deliverance; deliverance from the power of penalty and sin; redemption.

sin (Dictionary) transgression of divine law; an act regarded as such transgression, or any violation, especially a willful or deliberate one of some religious or moral principle; to offend against a principle, standard, etc.

transgression (Dictionary) violation of a law, command, etc.; sin.

redemption (Dictionary) deliverance; rescue; repurchase, as of something sold; recovery by payment, as of something pledged.

(7768) pronounced shaw-vah'; a prim. root; prop. to be free; but used only causat. and reflex. to halloo (for help, i.e. freedom from some trouble):- cry (aloud, out), shout.

halloo (Dictionary) an exclamation used to attract attention, to incite the dogs in hunting, etc.; to call with a loud voice: shout, cry, as after dogs; to incite or chase with shouts and cries of "halloo".

(3467) pronounced yaw-shah'; a prim. root; prop. to be open, wide or free, i.e. (by impl.) to be safe; causat. to free or succor: - x at all, avenging, defend, deliver (-er), help, preserve, rescue, be safe, bring (having) salvation, save (-iour), get victory.

succor (Dictionary) help, relief, aid, assistance in difficulty, need, or distress.

salvation (Dictionary) act of saving or delivering; a source, cause, or means of deliverance; deliverance from the power of penalty and sin; redemption.

sin (Dictionary) transgression of divine law; an act regarded as such transgression, or any violation, especially a willful or deliberate one of some religious or moral principle; to offend against a principle, standard, etc.

transgression (Dictionary) violation of a law, command, etc.; sin.

redemption (Dictionary) deliverance; rescue; repurchase, as of something sold; recovery by payment, as of something pledged.

Savior (Dictionary) one who saves, rescues, or delivers: the savior of the country; (cap.) a title of God, especially of Christ (commonly spelled Saviour).

O God, the rock wherein I take shelter: My shield, my mighty champion, my fortress and refuge! My savior, You who rescue me from violence. SH'MU'EL BET 22:3 (II SAMUEL 22:3)

God, the rock: Lit. "the God of my rock", Ps. 18:3 "my God, my rock" (TANAKH footnote)

mighty champion: Lit. "horn of rescue" (TANAKH footnote)

He said: I adore you, O LORD, my strength, O LORD, my crag, my fortress, my rescuer, my God, my rock in whom I seek refuge, my shield, my mighty champion, my haven. TEHILLIM 18:2-3 (PSALMS 18:2-3)

The LORD is my rock, and my fortress, and my deliverer; my God, my strength, in whom I will trust: my buckler, and the horn of my salvation, *and* my high tower. I will call upon the LORD *who is worthy* to be praised: so shall I be saved from mine enemies. PSALMS 18:2-3

The God of my rock: in Him will I trust*: he is* my shield, and the horn of my salvation (3468), my high tower, and my refuge, my saviour; thou savest me from violence. II SAMUEL 22:3

Salvation (3468) pronounced yeh'-shah; from 3467; liberty, deliverance, prosperity, safety, salvation, saving.

liberty (Dictionary) freedom from arbitrary or despotic government or, often, from other rule or law than that of a self-governing community; freedom from external or foreign rule; freedom from control, interference, obligation, restriction, hampering conditions, etc.; power or right of doing, thinking, speaking, etc., according to choice.

deliverance (Dictionary) the act of giving up or surrendering; giving into another's possession or keeping; to give forth in words; utter or pronounce; to deliver a verdict; setting free; disburden (oneself) of thoughts, opinions, etc.; Obsolete: to make known, assert; Obsolete or Archaic: agile, active, quick.

prosperity (Dictionary) flourishing or thriving condition; good fortune; success.

fortune (Dictionary) position in life as determined by wealth.

success (Dictionary) favorable or prosperous termination of attempts or endeavors; gaining of wealth, position, or the like; Obsolete: outcome.

(3467) pronounced yaw-shah'; a prim. root; prop. to be open, wide or free, i.e. (by impl.) to be safe; causat. to free or succor: - x at all, avenging, defend, deliver (-er), help, preserve, rescue, be safe, bring (having) salvation, save (-iour), get victory.

succor (Dictionary) help, relief, aid, assistance in difficulty, need, or distress.

salvation (Dictionary) act of saving or delivering; a source, cause, or means of deliverance; deliverance from the power of penalty and sin; redemption.

sin (Dictionary) transgression of divine law; an act regarded as such transgression, or any violation, especially a willful or deliberate one of some religious or moral principle; to offend against a principle, standard, etc.

transgression (Dictionary) violation of a law, command, etc.; sin.

redemption (Dictionary) deliverance; rescue; repurchase, as of something sold; recovery by payment, as of something pledged.

Savior (Dictionary) one who saves, rescues, or delivers: the savior of the country; (cap.) a title of God, especially of Christ (commonly spelled Saviour).

You have granted me the shield of Your protection and Your providence has made me great.
SH'MU'EL BET 22:36 (II SAMUEL 22:36)

Thou hast also given me the shield of thy salvation (3468) and thy gentleness hath made me great.
II SAMUEL 22:36

Salvation (3468) pronounced yeh'-shah; from 3467; liberty, deliverance, prosperity, safety, salvation, saving.

liberty (Dictionary) freedom from arbitrary or despotic government or, often, from other rule or law than that of a self-governing community; freedom from external or foreign rule; freedom from control, interference, obligation, restriction, hampering conditions, etc.; power or right of doing, thinking, speaking, etc., according to choice.

deliverance (Dictionary) the act of giving up or surrendering; giving into another's possession or keeping; to give forth in words; utter or pronounce; to deliver a verdict; setting free; disburden (oneself) of thoughts, opinions, etc.; Obsolete: to make known, assert; Obsolete or Archaic: agile, active, quick.

prosperity (Dictionary) flourishing or thriving condition; good fortune; success.

fortune (Dictionary) position in life as determined by wealth.

success (Dictionary) favorable or prosperous termination of attempts or endeavors; gaining of wealth, position, or the like; Obsolete: outcome.

(3467) pronounced yaw-shah'; a prim. root; prop. to be open, wide or free, i.e. (by impl.) to be safe; causat. to free or succor: - x at all, avenging, defend, deliver (-er), help, preserve, rescue, be safe, bring (having) salvation, save (-iour), get victory.

succor (Dictionary) help, relief, aid, assistance in difficulty, need, or distress.

salvation (Dictionary) act of saving or delivering; a source, cause, or means of deliverance; deliverance from the power of penalty and sin; redemption.

sin (Dictionary) transgression of divine law; an act regarded as such transgression, or any violation, especially a willful or deliberate one of some religious or moral principle; to offend against a principle, standard, etc.

transgression (Dictionary) violation of a law, command, etc.; sin.

redemption (Dictionary) deliverance; rescue; repurchase, as of something sold; recovery by payment, as of something pledged.

Savior (Dictionary) one who saves, rescues, or delivers: the savior of the country; (cap.) a title of God, especially of Christ (commonly spelled Saviour).

The LORD lives! Blessed is my rock! Exalted be God, the rock Who gives me victory;
SH'MU'EL BET 22:47 (II SAMUEL 22:47)

The LORD liveth; and blessed *be* my rock; and exalted be the God of the rock of my salvation (3468).
II SAMUEL 22:47

Salvation (3468) pronounced yeh'-shah; from 3467; liberty, deliverance, prosperity, safety, salvation, saving.

liberty (Dictionary) freedom from arbitrary or despotic government or, often, from other rule or law than that of a self-governing community; freedom from external or foreign rule; freedom from control, interference, obligation, restriction, hampering conditions, etc.; power or right of doing, thinking, speaking, etc., according to choice.

deliverance (Dictionary) the act of giving up or surrendering; giving into another's possession or keeping; to give forth in words; utter or pronounce; to deliver a verdict; setting free; disburden (oneself) of thoughts, opinions, etc.; Obsolete: to make known, assert; Obsolete or Archaic: agile, active, quick.

prosperity (Dictionary) flourishing or thriving condition; good fortune; success.

fortune (Dictionary) position in life as determined by wealth.

success (Dictionary) favorable or prosperous termination of attempts or endeavors; gaining of wealth, position, or the like; Obsolete: outcome.

(3467) pronounced yaw-shah'; a prim. root; prop. to be open, wide or free, i.e. (by impl.) to be safe; causat. to free or succor: - x at all, avenging, defend, deliver (-er), help, preserve, rescue, be safe, bring (having) salvation, save (-iour), get victory.

succor (Dictionary) help, relief, aid, assistance in difficulty, need, or distress.

salvation (Dictionary) act of saving or delivering; a source, cause, or means of deliverance; deliverance from the power of penalty and sin; redemption.

sin (Dictionary) transgression of divine law; an act regarded as such transgression, or any violation, especially a willful or deliberate one of some religious or moral principle; to offend against a principle, standard, etc.

transgression (Dictionary) violation of a law, command, etc.; sin.

redemption (Dictionary) deliverance; rescue; repurchase, as of something sold; recovery by payment, as of something pledged.

Savior (Dictionary) one who saves, rescues, or delivers: the savior of the country; (cap.) a title of God, especially of Christ (commonly spelled Saviour).

For this I sing Your praise among the nations and hymn Your name: Tower of victory to His king, who deals graciously with His anointed, with David and his offspring evermore. SH'MU'EL BET 22:50-51 (II SAMUEL 22:50-51)

Therefore I will give thanks unto thee, O LORD, among the heathen, and I will sing praises unto thy name. *He is* the tower of salvation (3444) for his king; and showeth mercy to his anointed unto David, and to his seed for evermore. II SAMUEL 22:50-51

Salvation (3444) pronounced yesh-oo'-aw; fem. pass. part. of 3467; something saved, i.e. (abstr.) deliverance; hence aid, victory, prosperity:- deliverance, health, help (-ing), salvation, save, saving (health), welfare.

deliverance (Dictionary) the act of giving up or surrendering; giving into another's possession or keeping; to give forth in words; utter or pronounce; to deliver a verdict; setting free; disburden (oneself) of thoughts, opinions, etc.; Obsolete: to make known, assert; Obsolete or Archaic: agile, active, quick.

prosperity (Dictionary) flourishing or thriving condition; good fortune; success.

fortune (Dictionary) position in life as determined by wealth.

success (Dictionary) favorable or prosperous termination of attempts or endeavors; gaining of wealth, position, or the like; Obsolete: outcome.

welfare (Dictionary) state of faring well; well-being; prosperity; success; happiness; weal.

happiness (2) (Dictionary) good fortune, pleasure, content or gladness.

weal (1) (Dictionary) Archaic: well-being, prosperity , or happiness.

(3467) pronounced yaw-shah'; a prim. root; prop. to be open, wide or free, i.e. (by impl.) to be safe; causat. to free or succor: - x at all, avenging, defend, deliver (-er), help, preserve, rescue, be safe, bring (having) salvation, save (-iour), get victory.

succor (Dictionary) help, relief, aid, assistance in difficulty, need, or distress.

salvation (Dictionary) act of saving or delivering; a source, cause, or means of deliverance; deliverance from the power of penalty and sin; redemption.

sin (Dictionary) transgression of divine law; an act regarded as such transgression, or any violation, especially a willful or deliberate one of some religious or moral principle; to offend against a principle, standard, etc.

transgression (Dictionary) violation of a law, command, etc.; sin.

redemption (Dictionary) deliverance; rescue; repurchase, as of something sold; recovery by payment, as of something pledged.

Savior (Dictionary) one who saves, rescues, or delivers: the savior of the country; (cap.) a title of God, especially of Christ (commonly spelled Saviour).

Is not my House established before God? For He has granted me an eternal pact, drawn up in full and secured. Will He not cause all my success and [my] every desire to blossom? SH'MU'EL BET 23:5 (II SAMUEL 23:5)

Although my house *be* not so with God: yet he hath made with me an everlasting covenant ordered in all *things*, and sure: for *this is* all my salvation (3468), and all *my* desire, although he make *it* not to grow. II SAMUEL 23:5

Salvation (3468) pronounced yeh'-shah; from 3467; liberty, deliverance, prosperity, safety, salvation, saving.

liberty (Dictionary) freedom from arbitrary or despotic government or, often, from other rule or law than that of a self-governing community; freedom from external or foreign rule; freedom from control, interference, obligation, restriction, hampering conditions, etc.; power or right of doing, thinking, speaking, etc., according to choice.

deliverance (Dictionary) the act of giving up or surrendering; giving into another's possession or keeping; to give forth in words; utter or pronounce; to deliver a verdict; setting free; disburden (oneself) of thoughts, opinions, etc.; Obsolete: to make known, assert; Obsolete or Archaic: agile, active, quick.

prosperity (Dictionary) flourishing or thriving condition; good fortune; success.

fortune (Dictionary) position in life as determined by wealth.

success (Dictionary) favorable or prosperous termination of attempts or endeavors; gaining of wealth, position, or the like; Obsolete: outcome.

(3467) pronounced yaw-shah'; a prim. root; prop. to be open, wide or free, i.e. (by impl.) to be safe; causat. to free or succor: - x at all, avenging, defend, deliver (-er), help, preserve, rescue, be safe, bring (having) salvation, save (-iour), get victory.

succor (Dictionary) help, relief, aid, assistance in difficulty, need, or distress.

salvation (Dictionary) act of saving or delivering; a source, cause, or means of deliverance; deliverance from the power of penalty and sin; redemption.

sin (Dictionary) transgression of divine law; an act regarded as such transgression, or any violation, especially a willful or deliberate one of some religious or moral principle; to offend against a principle, standard, etc.

transgression (Dictionary) violation of a law, command, etc.; sin.

redemption (Dictionary) deliverance; rescue; repurchase, as of something sold; recovery by payment, as of something pledged.

Savior (Dictionary) one who saves, rescues, or delivers: the savior of the country; (cap.) a title of God, especially of Christ (commonly spelled Saviour).

Sing to the LORD, all the earth. Proclaim His victory day after day. DIVREI-HAYAMIM ALEF 16:23 (I CHRONICLES 16:23)

Sing unto the LORD, all the earth; show forth from day to day his salvation (3444). I CHRONICLES 16:23

Salvation (3444) pronounced yesh-oo'-aw; fem. pass. part. of 3467; something saved, i.e. (abstr.) deliverance; hence aid, victory, prosperity:- deliverance, health, help (-ing), salvation, save, saving (health), welfare.

deliverance (Dictionary) the act of giving up or surrendering; giving into another's possession or keeping; to give forth in words; utter or pronounce; to deliver a verdict; setting free; disburden (oneself) of thoughts, opinions, etc.; Obsolete: to make known, assert; Obsolete or Archaic: agile, active, quick.

prosperity (Dictionary) flourishing or thriving condition; good fortune; success.

fortune (Dictionary) position in life as determined by wealth.

success (Dictionary) favorable or prosperous termination of attempts or endeavors; gaining of wealth, position, or the like; Obsolete: outcome.

welfare (Dictionary) state of faring well; well-being; prosperity; success; happiness; weal.

happiness (2) (Dictionary) good fortune, pleasure, content or gladness.

weal (1) (Dictionary) Archaic: well-being, prosperity , or happiness.

(3467) pronounced yaw-shah'; a prim. root; prop. to be open, wide or free, i.e. (by impl.) to be safe; causat. to free or succor: - x at all, avenging, defend, deliver (-er), help, preserve, rescue, be safe, bring (having) salvation, save (-iour), get victory.

succor (Dictionary) help, relief, aid, assistance in difficulty, need, or distress.

salvation (Dictionary) act of saving or delivering; a source, cause, or means of deliverance; deliverance from the power of penalty and sin; redemption.

sin (Dictionary) transgression of divine law; an act regarded as such transgression, or any violation, especially a willful or deliberate one of some religious or moral principle; to offend against a principle, standard, etc.

transgression (Dictionary) violation of a law, command, etc.; sin.

redemption (Dictionary) deliverance; rescue; repurchase, as of something sold; recovery by payment, as of something pledged.

Savior (Dictionary) one who saves, rescues, or delivers: the savior of the country; (cap.) a title of God, especially of Christ (commonly spelled Saviour).

Declare: Deliver us, O God, our deliverer, and gather us and save *us* from the nations, to acclaim Your holy name, to glory in Your praise. DIVREI-HAYAMIM ALEF 16:35 (I CHRONICLES 16:35)

And say ye, Save us, O God of our salvation (3468), and gather *us* together, and deliver *us* from the heathen, that we may give thanks to thy holy name, *and* glory in thy praise. I CHRONICLES 16:35

Salvation (3468) pronounced yeh'-shah; from 3467; liberty, deliverance, prosperity, safety, salvation, saving.

liberty (Dictionary) freedom from arbitrary or despotic government or, often, from other rule or law than that of a self-governing community; freedom from external or foreign rule; freedom from control, interference, obligation, restriction, hampering conditions, etc.; power or right of doing, thinking, speaking, etc., according to choice.

deliverance (Dictionary) the act of giving up or surrendering; giving into another's possession or keeping; to give forth in words; utter or pronounce; to deliver a verdict; setting free; disburden (oneself) of thoughts, opinions, etc.; Obsolete: to make known, assert; Obsolete or Archaic: agile, active, quick.

prosperity (Dictionary) flourishing or thriving condition; good fortune; success.

fortune (Dictionary) position in life as determined by wealth.

success (Dictionary) favorable or prosperous termination of attempts or endeavors; gaining of wealth, position, or the like; Obsolete: outcome.

(3467) pronounced yaw-shah'; a prim. root; prop. to be open, wide or free, i.e. (by impl.) to be safe; causat. to free or succor: - x at all, avenging, defend, deliver (-er), help, preserve, rescue, be safe, bring (having) salvation, save (-iour), get victory.

succor (Dictionary) help, relief, aid, assistance in difficulty, need, or distress.

salvation (Dictionary) act of saving or delivering; a source, cause, or means of deliverance; deliverance from the power of penalty and sin; redemption.

sin (Dictionary) transgression of divine law; an act regarded as such transgression, or any violation, especially a willful or deliberate one of some religious or moral principle; to offend against a principle, standard, etc.

transgression (Dictionary) violation of a law, command, etc.; sin.

redemption (Dictionary) deliverance; rescue; repurchase, as of something sold; recovery by payment, as of something pledged.

Savior (Dictionary) one who saves, rescues, or delivers: the savior of the country; (cap.) a title of God, especially of Christ (commonly spelled Saviour).

Advance, O LORD God, to your resting place, You and Your mighty Ark. Your priests, O LORD God, are clothed in triumph: your loyal ones will rejoice in [Your] goodness. DIVREI-HAYAMIM BET 6:41
(II CHRONICLES 6:41)

Now therefore arise, O LORD God, into thy resting place, thou and the ark of thy strength: let thy priests, O LORD God, be clothed with salvation (8668), and let thy saints rejoice in goodness.
II CHRONICLES 6:41

Salvation (8668) pronounced tesh-oo-aw'; from 7768 in the sense of 3467; rescue (lit. or fig., pers., national, or spir.):- deliverance, help, safety, salvation, victory.

deliverance (Dictionary) the act of giving up or surrendering; giving into another's possession or keeping; to give forth in words; utter or pronounce; to deliver a verdict; setting free; disburden (oneself) of thoughts, opinions, etc.; Obsolete: to make known, assert; Obsolete or Archaic: agile, active, quick.

salvation (Dictionary) act of saving or delivering; a source, cause, or means of deliverance; deliverance from the power of penalty and sin; redemption.

sin (Dictionary) transgression of divine law; an act regarded as such transgression, or any violation, especially a willful or deliberate one of some religious or moral principle; to offend against a principle, standard, etc.

transgression (Dictionary) violation of a law, command, etc.; sin.

redemption (Dictionary) deliverance; rescue; repurchase, as of something sold; recovery by payment, as of something pledged.

(7768) pronounced shaw-vah'; a prim. root; prop. to be free; but used only causat. and reflex. to halloo (for help, i.e. freedom from some trouble):- cry (aloud, out), shout.

halloo (Dictionary) an exclamation used to attract attention, to incite the dogs in hunting, etc.; to call with a loud voice: shout, cry, as after dogs; to incite or chase with shouts and cries of "halloo".

(3467) pronounced yaw-shah'; a prim. root; prop. to be open, wide or free, i.e. (by impl.) to be safe; causat. to free or succor: - x at all, avenging, defend, deliver (-er), help, preserve, rescue, be safe, bring (having) salvation, save (-iour), get victory.

succor (Dictionary) help, relief, aid, assistance in difficulty, need, or distress.

salvation (Dictionary) act of saving or delivering; a source, cause, or means of deliverance; deliverance from the power of penalty and sin; redemption.

sin (Dictionary) transgression of divine law; an act regarded as such transgression, or any violation, especially a willful or deliberate one of some religious or moral principle; to offend against a principle, standard, etc.

transgression (Dictionary) violation of a law, command, etc.; sin.

redemption (Dictionary) deliverance; rescue; repurchase, as of something sold; recovery by payment, as of something pledged.

Savior (Dictionary) one who saves, rescues, or delivers: the savior of the country; (cap.) a title of God, especially of Christ (commonly spelled Saviour).

It is not for you to fight this battle; stand by, wait, and witness your deliverance by the LORD, O Judah and Jerusalem; do not fear or be dismayed; go forth to meet them tomorrow and the LORD will be with you. DIVREI- HAYAMIM BET 20:17 (II CHRONICLES 20:17)

Ye shall not *need to* fight in this *battle*; set yourselves, stand ye *still,* and see the salvation (3444) of the LORD with you, O Judah and Jerusalem; fear not, nor be dismayed; tomorrow go out against them; for the LORD *will be* with you. II CHRONICLES 20:17

Salvation (3444) pronounced yesh-oo'-aw; fem. pass. part. of 3467; something saved, i.e. (abstr.) deliverance; hence aid, victory, prosperity:- deliverance, health, help (-ing), salvation, save, saving (health), welfare.

deliverance (Dictionary) the act of giving up or surrendering; giving into another's possession or keeping; to give forth in words; utter or pronounce; to deliver a verdict;

setting free; disburden (oneself) of thoughts, opinions, etc.; Obsolete: to make known, assert; Obsolete or Archaic: agile, active, quick.

prosperity (Dictionary) flourishing or thriving condition; good fortune; success.

fortune (Dictionary) position in life as determined by wealth.

success (Dictionary) favorable or prosperous termination of attempts or endeavors; gaining of wealth, position, or the like; Obsolete: outcome.

welfare (Dictionary) state of faring well; well-being; prosperity; success; happiness; weal.

happiness (2) (Dictionary) good fortune, pleasure, content or gladness.

weal (1) (Dictionary) Archaic: well-being, prosperity , or happiness.

(3467) pronounced yaw-shah'; a prim. root; prop. to be open, wide or free, i.e. (by impl.) to be safe; causat. to free or succor: - x at all, avenging, defend, deliver (-er), help, preserve, rescue, be safe, bring (having) salvation, save (-iour), get victory.

succor (Dictionary) help, relief, aid, assistance in difficulty, need, or distress.

salvation (Dictionary) act of saving or delivering; a source, cause, or means of deliverance; deliverance from the power of penalty and sin; redemption.

sin (Dictionary) transgression of divine law; an act regarded as such transgression, or any violation, especially a willful or deliberate one of some religious or moral principle; to offend against a principle, standard, etc.

transgression (Dictionary) violation of a law, command, etc.; sin.

redemption (Dictionary) deliverance; rescue; repurchase, as of something sold; recovery by payment, as of something pledged.

Savior (Dictionary) one who saves, rescues, or delivers: the savior of the country; (cap.) a title of God, especially of Christ (commonly spelled Saviour).

In this too is my salvation: that no impious man can come into His presence. IYOV 13:16 (JOB 13:16)

He also shall be my salvation (3444); for a hypocrite shall not come before him. JOB 13:16

Salvation (3444) pronounced yesh-oo'-aw; fem. pass. part. of 3467; something saved, i.e. (abstr.) deliverance; hence aid, victory, prosperity:- deliverance, health, help (-ing), salvation, save, saving (health), welfare.

deliverance (Dictionary) the act of giving up or surrendering; giving into another's possession or keeping; to give forth in words; utter or pronounce; to deliver a verdict;

setting free; disburden (oneself) of thoughts, opinions, etc.; Obsolete: to make known, assert; Obsolete or Archaic: agile, active, quick.

prosperity (Dictionary) flourishing or thriving condition; good fortune; success.

fortune (Dictionary) position in life as determined by wealth.

success (Dictionary) favorable or prosperous termination of attempts or endeavors; gaining of wealth, position, or the like; Obsolete: outcome.

welfare (Dictionary) state of faring well; well-being; prosperity; success; happiness; weal.

happiness (2) (Dictionary) good fortune, pleasure, content or gladness.

weal (1) (Dictionary) Archaic: well-being, prosperity , or happiness.

(3467) pronounced yaw-shah'; a prim. root; prop. to be open, wide or free, i.e. (by impl.) to be safe; causat. to free or succor: - x at all, avenging, defend, deliver (-er), help, preserve, rescue, be safe, bring (having) salvation, save (-iour), get victory.

succor (Dictionary) help, relief, aid, assistance in difficulty, need, or distress.

salvation (Dictionary) act of saving or delivering; a source, cause, or means of deliverance; deliverance from the power of penalty and sin; redemption.

sin Dictionary) transgression of divine law; an act regarded as such transgression, or any violation, especially a willful or deliberate one of some religious or moral principle; to offend against a principle, standard, etc.

transgression (Dictionary) violation of a law, command, etc.; sin.

redemption (Dictionary) deliverance; rescue; repurchase, as of something sold; recovery by payment, as of something pledged.

Savior (Dictionary) one who saves, rescues, or delivers: the savior of the country; (cap.) a title of God, especially of Christ (commonly spelled Saviour).

Rise, O LORD! Deliver me, O my God! For you slap all my enemies in the face; You break the teeth of the wicked. Deliverance is the LORD's; Your blessing be upon Your people! Selah. TEHILLIM 3:8-9 (PSALMS 3:7-8)

Arise, O LORD; save (3467) me, O my God: for thou hast smitten all mine enemies *upon* the cheek bone; thou hast broken the teeth of the ungodly. Salvation (3444) *belongeth* unto the LORD: thy blessing *is* upon thy people. Selah PSALMS 3:7-8

SALVATION

(3467) pronounced yaw-shah'; a prim. root; prop. to be open, wide or free, i.e. (by impl.) to be safe; causat. to free or succor: - x at all, avenging, defend, deliver (-er), help, preserve, rescue, be safe, bring (having) salvation, save (-iour), get victory.

succor (Dictionary) help, relief, aid, assistance in difficulty, need, or distress.

salvation (Dictionary) act of saving or delivering; a source, cause, or means of deliverance; deliverance from the power of penalty and sin; redemption.

sin (Dictionary) transgression of divine law; an act regarded as such transgression, or any violation, especially a willful or deliberate one of some religious or moral principle; to offend against a principle, standard, etc.

transgression (Dictionary) violation of a law, command, etc.; sin.

redemption (Dictionary) deliverance; rescue; repurchase, as of something sold; recovery by payment, as of something pledged.

Savior (Dictionary) one who saves, rescues, or delivers: the savior of the country; (cap.) a title of God, especially of Christ (commonly spelled Saviour).

Salvation (3444) pronounced yesh-oo'-aw; fem. pass. part. of 3467; something saved, i.e. (abstr.) deliverance; hence aid, victory, prosperity:- deliverance, health, help (-ing), salvation, save, saving (health), welfare.

deliverance (Dictionary) the act of giving up or surrendering; giving into another's possession or keeping; to give forth in words; utter or pronounce; to deliver a verdict; setting free; disburden (oneself) of thoughts, opinions, etc.; Obsolete: to make known, assert; Obsolete or Archaic: agile, active, quick.

prosperity (Dictionary) flourishing or thriving condition; good fortune; success.

fortune (Dictionary) position in life as determined by wealth.

success (Dictionary) favorable or prosperous termination of attempts or endeavors; gaining of wealth, position, or the like; Obsolete: outcome.

welfare (Dictionary) state of faring well; well-being; prosperity; success; happiness; weal.

happiness (2) (Dictionary) good fortune, pleasure, content or gladness.

weal (1) (Dictionary) Archaic: well-being, prosperity , or happiness.

Have mercy on me, O LORD; see my afflictions at the hands of my foes, You who lift me from the gates of death, so that in the gates of Fair Zion I might tell all Your praise. I might exult in Your deliverance. TEHILLIM 9:14-15 (PSALMS 9:13-14)

SALVATION

Fair Zion: Lit. "the Daughter of Zion" (TANAKH footnote)

Have mercy upon me, O LORD: consider my trouble *which I suffer* of them that hate me, thou that liftest me up from the gates of death: that I may show forth all thy praise in the gates of the daughter of Zion: I will rejoice in thy salvation (3444). PSALMS 9:13-14

Salvation (3444) pronounced yesh-oo'-aw; fem. pass. part. of 3467; something saved, i.e. (abstr.) deliverance; hence aid, victory, prosperity:- deliverance, health, help (-ing), salvation, save, saving (health), welfare.

deliverance (Dictionary) the act of giving up or surrendering; giving into another's possession or keeping; to give forth in words; utter or pronounce; to deliver a verdict; setting free; disburden (oneself) of thoughts, opinions, etc.; Obsolete: to make known, assert; Obsolete or Archaic: agile, active, quick.

prosperity (Dictionary) flourishing or thriving condition; good fortune; success.

fortune (Dictionary) position in life as determined by wealth.

success (Dictionary) favorable or prosperous termination of attempts or endeavors; gaining of wealth, position, or the like; Obsolete: outcome.

welfare (Dictionary) state of faring well; well-being; prosperity; success; happiness; weal.

happiness (2) (Dictionary) good fortune, pleasure, content or gladness.

weal (1) (Dictionary) Archaic: well-being, prosperity , or happiness.

(3467) pronounced yaw-shah'; a prim. root; prop. to be open, wide or free, i.e. (by impl.) to be safe; causat. to free or succor: - x at all, avenging, defend, deliver (-er), help, preserve, rescue, be safe, bring (having) salvation, save (-iour), get victory.

succor (Dictionary) help, relief, aid, assistance in difficulty, need, or distress.

salvation (Dictionary) act of saving or delivering; a source, cause, or means of deliverance; deliverance from the power of penalty and sin; redemption.

sin (Dictionary) transgression of divine law; an act regarded as such transgression, or any violation, especially a willful or deliberate one of some religious or moral principle; to offend against a principle, standard, etc.

transgression (Dictionary) violation of a law, command, etc.; sin.

redemption (Dictionary) deliverance; rescue; repurchase, as of something sold; recovery by payment, as of something pledged.

Savior (Dictionary) one who saves, rescues, or delivers: the savior of the country; (cap.) a title of God, especially of Christ (commonly spelled Saviour).

Look at me, answer me, O LORD, my God! Restore the luster to my eyes, lest I sleep the sleep of death; lest my enemy say, "I have overcome him," my foes exult when I totter, but I trust in Your faithfulness, my heart will exult in Your deliverance. I will sing to the LORD, for He has been good to me. TEHILLIM 13:4-6 (PSALMS 13:3-6)

Consider *and* hear me, O LORD my God: lighten mine eyes, lest I sleep the *sleep of* death; lest mine enemy say, I have prevailed against him; *and* those that trouble me rejoice when I am moved. But I have trusted in thy mercy; my heart shall rejoice in thy salvation (3444). I will sing unto the LORD, because he hath dealt bountifully with me. PSALMS 13:3-6

Salvation (3444) pronounced yesh-oo'-aw; fem. pass. part. of 3467; something saved, i.e. (abstr.) deliverance; hence aid, victory, prosperity:- deliverance, health, help (-ing), salvation, save, saving (health), welfare.

deliverance (Dictionary) the act of giving up or surrendering; giving into another's possession or keeping; to give forth in words; utter or pronounce; to deliver a verdict; setting free; disburden (oneself) of thoughts, opinions, etc.; Obsolete: to make known, assert; Obsolete or Archaic: agile, active, quick.

prosperity (Dictionary) flourishing or thriving condition; good fortune; success.

fortune (Dictionary) position in life as determined by wealth.

success (Dictionary) favorable or prosperous termination of attempts or endeavors; gaining of wealth, position, or the like; Obsolete: outcome.

welfare (Dictionary) state of faring well; well-being; prosperity; success; happiness; weal.

happiness (2) (Dictionary) good fortune, pleasure, content or gladness.

weal (1) (Dictionary) Archaic: well-being, prosperity , or happiness.

(3467) pronounced yaw-shah'; a prim. root; prop. to be open, wide or free, i.e. (by impl.) to be safe; causat. to free or succor: - x at all, avenging, defend, deliver (-er), help, preserve, rescue, be safe, bring (having) salvation, save (-iour), get victory.

succor (Dictionary) help, relief, aid, assistance in difficulty, need, or distress.

salvation (Dictionary) act of saving or delivering; a source, cause, or means of deliverance; deliverance from the power of penalty and sin; redemption.

sin (Dictionary) transgression of divine law; an act regarded as such transgression, or any violation, especially a willful or deliberate one of some religious or moral principle; to offend against a principle, standard, etc.

transgression (Dictionary) violation of a law, command, etc.; sin.

redemption (Dictionary) deliverance; rescue; repurchase, as of something sold; recovery by payment, as of something pledged.

Savior (Dictionary) one who saves, rescues, or delivers: the savior of the country; (cap.) a title of God, especially of Christ (commonly spelled Saviour).

O that the deliverance of Israel might come from Zion! When the LORD restores the fortunes of His people, Jacob will exult, Israel will rejoice. TEHILLIM 14:7 (PSALMS 14:7)

O that the salvation (3444) of Israel *were come* out of Zion! When the LORD bringeth back the captivity of his people, Jacob shall rejoice*, and* Israel shall be glad. PSALMS 14:7

Salvation (3444) pronounced yesh-oo'-aw; fem. pass. part. of 3467; something saved, i.e. (abstr.) deliverance; hence aid, victory, prosperity:- deliverance, health, help (-ing), salvation, save, saving (health), welfare.

deliverance (Dictionary) the act of giving up or surrendering; giving into another's possession or keeping; to give forth in words; utter or pronounce; to deliver a verdict; setting free; disburden (oneself) of thoughts, opinions, etc.; Obsolete: to make known, assert; Obsolete or Archaic: agile, active, quick.

prosperity (Dictionary) flourishing or thriving condition; good fortune; success.

fortune (Dictionary) position in life as determined by wealth.

success (Dictionary) favorable or prosperous termination of attempts or endeavors; gaining of wealth, position, or the like; Obsolete: outcome.

welfare (Dictionary) state of faring well; well-being; prosperity; success; happiness; weal.

happiness (2) (Dictionary) good fortune, pleasure, content or gladness.

weal (1) (Dictionary) Archaic: well-being, prosperity , or happiness.

(3467) pronounced yaw-shah'; a prim. root; prop. to be open, wide or free, i.e. (by impl.) to be safe; causat. to free or succor: - x at all, avenging, defend, deliver (-er), help, preserve, rescue, be safe, bring (having) salvation, save (-iour), get victory.

succor (Dictionary) help, relief, aid, assistance in difficulty, need, or distress.

salvation (Dictionary) act of saving or delivering; a source, cause, or means of deliverance; deliverance from the power of penalty and sin; redemption.

sin (Dictionary) transgression of divine law; an act regarded as such transgression, or any violation, especially a willful or deliberate one of some religious or moral principle; to offend against a principle, standard, etc.

transgression (Dictionary) violation of a law, command, etc.; sin.

redemption (Dictionary) deliverance; rescue; repurchase, as of something sold; recovery by payment, as of something pledged.

Savior (Dictionary) one who saves, rescues, or delivers: the savior of the country; (cap.) a title of God, especially of Christ (commonly spelled Saviour).

You have given me the shield of Your protection: Your right hand has sustained me. Your care has made me great. TEHILLIM 18:36 (PSALMS 18:35)

care: others "condescension" (TANAKH footnote)

Thou hast also given me the shield of thy salvation (3468) and thy right hand hath holden me up, and thy gentleness hath made me great. PSALMS 18:35

Salvation (3468) pronounced yeh'-shah; from 3467; liberty, deliverance, prosperity, safety, salvation, saving.

liberty (Dictionary) freedom from arbitrary or despotic government or, often, from other rule or law than that of a self-governing community; freedom from external or foreign rule; freedom from control, interference, obligation, restriction, hampering conditions, etc.; power or right of doing, thinking, speaking, etc., according to choice.

deliverance (Dictionary) the act of giving up or surrendering; giving into another's possession or keeping; to give forth in words; utter or pronounce; to deliver a verdict; setting free; disburden (oneself) of thoughts, opinions, etc.; Obsolete: to make known, assert; Obsolete or Archaic: agile, active, quick.

prosperity (Dictionary) flourishing or thriving condition; good fortune; success.

fortune (Dictionary) position in life as determined by wealth.

success (Dictionary) favorable or prosperous termination of attempts or endeavors; gaining of wealth, position, or the like; Obsolete: outcome.

(3467) pronounced yaw-shah'; a prim. root; prop. to be open, wide or free, i.e. (by impl.) to be safe; causat. to free or succor: - x at all, avenging, defend, deliver (-er), help, preserve, rescue, be safe, bring (having) salvation, save (-iour), get victory.

succor (Dictionary) help, relief, aid, assistance in difficulty, need, or distress.

salvation (Dictionary) act of saving or delivering; a source, cause, or means of deliverance; deliverance from the power of penalty and sin; redemption.

sin (Dictionary) transgression of divine law; an act regarded as such transgression, or any violation, especially a willful or deliberate one of some religious or moral principle; to offend against a principle, standard, etc.

transgression (Dictionary) violation of a law, command, etc.; sin.

redemption (Dictionary) deliverance; rescue; repurchase, as of something sold; recovery by payment, as of something pledged.

Savior (Dictionary) one who saves, rescues, or delivers: the savior of the country; (cap.) a title of God, especially of Christ (commonly spelled Saviour).

The LORD lives! Blessed is my rock! Exalted be God, my deliverer, the God who has vindicated me and made peoples subject to me, who rescued me from my enemies, who raised me clear of my adversaries, saved me from lawless men. TEHILLIM 18:47-49 (PSALMS 18:46-48)

The LORD liveth; and blessed *be* my Rock; and let the God of my salvation (3468) be exalted. It *is* God that avengeth me, and subdueth the people under me. He delivereth me from mine enemies. yea, thou liftest me up above those that rise up against me; thou hast delivered me from the violent man. PSALMS 18:46-48

Salvation (3468) pronounced yeh'-shah; from 3467; liberty, deliverance, prosperity, safety, salvation, saving.

liberty (Dictionary) freedom from arbitrary or despotic government or, often, from other rule or law than that of a self-governing community; freedom from external or foreign rule; freedom from control, interference, obligation, restriction, hampering conditions, etc.; power or right of doing, thinking, speaking, etc., according to choice.

deliverance (Dictionary) the act of giving up or surrendering; giving into another's possession or keeping; to give forth in words; utter or pronounce; to deliver a verdict; setting free; disburden (oneself) of thoughts, opinions, etc.; Obsolete: to make known, assert; Obsolete or Archaic: agile, active, quick.

prosperity (Dictionary) flourishing or thriving condition; good fortune; success.

fortune (Dictionary) position in life as determined by wealth.

success (Dictionary) favorable or prosperous termination of attempts or endeavors; gaining of wealth, position, or the like; Obsolete: outcome.

(3467) pronounced yaw-shah'; a prim. root; prop. to be open, wide or free, i.e. (by impl.) to be safe; causat. to free or succor: - x at all, avenging, defend, deliver (-er), help, preserve, rescue, be safe, bring (having) salvation, save (-iour), get victory.

succor (Dictionary) help, relief, aid, assistance in difficulty, need, or distress.

salvation (Dictionary) act of saving or delivering; a source, cause, or means of deliverance; deliverance from the power of penalty and sin; redemption.

sin (Dictionary) transgression of divine law; an act regarded as such transgression, or any violation, especially a willful or deliberate one of some religious or moral principle; to offend against a principle, standard, etc.

transgression (Dictionary) violation of a law, command, etc.; sin.

redemption (Dictionary) deliverance; rescue; repurchase, as of something sold; recovery by payment, as of something pledged.

Savior (Dictionary) one who saves, rescues, or delivers: the savior of the country; (cap.) a title of God, especially of Christ (commonly spelled Saviour).

May He grant you your desire, and fulfill your every plan. May we shout for joy in your victory arrayed by standards in the name of our God. May the LORD fulfill your every wish. Now I know that the LORD will give victory to His anointed, will answer him from His heavenly sanctuary with the mighty victories of His right arm. TEHILLIM 20:5-7 (PSALMS 20:5-6)

We will rejoice in thy salvation (3444), and in the name of our God we will set up *our* banners; the LORD fulfill all thy petitions. Now know I that the LORD saveth (3467) his anointed; he will hear him from his holy heaven with the saving (3468) strength of his right hand. PSALMS 20:5-6

Salvation (3444) pronounced yesh-oo'-aw; fem. pass. part. of 3467; something saved, i.e. (abstr.) deliverance; hence aid, victory, prosperity:- deliverance, health, help (-ing), salvation, save, saving (health), welfare.

deliverance (Dictionary) the act of giving up or surrendering; giving into another's possession or keeping; to give forth in words; utter or pronounce; to deliver a verdict; setting free; disburden (oneself) of thoughts, opinions, etc.; Obsolete: to make known, assert; Obsolete or Archaic: agile, active, quick.

prosperity (Dictionary) flourishing or thriving condition; good fortune; success.

fortune (Dictionary) position in life as determined by wealth.

success (Dictionary) favorable or prosperous termination of attempts or endeavors; gaining of wealth, position, or the like; Obsolete: outcome.

welfare (Dictionary) state of faring well; well-being; prosperity; success; happiness; weal.

happiness (2) (Dictionary) good fortune, pleasure, content or gladness.

weal (1) (Dictionary) Archaic: well-being, prosperity , or happiness.

(3467) pronounced yaw-shah'; a prim. root; prop. to be open, wide or free, i.e. (by impl.) to be safe; causat. to free or succor: - x at all, avenging, defend, deliver (-er), help, preserve, rescue, be safe, bring (having) salvation, save (-iour), get victory.

succor (Dictionary) help, relief, aid, assistance in difficulty, need, or distress.

salvation (Dictionary) act of saving or delivering; a source, cause, or means of deliverance; deliverance from the power of penalty and sin; redemption.

sin (Dictionary) transgression of divine law; an act regarded as such transgression, or any violation, especially a willful or deliberate one of some religious or moral principle; to offend against a principle, standard, etc.

transgression (Dictionary) violation of a law, command, etc.; sin.

redemption (Dictionary) deliverance; rescue; repurchase, as of something sold; recovery by payment, as of something pledged.

Savior (Dictionary) one who saves, rescues, or delivers: the savior of the country; (cap.) a title of God, especially of Christ (commonly spelled Saviour).

Salvation (3468) pronounced yeh'-shah; from 3467; liberty, deliverance, prosperity, safety, salvation, saving.

liberty (Dictionary) freedom from arbitrary or despotic government or, often, from other rule or law than that of a self-governing community; freedom from external or foreign rule; freedom from control, interference, obligation, restriction, hampering conditions, etc.; power or right of doing, thinking, speaking, etc., according to choice.

deliverance (Dictionary) the act of giving up or surrendering; giving into another's possession or keeping; to give forth in words; utter or pronounce; to deliver a verdict; setting free; disburden (oneself) of thoughts, opinions, etc.; Obsolete: to make known, assert; Obsolete or Archaic: agile, active, quick.

prosperity (Dictionary) flourishing or thriving condition; good fortune; success.

fortune (Dictionary) position in life as determined by wealth.

success (Dictionary) favorable or prosperous termination of attempts or endeavors; gaining of wealth, position, or the like; Obsolete: outcome.

O LORD, the king rejoices in Your strength; how greatly he exults in Your victory! TEHILLIM 21:2 (PSALMS 21:1)

The king shall joy in thy strength, O LORD; and in thy salvation (3444) how greatly shall he rejoice! PSALMS 21:1

Salvation (3444) pronounced yesh-oo'-aw; fem. pass. part. of 3467; something saved, i.e. (abstr.) deliverance; hence aid, victory, prosperity:- deliverance, health, help (-ing), salvation, save, saving (health), welfare.

deliverance (Dictionary) the act of giving up or surrendering; giving into another's possession or keeping; to give forth in words; utter or pronounce; to deliver a verdict; setting free; disburden (oneself) of thoughts, opinions, etc.; Obsolete: to make known, assert; Obsolete or Archaic: agile, active, quick.

prosperity (Dictionary) flourishing or thriving condition; good fortune; success.

fortune (Dictionary) position in life as determined by wealth.

success (Dictionary) favorable or prosperous termination of attempts or endeavors; gaining of wealth, position, or the like; Obsolete: outcome.

welfare (Dictionary) state of faring well; well-being; prosperity; success; happiness; weal.

happiness (2) (Dictionary) good fortune, pleasure, content or gladness.

weal (1) Dictionary) Archaic: well-being, prosperity , or happiness.

(3467) pronounced yaw-shah'; a prim. root; prop. to be open, wide or free, i.e. (by impl.) to be safe; causat. to free or succor: - x at all, avenging, defend, deliver (-er), help, preserve, rescue, be safe, bring (having) salvation, save (-iour), get victory.

succor (Dictionary) help, relief, aid, assistance in difficulty, need, or distress.

salvation (Dictionary) act of saving or delivering; a source, cause, or means of deliverance; deliverance from the power of penalty and sin; redemption.

sin (Dictionary) transgression of divine law; an act regarded as such transgression, or any violation, especially a willful or deliberate one of some religious or moral principle; to offend against a principle, standard, etc.

transgression (Dictionary) violation of a law, command, etc.; sin.

redemption (Dictionary) deliverance; rescue; repurchase, as of something sold; recovery by payment, as of something pledged.

Savior (Dictionary) one who saves, rescues, or delivers: the savior of the country; (cap.) a title of God, especially of Christ (commonly spelled Saviour).

Great is his glory through Your victory; You have endowed him with splendor and majesty.
TEHILLIM 21:6 (PSALMS 21:5)

His glory *is* great in thy salvation (3444); honour and majesty hast thou laid upon him. PSALMS 21:5

Salvation (3444) pronounced yesh-oo'-aw; fem. pass. part. of 3467; something saved, i.e. (abstr.) deliverance; hence aid, victory, prosperity:- deliverance, health, help (-ing), salvation, save, saving (health), welfare.

deliverance (Dictionary) the act of giving up or surrendering; giving into another's possession or keeping; to give forth in words; utter or pronounce; to deliver a verdict; setting free; disburden (oneself) of thoughts, opinions, etc.; Obsolete: to make known, assert; Obsolete or Archaic: agile, active, quick.

prosperity (Dictionary) flourishing or thriving condition; good fortune; success.

fortune (Dictionary) position in life as determined by wealth.

success (Dictionary) favorable or prosperous termination of attempts or endeavors; gaining of wealth, position, or the like; Obsolete: outcome.

welfare (Dictionary) state of faring well; well-being; prosperity; success; happiness; weal.

happiness (2) (Dictionary) good fortune, pleasure, content or gladness.

weal (1) (Dictionary) Archaic: well-being, prosperity , or happiness.

(3467) pronounced yaw-shah'; a prim. root; prop. to be open, wide or free, i.e. (by impl.) to be safe; causat. to free or succor: - x at all, avenging, defend, deliver (-er), help, preserve, rescue, be safe, bring (having) salvation, save (-iour), get victory.

succor (Dictionary) help, relief, aid, assistance in difficulty, need, or distress.

salvation (Dictionary) act of saving or delivering; a source, cause, or means of deliverance; deliverance from the power of penalty and sin; redemption.

sin (Dictionary) transgression of divine law; an act regarded as such transgression, or any violation, especially a willful or deliberate one of some religious or moral principle; to offend against a principle, standard, etc.

transgression (Dictionary) violation of a law, command, etc.; sin.

redemption (Dictionary) deliverance; rescue; repurchase, as of something sold; recovery by payment, as of something pledged.

Savior (Dictionary) one who saves, rescues, or delivers: the savior of the country; (cap.) a title of God, especially of Christ (commonly spelled Saviour).

Who may ascend the mountain of the LORD? Who may stand in His holy place? He who has clean hands and a pure heart, who has not taken a false oath by My life or sworn deceitfully. He shall carry away a blessing from the LORD, a just reward from God, his deliverer. Such is the circle of those who turn to Him, Jacob, who seek Your presence. TEHILLIM 24:3-6 (PSALMS 24:3-6)

My life: Ancient versions and some mss. read "His" (TANAKH footnote)

such is the circle: Lit. "generation" (TANAKH footnote)

Who shall ascend into the hill of the LORD? Or who shall stand in his holy place? He that hath clean hands and a pure heart who hath not lifted up his soul unto vanity nor sworn deceitfully. He shall receive the blessing from the LORD, and righteousness from the God of his salvation (3468). This is the generation of them that seek him, that seek thy face, O Jacob, Selah. PSALMS 24:3-6

Salvation (3468) pronounced yeh'-shah; from 3467; liberty, deliverance, prosperity, safety, salvation, saving.

liberty (Dictionary) freedom from arbitrary or despotic government or, often, from other rule or law than that of a self-governing community; freedom from external or foreign rule; freedom from control, interference, obligation, restriction, hampering conditions, etc.; power or right of doing, thinking, speaking, etc., according to choice.

deliverance (Dictionary) the act of giving up or surrendering; giving into another's possession or keeping; to give forth in words; utter or pronounce; to deliver a verdict; setting free; disburden (oneself) of thoughts, opinions, etc.; Obsolete: to make known, assert; Obsolete or Archaic: agile, active, quick.

prosperity (Dictionary) flourishing or thriving condition; good fortune; success.

fortune (Dictionary) position in life as determined by wealth.

success (Dictionary) favorable or prosperous termination of attempts or endeavors; gaining of wealth, position, or the like; Obsolete: outcome.

(3467) pronounced yaw-shah'; a prim. root; prop. to be open, wide or free, i.e. (by impl.) to be safe; causat. to free or succor: - x at all, avenging, defend, deliver (-er), help, preserve, rescue, be safe, bring (having) salvation, save (-iour), get victory.

succor (Dictionary) help, relief, aid, assistance in difficulty, need, or distress.

salvation (Dictionary) act of saving or delivering; a source, cause, or means of deliverance; deliverance from the power of penalty and sin; redemption.

sin (Dictionary) transgression of divine law; an act regarded as such transgression, or any violation, especially a willful or deliberate one of some religious or moral principle; to offend against a principle, standard, etc.

transgression (Dictionary) violation of a law, command, etc.; sin.

redemption (Dictionary) deliverance; rescue; repurchase, as of something sold; recovery by payment, as of something pledged.

Savior (Dictionary) one who saves, rescues, or delivers: the savior of the country; (cap.) a title of God, especially of Christ (commonly spelled Saviour).

Let me know Your paths, O LORD; teach me Your ways; guide me in Your true way and teach me; for You are God, my deliverer; it is You I look to at all times. TEHILLIM 25:4-5 (PSALMS 25:4-5)

Show me thy ways, O LORD; teach me thy paths. Lead me in thy truth and teach me: for thou *art* the God of my salvation (3468); on thee do I wait all the day. PSALMS 25:4-5

Salvation (3468) pronounced yeh'-shah; from 3467; liberty, deliverance, prosperity, safety, salvation, saving.

liberty (Dictionary) freedom from arbitrary or despotic government or, often, from other rule or law than that of a self-governing community; freedom from external or foreign rule; freedom from control, interference, obligation, restriction, hampering conditions, etc.; power or right of doing, thinking, speaking, etc., according to choice.

deliverance (Dictionary) the act of giving up or surrendering; giving into another's possession or keeping; to give forth in words; utter or pronounce; to deliver a verdict; setting free; disburden (oneself) of thoughts, opinions, etc.; Obsolete: to make known, assert; Obsolete or Archaic: agile, active, quick.

prosperity (Dictionary) flourishing or thriving condition; good fortune; success.

fortune (Dictionary) position in life as determined by wealth.

success (Dictionary) favorable or prosperous termination of attempts or endeavors; gaining of wealth, position, or the like; Obsolete: outcome.

(3467) pronounced yaw-shah'; a prim. root; prop. to be open, wide or free, i.e. (by impl.) to be safe; causat. to free or succor: - x at all, avenging, defend, deliver (-er), help, preserve, rescue, be safe, bring (having) salvation, save (-iour), get victory.

succor (Dictionary) help, relief, aid, assistance in difficulty, need, or distress.

salvation (Dictionary) act of saving or delivering; a source, cause, or means of deliverance; deliverance from the power of penalty and sin; redemption.

sin (Dictionary) transgression of divine law; an act regarded as such transgression, or any violation, especially a willful or deliberate one of some religious or moral principle; to offend against a principle, standard, etc.

transgression (Dictionary) violation of a law, command, etc.; sin.

redemption (Dictionary) deliverance; rescue; repurchase, as of something sold; recovery by payment, as of something pledged.

Savior (Dictionary) one who saves, rescues, or delivers: the savior of the country; (cap.) a title of God, especially of Christ (commonly spelled Saviour).

The LORD is my light and my help; whom should I fear? The LORD is the stronghold of my life, whom should I dread? TEHILLIM 27:1 (PSALMS 27:1)

The LORD is my light and my salvation (3468); whom shall I fear? The LORD is the strength of my life; of whom shall I be afraid? PSALMS 27:1

Salvation (3468) pronounced yeh'-shah; from 3467; liberty, deliverance, prosperity, safety, salvation, saving.

liberty (Dictionary) freedom from arbitrary or despotic government or, often, from other rule or law than that of a self-governing community; freedom from external or foreign rule; freedom from control, interference, obligation, restriction, hampering conditions, etc.; power or right of doing, thinking, speaking, etc., according to choice.

deliverance (Dictionary) the act of giving up or surrendering; giving into another's possession or keeping; to give forth in words; utter or pronounce; to deliver a verdict; setting free; disburden (oneself) of thoughts, opinions, etc.; Obsolete: to make known, assert; Obsolete or Archaic: agile, active, quick.

prosperity (Dictionary) flourishing or thriving condition; good fortune; success.

fortune (Dictionary) position in life as determined by wealth.

success (Dictionary) favorable or prosperous termination of attempts or endeavors; gaining of wealth, position, or the like; Obsolete: outcome.

(3467) pronounced yaw-shah'; a prim. root; prop. to be open, wide or free, i.e. (by impl.) to be safe; causat. to free or succor: - x at all, avenging, defend, deliver (-er), help, preserve, rescue, be safe, bring (having) salvation, save (-iour), get victory.

succor (Dictionary) help, relief, aid, assistance in difficulty, need, or distress.

salvation (Dictionary) act of saving or delivering; a source, cause, or means of deliverance; deliverance from the power of penalty and sin; redemption.

sin (Dictionary) transgression of divine law; an act regarded as such transgression, or any violation, especially a willful or deliberate one of some religious or moral principle; to offend against a principle, standard, etc.

transgression (Dictionary) violation of a law, command, etc.; sin.

redemption (Dictionary) deliverance; rescue; repurchase, as of something sold; recovery by payment, as of something pledged.

Savior (Dictionary) one who saves, rescues, or delivers: the savior of the country; (cap.) a title of God, especially of Christ (commonly spelled Saviour).

Do not hide Your face from me; do not thrust aside Your servant in anger; You have ever been my help. Do not forsake me, do not abandon me, O God my deliverer. TEHILLIM 27:9 (PSALMS 27:9)

Hide not thy face *far* from me; put not thy servant away in anger; thou hast been my help; leave me not, neither forsake me, O God of my salvation (3468). PSALMS 27:9

Salvation (3468) pronounced yeh'-shah; from 3467; liberty, deliverance, prosperity, safety, salvation, saving.

liberty (Dictionary) freedom from arbitrary or despotic government or, often, from other rule or law than that of a self-governing community; freedom from external or foreign rule; freedom from control, interference, obligation, restriction, hampering conditions, etc.; power or right of doing, thinking, speaking, etc., according to choice.

deliverance (Dictionary) the act of giving up or surrendering; giving into another's possession or keeping; to give forth in words; utter or pronounce; to deliver a verdict; setting free; disburden (oneself) of thoughts, opinions, etc.; Obsolete: to make known, assert; Obsolete or Archaic: agile, active, quick.

prosperity (Dictionary) flourishing or thriving condition; good fortune; success.

fortune (Dictionary) position in life as determined by wealth.

success (Dictionary) favorable or prosperous termination of attempts or endeavors; gaining of wealth, position, or the like; Obsolete: outcome.

(3467) pronounced yaw-shah'; a prim. root; prop. to be open, wide or free, i.e. (by impl.) to be safe; causat. to free or succor: - x at all, avenging, defend, deliver (-er), help, preserve, rescue, be safe, bring (having) salvation, save (-iour), get victory.

succor (Dictionary) help, relief, aid, assistance in difficulty, need, or distress.

salvation (Dictionary) act of saving or delivering; a source, cause, or means of deliverance; deliverance from the power of penalty and sin; redemption.

sin (Dictionary) transgression of divine law; an act regarded as such transgression, or any violation, especially a willful or deliberate one of some religious or moral principle; to offend against a principle, standard, etc.

transgression (Dictionary) violation of a law, command, etc.; sin.

redemption (Dictionary) deliverance; rescue; repurchase, as of something sold; recovery by payment, as of something pledged.

Savior (Dictionary) one who saves, rescues, or delivers: the savior of the country; (cap.) a title of God, especially of Christ (commonly spelled Saviour).

O LORD, strive with my adversaries, give battle to my foes, take up shield and buckler, and come to my defense; ready the spear and javelin against my pursuers; tell me, "I am your deliverance."
TEHILLIM 35:1-3 (PSALMS 35:1-3)

Plead *my cause*, O LORD, with them that strive with me; fight against them that fight against me. Take hold of shield and buckler and stand up for mine help. Draw out also the spear, and stop the *way* against them that persecute me; say unto my soul, I *am* thy salvation (3444). PSALMS 35:1-3

Salvation (3444) pronounced yesh-oo'-aw; fem. pass. part. of 3467; something saved, i.e. (abstr.) deliverance; hence aid, victory, prosperity:- deliverance, health, help (-ing), salvation, save, saving (health), welfare.

deliverance (Dictionary) the act of giving up or surrendering; giving into another's possession or keeping; to give forth in words; utter or pronounce; to deliver a verdict; setting free; disburden (oneself) of thoughts, opinions, etc.; Obsolete: to make known, assert; Obsolete or Archaic: agile, active, quick.

prosperity (Dictionary) flourishing or thriving condition; good fortune; success.

fortune (Dictionary) position in life as determined by wealth.

success (Dictionary) favorable or prosperous termination of attempts or endeavors; gaining of wealth, position, or the like; Obsolete: outcome.

welfare (Dictionary) state of faring well; well-being; prosperity; success; happiness; weal.

happiness (2) (Dictionary) good fortune, pleasure, content or gladness.

weal (1) (Dictionary) Archaic: well-being, prosperity , or happiness.

(3467) pronounced yaw-shah'; a prim. root; prop. to be open, wide or free, i.e. (by impl.) to be safe; causat. to free or succor: - x at all, avenging, defend, deliver (-er), help, preserve, rescue, be safe, bring (having) salvation, save (-iour), get victory.

succor (Dictionary) help, relief, aid, assistance in difficulty, need, or distress.

salvation (Dictionary) act of saving or delivering; a source, cause, or means of deliverance; deliverance from the power of penalty and sin; redemption.

sin (Dictionary) transgression of divine law; an act regarded as such transgression, or any violation, especially a willful or deliberate one of some religious or moral principle; to offend against a principle, standard, etc.

transgression (Dictionary) violation of a law, command, etc.; sin.

redemption (Dictionary) deliverance; rescue; repurchase, as of something sold; recovery by payment, as of something pledged.

Savior (Dictionary) one who saves, rescues, or delivers: the savior of the country; (cap.) a title of God, especially of Christ (commonly spelled Saviour).

Then shall I exult in the LORD, rejoice in His deliverance. TEHILLIM 35:9 (PSALMS 35:9)

And my soul shall be joyful in the LORD; it shall rejoice in his salvation (3444). PSALMS 35:9

Salvation (3444) pronounced yesh-oo'-aw; fem. pass. part. of 3467; something saved, i.e. (abstr.) deliverance; hence aid, victory, prosperity:- deliverance, health, help (-ing), salvation, save, saving (health), welfare.

deliverance (Dictionary) the act of giving up or surrendering; giving into another's possession or keeping; to give forth in words; utter or pronounce; to deliver a verdict; setting free; disburden (oneself) of thoughts, opinions, etc.; Obsolete: to make known, assert; Obsolete or Archaic: agile, active, quick.

prosperity (Dictionary) flourishing or thriving condition; good fortune; success.

fortune (Dictionary) position in life as determined by wealth.

success (Dictionary) favorable or prosperous termination of attempts or endeavors; gaining of wealth, position, or the like; Obsolete: outcome.

welfare (Dictionary) state of faring well; well-being; prosperity; success; happiness; weal.

happiness (2) (Dictionary) good fortune, pleasure, content or gladness.

weal (1) (Dictionary) Archaic: well-being, prosperity , or happiness.

(3467) pronounced yaw-shah'; a prim. root; prop. to be open, wide or free, i.e. (by impl.) to be safe; causat. to free or succor: - x at all, avenging, defend, deliver (-er), help, preserve, rescue, be safe, bring (having) salvation, save (-iour), get victory.

succor (Dictionary) help, relief, aid, assistance in difficulty, need, or distress.

salvation (Dictionary) act of saving or delivering; a source, cause, or means of deliverance; deliverance from the power of penalty and sin; redemption.

sin (Dictionary) transgression of divine law; an act regarded as such transgression, or any violation, especially a willful or deliberate one of some religious or moral principle; to offend against a principle, standard, etc.

transgression (Dictionary) violation of a law, command, etc.; sin.

redemption (Dictionary) deliverance; rescue; repurchase, as of something sold; recovery by payment, as of something pledged.

Savior (Dictionary) one who saves, rescues, or delivers: the savior of the country; (cap.) a title of God, especially of Christ (commonly spelled Saviour).

The deliverance of the righteous comes from the LORD, their stronghold in times of trouble.
TEHILLIM 37:39 (PSALMS 37:39)

But the salvation (8668) of the righteous *is* of the LORD; *he is* their strength in the time of trouble.
PSALMS 37:39

Salvation (8668) pronounced tesh-oo-aw'; from 7768 in the sense of 3467; rescue (lit. or fig., pers., national, or spir.):- deliverance, help, safety, salvation, victory.

deliverance (Dictionary) the act of giving up or surrendering; giving into another's possession or keeping; to give forth in words; utter or pronounce; to deliver a verdict; setting free; disburden (oneself) of thoughts, opinions, etc.; Obsolete: to make known, assert; Obsolete or Archaic: agile, active, quick.

salvation (Dictionary) act of saving or delivering; a source, cause, or means of deliverance; deliverance from the power of penalty and sin; redemption.

sin (Dictionary) transgression of divine law; an act regarded as such transgression, or any violation, especially a willful or deliberate one of some religious or moral principle; to offend against a principle, standard, etc.

transgression (Dictionary) violation of a law, command, etc.; sin.

redemption (Dictionary) deliverance; rescue; repurchase, as of something sold; recovery by payment, as of something pledged.

(7768) pronounced shaw-vah'; a prim. root; prop. to be free; but used only causat. and reflex. to halloo (for help, i.e. freedom from some trouble):- cry (aloud, out), shout.

halloo (Dictionary) an exclamation used to attract attention, to incite the dogs in hunting, etc.; to call with a loud voice: shout, cry, as after dogs; to incite or chase with shouts and cries of "halloo".

(3467) pronounced yaw-shah'; a prim. root; prop. to be open, wide or free, i.e. (by impl.) to be safe; causat. to free or succor: - x at all, avenging, defend, deliver (-er), help, preserve, rescue, be safe, bring (having) salvation, save (-iour), get victory.

succor (Dictionary) help, relief, aid, assistance in difficulty, need, or distress.

salvation (Dictionary) act of saving or delivering; a source, cause, or means of deliverance; deliverance from the power of penalty and sin; redemption.

sin (Dictionary) transgression of divine law; an act regarded as such transgression, or any violation, especially a willful or deliberate one of some religious or moral principle; to offend against a principle, standard, etc.

transgression (Dictionary) violation of a law, command, etc.; sin.

redemption (Dictionary) deliverance; rescue; repurchase, as of something sold; recovery by payment, as of something pledged.

Savior Dictionary) one who saves, rescues, or delivers: the savior of the country; (cap.) a title of God, especially of Christ (commonly spelled Saviour).

Do not abandon me, O LORD; my God, be not far from me; hasten to my aid, O LORD, my deliverance. TEHILLIM 38:22 (PSALMS 38:22)

Make haste to help me, O LORD my salvation (8668). PSALMS 38:22

Salvation (8668) pronounced tesh-oo-aw'; from 7768 in the sense of 3467; rescue (lit. or fig., pers., national, or spir.):- deliverance, help, safety, salvation, victory.

deliverance (Dictionary) the act of giving up or surrendering; giving into another's possession or keeping; to give forth in words; utter or pronounce; to deliver a verdict; setting free; disburden (oneself) of thoughts, opinions, etc.; Obsolete: to make known, assert; Obsolete or Archaic: agile, active, quick.

salvation (Dictionary) act of saving or delivering; a source, cause, or means of deliverance; deliverance from the power of penalty and sin; redemption.

sin (Dictionary) transgression of divine law; an act regarded as such transgression, or any violation, especially a willful or deliberate one of some religious or moral principle; to offend against a principle, standard, etc.

transgression (Dictionary) violation of a law, command, etc.; sin.

redemption (Dictionary) deliverance; rescue; repurchase, as of something sold; recovery by payment, as of something pledged.

(7768) pronounced shaw-vah'; a prim. root; prop. to be free; but used only causat. and reflex. to halloo (for help, i.e. freedom from some trouble):- cry (aloud, out), shout.

halloo (Dictionary) an exclamation used to attract attention, to incite the dogs in hunting, etc.; to call with a loud voice: shout, cry, as after dogs; to incite or chase with shouts and cries of "halloo".

(3467) pronounced yaw-shah'; a prim. root; prop. to be open, wide or free, i.e. (by impl.) to be safe; causat. to free or succor: - x at all, avenging, defend, deliver (-er), help, preserve, rescue, be safe, bring (having) salvation, save (-iour), get victory.

succor (Dictionary) help, relief, aid, assistance in difficulty, need, or distress.

salvation (Dictionary) act of saving or delivering; a source, cause, or means of deliverance; deliverance from the power of penalty and sin; redemption.

sin (Dictionary) transgression of divine law; an act regarded as such transgression, or any violation, especially a willful or deliberate one of some religious or moral principle; to offend against a principle, standard, etc.

transgression (Dictionary) violation of a law, command, etc.; sin.

redemption (Dictionary) deliverance; rescue; repurchase, as of something sold; recovery by payment, as of something pledged.

Savior (Dictionary) one who saves, rescues, or delivers: the savior of the country; (cap.) a title of God, especially of Christ (commonly spelled Saviour).

I proclaimed [Your} righteousness in a great congregation; see, I did not withhold my words; O Lord, You must know it. TEHILLIM 40:10 (PSALMS 40:10)

I have not hid thy righteousness within my heart; I have declared thy faithfulness and thy salvation (8668); I have not concealed thy lovingkindness and thy truth from the great congregation.
PSALMS 40:10

Salvation (8668) pronounced tesh-oo-aw'; from 7768 in the sense of 3467; rescue (lit. or fig., pers., national, or spir.):- deliverance, help, safety, salvation, victory.

deliverance (Dictionary) the act of giving up or surrendering; giving into another's possession or keeping; to give forth in words; utter or pronounce; to deliver a verdict; setting free; disburden (oneself) of thoughts, opinions, etc.; Obsolete: to make known, assert; Obsolete or Archaic: agile, active, quick.

salvation (Dictionary) act of saving or delivering; a source, cause, or means of deliverance; deliverance from the power of penalty and sin; redemption.

sin (Dictionary) transgression of divine law; an act regarded as such transgression, or any violation, especially a willful or deliberate one of some religious or moral principle; to offend against a principle, standard, etc.

transgression (Dictionary) violation of a law, command, etc.; sin.

redemption (Dictionary) deliverance; rescue; repurchase, as of something sold; recovery by payment, as of something pledged.

(7768) pronounced shaw-vah'; a prim. root; prop. to be free; but used only causat. and reflex. to halloo (for help, i.e. freedom from some trouble):- cry (aloud, out), shout.

halloo (Dictionary) an exclamation used to attract attention, to incite the dogs in hunting, etc.; to call with a loud voice: shout, cry, as after dogs; to incite or chase with shouts and cries of "halloo".

(3467) pronounced yaw-shah'; a prim. root; prop. to be open, wide or free, i.e. (by impl.) to be safe; causat. to free or succor: - x at all, avenging, defend, deliver (-er), help, preserve, rescue, be safe, bring (having) salvation, save (-iour), get victory.

succor (Dictionary) help, relief, aid, assistance in difficulty, need, or distress.

salvation (Dictionary) act of saving or delivering; a source, cause, or means of deliverance; deliverance from the power of penalty and sin; redemption.

sin (Dictionary) transgression of divine law; an act regarded as such transgression, or any violation, especially a willful or deliberate one of some religious or moral principle; to offend against a principle, standard, etc.

transgression (Dictionary) violation of a law, command, etc.; sin.

redemption (Dictionary) deliverance; rescue; repurchase, as of something sold; recovery by payment, as of something pledged.

Savior (Dictionary) one who saves, rescues, or delivers: the savior of the country; (cap.) a title of God, especially of Christ (commonly spelled Saviour).

But let all who seek You be glad and rejoice in You: let those who are eager for Your deliverance always say, "Extolled be the LORD!" But I am poor and needy; may the LORD devise [deliverance] for me. You are my help and my rescuer; my God, do not delay. TEHILLIM 40:17-18 (PSALMS 40:16-17)

Let all those that seek thee rejoice and be glad in thee: let such as love thy salvation (8668) say continually, The LORD be magnified. But I *am* poor and needy; *yet* the LORD thinketh upon me; thou *art* my help and my deliverer; make no tarrying, O my God. PSALMS 40:16-17

Salvation (8668) pronounced tesh-oo-aw'; from 7768 in the sense of 3467; rescue (lit. or fig., pers., national, or spir.):- deliverance, help, safety, salvation, victory.

> deliverance (Dictionary) the act of giving up or surrendering; giving into another's possession or keeping; to give forth in words; utter or pronounce; to deliver a verdict; setting free; disburden (oneself) of thoughts, opinions, etc.; Obsolete: to make known, assert; Obsolete or Archaic: agile, active, quick.
>
> salvation Dictionary) act of saving or delivering; a source, cause, or means of deliverance; deliverance from the power of penalty and sin; redemption.
>
> sin (Dictionary) transgression of divine law; an act regarded as such transgression, or any violation, especially a willful or deliberate one of some religious or moral principle; to offend against a principle, standard, etc.
>
> transgression (Dictionary) violation of a law, command, etc.; sin.
>
> redemption (Dictionary) deliverance; rescue; repurchase, as of something sold; recovery by payment, as of something pledged.

(7768) pronounced shaw-vah'; a prim. root; prop. to be free; but used only causat. and reflex. to halloo (for help, i.e. freedom from some trouble):- cry (aloud, out), shout.

> halloo (Dictionary) an exclamation used to attract attention, to incite the dogs in hunting, etc.; to call with a loud voice: shout, cry, as after dogs; to incite or chase with shouts and cries of "halloo".

(3467) pronounced yaw-shah'; a prim. root; prop. to be open, wide or free, i.e. (by impl.) to be safe; causat. to free or succor: - x at all, avenging, defend, deliver (-er), help, preserve, rescue, be safe, bring (having) salvation, save (-iour), get victory.

> succor (Dictionary) help, relief, aid, assistance in difficulty, need, or distress.
>
> salvation (Dictionary) act of saving or delivering; a source, cause, or means of deliverance; deliverance from the power of penalty and sin; redemption.
>
> sin (Dictionary) transgression of divine law; an act regarded as such transgression, or any violation, especially a willful or deliberate one of some religious or moral principle; to offend against a principle, standard, etc.
>
> transgression (Dictionary) violation of a law, command, etc.; sin.
>
> redemption (Dictionary) deliverance; rescue; repurchase, as of something sold; recovery by payment, as of something pledged.
>
> Savior (Dictionary) one who saves, rescues, or delivers: the savior of the country; (cap.) a title of God, especially of Christ (commonly spelled Saviour).

He who sacrifices a thank offering honors Me, and to him who improves his way I will show the salvation of God. TEHILLIM 50:23 (PSALMS 50:23)

Whoso offereth praise glorifieth me; and to him that ordereth *his* conversation *aright* will I show the salvation (3468) of God. PSALMS 50:23

Salvation (3468) pronounced yeh'-shah; from 3467; liberty, deliverance, prosperity, safety, salvation, saving.

liberty (Dictionary) freedom from arbitrary or despotic government or, often, from other rule or law than that of a self-governing community; freedom from external or foreign rule; freedom from control, interference, obligation, restriction, hampering conditions, etc.; power or right of doing, thinking, speaking, etc., according to choice.

deliverance (Dictionary) the act of giving up or surrendering; giving into another's possession or keeping; to give forth in words; utter or pronounce; to deliver a verdict; setting free; disburden (oneself) of thoughts, opinions, etc.; Obsolete: to make known, assert; Obsolete or Archaic: agile, active, quick.

prosperity (Dictionary) flourishing or thriving condition; good fortune; success.

fortune (Dictionary) position in life as determined by wealth.

success (Dictionary) favorable or prosperous termination of attempts or endeavors; gaining of wealth, position, or the like; Obsolete: outcome.

(3467) pronounced yaw-shah'; a prim. root; prop. to be open, wide or free, i.e. (by impl.) to be safe; causat. to free or succor: - x at all, avenging, defend, deliver (-er), help, preserve, rescue, be safe, bring (having) salvation, save (-iour), get victory.

succor (Dictionary) help, relief, aid, assistance in difficulty, need, or distress.

salvation (Dictionary) act of saving or delivering; a source, cause, or means of deliverance; deliverance from the power of penalty and sin; redemption.

sin (Dictionary) transgression of divine law; an act regarded as such transgression, or any violation, especially a willful or deliberate one of some religious or moral principle; to offend against a principle, standard, etc.

transgression (Dictionary) violation of a law, command, etc.; sin.

redemption (Dictionary) deliverance; rescue; repurchase, as of something sold; recovery by payment, as of something pledged.

Savior (Dictionary) one who saves, rescues, or delivers: the savior of the country; (cap.) a title of God, especially of Christ (commonly spelled Saviour).

SALVATION

Fashion a pure heart for me, O God; create in me a steadfast spirit. Do not cast me out of Your presence, or take Your holy spirit away from me. Let me again rejoice in Your help; let a vigorous spirit sustain me. I will teach transgressors Your ways, that sinners may return to You. TEHILLIM 51:12-15 (PSALMS 51:12-15)

Restore unto me the joy of thy salvation (3468), and uphold me *with thy* free Spirit. *Then* will I teach transgressors thy ways; and sinners shall be converted unto thee. Deliver me from blood guiltiness, O God, thou God of my salvation (8668); *and* my tongue shall sing aloud of thy righteousness. O LORD, open thou my lips; and my mouth shall show forth thy praise. PSALMS 51:12-15

Salvation (3468) pronounced yeh'-shah; from 3467; liberty, deliverance, prosperity, safety, salvation, saving.

liberty (Dictionary) freedom from arbitrary or despotic government or, often, from other rule or law than that of a self-governing community; freedom from external or foreign rule; freedom from control, interference, obligation, restriction, hampering conditions, etc.; power or right of doing, thinking, speaking, etc., according to choice.

deliverance (Dictionary) the act of giving up or surrendering; giving into another's possession or keeping; to give forth in words; utter or pronounce; to deliver a verdict; setting free; disburden (oneself) of thoughts, opinions, etc.; Obsolete: to make known, assert; Obsolete or Archaic: agile, active, quick.

prosperity (Dictionary) flourishing or thriving condition; good fortune; success.

fortune (Dictionary) position in life as determined by wealth.

success (Dictionary) favorable or prosperous termination of attempts or endeavors; gaining of wealth, position, or the like; Obsolete: outcome.

(3467) pronounced yaw-shah'; a prim. root; prop. to be open, wide or free, i.e. (by impl.) to be safe; causat. to free or succor: - x at all, avenging, defend, deliver (-er), help, preserve, rescue, be safe, bring (having) salvation, save (-iour), get victory.

succor (Dictionary) help, relief, aid, assistance in difficulty, need, or distress.

salvation (Dictionary) act of saving or delivering; a source, cause, or means of deliverance; deliverance from the power of penalty and sin; redemption.

sin (Dictionary) transgression of divine law; an act regarded as such transgression, or any violation, especially a willful or deliberate one of some religious or moral principle; to offend against a principle, standard, etc.

transgression (Dictionary) violation of a law, command, etc.; sin.

redemption (Dictionary) deliverance; rescue; repurchase, as of something sold; recovery by payment, as of something pledged.

Savior (Dictionary) one who saves, rescues, or delivers: the savior of the country; (cap.) a title of God, especially of Christ (commonly spelled Saviour).

Salvation (8668) pronounced tesh-oo-aw'; from 7768 in the sense of 3467; rescue (lit. or fig., pers., national, or spir.):- deliverance, help, safety, salvation, victory.

deliverance (Dictionary) the act of giving up or surrendering; giving into another's possession or keeping; to give forth in words; utter or pronounce; to deliver a verdict; setting free; disburden (oneself) of thoughts, opinions, etc.; Obsolete: to make known, assert; Obsolete or Archaic: agile, active, quick.

salvation (Dictionary) act of saving or delivering; a source, cause, or means of deliverance; deliverance from the power of penalty and sin; redemption.

sin (Dictionary) transgression of divine law; an act regarded as such transgression, or any violation, especially a willful or deliberate one of some religious or moral principle; to offend against a principle, standard, etc.

transgression (Dictionary) violation of a law, command, etc.; sin.

redemption (Dictionary) deliverance; rescue; repurchase, as of something sold; recovery by payment, as of something pledged.

(7768) pronounced shaw-vah'; a prim. root; prop. to be free; but used only causat. and reflex. to halloo (for help, i.e. freedom from some trouble):- cry (aloud, out), shout.

halloo (Dictionary) an exclamation used to attract attention, to incite the dogs in hunting, etc.; to call with a loud voice: shout, cry, as after dogs; to incite or chase with shouts and cries of "halloo".

O that the deliverance of Israel might come from Zion! When God restores the fortunes of His people, Jacob will exult, Israel will rejoice. TEHILLIM 53:7 (PSALMS 53:6)

O that the salvation (3444) of Israel *were come* out of Zion! When God bringeth back the captivity of His people, Jacob shall rejoice, *and* Israel shall be glad. PSALMS 53:6

Salvation (3444) pronounced yesh-oo'-aw; fem. pass. part. of 3467; something saved, i.e. (abstr.) deliverance; hence aid, victory, prosperity:- deliverance, health, help (-ing), salvation, save, saving (health), welfare.

deliverance (Dictionary) the act of giving up or surrendering; giving into another's possession or keeping; to give forth in words; utter or pronounce; to deliver a verdict;

setting free; disburden (oneself) of thoughts, opinions, etc.; Obsolete: to make known, assert; Obsolete or Archaic: agile, active, quick.

prosperity (Dictionary) flourishing or thriving condition; good fortune; success.

fortune (Dictionary) position in life as determined by wealth.

success (Dictionary) favorable or prosperous termination of attempts or endeavors; gaining of wealth, position, or the like; Obsolete: outcome.

welfare (Dictionary) state of faring well; well-being; prosperity; success; happiness; weal.

happiness (2) (Dictionary) good fortune, pleasure, content or gladness.

weal (1) (Dictionary) Archaic: well-being, prosperity , or happiness.

(3467) pronounced yaw-shah'; a prim. root; prop. to be open, wide or free, i.e. (by impl.) to be safe; causat. to free or succor: - x at all, avenging, defend, deliver (-er), help, preserve, rescue, be safe, bring (having) salvation, save (-iour), get victory.

succor (Dictionary) help, relief, aid, assistance in difficulty, need, or distress.

salvation (Dictionary) act of saving or delivering; a source, cause, or means of deliverance; deliverance from the power of penalty and sin; redemption.

sin (Dictionary) transgression of divine law; an act regarded as such transgression, or any violation, especially a willful or deliberate one of some religious or moral principle; to offend against a principle, standard, etc.

transgression (Dictionary) violation of a law, command, etc.; sin.

redemption (Dictionary) deliverance; rescue; repurchase, as of something sold; recovery by payment, as of something pledged.

Savior (Dictionary) one who saves, rescues, or delivers: the savior of the country; (cap.) a title of God, especially of Christ (commonly spelled Saviour).

Truly my soul waits quietly for God; my deliverance comes from Him. Truly He is my rock and deliverance, my haven; I shall never be shaken. TEHILLIM 62:2-3 (PSALMS 62:1-2)

Truly my soul waiteth upon God; from him *cometh* my salvation (3444). He only is my rock and my salvation (3444): *he is* my defense; I shall not be greatly moved. PSALMS 62:1-2

Salvation (3444) pronounced yesh-oo'-aw; fem. pass. part. of 3467; something saved, i.e. (abstr.) deliverance; hence aid, victory, prosperity:- deliverance, health, help (-ing), salvation, save, saving (health), welfare.

deliverance (Dictionary) the act of giving up or surrendering; giving into another's possession or keeping; to give forth in words; utter or pronounce; to deliver a verdict; setting free; disburden (oneself) of thoughts, opinions, etc.; Obsolete: to make known, assert; Obsolete or Archaic: agile, active, quick.

prosperity (Dictionary) flourishing or thriving condition; good fortune; success.

fortune (Dictionary) position in life as determined by wealth.

success: (Dictionary) favorable or prosperous termination of attempts or endeavors; gaining of wealth, position, or the like; Obsolete: outcome.

welfare (Dictionary) state of faring well; well-being; prosperity; success; happiness; weal.

happiness (2) (Dictionary) good fortune, pleasure, content or gladness.

weal (1) (Dictionary) Archaic: well-being, prosperity , or happiness.

(3467) pronounced yaw-shah'; a prim. root; prop. to be open, wide or free, i.e. (by impl.) to be safe; causat. to free or succor: - x at all, avenging, defend, deliver (-er), help, preserve, rescue, be safe, bring (having) salvation, save (-iour), get victory.

succor (Dictionary) help, relief, aid, assistance in difficulty, need, or distress.

salvation (Dictionary) act of saving or delivering; a source, cause, or means of deliverance; deliverance from the power of penalty and sin; redemption.

sin (Dictionary) transgression of divine law; an act regarded as such transgression, or any violation, especially a willful or deliberate one of some religious or moral principle; to offend against a principle, standard, etc.

transgression (Dictionary) violation of a law, command, etc.; sin.

redemption (Dictionary) deliverance; rescue; repurchase, as of something sold; recovery by payment, as of something pledged.

Savior (Dictionary) one who saves, rescues, or delivers: the savior of the country; (cap.) a title of God, especially of Christ (commonly spelled Saviour).

Truly wait quietly for God, O my soul, for my hope comes from Him. He is my rock and deliverance, my haven; I shall not be shaken; I rely on God, my deliverance and glory; my rock of strength; in God is my refuge. TEHILLIM 62:6-8 (PSALMS 62:6-8)

He only *is* my rock and my salvation (3444); *he is* my defense; I shall not be moved. In God is my salvation (3468) and my glory: the rock of my strength, and my refuge, *is* in God. Trust in him at all times; ye people pour out your heart before him: God is a refuge for us. Selah. PSALMS 62:6-8

Salvation (3444) pronounced yesh-oo'-aw; fem. pass. part. of 3467; something saved, i.e. (abstr.) deliverance; hence aid, victory, prosperity:- deliverance, health, help (-ing), salvation, save, saving (health), welfare.

deliverance (Dictionary) the act of giving up or surrendering; giving into another's possession or keeping; to give forth in words; utter or pronounce; to deliver a verdict; setting free; disburden (oneself) of thoughts, opinions, etc.; Obsolete: to make known, assert; Obsolete or Archaic: agile, active, quick.

prosperity (Dictionary) flourishing or thriving condition; good fortune; success.

fortune (Dictionary) position in life as determined by wealth.

success (Dictionary) favorable or prosperous termination of attempts or endeavors; gaining of wealth, position, or the like; Obsolete: outcome.

welfare (Dictionary) state of faring well; well-being; prosperity; success; happiness; weal.

happiness (2) (Dictionary) good fortune, pleasure, content or gladness.

weal (1) (Dictionary) Archaic: well-being, prosperity , or happiness.

(3467) pronounced yaw-shah'; a prim. root; prop. to be open, wide or free, i.e. (by impl.) to be safe; causat. to free or succor: - x at all, avenging, defend, deliver (-er), help, preserve, rescue, be safe, bring (having) salvation, save (-iour), get victory.

succor (Dictionary) help, relief, aid, assistance in difficulty, need, or distress.

salvation (Dictionary) act of saving or delivering; a source, cause, or means of deliverance; deliverance from the power of penalty and sin; redemption.

sin (Dictionary) transgression of divine law; an act regarded as such transgression, or any violation, especially a willful or deliberate one of some religious or moral principle; to offend against a principle, standard, etc.

transgression (Dictionary) violation of a law, command, etc.; sin.

redemption (Dictionary) deliverance; rescue; repurchase, as of something sold; recovery by payment, as of something pledged.

Savior (Dictionary) one who saves, rescues, or delivers: the savior of the country; (cap.) a title of God, especially of Christ (commonly spelled Saviour).

Salvation (3468) pronounced yeh'-shah; from 3467; liberty, deliverance, prosperity, safety, salvation, saving.

liberty (Dictionary) freedom from arbitrary or despotic government or, often, from other rule or law than that of a self-governing community; freedom from external or foreign rule; freedom from control, interference, obligation, restriction, hampering conditions, etc.; power or right of doing, thinking, speaking, etc., according to choice.

deliverance (Dictionary) the act of giving up or surrendering; giving into another's possession or keeping; to give forth in words; utter or pronounce; to deliver a verdict; setting free; disburden (oneself) of thoughts, opinions, etc.; Obsolete: to make known, assert; Obsolete or Archaic: agile, active, quick.

prosperity (Dictionary) flourishing or thriving condition; good fortune; success.

fortune (Dictionary) position in life as determined by wealth.

success (Dictionary) favorable or prosperous termination of attempts or endeavors; gaining of wealth, position, or the like; Obsolete: outcome.

Happy is the man You choose and bring near to dwell in Your courts; may we be sated with the blessings of Your house, Your holy temple. Answer us with victory through awesome deeds, O God, our deliverer, in whom all the ends of the earth and the distant seas put their trust; TEHILLIM 65:5-6 (PSALMS 65:4-5)

Blessed *is the man whom* thou choosest, and causest to approach *unto thee*, *that* he may dwell in thy courts: we shall be satisfied with the goodness of thy house, *even* of thy holy temple. By terrible things in righteousness wilt thou answer us, O God of our salvation (3468); who *art* the confidence of all the ends of the earth, and of them that are afar off *upon* the sea: PSALMS 65:4-5

Salvation (3468) pronounced yeh'-shah; from 3467; liberty, deliverance, prosperity, safety, salvation, saving.

liberty (Dictionary) freedom from arbitrary or despotic government or, often, from other rule or law than that of a self-governing community; freedom from external or foreign rule; freedom from control, interference, obligation, restriction, hampering conditions, etc.; power or right of doing, thinking, speaking, etc., according to choice.

deliverance (Dictionary) the act of giving up or surrendering; giving into another's possession or keeping; to give forth in words; utter or pronounce; to deliver a verdict; setting free; disburden (oneself) of thoughts, opinions, etc.; Obsolete: to make known, assert; Obsolete or Archaic: agile, active, quick.

prosperity (Dictionary) flourishing or thriving condition; good fortune; success.

fortune (Dictionary) position in life as determined by wealth.

success (Dictionary) favorable or prosperous termination of attempts or endeavors; gaining of wealth, position, or the like; Obsolete: outcome.

(3467) pronounced yaw-shah'; a prim. root; prop. to be open, wide or free, i.e. (by impl.) to be safe; causat. to free or succor: - x at all, avenging, defend, deliver (-er), help, preserve, rescue, be safe, bring (having) salvation, save (-iour), get victory.

succor (Dictionary) help, relief, aid, assistance in difficulty, need, or distress.

salvation (Dictionary) act of saving or delivering; a source, cause, or means of deliverance; deliverance from the power of penalty and sin; redemption.

sin (Dictionary) transgression of divine law; an act regarded as such transgression, or any violation, especially a willful or deliberate one of some religious or moral principle; to offend against a principle, standard, etc.

transgression (Dictionary) violation of a law, command, etc.; sin.

redemption (Dictionary) deliverance; rescue; repurchase, as of something sold; recovery by payment, as of something pledged.

Savior (Dictionary) one who saves, rescues, or delivers: the savior of the country; (cap.) a title of God, especially of Christ (commonly spelled Saviour).

Blessed is the LORD. Day by day, He supports us, God, our deliverance. God is for us a God of deliverance; God the LORD provides an escape from death. TEHILLIM 68:20-21 (PSALMS 68:19-20)

Blessed *be* the LORD, *who* daily loadeth us *with benefits, even* the God of our salvation (3444). Selah. *He that is* our God *is* the God of salvation (4190); and unto God the LORD *belong* the issues from death. PSALMS 68:19-20

Salvation (3444) pronounced yesh-oo'-aw; fem. pass. part. of 3467; something saved, i.e. (abstr.) deliverance; hence aid, victory, prosperity:- deliverance, health, help (-ing), salvation, save, saving (health), welfare.

deliverance (Dictionary) the act of giving up or surrendering; giving into another's possession or keeping; to give forth in words; utter or pronounce; to deliver a verdict; setting free; disburden (oneself) of thoughts, opinions, etc.; Obsolete: to make known, assert; Obsolete or Archaic: agile, active, quick.

prosperity (Dictionary) flourishing or thriving condition; good fortune; success.

fortune (Dictionary) position in life as determined by wealth.

success (Dictionary) favorable or prosperous termination of attempts or endeavors; gaining of wealth, position, or the like; Obsolete: outcome.

welfare (Dictionary) state of faring well; well-being; prosperity; success; happiness; weal.

happiness (2) (Dictionary) good fortune, pleasure, content or gladness.

weal (1) (Dictionary) Archaic: well-being, prosperity , or happiness.

(3467) pronounced yaw-shah'; a prim. root; prop. to be open, wide or free, i.e. (by impl.) to be safe; causat. to free or succor: - x at all, avenging, defend, deliver (-er), help, preserve, rescue, be safe, bring (having) salvation, save (-iour), get victory.

succor (Dictionary) help, relief, aid, assistance in difficulty, need, or distress.

salvation (Dictionary) act of saving or delivering; a source, cause, or means of deliverance; deliverance from the power of penalty and sin; redemption.

sin (Dictionary) transgression of divine law; an act regarded as such transgression, or any violation, especially a willful or deliberate one of some religious or moral principle; to offend against a principle, standard, etc.

transgression (Dictionary) violation of a law, command, etc.; sin.

redemption (Dictionary) deliverance; rescue; repurchase, as of something sold; recovery by payment, as of something pledged.

Savior (Dictionary) one who saves, rescues, or delivers: the savior of the country; (cap.) a title of God, especially of Christ (commonly spelled Saviour).

Salvation (4190) pronounced mo-shaw-aw'; from 3467; deliverance:-salvation.

deliverance (Dictionary) the act of giving up or surrendering; giving into another's possession or keeping; to give forth in words; utter or pronounce; to deliver a verdict; setting free; disburden (oneself) of thoughts, opinions, etc.; Obsolete: to make known, assert; Obsolete or Archaic: agile, active, quick.

As for me, may my prayer come to You, O LORD, at a favorable moment; O God, in Your abundant faithfulness, answer me with Your sure deliverance. TEHILLIM 69:14 (PSALMS 69:13)

But as for me, my prayer *is* unto thee, O LORD*, in* an acceptable time: O God, in the multitude of thy mercy hear me, in the truth of thy salvation (3468). PSALMS 69:13

Salvation (3468) pronounced yeh'-shah; from 3467; liberty, deliverance, prosperity, safety, salvation, saving.

liberty (Dictionary) freedom from arbitrary or despotic government or, often, from other rule or law than that of a self-governing community; freedom from external or foreign rule; freedom from control, interference, obligation, restriction, hampering conditions, etc.; power or right of doing, thinking, speaking, etc., according to choice.

deliverance (Dictionary) the act of giving up or surrendering; giving into another's possession or keeping; to give forth in words; utter or pronounce; to deliver a verdict; setting free; disburden (oneself) of thoughts, opinions, etc.; Obsolete: to make known, assert; Obsolete or Archaic: agile, active, quick.

prosperity (Dictionary) flourishing or thriving condition; good fortune; success.

fortune (Dictionary) position in life as determined by wealth.

success (Dictionary) favorable or prosperous termination of attempts or endeavors; gaining of wealth, position, or the like; Obsolete: outcome.

(3467) pronounced yaw-shah'; a prim. root; prop. to be open, wide or free, i.e. (by impl.) to be safe; causat. to free or succor: - x at all, avenging, defend, deliver (-er), help, preserve, rescue, be safe, bring (having) salvation, save (-iour), get victory.

succor (Dictionary) help, relief, aid, assistance in difficulty, need, or distress.

salvation (Dictionary) act of saving or delivering; a source, cause, or means of deliverance; deliverance from the power of penalty and sin; redemption.

sin (Dictionary) transgression of divine law; an act regarded as such transgression, or any violation, especially a willful or deliberate one of some religious or moral principle; to offend against a principle, standard, etc.

transgression (Dictionary) violation of a law, command, etc.; sin.

redemption (Dictionary) deliverance; rescue; repurchase, as of something sold; recovery by payment, as of something pledged.

Savior (Dictionary) one who saves, rescues, or delivers: the savior of the country; (cap.) a title of God, especially of Christ (commonly spelled Saviour).

But I am lowly and in pain; Your help, O God, keeps me safe. TEHILLIM 69:30 (PSALMS 69:29)

But I *am* poor and sorrowful: let thy salvation (3444), O God, set me up on high. PSALMS 69:29

Salvation (3444) pronounced yesh-oo'-aw; fem. pass. part. of 3467; something saved, i.e. (abstr.) deliverance; hence aid, victory, prosperity:- deliverance, health, help (-ing), salvation, save, saving (health), welfare.

deliverance (Dictionary) the act of giving up or surrendering; giving into another's possession or keeping; to give forth in words; utter or pronounce; to deliver a verdict; setting free; disburden (oneself) of thoughts, opinions, etc.; Obsolete: to make known, assert; Obsolete or Archaic: agile, active, quick.

prosperity (Dictionary) flourishing or thriving condition; good fortune; success.

fortune (Dictionary) position in life as determined by wealth.

success (Dictionary) favorable or prosperous termination of attempts or endeavors; gaining of wealth, position, or the like; Obsolete: outcome.

welfare (Dictionary) state of faring well; well-being; prosperity; success; happiness; weal.

happiness (2) (Dictionary) good fortune, pleasure, content or gladness.

weal (1) (Dictionary) Archaic: well-being, prosperity , or happiness.

(3467) pronounced yaw-shah'; a prim. root; prop. to be open, wide or free, i.e. (by impl.) to be safe; causat. to free or succor: - x at all, avenging, defend, deliver (-er), help, preserve, rescue, be safe, bring (having) salvation, save (-iour), get victory.

succor (Dictionary) help, relief, aid, assistance in difficulty, need, or distress.

salvation (Dictionary) act of saving or delivering; a source, cause, or means of deliverance; deliverance from the power of penalty and sin; redemption.

sin (Dictionary) transgression of divine law; an act regarded as such transgression, or any violation, especially a willful or deliberate one of some religious or moral principle; to offend against a principle, standard, etc.

transgression (Dictionary) violation of a law, command, etc.; sin.

redemption (Dictionary) deliverance; rescue; repurchase, as of something sold; recovery by payment, as of something pledged.

Savior (Dictionary) one who saves, rescues, or delivers: the savior of the country; (cap.) a title of God, especially of Christ (commonly spelled Saviour).

But let all who seek You be glad and rejoice in You; let those who are eager for Your deliverance always say, "Extolled be God!" TEHILLIM 70:5 (PSALMS 70:4)

Let all those that seek thee rejoice and be glad in thee: and let such as love thy salvation (3444) say continually, Let God be magnified. PSALMS 70:4

Salvation (3444) pronounced yesh-oo'-aw; fem. pass. part. of 3467; something saved, i.e. (abstr.) deliverance; hence aid, victory, prosperity:- deliverance, health, help (-ing), salvation, save, saving (health), welfare.

deliverance (Dictionary) the act of giving up or surrendering; giving into another's possession or keeping; to give forth in words; utter or pronounce; to deliver a verdict; setting free; disburden (oneself) of thoughts, opinions, etc.; Obsolete: to make known, assert; Obsolete or Archaic: agile, active, quick.

prosperity (Dictionary) flourishing or thriving condition; good fortune; success.

fortune (Dictionary) position in life as determined by wealth.

success (Dictionary) favorable or prosperous termination of attempts or endeavors; gaining of wealth, position, or the like; Obsolete: outcome.

welfare (Dictionary) state of faring well; well-being; prosperity; success; happiness; weal.

happiness (2) (Dictionary) good fortune, pleasure, content or gladness.

weal (1) (Dictionary) Archaic: well-being, prosperity , or happiness.

(3467) pronounced yaw-shah'; a prim. root; prop. to be open, wide or free, i.e. (by impl.) to be safe; causat. to free or succor: - x at all, avenging, defend, deliver (-er), help, preserve, rescue, be safe, bring (having) salvation, save (-iour), get victory.

succor (Dictionary) help, relief, aid, assistance in difficulty, need, or distress.

salvation (Dictionary) act of saving or delivering; a source, cause, or means of deliverance; deliverance from the power of penalty and sin; redemption.

sin (Dictionary) transgression of divine law; an act regarded as such transgression, or any violation, especially a willful or deliberate one of some religious or moral principle; to offend against a principle, standard, etc.

transgression (Dictionary) violation of a law, command, etc.; sin.

redemption (Dictionary) deliverance; rescue; repurchase, as of something sold; recovery by payment, as of something pledged.

Savior (Dictionary) one who saves, rescues, or delivers: the savior of the country; (cap.) a title of God, especially of Christ (commonly spelled Saviour).

My mouth tells of Your beneficence, of Your deliverance all day long, though I know not how to tell it. TEHILLIM 71:15 (PSALMS 71:15)

My mouth shall show forth thy righteousness *and* thy salvation (8668) all the day; for I know not the numbers *thereof*., PSALMS 71:15

Salvation (8668) pronounced tesh-oo-aw'; from 7768 in the sense of 3467; rescue (lit. or fig., pers., national, or spir.):- deliverance, help, safety, salvation, victory.

deliverance (Dictionary) the act of giving up or surrendering; giving into another's possession or keeping; to give forth in words; utter or pronounce; to deliver a verdict;

setting free; disburden (oneself) of thoughts, opinions, etc.; Obsolete: to make known, assert; Obsolete or Archaic: agile, active, quick.

salvation (Dictionary) act of saving or delivering; a source, cause, or means of deliverance; deliverance from the power of penalty and sin; redemption.

sin (Dictionary) transgression of divine law; an act regarded as such transgression, or any violation, especially a willful or deliberate one of some religious or moral principle; to offend against a principle, standard, etc.

transgression (Dictionary) violation of a law, command, etc.; sin.

redemption (Dictionary) deliverance; rescue; repurchase, as of something sold; recovery by payment, as of something pledged.

(7768) pronounced shaw-vah'; a prim. root; prop. to be free; but used only causat. and reflex. to halloo (for help, i.e. freedom from some trouble):- cry (aloud, out), shout.

halloo (Dictionary) an exclamation used to attract attention, to incite the dogs in hunting, etc.; to call with a loud voice: shout, cry, as after dogs; to incite or chase with shouts and cries of "halloo".

(3467) pronounced yaw-shah'; a prim. root; prop. to be open, wide or free, i.e. (by impl.) to be safe; causat. to free or succor: - x at all, avenging, defend, deliver (-er), help, preserve, rescue, be safe, bring (having) salvation, save (-iour), get victory.

succor (Dictionary) help, relief, aid, assistance in difficulty, need, or distress.

salvation (Dictionary) act of saving or delivering; a source, cause, or means of deliverance; deliverance from the power of penalty and sin; redemption.

sin (Dictionary) transgression of divine law; an act regarded as such transgression, or any violation, especially a willful or deliberate one of some religious or moral principle; to offend against a principle, standard, etc.

transgression (Dictionary) violation of a law, command, etc.; sin.

redemption (Dictionary) deliverance; rescue; repurchase, as of something sold; recovery by payment, as of something pledged.

Savior (Dictionary) one who saves, rescues, or delivers: the savior of the country; (cap.) a title of God, especially of Christ (commonly spelled Saviour).

O God, my king from of old, who brings deliverance throughout the land; TEHILLIM 74:12 (PSALMS 74:12)

For God *is* my King of old, working salvation (3444) in the midst of the earth. PSALMS 74:12

Salvation (3444) pronounced yesh-oo'-aw; fem. pass. part. of 3467; something saved, i.e. (abstr.) deliverance; hence aid, victory, prosperity:- deliverance, health, help (-ing), salvation, save, saving (health), welfare.

deliverance (Dictionary) the act of giving up or surrendering; giving into another's possession or keeping; to give forth in words; utter or pronounce; to deliver a verdict; setting free; disburden (oneself) of thoughts, opinions, etc.; Obsolete: to make known, assert; Obsolete or Archaic: agile, active, quick.

prosperity (Dictionary) flourishing or thriving condition; good fortune; success.

fortune (Dictionary) position in life as determined by wealth.

success (Dictionary) favorable or prosperous termination of attempts or endeavors; gaining of wealth, position, or the like; Obsolete: outcome.

welfare (Dictionary) state of faring well; well-being; prosperity; success; happiness; weal.

happiness (2) (Dictionary) good fortune, pleasure, content or gladness.

weal (1) (Dictionary) Archaic: well-being, prosperity , or happiness.

(3467) pronounced yaw-shah'; a prim. root; prop. to be open, wide or free, i.e. (by impl.) to be safe; causat. to free or succor: - x at all, avenging, defend, deliver (-er), help, preserve, rescue, be safe, bring (having) salvation, save (-iour), get victory.

succor (Dictionary) help, relief, aid, assistance in difficulty, need, or distress.

salvation (Dictionary) act of saving or delivering; a source, cause, or means of deliverance; deliverance from the power of penalty and sin; redemption.

sin (Dictionary) transgression of divine law; an act regarded as such transgression, or any violation, especially a willful or deliberate one of some religious or moral principle; to offend against a principle, standard, etc.

transgression (Dictionary) violation of a law, command, etc.; sin.

redemption (Dictionary) deliverance; rescue; repurchase, as of something sold; recovery by payment, as of something pledged.

Savior (Dictionary) one who saves, rescues, or delivers: the savior of the country; (cap.) a title of God, especially of Christ (commonly spelled Saviour).

The LORD heard and He raged; fire broke out against Jacob, anger flared up at Israel, because they did not put their trust in God, did not rely on His deliverance. TEHILLIM 78:21-22 (PSALMS 78:21-22)

SALVATION

Therefore the LORD heard this, and was wroth: so a fire was kindled against Jacob, and anger also came up against Israel; because they believed not in God, and trusted not in his salvation (3444). PSALMS 78:21-22

Salvation (3444) pronounced yesh-oo'-aw; fem. pass. part. of 3467; something saved, i.e. (abstr.) deliverance; hence aid, victory, prosperity:- deliverance, health, help (-ing), salvation, save, saving (health), welfare.

deliverance (Dictionary) the act of giving up or surrendering; giving into another's possession or keeping; to give forth in words; utter or pronounce; to deliver a verdict; setting free; disburden (oneself) of thoughts, opinions, etc.; Obsolete: to make known, assert; Obsolete or Archaic: agile, active, quick.

prosperity (Dictionary) flourishing or thriving condition; good fortune; success.

fortune (Dictionary) position in life as determined by wealth.

success (Dictionary) favorable or prosperous termination of attempts or endeavors; gaining of wealth, position, or the like; Obsolete: outcome.

welfare (Dictionary) state of faring well; well-being; prosperity; success; happiness; weal.

happiness (2) (Dictionary) good fortune, pleasure, content or gladness.

weal (1) (Dictionary) Archaic: well-being, prosperity , or happiness.

(3467) pronounced yaw-shah'; a prim. root; prop. to be open, wide or free, i.e. (by impl.) to be safe; causat. to free or succor: - x at all, avenging, defend, deliver (-er), help, preserve, rescue, be safe, bring (having) salvation, save (-iour), get victory.

succor (Dictionary) help, relief, aid, assistance in difficulty, need, or distress.

salvation (Dictionary) act of saving or delivering; a source, cause, or means of deliverance; deliverance from the power of penalty and sin; redemption.

sin (Dictionary) transgression of divine law; an act regarded as such transgression, or any violation, especially a willful or deliberate one of some religious or moral principle; to offend against a principle, standard, etc.

transgression (Dictionary) violation of a law, command, etc.; sin.

redemption (Dictionary) deliverance; rescue; repurchase, as of something sold; recovery by payment, as of something pledged.

Savior (Dictionary) one who saves, rescues, or delivers: the savior of the country; (cap.) a title of God, especially of Christ (commonly spelled Saviour).

SALVATION

Help us, O God, our deliverer, for the sake of the glory of Your name. Save us and forgive our sin, for the sake of Your name. TEHILLIM 79:9 (PSALMS 79:9)

Help us, O God of our salvation (3468), for the glory of thy name; and deliver us, and purge away our sins, for thy name's sake. PSALMS 79:9

Salvation (3468) pronounced yeh'-shah; from 3467; liberty, deliverance, prosperity, safety, salvation, saving.

liberty (Dictionary) freedom from arbitrary or despotic government or, often, from other rule or law than that of a self-governing community; freedom from external or foreign rule; freedom from control, interference, obligation, restriction, hampering conditions, etc.; power or right of doing, thinking, speaking, etc., according to choice.

deliverance (Dictionary) the act of giving up or surrendering; giving into another's possession or keeping; to give forth in words; utter or pronounce; to deliver a verdict; setting free; disburden (oneself) of thoughts, opinions, etc.; Obsolete: to make known, assert; Obsolete or Archaic: agile, active, quick.

prosperity (Dictionary) flourishing or thriving condition; good fortune; success.

fortune (Dictionary) position in life as determined by wealth.

success (Dictionary) favorable or prosperous termination of attempts or endeavors; gaining of wealth, position, or the like; Obsolete: outcome.

(3467) pronounced yaw-shah'; a prim. root; prop. to be open, wide or free, i.e. (by impl.) to be safe; causat. to free or succor: - x at all, avenging, defend, deliver (-er), help, preserve, rescue, be safe, bring (having) salvation, save (-iour), get victory.

succor (Dictionary) help, relief, aid, assistance in difficulty, need, or distress.

salvation (Dictionary) act of saving or delivering; a source, cause, or means of deliverance; deliverance from the power of penalty and sin; redemption.

sin (Dictionary) transgression of divine law; an act regarded as such transgression, or any violation, especially a willful or deliberate one of some religious or moral principle; to offend against a principle, standard, etc.

transgression (Dictionary) violation of a law, command, etc.; sin.

redemption (Dictionary) deliverance; rescue; repurchase, as of something sold; recovery by payment, as of something pledged.

Savior (Dictionary) one who saves, rescues, or delivers: the savior of the country; (cap.) a title of God, especially of Christ (commonly spelled Saviour).

Turn again, O God, our helper, revoke Your displeasure with us. Will you be angry with us forever, prolong Your wrath for all generations? Surely You will revive us again, so that Your people may rejoice in You. Show us, O LORD, Your faithfulness; grant us Your deliverance. Let me hear what God, the LORD, will speak: He will promise well-being to His people, His faithful ones; may they not turn to folly. His help is very near to those who fear Him, to make His glory dwell in our land. TEHILLIM 85:5-10 (PSALMS 85:4-9)

Turn us, O God of our salvation (3468), and cause thine anger toward us to cease. Wilt thou be angry with us forever? Wilt thou draw out thine anger to all generations? Wilt thou not revive us again: that thy people may rejoice in thee? Show us thy mercy, O LORD, and grant us thy salvation (3468). I will hear what God the LORD will speak: for he will speak peace unto his people, and to his saints; but let them not turn again to folly. Surely his salvation (3468) is nigh them that fear him; that glory may dwell in our land. PSALMS 85:4-9

> Salvation (3468) pronounced yeh'-shah; from 3467; liberty, deliverance, prosperity, safety, salvation, saving.
>
> > liberty (Dictionary) freedom from arbitrary or despotic government or, often, from other rule or law than that of a self-governing community; freedom from external or foreign rule; freedom from control, interference, obligation, restriction, hampering conditions, etc.; power or right of doing, thinking, speaking, etc., according to choice.
> >
> > deliverance (Dictionary) the act of giving up or surrendering; giving into another's possession or keeping; to give forth in words; utter or pronounce; to deliver a verdict; setting free; disburden (oneself) of thoughts, opinions, etc.; Obsolete: to make known, assert; Obsolete or Archaic: agile, active, quick.
> >
> > prosperity (Dictionary) flourishing or thriving condition; good fortune; success.
> >
> > fortune (Dictionary) position in life as determined by wealth.
> >
> > success (Dictionary) favorable or prosperous termination of attempts or endeavors; gaining of wealth, position, or the like; Obsolete: outcome.
>
> (3467) pronounced yaw-shah'; a prim. root; prop. to be open, wide or free, i.e. (by impl.) to be safe; causat. to free or succor: - x at all, avenging, defend, deliver (-er), help, preserve, rescue, be safe, bring (having) salvation, save (-iour), get victory.
>
> > succor (Dictionary) help, relief, aid, assistance in difficulty, need, or distress.
> >
> > salvation (Dictionary) act of saving or delivering; a source, cause, or means of deliverance; deliverance from the power of penalty and sin; redemption.

sin (Dictionary) transgression of divine law; an act regarded as such transgression, or any violation, especially a willful or deliberate one of some religious or moral principle; to offend against a principle, standard, etc.

transgression (Dictionary) violation of a law, command, etc.; sin.

redemption (Dictionary) deliverance; rescue; repurchase, as of something sold; recovery by payment, as of something pledged.

Savior (Dictionary) one who saves, rescues, or delivers: the savior of the country; (cap.) a title of God, especially of Christ (commonly spelled Saviour).

O LORD, God of my deliverance, when I cry out in the night before You, let my prayer reach you; incline Your ear to my cry. TEHILLIM 88:2-3 (PSALMS 88:1-2)

O LORD God of my salvation (3444), I have cried day *and* night before thee: Let my prayer come before thee; incline thine ear unto my cry; PSALMS 88:1-2

Salvation (3444) pronounced yesh-oo'-aw; fem. pass. part. of 3467; something saved, i.e. (abstr.) deliverance; hence aid, victory, prosperity:- deliverance, health, help (-ing), salvation, save, saving (health), welfare.

deliverance (Dictionary) the act of giving up or surrendering; giving into another's possession or keeping; to give forth in words; utter or pronounce; to deliver a verdict; setting free; disburden (oneself) of thoughts, opinions, etc.; Obsolete: to make known, assert; Obsolete or Archaic: agile, active, quick.

prosperity (Dictionary) flourishing or thriving condition; good fortune; success.

fortune (Dictionary) position in life as determined by wealth.

success (Dictionary) favorable or prosperous termination of attempts or endeavors; gaining of wealth, position, or the like; Obsolete: outcome.

welfare (Dictionary) state of faring well; well-being; prosperity; success; happiness; weal.

happiness (2) (Dictionary) good fortune, pleasure, content or gladness.

weal (1) (Dictionary) Archaic: well-being, prosperity , or happiness.

(3467) pronounced yaw-shah'; a prim. root; prop. to be open, wide or free, i.e. (by impl.) to be safe; causat. to free or succor: - x at all, avenging, defend, deliver (-er), help, preserve, rescue, be safe, bring (having) salvation, save (-iour), get victory.

succor (Dictionary) help, relief, aid, assistance in difficulty, need, or distress.

salvation (Dictionary) act of saving or delivering; a source, cause, or means of deliverance; deliverance from the power of penalty and sin; redemption.

sin Dictionary) transgression of divine law; an act regarded as such transgression, or any violation, especially a willful or deliberate one of some religious or moral principle; to offend against a principle, standard, etc.

transgression (Dictionary) violation of a law, command, etc.; sin.

redemption (Dictionary) deliverance; rescue; repurchase, as of something sold; recovery by payment, as of something pledged.

Savior (Dictionary) one who saves, rescues, or delivers: the savior of the country; (cap.) a title of God, especially of Christ (commonly spelled Saviour).

He shall say to Me, You are my father, my God, the rock of my deliverance. TEHILLIM 89:27 (PSALMS 89:26)

He shall cry unto me, Thou *art* my father, my God, and the rock of my salvation (3444). PSALMS 89:26

Salvation (3444) pronounced yesh-oo'-aw; fem. pass. part. of 3467; something saved, i.e. (abstr.) deliverance; hence aid, victory, prosperity:- deliverance, health, help (-ing), salvation, save, saving (health), welfare.

deliverance (Dictionary) the act of giving up or surrendering; giving into another's possession or keeping; to give forth in words; utter or pronounce; to deliver a verdict; setting free; disburden (oneself) of thoughts, opinions, etc.; Obsolete: to make known, assert; Obsolete or Archaic: agile, active, quick.

prosperity (Dictionary) flourishing or thriving condition; good fortune; success.

fortune (Dictionary) position in life as determined by wealth.

success (Dictionary) favorable or prosperous termination of attempts or endeavors; gaining of wealth, position, or the like; Obsolete: outcome.

welfare (Dictionary) state of faring well; well-being; prosperity; success; happiness; weal.

happiness (2) (Dictionary) good fortune, pleasure, content or gladness.

weal (1) (Dictionary) Archaic: well-being, prosperity , or happiness.

(3467) pronounced yaw-shah'; a prim. root; prop. to be open, wide or free, i.e. (by impl.) to be safe; causat. to free or succor: - x at all, avenging, defend, deliver (-er), help, preserve, rescue, be safe, bring (having) salvation, save (-iour), get victory.

succor (Dictionary) help, relief, aid, assistance in difficulty, need, or distress.

salvation (Dictionary) act of saving or delivering; a source, cause, or means of deliverance; deliverance from the power of penalty and sin; redemption.

sin (Dictionary) transgression of divine law; an act regarded as such transgression, or any violation, especially a willful or deliberate one of some religious or moral principle; to offend against a principle, standard, etc.

transgression (Dictionary) violation of a law, command, etc.; sin.

redemption (Dictionary) deliverance; rescue; repurchase, as of something sold; recovery by payment, as of something pledged.

Savior (Dictionary) one who saves, rescues, or delivers: the savior of the country; (cap.) a title of God, especially of Christ (commonly spelled Saviour).

"Because he is devoted to Me I will deliver him: I will keep him safe, for he knows My name. When he calls on me, I will answer him; I will be with him in distress; I will rescue him and make him honored; I will let him live to a ripe old age, and show him My salvation. " TEHILLIM 91:14-16 (PSALMS 91:14-16)

Because he hath set his love upon me, therefore will I deliver him: I will set him on high, because he hath known my name. He shall call upon me, and I will answer him: I *will be* with him in trouble; I will deliver him, and honor him. With long life will I satisfy him, and show him my salvation (3444). PSALMS 91:14-16

Salvation (3444) pronounced yesh-oo'-aw; fem. pass. part. of 3467; something saved, i.e. (abstr.) deliverance; hence aid, victory, prosperity:- deliverance, health, help (-ing), salvation, save, saving (health), welfare.

deliverance (Dictionary) the act of giving up or surrendering; giving into another's possession or keeping; to give forth in words; utter or pronounce; to deliver a verdict; setting free; disburden (oneself) of thoughts, opinions, etc.; Obsolete: to make known, assert; Obsolete or Archaic: agile, active, quick.

prosperity (Dictionary) flourishing or thriving condition; good fortune; success.

fortune (Dictionary) position in life as determined by wealth.

success (Dictionary) favorable or prosperous termination of attempts or endeavors; gaining of wealth, position, or the like; Obsolete: outcome.

welfare (Dictionary) state of faring well; well-being; prosperity; success; happiness; weal.

happiness (2) (Dictionary) good fortune, pleasure, content or gladness.

weal (1) (Dictionary) Archaic: well-being, prosperity , or happiness.

(3467) pronounced yaw-shah'; a prim. root; prop. to be open, wide or free, i.e. (by impl.) to be safe; causat. to free or succor: - x at all, avenging, defend, deliver (-er), help, preserve, rescue, be safe, bring (having) salvation, save (-iour), get victory.

succor (Dictionary) help, relief, aid, assistance in difficulty, need, or distress.

salvation (Dictionary) act of saving or delivering; a source, cause, or means of deliverance; deliverance from the power of penalty and sin; redemption.

sin (Dictionary) transgression of divine law; an act regarded as such transgression, or any violation, especially a willful or deliberate one of some religious or moral principle; to offend against a principle, standard, etc.

transgression (Dictionary) violation of a law, command, etc.; sin.

redemption (Dictionary) deliverance; rescue; repurchase, as of something sold; recovery by payment, as of something pledged.

Savior (Dictionary) one who saves, rescues, or delivers: the savior of the country; (cap.) a title of God, especially of Christ (commonly spelled Saviour).

Come, let us sing joyously to the LORD, raise a shout for our rock and deliverer; TEHILLIM 95:1 (PSALMS 95:1)

O come, let us sing unto the LORD; let us make a joyful noise to the rock of our salvation (3468). PSALMS 95:1

Salvation (3468) pronounced yeh'-shah; from 3467; liberty, deliverance, prosperity, safety, salvation, saving.

liberty (Dictionary) freedom from arbitrary or despotic government or, often, from other rule or law than that of a self-governing community; freedom from external or foreign rule; freedom from control, interference, obligation, restriction, hampering conditions, etc.; power or right of doing, thinking, speaking, etc., according to choice.

deliverance (Dictionary) the act of giving up or surrendering; giving into another's possession or keeping; to give forth in words; utter or pronounce; to deliver a verdict; setting free; disburden (oneself) of thoughts, opinions, etc.; Obsolete: to make known, assert; Obsolete or Archaic: agile, active, quick.

prosperity (Dictionary) flourishing or thriving condition; good fortune; success.

fortune (Dictionary) position in life as determined by wealth.

success (Dictionary) favorable or prosperous termination of attempts or endeavors; gaining of wealth, position, or the like; Obsolete: outcome.

(3467) pronounced yaw-shah'; a prim. root; prop. to be open, wide or free, i.e. (by impl.) to be safe; causat. to free or succor: - x at all, avenging, defend, deliver (-er), help, preserve, rescue, be safe, bring (having) salvation, save (-iour), get victory.

succor (Dictionary) help, relief, aid, assistance in difficulty, need, or distress.

salvation (Dictionary) act of saving or delivering; a source, cause, or means of deliverance; deliverance from the power of penalty and sin; redemption.

sin (Dictionary) transgression of divine law; an act regarded as such transgression, or any violation, especially a willful or deliberate one of some religious or moral principle; to offend against a principle, standard, etc.

transgression (Dictionary) violation of a law, command, etc.; sin.

redemption (Dictionary) deliverance; rescue; repurchase, as of something sold; recovery by payment, as of something pledged.

Savior (Dictionary) one who saves, rescues, or delivers: the savior of the country; (cap.) a title of God, especially of Christ (commonly spelled Saviour).

Sing to the LORD, bless His name, proclaim His victory day after day. TEHILLIM 96:2 (PSALMS 96:2)

Sing unto the LORD, bless his name; show forth his salvation (3444) from day to day. PSALMS 96:2

Salvation (3444) pronounced yesh-oo'-aw; fem. pass. part. of 3467; something saved, i.e. (abstr.) deliverance; hence aid, victory, prosperity:- deliverance, health, help (-ing), salvation, save, saving (health), welfare.

deliverance (Dictionary) the act of giving up or surrendering; giving into another's possession or keeping; to give forth in words; utter or pronounce; to deliver a verdict; setting free; disburden (oneself) of thoughts, opinions, etc.; Obsolete: to make known, assert; Obsolete or Archaic: agile, active, quick.

prosperity (Dictionary) flourishing or thriving condition; good fortune; success.

fortune (Dictionary) position in life as determined by wealth.

success (Dictionary) favorable or prosperous termination of attempts or endeavors; gaining of wealth, position, or the like; Obsolete: outcome.

welfare Dictionary) state of faring well; well-being; prosperity; success; happiness; weal.

happiness (2) (Dictionary) good fortune, pleasure, content or gladness.

weal (1) (Dictionary) Archaic: well-being, prosperity , or happiness.

(3467) pronounced yaw-shah'; a prim. root; prop. to be open, wide or free, i.e. (by impl.) to be safe; causat. to free or succor: - x at all, avenging, defend, deliver (-er), help, preserve, rescue, be safe, bring (having) salvation, save (-iour), get victory.

succor (Dictionary) help, relief, aid, assistance in difficulty, need, or distress.

salvation (Dictionary) act of saving or delivering; a source, cause, or means of deliverance; deliverance from the power of penalty and sin; redemption.

sin (Dictionary) transgression of divine law; an act regarded as such transgression, or any violation, especially a willful or deliberate one of some religious or moral principle; to offend against a principle, standard, etc.

transgression (Dictionary) violation of a law, command, etc.; sin.

redemption (Dictionary) deliverance; rescue; repurchase, as of something sold; recovery by payment, as of something pledged.

Savior (Dictionary) one who saves, rescues, or delivers: the savior of the country; (cap.) a title of God, especially of Christ (commonly spelled Saviour).

The LORD has manifested His victory, has displayed His triumph in the sight of the nations. He was mindful of His steadfast love and faithfulness toward the house of Israel; all the ends of the earth beheld the victory of our God. TEHILLIM 98:2-3 (PSALMS 98:2-3)

The LORD hath made known his salvation (3444): his righteousness hath he openly shown in the sight of the heathen. He hath remembered his mercy and his truth toward the house of Israel: all the ends of the earth have seen the salvation (3444) of our God. PSALMS 98:2-3

Salvation (3444) pronounced yesh-oo'-aw; fem. pass. part. of 3467; something saved, i.e. (abstr.) deliverance; hence aid, victory, prosperity:- deliverance, health, help (-ing), salvation, save, saving (health), welfare.

deliverance (Dictionary) the act of giving up or surrendering; giving into another's possession or keeping; to give forth in words; utter or pronounce; to deliver a verdict; setting free; disburden (oneself) of thoughts, opinions, etc.; Obsolete: to make known, assert; Obsolete or Archaic: agile, active, quick.

prosperity (Dictionary) flourishing or thriving condition; good fortune; success.

fortune (Dictionary) position in life as determined by wealth.

success (Dictionary) favorable or prosperous termination of attempts or endeavors; gaining of wealth, position, or the like; Obsolete: outcome.

welfare (Dictionary) state of faring well; well-being; prosperity; success; happiness; weal.

happiness (2) (Dictionary) good fortune, pleasure, content or gladness.

weal (1) (Dictionary) Archaic: well-being, prosperity , or happiness.

(3467) pronounced yaw-shah'; a prim. root; prop. to be open, wide or free, i.e. (by impl.) to be safe; causat. to free or succor: - x at all, avenging, defend, deliver (-er), help, preserve, rescue, be safe, bring (having) salvation, save (-iour), get victory.

succor (Dictionary) help, relief, aid, assistance in difficulty, need, or distress.

salvation (Dictionary) act of saving or delivering; a source, cause, or means of deliverance; deliverance from the power of penalty and sin; redemption.

sin (Dictionary) transgression of divine law; an act regarded as such transgression, or any violation, especially a willful or deliberate one of some religious or moral principle; to offend against a principle, standard, etc.

transgression (Dictionary) violation of a law, command, etc.; sin.

redemption (Dictionary) deliverance; rescue; repurchase, as of something sold; recovery by payment, as of something pledged.

Savior (Dictionary) one who saves, rescues, or delivers: the savior of the country; (cap.) a title of God, especially of Christ (commonly spelled Saviour).

Be mindful of me, O LORD, when You favor Your people; take note of me when You deliver them, that I may enjoy the prosperity of Your chosen ones, share the joy of Your nation, glory in Your very own people. TEHILLIM 106:4-5 (PSALMS 106:4-5)

Remember me, O LORD, with the favour *that thou bearest unto* thy people: O visit me with thy salvation (3444); that I may see the good of thy chosen, that I may rejoice in the gladness of thy nation, that I may glory with thine inheritance. PSALMS 106:4-5

Salvation (3444) pronounced yesh-oo'-aw; fem. pass. part. of 3467; something saved, i.e. (abstr.) deliverance; hence aid, victory, prosperity:- deliverance, health, help (-ing), salvation, save, saving (health), welfare.

deliverance (Dictionary) the act of giving up or surrendering; giving into another's possession or keeping; to give forth in words; utter or pronounce; to deliver a verdict; setting free; disburden (oneself) of thoughts, opinions, etc.; Obsolete: to make known, assert; Obsolete or Archaic: agile, active, quick.

prosperity (Dictionary) flourishing or thriving condition; good fortune; success.

fortune (Dictionary) position in life as determined by wealth.

success (Dictionary) favorable or prosperous termination of attempts or endeavors; gaining of wealth, position, or the like; Obsolete: outcome.

welfare (Dictionary) state of faring well; well-being; prosperity; success; happiness; weal.

happiness (2) (Dictionary) good fortune, pleasure, content or gladness.

weal (1) (Dictionary) Archaic: well-being, prosperity , or happiness.

(3467) pronounced yaw-shah'; a prim. root; prop. to be open, wide or free, i.e. (by impl.) to be safe; causat. to free or succor: - x at all, avenging, defend, deliver (-er), help, preserve, rescue, be safe, bring (having) salvation, save (-iour), get victory.

succor (Dictionary) help, relief, aid, assistance in difficulty, need, or distress.

salvation (Dictionary) act of saving or delivering; a source, cause, or means of deliverance; deliverance from the power of penalty and sin; redemption.

sin (Dictionary) transgression of divine law; an act regarded as such transgression, or any violation, especially a willful or deliberate one of some religious or moral principle; to offend against a principle, standard, etc.

transgression (Dictionary) violation of a law, command, etc.; sin.

redemption (Dictionary) deliverance; rescue; repurchase, as of something sold; recovery by payment, as of something pledged.

Savior (Dictionary) one who saves, rescues, or delivers: the savior of the country; (cap.) a title of God, especially of Christ (commonly spelled Saviour).

I raise the cup of deliverance and invoke the name of the LORD. TEHILLIM 116:13 (PSALMS 116:13)

I will take the cup of salvation (3444), and call upon the name of the LORD. PSALMS 116:13

Salvation (3444) pronounced yesh-oo'-aw; fem. pass. part. of 3467; something saved, i.e. (abstr.) deliverance; hence aid, victory, prosperity:- deliverance, health, help (-ing), salvation, save, saving (health), welfare.

deliverance (Dictionary) the act of giving up or surrendering; giving into another's possession or keeping; to give forth in words; utter or pronounce; to deliver a verdict; setting free; disburden (oneself) of thoughts, opinions, etc.; Obsolete: to make known, assert; Obsolete or Archaic: agile, active, quick.

prosperity (Dictionary) flourishing or thriving condition; good fortune; success.

fortune (Dictionary) position in life as determined by wealth.

success (Dictionary) favorable or prosperous termination of attempts or endeavors; gaining of wealth, position, or the like; Obsolete: outcome.

welfare (Dictionary) state of faring well; well-being; prosperity; success; happiness; weal.

happiness (2) (Dictionary) good fortune, pleasure, content or gladness.

weal (1) (Dictionary) Archaic: well-being, prosperity , or happiness.

(3467) pronounced yaw-shah'; a prim. root; prop. to be open, wide or free, i.e. (by impl.) to be safe; causat. to free or succor: - x at all, avenging, defend, deliver (-er), help, preserve, rescue, be safe, bring (having) salvation, save (-iour), get victory.

succor (Dictionary) help, relief, aid, assistance in difficulty, need, or distress.

salvation (Dictionary) act of saving or delivering; a source, cause, or means of deliverance; deliverance from the power of penalty and sin; redemption.

sin (Dictionary) transgression of divine law; an act regarded as such transgression, or any violation, especially a willful or deliberate one of some religious or moral principle; to offend against a principle, standard, etc.

transgression (Dictionary) violation of a law, command, etc.; sin.

redemption (Dictionary) deliverance; rescue; repurchase, as of something sold; recovery by payment, as of something pledged.

Savior (Dictionary) one who saves, rescues, or delivers: the savior of the country; (cap.) a title of God, especially of Christ (commonly spelled Saviour).

The LORD is my strength and might; He has become my deliverance. The tents of the victorious resound with joyous shouts of deliverance. The right hand of the LORD is triumphant! TEHILLIM 118:14-15 (PSALMS 118:14-15)

might: Others "song" (TANAKH footnote)

victorious: *"righteous" (TANAKH footnote)*

The LORD is *my strength and song, and* is *become my salvation (3444). The voice of rejoicing and salvation (3444) is in the tabernacles of the righteous; the right hand of the LORD doeth valiantly. PSALMS 118:14-15*

Salvation (3444) pronounced yesh-oo'-aw; fem. pass. part. of 3467; something saved, i.e. (abstr.) deliverance; hence aid, victory, prosperity:- deliverance, health, help (-ing), salvation, save, saving (health), welfare.

deliverance (Dictionary) the act of giving up or surrendering; giving into another's possession or keeping; to give forth in words; utter or pronounce; to deliver a verdict; setting free; disburden (oneself) of thoughts, opinions, etc.; Obsolete: to make known, assert; Obsolete or Archaic: agile, active, quick.

prosperity (Dictionary) flourishing or thriving condition; good fortune; success.

fortune (Dictionary) position in life as determined by wealth.

success (Dictionary) favorable or prosperous termination of attempts or endeavors; gaining of wealth, position, or the like; Obsolete: outcome.

welfare (Dictionary) state of faring well; well-being; prosperity; success; happiness; weal.

happiness (2) (Dictionary) good fortune, pleasure, content or gladness.

weal (1) (Dictionary) Archaic: well-being, prosperity , or happiness.

(3467) pronounced yaw-shah'; a prim. root; prop. to be open, wide or free, i.e. (by impl.) to be safe; causat. to free or succor: - x at all, avenging, defend, deliver (-er), help, preserve, rescue, be safe, bring (having) salvation, save (-iour), get victory.

succor (Dictionary) help, relief, aid, assistance in difficulty, need, or distress.

salvation (Dictionary) act of saving or delivering; a source, cause, or means of deliverance; deliverance from the power of penalty and sin; redemption.

sin (Dictionary) transgression of divine law; an act regarded as such transgression, or any violation, especially a willful or deliberate one of some religious or moral principle; to offend against a principle, standard, etc.

transgression (Dictionary) violation of a law, command, etc.; sin.

redemption (Dictionary) deliverance; rescue; repurchase, as of something sold; recovery by payment, as of something pledged.

Savior (Dictionary) one who saves, rescues, or delivers: the savior of the country; (cap.) a title of God, especially of Christ (commonly spelled Saviour).

I praise You, for You have answered me, and have become my deliverance. TEHILLIM 118:21 (PSALMS 118:21)

SALVATION

I will praise thee; for thou hast heard me, and art become my salvation (3444). PSALMS 118:21

Salvation (3444) pronounced yesh-oo'-aw; fem. pass. part. of 3467; something saved, i.e. (abstr.) deliverance; hence aid, victory, prosperity:- deliverance, health, help (-ing), salvation, save, saving (health), welfare.

deliverance (Dictionary) the act of giving up or surrendering; giving into another's possession or keeping; to give forth in words; utter or pronounce; to deliver a verdict; setting free; disburden (oneself) of thoughts, opinions, etc.; Obsolete: to make known, assert; Obsolete or Archaic: agile, active, quick.

prosperity (Dictionary) flourishing or thriving condition; good fortune; success.

fortune (Dictionary) position in life as determined by wealth.

success (Dictionary) favorable or prosperous termination of attempts or endeavors; gaining of wealth, position, or the like; Obsolete: outcome.

welfare (Dictionary) state of faring well; well-being; prosperity; success; happiness; weal.

happiness (2) (Dictionary) good fortune, pleasure, content or gladness.

weal (1) (Dictionary) Archaic: well-being, prosperity , or happiness.

(3467) pronounced yaw-shah'; a prim. root; prop. to be open, wide or free, i.e. (by impl.) to be safe; causat. to free or succor: - x at all, avenging, defend, deliver (-er), help, preserve, rescue, be safe, bring (having) salvation, save (-iour), get victory.

succor (Dictionary) help, relief, aid, assistance in difficulty, need, or distress.

salvation (Dictionary) act of saving or delivering; a source, cause, or means of deliverance; deliverance from the power of penalty and sin; redemption.

sin (Dictionary) transgression of divine law; an act regarded as such transgression, or any violation, especially a willful or deliberate one of some religious or moral principle; to offend against a principle, standard, etc.

transgression (Dictionary) violation of a law, command, etc.; sin.

redemption (Dictionary) deliverance; rescue; repurchase, as of something sold; recovery by payment, as of something pledged.

Savior (Dictionary) one who saves, rescues, or delivers: the savior of the country; (cap.) a title of God, especially of Christ (commonly spelled Saviour).

SALVATION

May Your steadfast love reach me, O LORD, Your deliverance; as You have promised. TEHILLIM 119:41 (PSALMS 119:41)

Let thy mercies come also unto me, O LORD, *even* thy salvation (8668), according to thy word. PSALMS 119:41

Salvation (8668) pronounced tesh-oo-aw'; from 7768 in the sense of 3467; rescue (lit. or fig., pers., national, or spir.):- deliverance, help, safety, salvation, victory.

deliverance (Dictionary) the act of giving up or surrendering; giving into another's possession or keeping; to give forth in words; utter or pronounce; to deliver a verdict; setting free; disburden (oneself) of thoughts, opinions, etc.; Obsolete: to make known, assert; Obsolete or Archaic: agile, active, quick.

salvation (Dictionary) act of saving or delivering; a source, cause, or means of deliverance; deliverance from the power of penalty and sin; redemption.

sin (Dictionary) transgression of divine law; an act regarded as such transgression, or any violation, especially a willful or deliberate one of some religious or moral principle; to offend against a principle, standard, etc.

transgression (Dictionary) violation of a law, command, etc.; sin.

redemption (Dictionary) deliverance; rescue; repurchase, as of something sold; recovery by payment, as of something pledged.

(7768) pronounced shaw-vah'; a prim. root; prop. to be free; but used only causat. and reflex. to halloo (for help, i.e. freedom from some trouble):- cry (aloud, out), shout.

halloo (Dictionary) an exclamation used to attract attention, to incite the dogs in hunting, etc.; to call with a loud voice: shout, cry, as after dogs; to incite or chase with shouts and cries of "halloo".

(3467) pronounced yaw-shah'; a prim. root; prop. to be open, wide or free, i.e. (by impl.) to be safe; causat. to free or succor: - x at all, avenging, defend, deliver (-er), help, preserve, rescue, be safe, bring (having) salvation, save (-iour), get victory.

succor (Dictionary) help, relief, aid, assistance in difficulty, need, or distress.

salvation (Dictionary) act of saving or delivering; a source, cause, or means of deliverance; deliverance from the power of penalty and sin; redemption.

sin (Dictionary) transgression of divine law; an act regarded as such transgression, or any violation, especially a willful or deliberate one of some religious or moral principle; to offend against a principle, standard, etc.

transgression (Dictionary) violation of a law, command, etc.; sin.

redemption (Dictionary) deliverance; rescue; repurchase, as of something sold; recovery by payment, as of something pledged.

Savior (Dictionary) one who saves, rescues, or delivers: the savior of the country; (cap.) a title of God, especially of Christ (commonly spelled Saviour).

I long for Your deliverance; I hope for Your word. TEHILLIM 119:81 (PSALMS 119:81)

My soul fainteth for thy salvation (8668): *but* I hope in thy word. PSALMS 119:81

Salvation (8668) pronounced tesh-oo-aw'; from 7768 in the sense of 3467; rescue (lit. or fig., pers., national, or spir.):- deliverance, help, safety, salvation, victory.

deliverance (Dictionary) the act of giving up or surrendering; giving into another's possession or keeping; to give forth in words; utter or pronounce; to deliver a verdict; setting free; disburden (oneself) of thoughts, opinions, etc.; Obsolete: to make known, assert; Obsolete or Archaic: agile, active, quick.

salvation (Dictionary) act of saving or delivering; a source, cause, or means of deliverance; deliverance from the power of penalty and sin; redemption.

sin (Dictionary) transgression of divine law; an act regarded as such transgression, or any violation, especially a willful or deliberate one of some religious or moral principle; to offend against a principle, standard, etc.

transgression (Dictionary) violation of a law, command, etc.; sin.

redemption (Dictionary) deliverance; rescue; repurchase, as of something sold; recovery by payment, as of something pledged.

(7768) pronounced shaw-vah'; a prim. root; prop. to be free; but used only causat. and reflex. to halloo (for help, i.e. freedom from some trouble):- cry (aloud, out), shout.

halloo (Dictionary) an exclamation used to attract attention, to incite the dogs in hunting, etc.; to call with a loud voice: shout, cry, as after dogs; to incite or chase with shouts and cries of "halloo".

(3467) pronounced yaw-shah'; a prim. root; prop. to be open, wide or free, i.e. (by impl.) to be safe; causat. to free or succor: - x at all, avenging, defend, deliver (-er), help, preserve, rescue, be safe, bring (having) salvation, save (-iour), get victory.

succor (Dictionary) help, relief, aid, assistance in difficulty, need, or distress.

salvation (Dictionary) act of saving or delivering; a source, cause, or means of deliverance; deliverance from the power of penalty and sin; redemption.

sin (Dictionary) transgression of divine law; an act regarded as such transgression, or any violation, especially a willful or deliberate one of some religious or moral principle; to offend against a principle, standard, etc.

transgression (Dictionary) violation of a law, command, etc.; sin.

redemption (Dictionary) deliverance; rescue; repurchase, as of something sold; recovery by payment, as of something pledged.

Savior (Dictionary) one who saves, rescues, or delivers: the savior of the country; (cap.) a title of God, especially of Christ (commonly spelled Saviour).

My eyes pine away for Your deliverance, for Your promise of victory. TEHILLIM 119:123 (PSALMS 119:123)

Mine eyes fail for thy salvation (3444), and for the word of thy righteousness. PSALMS 119:123

Salvation (3444) pronounced yesh-oo'-aw; fem. pass. part. of 3467; something saved, i.e. (abstr.) deliverance; hence aid, victory, prosperity:- deliverance, health, help (-ing), salvation, save, saving (health), welfare.

deliverance (Dictionary) the act of giving up or surrendering; giving into another's possession or keeping; to give forth in words; utter or pronounce; to deliver a verdict; setting free; disburden (oneself) of thoughts, opinions, etc.; Obsolete: to make known, assert; Obsolete or Archaic: agile, active, quick.

prosperity (Dictionary) flourishing or thriving condition; good fortune; success.

fortune (Dictionary) position in life as determined by wealth.

success (Dictionary) favorable or prosperous termination of attempts or endeavors; gaining of wealth, position, or the like; Obsolete: outcome.

welfare (Dictionary) state of faring well; well-being; prosperity; success; happiness; weal.

happiness (2) (Dictionary) good fortune, pleasure, content or gladness.

weal (1) (Dictionary) Archaic: well-being, prosperity , or happiness.

(3467) pronounced yaw-shah'; a prim. root; prop. to be open, wide or free, i.e. (by impl.) to be safe; causat. to free or succor: - x at all, avenging, defend, deliver (-er), help, preserve, rescue, be safe, bring (having) salvation, save (-iour), get victory.

succor (Dictionary) help, relief, aid, assistance in difficulty, need, or distress.

salvation (Dictionary) act of saving or delivering; a source, cause, or means of deliverance; deliverance from the power of penalty and sin; redemption.

sin (Dictionary) transgression of divine law; an act regarded as such transgression, or any violation, especially a willful or deliberate one of some religious or moral principle; to offend against a principle, standard, etc.

transgression (Dictionary) violation of a law, command, etc.; sin.

redemption (Dictionary) deliverance; rescue; repurchase, as of something sold; recovery by payment, as of something pledged.

Savior (Dictionary) one who saves, rescues, or delivers: the savior of the country; (cap.) a title of God, especially of Christ (commonly spelled Saviour).

Deliverance is far from the wicked, for they have not turned to Your laws. TEHILLIM 119:155 (PSALMS 119:155)

Salvation (3444) *is* far from the wicked; for they seek not thy statutes. PSALMS 119:155

Salvation (3444) pronounced yesh-oo'-aw; fem. pass. part. of 3467; something saved, i.e. (abstr.) deliverance; hence aid, victory, prosperity:- deliverance, health, help (-ing), salvation, save, saving (health), welfare.

deliverance (Dictionary) the act of giving up or surrendering; giving into another's possession or keeping; to give forth in words; utter or pronounce; to deliver a verdict; setting free; disburden (oneself) of thoughts, opinions, etc.; Obsolete: to make known, assert; Obsolete or Archaic: agile, active, quick.

prosperity (Dictionary) flourishing or thriving condition; good fortune; success.

fortune (Dictionary) position in life as determined by wealth.

success (Dictionary) favorable or prosperous termination of attempts or endeavors; gaining of wealth, position, or the like; Obsolete: outcome.

welfare (Dictionary) state of faring well; well-being; prosperity; success; happiness; weal.

happiness (2) (Dictionary) good fortune, pleasure, content or gladness.

weal (1) (Dictionary) Archaic: well-being, prosperity , or happiness.

(3467) pronounced yaw-shah'; a prim. root; prop. to be open, wide or free, i.e. (by impl.) to be safe; causat. to free or succor: - x at all, avenging, defend, deliver (-er), help, preserve, rescue, be safe, bring (having) salvation, save (-iour), get victory.

succor (Dictionary) help, relief, aid, assistance in difficulty, need, or distress.

salvation (Dictionary) act of saving or delivering; a source, cause, or means of deliverance; deliverance from the power of penalty and sin; redemption.

sin (Dictionary) transgression of divine law; an act regarded as such transgression, or any violation, especially a willful or deliberate one of some religious or moral principle; to offend against a principle, standard, etc.

transgression (Dictionary) violation of a law, command, etc.; sin.

redemption (Dictionary) deliverance; rescue; repurchase, as of something sold; recovery by payment, as of something pledged.

Savior (Dictionary) one who saves, rescues, or delivers: the savior of the country; (cap.) a title of God, especially of Christ (commonly spelled Saviour).

I hope for Your deliverance, O LORD; I observe Your commandments. TEHILLIM 119:166 (PSALMS 119:166)

LORD, I have hoped for thy salvation (3444), and done thy commandments. PSALMS 119:166

Salvation (3444) pronounced yesh-oo'-aw; fem. pass. part. of 3467; something saved, i.e. (abstr.) deliverance; hence aid, victory, prosperity:- deliverance, health, help (-ing), salvation, save, saving (health), welfare.

deliverance (Dictionary) the act of giving up or surrendering; giving into another's possession or keeping; to give forth in words; utter or pronounce; to deliver a verdict; setting free; disburden (oneself) of thoughts, opinions, etc.; Obsolete: to make known, assert; Obsolete or Archaic: agile, active, quick.

prosperity (Dictionary) flourishing or thriving condition; good fortune; success.

fortune (Dictionary) position in life as determined by wealth.

success (Dictionary) favorable or prosperous termination of attempts or endeavors; gaining of wealth, position, or the like; Obsolete: outcome.

welfare (Dictionary) state of faring well; well-being; prosperity; success; happiness; weal.

happiness (2) (Dictionary) good fortune, pleasure, content or gladness.

weal (1) (Dictionary) Archaic: well-being, prosperity , or happiness.

(3467) pronounced yaw-shah'; a prim. root; prop. to be open, wide or free, i.e. (by impl.) to be safe; causat. to free or succor: - x at all, avenging, defend, deliver (-er), help, preserve, rescue, be safe, bring (having) salvation, save (-iour), get victory.

succor (Dictionary) help, relief, aid, assistance in difficulty, need, or distress.

salvation (Dictionary) act of saving or delivering; a source, cause, or means of deliverance; deliverance from the power of penalty and sin; redemption.

sin (Dictionary) transgression of divine law; an act regarded as such transgression, or any violation, especially a willful or deliberate one of some religious or moral principle; to offend against a principle, standard, etc.

transgression (Dictionary) violation of a law, command, etc.; sin.

redemption (Dictionary) deliverance; rescue; repurchase, as of something sold; recovery by payment, as of something pledged.

Savior (Dictionary) one who saves, rescues, or delivers: the savior of the country; (cap.) a title of God, especially of Christ (commonly spelled Saviour).

I have longed for Your deliverance, O LORD; Your teaching is my delight. TEHILLIM 119:174 (PSALMS 119:174)

I have longed for thy salvation (3444), O LORD; and thy law *is* my delight. PSALMS 119:174

Salvation (3444) pronounced yesh-oo'-aw; fem. pass. part. of 3467; something saved, i.e. (abstr.) deliverance; hence aid, victory, prosperity:- deliverance, health, help (-ing), salvation, save, saving (health), welfare.

deliverance (Dictionary) the act of giving up or surrendering; giving into another's possession or keeping; to give forth in words; utter or pronounce; to deliver a verdict; setting free; disburden (oneself) of thoughts, opinions, etc.; Obsolete: to make known, assert; Obsolete or Archaic: agile, active, quick.

prosperity (Dictionary) flourishing or thriving condition; good fortune; success.

fortune (Dictionary) position in life as determined by wealth.

success (Dictionary) favorable or prosperous termination of attempts or endeavors; gaining of wealth, position, or the like; Obsolete: outcome.

welfare (Dictionary) state of faring well; well-being; prosperity; success; happiness; weal.

happiness (2) (Dictionary) good fortune, pleasure, content or gladness.

weal (1) (Dictionary) Archaic: well-being, prosperity , or happiness.

(3467) pronounced yaw-shah'; a prim. root; prop. to be open, wide or free, i.e. (by impl.) to be safe; causat. to free or succor: - x at all, avenging, defend, deliver (-er), help, preserve, rescue, be safe, bring (having) salvation, save (-iour), get victory.

succor (Dictionary) help, relief, aid, assistance in difficulty, need, or distress.

salvation (Dictionary) act of saving or delivering; a source, cause, or means of deliverance; deliverance from the power of penalty and sin; redemption.

sin (Dictionary) transgression of divine law; an act regarded as such transgression, or any violation, especially a willful or deliberate one of some religious or moral principle; to offend against a principle, standard, etc.

transgression (Dictionary) violation of a law, command, etc.; sin.

redemption (Dictionary) deliverance; rescue; repurchase, as of something sold; recovery by payment, as of something pledged.

Savior (Dictionary) one who saves, rescues, or delivers: the savior of the country; (cap.) a title of God, especially of Christ (commonly spelled Saviour).

I will clothe its priests in victory, its loyal ones shall sing for joy. TEHILLIM 132:16 (PSALMS 132:16)

I will also clothe her priests with salvation (3468): and her saints shall shout aloud for joy. PSALMS 132:16

Salvation (3468) pronounced yeh'-shah; from 3467; liberty, deliverance, prosperity, safety, salvation, saving.

liberty (Dictionary) freedom from arbitrary or despotic government or, often, from other rule or law than that of a self-governing community; freedom from external or foreign rule; freedom from control, interference, obligation, restriction, hampering conditions, etc.; power or right of doing, thinking, speaking, etc., according to choice.

deliverance (Dictionary) the act of giving up or surrendering; giving into another's possession or keeping; to give forth in words; utter or pronounce; to deliver a verdict; setting free; disburden (oneself) of thoughts, opinions, etc.; Obsolete: to make known, assert; Obsolete or Archaic: agile, active, quick.

prosperity (Dictionary) flourishing or thriving condition; good fortune; success.

fortune (Dictionary) position in life as determined by wealth.

success (Dictionary) favorable or prosperous termination of attempts or endeavors; gaining of wealth, position, or the like; Obsolete: outcome.

(3467) pronounced yaw-shah'; a prim. root; prop. to be open, wide or free, i.e. (by impl.) to be safe; causat. to free or succor: - x at all, avenging, defend, deliver (-er), help, preserve, rescue, be safe, bring (having) salvation, save (-iour), get victory.

succor (Dictionary) help, relief, aid, assistance in difficulty, need, or distress.

salvation (Dictionary) act of saving or delivering; a source, cause, or means of deliverance; deliverance from the power of penalty and sin; redemption.

sin (Dictionary) transgression of divine law; an act regarded as such transgression, or any violation, especially a willful or deliberate one of some religious or moral principle; to offend against a principle, standard, etc.

transgression (Dictionary) violation of a law, command, etc.; sin.

redemption (Dictionary) deliverance; rescue; repurchase, as of something sold; recovery by payment, as of something pledged.

Savior (Dictionary) one who saves, rescues, or delivers: the savior of the country; (cap.) a title of God, especially of Christ (commonly spelled Saviour).

O God, my LORD, the strength of my deliverance, You protected my head on the day of battle.
TEHILLIM 140:8 (PSALMS 140:7)

battle: Lit. "arms" (TANAKH footnote)

O God, the LORD, the strength of my salvation (3444), thou hast covered my head in the day of battle.
PSALMS 140:7

Salvation (3444) pronounced yesh-oo'-aw; fem. pass. part. of 3467; something saved, i.e. (abstr.) deliverance; hence aid, victory, prosperity:- deliverance, health, help (-ing), salvation, save, saving (health), welfare.

deliverance (Dictionary) the act of giving up or surrendering; giving into another's possession or keeping; to give forth in words; utter or pronounce; to deliver a verdict; setting free; disburden (oneself) of thoughts, opinions, etc.; Obsolete: to make known, assert; Obsolete or Archaic: agile, active, quick.

prosperity (Dictionary) flourishing or thriving condition; good fortune; success.

fortune (Dictionary) position in life as determined by wealth.

success (Dictionary) favorable or prosperous termination of attempts or endeavors; gaining of wealth, position, or the like; Obsolete: outcome.

welfare (Dictionary) state of faring well; well-being; prosperity; success; happiness; weal.

happiness (2) (Dictionary) good fortune, pleasure, content or gladness.

weal (1) (Dictionary) Archaic: well-being, prosperity , or happiness.

(3467) pronounced yaw-shah'; a prim. root; prop. to be open, wide or free, i.e. (by impl.) to be safe; causat. to free or succor: - x at all, avenging, defend, deliver (-er), help, preserve, rescue, be safe, bring (having) salvation, save (-iour), get victory.

succor (Dictionary) help, relief, aid, assistance in difficulty, need, or distress.

salvation (Dictionary) act of saving or delivering; a source, cause, or means of deliverance; deliverance from the power of penalty and sin; redemption.

sin (Dictionary) transgression of divine law; an act regarded as such transgression, or any violation, especially a willful or deliberate one of some religious or moral principle; to offend against a principle, standard, etc.

transgression (Dictionary) violation of a law, command, etc.; sin.

redemption (Dictionary) deliverance; rescue; repurchase, as of something sold; recovery by payment, as of something pledged.

Savior (Dictionary) one who saves, rescues, or delivers: the savior of the country; (cap.) a title of God, especially of Christ (commonly spelled Saviour).

...to You who give victory to kings, who rescue His servant David from the deadly sword.
TEHILLIM 144:10 (PSALMS 144:10)

It *is he* that giveth salvation (8668) unto kings; who delivereth David his servant from the hurtful sword.
PSALMS 144:10

Salvation (8668) pronounced tesh-oo-aw'; from 7768 in the sense of 3467; rescue (lit. or fig., pers., national, or spir.):- deliverance, help, safety, salvation, victory.

deliverance (Dictionary) the act of giving up or surrendering; giving into another's possession or keeping; to give forth in words; utter or pronounce; to deliver a verdict; setting free; disburden (oneself) of thoughts, opinions, etc.; Obsolete: to make known, assert; Obsolete or Archaic: agile, active, quick.

salvation (Dictionary) act of saving or delivering; a source, cause, or means of deliverance; deliverance from the power of penalty and sin; redemption.

sin (Dictionary) transgression of divine law; an act regarded as such transgression, or any violation, especially a willful or deliberate one of some religious or moral principle; to offend against a principle, standard, etc.

transgression (Dictionary) violation of a law, command, etc.; sin.

redemption (Dictionary) deliverance; rescue; repurchase, as of something sold; recovery by payment, as of something pledged.

(7768) pronounced shaw-vah'; a prim. root; prop. to be free; but used only causat. and reflex. to halloo (for help, i.e. freedom from some trouble):- cry (aloud, out), shout.

halloo (Dictionary) an exclamation used to attract attention, to incite the dogs in hunting, etc.; to call with a loud voice: shout, cry, as after dogs; to incite or chase with shouts and cries of "halloo".

(3467) pronounced yaw-shah'; a prim. root; prop. to be open, wide or free, i.e. (by impl.) to be safe; causat. to free or succor: - x at all, avenging, defend, deliver (-er), help, preserve, rescue, be safe, bring (having) salvation, save (-iour), get victory.

succor (Dictionary) help, relief, aid, assistance in difficulty, need, or distress.

salvation (Dictionary) act of saving or delivering; a source, cause, or means of deliverance; deliverance from the power of penalty and sin; redemption.

sin (Dictionary) transgression of divine law; an act regarded as such transgression, or any violation, especially a willful or deliberate one of some religious or moral principle; to offend against a principle, standard, etc.

transgression (Dictionary) violation of a law, command, etc.; sin.

redemption (Dictionary) deliverance; rescue; repurchase, as of something sold; recovery by payment, as of something pledged.

Savior (Dictionary) one who saves, rescues, or delivers: the savior of the country; (cap.) a title of God, especially of Christ (commonly spelled Saviour).

For the LORD delights in His people; He adorns the lowly with victory. TEHILLIM 149:4 (PSALMS 149:4)

For the LORD taketh pleasure in His people: he will beautify the meek with salvation (3444). PSALMS 149:4

Salvation (3444) pronounced yesh-oo'-aw; fem. pass. part. of 3467; something saved, i.e. (abstr.) deliverance; hence aid, victory, prosperity:- deliverance, health, help (-ing), salvation, save, saving (health), welfare.

deliverance (Dictionary) the act of giving up or surrendering; giving into another's possession or keeping; to give forth in words; utter or pronounce; to deliver a verdict; setting free; disburden (oneself) of thoughts, opinions, etc.; Obsolete: to make known, assert; Obsolete or Archaic: agile, active, quick.

prosperity (Dictionary) flourishing or thriving condition; good fortune; success.

fortune (Dictionary) position in life as determined by wealth.

success (Dictionary) favorable or prosperous termination of attempts or endeavors; gaining of wealth, position, or the like; Obsolete: outcome.

welfare (Dictionary) state of faring well; well-being; prosperity; success; happiness; weal.

happiness (2) (Dictionary) good fortune, pleasure, content or gladness.

weal (1) (Dictionary) Archaic: well-being, prosperity , or happiness.

(3467) pronounced yaw-shah'; a prim. root; prop. to be open, wide or free, i.e. (by impl.) to be safe; causat. to free or succor: - x at all, avenging, defend, deliver (-er), help, preserve, rescue, be safe, bring (having) salvation, save (-iour), get victory.

succor (Dictionary) help, relief, aid, assistance in difficulty, need, or distress.

salvation (Dictionary) act of saving or delivering; a source, cause, or means of deliverance; deliverance from the power of penalty and sin; redemption.

sin (Dictionary) transgression of divine law; an act regarded as such transgression, or any violation, especially a willful or deliberate one of some religious or moral principle; to offend against a principle, standard, etc.

transgression (Dictionary) violation of a law, command, etc.; sin.

redemption (Dictionary) deliverance; rescue; repurchase, as of something sold; recovery by payment, as of something pledged.

Savior (Dictionary) one who saves, rescues, or delivers: the savior of the country; (cap.) a title of God, especially of Christ (commonly spelled Saviour).

In that day, you shall say: " I give thanks to You, O LORD! Although You were wroth with me, Your wrath has turned back and You comfort me. Behold the God who gives me triumph! I am confident, unafraid; for Yah the LORD is my strength and might, and He has been my deliverance." Joyfully shall you draw water from the fountains of triumph. YESHA'YAHU 12:1-3 (ISAIAH 12:1-3)

might: "song" (TANAKH footnote)

And in that day thou shalt say, O LORD, I will praise thee; though thou wast angry with me, thine anger is turned away, and thou comfortedst me. Behold, God *is* my salvation (3444); I will trust, and not be afraid; for the LORD JEHOVAH *is* my strength and *my* song; he also is become my salvation (3444). Therefore with joy shall ye draw water out of the wells of salvation (3444). ISAIAH 12:1-3

SALVATION

Salvation (3444) pronounced yesh-oo'-aw; fem. pass. part. of 3467; something saved, i.e. (abstr.) deliverance; hence aid, victory, prosperity:- deliverance, health, help (-ing), salvation, save, saving (health), welfare.

> deliverance (Dictionary) the act of giving up or surrendering; giving into another's possession or keeping; to give forth in words; utter or pronounce; to deliver a verdict; setting free; disburden (oneself) of thoughts, opinions, etc.; Obsolete: to make known, assert; Obsolete or Archaic: agile, active, quick.
>
> prosperity (Dictionary) flourishing or thriving condition; good fortune; success.
>
> fortune (Dictionary) position in life as determined by wealth.
>
> success (Dictionary) favorable or prosperous termination of attempts or endeavors; gaining of wealth, position, or the like; Obsolete: outcome.
>
> welfare (Dictionary) state of faring well; well-being; prosperity; success; happiness; weal.
>
> happiness (2) (Dictionary) good fortune, pleasure, content or gladness.
>
> weal (1) (Dictionary) Archaic: well-being, prosperity , or happiness.

(3467) pronounced yaw-shah'; a prim. root; prop. to be open, wide or free, i.e. (by impl.) to be safe; causat. to free or succor: - x at all, avenging, defend, deliver (-er), help, preserve, rescue, be safe, bring (having) salvation, save (-iour), get victory.

> succor (Dictionary) help, relief, aid, assistance in difficulty, need, or distress.
>
> salvation (Dictionary) act of saving or delivering; a source, cause, or means of deliverance; deliverance from the power of penalty and sin; redemption.
>
> sin (Dictionary) transgression of divine law; an act regarded as such transgression, or any violation, especially a willful or deliberate one of some religious or moral principle; to offend against a principle, standard, etc.
>
> transgression (Dictionary) violation of a law, command, etc.; sin.
>
> redemption (Dictionary) deliverance; rescue; repurchase, as of something sold; recovery by payment, as of something pledged.
>
> Savior (Dictionary) one who saves, rescues, or delivers: the savior of the country; (cap.) a title of God, especially of Christ (commonly spelled Saviour).

Truly, you have forgotten the God who saves you and have not remembered the Rock who shelters you: that is why, though you plant a delightful sapling, what you sow proves a disappointing slip.
YESHA"YAHU 17:10 (ISAIAH 17:10)

delightful: Emendation yields "true" So Vulgate (cf. Septuagint); cf. Jer. 2:21 (TANAKH footnote)

I planted you with noble vines, all with choicest seed; alas, I find you changed into a base, an alien vine! YIRMEYAHU 2:21 (JEREMIAH 2:21)

Yet I had planted thee a noble vine, wholly a right seed: how then art thou turned into the degenerate plant of a strange vine unto me? JEREMIAH 2:21

Because thou hast forgotten the God of thy salvation (3468) and hast not been mindful of the Rock of thy strength, therefore shalt thou plant pleasant plants, and shalt set it with strange slips;...
ISAIAH 17:10

Salvation (3468) pronounced yeh'-shah; from 3467; liberty, deliverance, prosperity, safety, salvation, saving.

liberty (Dictionary) freedom from arbitrary or despotic government or, often, from other rule or law than that of a self-governing community; freedom from external or foreign rule; freedom from control, interference, obligation, restriction, hampering conditions, etc.; power or right of doing, thinking, speaking, etc., according to choice.

deliverance (Dictionary) the act of giving up or surrendering; giving into another's possession or keeping; to give forth in words; utter or pronounce; to deliver a verdict; setting free; disburden (oneself) of thoughts, opinions, etc.; Obsolete: to make known, assert; Obsolete or Archaic: agile, active, quick.

prosperity (Dictionary) flourishing or thriving condition; good fortune; success.

fortune (Dictionary) position in life as determined by wealth.

success (Dictionary) favorable or prosperous termination of attempts or endeavors; gaining of wealth, position, or the like; Obsolete: outcome.

(3467) pronounced yaw-shah'; a prim. root; prop. to be open, wide or free, i.e. (by impl.) to be safe; causat. to free or succor: - x at all, avenging, defend, deliver (-er), help, preserve, rescue, be safe, bring (having) salvation, save (-iour), get victory.

succor (Dictionary) help, relief, aid, assistance in difficulty, need, or distress.

salvation (Dictionary) act of saving or delivering; a source, cause, or means of deliverance; deliverance from the power of penalty and sin; redemption.

sin (Dictionary) transgression of divine law; an act regarded as such transgression, or any violation, especially a willful or deliberate one of some religious or moral principle; to offend against a principle, standard, etc.

transgression (Dictionary) violation of a law, command, etc.; sin.

redemption (Dictionary) deliverance; rescue; repurchase, as of something sold; recovery by payment, as of something pledged.

Savior (Dictionary) one who saves, rescues, or delivers: the savior of the country; (cap.) a title of God, especially of Christ (commonly spelled Saviour).

In that day they shall say: This is our God; we trusted in Him, and He delivered us. This is the LORD, in whom we trusted; let us rejoice and exult in His deliverance! YESHA'YAHU 25:9 (ISAIAH 25:9)

And it shall be said in that day, Lo, this *is* our God: we have waited for him; and he will save (3467) us; this *is* the LORD, we have waited for him, we will be glad and rejoice in his salvation (3444). ISAIAH 25:9

(3467) pronounced yaw-shah'; a prim. root; prop. to be open, wide or free, i.e. (by impl.) to be safe; causat. to free or succor: - x at all, avenging, defend, deliver (-er), help, preserve, rescue, be safe, bring (having) salvation, save (-iour), get victory.

succor (Dictionary) help, relief, aid, assistance in difficulty, need, or distress.

salvation (Dictionary) act of saving or delivering; a source, cause, or means of deliverance; deliverance from the power of penalty and sin; redemption.

sin (Dictionary) transgression of divine law; an act regarded as such transgression, or any violation, especially a willful or deliberate one of some religious or moral principle; to offend against a principle, standard, etc.

transgression (Dictionary) violation of a law, command, etc.; sin.

redemption (Dictionary) deliverance; rescue; repurchase, as of something sold; recovery by payment, as of something pledged.

Savior (Dictionary) one who saves, rescues, or delivers: the savior of the country; (cap.) a title of God, especially of Christ (commonly spelled Saviour).

Salvation (3444) pronounced yesh-oo'-aw; fem. pass. part. of 3467; something saved, i.e. (abstr.) deliverance; hence aid, victory, prosperity:- deliverance, health, help (-ing), salvation, save, saving (health), welfare.

deliverance (Dictionary) the act of giving up or surrendering; giving into another's possession or keeping; to give forth in words; utter or pronounce; to deliver a verdict; setting free; disburden (oneself) of thoughts, opinions, etc.; Obsolete: to make known, assert; Obsolete or Archaic: agile, active, quick.

prosperity (Dictionary) flourishing or thriving condition; good fortune; success.

fortune (Dictionary) position in life as determined by wealth.

success (Dictionary) favorable or prosperous termination of attempts or endeavors; gaining of wealth, position, or the like; Obsolete: outcome.

welfare (Dictionary) state of faring well; well-being; prosperity; success; happiness; weal.

happiness (2) (Dictionary) good fortune, pleasure, content or gladness.

weal (1) (Dictionary) Archaic: well-being, prosperity , or happiness.

In that day, this song shall be sung in the land of Judah: Ours is a mighty city; He makes victory our inner and outer wall. YESHA'YAHU 26:1 (ISAIAH 26:1)

In that day shall this song be sung in the land of Judah: We have a strong city; salvation (3444) will God appoint *for* walls and bulwarks. ISAIAH 26:1

Salvation (3444) pronounced yesh-oo'-aw; fem. pass. part. of 3467; something saved, i.e. (abstr.) deliverance; hence aid, victory, prosperity:- deliverance, health, help (-ing), salvation, save, saving (health), welfare.

deliverance (Dictionary) the act of giving up or surrendering; giving into another's possession or keeping; to give forth in words; utter or pronounce; to deliver a verdict; setting free; disburden (oneself) of thoughts, opinions, etc.; Obsolete: to make known, assert; Obsolete or Archaic: agile, active, quick.

prosperity (Dictionary) flourishing or thriving condition; good fortune; success.

fortune (Dictionary) position in life as determined by wealth.

success (Dictionary) favorable or prosperous termination of attempts or endeavors; gaining of wealth, position, or the like; Obsolete: outcome.

welfare (Dictionary) state of faring well; well-being; prosperity; success; happiness; weal.

happiness (2) (Dictionary) good fortune, pleasure, content or gladness.

weal (1) (Dictionary) Archaic: well-being, prosperity , or happiness.

(3467) pronounced yaw-shah'; a prim. root; prop. to be open, wide or free, i.e. (by impl.) to be safe; causat. to free or succor: - x at all, avenging, defend, deliver (-er), help, preserve, rescue, be safe, bring (having) salvation, save (-iour), get victory.

succor (Dictionary) help, relief, aid, assistance in difficulty, need, or distress.

salvation (Dictionary) act of saving or delivering; a source, cause, or means of deliverance; deliverance from the power of penalty and sin; redemption.

sin (Dictionary) transgression of divine law; an act regarded as such transgression, or any violation, especially a willful or deliberate one of some religious or moral principle; to offend against a principle, standard, etc.

transgression (Dictionary) violation of a law, command, etc.; sin.

redemption (Dictionary) deliverance; rescue; repurchase, as of something sold; recovery by payment, as of something pledged.

Savior (Dictionary) one who saves, rescues, or delivers: the savior of the country; (cap.) a title of God, especially of Christ (commonly spelled Saviour).

O LORD, be gracious unto us! It is to You we have looked; Be their arm every morning, also our deliverance in time of stress. YESHA'YAHU 33:2 (ISAIAH 33:2)

be their arm: Emendation yields "You have been our help." (TANAKH footnote)

O LORD, be gracious unto us; we have waited for thee: be thou their arm every morning, our salvation (3444) also in the time of trouble. ISAIAH 33:2

Salvation (3444) pronounced yesh-oo'-aw; fem. pass. part. of 3467; something saved, i.e. (abstr.) deliverance; hence aid, victory, prosperity:- deliverance, health, help (-ing), salvation, save, saving (health), welfare.

deliverance (Dictionary) the act of giving up or surrendering; giving into another's possession or keeping; to give forth in words; utter or pronounce; to deliver a verdict; setting free; disburden (oneself) of thoughts, opinions, etc.; Obsolete: to make known, assert; Obsolete or Archaic: agile, active, quick.

prosperity (Dictionary) flourishing or thriving condition; good fortune; success.

fortune (Dictionary) position in life as determined by wealth.

success (Dictionary) favorable or prosperous termination of attempts or endeavors; gaining of wealth, position, or the like; Obsolete: outcome.

welfare (Dictionary) state of faring well; well-being; prosperity; success; happiness; weal.

happiness (2) (Dictionary) good fortune, pleasure, content or gladness.

weal (1) (Dictionary) Archaic: well-being, prosperity , or happiness.

(3467) pronounced yaw-shah'; a prim. root; prop. to be open, wide or free, i.e. (by impl.) to be safe; causat. to free or succor: - x at all, avenging, defend, deliver (-er), help, preserve, rescue, be safe, bring (having) salvation, save (-iour), get victory.

succor (Dictionary) help, relief, aid, assistance in difficulty, need, or distress.

salvation (Dictionary) act of saving or delivering; a source, cause, or means of deliverance; deliverance from the power of penalty and sin; redemption.

sin (Dictionary) transgression of divine law; an act regarded as such transgression, or any violation, especially a willful or deliberate one of some religious or moral principle; to offend against a principle, standard, etc.

transgression (Dictionary) violation of a law, command, etc.; sin.

redemption (Dictionary) deliverance; rescue; repurchase, as of something sold; recovery by payment, as of something pledged.

Savior (Dictionary) one who saves, rescues, or delivers: the savior of the country; (cap.) a title of God, especially of Christ (commonly spelled Saviour).

Faithfulness to Your charge was [her] wealth, wisdom and devotion [her] triumph, reverence for the LORD-that was her treasure. YESHA'YAHU 33:6 (ISAIAH 33:6)

her: Heb. "his" (TANAKH footnote)

And wisdom and knowledge shall be the stability of thy times, *and* strength of salvation (3444): the fear of the LORD *is* his treasure. ISAIAH 33:6

Salvation (3444) pronounced yesh-oo'-aw; fem. pass. part. of 3467; something saved, i.e. (abstr.) deliverance; hence aid, victory, prosperity:- deliverance, health, help (-ing), salvation, save, saving (health), welfare.

deliverance (Dictionary) the act of giving up or surrendering; giving into another's possession or keeping; to give forth in words; utter or pronounce; to deliver a verdict; setting free; disburden (oneself) of thoughts, opinions, etc.; Obsolete: to make known, assert; Obsolete or Archaic: agile, active, quick.

prosperity (Dictionary) flourishing or thriving condition; good fortune; success.

fortune (Dictionary) position in life as determined by wealth.

success (Dictionary) favorable or prosperous termination of attempts or endeavors; gaining of wealth, position, or the like; Obsolete: outcome.

welfare (Dictionary) state of faring well; well-being; prosperity; success; happiness; weal.

happiness (2) (Dictionary) good fortune, pleasure, content or gladness.

weal (1) (Dictionary) Archaic: well-being, prosperity , or happiness.

(3467) pronounced yaw-shah'; a prim. root; prop. to be open, wide or free, i.e. (by impl.) to be safe; causat. to free or succor: - x at all, avenging, defend, deliver (-er), help, preserve, rescue, be safe, bring (having) salvation, save (-iour), get victory.

succor (Dictionary) help, relief, aid, assistance in difficulty, need, or distress.

salvation (Dictionary) act of saving or delivering; a source, cause, or means of deliverance; deliverance from the power of penalty and sin; redemption.

sin (Dictionary) transgression of divine law; an act regarded as such transgression, or any violation, especially a willful or deliberate one of some religious or moral principle; to offend against a principle, standard, etc.

transgression (Dictionary) violation of a law, command, etc.; sin.

redemption (Dictionary) deliverance; rescue; repurchase, as of something sold; recovery by payment, as of something pledged.

Savior (Dictionary) one who saves, rescues, or delivers: the savior of the country; (cap.) a title of God, especially of Christ (commonly spelled Saviour).

Pour down, O skies, from above! Let the heavens rain down victory! Let the earth open up and triumph sprout, yes, let vindication spring up; I the LORD have created it. YESHA'YAHU 45:8 (ISAIAH 45:8)

Drop down, ye heavens from above, and let the skies pour down righteousness: let the earth open, and let them bring forth salvation (3468), and let righteousness spring up together; I the LORD have created it. ISAIAH 45:8

Salvation (3468) pronounced yeh'-shah; from 3467; liberty, deliverance, prosperity, safety, salvation, saving.

liberty (Dictionary) freedom from arbitrary or despotic government or, often, from other rule or law than that of a self-governing community; freedom from external or foreign rule; freedom from control, interference, obligation, restriction, hampering conditions, etc.; power or right of doing, thinking, speaking, etc., according to choice.

deliverance (Dictionary) the act of giving up or surrendering; giving into another's possession or keeping; to give forth in words; utter or pronounce; to deliver a verdict; setting free; disburden (oneself) of thoughts, opinions, etc.; Obsolete: to make known, assert; Obsolete or Archaic: agile, active, quick.

prosperity (Dictionary) flourishing or thriving condition; good fortune; success.

fortune (Dictionary) position in life as determined by wealth.

success (Dictionary) favorable or prosperous termination of attempts or endeavors; gaining of wealth, position, or the like; Obsolete: outcome.

(3467) pronounced yaw-shah'; a prim. root; prop. to be open, wide or free, i.e. (by impl.) to be safe; causat. to free or succor: - x at all, avenging, defend, deliver (-er), help, preserve, rescue, be safe, bring (having) salvation, save (-iour), get victory.

succor (Dictionary) help, relief, aid, assistance in difficulty, need, or distress.

salvation (Dictionary) act of saving or delivering; a source, cause, or means of deliverance; deliverance from the power of penalty and sin; redemption.

sin (Dictionary) transgression of divine law; an act regarded as such transgression, or any violation, especially a willful or deliberate one of some religious or moral principle; to offend against a principle, standard, etc.

transgression (Dictionary) violation of a law, command, etc.; sin.

redemption (Dictionary) deliverance; rescue; repurchase, as of something sold; recovery by payment, as of something pledged.

Savior (Dictionary) one who saves, rescues, or delivers: the savior of the country; (cap.) a title of God, especially of Christ (commonly spelled Saviour).

But Israel has won through the LORD triumph everlasting. You shall not be shamed or disgraced in all the ages to come! YESHA'YAHU 45:17 (ISAIAH 45:17)

But Israel shall be saved (3467) in the LORD with an everlasting salvation (8668): ye shall not be ashamed nor confounded world without end. ISAIAH 45:17

(3467) pronounced yaw-shah'; a prim. root; prop. to be open, wide or free, i.e. (by impl.) to be safe; causat. to free or succor: - x at all, avenging, defend, deliver (-er), help, preserve, rescue, be safe, bring (having) salvation, save (-iour), get victory.

succor (Dictionary) help, relief, aid, assistance in difficulty, need, or distress.

salvation (Dictionary) act of saving or delivering; a source, cause, or means of deliverance; deliverance from the power of penalty and sin; redemption.

sin (Dictionary) transgression of divine law; an act regarded as such transgression, or any violation, especially a willful or deliberate one of some religious or moral principle; to offend against a principle, standard, etc.

transgression (Dictionary) violation of a law, command, etc.; sin.

redemption (Dictionary) deliverance; rescue; repurchase, as of something sold; recovery by payment, as of something pledged.

Savior (Dictionary) one who saves, rescues, or delivers: the savior of the country; (cap.) a title of God, especially of Christ (commonly spelled Saviour).

SALVATION

Salvation (8668) pronounced tesh-oo-aw'; from 7768 in the sense of 3467; rescue (lit. or fig., pers., national, or spir.):- deliverance, help, safety, salvation, victory.

deliverance (Dictionary) the act of giving up or surrendering; giving into another's possession or keeping; to give forth in words; utter or pronounce; to deliver a verdict; setting free; disburden (oneself) of thoughts, opinions, etc.; Obsolete: to make known, assert; Obsolete or Archaic: agile, active, quick.

salvation (Dictionary) act of saving or delivering; a source, cause, or means of deliverance; deliverance from the power of penalty and sin; redemption.

sin (Dictionary) transgression of divine law; an act regarded as such transgression, or any violation, especially a willful or deliberate one of some religious or moral principle; to offend against a principle, standard, etc.

transgression (Dictionary) violation of a law, command, etc.; sin.

redemption (Dictionary) deliverance; rescue; repurchase, as of something sold; recovery by payment, as of something pledged.

(7768) pronounced shaw-vah'; a prim. root; prop. to be free; but used only causat. and reflex. to halloo (for help, i.e. freedom from some trouble):- cry (aloud, out), shout.

halloo (Dictionary) an exclamation used to attract attention, to incite the dogs in hunting, etc.; to call with a loud voice: shout, cry, as after dogs; to incite or chase with shouts and cries of "halloo".

I am bringing My victory close; it shall not be far, and My triumph shall not be delayed. I will grant triumph in Zion to Israel, in whom I glory. YESHA'YAHU 46:13 (ISAIAH 46:13)

I bring near my righteousness; it shall not be far off, and my salvation (8668) shall not tarry; and I will place salvation (8668) in Zion for Israel my glory. ISAIAH 46:13

Salvation (8668) pronounced tesh-oo-aw'; from 7768 in the sense of 3467; rescue (lit. or fig., pers., national, or spir.):- deliverance, help, safety, salvation, victory.

deliverance (Dictionary) the act of giving up or surrendering; giving into another's possession or keeping; to give forth in words; utter or pronounce; to deliver a verdict; setting free; disburden (oneself) of thoughts, opinions, etc.; Obsolete: to make known, assert; Obsolete or Archaic: agile, active, quick.

salvation (Dictionary) act of saving or delivering; a source, cause, or means of deliverance; deliverance from the power of penalty and sin; redemption.

sin (Dictionary) transgression of divine law; an act regarded as such transgression, or any violation, especially a willful or deliberate one of some religious or moral principle; to offend against a principle, standard, etc.

transgression (Dictionary) violation of a law, command, etc.; sin.

redemption (Dictionary) deliverance; rescue; repurchase, as of something sold; recovery by payment, as of something pledged.

(7768) pronounced shaw-vah'; a prim. root; prop. to be free; but used only causat. and reflex. to halloo (for help, i.e. freedom from some trouble):- cry (aloud, out), shout.

halloo (Dictionary) an exclamation used to attract attention, to incite the dogs in hunting, etc.; to call with a loud voice: shout, cry, as after dogs; to incite or chase with shouts and cries of "halloo".

(3467) pronounced yaw-shah'; a prim. root; prop. to be open, wide or free, i.e. (by impl.) to be safe; causat. to free or succor: - x at all, avenging, defend, deliver (-er), help, preserve, rescue, be safe, bring (having) salvation, save (-iour), get victory.

succor (Dictionary) help, relief, aid, assistance in difficulty, need, or distress.

salvation (Dictionary) act of saving or delivering; a source, cause, or means of deliverance; deliverance from the power of penalty and sin; redemption.

sin (Dictionary) transgression of divine law; an act regarded as such transgression, or any violation, especially a willful or deliberate one of some religious or moral principle; to offend against a principle, standard, etc.

transgression (Dictionary) violation of a law, command, etc.; sin.

redemption (Dictionary) deliverance; rescue; repurchase, as of something sold; recovery by payment, as of something pledged.

Savior (Dictionary) one who saves, rescues, or delivers: the savior of the country; (cap.) a title of God, especially of Christ (commonly spelled Saviour).

For He has said: "It is too little that you should be My servant in that I raise up the tribes of Jacob and restore the survivors of Israel; I will also make you a light of nations, that My salvation may reach the ends of the earth." Thus said the LORD, the Redeemer of Israel, his Holy One, to the despised one, to the abhorred nations, to the slave of rulers: kings shall see and stand up; nobles, and they shall prostrate themselves-to the honor of the LORD, who is faithful, to the Holy One of Israel who chose you. Thus said the LORD: In an hour of favor I answer you, and on a day of salvation I help you - I created you and appointed you a covenant people, restoring the land, allotting anew the desolate holdings. YESHA'YAHU 49:6-8 (ISAIAH 49:6-8)

light: i.e., the agent of good fortune; cf. 42:1-4, 51:4-5. (TANAKH footnote)

abhorred nations: Meaning of Heb. Uncertain. Emendation yields "Whose being is despised./ Whose body is detested"; cf. 51:23. (TANAKH footnote)

a covenant people: Lit. "covenants of a people", meaning of Heb. uncertain. (TANAKH footnote)

> This is My servant, whom I uphold, My chosen one, in whom I delight. I have put My spirit upon him. He shall teach the true way to the nations. He shall not cry out or shout aloud, or make his voice heard in the streets. He shall not break even a bruised reed, or snuff out even a dim wick. He shall bring forth the true way. He shall not grow dim or be bruised till he has established the true way on earth; and the coastlands shall await his teaching. YESHA'YAHU 42:1-4 (ISAIAH 42:1-4)
>
> > He shall not break even a bruised reed, or snuff out even a dim wick: Or "A bruised reed, he shall not be broken;/ A dim wick, he shall not be snuffed out." (TANAKH footnote)
>
> Behold my servant, whom I uphold; mine elect*, in whom* my soul delighteth; I have put my Spirit upon him: he shall bring forth judgment to the Gentiles. He shall not cry, nor lift up, nor cause his voice to be heard in the street. A bruised reed shall he not break, and the smoking flax shall he not quench: he shall bring forth judgment unto truth. He shall not fail nor be discouraged till he have set judgment in the earth: and the isles shall wait for his law. ISAIAH 42:1-4
>
> Hearken to Me, My people, and give ear to Me, O My nation, for teaching shall go forth from Me, My way for the light of peoples. In a moment I will bring it: the triumph I grant is near, the success I give has gone forth. My arms shall provide for the peoples; the coastlands shall trust in Me, they shall look to My arm. YESHA'YAHU 51:4-5 (ISAIAH 51:4-5)
>
> > My people: Several mss. read "O peoples...O nations"; cf. end of this verse and v.5. (TANAKH footnote)
> >
> > from Me: i.e., through My servant Israel; cf. 42:14. (TANAKH footnote)
> >
> > provide for: Lit. "judge". (TANAKH footnote)
>
> Hearken unto me, my people; and give ear unto me, O my nation: for a law shall proceed from me, and I will make my judgment to rest for a light to the people. My righteousness is near; my salvation is gone forth, and mine arms shall judge the people; the isles shall wait upon me, and on mine arm shall they trust. ISAIAH 51:4-5

> Thus said the LORD, your LORD, your God who champions His people: Herewith I take from your hand the cup of reeling, the bowl, the cup of My wrath; you shall never drink it again. I will put it in the hand of your tormentors, who have commanded you, "Get down, that we may walk over you"- so that you made your back like the ground, like a street for passerby. YESHA'YAHU 51:22-23 (ISAIAH 51:22-23)
>
> Thus saith the LORD the LORD, and thy God that pleadeth the cause of his people, Behold, I have taken out of thine hand the cup of trembling, even the dregs of the cup of my fury; thou shalt no more drink it again: but I will put it into the hand of them that afflict thee; which have said to thy soul, Bow down, that we may go over: and thou hast laid thy body as the ground, and as the street, to them that went over. ISAIAH 51:22-23

And he said, It is a light thing that thou shouldest be my servant to raise up the tribes of Jacob, and to restore the preserved of Israel: I will also give thee for a light to the Gentiles, that thou mayest be my salvation (3444) unto the end of the earth. Thus saith the LORD, the Redeemer of Israel, and his Holy One, to him whom man despiseth, to him whom the nation abhorreth, to a servant of rulers. Kings shall see and arise, princes also shall worship, because of the LORD that is faithful, and the Holy One of Israel, and he shall choose thee. Thus saith the LORD, In an acceptable time have I heard thee, and in a day of salvation (3444) have I helped thee; and I will preserve thee, and give thee for a covenant of the people, to establish the earth, to cause to inherit the desolate heritages: ISAIAH 49:6-8

> Salvation (3444) pronounced yesh-oo'-aw; fem. pass. part. of 3467; something saved, i.e. (abstr.) deliverance; hence aid, victory, prosperity:- deliverance, health, help (-ing), salvation, save, saving (health), welfare.
>
> > deliverance (Dictionary) the act of giving up or surrendering; giving into another's possession or keeping; to give forth in words; utter or pronounce; to deliver a verdict; setting free; disburden (oneself) of thoughts, opinions, etc.; Obsolete: to make known, assert; Obsolete or Archaic: agile, active, quick.
> >
> > prosperity (Dictionary) flourishing or thriving condition; good fortune; success.
> >
> > fortune (Dictionary) position in life as determined by wealth.
> >
> > success (Dictionary) favorable or prosperous termination of attempts or endeavors; gaining of wealth, position, or the like; Obsolete: outcome.
> >
> > welfare (Dictionary) state of faring well; well-being; prosperity; success; happiness; weal.
> >
> > happiness (2) (Dictionary) good fortune, pleasure, content or gladness.
> >
> > weal (1) (Dictionary) Archaic: well-being, prosperity , or happiness.

(3467) pronounced yaw-shah'; a prim. root; prop. to be open, wide or free, i.e. (by impl.) to be safe; causat. to free or succor: - x at all, avenging, defend, deliver (-er), help, preserve, rescue, be safe, bring (having) salvation, save (-iour), get victory.

succor (Dictionary) help, relief, aid, assistance in difficulty, need, or distress.

salvation (Dictionary) act of saving or delivering; a source, cause, or means of deliverance; deliverance from the power of penalty and sin; redemption.

sin (Dictionary) transgression of divine law; an act regarded as such transgression, or any violation, especially a willful or deliberate one of some religious or moral principle; to offend against a principle, standard, etc.

transgression (Dictionary) violation of a law, command, etc.; sin.

redemption (Dictionary) deliverance; rescue; repurchase, as of something sold; recovery by payment, as of something pledged.

Savior (Dictionary) one who saves, rescues, or delivers: the savior of the country; (cap.) a title of God, especially of Christ (commonly spelled Saviour).

Raise your eyes to the heavens, and look upon the earth beneath: though the heavens should melt away like smoke, and the earth wear out like a garment, and its inhabitants die out as well, My victory shall stand forever, my triumph shall remain unbroken. Listen to Me, you who care for the right, O people who lay My instruction to heart! Fear not the insults of men, and be not dismayed at their jeers; for the moth shall eat them up like a garment. The worm shall eat them up like wool. But my triumph shall endure forever, My salvation through all the ages. YESHA'YAHU 51:6-8 (ISAIAH 51:6-8)

as well: Emendation yields "like gnats" (TANAKH footnote)

worm: Heb. sas, another word for "moth" (TANAKH footnote)

Lift up your eyes to the heavens, and look upon the earth beneath; for the heavens shall vanish away like smoke, and the earth shall wax old like a garment, and they that dwell therein shall die in like manner: but my salvation (3444) shall be forever, and my righteousness shall not be abolished. Hearken unto me, ye that know righteousness, the people in whose heart *is* my law; fear ye not the reproach of men, neither be ye afraid of their revilings. For the moth shall eat them up like a garment, and the worm shall eat them like wool; but my righteousness shall be forever, and my salvation (3444) from generation to generation. ISAIAH 51:6-8

Salvation (3444) pronounced yesh-oo'-aw; fem. pass. part. of 3467; something saved, i.e. (abstr.) deliverance; hence aid, victory, prosperity:- deliverance, health, help (-ing), salvation, save, saving (health), welfare.

deliverance (Dictionary) the act of giving up or surrendering; giving into another's possession or keeping; to give forth in words; utter or pronounce; to deliver a verdict;

setting free; disburden (oneself) of thoughts, opinions, etc.; Obsolete: to make known, assert; Obsolete or Archaic: agile, active, quick.

prosperity (Dictionary) flourishing or thriving condition; good fortune; success.

fortune (Dictionary) position in life as determined by wealth.

success (Dictionary) favorable or prosperous termination of attempts or endeavors; gaining of wealth, position, or the like; Obsolete: outcome.

welfare (Dictionary) state of faring well; well-being; prosperity; success; happiness; weal.

happiness (2) (Dictionary) good fortune, pleasure, content or gladness.

weal (1) (Dictionary) Archaic: well-being, prosperity , or happiness.

(3467) pronounced yaw-shah'; a prim. root; prop. to be open, wide or free, i.e. (by impl.) to be safe; causat. to free or succor: - x at all, avenging, defend, deliver (-er), help, preserve, rescue, be safe, bring (having) salvation, save (-iour), get victory.

succor (Dictionary) help, relief, aid, assistance in difficulty, need, or distress.

salvation (Dictionary) act of saving or delivering; a source, cause, or means of deliverance; deliverance from the power of penalty and sin; redemption.

sin (Dictionary) transgression of divine law; an act regarded as such transgression, or any violation, especially a willful or deliberate one of some religious or moral principle; to offend against a principle, standard, etc.

transgression (Dictionary) violation of a law, command, etc.; sin.

redemption (Dictionary) deliverance; rescue; repurchase, as of something sold; recovery by payment, as of something pledged.

Savior (Dictionary) one who saves, rescues, or delivers: the savior of the country; (cap.) a title of God, especially of Christ (commonly spelled Saviour).

How welcome on the mountains are the footsteps of the herald announcing happiness, heralding good fortune, announcing victory, telling Zion, "Your God is King!" YESHA'YAHU 52:7 (ISAIAH 52:7)

How beautiful upon the mountains are the feet of him that bringeth good tidings, that publisheth peace; that bringeth good tidings of good, that publisheth salvation (3444); that saith unto Zion, Thy God reigneth! ISAIAH 52:7

Salvation (3444) pronounced yesh-oo'-aw; fem. pass. part. of 3467; something saved, i.e. (abstr.) deliverance; hence aid, victory, prosperity:- deliverance, health, help (-ing), salvation, save, saving (health), welfare.

> deliverance (Dictionary) the act of giving up or surrendering; giving into another's possession or keeping; to give forth in words; utter or pronounce; to deliver a verdict; setting free; disburden (oneself) of thoughts, opinions, etc.; Obsolete: to make known, assert; Obsolete or Archaic: agile, active, quick.
>
> prosperity (Dictionary) flourishing or thriving condition; good fortune; success.
>
> fortune (Dictionary) position in life as determined by wealth.
>
> success (Dictionary) favorable or prosperous termination of attempts or endeavors; gaining of wealth, position, or the like; Obsolete: outcome.
>
> welfare (Dictionary) state of faring well; well-being; prosperity; success; happiness; weal.
>
> happiness (2) (Dictionary) good fortune, pleasure, content or gladness.
>
> weal (1) (Dictionary) Archaic: well-being, prosperity , or happiness.

(3467) pronounced yaw-shah'; a prim. root; prop. to be open, wide or free, i.e. (by impl.) to be safe; causat. to free or succor: - x at all, avenging, defend, deliver (-er), help, preserve, rescue, be safe, bring (having) salvation, save (-iour), get victory.

> succor (Dictionary) help, relief, aid, assistance in difficulty, need, or distress.
>
> salvation (Dictionary) act of saving or delivering; a source, cause, or means of deliverance; deliverance from the power of penalty and sin; redemption.
>
> sin (Dictionary) transgression of divine law; an act regarded as such transgression, or any violation, especially a willful or deliberate one of some religious or moral principle; to offend against a principle, standard, etc.
>
> transgression (Dictionary) violation of a law, command, etc.; sin.
>
> redemption (Dictionary) deliverance; rescue; repurchase, as of something sold; recovery by payment, as of something pledged.
>
> Savior (Dictionary) one who saves, rescues, or delivers: the savior of the country; (cap.) a title of God, especially of Christ (commonly spelled Saviour).

The LORD will bare His holy arm in the sight of all the nations, and the very ends of earth shall see the victory of our God. YESHA'YAHU 52:10 (ISAIAH 52:10)

The LORD hath made bare his holy arm in the eyes of all the nations; and all the ends of the earth shall see the salvation (3444) of our God. ISAIAH 52:10

Salvation (3444) pronounced yesh-oo'-aw; fem. pass. part. of 3467; something saved, i.e. (abstr.) deliverance; hence aid, victory, prosperity:- deliverance, health, help (-ing), salvation, save, saving (health), welfare.

deliverance (Dictionary) the act of giving up or surrendering; giving into another's possession or keeping; to give forth in words; utter or pronounce; to deliver a verdict; setting free; disburden (oneself) of thoughts, opinions, etc.; Obsolete: to make known, assert; Obsolete or Archaic: agile, active, quick.

prosperity (Dictionary) flourishing or thriving condition; good fortune; success.

fortune (Dictionary) position in life as determined by wealth.

success (Dictionary) favorable or prosperous termination of attempts or endeavors; gaining of wealth, position, or the like; Obsolete: outcome.

welfare (Dictionary) state of faring well; well-being; prosperity; success; happiness; weal.

happiness (2) (Dictionary) good fortune, pleasure, content or gladness.

weal (1) (Dictionary) Archaic: well-being, prosperity , or happiness.

(3467) pronounced yaw-shah'; a prim. root; prop. to be open, wide or free, i.e. (by impl.) to be safe; causat. to free or succor: - x at all, avenging, defend, deliver (-er), help, preserve, rescue, be safe, bring (having) salvation, save (-iour), get victory.

succor (Dictionary) help, relief, aid, assistance in difficulty, need, or distress.

salvation (Dictionary) act of saving or delivering; a source, cause, or means of deliverance; deliverance from the power of penalty and sin; redemption.

sin (Dictionary) transgression of divine law; an act regarded as such transgression, or any violation, especially a willful or deliberate one of some religious or moral principle; to offend against a principle, standard, etc.

transgression (Dictionary) violation of a law, command, etc.; sin.

redemption (Dictionary) deliverance; rescue; repurchase, as of something sold; recovery by payment, as of something pledged.

Savior (Dictionary) one who saves, rescues, or delivers: the savior of the country; (cap.) a title of God, especially of Christ (commonly spelled Saviour).

SALVATION

Thus said the LORD: Observe what is right and do what is just; for soon My salvation shall come, and My deliverance be revealed. YESHA'YAHU 56:1 (ISAIAH 56:1)

Thus saith the LORD, Keep ye judgment, and do justice: for my salvation (3444) is near to come, and my righteousness to be revealed. ISAIAH 56:1

Salvation (3444) pronounced yesh-oo'-aw; fem. pass. part. of 3467; something saved, i.e. (abstr.) deliverance; hence aid, victory, prosperity:- deliverance, health, help (-ing), salvation, save, saving (health), welfare.

deliverance (Dictionary) the act of giving up or surrendering; giving into another's possession or keeping; to give forth in words; utter or pronounce; to deliver a verdict; setting free; disburden (oneself) of thoughts, opinions, etc.; Obsolete: to make known, assert; Obsolete or Archaic: agile, active, quick.

prosperity (Dictionary) flourishing or thriving condition; good fortune; success.

fortune (Dictionary) position in life as determined by wealth.

success (Dictionary) favorable or prosperous termination of attempts or endeavors; gaining of wealth, position, or the like; Obsolete: outcome.

welfare (Dictionary) state of faring well; well-being; prosperity; success; happiness; weal.

happiness (2) (Dictionary) good fortune, pleasure, content or gladness.

weal (1) (Dictionary) Archaic: well-being, prosperity , or happiness.

(3467) pronounced yaw-shah'; a prim. root; prop. to be open, wide or free, i.e. (by impl.) to be safe; causat. to free or succor: - x at all, avenging, defend, deliver (-er), help, preserve, rescue, be safe, bring (having) salvation, save (-iour), get victory.

succor (Dictionary) help, relief, aid, assistance in difficulty, need, or distress.

salvation (Dictionary) act of saving or delivering; a source, cause, or means of deliverance; deliverance from the power of penalty and sin; redemption.

sin (Dictionary) transgression of divine law; an act regarded as such transgression, or any violation, especially a willful or deliberate one of some religious or moral principle; to offend against a principle, standard, etc.

transgression (Dictionary) violation of a law, command, etc.; sin.

redemption (Dictionary) deliverance; rescue; repurchase, as of something sold; recovery by payment, as of something pledged.

SALVATION

Savior (Dictionary) one who saves, rescues, or delivers: the savior of the country; (cap.) a title of God, especially of Christ (commonly spelled Saviour).

We all growl like bears and moan like doves. We hope for redress, and there is none; for victory, and it is far from us. YESHA'YAHU 59:11 (ISAIAH 59:11)

We roar all like bears, and mourn sore like doves: we look for judgment, but *there is none*; for salvation (3444), *but* it is far off from us. ISAIAH 59:11

Salvation (3444) pronounced yesh-oo'-aw; fem. pass. part. of 3467; something saved, i.e. (abstr.) deliverance; hence aid, victory, prosperity:- deliverance, health, help (-ing), salvation, save, saving (health), welfare.

deliverance (Dictionary) the act of giving up or surrendering; giving into another's possession or keeping; to give forth in words; utter or pronounce; to deliver a verdict; setting free; disburden (oneself) of thoughts, opinions, etc.; Obsolete: to make known, assert; Obsolete or Archaic: agile, active, quick.

prosperity (Dictionary) flourishing or thriving condition; good fortune; success.

fortune (Dictionary) position in life as determined by wealth.

success (Dictionary) favorable or prosperous termination of attempts or endeavors; gaining of wealth, position, or the like; Obsolete: outcome.

welfare (Dictionary) state of faring well; well-being; prosperity; success; happiness; weal.

happiness (2) (Dictionary) good fortune, pleasure, content or gladness.

weal (1) (Dictionary) Archaic: well-being, prosperity , or happiness.

(3467) pronounced yaw-shah'; a prim. root; prop. to be open, wide or free, i.e. (by impl.) to be safe; causat. to free or succor: - x at all, avenging, defend, deliver (-er), help, preserve, rescue, be safe, bring (having) salvation, save (-iour), get victory.

succor (Dictionary) help, relief, aid, assistance in difficulty, need, or distress.

salvation (Dictionary) act of saving or delivering; a source, cause, or means of deliverance; deliverance from the power of penalty and sin; redemption.

sin (Dictionary) transgression of divine law; an act regarded as such transgression, or any violation, especially a willful or deliberate one of some religious or moral principle; to offend against a principle, standard, etc.

transgression (Dictionary) violation of a law, command, etc.; sin.

redemption (Dictionary) deliverance; rescue; repurchase, as of something sold; recovery by payment, as of something pledged.

Savior (Dictionary) one who saves, rescues, or delivers: the savior of the country; (cap.) a title of God, especially of Christ (commonly spelled Saviour).

He saw that there was no man. He gazed long, but no one intervened. Then His own arm won Him triumph. His victorious right hand supported Him. He donned victory like a coat of mail, with a helmet of triumph on His head; He clothed Himself with garments of retribution, wrapped Himself in zeal as in a robe. YESHA'YAHU 59:16-17 (ISAIAH 59:16-17)

And he saw that *there was* no man, and wondered that *there was* no intercessor: therefore his arm brought salvation (3467) unto him; and his righteousness, it sustained him. For he put on righteousness as a breastplate, and a helmet of salvation (3444) upon his head; and he put on the garments of vengeance for clothing, and was clad with zeal as a cloak. ISAIAH 59:16-17

(3467) pronounced yaw-shah'; a prim. root; prop. to be open, wide or free, i.e. (by impl.) to be safe; causat. to free or succor: - x at all, avenging, defend, deliver (-er), help, preserve, rescue, be safe, bring (having) salvation, save (-iour), get victory.

succor (Dictionary) help, relief, aid, assistance in difficulty, need, or distress.

salvation (Dictionary) act of saving or delivering; a source, cause, or means of deliverance; deliverance from the power of penalty and sin; redemption.

sin (Dictionary) transgression of divine law; an act regarded as such transgression, or any violation, especially a willful or deliberate one of some religious or moral principle; to offend against a principle, standard, etc.

transgression (Dictionary) violation of a law, command, etc.; sin.

redemption (Dictionary) deliverance; rescue; repurchase, as of something sold; recovery by payment, as of something pledged.

Savior (Dictionary) one who saves, rescues, or delivers: the savior of the country; (cap.) a title of God, especially of Christ (commonly spelled Saviour).

Salvation (3444) pronounced yesh-oo'-aw; fem. pass. part. of 3467; something saved, i.e. (abstr.) deliverance; hence aid, victory, prosperity:- deliverance, health, help (-ing), salvation, save, saving (health), welfare.

deliverance (Dictionary) the act of giving up or surrendering; giving into another's possession or keeping; to give forth in words; utter or pronounce; to deliver a verdict; setting free; disburden (oneself) of thoughts, opinions, etc.; Obsolete: to make known, assert; Obsolete or Archaic: agile, active, quick.

prosperity (Dictionary) flourishing or thriving condition; good fortune; success.

fortune (Dictionary) position in life as determined by wealth.

success (Dictionary) favorable or prosperous termination of attempts or endeavors; gaining of wealth, position, or the like; Obsolete: outcome.

welfare (Dictionary) state of faring well; well-being; prosperity; success; happiness; weal.

happiness (2) (Dictionary) good fortune, pleasure, content or gladness.

weal (1) (Dictionary) Archaic: well-being, prosperity , or happiness.

The cry "Violence!" shall no more be heard in your land, nor "Wrack and ruin!" within your borders. And you shall name your walls "Victory" and your gates "Renown." YESHA'YAHU 60:18 (ISAIAH 60:18)

Violence shall no more be heard in thy land, wasting nor destruction within thy borders; but thou shalt call thy walls Salvation (3468), and thy gates Praise. ISAIAH 60:18

Salvation (3468) pronounced yeh'-shah; from 3467; liberty, deliverance, prosperity, safety, salvation, saving.

liberty (Dictionary) freedom from arbitrary or despotic government or, often, from other rule or law than that of a self-governing community; freedom from external or foreign rule; freedom from control, interference, obligation, restriction, hampering conditions, etc.; power or right of doing, thinking, speaking, etc., according to choice.

deliverance (Dictionary) the act of giving up or surrendering; giving into another's possession or keeping; to give forth in words; utter or pronounce; to deliver a verdict; setting free; disburden (oneself) of thoughts, opinions, etc.; Obsolete: to make known, assert; Obsolete or Archaic: agile, active, quick.

prosperity (Dictionary) flourishing or thriving condition; good fortune; success.

fortune (Dictionary) position in life as determined by wealth.

success (Dictionary) favorable or prosperous termination of attempts or endeavors; gaining of wealth, position, or the like; Obsolete: outcome.

(3467) pronounced yaw-shah'; a prim. root; prop. to be open, wide or free, i.e. (by impl.) to be safe; causat. to free or succor: - x at all, avenging, defend, deliver (-er), help, preserve, rescue, be safe, bring (having) salvation, save (-iour), get victory.

succor (Dictionary) help, relief, aid, assistance in difficulty, need, or distress.

salvation (Dictionary) act of saving or delivering; a source, cause, or means of deliverance; deliverance from the power of penalty and sin; redemption.

sin (Dictionary) transgression of divine law; an act regarded as such transgression, or any violation, especially a willful or deliberate one of some religious or moral principle; to offend against a principle, standard, etc.

transgression (Dictionary) violation of a law, command, etc.; sin.

redemption (Dictionary) deliverance; rescue; repurchase, as of something sold; recovery by payment, as of something pledged.

Savior (Dictionary) one who saves, rescues, or delivers: the savior of the country; (cap.) a title of God, especially of Christ (commonly spelled Saviour).

I greatly rejoice in the LORD, my whole being exults in my God. For He has clothed me in garments of triumph, wrapped me in a robe of victory, like a bridegroom adorned with a turban, like a bride bedecked with her finery. YESHA'YAHU 61:10 (ISAIAH 61:10)

I will greatly rejoice in the LORD, my soul shall be joyful in my God; for he hath clothed me with the garments of salvation (3468), he hath covered me with the robe of righteousness, as a bridegroom decketh *himself* with ornaments, and as a bride adorneth *herself* with her jewels. ISAIAH 61:10

Salvation (3468) pronounced yeh'-shah; from 3467; liberty, deliverance, prosperity, safety, salvation, saving.

liberty (Dictionary) freedom from arbitrary or despotic government or, often, from other rule or law than that of a self-governing community; freedom from external or foreign rule; freedom from control, interference, obligation, restriction, hampering conditions, etc.; power or right of doing, thinking, speaking, etc., according to choice.

deliverance (Dictionary) the act of giving up or surrendering; giving into another's possession or keeping; to give forth in words; utter or pronounce; to deliver a verdict; setting free; disburden (oneself) of thoughts, opinions, etc.; Obsolete: to make known, assert; Obsolete or Archaic: agile, active, quick.

prosperity (Dictionary) flourishing or thriving condition; good fortune; success.

fortune (Dictionary) position in life as determined by wealth.

success (Dictionary) favorable or prosperous termination of attempts or endeavors; gaining of wealth, position, or the like; Obsolete: outcome.

(3467) pronounced yaw-shah'; a prim. root; prop. to be open, wide or free, i.e. (by impl.) to be safe; causat. to free or succor: - x at all, avenging, defend, deliver (-er), help, preserve, rescue, be safe, bring (having) salvation, save (-iour), get victory.

succor (Dictionary) help, relief, aid, assistance in difficulty, need, or distress.

salvation (Dictionary) act of saving or delivering; a source, cause, or means of deliverance; deliverance from the power of penalty and sin; redemption.

sin (Dictionary) transgression of divine law; an act regarded as such transgression, or any violation, especially a willful or deliberate one of some religious or moral principle; to offend against a principle, standard, etc.

transgression (Dictionary) violation of a law, command, etc.; sin.

redemption (Dictionary) deliverance; rescue; repurchase, as of something sold; recovery by payment, as of something pledged.

Savior (Dictionary) one who saves, rescues, or delivers: the savior of the country; (cap.) a title of God, especially of Christ (commonly spelled Saviour).

For the sake of Zion I will not be silent, for the sake of Jerusalem I will not be still, till her victory emerge resplendent and her triumph like a flaming torch. YESHA'YAHU 62:1 (ISAIAH 62:1)

For Zion's sake will I not hold my peace, and for Jerusalem's sake I will not rest, until the righteousness thereof go forth as brightness, and the salvation (3444) thereof as a lamp *that* burneth. ISAIAH 62:1

Salvation (3444) pronounced yesh-oo'-aw; fem. pass. part. of 3467; something saved, i.e. (abstr.) deliverance; hence aid, victory, prosperity:- deliverance, health, help (-ing), salvation, save, saving (health), welfare.

deliverance (Dictionary) the act of giving up or surrendering; giving into another's possession or keeping; to give forth in words; utter or pronounce; to deliver a verdict; setting free; disburden (oneself) of thoughts, opinions, etc.; Obsolete: to make known, assert; Obsolete or Archaic: agile, active, quick.

prosperity (Dictionary) flourishing or thriving condition; good fortune; success.

fortune (Dictionary) position in life as determined by wealth.

success (Dictionary) favorable or prosperous termination of attempts or endeavors; gaining of wealth, position, or the like; Obsolete: outcome.

welfare (Dictionary) state of faring well; well-being; prosperity; success; happiness; weal.

happiness (2) (Dictionary) good fortune, pleasure, content or gladness.

weal (1) (Dictionary) Archaic: well-being, prosperity , or happiness.

(3467) pronounced yaw-shah'; a prim. root; prop. to be open, wide or free, i.e. (by impl.) to be safe; causat. to free or succor: - x at all, avenging, defend, deliver (-er), help, preserve, rescue, be safe, bring (having) salvation, save (-iour), get victory.

succor (Dictionary) help, relief, aid, assistance in difficulty, need, or distress.

salvation (Dictionary) act of saving or delivering; a source, cause, or means of deliverance; deliverance from the power of penalty and sin; redemption.

sin (Dictionary) transgression of divine law; an act regarded as such transgression, or any violation, especially a willful or deliberate one of some religious or moral principle; to offend against a principle, standard, etc.

transgression (Dictionary) violation of a law, command, etc.; sin.

redemption (Dictionary) deliverance; rescue; repurchase, as of something sold; recovery by payment, as of something pledged.

Savior (Dictionary) one who saves, rescues, or delivers: the savior of the country; (cap.) a title of God, especially of Christ (commonly spelled Saviour).

See, the LORD has proclaimed to the end of the earth: Announce to Fair Zion, Your Deliverer is coming! See, His reward is with Him, His recompense before Him. YESHA'YAHU 62:11 (ISAIAH 62:11)

recompense: see note at 40:10. (TANAKH footnote)

(40:10): the reward and recompense to the cities of Judah; cf. Jer. 31:14, 16

I will give the priests their fill of fatness, and My people shall enjoy My full bounty declares the LORD. YIRMEYAHU 31:14 (JEREMIAH 31:14)

And I will satiate the soul of the priests with fatness, and my people shall be satisfied with my goodness, saith the LORD. JEREMIAH 31:14

Thus said the LORD: restrain your voice from weeping, your eyes from shedding tears; for there is a reward for your labor declares the LORD. YIRMEYAHU 31:16 (JEREMIAH 31:16)

Thus saith the LORD: Refrain thy voice from weeping, and thine eyes from tears; for thy work shall be rewarded, saith the LORD; and they shall come again from the land of the enemy. JEREMIAH 31:16

Behold, the LORD hath proclaimed unto the end of the world, Say ye to the daughter of Zion, Behold, thy salvation (3468) cometh; behold, his reward *is* with him, and his work before him. ISAIAH 62:11

SALVATION

Salvation (3468) pronounced yeh'-shah; from 3467; liberty, deliverance, prosperity, safety, salvation, saving.

> liberty (Dictionary) freedom from arbitrary or despotic government or, often, from other rule or law than that of a self-governing community; freedom from external or foreign rule; freedom from control, interference, obligation, restriction, hampering conditions, etc.; power or right of doing, thinking, speaking, etc., according to choice.
>
> deliverance (Dictionary) the act of giving up or surrendering; giving into another's possession or keeping; to give forth in words; utter or pronounce; to deliver a verdict; setting free; disburden (oneself) of thoughts, opinions, etc.; Obsolete: to make known, assert; Obsolete or Archaic: agile, active, quick.
>
> prosperity (Dictionary) flourishing or thriving condition; good fortune; success.
>
> fortune (Dictionary) position in life as determined by wealth.
>
> success (Dictionary) favorable or prosperous termination of attempts or endeavors; gaining of wealth, position, or the like; Obsolete: outcome.

(3467) pronounced yaw-shah'; a prim. root; prop. to be open, wide or free, i.e. (by impl.) to be safe; causat. to free or succor: - x at all, avenging, defend, deliver (-er), help, preserve, rescue, be safe, bring (having) salvation, save (-iour), get victory.

> succor (Dictionary) help, relief, aid, assistance in difficulty, need, or distress.
>
> salvation (Dictionary) act of saving or delivering; a source, cause, or means of deliverance; deliverance from the power of penalty and sin; redemption.
>
> sin (Dictionary) transgression of divine law; an act regarded as such transgression, or any violation, especially a willful or deliberate one of some religious or moral principle; to offend against a principle, standard, etc.
>
> transgression (Dictionary) violation of a law, command, etc.; sin.
>
> redemption (Dictionary) deliverance; rescue; repurchase, as of something sold; recovery by payment, as of something pledged.
>
> Savior (Dictionary) one who saves, rescues, or delivers: the savior of the country; (cap.) a title of God, especially of Christ (commonly spelled Saviour).

Then I looked, but there was none to help; I stared, but there was none to aid- so my own arm wrought the triumph, and My own rage was My aid. YESHA'YAHU 63:5 (ISAIAH 63:5)

> My own rage: Many mss. read wesidqathi "My victorious [right hand]", cf. 59:16 (TANAKH footnote)

> He saw that there was no man. He gazed long, but no one intervened. Then His own arm won Him triumph. His victorious right hand supported Him. YESHA'YAHU 59:16 (ISAIAH 59:16)
>
> And he saw that there was no man, and wondered that *there was* no intercessor: therefore his arm brought salvation (3467) unto him; and his righteousness, it sustained him. ISAIAH 59:16

And I looked and *there was* none to help; and I wondered that *there was* none to uphold: therefore mine own arm brought salvation (3467) unto me; and my fury, it upheld me. ISAIAH 63:5

(3467) pronounced yaw-shah'; a prim. root; prop. to be open, wide or free, i.e. (by impl.) to be safe; causat. to free or succor: - x at all, avenging, defend, deliver (-er), help, preserve, rescue, be safe, bring (having) salvation, save (-iour), get victory.

succor (Dictionary) help, relief, aid, assistance in difficulty, need, or distress.

salvation (Dictionary) act of saving or delivering; a source, cause, or means of deliverance; deliverance from the power of penalty and sin; redemption.

sin (Dictionary) transgression of divine law; an act regarded as such transgression, or any violation, especially a willful or deliberate one of some religious or moral principle; to offend against a principle, standard, etc.

transgression (Dictionary) violation of a law, command, etc.; sin.

redemption (Dictionary) deliverance; rescue; repurchase, as of something sold; recovery by payment, as of something pledged.

Savior (Dictionary) one who saves, rescues, or delivers: the savior of the country; (cap.) a title of God, especially of Christ (commonly spelled Saviour).

It is good to wait patiently till rescue comes from the LORD. EIKHAH 3:26 (LAMENTATIONS 3:26)

It *is good* that *a man* should both hope and quietly wait for the salvation (8668) of the LORD. LAMENTATIONS 3:26

Salvation (8668) pronounced tesh-oo-aw'; from 7768 in the sense of 3467; rescue (lit. or fig., pers., national, or spir.):- deliverance, help, safety, salvation, victory.

deliverance (Dictionary) the act of giving up or surrendering; giving into another's possession or keeping; to give forth in words; utter or pronounce; to deliver a verdict; setting free; disburden (oneself) of thoughts, opinions, etc.; Obsolete: to make known, assert; Obsolete or Archaic: agile, active, quick.

salvation (Dictionary) act of saving or delivering; a source, cause, or means of deliverance; deliverance from the power of penalty and sin; redemption.

sin (Dictionary) transgression of divine law; an act regarded as such transgression, or any violation, especially a willful or deliberate one of some religious or moral principle; to offend against a principle, standard, etc.

transgression (Dictionary) violation of a law, command, etc.; sin.

redemption (Dictionary) deliverance; rescue; repurchase, as of something sold; recovery by payment, as of something pledged.

(7768) pronounced shaw-vah'; a prim. root; prop. to be free; but used only causat. and reflex. to halloo (for help, i.e. freedom from some trouble):- cry (aloud, out), shout.

halloo (Dictionary) an exclamation used to attract attention, to incite the dogs in hunting, etc.; to call with a loud voice: shout, cry, as after dogs; to incite or chase with shouts and cries of "halloo".

(3467) pronounced yaw-shah'; a prim. root; prop. to be open, wide or free, i.e. (by impl.) to be safe; causat. to free or succor: - x at all, avenging, defend, deliver (-er), help, preserve, rescue, be safe, bring (having) salvation, save (-iour), get victory.

succor (Dictionary) help, relief, aid, assistance in difficulty, need, or distress.

salvation (Dictionary) act of saving or delivering; a source, cause, or means of deliverance; deliverance from the power of penalty and sin; redemption.

sin (Dictionary) transgression of divine law; an act regarded as such transgression, or any violation, especially a willful or deliberate one of some religious or moral principle; to offend against a principle, standard, etc.

transgression (Dictionary) violation of a law, command, etc.; sin.

redemption (Dictionary) deliverance; rescue; repurchase, as of something sold; recovery by payment, as of something pledged.

Savior (Dictionary) one who saves, rescues, or delivers: the savior of the country; (cap.) a title of God, especially of Christ (commonly spelled Saviour).

Book Two

Walking the Same Sure Foundation of Righteousness

Introduction

This is the second of five books in a mini-series with a unique purpose. Each book provides a verse to verse comparison of *TANAKH THE HOLY SCRIPTURES* (hereafter referred to as *Tanakh*) and the *AUTHORIZED KING JAMES VERSION* (hereafter referred to as *KJV*, Old Testament only) on a particular subject. The subject of Book One is *SALVATION*. Book Two, *RIGHTEOUSNESS,* provides references from *TANAKH* footnotes and *STRONG'S CONCORDANCE*. Readers will quickly discover that all spiritual concepts presented on the following pages have physical actions that can be observed and experienced. This series is about relationship, not religion.

Each of the five books are in the same order and format for ease of use. Format, as well as use of *TANAKH* footnotes and *STRONG'S CONCORDANCE* will be discussed in the section *How This Book is Organized*. Yeshua (Jesus) spoke about each of these subjects often before the New Testament was written. Modern-day readers who grasp these truths will be able to understand the teachings of the New Testament in the same way as people of Yeshua's (Jesus's) generation.

How This Book is Organized

TANAKH verse followed by TANAKH reference (each letter capitalized) with corresponding KJV reference (also capitalized) in parenthesis. Sometimes numbers will not match exactly but will be close. TANAKH reference will be highlighted in gray.

Example:

Offer sacrifices in righteousness and trust in the LORD. TEHILLIM 4:6 (PSALMS 4:5)

Spelling of highlighted *TANAKH* references is the same as the *COMPLETE JEWISH BIBLE* throughout the book to maintain its sense of Jewishness. Refer to *Works Cited* for additional information.

KJV will include the word righteousness followed by a highlighted number in parenthesis within the verse. The highlighted number will be a reference number to *STRONG'S CONCORDANCE* (original Hebrew or Chaldee). The verse will be followed by the highlighted KJV reference only. Words in italic in the original text will be in italics. Archaic spelling of words will also be presented as the original authors intended.

Example:

Offer the sacrifices of righteousness (6664), and put your trust in the LORD. PSALMS 4:5

righteousness (6664) pronounced tseh'-dek; from 6663; the right (nat., mor., or legal); also (abstr.) equity or (fig.) prosperity:- x even, (x that which is altogether) just (-ice), ({un-}) right (-eous) (cause, -ly, -ness).

Pronunciation is provided with the complete definition by *STRONG'S CONCORDANCE* . Readers will notice a second highlighted number in the above example. This is the primitive root word. It will be shown with pronunciation and complete definition by *STRONG'S CONCORDANCE* also.

The primitive root will usually be listed last unless it is the only reference or the first of several references. The number of the root will be indented, under the verse, lining up with the first reference.

Example:

righteousness (6664)...

(6663) pronounced tsaw-dak'; prim. root; to be (causat., make) right (in a moral or forensic sense):- cleanse, clear self (be, do) just (-ice, -ify, -ify self), (be, turn to) righteous (-ness).

Abbreviations such as prim. and causat. will be identified in *Abbreviations Employed,* the next section of the book.

Occasionally, footnotes will be provided in *TANAKH*. When this occurs, the footnote will be noted exactly as referenced. If scripture references are available, they will also be included in the same format as above so that readers may be able to have immediate access to as much information as possible without turning pages.

The first of two examples below supplies a literal explanation as to how the original context would have been understood by its listeners.

Are Your wonders made known in the netherworld, Your beneficent deeds in the land of oblivion? TEHILLIM 88:13 (PSALMS 88:12)

netherworld: Lit. "darkness" (TANAKH footnote)

The second example directs the reader's attention to additional scriptures for more information.

"I will restore your magistrates as of old, and your counselors as of yore. After that you shall be called City of Righteousness, Faithful City." Zion shall be saved in the judgment; her repentant ones, in the retribution. YESHA'YAHU 1:26-27 (ISAIAH 1:26-27)

retribution: for this meaning cf. 5.16, 10.22. (TANAKH footnote)

And the LORD of Hosts is exalted by judgment, the Holy God proved holy by retribution. YESHA'YAHU 5:16 (ISAIAH 5:16)

But the LORD of hosts shall be exalted in judgment, and God that is holy shall be sanctified in righteousness. ISAIAH 5:16

Even if your people, O Israel, should be as the sands of the sea, only a remnant of it shall return. Destruction is decreed; retribution comes like a flood! YESHA'YAHU 10:22 (ISAIAH 10:22)

For though thy people Israel be as the sand of the sea, *yet* a remnant of them shall return: the consumption decreed shall overflow with righteousness. ISAIAH 10:22

KJV reference will always be added for comparison and continuity of the *TANAKH* footnote before continuing on to the corresponding KJV. In this example , ISAIAH 1:26-27 will be the next entry.

Abbreviations Employed

Abstr.: abstract, abstractly

Adv.: adverb, adverbial, adverbially

Art.: article

Caus., causat.: causative, causatively

Cf.: confer, compare

Chald.: Chaldee, Chaldaism

Coll., collect.: collective, collectively

Concr.: concrete, concretely

Corresp.: corresponding, correspondingly

Esp., espec.: especial, especially

Ext., extens.: extension

Fem.: feminine

Fig.: figurative, figuratively

i.e.: id est, that is

impl.: implication, implied

incl., includ.: including, inclusive, inclusively

intr., intrans.: intransitive, intransitively

lit.: literal, literally

mean.: meaning

mor.: moral, morally

nat.: native, natural, naturally, nature

obj.: object, objection, objective

part., partic.: participle, particular

pl., plur.: plural

pref.: preface, preference, preferred, prefix

prim.: primitive, primary

prop.: proper, properly

subj.: subject, subjective, subjectively

te., techn.: technical, technically

trans. transit.: transitive, transitively

v.: verse

viz.: videlicet, namely, that is to say; used to introduce examples, details, lists, etc.

And because he put his trust in the LORD, He reckoned it to his merit. B'RESHEET 15:6 (GENESIS 15:6)

And he believed in the LORD; and he counted it to him for righteousness (6666). (GENESIS 15:6)

> righteousness (6666) pronounced tsed-aw-kaw'; from 6663; rightness (abstr.), subj. (rectitude); obj. (justice) , mor. (virtue) or fig. (prosperity):- justice, moderately, right (-eous) (act, -ly, -ness)
>
> (6663) pronounced tsaw-dak'; prim. root; to be (causat., make) right (in a moral or forensic sense):- cleanse, clear self (be, do) just (-ice, -ify, -ify self), (be, turn to) righteous (-ness).

In the future when you go over my wages, let my honesty toward you testify for me: If there are among my goats any that are not speckled or spotted or any sheep that are not dark-colored, they got there by theft. B'RESHEET 30:33 (GENESIS 30:33)

So shall my righteousness (6666) answer for me in time to come, when it shall come for my hire before thy face: every one that is not speckled and spotted among the goats, and brown among the sheep, that shall be counted stolen with me. GENESIS 30:33

> righteousness (6666) pronounced tsed-aw-kaw'; from 6663; rightness (abstr.), subj. (rectitude); obj. (justice) , mor. (virtue) or fig. (prosperity):- justice, moderately, right (-eous) (act, -ly, -ness)
>
> (6663) pronounced tsaw-dak'; prim. root; to be (causat., make) right (in a moral or forensic sense):- cleanse, clear self (be, do) just (-ice, -ify, -ify self), (be, turn to) righteous (-ness).

You shall not render an unfair decision: do not favor the poor or show deference to the rich; judge your kinsman fairly. VAYIKRA 19:15 (LEVITICUS 19:15)

Ye shall do no unrighteousness (5766) in judgment: thou shalt not respect the person of the poor, nor honour the person of the mighty: but in righteousness (6664) shalt thou judge thy neighbour. LEVITICUS 19:15

> unrighteousness (5766) pronounced eh'-vel; or aw'-vel; and (fem.) av-law'; or o-law', from 5765; (moral) evil:- iniquity, perverseness, unjust (-ly), unrighteous (-ly), wicked (-ness).
>
> (5765) pronounced aw-val'; a prim. root; to distort (morally):- deal unjustly, unrighteous.
>
> righteousness (6664) pronounced tseh'-dek; from 6663; the right (nat., mor., or legal); also (abstr.) equity or (fig.) prosperity:- x even, (x that which is altogether) just (-ice), ([un-]) right (-eous) (cause, -ly, -ness).
>
> (6663) pronounced tsaw-dak'; prim. root; to be (causat., make) right (in a moral or forensic sense):- cleanse, clear self (be, do) just (-ice, -ify, -ify self), (be, turn to) righteous (-ness).

It will be therefore to our merit before the LORD our God to observe faithfully this whole Instruction, as He has commanded us. D'VARIM 6:25 (DEUTERONOMY 6:25)

And it shall be our righteousness (6666), if we observe to do all these commandments before the LORD our God, as he hath commanded us. DEUTERONOMY 6:25

> righteousness (6666) pronounced tsed-aw-kaw'; from 6663; rightness (abstr.), subj. (rectitude); obj. (justice) , mor. (virtue) or fig. (prosperity):- justice, moderately, right (-eous) (act, -ly, -ness)
>
> (6663) pronounced tsaw-dak'; prim. root; to be (causat., make) right (in a moral or forensic sense):- cleanse, clear self (be, do) just (-ice, -ify, -ify self), (be, turn to) righteous (-ness).

And when the LORD your God has thrust them from your path, say not to yourselves, "The LORD has enabled us to possess this land because of our virtues." It is rather because of the wickedness of those nations that the LORD is dispossessing them before you. It is not because of your virtues and rectitude that you will be able to possess their country; but it is because of their wickedness that the LORD your God is dispossessing those nations before you, and in order to fulfill the oath that the LORD made to your fathers, Abraham, Isaac, and Jacob. Know then, that it is not for any virtue of yours that the LORD your God is giving you this good land to possess; for you are a stiffnecked people. D'VARIM 9:4-6 (DEUTERONOMY 9:4-6)

Speak not thou in thine heart, after that the LORD thy God hath cast them out from before thee, saying, For my righteousness (6666) the LORD hath brought me in to possess this land: but for the wickedness of these nations the LORD doth drive them out from before thee. Not for thy righteousness (6666), or for the uprightness (3476) of thine heart, dost thou go to possess their land: but for the wickedness of these nations the LORD thy God doth drive them out from before thee, and that he may perform the word which the LORD sware unto thy fathers, Abraham, Isaac, and Jacob. Understand therefore, that the LORD thy God giveth thee not this good land to possess it for thy righteousness (6666); for thou *art* a stiffnecked people. DEUTERONOMY 9:4-6

> righteousness (6666) pronounced tsed-aw-kaw'; from 6663; rightness (abstr.), subj. (rectitude); obj. (justice) , mor. (virtue) or fig. (prosperity):- justice, moderately, right (-eous) (act, -ly, -ness)
>
> (6663) pronounced tsaw-dak'; prim. root; to be (causat., make) right (in a moral or forensic sense):- cleanse, clear self (be, do) just (-ice, -ify, -ify self), (be, turn to) righteous (-ness).
>
> uprightness (3476) pronounced yo-sher'; from 3474; the right:- equity, meet, right, upright (-ness).
>
> (3474) pronounced yaw-shar'; a prim. root; to be straight or even; fig. to be (causat. to make) right, pleasant, prosperous:- direct, fit, seem good (meet), + please (well), be (esteem, go) right (on), bring (look, make, take the) straight (way), be upright (-ly).

You must return the pledge to him at sundown, that he may sleep in his cloth and bless you; and it will be to your merit before the LORD your God. D'VARIM 24:13 (DEUTERONOMY 24:13)

In any case thou shalt deliver him the pledge again when the sun goeth down, that he may sleep in his own raiment, and bless thee: and it shall be righteousness (6666) unto thee before the LORD thy God. DEUTERONOMY 24:13

> righteousness (6666) pronounced tsed-aw-kaw'; from 6663; rightness (abstr.), subj. (rectitude); obj. (justice) , mor. (virtue) or fig. (prosperity):- justice, moderately, right (-eous) (act, -ly, -ness)
>
> (6663) pronounced tsaw-dak'; prim. root; to be (causat., make) right (in a moral or forensic sense):- cleanse, clear self (be, do) just (-ice, -ify, -ify self), (be, turn to) righteous (-ness).

They invite their kin to the mountain, where they offer sacrifices of success. For they draw from the riches of the sea and the hidden hoards of the sand. D'VARIM 33:19 (DEUTERONOMY 33:19)

They shall call the people unto the mountain, there they shall offer sacrifices of righteousness (6664) for they shall suck *of* the abundance *of* the seas and *of* treasures hid in the sand. DEUTERONOMY 33:19

> righteousness (6664) pronounced tseh'-dek; from 6663; the right (nat., mor., or legal); also (abstr.) equity or (fig.) prosperity:- x even, (x that which is altogether) just (-ice), ([un-]) right (-eous) (cause, -ly, -ness).
>
> (6663) pronounced tsaw-dak'; prim. root; to be (causat., make) right (in a moral or forensic sense):- cleanse, clear self (be, do) just (-ice, -ify, -ify self), (be, turn to) righteous (-ness).

And the LORD will requite every man for his right conduct and loyalty- for this day the LORD delivered you into *my* hands and I would not raise a hand against the LORD's anointed. SH'MU'EL ALEF 26:23 (I SAMUEL 26:23)

The LORD render to every man his righteousness (6666) and his faithfulness: for the LORD delivered thee into my hand today, but I would not stretch forth mine hand against the LORD's anointed. I SAMUEL 26:23

> righteousness (6666) pronounced tsed-aw-kaw'; from 6663; rightness (abstr.), subj. (rectitude); obj. (justice) , mor. (virtue) or fig. (prosperity):- justice, moderately, right (-eous) (act, -ly, -ness)
>
> (6663) pronounced tsaw-dak'; prim. root; to be (causat., make) right (in a moral or forensic sense):- cleanse, clear self (be, do) just (-ice, -ify, -ify self), (be, turn to) righteous (-ness).

The LORD rewarded me according to my merit. He requited the cleanness of my hands. For I have kept the ways of the LORD and have not been guilty before my God: I am mindful of all His rules, and have not departed from His laws. I have been blameless before Him, and have guarded myself against sinning- and the LORD has requited my merit, according to my purity in His sight. SH'MU'EL BET 22:21-25 (II SAMUEL 22:21-25)

The LORD rewarded me according to my righteousness (6666); according to the cleanness of my hands hath he recompensed me. For I have kept the ways of the LORD, and have not wickedly departed from my God. For all his judgments *were* before me: and *as for* his statutes, I did not depart from them. I was also upright (8549) before him, and have kept myself from mine iniquity. Therefore the LORD hath recompensed me according to my righteousness (6666); according to my cleanness in his eyesight. II SAMUEL 22:21-25

> righteousness (6666) pronounced tsed-aw-kaw'; from 6663; rightness (abstr.), subj. (rectitude); obj. (justice) , mor. (virtue) or fig. (prosperity):- justice, moderately, right (-eous) (act, -ly, -ness)
>
> (6663) pronounced tsaw-dak'; prim. root; to be (causat., make) right (in a moral or forensic sense):- cleanse, clear self (be, do) just (-ice, -ify, -ify self), (be, turn to) righteous (-ness).
>
> upright (8549) pronounced taw-meem'; from 8552; entire (lit., fig., or mor.); also (as noun) integrity, truth:- without blemish, complete, full, perfect, sincerely (-ity), sound, without spot, undefiled, upright (-ly), whole.
>
> (8552) pronounced taw-mam'; a prim. root; to complete, in a good or a bad sense, lit. or fig., trans. or intrans. (as follows):- accomplish, cease, be clean, [pass-] ed, consume, have done, (come to an, have an, make an) end, fail, come to the full, be all gone, x be all here, be (make) perfect, be spent, sum, be (shew self) upright, be wasted, whole.

Solomon said, "You dealt most graciously with Your servant my father, David, because he walked before You in faithfulness and righteousness and in integrity of heart. You have continued this great kindness to him by giving him a son to occupy his throne, as is now the case." M'LAKHIM ALEF 3:6 (I KINGS 3:6)

And Solomon said, Thou hast shown unto thy servant David my father great mercy, according as he walked before thee in truth, and in righteousness (6666), and in uprightness (3483) of heart with thee; and thou hast kept for him this great kindness, that thou hast given him a son to sit on his throne, as *it is* this day. I KINGS 3:6

> righteousness (6666) pronounced tsed-aw-kaw'; from 6663; rightness (abstr.), subj. (rectitude); obj. (justice) , mor. (virtue) or fig. (prosperity):- justice, moderately, right (-eous) (act, -ly, -ness)
>
> (6663) pronounced tsaw-dak'; prim. root; to be (causat., make) right (in a moral or forensic sense):- cleanse, clear self (be, do) just (-ice, -ify, -ify self), (be, turn to) righteous (-ness).
>
> uprightness (3483) pronounced yish-raw'; fem. of 3477; rectitude:-uprightness.
>
> (3477) pronounced yaw-shawr'; from 3474-straight (lit. or fig.)-convenient, equity, Jasher, just, meet (-est), + pleased well, right (-eous), straight, (most) upright (-ly, -ness).
>
> (3474) pronounced yaw-shar'; a prim. root; to be straight or even; fig. to be (causat. to make) right, pleasant, prosperous:- direct, fit, seem good (meet), + please (well), be (esteem, go) right (on), bring (look, make, take the) straight (way), be upright (-ly).

Whenever one man commits an offense against another, and the latter utters an imprecation to bring a curse upon him, and comes with his imprecation before Your altar in this House, oh, hear in heaven and take action to judge Your servants, condemning him who is in the wrong and bringing down the punishment of his conduct on his head, vindicating him who is in the right by rewarding him according to his righteousness. M'LAKHIM ALEF 8:31-32 (I KINGS 8:31-32)

If any man trespass against his neighbor, and an oath be laid upon him to cause him to swear, and the oath come before thine altar in this house; then hear thou in heaven, and do, and judge thy servants, condemning the wicked, to bring his way upon his head; and justifying the righteous (6662) to give him according to his righteousness (6666). I KINGS 8:31-32

righteous (6662) pronounced tsad-deek'; from 6663; just:- just, lawful, righteous (man).

(6663) pronounced tsaw-dak'; prim. root; to be (causat., make) right (in a moral or forensic sense):- cleanse, clear self (be, do) just (-ice, -ify, -ify self), (be, turn to) righteous (-ness).

righteousness (6666) pronounced tsed-aw-kaw'; from 6663; rightness (abstr.), subj. (rectitude); obj. (justice) , mor. (virtue) or fig. (prosperity):- justice, moderately, right (-eous) (act, -ly, -ness)

If a man commits an offense against his fellow, and an oath is exacted from him, causing him to utter an imprecation against himself, and he comes with his imprecation before Your altar in this House, may You hear in heaven and take action to judge Your servants, requiting him who is in the wrong by bringing down the punishment of his conduct on his head, vindicating him who is in the right by rewarding him according to his righteousness. DIVREI-HAYAMIM BET 6:22-23 (II CHRONICLES 6:22-23)

If a man sin against his neighbour, and an oath be laid upon him to make him swear, and the oath come before thine altar in this house; then hear thou from heaven, and do, and judge thy servants, by requiting the wicked, by recompensing his way upon his own head; and by justifying the righteous (6662), by giving him according to his righteousness (6666). II CHRONICLES 6:22-23

righteous (6662) pronounced tsad-deek'; from 6663; just:- just, lawful, righteous (man).

(6663) pronounced tsaw-dak'; prim. root; to be (causat., make) right (in a moral or forensic sense):- cleanse, clear self (be, do) just (-ice, -ify, -ify self), (be, turn to) righteous (-ness).

righteousness (6666) pronounced tsed-aw-kaw'; from 6663; rightness (abstr.), subj. (rectitude); obj. (justice) , mor. (virtue) or fig. (prosperity):- justice, moderately, right (-eous) (act, -ly, -ness)

Relent! Let there not be injustice; Relent! I am still in the right. IYOV 6:29 (JOB 6:29)

Return, I pray you, let it not be iniquity; yea, return again, my righteousness (6664) *is* in it. JOB 6:29

righteousness (6664) pronounced tseh'-dek; from 6663; the right (nat., mor., or legal); also (abstr.) equity or (fig.) prosperity:- x even, (x that which is altogether) just (-ice), ([un-]) right (-eous) (cause, -ly, -ness).

(6663) pronounced tsaw-dak'; prim. root; to be (causat., make) right (in a moral or forensic sense):- cleanse, clear self (be, do) just (-ice, -ify, -ify self), (be, turn to) righteous (-ness).

If you are blameless and upright, He will protect you, and grant well-being to your righteous home. IYOV 8:6 (JOB 8:6)

If thou *wert* pure and upright (3477); surely now he would awake for thee, and make the habitation of thy righteousness (6664) prosperous. JOB 8:6

> upright (3477) pronounced yaw-shawr'; from 3474-straight (lit. or fig.)-convenient, equity, Jasher, just, meet (-est), + pleased well, right (-eous), straight, (most) upright (-ly, -ness).
>
> (3474) pronounced yaw-shar'; a prim. root; to be straight or even; fig. to be (causat. to make) right, pleasant, prosperous:- direct, fit, seem good (meet), + please (well), be (esteem, go) right (on), bring (look, make, take the) straight (way), be upright (-ly).
>
> righteousness (6664) pronounced tseh'-dek; from 6663; the right (nat., mor., or legal); also (abstr.) equity or (fig.) prosperity:- x even, (x that which is altogether) just (-ice), ([un-]) right (-eous) (cause, -ly, -ness).
>
> (6663) pronounced tsaw-dak'; prim. root; to be (causat., make) right (in a moral or forensic sense):- cleanse, clear self (be, do) just (-ice, -ify, -ify self), (be, turn to) righteous (-ness).

I persist in my righteousness and will not yield; I shall be free of reproach as long as I live. IYOV 27:6 (JOB 27:6)

My righteousness (6666) I hold fast, and will not let it go: my heart shall not reproach *me* so long as I live. JOB 27:6

> righteousness (6666) pronounced tsed-aw-kaw'; from 6663; rightness (abstr.), subj. (rectitude); obj. (justice) , mor. (virtue) or fig. (prosperity):- justice, moderately, right (-eous) (act, -ly, -ness)
>
> (6663) pronounced tsaw-dak'; prim. root; to be (causat., make) right (in a moral or forensic sense):- cleanse, clear self (be, do) just (-ice, -ify, -ify self), (be, turn to) righteous (-ness).

I clothed myself in righteousness and it robed me; justice was my cloak and turban. IYOV 29:14 (JOB 29:14)

I put on righteousness (6664) and it clothed me; my judgment was as a robe and a diadem. JOB 29:14

> righteousness (6664) pronounced tseh'-dek; from 6663; the right (nat., mor., or legal); also (abstr.) equity or (fig.) prosperity:- x even, (x that which is altogether) just (-ice), ([un-]) right (-eous) (cause, -ly, -ness).
>
> (6663) pronounced tsaw-dak'; prim. root; to be (causat., make) right (in a moral or forensic sense):- cleanse, clear self (be, do) just (-ice, -ify, -ify self), (be, turn to) righteous (-ness).

He prays to God and is accepted by Him; he enters His presence with shouts of joy; for He requites a man for his righteousness. IYOV 33:26 (JOB 33:26)

He shall pray unto God, and he will be favourable unto him: and he shall see his face with joy: for he will render unto man his righteousness (6666). JOB 33:26

> righteousness (6666) pronounced tsed-aw-kaw'; from 6663; rightness (abstr.), subj. (rectitude); obj. (justice) , mor. (virtue) or fig. (prosperity):- justice, moderately, right (-eous) (act, -ly, -ness)
>
> (6663) pronounced tsaw-dak'; prim. root; to be (causat., make) right (in a moral or forensic sense):- cleanse, clear self (be, do) just (-ice, -ify, -ify self), (be, turn to) righteous (-ness).

Elihu said in reply: Do you think it just to say, "I am right against God?" IYOV 35:1-2 (JOB 35:1-2)

Elihu spake moreover, and said, thinkest thou this to be right, *that* thou saidst, My righteousness (6664) *is* more than God's? JOB 35:1-2

> righteousness (6664) pronounced tseh'-dek; from 6663; the right (nat., mor., or legal); also (abstr.) equity or (fig.) prosperity:- x even, (x that which is altogether) just (-ice), ([un-]) right (-eous) (cause, -ly, -ness).
>
> (6663) pronounced tsaw-dak'; prim. root; to be (causat., make) right (in a moral or forensic sense):- cleanse, clear self (be, do) just (-ice, -ify, -ify self), (be, turn to) righteous (-ness).

Your wickedness affects men like yourself; your righteousness, mortals. IYOV 35:8 (JOB 35:8)

Thy wickedness *may hurt a* man as thou *art;* and thy righteousness (6666) *may profit* the son of man. JOB 35:8

> righteousness (6666) pronounced tsed-aw-kaw'; from 6663; rightness (abstr.), subj. (rectitude); obj. (justice) , mor. (virtue) or fig. (prosperity):- justice, moderately, right (-eous) (act, -ly, -ness)
>
> (6663) pronounced tsaw-dak'; prim. root; to be (causat., make) right (in a moral or forensic sense):- cleanse, clear self (be, do) just (-ice, -ify, -ify self), (be, turn to) righteous (-ness).

Then Elihu spoke once more. Wait a little and let me hold forth; there is still more to say for God. I will make my opinions widely known; I will justify my Maker. IYOV 36:1-3 (JOB 36:1-3)

Elihu also proceeded, and said, suffer me a little, and I will show thee that I *have* yet to speak on God's behalf. I will fetch my knowledge from afar, and will ascribe righteousness (6664) to my Maker. JOB 36:1-3

> righteousness (6664) pronounced tseh'-dek; from 6663; the right (nat., mor., or legal); also (abstr.) equity or (fig.) prosperity:- x even, (x that which is altogether) just (-ice), ([un-]) right (-eous) (cause, -ly, -ness).
>
> (6663) pronounced tsaw-dak'; prim. root; to be (causat., make) right (in a moral or forensic sense):- cleanse, clear self (be, do) just (-ice, -ify, -ify self), (be, turn to) righteous (-ness).

Answer me when I call, O God, my vindicator! You freed me from distress; have mercy on me and hear my prayer. TEHILLIM 4:2 (PSALMS 4:1)

Hear me when I call, O God of my righteousness (6664); thou hast enlarged me *when I was* in distress; have mercy upon me, and hear my prayer. PSALMS 4:1

> righteousness (6664) pronounced tseh'-dek; from 6663; the right (nat., mor., or legal); also (abstr.) equity or (fig.) prosperity:- x even, (x that which is altogether) just (-ice), ([un-]) right (-eous) (cause, -ly, -ness).
>
> (6663) pronounced tsaw-dak'; prim. root; to be (causat., make) right (in a moral or forensic sense):- cleanse, clear self (be, do) just (-ice, -ify, -ify self), (be, turn to) righteous (-ness).

Offer sacrifices in righteousness and trust in the LORD. TEHILLIM 4:6 (PSALMS 4:5)

Offer the sacrifices of righteousness (6664), and put your trust in the LORD. PSALMS 4:5

> righteousness (6664) pronounced tseh'-dek; from 6663; the right (nat., mor., or legal); also (abstr.) equity or (fig.) prosperity:- x even, (x that which is altogether) just (-ice), ([un-]) right (-eous) (cause, -ly, -ness).
>
> (6663) pronounced tsaw-dak'; prim. root; to be (causat., make) right (in a moral or forensic sense):- cleanse, clear self (be, do) just (-ice, -ify, -ify self), (be, turn to) righteous (-ness).

O LORD, lead me along Your righteous [path] because of my watchful foes; make Your way straight before me. TEHILLIM 5:9 (PSALMS 5:8)

> [path]: Or "as You are righteous, lead me." (TANAKH footnote)

Lead me, O LORD, in thy righteousness (6666) because of mine enemies; make thy way straight before my face. PSALMS 5:8

> righteousness (6666) pronounced tsed-aw-kaw'; from 6663; rightness (abstr.), subj. (rectitude); obj. (justice) , mor. (virtue) or fig. (prosperity):- justice, moderately, right (-eous) (act, -ly, -ness)
>
> (6663) pronounced tsaw-dak'; prim. root; to be (causat., make) right (in a moral or forensic sense):- cleanse, clear self (be, do) just (-ice, -ify, -ify self), (be, turn to) righteous (-ness).

The LORD judges the peoples; vindicate me, O LORD, for the righteousness and blamelessness that are mine. TEHILLIM 7:9 (PSALMS 7:8)

The LORD shall judge the people: judge me, O LORD, according to my righteousness (6664), and according to mine integrity *that is* in me. PSALMS 7:8

> righteousness (6664) pronounced tseh'-dek; from 6663; the right (nat., mor., or legal); also (abstr.) equity or (fig.) prosperity:- x even, (x that which is altogether) just (-ice), ([un-]) right (-eous) (cause, -ly, -ness).

(6663) pronounced tsaw-dak'; prim. root; to be (causat., make) right (in a moral or forensic sense):- cleanse, clear self (be, do) just (-ice, -ify, -ify self), (be, turn to) righteous (-ness).

I will praise the LORD for His righteousness, and sing a hymn to the name of the LORD Most High. TEHILLIM 7:18 (PSALMS 7:17)

I will praise the LORD according to his righteousness (6664): and will sing praise to the name of the LORD most high. PSALMS 7:17

righteousness (6664) pronounced tseh'-dek; from 6663; the right (nat., mor., or legal); also (abstr.) equity or (fig.) prosperity:- x even, (x that which is altogether) just (-ice), ([un-]) right (-eous) (cause, -ly, -ness).

(6663) pronounced tsaw-dak'; prim. root; to be (causat., make) right (in a moral or forensic sense):- cleanse, clear self (be, do) just (-ice, -ify, -ify self), (be, turn to) righteous (-ness).

It is He who judges the world with righteousness, rules the people with equity. TEHILLIM 9:9 (PSALMS 9:8)

And he shall judge the world in righteousness (6664), he shall minister judgment to the people in uprightness (4334). PSALMS 9:8

righteousness (6664) pronounced tseh'-dek; from 6663; the right (nat., mor., or legal); also (abstr.) equity or (fig.) prosperity:- x even, (x that which is altogether) just (-ice), ([un-]) right (-eous) (cause, -ly, -ness).

(6663) pronounced tsaw-dak'; prim. root; to be (causat., make) right (in a moral or forensic sense):- cleanse, clear self (be, do) just (-ice, -ify, -ify self), (be, turn to) righteous (-ness).

uprightness (4334) pronounced mee-shore'; from 3474; a level, i.e. a plain (often used [with the art. pref.] as a prop. name of certain districts; fig. Concord): also straightness i.e. (fig.) justice (sometimes adv. Justly):- equity, even place, plain, right (-eously), (made) straight, uprightness.

(3474) pronounced yaw-shar'; a prim. root; to be straight or even; fig. to be (causat. to make) right, pleasant, prosperous:- direct, fit, seem good (meet), + please (well), be (esteem, go) right (on), bring (look, make, take the) straight (way), be upright (-ly).

For the LORD is righteous; He loves righteous deeds; the upright shall behold His face. TEHILLIM 11:7 (PSALMS 11:7)

For the righteous (6662) LORD loveth righteousness (6666); his countenance doth behold the upright. PSALMS 11:7

righteous (6662) pronounced tsad-deek'; from 6663; just:- just, lawful, righteous (man).

(6663) pronounced tsaw-dak'; prim. root; to be (causat., make) right (in a moral or forensic sense):- cleanse, clear self (be, do) just (-ice, -ify, -ify self), (be, turn to) righteous (-ness).

righteousness (6666) pronounced tsed-aw-kaw'; from 6663; rightness (abstr.), subj. (rectitude); obj. (justice) , mor. (virtue) or fig. (prosperity):- justice, moderately, right (-eous) (act, -ly, -ness)

LORD, who may sojourn in Your tent, who may dwell on Your holy mountain? He who lives without blame, who does what is right, and in his heart acknowledges the truth: TEHILLIM 15:1-2 (PSALMS 15:1-2)

LORD, who shall abide in thy tabernacle? Who shall dwell in thy holy hill? He that walketh uprightly (8549), and worketh righteousness (6664), and speaketh the truth in his heart. PSALMS 15:1-2

uprightly (8549) pronounced taw-meem'; from 8552; entire (lit., fig., or mor.); also (as noun) integrity, truth:- without blemish, complete, full, perfect, sincerely (-ity), sound, without spot, undefiled, upright (-ly), whole.

(8552) pronounced taw-mam'; a prim. root; to complete, in a good or a bad sense, lit. or fig., trans. or intrans. (as follows):- accomplish, cease, be clean, [pass-] ed, consume, have done, (come to an, have an, make an) end, fail, come to the full, be all gone, x be all here, be (make) perfect, be spent, sum, be (shew self) upright, be wasted, whole.

righteousness (6664) pronounced tseh'-dek; from 6663; the right (nat., mor., or legal); also (abstr.) equity or (fig.) prosperity:- x even, (x that which is altogether) just (-ice), ([un-]) right (-eous) (cause, -ly, -ness).

(6663) pronounced tsaw-dak'; prim. root; to be (causat., make) right (in a moral or forensic sense):- cleanse, clear self (be, do) just (-ice, -ify, -ify self), (be, turn to) righteous (-ness).

Then I, justified, will behold Your face: awake, I am filled with the vision of You. TEHILLIM 17:15 (PSALMS 17:15)

As for me, I will behold thy face in righteousness (6664): I shall be satisfied when I awake, with thy likeness. PSALMS 17:15

righteousness (6664) pronounced tseh'-dek; from 6663; the right (nat., mor., or legal); also (abstr.) equity or (fig.) prosperity:- x even, (x that which is altogether) just (-ice), ([un-]) right (-eous) (cause, -ly, -ness).

(6663) pronounced tsaw-dak'; prim. root; to be (causat., make) right (in a moral or forensic sense):- cleanse, clear self (be, do) just (-ice, -ify, -ify self), (be, turn to) righteous (-ness).

The LORD rewarded me according to my merit; He requited the cleanness of my hands; for I have kept to the ways of the LORD, and have not been guilty before my God; for I am mindful of all His rules; I have not disregarded His laws. I have been blameless toward Him, and have guarded myself against sinning; and the LORD has requited me according to my merit, the cleanness of my hands in His sight. TEHILLIM 18:21-25 (PSALMS 18:20-24)

The LORD rewarded me according to my righteousness (6664); according to the cleanness of my hands hath he recompensed me. For I have kept the ways of the LORD, and have not wickedly departed from my God. For all his judgments *were* before me, and I did not put away his statutes from me. I was also upright (8549) before him, and I kept myself from mine iniquity. Therefore hath the LORD recompensed me according to my righteousness (6664), according to the cleanness of my hands in his eyesight. PSALMS 18:20-24

> righteousness (6664) pronounced tseh'-dek; from 6663; the right (nat., mor., or legal); also (abstr.) equity or (fig.) prosperity:- x even, (x that which is altogether) just (-ice), ([un-]) right (-eous) (cause, -ly, -ness).
>
> (6663) pronounced tsaw-dak'; prim. root; to be (causat., make) right (in a moral or forensic sense):- cleanse, clear self (be, do) just (-ice, -ify, -ify self), (be, turn to) righteous (-ness).
>
> upright (8549) pronounced taw-meem'; from 8552; entire (lit., fig., or mor.); also (as noun) integrity, truth:- without blemish, complete, full, perfect, sincerely (-ity), sound, without spot, undefiled, upright (-ly), whole.
>
> (8552) pronounced taw-mam'; a prim. root; to complete, in a good or a bad sense, lit. or fig., trans. or intrans. (as follows):- accomplish, cease, be clean, [pass-] ed, consume, have done, (come to an, have an, make an) end, fail, come to the full, be all gone, x be all here, be (make) perfect, be spent, sum, be (shew self) upright, be wasted, whole.

Offspring shall serve Him; the LORD's fame shall be proclaimed to the generation to come; they shall tell of His beneficence to people yet to be born, for He has acted. TEHILLIM 22:31-32 (PSALMS 22:30-31)

A seed shall serve him; it shall be accounted to the LORD for a generation. They shall come, and shall declare his righteousness (6666) unto a people that shall be born, that he hath done *this*. PSALMS 22:30-31

> righteousness (6666) pronounced tsed-aw-kaw'; from 6663; rightness (abstr.), subj. (rectitude); obj. (justice) , mor. (virtue) or fig. (prosperity):- justice, moderately, right (-eous) (act, -ly, -ness)
>
> (6663) pronounced tsaw-dak'; prim. root; to be (causat., make) right (in a moral or forensic sense):- cleanse, clear self (be, do) just (-ice, -ify, -ify self), (be, turn to) righteous (-ness).

He renews my life; He guides me in right paths as befits His name. TEHILLIM 23:3 (PSALMS 23:3)

He restoreth my soul: He leadeth me in the paths of righteousness (6664) for His name's sake. PSALMS 23:3

> righteousness (6664) pronounced tseh'-dek; from 6663; the right (nat., mor., or legal); also (abstr.) equity or (fig.) prosperity:- x even, (x that which is altogether) just (-ice), ([un-]) right (-eous) (cause, -ly, -ness).

(6663) pronounced tsaw-dak'; prim. root; to be (causat., make) right (in a moral or forensic sense):- cleanse, clear self (be, do) just (-ice, -ify, -ify self), (be, turn to) righteous (-ness).

He shall carry away a blessing from the LORD, a just reward from God, his deliverer. TEHILLIM 24:5 (PSALMS 24:5)

He shall receive the blessing from the LORD, and righteousness (6666) from the God of his salvation. PSALMS 24:5

righteousness (6666) pronounced tsed-aw-kaw'; from 6663; rightness (abstr.), subj. (rectitude); obj. (justice) , mor. (virtue) or fig. (prosperity):- justice, moderately, right (-eous) (act, -ly, -ness)

(6663) pronounced tsaw-dak'; prim. root; to be (causat., make) right (in a moral or forensic sense):- cleanse, clear self (be, do) just (-ice, -ify, -ify self), (be, turn to) righteous (-ness).

I seek refuge in You, O LORD; may I never be disappointed; as You are righteous, rescue me. TEHILLIM 31:2 (PSALMS 31:1)

In thee, O LORD, do I put my trust; let me never be ashamed: deliver me in thy righteousness (6666). PSALMS 31:1

righteousness (6666) pronounced tsed-aw-kaw'; from 6663; rightness (abstr.), subj. (rectitude); obj. (justice) , mor. (virtue) or fig. (prosperity):- justice, moderately, right (-eous) (act, -ly, -ness)

(6663) pronounced tsaw-dak'; prim. root; to be (causat., make) right (in a moral or forensic sense):- cleanse, clear self (be, do) just (-ice, -ify, -ify self), (be, turn to) righteous (-ness).

He loves what is right and just; the earth is full of the LORD's faithful care. TEHILLIM 33:5 (PSALMS 33:5)

He loveth righteousness (6666) and judgment: the earth is full of the goodness of the LORD. PSALMS 33:5

righteousness (6666) pronounced tsed-aw-kaw'; from 6663; rightness (abstr.), subj. (rectitude); obj. (justice) , mor. (virtue) or fig. (prosperity):- justice, moderately, right (-eous) (act, -ly, -ness)

(6663) pronounced tsaw-dak'; prim. root; to be (causat., make) right (in a moral or forensic sense):- cleanse, clear self (be, do) just (-ice, -ify, -ify self), (be, turn to) righteous (-ness).

Take up my cause, O LORD, my God, as You are beneficent, and let them not rejoice over me. TEHILLIM 35:24 (PSALMS 35:24)

Judge me, O LORD my God, according to thy righteousness (6664); and let them not rejoice over me. PSALMS 35:24

righteousness (6664) pronounced tseh'-dek; from 6663; the right (nat., mor., or legal); also (abstr.) equity or (fig.) prosperity:- x even, (x that which is altogether) just (-ice), ([un-]) right (-eous) (cause, -ly, -ness).

(6663) pronounced tsaw-dak'; prim. root; to be (causat., make) right (in a moral or forensic sense):- cleanse, clear self (be, do) just (-ice, -ify, -ify self), (be, turn to) righteous (-ness).

May those who desire my vindication sing forth joyously; may they always say, "Extolled be the LORD who desires the well-being of His servant," while my tongue shall recite Your beneficent acts, Your praises all day long. TEHILLIM 35;27-28 (PSALMS 35:27-28)

Let them shout for joy, and be glad, that favour my righteous (6664) cause: yea, let them say continually, Let the LORD be magnified, which hath pleasure in the prosperity of his servant. And my tongue shall speak of thy righteousness (6664) *and* of thy praise all the day long. PSALMS 35:27-28

righteousness (6664) pronounced tseh'-dek; from 6663; the right (nat., mor., or legal); also (abstr.) equity or (fig.) prosperity:- x even, (x that which is altogether) just (-ice), ([un-]) right (-eous) (cause, -ly, -ness).

(6663) pronounced tsaw-dak'; prim. root; to be (causat., make) right (in a moral or forensic sense):- cleanse, clear self (be, do) just (-ice, -ify, -ify self), (be, turn to) righteous (-ness).

Your beneficence is like the high mountains; Your justice like the great deep; man and beast You deliver, O LORD. TEHILLIM 36:7 (PSALMS 36:6)

Thy righteousness (6666) *is* like the great mountains; thy judgments *are* a great deep: O LORD, thou preservest man and beast. PSALMS 36:6

righteousness (6666) pronounced tsed-aw-kaw'; from 6663; rightness (abstr.), subj. (rectitude); obj. (justice) , mor. (virtue) or fig. (prosperity):- justice, moderately, right (-eous) (act, -ly, -ness)

(6663) pronounced tsaw-dak'; prim. root; to be (causat., make) right (in a moral or forensic sense):- cleanse, clear self (be, do) just (-ice, -ify, -ify self), (be, turn to) righteous (-ness).

Bestow Your faithful care on those devoted to You, and Your beneficence on upright men.
TEHILLIM 36:11 (PSALMS 36:10)

O continue thy lovingkindness unto them that know thee; and thy righteousness (6666) to the upright (3477) in heart. PSALMS 36:10

righteousness (6666) pronounced tsed-aw-kaw'; from 6663; rightness (abstr.), subj. (rectitude); obj. (justice) , mor. (virtue) or fig. (prosperity):- justice, moderately, right (-eous) (act, -ly, -ness)

(6663) pronounced tsaw-dak'; prim. root; to be (causat., make) right (in a moral or forensic sense):- cleanse, clear self (be, do) just (-ice, -ify, -ify self), (be, turn to) righteous (-ness).

> upright (3477) pronounced yaw-shawr'; from 3474; straight (lit. or fig.):- convenient, equity, Jasher, just, meet (-est), + pleased well, right (-eous), straight (most) upright (-ly, -ness)
>
> (3474) pronounced yaw-shar'; a prim. root; to be straight or even; fig. to be (causat. to make) right, pleasant, prosperous:- direct, fit, seem good (meet), + please (well), be (esteem, go) right (on), bring (look, make, take the) straight (way), be upright (-ly).

He will cause your vindication to shine forth like the light, the justice of your case, like the noonday sun. TEHILLIM 37:6 (PSALMS 37:6)

And he shall bring forth thy righteousness (6664) as the light, and thy judgment as the noonday. PSALMS 37:6

> righteousness (6664) pronounced tseh'-dek; from 6663; the right (nat., mor., or legal); also (abstr.) equity or (fig.) prosperity:- x even, (x that which is altogether) just (-ice), ([un-]) right (-eous) (cause, -ly, -ness).
>
> (6663) pronounced tsaw-dak'; prim. root; to be (causat., make) right (in a moral or forensic sense):- cleanse, clear self (be, do) just (-ice, -ify, -ify self), (be, turn to) righteous (-ness).

I proclaimed [Your] righteousness in a great congregation; see, I did not withhold my words; O LORD, You must know it. I did not keep Your beneficence to myself; I declared Your faithful deliverance; I did not fail to speak of Your steadfast love in a great congregation. TEHILLIM 40:10-11 (PSALMS 40:9-10)

I have preached righteousness (6664) in the great congregation: lo, I have not refrained my lips, O LORD, thou knowest. I have not hid thy righteousness (6666) within my heart; I have declared thy faithfulness and thy salvation: I have not concealed thy lovingkindness and thy truth from the great congregation. PSALMS 40:9-10

> righteousness (6664) pronounced tseh'-dek; from 6663; the right (nat., mor., or legal); also (abstr.) equity or (fig.) prosperity:- x even, (x that which is altogether) just (-ice), ([un-]) right (-eous) (cause, -ly, -ness).
>
> (6663) pronounced tsaw-dak'; prim. root; to be (causat., make) right (in a moral or forensic sense):- cleanse, clear self (be, do) just (-ice, -ify, -ify self), (be, turn to) righteous (-ness).
>
> righteousness (6666) pronounced tsed-aw-kaw'; from 6663; rightness (abstr.), subj. (rectitude); obj. (justice) , mor. (virtue) or fig. (prosperity):- justice, moderately, right (-eous) (act, -ly, -ness)

Gird your sword upon your thigh, O hero, in your splendor and glory; in your glory, win success; ride on in the cause of truth and meekness and right; and let your right hand lead you to awesome deeds. Your arrows, sharpened, [pierce] the breast of the king's enemies; peoples fall at your feet. Your divine throne is everlasting; your royal scepter is a scepter of equity. You love righteousness and hate wickedness; rightly has God, your God, chosen to anoint you with oil of gladness over all your peers. TEHILLIM 45:4-8 (PSALMS 45:3-7)

[pierce] the breast of the king's enemies; peoples fall at your feet: Order of Heb. clauses inverted for clarity. (TANAKH footnote).

divine throne: cf. I Chron. 29.23 (TANAKH footnote)

Solomon successfully took over the throne of the LORD as king instead of his father David, and all went well with him. DIVREI –HAYAMIM ALEF 29:23 (I CHRONICLES 29:23)

Then Solomon sat on the throne of the LORD as king instead of David his father, and prospered; and all Israel obeyed him. I CHRONICLES 29:23

Gird thy sword upon *thy* thigh, O *most* mighty, with thy glory and thy majesty. And in thy majesty ride prosperously, because of truth and meekness and righteousness (6664); *and* thy right hand shall teach *thee* terrible things. Thine arrows *are* sharp in the heart of the King's enemies; *whereby* the people fall under thee. Thy throne, O God, is for ever and ever: the scepter of thy kingdom *is* a right scepter. Thou lovest righteousness (6664) and hatest wickedness: therefore God, thy God, hath anointed thee with the oil of gladness above thy fellows. PSALMS 45:3-7

righteousness (6664) pronounced tseh'-dek; from 6663; the right (nat., mor., or legal); also (abstr.) equity or (fig.) prosperity:- x even, (x that which is altogether) just (-ice), ([un-]) right (-eous) (cause, -ly, -ness).

(6663) pronounced tsaw-dak'; prim. root; to be (causat., make) right (in a moral or forensic sense):- cleanse, clear self (be, do) just (-ice, -ify, -ify self), (be, turn to) righteous (-ness).

The praise of You, God, like Your name, reaches to the ends of the earth; Your right hand is filled with beneficence. TEHILLIM 48:11 (PSALMS 48:10)

According to thy name, O God, *so is* thy praise unto the ends of the earth: thy right hand is full of righteousness (6664). PSALMS 48:10

righteousness (6664) pronounced tseh'-dek; from 6663; the right (nat., mor., or legal); also (abstr.) equity or (fig.) prosperity:- x even, (x that which is altogether) just (-ice), ([un-]) right (-eous) (cause, -ly, -ness).

(6663) pronounced tsaw-dak'; prim. root; to be (causat., make) right (in a moral or forensic sense):- cleanse, clear self (be, do) just (-ice, -ify, -ify self), (be, turn to) righteous (-ness).

Then the heavens proclaimed His righteousness, for He is a God who judges. TEHILLIM 50:6 (PSALMS 50:6)

And the heavens shall declare his righteousness (6664): for God *is* judge himself. Selah. PSALMS 50:6

righteousness (6664) pronounced tseh'-dek; from 6663; the right (nat., mor., or legal); also (abstr.) equity or (fig.) prosperity:- x even, (x that which is altogether) just (-ice), ([un-]) right (-eous) (cause, -ly, -ness).

(6663) pronounced tsaw-dak'; prim. root; to be (causat., make) right (in a moral or forensic sense):- cleanse, clear self (be, do) just (-ice, -ify, -ify self), (be, turn to) righteous (-ness).

Save me from bloodguilt, O God, God, my deliverer, that I may sing forth Your beneficence. TEHILLIM 51:16 (PSALMS 51:14)

Deliver me from bloodguiltiness, O God, thou God of my salvation: and my tongue shall sing aloud of thy righteousness (6666). PSALMS 51:14

righteousness (6666) pronounced tsed-aw-kaw'; from 6663; rightness (abstr.), subj. (rectitude); obj. (justice) , mor. (virtue) or fig. (prosperity):- justice, moderately, right (-eous) (act, -ly, -ness)

(6663) pronounced tsaw-dak'; prim. root; to be (causat., make) right (in a moral or forensic sense):- cleanse, clear self (be, do) just (-ice, -ify, -ify self), (be, turn to) righteous (-ness).

Then You will want sacrifices offered in righteousness, burnt and whole offerings; then bulls will be offered on Your altar. TEHILLIM 51:21 (PSALMS 51:19)

Then shalt thou be pleased with the sacrifices of righteousness (6664), with burnt offering and whole burnt offering; then shall they offer bullocks upon thine altar. PSALMS 51:19

righteousness (6664) pronounced tseh'-dek; from 6663; the right (nat., mor., or legal); also (abstr.) equity or (fig.) prosperity:- x even, (x that which is altogether) just (-ice), ([un-]) right (-eous) (cause, -ly, -ness).

(6663) pronounced tsaw-dak'; prim. root; to be (causat., make) right (in a moral or forensic sense):- cleanse, clear self (be, do) just (-ice, -ify, -ify self), (be, turn to) righteous (-ness).

You prefer evil to good, the lie, to speaking truthfully. TEHILLIM 52:5 (PSALMS 52:3)

Thou lovest evil more than good; and lying rather than to speak righteousness (6664). Selah. PSALMS 52:3

righteousness (6664) pronounced tseh'-dek; from 6663; the right (nat., mor., or legal); also (abstr.) equity or (fig.) prosperity:- x even, (x that which is altogether) just (-ice), ([un-]) right (-eous) (cause, -ly, -ness).

(6663) pronounced tsaw-dak'; prim. root; to be (causat., make) right (in a moral or forensic sense):- cleanse, clear self (be, do) just (-ice, -ify, -ify self), (be, turn to) righteous (-ness).

O mighty ones, do you really decree what is just? Do you judge mankind with equity? TEHILLIM 58:2 (PSALMS 58:1)

Do ye indeed speak righteousness (6664), O congregation? Do ye judge uprightly (4334), O ye sons of men? PSALMS 58:1

> righteousness (6664) pronounced tseh'-dek; from 6663; the right (nat., mor., or legal); also (abstr.) equity or (fig.) prosperity:- x even, (x that which is altogether) just (-ice), ([un-]) right (-eous) (cause, -ly, -ness).
>
> (6663) pronounced tsaw-dak'; prim. root; to be (causat., make) right (in a moral or forensic sense):- cleanse, clear self (be, do) just (-ice, -ify, -ify self), (be, turn to) righteous (-ness).
>
> uprightly (4334) pronounced mee-shore'; from 3474; a level, i.e. a plain (often used [with the art. pref.] as a prop. name of certain districts; fig. Concord): also straightness i.e. (fig.) justice (sometimes adv. Justly):- equity, even place, plain, right (-eously), (made) straight, uprightness.
>
> (3474) pronounced yaw-shar'; a prim. root; to be straight or even; fig. to be (causat. to make) right, pleasant, prosperous:- direct, fit, seem good (meet), + please (well), be (esteem, go) right (on), bring (look, make, take the) straight (way), be upright (-ly).

Answer us with victory through awesome deeds, O God, our deliverer, in whom all the ends of the earth and the distant seas put their trust; TEHILLIM 65:6 (PSALMS 65:5)

By terrible things in righteousness (6664) wilt thou answer us, O God of our salvation; *who art* the confidence of all the ends of the earth, and of them that are afar off *upon* the sea PSALMS 65:5

> righteousness (6664) pronounced tseh'-dek; from 6663; the right (nat., mor., or legal); also (abstr.) equity or (fig.) prosperity:- x even, (x that which is altogether) just (-ice), ([un-]) right (-eous) (cause, -ly, -ness).
>
> (6663) pronounced tsaw-dak'; prim. root; to be (causat., make) right (in a moral or forensic sense):- cleanse, clear self (be, do) just (-ice, -ify, -ify self), (be, turn to) righteous (-ness).

For they persecute those You have struck; they talk about the pain of those You have felled. Add that to their guilt; let them have no share of Your beneficence; may they be erased from the book of life, and not be inscribed with the righteous. TEHILLIM 69:27-29 (PSALMS 69:26-28)

For they persecute *him* whom thou hast smitten; and they talk to the grief of those whom thou hast wounded. Add iniquity unto their iniquity: and let them not come into thy righteousness (6666). Let them be blotted out of the book of the living, and not be written with the righteous (6662).
PSALMS 69:26-28

> righteousness (6666) pronounced tsed-aw-kaw'; from 6663; rightness (abstr.), subj. (rectitude); obj. (justice) , mor. (virtue) or fig. (prosperity):- justice, moderately, right (-eous) (act, -ly, -ness)
>
> (6663) pronounced tsaw-dak'; prim. root; to be (causat., make) right (in a moral or forensic sense):- cleanse, clear self (be, do) just (-ice, -ify, -ify self), (be, turn to) righteous (-ness).

righteous (6662) pronounced tsad-deek'; from 6663; just:- just, lawful, righteous (man).

As You are beneficent, save me and rescue me; incline Your ear to me and deliver me. TEHILLIM 71:2 (PSALMS 71:2)

Deliver me in thy righteousness (6666), and cause me to escape: incline thine ear unto me, and save me. PSALMS 71:2

righteousness (6666) pronounced tsed-aw-kaw'; from 6663; rightness (abstr.), subj. (rectitude); obj. (justice) , mor. (virtue) or fig. (prosperity):- justice, moderately, right (-eous) (act, -ly, -ness)

(6663) pronounced tsaw-dak'; prim. root; to be (causat., make) right (in a moral or forensic sense):- cleanse, clear self (be, do) just (-ice, -ify, -ify self), (be, turn to) righteous (-ness).

My mouth tells of Your beneficence, of Your deliverance all day long, though I know not how to tell it. I come with praise of Your mighty acts, O LORD God; I celebrate Your beneficence, Yours alone. TEHILLIM 71:15-16 (PSALMS 71:15-16)

My mouth shall show forth thy righteousness (6666) *and* thy salvation all the day; for I know not the numbers *thereof*. I will go in the strength of the LORD God; I will make mention of thy righteousness (6666), *even* of thine only. PSALMS 71:15-16

righteousness (6666) pronounced tsed-aw-kaw'; from 6663; rightness (abstr.), subj. (rectitude); obj. (justice) , mor. (virtue) or fig. (prosperity):- justice, moderately, right (-eous) (act, -ly, -ness)

(6663) pronounced tsaw-dak'; prim. root; to be (causat., make) right (in a moral or forensic sense):- cleanse, clear self (be, do) just (-ice, -ify, -ify self), (be, turn to) righteous (-ness).

Your mighty acts, to all who are to come, Your beneficence, high as the heavens, O God, You who have done great things; O God, who is Your peer! TEHILLIM 71:19 (PSALMS 71:19)

Thy righteousness (6666) also, O God, *is* very high, who hast done great things: O God, who *is* like unto thee! PSALMS 71:19

righteousness (6666) pronounced tsed-aw-kaw'; from 6663; rightness (abstr.), subj. (rectitude); obj. (justice) , mor. (virtue) or fig. (prosperity):- justice, moderately, right (-eous) (act, -ly, -ness)

(6663) pronounced tsaw-dak'; prim. root; to be (causat., make) right (in a moral or forensic sense):- cleanse, clear self (be, do) just (-ice, -ify, -ify self), (be, turn to) righteous (-ness).

All day long my tongue shall recite Your beneficent acts; how those who sought my ruin were frustrated and disgraced. TEHILLIM 71:24 (PSALMS 71:24)

My tongue also shall talk of thy righteousness (6666) all the day long: for they are confounded, for they are brought unto shame, that seek my hurt. PSALMS 71:24

righteousness (6666) pronounced tsed-aw-kaw'; from 6663; rightness (abstr.), subj. (rectitude); obj. (justice) , mor. (virtue) or fig. (prosperity):- justice, moderately, right (-eous) (act, -ly, -ness)

(6663) pronounced tsaw-dak'; prim. root; to be (causat., make) right (in a moral or forensic sense):- cleanse, clear self (be, do) just (-ice, -ify, -ify self), (be, turn to) righteous (-ness).

O God, endow the king with Your judgments, the king's son with Your righteousness; that he may judge Your people rightly, Your lowly ones justly. Let the mountains produce well-being for the people, the hills, the reward of justice. Let him champion the lowly among the people, deliver the needy folk, and crush those who wrong them. TEHILLIM 72:2-4 (PSALMS 72:1-3)

Give the king thy judgments, O God, and thy righteousness (6666) unto the king's son. He shall judge thy people with righteousness (6664), and thy poor with judgment. The mountains shall bring peace to the people, and the little hills, by righteousness (6666). PSALMS 72:1-3

righteousness (6666) pronounced tsed-aw-kaw'; from 6663; rightness (abstr.), subj. (rectitude); obj. (justice) , mor. (virtue) or fig. (prosperity):- justice, moderately, right (-eous) (act, -ly, -ness)

(6663) pronounced tsaw-dak'; prim. root; to be (causat., make) right (in a moral or forensic sense):- cleanse, clear self (be, do) just (-ice, -ify, -ify self), (be, turn to) righteous (-ness).

righteousness (6664) pronounced tseh'-dek; from 6663; the right (nat., mor., or legal); also (abstr.) equity or (fig.) prosperity:- x even, (x that which is altogether) just (-ice), ([un-]) right (-eous) (cause, -ly, -ness).

Faithfulness and truth meet; justice and well-being kiss. Truth springs up from the earth; justice looks down from heaven. The LORD also bestows His bounty; our land yields its produce. Justice goes before Him as He sets out on His way. TEHILLIM 85:11-14 (PSALMS 85:10-13)

Mercy and truth are met together; righteousness (6664) and peace have kissed *each other*. Truth shall spring out of the earth; and righteousness (6664) shall look down from heaven. Yea, the LORD shall give *that which is good*; and our land shall yield her increase. Righteousness (6664) shall go before him; and shall set *us* in the way of his steps. PSALMS 85:10-13

righteousness (6664) pronounced tseh'-dek; from 6663; the right (nat., mor., or legal); also (abstr.) equity or (fig.) prosperity:- x even, (x that which is altogether) just (-ice), ([un-]) right (-eous) (cause, -ly, -ness).

(6663) pronounced tsaw-dak'; prim. root; to be (causat., make) right (in a moral or forensic sense):- cleanse, clear self (be, do) just (-ice, -ify, -ify self), (be, turn to) righteous (-ness).

Are Your wonders made known in the netherworld, Your beneficent deeds in the land of oblivion? TEHILLIM 88:13 (PSALMS 88:12)

netherworld: Lit. "darkness" (TANAKH footnote)

Shall thy wonders be known in the dark? and thy righteousness (6666) in the land of forgetfulness? PSALMS 88:12

> righteousness (6666) pronounced tsed-aw-kaw'; from 6663; rightness (abstr.), subj. (rectitude); obj. (justice) , mor. (virtue) or fig. (prosperity):- justice, moderately, right (-eous) (act, -ly, -ness)
>
> (6663) pronounced tsaw-dak'; prim. root; to be (causat., make) right (in a moral or forensic sense):- cleanse, clear self (be, do) just (-ice, -ify, -ify self), (be, turn to) righteous (-ness).

They rejoice in Your name all day long; they are exalted through Your righteousness. TEHILLIM 89:17 (PSALMS 89:16)

In thy name shall they rejoice all the day and in thy righteousness (6666) shall they be exalted. PSALMS 89:16

> righteousness (6666) pronounced tsed-aw-kaw'; from 6663; rightness (abstr.), subj. (rectitude); obj. (justice) , mor. (virtue) or fig. (prosperity):- justice, moderately, right (-eous) (act, -ly, -ness)
>
> (6663) pronounced tsaw-dak'; prim. root; to be (causat., make) right (in a moral or forensic sense):- cleanse, clear self (be, do) just (-ice, -ify, -ify self), (be, turn to) righteous (-ness).

Judgment shall again accord with justice and all the upright shall rally to it. TEHILLIM 94:15 (PSALMS 94:15)

But judgment shall return unto righteousness (6664): and all the upright (3477) in heart shall follow it. PSALMS 94:15

> righteousness (6664) pronounced tseh'-dek; from 6663; the right (nat., mor., or legal); also (abstr.) equity or (fig.) prosperity:- x even, (x that which is altogether) just (-ice), ([un-]) right (-eous) (cause, -ly, -ness).
>
> (6663) pronounced tsaw-dak'; prim. root; to be (causat., make) right (in a moral or forensic sense):- cleanse, clear self (be, do) just (-ice, -ify, -ify self), (be, turn to) righteous (-ness).
>
> upright (3477) pronounced yaw-shawr'; from 3474; straight (lit. or fig.):- convenient, equity, Jasher, just, meet (-est), + pleased well, right (-eous), straight (most) upright (-ly, -ness)
>
> (3474) pronounced yaw-shar'; a prim. root; to be straight or even; fig. to be (causat. to make) right, pleasant, prosperous:- direct, fit, seem good (meet), + please (well), be (esteem, go) right (on), bring (look, make, take the) straight (way), be upright (-ly).

Let the heavens rejoice and the earth exult; let the sea and all within it thunder, the fields and everything in them exult; then shall all the trees of the forest shout for joy at the presence of the LORD, for He is coming, for He is coming to rule the earth; He will rule the world justly, and its peoples in faithfulness. TEHILLIM 96:11-13 (PSALMS 96:11-13)

Let the heavens rejoice, and let the earth be glad; let the sea roar, and the fullness thereof. Let the field be joyful, and all that *is* therein: then shall all the trees of the wood rejoice before the LORD: for he cometh, for he cometh to judge the earth: he shall judge the world with righteousness (6664), and the people with his truth. PSALMS 96:11-13

> righteousness (6664) pronounced tseh'-dek; from 6663; the right (nat., mor., or legal); also (abstr.) equity or (fig.) prosperity:- x even, (x that which is altogether) just (-ice), ([un-]) right (-eous) (cause, -ly, -ness).
>
> (6663) pronounced tsaw-dak'; prim. root; to be (causat., make) right (in a moral or forensic sense):- cleanse, clear self (be, do) just (-ice, -ify, -ify self), (be, turn to) righteous (-ness).

Dense clouds are around Him, righteousness and justice are the base of His throne. TEHILLIM 97:2 (PSALMS 97:2)

Clouds and darkness *are* round about him: righteousness (6664) and judgment *are* the habitation of his throne. PSALMS 97:2

> righteousness (6664) pronounced tseh'-dek; from 6663; the right (nat., mor., or legal); also (abstr.) equity or (fig.) prosperity:- x even, (x that which is altogether) just (-ice), ([un-]) right (-eous) (cause, -ly, -ness).
>
> (6663) pronounced tsaw-dak'; prim. root; to be (causat., make) right (in a moral or forensic sense):- cleanse, clear self (be, do) just (-ice, -ify, -ify self), (be, turn to) righteous (-ness).

The heavens proclaim His righteousness and all peoples see His glory. TEHILLIM 97:6 (PSALMS 97:6)

The heavens declare his righteousness (6664), and all the people see his glory. PSALMS 97:6

> righteousness (6664) pronounced tseh'-dek; from 6663; the right (nat., mor., or legal); also (abstr.) equity or (fig.) prosperity:- x even, (x that which is altogether) just (-ice), ([un-]) right (-eous) (cause, -ly, -ness).
>
> (6663) pronounced tsaw-dak'; prim. root; to be (causat., make) right (in a moral or forensic sense):- cleanse, clear self (be, do) just (-ice, -ify, -ify self), (be, turn to) righteous (-ness).

The LORD has manifested His victory, has displayed His triumph in the sight of the nations. TEHILLIM 98:2 (PSALMS 98:2)

The LORD hath made known his salvation: his righteousness (6666) hath he openly shown in the sight of the heathen. PSALMS 98:2

> righteousness (6666) pronounced tsed-aw-kaw'; from 6663; rightness (abstr.), subj. (rectitude); obj. (justice) , mor. (virtue) or fig. (prosperity):- justice, moderately, right (-eous) (act, -ly, -ness)
>
> (6663) pronounced tsaw-dak'; prim. root; to be (causat., make) right (in a moral or forensic sense):- cleanse, clear self (be, do) just (-ice, -ify, -ify self), (be, turn to) righteous (-ness).

Let the sea and all within it thunder, the world and its inhabitants; let the rivers clap their hands, the mountains sing joyously together at the presence of the LORD, for He is coming to rule the earth; He will rule the world justly, and its people with equity. TEHILLIM 98:7-9 (PSALMS 98:7-9)

Let the sea roar, and the fulness thereof; the world, and they that dwell therein. Let the floods clap *their* hands; let the hills be joyful together before the LORD; for he cometh to judge the earth: with righteousness (6664) shall he judge the world, and the people with equity. PSALMS 98:7-9

> righteousness (6664) pronounced tseh'-dek; from 6663; the right (nat., mor., or legal); also (abstr.) equity or (fig.) prosperity:- x even, (x that which is altogether) just (-ice), ([un-]) right (-eous) (cause, -ly, -ness).
>
> (6663) pronounced tsaw-dak'; prim. root; to be (causat., make) right (in a moral or forensic sense):- cleanse, clear self (be, do) just (-ice, -ify, -ify self), (be, turn to) righteous (-ness).

Mighty king who loves justice, it was You who established equity, You who worked righteous judgment in Jacob. TEHILLIM 99:4 (PSALMS 99:4)

The king's strength also loveth judgment; thou dost establish equity, thou executest judgment and righteousness (6666) in Jacob. PSALMS 99:4

> righteousness (6666) pronounced tsed-aw-kaw'; from 6663; rightness (abstr.), subj. (rectitude); obj. (justice) , mor. (virtue) or fig. (prosperity):- justice, moderately, right (-eous) (act, -ly, -ness)
>
> (6663) pronounced tsaw-dak'; prim. root; to be (causat., make) right (in a moral or forensic sense):- cleanse, clear self (be, do) just (-ice, -ify, -ify self), (be, turn to) righteous (-ness).

The LORD executes righteous acts and judgments for all who are wronged. TEHILLIM 103:6 (PSALMS 103:6)

The LORD executeth righteousness (6666) and judgment for all that are oppressed. PSALMS 103:6

> righteousness (6666) pronounced tsed-aw-kaw'; from 6663; rightness (abstr.), subj. (rectitude); obj. (justice) , mor. (virtue) or fig. (prosperity):- justice, moderately, right (-eous) (act, -ly, -ness)
>
> (6663) pronounced tsaw-dak'; prim. root; to be (causat., make) right (in a moral or forensic sense):- cleanse, clear self (be, do) just (-ice, -ify, -ify self), (be, turn to) righteous (-ness).

But the LORD's steadfast love is for all eternity toward those who fear Him, and His beneficence is for the children's children of those who keep His covenant and remember to observe His precepts. TEHILLIM 103:17-18 (PSALMS 103:17-18)

But the mercy of the LORD *is* from everlasting to everlasting upon them that fear him, and his righteousness (6666) unto children's children: to such as keep his covenant, and to those that remember his commandments to do them. PSALMS 103:17-18

righteousness (6666) pronounced tsed-aw-kaw'; from 6663; rightness (abstr.), subj. (rectitude); obj. (justice) , mor. (virtue) or fig. (prosperity):- justice, moderately, right (-eous) (act, -ly, -ness)

(6663) pronounced tsaw-dak'; prim. root; to be (causat., make) right (in a moral or forensic sense):- cleanse, clear self (be, do) just (-ice, -ify, -ify self), (be, turn to) righteous (-ness).

Happy are those who act justly, who do right at all times. TEHILLIM 106:3 (PSALMS 106:3)

Blessed *are* they that keep judgment, *and* he that doeth righteousness (6666) at all times.
PSALMS 106:3

righteousness (6666) pronounced tsed-aw-kaw'; from 6663; rightness (abstr.), subj. (rectitude); obj. (justice) , mor. (virtue) or fig. (prosperity):- justice, moderately, right (-eous) (act, -ly, -ness)

(6663) pronounced tsaw-dak'; prim. root; to be (causat., make) right (in a moral or forensic sense):- cleanse, clear self (be, do) just (-ice, -ify, -ify self), (be, turn to) righteous (-ness).

It was reckoned to his merit for all generations, to eternity. TEHILLIM 106:31 (PSALMS 106:31)

And that was counted unto him for righteousness (6666) unto all generations for evermore.
PSALMS 106:31

righteousness (6666) pronounced tsed-aw-kaw'; from 6663; rightness (abstr.), subj. (rectitude); obj. (justice) , mor. (virtue) or fig. (prosperity):- justice, moderately, right (-eous) (act, -ly, -ness)

(6663) pronounced tsaw-dak'; prim. root; to be (causat., make) right (in a moral or forensic sense):- cleanse, clear self (be, do) just (-ice, -ify, -ify self), (be, turn to) righteous (-ness).

His deeds are splendid and glorious; His beneficence is everlasting; TEHILLIM 111:3 (PSALMS 111:3)

His work *is* honourable and glorious; and his righteousness (6666) endureth for ever. PSALMS 111:3

righteousness (6666) pronounced tsed-aw-kaw'; from 6663; rightness (abstr.), subj. (rectitude); obj. (justice) , mor. (virtue) or fig. (prosperity):- justice, moderately, right (-eous) (act, -ly, -ness)

(6663) pronounced tsaw-dak'; prim. root; to be (causat., make) right (in a moral or forensic sense):- cleanse, clear self (be, do) just (-ice, -ify, -ify self), (be, turn to) righteous (-ness).

Wealth and riches are in his house, and his beneficence lasts forever. TEHILLIM 112:3 (PSALMS 112:3)

Wealth and riches *shall be* in his house: and his righteousness (6666) endureth for ever. PSALMS 112:3

righteousness (6666) pronounced tsed-aw-kaw'; from 6663; rightness (abstr.), subj. (rectitude); obj. (justice) , mor. (virtue) or fig. (prosperity):- justice, moderately, right (-eous) (act, -ly, -ness)

(6663) pronounced tsaw-dak'; prim. root; to be (causat., make) right (in a moral or forensic sense):- cleanse, clear self (be, do) just (-ice, -ify, -ify self), (be, turn to) righteous (-ness).

He gives freely to the poor; his beneficence lasts forever; his horn is exalted in honor. TEHILLIM 112:9 (PSALMS 112:9)

He hath dispersed, he hath given to the poor; his righteousness (6666) endureth for ever; his horn shall be exalted with honour. PSALMS 112:9

> righteousness (6666) pronounced tsed-aw-kaw'; from 6663; rightness (abstr.), subj. (rectitude); obj. (justice) , mor. (virtue) or fig. (prosperity):- justice, moderately, right (-eous) (act, -ly, -ness)
>
> (6663) pronounced tsaw-dak'; prim. root; to be (causat., make) right (in a moral or forensic sense):- cleanse, clear self (be, do) just (-ice, -ify, -ify self), (be, turn to) righteous (-ness).

Open the gates of victory for me that I may enter them and praise the LORD. TEHILLIM 118:19 (PSALMS 118:19)

Open to me the gates of righteousness (6664); I will go into them, *and* I will praise the LORD: PSALMS 118:19

> righteousness (6664) pronounced tseh'-dek; from 6663; the right (nat., mor., or legal); also (abstr.) equity or (fig.) prosperity:- x even, (x that which is altogether) just (-ice), ([un-]) right (-eous) (cause, -ly, -ness).
>
> (6663) pronounced tsaw-dak'; prim. root; to be (causat., make) right (in a moral or forensic sense):- cleanse, clear self (be, do) just (-ice, -ify, -ify self), (be, turn to) righteous (-ness).

See, I have longed for Your precepts; by Your righteousness preserve me. TEHILLIM 119:40 (PSALMS 119:40)

Behold, I have longed after thy precepts: quicken me in thy righteousness (6666). PSALMS 119:40

> righteousness (6666) pronounced tsed-aw-kaw'; from 6663; rightness (abstr.), subj. (rectitude); obj. (justice) , mor. (virtue) or fig. (prosperity):- justice, moderately, right (-eous) (act, -ly, -ness)
>
> (6663) pronounced tsaw-dak'; prim. root; to be (causat., make) right (in a moral or forensic sense):- cleanse, clear self (be, do) just (-ice, -ify, -ify self), (be, turn to) righteous (-ness).

My eyes pine away for Your deliverance, for Your promise of victory. TEHILLIM 119:123 (PSALMS 119:123)

Mine eyes fail for thy salvation, and for the word of thy righteousness (6664). PSALMS 119:123

> righteousness (6664) pronounced tseh'-dek; from 6663; the right (nat., mor., or legal); also (abstr.) equity or (fig.) prosperity:- x even, (x that which is altogether) just (-ice), ([un-]) right (-eous) (cause, -ly, -ness).
>
> (6663) pronounced tsaw-dak'; prim. root; to be (causat., make) right (in a moral or forensic sense):- cleanse, clear self (be, do) just (-ice, -ify, -ify self), (be, turn to) righteous (-ness).

Your righteousness is eternal; Your teaching is true. Though anguish and distress come upon me, Your commandments are my delight. Your righteous decrees are eternal; give me understanding that I might live. TEHILLIM 119:142-144 (PSALMS 119:142-144)

Thy righteousness (6666) *is* an everlasting righteousness (6664), and thy law *is* the truth. Trouble and anguish have taken hold on me: *yet* thy commandments *are* my delights. The righteousness (6664) of thy testimonies *is* everlasting: give me understanding, and I shall live. PSALMS 119:142-144

> righteousness (6666) pronounced tsed-aw-kaw'; from 6663; rightness (abstr.), subj. (rectitude); obj. (justice) , mor. (virtue) or fig. (prosperity):- justice, moderately, right (-eous) (act, -ly, -ness)
>
> (6663) pronounced tsaw-dak'; prim. root; to be (causat., make) right (in a moral or forensic sense):- cleanse, clear self (be, do) just (-ice, -ify, -ify self), (be, turn to) righteous (-ness).
>
> righteousness (6664) pronounced tseh'-dek; from 6663; the right (nat., mor., or legal); also (abstr.) equity or (fig.) prosperity:- x even, (x that which is altogether) just (-ice), ([un-]) right (-eous) (cause, -ly, -ness).

My tongue shall declare Your promise, for all Your commandments are just. TEHILLIM 119:172 (PSALMS 119:172)

My tongue shall speak of thy word; for all thy commandments *are* righteousness (6664). PSALMS 119:172

> righteousness (6664) pronounced tseh'-dek; from 6663; the right (nat., mor., or legal); also (abstr.) equity or (fig.) prosperity:- x even, (x that which is altogether) just (-ice), ([un-]) right (-eous) (cause, -ly, -ness).
>
> (6663) pronounced tsaw-dak'; prim. root; to be (causat., make) right (in a moral or forensic sense):- cleanse, clear self (be, do) just (-ice, -ify, -ify self), (be, turn to) righteous (-ness).

Your priests are clothed in triumph; Your loyal ones sing for joy. TEHILLIM 132:9 (PSALMS 132:9)

Let thy priests be clothed with righteousness (6664); and let thy saints shout for joy. PSALMS 132:9

> righteousness (6664) pronounced tseh'-dek; from 6663; the right (nat., mor., or legal); also (abstr.) equity or (fig.) prosperity:- x even, (x that which is altogether) just (-ice), ([un-]) right (-eous) (cause, -ly, -ness).
>
> (6663) pronounced tsaw-dak'; prim. root; to be (causat., make) right (in a moral or forensic sense):- cleanse, clear self (be, do) just (-ice, -ify, -ify self), (be, turn to) righteous (-ness).

O LORD, hear my prayer; give ear to my plea, as You are faithful: answer me, as You are beneficent. TEHILLIM 143:1 (PSALMS 143:1)

Hear my prayer, O LORD, give ear to my supplications: in thy faithfulness answer me, in thy righteousness (6666). PSALMS 143:1

righteousness (6666) pronounced tsed-aw-kaw'; from 6663; rightness (abstr.), subj. (rectitude); obj. (justice) , mor. (virtue) or fig. (prosperity):- justice, moderately, right (-eous) (act, -ly, -ness)

(6663) pronounced tsaw-dak'; prim. root; to be (causat., make) right (in a moral or forensic sense):- cleanse, clear self (be, do) just (-ice, -ify, -ify self), (be, turn to) righteous (-ness).

They should celebrate Your abundant goodness, and sing joyously of Your beneficence. TEHILLIM 145:7 (PSALMS 145:7)

They shall abundantly utter the memory of thy great goodness, and shall sing of thy righteousness (6666). PSALMS 145:7

righteousness (6666) pronounced tsed-aw-kaw'; from 6663; rightness (abstr.), subj. (rectitude); obj. (justice) , mor. (virtue) or fig. (prosperity):- justice, moderately, right (-eous) (act, -ly, -ness)

(6663) pronounced tsaw-dak'; prim. root; to be (causat., make) right (in a moral or forensic sense):- cleanse, clear self (be, do) just (-ice, -ify, -ify self), (be, turn to) righteous (-ness).

For the LORD grants wisdom; knowledge and discernment are by His decree. He reserves ability for the upright and is a shield for those who live blamelessly, guarding the paths of justice, protecting the way of those loyal to Him. You will then understand what is right, just, and equitable- every good course. MISHLEI 2:6-9 (PROVERBS 2:6-9)

For the LORD giveth wisdom: out of his mouth *cometh* knowledge and understanding. He layeth up sound wisdom for the righteous (3477); he is a buckler to them that walk uprightly (8537). He keepeth the paths of judgment, and preserveth the way of his saints. Then shalt thou understand righteousness (6664), and judgment, and equity; *yea*, every good path., PROVERBS 2:6-9

righteous (3477) pronounced yaw-shawr'; from 3474; straight (lit. or fig.):- convenient, equity, Jasher, just, meet (-est), + pleased well, right (-eous), straight (most) upright (-ly, -ness)

(3474) pronounced yaw-shar'; a prim. root; to be straight or even; fig. to be (causat. to make) right, pleasant, prosperous:- direct, fit, seem good (meet), + please (well), be (esteem, go) right (on), bring (look, make, take the) straight (way), be upright (-ly).

uprightly (8537) pronounced tome; from 8552; completeness; fig. prosperity; usually (mor.) innocence:- full, integrity, perfect (-ion), simplicity, upright (-ly, -ness), at a venture. See 8550.

(8552) pronounced taw-mam'; a prim. root; to complete, in a good or a bad sense, lit. or fig., trans. or intrans. (as follows):- accomplish, cease, be clean, [pass-] ed, consume, have done, (come to an, have an, make an) end, fail, come to the full, be all gone, x be all here, be (make) perfect, be spent, sum, be (shew self) upright, be wasted, whole.

(8550) pronounced toom-meem'; plur. of 8537; perfections, i.e. (techn.) one of the epithets of the objects in the high-priest's breastplate as an emblem of complete Truth:-Thummim.

righteousness (6664) pronounced tseh'-dek; from 6663; the right (nat., mor., or legal); also (abstr.) equity or (fig.) prosperity:- x even, (x that which is altogether) just (-ice), ([un-]) right (-eous) (cause, -ly, -ness).

(6663) pronounced tsaw-dak'; prim. root; to be (causat., make) right (in a moral or forensic sense):- cleanse, clear self (be, do) just (-ice, -ify, -ify self), (be, turn to) righteous (-ness).

All my words are just, none of them perverse or crooked; MISHLEI 8:8 (PROVERBS 8:8)

All the words of my mouth *are* in righteousness (6664); *there is* nothing forward or perverse in them. PROVERBS 8:8

righteousness (6664) pronounced tseh'-dek; from 6663; the right (nat., mor., or legal); also (abstr.) equity or (fig.) prosperity:- x even, (x that which is altogether) just (-ice), ([un-]) right (-eous) (cause, -ly, -ness).

(6663) pronounced tsaw-dak'; prim. root; to be (causat., make) right (in a moral or forensic sense):- cleanse, clear self (be, do) just (-ice, -ify, -ify self), (be, turn to) righteous (-ness).

Riches and honor belong to me, enduring wealth and success. My fruit is better than gold, fine gold, and my produce better than choice silver. I walk on the way of righteousness, on the paths of justice. MISHLEI 8:18-20 (PROVERBS 8:18-20)

Riches and honour *are* with me; *yea*, durable riches and righteousness (6666). My fruit is better than gold, *yea*, than fine gold; and my revenue than choice silver. I lead in the way of righteousness (6666), in the midst of the paths of judgment. PROVERBS 8:18-20

righteousness (6666) pronounced tsed-aw-kaw'; from 6663; rightness (abstr.), subj. (rectitude); obj. (justice) , mor. (virtue) or fig. (prosperity):- justice, moderately, right (-eous) (act, -ly, -ness)

(6663) pronounced tsaw-dak'; prim. root; to be (causat., make) right (in a moral or forensic sense):- cleanse, clear self (be, do) just (-ice, -ify, -ify self), (be, turn to) righteous (-ness).

Ill-gotten wealth is of no avail, but righteousness saves from death. MISHLEI 10:2 (PROVERBS 10:2)

Treasures of wickedness profit nothing: but righteousness (6666) delivereth from death. PROVERBS 10:2

righteousness (6666) pronounced tsed-aw-kaw'; from 6663; rightness (abstr.), subj. (rectitude); obj. (justice) , mor. (virtue) or fig. (prosperity):- justice, moderately, right (-eous) (act, -ly, -ness)

(6663) pronounced tsaw-dak'; prim. root; to be (causat., make) right (in a moral or forensic sense):- cleanse, clear self (be, do) just (-ice, -ify, -ify self), (be, turn to) righteous (-ness).

Wealth is of no avail on the day of wrath, but righteousness saves from death. The righteousness of a blameless man smooths his way, but the wicked man is felled by his wickedness. The righteousness of the upright saves them, but the treacherous are trapped by their malice. MISHLEI 11:4-6 (PROVERBS 11:4-6)

Riches profit not in the day of wrath: but righteousness (6666) delivereth from death. The righteousness (6666) of the perfect shall direct his way: but the wicked shall fall by his own wickedness. The righteousness (6666) of the upright (3477) shall deliver them: but transgressors shall be taken in *their own* naughtiness. PROVERBS 11:4-6

> righteousness (6666) pronounced tsed-aw-kaw'; from 6663; rightness (abstr.), subj. (rectitude); obj. (justice) , mor. (virtue) or fig. (prosperity):- justice, moderately, right (-eous) (act, -ly, -ness)
>
> (6663) pronounced tsaw-dak'; prim. root; to be (causat., make) right (in a moral or forensic sense):- cleanse, clear self (be, do) just (-ice, -ify, -ify self), (be, turn to) righteous (-ness).
>
> upright (3477) pronounced yaw-shawr'; from 3474; straight (lit. or fig.):- convenient, equity, Jasher, just, meet (-est), + pleased well, right (-eous), straight (most) upright (-ly, -ness)
>
> (3474) pronounced yaw-shar'; a prim. root; to be straight or even; fig. to be (causat. to make) right, pleasant, prosperous:- direct, fit, seem good (meet), + please (well), be (esteem, go) right (on), bring (look, make, take the) straight (way), be upright (-ly).

The wicked man earns illusory wages, but he who sows righteousness has a true reward. Righteousness is a prop of life, but to pursue evil leads to death. MISHLEI 11:18-19 (PROVERBS 11:18-19)

The wicked worketh a deceitful work: but to him that soweth righteousness (6666) *shall be* a sure reward. As righteousness (6666) *tendeth* to life; so he that pursueth evil *pursueth it* to his own death. PROVERBS 11:18-19

> righteousness (6666) pronounced tsed-aw-kaw'; from 6663; rightness (abstr.), subj. (rectitude); obj. (justice) , mor. (virtue) or fig. (prosperity):- justice, moderately, right (-eous) (act, -ly, -ness)
>
> (6663) pronounced tsaw-dak'; prim. root; to be (causat., make) right (in a moral or forensic sense):- cleanse, clear self (be, do) just (-ice, -ify, -ify self), (be, turn to) righteous (-ness).

He who testifies faithfully tells the truth, but a false witness, deceit. MISHLEI 12:17 (PROVERBS 12:17)

He *that* speaketh truth showeth forth righteousness (6664): but a false witness deceit. PROVERBS 12:17

> righteousness (6664) pronounced tseh'-dek; from 6663; the right (nat., mor., or legal); also (abstr.) equity or (fig.) prosperity:- x even, (x that which is altogether) just (-ice), ([un-]) right (-eous) (cause, -ly, -ness).
>
> (6663) pronounced tsaw-dak'; prim. root; to be (causat., make) right (in a moral or forensic sense):- cleanse, clear self (be, do) just (-ice, -ify, -ify self), (be, turn to) righteous (-ness).

The road of righteousness leads to life; by way of its path there is no death. MISHLEI 12:28 (PROVERBS 12:28)

In the way of righteousness (6666) is life; and in the pathway *thereof there* is no death. PROVERBS 12:28

righteousness (6666) pronounced tsed-aw-kaw'; from 6663; rightness (abstr.), subj. (rectitude); obj. (justice) , mor. (virtue) or fig. (prosperity):- justice, moderately, right (-eous) (act, -ly, -ness)

(6663) pronounced tsaw-dak'; prim. root; to be (causat., make) right (in a moral or forensic sense):- cleanse, clear self (be, do) just (-ice, -ify, -ify self), (be, turn to) righteous (-ness).

Righteousness protects him whose way is blameless; wickedness subverts the sinner. MISHLEI 13:6 (PROVERBS 13:6)

Righteousness (6666) keepeth *him that is* upright (8537) in the way: but wickedness overthroweth the sinner. PROVERBS 13:6

righteousness (6666) pronounced tsed-aw-kaw'; from 6663; rightness (abstr.), subj. (rectitude); obj. (justice) , mor. (virtue) or fig. (prosperity):- justice, moderately, right (-eous) (act, -ly, -ness)

(6663) pronounced tsaw-dak'; prim. root; to be (causat., make) right (in a moral or forensic sense):- cleanse, clear self (be, do) just (-ice, -ify, -ify self), (be, turn to) righteous (-ness).

upright (8537) pronounced tome; from 8552; completeness; fig. prosperity; usually (mor.) innocence:- full, integrity, perfect (-ion), simplicity, upright (-ly, -ness), at a venture. See 8550.

(8552) pronounced taw-mam'; a prim. root; to complete, in a good or a bad sense, lit. or fig., trans. or intrans. (as follows):- accomplish, cease, be clean, [pass-] ed, consume, have done, (come to an, have an, make an) end, fail, come to the full, be all gone, x be all here, be (make) perfect, be spent, sum, be (shew self) upright, be wasted, whole.

(8550) pronounced toom-meem'; plur. of 8537; perfections, i.e. (techn.) one of the epithets of the objects in the high-priest's breastplate as an emblem of complete Truth:-Thummim.

Righteousness exalts a nation; sin is a reproach to any people. MISHLEI 14:34 (PROVERBS 14:34)

Righteousness (6666) exalteth a nation: but sin is a reproach to any people. PROVERBS 14:34

righteousness (6666) pronounced tsed-aw-kaw'; from 6663; rightness (abstr.), subj. (rectitude); obj. (justice) , mor. (virtue) or fig. (prosperity):- justice, moderately, right (-eous) (act, -ly, -ness)

(6663) pronounced tsaw-dak'; prim. root; to be (causat., make) right (in a moral or forensic sense):- cleanse, clear self (be, do) just (-ice, -ify, -ify self), (be, turn to) righteous (-ness).

The way of the wicked is an abomination to the LORD, but He loves him who pursues righteousness. MISHLEI 15:9 (PROVERBS 15:9)

The way of the wicked is an abomination unto the LORD: but he loveth him that followeth after righteousness (6666). PROVERBS 15:9

> righteousness (6666) pronounced tsed-aw-kaw'; from 6663; rightness (abstr.), subj. (rectitude); obj. (justice) , mor. (virtue) or fig. (prosperity):- justice, moderately, right (-eous) (act, -ly, -ness)
>
> (6663) pronounced tsaw-dak'; prim. root; to be (causat., make) right (in a moral or forensic sense):- cleanse, clear self (be, do) just (-ice, -ify, -ify self), (be, turn to) righteous (-ness).

Better a little with righteousness than a large income with injustice. MISHLEI 16:8 (PROVERBS 16:8)

Better is a little with righteousness (6666) than great revenues without right (4941). PROVERBS 16:8

> righteousness (6666) pronounced tsed-aw-kaw'; from 6663; rightness (abstr.), subj. (rectitude); obj. (justice) , mor. (virtue) or fig. (prosperity):- justice, moderately, right (-eous) (act, -ly, -ness)
>
> (6663) pronounced tsaw-dak'; prim. root; to be (causat., make) right (in a moral or forensic sense):- cleanse, clear self (be, do) just (-ice, -ify, -ify self), (be, turn to) righteous (-ness).
>
> right (4941) pronounced mish-pawt'; from 8199; prop. a verdict (favorable or unfavorable) pronounced judicially, espec. a sentence or formal decree (human or [partic.] divine law, individual or collect.) includ. the act, the place, the suit, the crime, and the penalty; abstr. Justice includ. a partic. right, or privilege (statutory or customary), or even a style:- + adversary, ceremony, charge, x crime, custom, desert, determination, discretion, disposing, due, fashion, form, to be judged, judgment, just (-ice, -ly), (manner of) law (-ful), manner, measure, (due) order, ordinance, right, sentence, usest, x worthy, + wrong.
>
> (8199) pronounced shaw-fat'; a prim. root; to judge; i.e. pronounce sentence (for or against):- by impl. to vindicate or punish; by extens. to govern; pass. to litigate (lit. or fig.):- + avenge, x that condemn, contend, defend, execute (judgment), (be a) judge (-ment), x needs, plead, reason, rule.

Wicked deeds are an abomination to kings, for the throne is established by righteousness. MISHLEI 16:12 (PROVERBS 16:12)

It is an abomination to kings to commit wickedness; for the throne is established by righteousness (6666). PROVERBS 16:12

> righteousness (6666) pronounced tsed-aw-kaw'; from 6663; rightness (abstr.), subj. (rectitude); obj. (justice) , mor. (virtue) or fig. (prosperity):- justice, moderately, right (-eous) (act, -ly, -ness)
>
> (6663) pronounced tsaw-dak'; prim. root; to be (causat., make) right (in a moral or forensic sense):- cleanse, clear self (be, do) just (-ice, -ify, -ify self), (be, turn to) righteous (-ness).

Gray hair is a crown of glory; it is attained by the way of righteousness. MISHLEI 16:31 (PROVERBS 16:31)

The hoary head *is* a crown of glory, *if* it be found in the way of righteousness (6666). PROVERBS 16:31

> righteousness (6666) pronounced tsed-aw-kaw'; from 6663; rightness (abstr.), subj. (rectitude); obj. (justice) , mor. (virtue) or fig. (prosperity):- justice, moderately, right (-eous) (act, -ly, -ness)
>
> (6663) pronounced tsaw-dak'; prim. root; to be (causat., make) right (in a moral or forensic sense):- cleanse, clear self (be, do) just (-ice, -ify, -ify self), (be, turn to) righteous (-ness).

He who strives to do good and kind deeds attains life, success, and honor. MISHLEI 21:21 (PROVERBS 21:21)

He that followeth after righteousness (6666) and mercy findeth life, righteousness (6666), and honour. PROVERBS 21:21

> righteousness (6666) pronounced tsed-aw-kaw'; from 6663; rightness (abstr.), subj. (rectitude); obj. (justice) , mor. (virtue) or fig. (prosperity):- justice, moderately, right (-eous) (act, -ly, -ness)
>
> (6663) pronounced tsaw-dak'; prim. root; to be (causat., make) right (in a moral or forensic sense):- cleanse, clear self (be, do) just (-ice, -ify, -ify self), (be, turn to) righteous (-ness).

Remove the wicked from the king's presence, and his throne will be established in justice. MISHLEI 25:5 (PROVERBS 25:5)

Take away the wicked *from* before the king, and his throne shall be established in righteousness (6664). PROVERBS 25:5

> righteousness (6664) pronounced tseh'-dek; from 6663; the right (nat., mor., or legal); also (abstr.) equity or (fig.) prosperity:- x even, (x that which is altogether) just (-ice), ([un-]) right (-eous) (cause, -ly, -ness).
>
> (6663) pronounced tsaw-dak'; prim. root; to be (causat., make) right (in a moral or forensic sense):- cleanse, clear self (be, do) just (-ice, -ify, -ify self), (be, turn to) righteous (-ness).

And, indeed, I have observed under the sun: alongside justice there is wickedness. Alongside righteousness there is wickedness. KOHELET 3:16 (ECCLESIASTES 3:16)

And moreover I saw under the sun the place of judgment*, that* wickedness was there; *and* the place of righteousness (6664), that iniquity *was* there. ECCLESIASTES 3:16

> righteousness (6664) pronounced tseh'-dek; from 6663; the right (nat., mor., or legal); also (abstr.) equity or (fig.) prosperity:- x even, (x that which is altogether) just (-ice), ([un-]) right (-eous) (cause, -ly, -ness).
>
> (6663) pronounced tsaw-dak'; prim. root; to be (causat., make) right (in a moral or forensic sense):- cleanse, clear self (be, do) just (-ice, -ify, -ify self), (be, turn to) righteous (-ness).

RIGHTEOUSNESS

In my own brief span of life, I have seen both these things: sometimes a good man perishes in spite of his goodness, and sometimes a wicked one endures in spite of his wickedness. KOHELET 7:15 (ECCLESIASTES 7:15)

All *things* have I seen in the days of my vanity: there is a just *man* that perisheth in his righteousness (6664), and there is a wicked *man* that prolongeth *his life* in his wickedness. ECCLESIASTES 7:15

> righteousness (6664) pronounced tseh'-dek; from 6663; the right (nat., mor., or legal); also (abstr.) equity or (fig.) prosperity:- x even, (x that which is altogether) just (-ice), ([un-]) right (-eous) (cause, -ly, -ness).
>
> (6663) pronounced tsaw-dak'; prim. root; to be (causat., make) right (in a moral or forensic sense):- cleanse, clear self (be, do) just (-ice, -ify, -ify self), (be, turn to) righteous (-ness).

Alas, she has become a harlot, the faithful city that was filled with justice, where righteousness dwelt but now murderers. YESHA' YAHU 1:21 (ISAIAH 1:21)

How is the faithful city become a harlot! It was full of judgment; righteousness (6664) lodged in it; but now murderers. ISAIAH 1:21

> righteousness (6664) pronounced tseh'-dek; from 6663; the right (nat., mor., or legal); also (abstr.) equity or (fig.) prosperity:- x even, (x that which is altogether) just (-ice), ([un-]) right (-eous) (cause, -ly, -ness).
>
> (6663) pronounced tsaw-dak'; prim. root; to be (causat., make) right (in a moral or forensic sense):- cleanse, clear self (be, do) just (-ice, -ify, -ify self), (be, turn to) righteous (-ness).

"I will restore your magistrates as of old, and your counselors as of yore. After that you shall be called City of Righteousness, Faithful City." Zion shall be saved in the judgment; her repentant ones, in the retribution. YESHA' YAHU 1:26-27 (ISAIAH 1:26-27)

> retribution: for this meaning cf. 5.16, 10.22. (TANAKH footnote)
>
> > And the LORD of Hosts is exalted by judgment, the Holy God proved holy by retribution. YESHA' YAHU 5:16 (ISAIAH 5:16)
> >
> > But the LORD of hosts shall be exalted in judgment, and God that is holy shall be sanctified in righteousness. ISAIAH 5:16
> >
> > Even if your people, O Israel, should be as the sands of the sea, only a remnant of it shall return. Destruction is decreed; retribution comes like a flood! YESHA' YAHU 10:22 (ISAIAH 10:22)
> >
> > For though thy people Israel be as the sand of the sea, *yet* a remnant of them shall return: the consumption decreed shall overflow with righteousness. ISAIAH 10:22

And I will restore thy judges as at the first and thy counselors as at the beginning: afterward thou shalt be called The city of righteousness (6664), the faithful city. Zion shall be redeemed with judgment, and her converts with righteousness (6666). ISAIAH 1:26-27

> righteousness (6664) pronounced tseh'-dek; from 6663; the right (nat., mor., or legal); also (abstr.) equity or (fig.) prosperity:- x even, (x that which is altogether) just (-ice), ([un-]) right (-eous) (cause, -ly, -ness).
>
> (6663) pronounced tsaw-dak'; prim. root; to be (causat., make) right (in a moral or forensic sense):- cleanse, clear self (be, do) just (-ice, -ify, -ify self), (be, turn to) righteous (-ness).
>
> righteousness (6666) pronounced tsed-aw-kaw'; from 6663; rightness (abstr.), subj. (rectitude); obj. (justice) , mor. (virtue) or fig. (prosperity):- justice, moderately, right (-eous) (act, -ly, -ness)

For the vineyard of the LORD of Hosts is the House of Israel, and the seedlings He lovingly tended are the men of Judah. And He hoped for justice, but behold, injustice; for equity, but behold, iniquity!
YESHA' YAHU 5:7 (ISAIAH 5:7)

For the vineyard of the LORD of hosts *is* the house of Israel, and the men of Judah his pleasant plant: and he looked for judgment but behold oppression; for righteousness (6666), but behold a cry.
ISAIAH 5:7

> righteousness (6666) pronounced tsed-aw-kaw'; from 6663; rightness (abstr.), subj. (rectitude); obj. (justice) , mor. (virtue) or fig. (prosperity):- justice, moderately, right (-eous) (act, -ly, -ness)
>
> (6663) pronounced tsaw-dak'; prim. root; to be (causat., make) right (in a moral or forensic sense):- cleanse, clear self (be, do) just (-ice, -ify, -ify self), (be, turn to) righteous (-ness).

And the LORD of Hosts is exalted by judgment, the Holy God proved holy by retribution.
YESHA' YAHU 5:16 (ISAIAH 5:16)

But the LORD of hosts shall be exalted in judgment, and God that is holy shall be sanctified in righteousness (6666). ISAIAH 5:16

> righteousness (6666) pronounced tsed-aw-kaw'; from 6663; rightness (abstr.), subj. (rectitude); obj. (justice) , mor. (virtue) or fig. (prosperity):- justice, moderately, right (-eous) (act, -ly, -ness)
>
> (6663) pronounced tsaw-dak'; prim. root; to be (causat., make) right (in a moral or forensic sense):- cleanse, clear self (be, do) just (-ice, -ify, -ify self), (be, turn to) righteous (-ness).

Ah, those who are so doughty- as drinkers of wine, and so valiant- as mixers of drink! Who vindicate him who is in the wrong in return for a bribe, and withhold vindication from him who is in the right.
YESHA' YAHU 5:22-23 (ISAIAH 5:22-23)

Woe unto *them that are* mighty to drink wine, and men of strength to mingle strong drink; which justify the wicked for reward, and take away the righteousness (6666) of the righteous (6662) from him! ISAIAH 5:22-23

> righteousness (6666) pronounced tsed-aw-kaw'; from 6663; rightness (abstr.), subj. (rectitude); obj. (justice) , mor. (virtue) or fig. (prosperity):- justice, moderately, right (-eous) (act, -ly, -ness)
>
> (6663) pronounced tsaw-dak'; prim. root; to be (causat., make) right (in a moral or forensic sense):- cleanse, clear self (be, do) just (-ice, -ify, -ify self), (be, turn to) righteous (-ness).
>
> righteous (6662) pronounced tsad-deek'; from 6663; just:- just, lawful, righteous (man).

Thus he shall judge the poor with equity and decide with justice for the lowly of the land. He shall strike down a land with the rod of his mouth and slay the wicked with the breath of his lips. Justice shall be the girdle of his loins, and faithfulness the girdle of his waist. YESHA' YAHU 11:4-5 (ISAIAH 11:4-5)

> a land: Emendation yields "the ruthless". (TANAKH footnote)

But with righteousness (6664) shall he judge the poor, and reprove with equity for the meek of the earth: and he shall smite the earth with the rod of his mouth and with the breath of his lips shall he slay the wicked. And righteousness (6664) shall be the girdle of his loins, and faithfulness the girdle of his reins. ISAIAH 11:4-5

> righteousness (6664) pronounced tseh'-dek; from 6663; the right (nat., mor., or legal); also (abstr.) equity or (fig.) prosperity:- x even, (x that which is altogether) just (-ice), ([un-]) right (-eous) (cause, -ly, -ness).
>
> (6663) pronounced tsaw-dak'; prim. root; to be (causat., make) right (in a moral or forensic sense):- cleanse, clear self (be, do) just (-ice, -ify, -ify self), (be, turn to) righteous (-ness).

And a throne shall be established in goodness in the tent of David, and on it shall sit in faithfulness a ruler devoted to justice and zealous for equity. YESHA' YAHU 16:5 (ISAIAH 16:5)

> 14.32 above would read well here. (TANAKH footnote)
>
> > And what would he answer the messengers of any nation? That Zion has been established by the LORD: in it, the needy of His people shall find shelter. YESHA' YAHU 14:32 (ISAIAH 14:32)
> >
> > What shall *one* then answer the messengers of the nation? That the LORD hath founded Zion, and the poor of his people shall trust in it. ISAIAH 14:32

And in mercy shall the throne be established: and he shall sit upon it in truth in the tabernacle of David, judging, and seeking judgment, and hasting righteousness (6664). ISAIAH 16:5

righteousness (6664) pronounced tseh'-dek; from 6663; the right (nat., mor., or legal); also (abstr.) equity or (fig.) prosperity:- x even, (x that which is altogether) just (-ice), ([un-]) right (-eous) (cause, -ly, -ness).

(6663) pronounced tsaw-dak'; prim. root; to be (causat., make) right (in a moral or forensic sense):- cleanse, clear self (be, do) just (-ice, -ify, -ify self), (be, turn to) righteous (-ness).

I seek You with all the spirit within me. For when Your judgments are wrought on earth, the inhabitants of the world learn righteousness. But when the scoundrel is spared, he learns not righteousness; in a place of integrity, he does wrong! He ignores the majesty of the LORD. YESHA' YAHU 26:9-10 (ISAIAH 26:9-10)

the spirit within me: Emendation yields "my spirit in the morning." (TANAKH footnote)

With my soul have I desired thee in the night; yea, with my spirit within me will I seek thee early: for when thy judgments *are* in the earth, the inhabitants of the world will learn righteousness (6664). Let favour be showed to the wicked, *yet* will he not learn righteousness (6664); in the land of uprightness (5229) will he deal unjustly, and will not behold the majesty of the LORD. ISAIAH 26:9-10

righteousness (6664) pronounced tseh'-dek; from 6663; the right (nat., mor., or legal); also (abstr.) equity or (fig.) prosperity:- x even, (x that which is altogether) just (-ice), ([un-]) right (-eous) (cause, -ly, -ness).

(6663) pronounced tsaw-dak'; prim. root; to be (causat., make) right (in a moral or forensic sense):- cleanse, clear self (be, do) just (-ice, -ify, -ify self), (be, turn to) righteous (-ness).

uprightness (5229) pronounced nek-o-khaw'; fem. of 5228; prop. straightforwardness; i.e. (fig.) integrity , or (concr.) a truth:- equity, right (thing), uprightness.

(5228) pronounced naw-ko'-akh; from the same as 5226; straightforward; i.e. (fig.) equitable, correct, or (abstr.) integrity:- plain, right, uprightness.

(5226) pronounced nay-kakh; from an unused root mean. to be straightforward; prop. the fore part; used adv., opposite:- before, over, against.

But I will apply judgment as a measuring line and retribution of weights: hail shall sweep away the refuge of falsehood, and flood-waters engulf your shelter. YESHA' YAHU 28:17 (ISAIAH 28:17)

retribution: as in 1.27; 5.16; 10.22. (TANAKH footnote)

Zion shall be saved in the judgment; her repentant ones, in the retribution. YESHA' YAHU 1:27 (ISAIAH 1:27)

Zion shall be redeemed with judgment, and her converts with righteousness (6666). ISAIAH 1:27

> righteousness (6666) pronounced tsed-aw-kaw'; from 6663; rightness (abstr.), subj. (rectitude); obj. (justice) , mor. (virtue) or fig. (prosperity):- justice, moderately, right (-eous) (act, -ly, -ness)
>
> (6663) pronounced tsaw-dak'; prim. root; to be (causat., make) right (in a moral or forensic sense):- cleanse, clear self (be, do) just (-ice, -ify, -ify self), (be, turn to) righteous (-ness).

And the LORD of Hosts is exalted by judgment, the Holy God proved holy by retribution. YESHA' YAHU 5:16 (ISAIAH 5:16)

But the LORD of hosts shall be exalted in judgment, and God that is holy shall be sanctified in righteousness (6666). ISAIAH 5:16

> righteousness (6666) pronounced tsed-aw-kaw'; from 6663; rightness (abstr.), subj. (rectitude); obj. (justice) , mor. (virtue) or fig. (prosperity):- justice, moderately, right (-eous) (act, -ly, -ness)
>
> (6663) pronounced tsaw-dak'; prim. root; to be (causat., make) right (in a moral or forensic sense):- cleanse, clear self (be, do) just (-ice, -ify, -ify self), (be, turn to) righteous (-ness).

Even if your people, O Israel, should be as the sands of the sea, only a remnant of it shall return. Destruction is decreed; retribution comes like a flood!
YESHA' YAHU 10:22 (ISAIAH 10:22)

For though thy people Israel be as the sand of the sea, *yet* a remnant of them shall return; the consumption decreed shall overflow with righteousness (6666).
ISAIAH 10:22

> righteousness (6666) pronounced tsed-aw-kaw'; from 6663; rightness (abstr.), subj. (rectitude); obj. (justice) , mor. (virtue) or fig. (prosperity):- justice, moderately, right (-eous) (act, -ly, -ness)
>
> (6663) pronounced tsaw-dak'; prim. root; to be (causat., make) right (in a moral or forensic sense):- cleanse, clear self (be, do) just (-ice, -ify, -ify self), (be, turn to) righteous (-ness).

weights: i.e. , I will make judgment and retribution My plan of action; cf. 34.11; 2 Kings 21.13 (TANAKH footnote)

Jackdaws and owls shall possess it; great owls and ravens shall dwell there. He shall measure it with a line of chaos and with weights of emptiness.
YESHA' YAHU 34:11 (ISAIAH 34:11)

> But the cormorant and the bittern shall possess it; the owl also and the raven shall dwell in it: and he shall stretch out upon it the line of confusion, and the stones of emptiness. ISAIAH 34:11
>
> I will apply to Jerusalem the measuring line of Samaria and the weights of the House of Ahab; I will wipe Jerusalem clean as one wipes a dish and turns it upside down. M'LAKHIM BET 21:13 (II KINGS 21:13)
>
> And I will stretch over Jerusalem the line of Samaria, and the plummet of the house of Ahab: and I will wipe Jerusalem *as a man* wipeth a dish, wiping *it*, and turning *it* upside down. II KINGS 21:13

Judgment also will I lay to the line, and righteousness (6666) to the plummet: and the hail shall sweep away the refuge of lies, and the waters shall overflow the hiding place. ISAIAH 28:17

> righteousness (6666) pronounced tsed-aw-kaw'; from 6663; rightness (abstr.), subj. (rectitude); obj. (justice) , mor. (virtue) or fig. (prosperity):- justice, moderately, right (-eous) (act, -ly, -ness).
>
> (6663) pronounced tsaw-dak'; prim. root; to be (causat., make) right (in a moral or forensic sense):- cleanse, clear self (be, do) just (-ice, -ify, -ify self), (be, turn to) righteous (-ness).

Behold a king shall reign in righteousness, and ministers shall govern with justice. YESHA' YAHU 32:1 (ISAIAH 32:1)

Behold, a King shall reign in righteousness (6664), and princes shall rule in judgment. ISAIAH 32:1

> righteousness (6664) pronounced tseh'-dek; from 6663; the right (nat., mor., or legal); also (abstr.) equity or (fig.) prosperity:- x even, (x that which is altogether) just (-ice), ([un-]) right (-eous) (cause, -ly, -ness).
>
> (6663) pronounced tsaw-dak'; prim. root; to be (causat., make) right (in a moral or forensic sense):- cleanse, clear self (be, do) just (-ice, -ify, -ify self), (be, turn to) righteous (-ness).

Then justice shall abide in the wilderness and righteousness shall dwell on the farm land. For the work of righteousness shall be peace, and the effect of righteousness, calm and confidence forever. YESHA' YAHU 32:16-17 (ISAIAH 32:16-17)

Then judgment shall dwell in the wilderness, and righteousness (6666) remain in the fruitful field. And the work of righteousness (6666) shall be peace; and the effect of righteousness (6666), quietness and assurance for ever. ISAIAH 32:16-17

> righteousness (6666) pronounced tsed-aw-kaw'; from 6663; rightness (abstr.), subj. (rectitude); obj. (justice) , mor. (virtue) or fig. (prosperity):- justice, moderately, right (-eous) (act, -ly, -ness).
>
> (6663) pronounced tsaw-dak'; prim. root; to be (causat., make) right (in a moral or forensic sense):- cleanse, clear self (be, do) just (-ice, -ify, -ify self), (be, turn to) righteous (-ness).

The LORD is exalted, He dwells on high! [Of old] He filled Zion with justice and righteousness. YESHA' YAHU 33:5 (ISAIAH 33:5)

The LORD is exalted; for he dwelleth on high: he hath filled Zion with judgment and righteousness (6666). ISAIAH 33:5

> righteousness (6666) pronounced tsed-aw-kaw'; from 6663; rightness (abstr.), subj. (rectitude); obj. (justice) , mor. (virtue) or fig. (prosperity):- justice, moderately, right (-eous) (act, -ly, -ness).
>
> (6663) pronounced tsaw-dak'; prim. root; to be (causat., make) right (in a moral or forensic sense):- cleanse, clear self (be, do) just (-ice, -ify, -ify self), (be, turn to) righteous (-ness).

Fear not, for I am with you. Be not frightened, for I am your God; I strengthen you and I help you. I uphold you with My victorious right hand. YESHA' YAHU 41:10 (ISAIAH 41:10)

Fear thou not; for I *am* with thee: be not dismayed; for I *am* thy God: I will strengthen thee; yea, I will help thee; yea, I will uphold thee with the right hand of my righteousness (6664). ISAIAH 41:10

> righteousness (6664) pronounced tseh'-dek; from 6663; the right (nat., mor., or legal); also (abstr.) equity or (fig.) prosperity:- x even, (x that which is altogether) just (-ice), ([un-]) right (-eous) (cause, -ly, -ness).
>
> (6663) pronounced tsaw-dak'; prim. root; to be (causat., make) right (in a moral or forensic sense):- cleanse, clear self (be, do) just (-ice, -ify, -ify self), (be, turn to) righteous (-ness).

I, the LORD, in My grace, have summoned you, and I have grasped you by the hand. I created you, and appointed you a covenant people, a light of nations- YESHA' YAHU 42:6 (ISAIAH 42:6)

> > Covenant people: Lit. "covenants of a people," meaning of Heb. uncertain (TANAKH footnote)
> >
> > light of nations: See 49.6 and note. (TANAKH footnote)
> >
> > > For He has said: "It is too little that you should be My servant in that I raise up the tribes of Jacob and restore the survivors of Israel: I will also make you a light of nations, that My salvation may reach the ends of the earth." YESHA' YAHU 49:6 (ISAIAH 49:6)
> > >
> > > > note: i.e. the agent of good fortune: cf. 42.1-4, 51.4-5.
> > >
> > > And he said, it is a light thing that thou shouldest be my servant to raise up the tribes of Jacob, and to restore the preserved of Israel: I will also give thee for a light to the Gentiles, that thou mayest be my salvation unto the end of the earth. ISAIAH 49:6
> > >
> > > This is My servant, whom I uphold, My chosen one, in whom I delight. I have put My spirit upon him. He shall teach the true way to the nations. He shall not

> cry out or shout aloud, or make his voice heard in the streets. He shall not break even a bruised reed, or snuff out even a dim wick. He shall bring forth the true way. He shall not grow dim or be bruised till he has established the true way on earth; and the coastlands shall await his teaching. YESHA' YAHU 42:1-4 (ISAIAH 42:1-4)
>
> Behold my servant, whom I uphold; mine elect, *in whom* my soul delighteth; I have put my Spirit upon him: he shall bring forth judgment to the Gentiles. He shall not cry, nor lift up, nor cause his voice to be heard in the street. A bruised reed shall he not break, and the smoking flax shall he not quench: he shall bring forth judgment unto truth. He shall not fail nor be discouraged, till he have set judgment in the earth; and the isles shall wait for his law. ISAIAH 42:1-4
>
> Hearken to Me, My people, and give ear to Me, O My nation, for teaching shall go forth from Me, My way for the light of peoples. In a moment, I will bring it: the triumph I grant is near, the success I give has gone forth. My arms shall provide for the peoples: the coastlands shall trust in Me, they shall look to my arm. YESHA' YAHU 51:4-5 (ISAIAH 51:4-5)
>
> Hearken unto me, my people, and give ear unto me, o my nation; for a law shall proceed from me, and I will make my judgment to rest for a light of the people. My righteousness is near; my salvation is gone forth, and mine arms shall judge the people; the isles shall wait upon me, and on mine arm shall they trust. ISAIAH 51:4-5

I the LORD have called thee in righteousness (6664), and will hold thine hand, and will keep thee, and give thee for a covenant of the people, for a light of the Gentiles. ISAIAH 42:6

> righteousness (6664) pronounced tseh'-dek; from 6663; the right (nat., mor., or legal); also (abstr.) equity or (fig.) prosperity:- x even, (x that which is altogether) just (-ice), ([un-]) right (-eous) (cause, -ly, -ness).
>
> (6663) pronounced tsaw-dak'; prim. root; to be (causat., make) right (in a moral or forensic sense):- cleanse, clear self (be, do) just (-ice, -ify, -ify self), (be, turn to) righteous (-ness).

I form light and create darkness. I make weal and create woe. I the LORD do all these things. Pour down, O skies, from above! Let the heavens rain down victory! Let the earth open up and triumph sprout, yes, let vindication spring up: I the LORD have created it. YESHA' YAHU 45:7-8 (ISAIAH 45:7-8)

I form the light and create darkness: I make peace and create evil: I the LORD do all these *things.* Drop down, ye heavens from above, and let the skies pour down righteousness (6664); let the earth open, and let them bring forth salvation, and let righteousness (6666) spring up together; I the LORD have created it. ISAIAH 45:7-8

righteousness (6664) pronounced tseh'-dek; from 6663; the right (nat., mor., or legal); also (abstr.) equity or (fig.) prosperity:- x even, (x that which is altogether) just (-ice), ([un-]) right (-eous) (cause, -ly, -ness).

(6663) pronounced tsaw-dak'; prim. root; to be (causat., make) right (in a moral or forensic sense):- cleanse, clear self (be, do) just (-ice, -ify, -ify self), (be, turn to) righteous (-ness).

righteousness (6666) pronounced tsed-aw-kaw'; from 6663; rightness (abstr.), subj. (rectitude); obj. (justice) , mor. (virtue) or fig. (prosperity):- justice, moderately, right (-eous) (act, -ly, -ness).

It was I who roused him for victory and who level all roads for him. He shall rebuild My city and let My exiled people go without price and without payment said the LORD of Hosts. YESHA' YAHU 45:13 (ISAIAH 45:13)

him: i.e. Cyrus. (TANAKH footnote).

I have raised him up in righteousness (6664), and I will direct all his ways: he shall build my city, and he shall let go my captives, not for price nor reward, saith the LORD of hosts. ISAIAH 45:13

righteousness (6664) pronounced tseh'-dek; from 6663; the right (nat., mor., or legal); also (abstr.) equity or (fig.) prosperity:- x even, (x that which is altogether) just (-ice), ([un-]) right (-eous) (cause, -ly, -ness).

(6663) pronounced tsaw-dak'; prim. root; to be (causat., make) right (in a moral or forensic sense):- cleanse, clear self (be, do) just (-ice, -ify, -ify self), (be, turn to) righteous (-ness).

I did not speak in secret, at a site in a land of darkness; I did not say to the stock of Jacob, "seek Me out in a wasteland." I, the LORD, who foretell reliably, who announce what is true. YESHA' YAHU 45:19 (ISAIAH 45:19)

I have not spoken in secret, in a dark place of the earth: I said not unto the seed of Jacob, Seek ye me in vain: I the LORD speak righteousness (6664). I declare things that are right (4334). ISAIAH 45:19

righteousness (6664) pronounced tseh'-dek; from 6663; the right (nat., mor., or legal); also (abstr.) equity or (fig.) prosperity:- x even, (x that which is altogether) just (-ice), ([un-]) right (-eous) (cause, -ly, -ness).

(6663) pronounced tsaw-dak'; prim. root; to be (causat., make) right (in a moral or forensic sense):- cleanse, clear self (be, do) just (-ice, -ify, -ify self), (be, turn to) righteous (-ness).

right (4334) pronounced mee-shore'; from 3474; a level, i.e. a plain (often used [with the art. pref.] as a prop. name of certain districts; fig. Concord): also straightness i.e. (fig.) justice (sometimes adv. Justly):- equity, even place, plain, right (-eously), (made) straight, uprightness.

(3474) pronounced yaw-shar'; a prim. root; to be straight or even; fig. to be (causat. to make) right, pleasant, prosperous:- direct, fit, seem good (meet), + please (well), be (esteem, go) right (on), bring (look, make, take the) straight (way), be upright (-ly).

By Myself have I sworn, from My mouth has issued truth, a word that shall not turn back: To Me every knee shall bend, every tongue swear loyalty. They shall say: "Only through the LORD can I find victory and might. When people trust in Him, all their adversaries are put to shame: it is through the LORD that all the offspring of Israel have vindication and glory." YESHA' YAHU 45:23-25 (ISAIAH 45:23-25)

might: Emendation yields "Only in the LORD/Are there victory and might for man." (TANAKH footnote)

trust in: Lit. "come to"; for this idiom cf. Ps. 65.3, Job 6.20. (TANAKH footnote)

All mankind comes to You, You who hear prayer. TEHILLIM 65:3 (PSALMS 65:2)

O thou that hearest prayer, unto thee shall all flesh come. PSALMS 65:2

They are disappointed in their hopes; when they reach the place, they stand aghast. IYOV 6:20 (JOB 6:20)

They were confounded because they had hoped; they came thither, and were ashamed. JOB 6:20

I have sworn by myself, the word is gone out of my mouth *in* righteousness (6666), and shall not return, That unto me every knee shall bow, every tongue shall swear. Surely shall *one* say, in the LORD have I righteousness (6666) and strength: *even* to him shall *men* come: and all that are incensed against him shall be ashamed. In the LORD shall all the seed of Israel be justified, and shall glory.
ISAIAH 45:23-25

righteousness (6666) pronounced tsed-aw-kaw'; from 6663; rightness (abstr.), subj. (rectitude); obj. (justice) , mor. (virtue) or fig. (prosperity):- justice, moderately, right (-eous) (act, -ly, -ness).

(6663) pronounced tsaw-dak'; prim. root; to be (causat., make) right (in a moral or forensic sense):- cleanse, clear self (be, do) just (-ice, -ify, -ify self), (be, turn to) righteous (-ness).

Listen to Me, you stubborn of heart, who are far from victory: I am bringing My victory close; it shall not be far, and My triumph shall not be delayed. I will grant triumph in Zion to Israel, in whom I glory.
YESHA' YAHU 46:12-13 (ISAIAH 46:12-13)

stubborn of heart: Septuagint reads "who have lost heart." (TANAKH footnote)

Hearken unto me, ye stouthearted, that *are* far from righteousness (6666): I bring near my righteousness (6666); it shall not be far off, and my salvation shall not tarry: and I will place salvation in Zion for Israel my glory. ISAIAH 46:12-13

righteousness (6666) pronounced tsed-aw-kaw'; from 6663; rightness (abstr.), subj. (rectitude); obj. (justice) , mor. (virtue) or fig. (prosperity):- justice, moderately, right (-eous) (act, -ly, -ness).

(6663) pronounced tsaw-dak'; prim. root; to be (causat., make) right (in a moral or forensic sense):- cleanse, clear self (be, do) just (-ice, -ify, -ify self), (be, turn to) righteous (-ness).

Listen to this, O House of Jacob, who bear the name Israel and have issued from the waters of Judah, who swear by the name of the LORD and invoke the God of Israel- though not in truth and sincerity- for you are called after the Holy City and you do lean on the God of Israel, whose name is the LORD of Hosts: YESHA' YAHU 48:1-2 (ISAIAH 48:1-2)

you: Heb. "they." (TANAKH footnote)

the Holy City: Emendation yields "the holy people." (TANAKH footnote)

Hear ye this, O house of Jacob, which are called by the name of Israel, and are come forth out of the waters of Judah, which swear by the name of the LORD, and make mention of the God of Israel, *but* not in truth, nor in righteousness (6666). For they call themselves of the holy city, and stay themselves upon the God of Israel: The LORD of hosts is his name. ISAIAH 48:1-2

righteousness (6666) pronounced tsed-aw-kaw'; from 6663; rightness (abstr.), subj. (rectitude); obj. (justice) , mor. (virtue) or fig. (prosperity):- justice, moderately, right (-eous) (act, -ly, -ness).

(6663) pronounced tsaw-dak'; prim. root; to be (causat., make) right (in a moral or forensic sense):- cleanse, clear self (be, do) just (-ice, -ify, -ify self), (be, turn to) righteous (-ness).

If only you would heed My commands! Then your prosperity would be like a river, your triumph like the waves of the sea. YESHA' YAHU 48:18 (ISAIAH 48:18)

O that thou hadst hearkened to my commandments! Then had thy peace been as a river, and thy righteousness (6666) as the waves of the sea. ISAIAH 48:18

righteousness (6666) pronounced tsed-aw-kaw'; from 6663; rightness (abstr.), subj. (rectitude); obj. (justice) , mor. (virtue) or fig. (prosperity):- justice, moderately, right (-eous) (act, -ly, -ness).

(6663) pronounced tsaw-dak'; prim. root; to be (causat., make) right (in a moral or forensic sense):- cleanse, clear self (be, do) just (-ice, -ify, -ify self), (be, turn to) righteous (-ness).

Listen to Me, you who pursue justice, you who seek the LORD: look to the rock you were hewn from, to the quarry you were dug from. YESHA' YAHU 51:1 (ISAIAH 51:1)

Hearken to me, ye that follow after righteousness (6666), ye that seek the LORD: look unto the rock *whence* you are hewn, and to the hole of the pit *whence* ye are digged. ISAIAH 51:1

righteousness (6666) pronounced tsed-aw-kaw'; from 6663; rightness (abstr.), subj. (rectitude); obj. (justice) , mor. (virtue) or fig. (prosperity):- justice, moderately, right (-eous) (act, -ly, -ness).

(6663) pronounced tsaw-dak'; prim. root; to be (causat., make) right (in a moral or forensic sense):- cleanse, clear self (be, do) just (-ice, -ify, -ify self), (be, turn to) righteous (-ness).

The triumph I grant is near, the success I give has gone forth. My arms shall provide for the peoples: the coastlands shall trust in Me, they shall look to My arm. Raise your eyes to the heavens, and look upon the earth beneath: Though the heavens should melt away like smoke, and the earth wear out like a garment, and its inhabitants die out as well, My victory shall stand forever, My triumph shall remain unbroken. Listen to me, you who care for the right, O people who lay My instruction to heart! Fear not the insults of men, and be not dismayed at their jeers; for the moth shall eat them up like a garment, the worm shall eat them up like wool. But my triumph shall endure forever, My salvation through all the ages. YESHA' YAHU 51:5-8 (ISAIAH 51:5-8)

provide for: Lit. "judge." (TANAKH footnote)

as well: Emendation yields "like gnats." (TANAKH footnote)

worm: Heb. sas, another word for "moth." (TANAKH footnote)

My righteousness (6664) *is* near; my salvation is gone forth, and mine arms shall judge the people; the isles shall wait upon me, and on mine arm shall they trust. Lift up your eyes to the heavens, and look upon the earth beneath: for the heavens shall vanish away like smoke, and the earth shall wax old like a garment, and they that dwell therein shall die in like manner: but my salvation shall be for ever, and my righteousness (6666) shall not be abolished. Hearken unto me, ye that know righteousness (6664), the people in whose heart is my law; fear ye not the reproach of men, neither be ye afraid of their revilings. For the moth shall eat them up like a garment, and the worm shall eat them like wool; but my righteousness (6666) shall be for ever, and my salvation from generation to generation. ISAIAH 51:5-8

righteousness (6664) pronounced tseh'-dek; from 6663; the right (nat., mor., or legal); also (abstr.) equity or (fig.) prosperity:- x even, (x that which is altogether) just (-ice), ([un-]) right (-eous) (cause, -ly, -ness).

(6663) pronounced tsaw-dak'; prim. root; to be (causat., make) right (in a moral or forensic sense):- cleanse, clear self (be, do) just (-ice, -ify, -ify self), (be, turn to) righteous (-ness).

righteousness (6666) pronounced tsed-aw-kaw'; from 6663; rightness (abstr.), subj. (rectitude); obj. (justice) , mor. (virtue) or fig. (prosperity):- justice, moderately, right (-eous) (act, -ly, -ness).

You shall be established through righteousness. You shall be safe from oppression, and shall have no fear from ruin, and it shall not come near you. Surely no harm can be done without My consent: whoever would harm you shall fall because of you. It is I who created the smith to fan the charcoal fire and produce the tools for his work; so it is I who create the instruments of havoc. No weapon formed against you shall succeed, and every tongue that contends with you at law, you shall defeat. Such is the lot of the servants of the LORD, such their triumph through Me declares the LORD.
YESHA' YAHU 54:14-17 (ISAIAH 54:14-17)

In righteousness (6666) shalt thou be established: thou shalt be far from oppression: for thou shall not fear: and *from* terror; for it shall not come near thee. Behold, they shall surely gather together, *but* not by me: whosoever shall gather together against thee shall fall for thy sake. Behold I have created the smith that bloweth the coals in the fire, and that bringeth forth an instrument for his work; and I have created the waster to destroy. No weapon that is formed against thee shall prosper; and every tongue *that* shall rise against thee in judgment thou shalt condemn. This is the heritage of the servants of the LORD, and their righteousness (6666*) is* of me, saith the LORD. ISAIAH 54:14-17

righteousness (6666) pronounced tsed-aw-kaw'; from 6663; rightness (abstr.), subj. (rectitude); obj. (justice) , mor. (virtue) or fig. (prosperity):- justice, moderately, right (-eous) (act, -ly, -ness).

(6663) pronounced tsaw-dak'; prim. root; to be (causat., make) right (in a moral or forensic sense):- cleanse, clear self (be, do) just (-ice, -ify, -ify self), (be, turn to) righteous (-ness).

Thus said the LORD: observe what is right and do what is just; for soon My salvation shall come, and My deliverance be revealed. YESHA' YAHU 56:1 (ISAIAH 56:1)

Thus saith the LORD, Keep ye judgment, and do justice: for my salvation *is* near to come, and my righteousness (6666) to be revealed. ISAIAH 56:1

righteousness (6666) pronounced tsed-aw-kaw'; from 6663; rightness (abstr.), subj. (rectitude); obj. (justice) , mor. (virtue) or fig. (prosperity):- justice, moderately, right (-eous) (act, -ly, -ness).

(6663) pronounced tsaw-dak'; prim. root; to be (causat., make) right (in a moral or forensic sense):- cleanse, clear self (be, do) just (-ice, -ify, -ify self), (be, turn to) righteous (-ness).

I hereby pronounce judgment upon your deeds your assorted [idols] shall not avail you,
YESHA' YAHU 57:12 (ISAIAH 57:12)

judgment upon your deeds: Lit. "your retribution and your deeds." (TANAKH footnote)

your assorted [idols]: brought up from v. 13 for clarity. (TANAKH footnote)

Shall not save you when you cry out. They shall all be borne off by the wind, snatched away by a breeze. But those who trust in Me shall inherit the land and possess My sacred mount. YESHA' YAHU 57:13 (ISAIAH 57:13)

When thou criest, let thy companies deliver thee; but the wind shall carry them all away; vanity shall take them: but he that putteth his trust in me shall possess the land, and shall inherit my holy mountain. ISAIAH 57:13

I will declare thy righteousness (6666), and thy works; for they shall not profit thee. ISAIAH 57:12

righteousness (6666) pronounced tsed-aw-kaw'; from 6663; rightness (abstr.), subj. (rectitude); obj. (justice) , mor. (virtue) or fig. (prosperity):- justice, moderately, right (-eous) (act, -ly, -ness).

(6663) pronounced tsaw-dak'; prim. root; to be (causat., make) right (in a moral or forensic sense):- cleanse, clear self (be, do) just (-ice, -ify, -ify self), (be, turn to) righteous (-ness).

To be sure, they seek Me daily, eager to learn My ways. Like a nation that does what is right, that has not abandoned the laws of its God, they ask Me for the right way, they are eager for the nearness of God: YESHA' YAHU 58:2 (ISAIAH 58:2)

Yet they seek me daily, and delight to know my ways, as a nation that did righteousness (6666), and forsook not the ordinance of their God; they ask of me the ordinances of justice; they take delight in approaching to God. ISAIAH 58:2

righteousness (6666) pronounced tsed-aw-kaw'; from 6663; rightness (abstr.), subj. (rectitude); obj. (justice) , mor. (virtue) or fig. (prosperity):- justice, moderately, right (-eous) (act, -ly, -ness).

(6663) pronounced tsaw-dak'; prim. root; to be (causat., make) right (in a moral or forensic sense):- cleanse, clear self (be, do) just (-ice, -ify, -ify self), (be, turn to) righteous (-ness).

Then shall your light burst through like the dawn and your healing spring up quickly; your vindicator shall march before you. The Presence of the LORD shall be your rear guard. YESHA' YAHU 58:8 (ISAIAH 58:8)

Then shall thy light break forth as the morning, and thine health shall spring forth speedily: and thy righteousness (6664) shall go before thee; the glory of the LORD shall be thy reward. ISAIAH 58:8

righteousness (6664) pronounced tseh'-dek; from 6663; the right (nat., mor., or legal); also (abstr.) equity or (fig.) prosperity:- x even, (x that which is altogether) just (-ice), ([un-]) right (-eous) (cause, -ly, -ness).

(6663) pronounced tsaw-dak'; prim. root; to be (causat., make) right (in a moral or forensic sense):- cleanse, clear self (be, do) just (-ice, -ify, -ify self), (be, turn to) righteous (-ness).

He saw that there was no man, he gazed long, but no one intervened. Then His own arm won Him triumph, His victorious right hand supported Him. He donned victory like a coat of mail, with a helmet of triumph on His head; He clothed Himself with garments of retribution, wrapped Himself in zeal as in a robe. YESHA' YAHU 59:16-17 (ISAIAH 59:16-17)

right hand: cf. Ps. 98.1-2. (TANAKH footnote)

Sing to the LORD a new song, for He has worked wonders; His right hand, His holy arm, has won Him victory. The LORD has manifested His victory, has displayed His triumph in the sight of the nations. TEHILLIM 98:1-2 (PSALMS 98:1-2)

O sing unto the LORD a new song; for he hath done marvelous things; his right hand, and his holy arm, hath gotten him the victory. The LORD hath made known his salvation: his righteousness hath he openly shown in the sight of the heathen. PSALMS 98:1-2

And he saw that *there was* no man, and wondered that *there was* no intercessor: therefore his arm brought salvation unto him; and his righteousness (6666), it sustained him. For he put on righteousness (6666) as a breastplate, and a helmet of salvation upon his head; and he put on the garments of vengeance for clothing, and was clad with zeal as a cloak. ISAIAH 59:16-17

righteousness (6666) pronounced tsed-aw-kaw'; from 6663; rightness (abstr.), subj. (rectitude); obj. (justice) , mor. (virtue) or fig. (prosperity):- justice, moderately, right (-eous) (act, -ly, -ness).

(6663) pronounced tsaw-dak'; prim. root; to be (causat., make) right (in a moral or forensic sense):- cleanse, clear self (be, do) just (-ice, -ify, -ify self), (be, turn to) righteous (-ness).

Instead of copper I will bring gold, instead of iron I will bring silver; instead of wood, copper; and instead of stone, iron. And I will appoint Well-being as your government, Prosperity as your officials.
YESHA' YAHU 60:17 (ISAIAH 60:17)

For brass I will bring gold, and for iron I will bring silver, and for wood brass, and for stones iron: I will also make thy officers peace, and thine exactors righteousness (6666). ISAIAH 60:17

righteousness (6666) pronounced tsed-aw-kaw'; from 6663; rightness (abstr.), subj. (rectitude); obj. (justice) , mor. (virtue) or fig. (prosperity):- justice, moderately, right (-eous) (act, -ly, -ness).

(6663) pronounced tsaw-dak'; prim. root; to be (causat., make) right (in a moral or forensic sense):- cleanse, clear self (be, do) just (-ice, -ify, -ify self), (be, turn to) righteous (-ness).

To provide for the mourners in Zion to give them a turban instead of ashes, the festive ointment instead of mourning, a garment of splendor instead of a drooping spirit; they shall be called terebinths of victory, planted by the LORD for His glory. YESHA' YAHU 61:3 (ISAIAH 61:3)

To appoint unto them that mourn in Zion, to give unto them beauty for ashes, the oil of joy for mourning, the garment of praise for the spirit of heaviness: that they might be called Trees of righteousness (6664), The planting of the LORD, that he might be glorified. ISAIAH 61:3

righteousness (6664) pronounced tseh'-dek; from 6663; the right (nat., mor., or legal); also (abstr.) equity or (fig.) prosperity:- x even, (x that which is altogether) just (-ice), ([un-]) right (-eous) (cause, -ly, -ness).

(6663) pronounced tsaw-dak'; prim. root; to be (causat., make) right (in a moral or forensic sense):- cleanse, clear self (be, do) just (-ice, -ify, -ify self), (be, turn to) righteous (-ness).

I greatly rejoice in the LORD, my whole being exults in my God. For he has clothed me with garments of triumph, wrapped me in a robe of victory, like a bridegroom adorned with a turban, like a bride bedecked with her finery. For as the earth brings forth her growth and a garden makes the seed shoot

up, so the LORD God will make victory and renown shoot up in the presence of all the nations.
YESHA' YAHU 61:10-11 (ISAIAH 61:10-11)

I will greatly rejoice in the LORD, my soul shall be joyful in my God: for he hath clothed me with the garments of salvation; he hath covered me with the robe of righteousness (6666), as a bridegroom decketh *himself* with ornaments, and as a bride adorneth *herself* with her jewels. For as the earth bringeth forth her bud, and as the garden causeth the things that are sown in it to spring forth; so the LORD God will cause righteousness (6666) and praise to spring forth before all the nations.
ISAIAH 61:10-11

> righteousness (6666) pronounced tsed-aw-kaw'; from 6663; rightness (abstr.), subj. (rectitude); obj. (justice) , mor. (virtue) or fig. (prosperity):- justice, moderately, right (-eous) (act, -ly, -ness).
>
> (6663) pronounced tsaw-dak'; prim. root; to be (causat., make) right (in a moral or forensic sense):- cleanse, clear self (be, do) just (-ice, -ify, -ify self), (be, turn to) righteous (-ness).

For the sake of Zion, I will not be silent, for the sake of Jerusalem I will not be still, till her victory emerge resplendent and her triumph like a flaming torch. Nations shall see your victory, and every king your majesty; and you shall be called by a new name which the LORD himself shall bestow.
YESHA' YAHU 62:1-2 (ISAIAH 62:1-2)

For Zion's sake will I not hold my peace, and for Jerusalem's sake I will not rest, until the righteousness (6664) thereof go forth as the brightness, and the salvation thereof as a lamp *that* burneth. And the Gentiles shall see thy righteousness (6664), and all kings thy glory: and thou shalt be called by a new name, which the mouth of the LORD shall name. ISAIAH 62:1-2

> righteousness (6664) pronounced tseh'-dek; from 6663; the right (nat., mor., or legal); also (abstr.) equity or (fig.) prosperity:- x even, (x that which is altogether) just (-ice), ([un-]) right (-eous) (cause, -ly, -ness).
>
> (6663) pronounced tsaw-dak'; prim. root; to be (causat., make) right (in a moral or forensic sense):- cleanse, clear self (be, do) just (-ice, -ify, -ify self), (be, turn to) righteous (-ness).

Who is this coming from Edom, in crimsoned garments from Bozrah- who is this, majestic in attire, pressing forward in His great might? It is I, who contend victoriously, powerful to give triumph.
YESHA' YAHU 63:1 (ISAIAH 63:1)

> pressing forward: Meaning of Heb. uncertain; emendation yields "striding." (TANAKH footnote)
>
> give triumph: change of vocalization yields "Who contest triumphantly"; cf. 19.20. (TANAKH footnote)
>
>> In that day, there shall be an altar to the LORD inside the land of Egypt and a pillar to the LORD at its border. They shall serve as a symbol and reminder of

> the LORD of Hosts in the land of Egypt, so that when the Egyptians cry out to the LORD against oppressors, He will send them a savior and champion to deliver them. YESHA' YAHU 19:19-20 (ISAIAH 19:19-20)
>
> In that day shall there be an altar to the LORD in the midst of the land of Egypt, and a pillar at the border thereof to the LORD. And it shall be for a sign and for a witness unto the LORD of hosts in the land of Egypt: for they shall cry unto the LORD because of the oppressors, and he shall send them a savior, and a great one, and he shall deliver them. ISAIAH 19:19-20

Who *is* this that cometh from Edom, with dyed garments from Bozrah? This *that is* glorious in his apparel, traveling in the greatness of his strength? I that speak in righteousness (6666), mighty to save. ISAIAH 63:1

> righteousness (6666) pronounced tsed-aw-kaw'; from 6663; rightness (abstr.), subj. (rectitude); obj. (justice) , mor. (virtue) or fig. (prosperity):- justice, moderately, right (-eous) (act, -ly, -ness).
>
> (6663) pronounced tsaw-dak'; prim. root; to be (causat., make) right (in a moral or forensic sense):- cleanse, clear self (be, do) just (-ice, -ify, -ify self), (be, turn to) righteous (-ness).

Yet you have struck him who would gladly do justice, and remember You in Your ways. It is because You are angry that we have sinned: we have been steeped in them from of old, and can we be saved? We have all become like an unclean thing, and all our virtues like a filthy rag. We are all withering like leaves, and our iniquities, like a wind, carry us off. YESHA' YAHU 64:4-5 (ISAIAH 64:5-6)

Thou meetest him that rejoiceth and worketh righteousness (6664), *those that* remember thee in thy ways: behold, thou art wroth; for we have sinned: in those is continuance, and we shall be saved. But we are all as an unclean *thing*, and all our righteousnesses (6664) *are* as filthy rags; and we all do fade as a leaf; and our iniquities, like the wind, have taken us away. ISAIAH 64;5-6

> righteousness (6664) pronounced tseh'-dek; from 6663; the right (nat., mor., or legal); also (abstr.) equity or (fig.) prosperity:- x even, (x that which is altogether) just (-ice), ([un-]) right (-eous) (cause, -ly, -ness).
>
> (6663) pronounced tsaw-dak'; prim. root; to be (causat., make) right (in a moral or forensic sense):- cleanse, clear self (be, do) just (-ice, -ify, -ify self), (be, turn to) righteous (-ness).

And swear, "As the LORD lives," in sincerity, justice, and righteousness nations shall bless themselves by you and praise themselves by you. YIRMEYAHU 4:2 (JEREMIAH 4:2)

> swear, "As the LORD lives,": i.e. profess the worship of the LORD. (TANAKH footnote)
>
> you: Heb. "him." (TANAKH footnote)

And thou shalt swear, The LORD liveth, in truth, in judgment, and in righteousness (6666): and the nations shall bless themselves in him, and in him shall they glory. JEREMIAH 4:2

righteousness (6666) pronounced tsed-aw-kaw'; from 6663; rightness (abstr.), subj. (rectitude); obj. (justice) , mor. (virtue) or fig. (prosperity):- justice, moderately, right (-eous) (act, -ly, -ness).

(6663) pronounced tsaw-dak'; prim. root; to be (causat., make) right (in a moral or forensic sense):- cleanse, clear self (be, do) just (-ice, -ify, -ify self), (be, turn to) righteous (-ness).

Lo, days are coming- declares the LORD- when I will take note of everyone circumcised in the foreskin: of Egypt, Judah, Edom, the Ammonites, Moab, and all the desert dwellers who have the hair of their temples clipped. For all these nations are uncircumcised, but all the House of Israel are uncircumcised of heart. YIRMEYAHU 9:24-25 (JEREMIAH 9:24-26)

circumcised in the foreskin: Force of Heb. uncertain, (TANAKH footnote)

uncircumcised of heart: i.e. their minds are blocked to God's commandments. (TANAKH footnote)

But let him that glorieth glory in this, that he understandeth and knoweth me, that I *am* the LORD which exercise loving-kindness, judgment, and righteousness (6666) in the earth: for in these *things* I delight, saith the LORD. Behold the days come, saith the LORD, that I will punish all *them which are* circumcised with the uncircumcised: Egypt, and Judah, and Edom, and the children of Ammon, and Moab, and all *that are* in the utmost corners, that dwell in the wilderness: for all *these* nations are uncircumcised, and all the house of Israel *are* uncircumcised in the heart. JEREMIAH 9:24-26

righteousness (6666) pronounced tsed-aw-kaw'; from 6663; rightness (abstr.), subj. (rectitude); obj. (justice) , mor. (virtue) or fig. (prosperity):- justice, moderately, right (-eous) (act, -ly, -ness).

(6663) pronounced tsaw-dak'; prim. root; to be (causat., make) right (in a moral or forensic sense):- cleanse, clear self (be, do) just (-ice, -ify, -ify self), (be, turn to) righteous (-ness).

Thus said the LORD: do what is just and right; rescue from the defrauder him who is robbed; do not wrong the stranger, the fatherless, and the widow; commit no lawless act, and do not shed the blood of the innocent in this place. YIRMEYAHU 22:3 (JEREMIAH 22:3)

Thus saith the LORD: Execute ye judgment and righteousness (6666), and deliver the spoiled out of the hand of the oppressor: and do no wrong, do no violence to the stranger, the fatherless, nor the widow, neither shed innocent blood in this place. JEREMIAH 22:3

righteousness (6666) pronounced tsed-aw-kaw'; from 6663; rightness (abstr.), subj. (rectitude); obj. (justice) , mor. (virtue) or fig. (prosperity):- justice, moderately, right (-eous) (act, -ly, -ness).

(6663) pronounced tsaw-dak'; prim. root; to be (causat., make) right (in a moral or forensic sense):- cleanse, clear self (be, do) just (-ice, -ify, -ify self), (be, turn to) righteous (-ness).

In his days Judah shall be delivered and Israel shall dwell secure. And this is the name by which he shall be called: "The LORD is our Vindicator." YIRMEYAHU 23:6 (JEREMIAH 23:6)

In his days Judah shall be saved, and Israel shall dwell safely: and this *is* his name whereby he shall be called, THE LORD OUR RIGHTEOUSNESS (6664). JEREMIAH 23:6

> righteousness (6664) pronounced tseh'-dek; from 6663; the right (nat., mor., or legal); also (abstr.) equity or (fig.) prosperity:- x even, (x that which is altogether) just (-ice), ([un-]) right (-eous) (cause, -ly, -ness).
>
> (6663) pronounced tsaw-dak'; prim. root; to be (causat., make) right (in a moral or forensic sense):- cleanse, clear self (be, do) just (-ice, -ify, -ify self), (be, turn to) righteous (-ness).

In those days and at that time, I will raise up a true branch of David's line, and he shall do what is just and right in the land. In those days Judah shall be delivered and Israel shall dwell secure. And this is what she shall be called: "The LORD is our Vindicator." YIRMEYAHU 33:15-16 (JEREMIAH 33:15-16)

In those days and at that time, will I cause the Branch of righteousness (6666) to grow up unto David; and he shall execute judgment and righteousness (6666) in the land. In those days shall Judah be saved, and Jerusalem shall dwell safely: and this is *the name* wherewith she shall be called, The LORD our righteousness (6664). JEREMIAH 33:15-16

> righteousness (6666) pronounced tsed-aw-kaw'; from 6663; rightness (abstr.), subj. (rectitude); obj. (justice) , mor. (virtue) or fig. (prosperity):- justice, moderately, right (-eous) (act, -ly, -ness).
>
> (6663) pronounced tsaw-dak'; prim. root; to be (causat., make) right (in a moral or forensic sense):- cleanse, clear self (be, do) just (-ice, -ify, -ify self), (be, turn to) righteous (-ness).
>
> righteousness (6664) pronounced tseh'-dek; from 6663; the right (nat., mor., or legal); also (abstr.) equity or (fig.) prosperity:- x even, (x that which is altogether) just (-ice), ([un-]) right (-eous) (cause, -ly, -ness).

The LORD has proclaimed our vindication; come, let us recount in Zion the deeds of the LORD our God. YIRMEYAHU 51:10 (JEREMIAH 51:10)

The LORD hath brought forth our righteousness (6666): come, and let us declare in Zion the work of the LORD our God. JEREMIAH 51:10

> righteousness (6666) pronounced tsed-aw-kaw'; from 6663; rightness (abstr.), subj. (rectitude); obj. (justice) , mor. (virtue) or fig. (prosperity):- justice, moderately, right (-eous) (act, -ly, -ness).
>
> (6663) pronounced tsaw-dak'; prim. root; to be (causat., make) right (in a moral or forensic sense):- cleanse, clear self (be, do) just (-ice, -ify, -ify self), (be, turn to) righteous (-ness).

Again, if a righteous man abandons his righteousness and does wrong, when I put a stumbling block before him, he shall die. He shall die for his sins; the righteous deeds that he did shall not be remembered; but because you did not warn him, I will require a reckoning for his blood from you. YECHEZK'EL 3:20 (EZEKIEL 3:20)

Again, when a righteous (6662) *man* doth turn from his righteousness (6664), and commit iniquity, and I lay a stumbling block before him, he shall die: because thou hast not given him warning, he shall die in his sin, and his righteousness (6666) which he hath done shall not be remembered: but his blood will I require at thine hand. EZEKIEL 3:20

> righteous (6662) pronounced tsad-deek'; from 6663; just:-just, lawful, righteous (man).
>
> (6663) pronounced tsaw-dak'; prim. root; to be (causat., make) right (in a moral or forensic sense):- cleanse, clear self (be, do) just (-ice, -ify, -ify self), (be, turn to) righteous (-ness).
>
> righteousness (6664) pronounced tseh'-dek; from 6663; the right (nat., mor., or legal); also (abstr.) equity or (fig.) prosperity:- x even, (x that which is altogether) just (-ice), ([un-]) right (-eous) (cause, -ly, -ness).
>
> righteousness (6666) pronounced tsed-aw-kaw'; from 6663; rightness (abstr.), subj. (rectitude); obj. (justice) , mor. (virtue) or fig. (prosperity):- justice, moderately, right (-eous) (act, -ly, -ness).

Even if these three men- Noah, Daniel, and Job- should be in it, they would by their righteousness save only themselves- declares the LORD God. YECHEZK'EL 14:14 (EZEKIEL 14:14)

Though these three men, Noah, Daniel, and Job, were in it, they should deliver *but* their own souls by their righteousness (6666), saith the LORD God. EZEKIEL 14:14

> righteousness (6666) pronounced tsed-aw-kaw'; from 6663; rightness (abstr.), subj. (rectitude); obj. (justice) , mor. (virtue) or fig. (prosperity):- justice, moderately, right (-eous) (act, -ly, -ness).
>
> (6663) pronounced tsaw-dak'; prim. root; to be (causat., make) right (in a moral or forensic sense):- cleanse, clear self (be, do) just (-ice, -ify, -ify self), (be, turn to) righteous (-ness).

Should Noah, Daniel, and Job be in it, as I live- declares the LORD God- they would save neither son nor daughter; they would save themselves alone by their righteousness. YECHEZK'EL 14:20 (EZEKIEL 14:20)

Though Noah, Daniel, and Job *were* in it, *as* I live, saith the LORD God, they shall deliver neither son nor daughter; they shall but deliver their own souls by their righteousness (6666). EZEKIEL 14:20

> righteousness (6666) pronounced tsed-aw-kaw'; from 6663; rightness (abstr.), subj. (rectitude); obj. (justice) , mor. (virtue) or fig. (prosperity):- justice, moderately, right (-eous) (act, -ly, -ness).
>
> (6663) pronounced tsaw-dak'; prim. root; to be (causat., make) right (in a moral or forensic sense):- cleanse, clear self (be, do) just (-ice, -ify, -ify self), (be, turn to) righteous (-ness).

The person who sins, he alone shall die. A child shall not share the burden of a parent's guilt, nor shall a parent share the burden of a child's guilt; the righteousness of the righteous shall be accounted to him alone, and the wickedness of the wicked shall be accounted to him alone. YECHEZK'EL 18:20 (EZEKIEL 18:20)

The soul that sinneth, it shall die. The son shall not bear the iniquity of the father, neither shall the father bear the iniquity of the son: the righteousness (6666) of the righteous (6662) shall be upon him, and the wickedness of the wicked shall be upon him. EZEKIEL 18:20

> righteousness (6666) pronounced tsed-aw-kaw'; from 6663; rightness (abstr.), subj. (rectitude); obj. (justice) , mor. (virtue) or fig. (prosperity):- justice, moderately, right (-eous) (act, -ly, -ness).
>
> (6663) pronounced tsaw-dak'; prim. root; to be (causat., make) right (in a moral or forensic sense):- cleanse, clear self (be, do) just (-ice, -ify, -ify self), (be, turn to) righteous (-ness).
>
> righteous (6662) pronounced tsad-deek'; from 6663; just:- just, lawful, righteous (man).

None of the transgressions he committed shall be remembered against him, because of the righteousness he has practiced, he shall live. YECHEZK'EL 18:22 (EZEKIEL 18:22)

All his transgressions that he hath committed, they shall not be mentioned unto him: in his righteousness (6666) that he hath done he shall live. EZEKIEL 18:22

> righteousness (6666) pronounced tsed-aw-kaw'; from 6663; rightness (abstr.), subj. (rectitude); obj. (justice) , mor. (virtue) or fig. (prosperity):- justice, moderately, right (-eous) (act, -ly, -ness).
>
> (6663) pronounced tsaw-dak'; prim. root; to be (causat., make) right (in a moral or forensic sense):- cleanse, clear self (be, do) just (-ice, -ify, -ify self), (be, turn to) righteous (-ness).

So, too, if a righteous person turns away from his righteousness and does wrong, practicing the very abominations that the wicked person practiced, shall he live? None of the righteous deeds that he did shall be remembered; because of the treachery he has practiced and the sins he has committed- because of these, he shall die. YECHEZK'EL 18:24 (EZEKIEL 18:24)

But when the righteous (6662) turneth away from his righteousness (6666), and committeth iniquity, *and* doeth according to all the abominations that the wicked *man* doeth, shall he live? All his righteousness (6666) that he hath done shall not be mentioned: in his trespass that he hath trespassed, and in his sin that he hath sinned, in them shall he die. EZEKIEL 18:24

> righteous (6662) pronounced tsad-deek'; from 6663; just:- just, lawful, righteous (man).
>
> (6663) pronounced tsaw-dak'; prim. root; to be (causat., make) right (in a moral or forensic sense):- cleanse, clear self (be, do) just (-ice, -ify, -ify self), (be, turn to) righteous (-ness).
>
> righteousness (6666) pronounced tsed-aw-kaw'; from 6663; rightness (abstr.), subj. (rectitude); obj. (justice) , mor. (virtue) or fig. (prosperity):- justice, moderately, right (-eous) (act, -ly, -ness).

When a righteous person turns away from his righteousness and does wrong, he shall die for it; he shall die for the wrong he has done. YECHEZK'EL 18:26 (EZEKIEL 18:26)

When a righteous (6662) *man* turneth away from his righteousness (6666), and committeth iniquity, and dieth in them; for his iniquity that he hath done shall he die. EZEKIEL 18:26

righteous (6662) pronounced tsad-deek'; from 6663; just:- just, lawful, righteous (man).

(6663) pronounced tsaw-dak'; prim. root; to be (causat., make) right (in a moral or forensic sense):- cleanse, clear self (be, do) just (-ice, -ify, -ify self), (be, turn to) righteous (-ness).

righteousness (6666) pronounced tsed-aw-kaw'; from 6663; rightness (abstr.), subj. (rectitude); obj. (justice) , mor. (virtue) or fig. (prosperity):- justice, moderately, right (-eous) (act, -ly, -ness).

Now, O mortal, say to your fellow countrymen: The righteousness of the righteous shall not save him when he transgresses, nor shall the wickedness of the wicked cause him to stumble when he turns back from his wickedness. The righteous shall not survive through his righteousness when he sins. When I say of the righteous "He shall surely live," and relying on his righteousness, he commits iniquity, none of his righteous deeds shall be remembered; but for the iniquity that he has committed he shall die. YECHEZK'EL 33:12-13 (EZEKIEL 33:12-13)

his righteousness: Heb. "it." (TANAKH footnote)

Therefore, thou son of man, say unto the children of thy people, The righteousness (6666) of the righteous (6662) shall not deliver him in the day of his transgression: as for the wickedness of the wicked, he shall not fall thereby in the day that he turneth from his wickedness; neither shall the righteous (6662) be able to live for his *righteousness* (6666) in the day that he sinneth. When I shall say to the righteous (6662), *that* he shall surely live; if he trust to his own righteousness (6666), and commit iniquity, all his righteousnesses (6666) shall not be remembered; but for his iniquity that he hath committed, he shall die for it. EZEKIEL 33:12-13

righteousness (6666) pronounced tsed-aw-kaw'; from 6663; rightness (abstr.), subj. (rectitude); obj. (justice) , mor. (virtue) or fig. (prosperity):- justice, moderately, right (-eous) (act, -ly, -ness).

(6663) pronounced tsaw-dak'; prim. root; to be (causat., make) right (in a moral or forensic sense):- cleanse, clear self (be, do) just (-ice, -ify, -ify self), (be, turn to) righteous (-ness).

righteous (6662) pronounced tsad-deek'; from 6663; just:- just, lawful, righteous (man).

When a righteous man turns away from his righteous deeds and commits iniquity, he shall die for it. YECHEZK'EL 33:18 (EZEKIEL 33:18)

When the righteous turneth from his righteousness (6666), and committeth iniquity, he shall even die thereby. EZEKIEL 33:18

righteousness (6666) pronounced tsed-aw-kaw'; from 6663; rightness (abstr.), subj. (rectitude); obj. (justice) , mor. (virtue) or fig. (prosperity):- justice, moderately, right (-eous) (act, -ly, -ness).

(6663) pronounced tsaw-dak'; prim. root; to be (causat., make) right (in a moral or forensic sense):- cleanse, clear self (be, do) just (-ice, -ify, -ify self), (be, turn to) righteous (-ness).

Therefore, O King; may my advice be acceptable to you. Redeem our sins by beneficence and your iiniquities by generosity to the poor; then your serenity may be extended. All this befell King Nebuchadnezzar. DANI'EL 4:24-25 (DANIEL 4:27-28)

Wherefore, O king, let my counsel be acceptable unto thee, and break off thy sins by righteousness (6665), and thine iniquities by showing mercy to the poor; if it may be a lengthening of thy tranquility. All this came upon the king Nebuchadnezzar. DANIEL 4:27-28

> righteousness (6665) (Chald.) pronounced tsid-kaw'; corresp. To 6666; beneficence:- righteousness.
>
> righteousness (6666) pronounced tsed-aw-kaw'; from 6663; rightness (abstr.), subj. (rectitude); obj. (justice) , mor. (virtue) or fig. (prosperity):- justice, moderately, right (-eous) (act, -ly, -ness).
>
> (6663) pronounced tsaw-dak'; prim. root; to be (causat., make) right (in a moral or forensic sense):- cleanse, clear self (be, do) just (-ice, -ify, -ify self), (be, turn to) righteous (-ness).

With you, O LORD, is the right, and the shame is on us to this very day, on the men of Judah and the inhabitants of Jerusalem, all Israel, near and far, in all the lands where You have banished them, for the trespass they committed against You. DANI'EL 9:7 (DANIEL 9:7)

O LORD, righteousness (6666) *belongeth* unto thee, but unto us confusion of faces, as at this day; to the men of Judah, and to the inhabitants of Jerusalem, and unto all Israel, *that are* near, and *that are* far off, through all the countries whither thou hast driven them, because of their trespass that they have trespassed against thee. DANIEL 9:7

> righteousness (6666) pronounced tsed-aw-kaw'; from 6663; rightness (abstr.), subj. (rectitude); obj. (justice) , mor. (virtue) or fig. (prosperity):- justice, moderately, right (-eous) (act, -ly, -ness).
>
> (6663) pronounced tsaw-dak'; prim. root; to be (causat., make) right (in a moral or forensic sense):- cleanse, clear self (be, do) just (-ice, -ify, -ify self), (be, turn to) righteous (-ness).

O LORD, as befits Your abundant benevolence, let Your wrathful fury turn back from Your city, Jerusalem, Your holy mountain; for because of our sins and the iniquities of our fathers, Jerusalem and Your people have become a mockery among all who are around us. DANI'EL 9:16 (DANIEL 9:16)

O LORD, according to all thy righteousness (6666), I beseech thee, let thine anger and thy fury be turned away from thy city Jerusalem, thy holy mountain: because for our sins and the iniquities of our fathers, Jerusalem and thy people are *become* a reproach to all *that are* about us. DANIEL 9:16

> righteousness (6666) pronounced tsed-aw-kaw'; from 6663; rightness (abstr.), subj. (rectitude); obj. (justice) , mor. (virtue) or fig. (prosperity):- justice, moderately, right (-eous) (act, -ly, -ness).
>
> (6663) pronounced tsaw-dak'; prim. root; to be (causat., make) right (in a moral or forensic sense):- cleanse, clear self (be, do) just (-ice, -ify, -ify self), (be, turn to) righteous (-ness).

Seventy weeks have been decreed for your people and your holy city until the measure of transgression is filled and that of sin complete, until iniquity is expiated, and eternal righteousness ushered in; and prophetic vision ratified, and the Holy of Holies anointed. DANI'EL 9:24 (DANIEL 9:24)

> seventy weeks: Viz. of years. (TANAKH footnote)
>
> ratified: Lit. "sealed." (TANAKH footnote)

Seventy weeks are determined upon thy people and upon thy holy city, to finish the transgression, and to make an end of sins, and to make reconciliation for iniquity, and to bring in everlasting righteousness (6664), and to seal up the vision and prophecy, and to anoint the Most Holy. DANIEL 9:24

> righteousness (6664) pronounced tseh'-dek; from 6663; the right (nat., mor., or legal); also (abstr.) equity or (fig.) prosperity:- x even, (x that which is altogether) just (-ice), ([un-]) right (-eous) (cause, -ly, -ness).
>
> (6663) pronounced tsaw-dak'; prim. root; to be (causat., make) right (in a moral or forensic sense):- cleanse, clear self (be, do) just (-ice, -ify, -ify self), (be, turn to) righteous (-ness).

And the knowledgeable will be radiant like the bright expanse of sky, and those who lead the many to righteousness will be like the stars forever and ever. DANI'EL 12:3 (DANIEL 12:3)

And they that be wise shall shine as the brightness of the firmament; and they that turn many to righteousness (6663), as the stars for ever and ever. DANIEL 12:3

> righteousness (6663) pronounced tsaw-dak'; prim. root; to be (causat., make) right (in a moral or forensic sense):- cleanse, clear self (be, do) just (-ice, -ify, -ify self), (be, turn to) righteous (-ness).

And I will espouse you forever; I will espouse you with righteousness and justice, and with goodness and mercy, and I will espouse you with faithfulness; then you shall be devoted to the LORD.
HOSHEA 2:21-22 (HOSEA 2:19-20):

> faithfulness: As the bride-price which the bridegroom will pay, He will confer these qualities on her, so that she will never offend again. (TANAKH footnote)

And I will betroth thee unto me for ever; yea, I will betroth thee unto me in righteousness (6664), and in judgment, and in loving-kindness, and in mercies. I will even betroth thee unto me in faithfulness; and thou shalt know the LORD. HOSEA 2:19-20

> righteousness (6664) pronounced tseh'-dek; from 6663; the right (nat., mor., or legal); also (abstr.) equity or (fig.) prosperity:- x even, (x that which is altogether) just (-ice), ([un-]) right (-eous) (cause, -ly, -ness).
>
> (6663) pronounced tsaw-dak'; prim. root; to be (causat., make) right (in a moral or forensic sense):- cleanse, clear self (be, do) just (-ice, -ify, -ify self), (be, turn to) righteous (-ness).

"Sow righteousness for yourselves; reap the fruits of goodness; break for yourselves betimes fresh ground of seeking the LORD so that you may obtain a teacher of righteousness." HOSHEA 10:12 (HOSEA 10:12)

Sow to yourselves in righteousness (6666), reap in mercy; break up your fallow ground; for *it is* time to seek the LORD, till he come and rain righteousness (6664) upon youl. HOSEA 10:12

> righteousness (6666) pronounced tsed-aw-kaw'; from 6663; rightness (abstr.), subj. (rectitude); obj. (justice) , mor. (virtue) or fig. (prosperity):- justice, moderately, right (-eous) (act, -ly, -ness).
>
> (6663) pronounced tsaw-dak'; prim. root; to be (causat., make) right (in a moral or forensic sense):- cleanse, clear self (be, do) just (-ice, -ify, -ify self), (be, turn to) righteous (-ness).
>
> righteousness (6664) pronounced tseh'-dek; from 6663; the right (nat., mor., or legal); also (abstr.) equity or (fig.) prosperity:- x even, (x that which is altogether) just (-ice), ([un-]) right (-eous) (cause, -ly, -ness).

[Ah], you who turn justice into wormwood and hurl righteousness to the ground! [Seek the LORD.] 'AMOS 5:7 (AMOS 5:7)

Ye who turn judgment to wormwood, and leave off righteousness (6666) in the earth. AMOS 5:7

> righteousness (6666) pronounced tsed-aw-kaw'; from 6663; rightness (abstr.), subj. (rectitude); obj. (justice) , mor. (virtue) or fig. (prosperity):- justice, moderately, right (-eous) (act, -ly, -ness).
>
> (6663) pronounced tsaw-dak'; prim. root; to be (causat., make) right (in a moral or forensic sense):- cleanse, clear self (be, do) just (-ice, -ify, -ify self), (be, turn to) righteous (-ness).

But let justice well up like water, righteousness like an unfailing stream. 'AMOS 5:24 (AMOS 5:24)

But let judgment run down as waters, and righteousness (6666) as a mighty stream. AMOS 5:24

> righteousness (6666) pronounced tsed-aw-kaw'; from 6663; rightness (abstr.), subj. (rectitude); obj. (justice) , mor. (virtue) or fig. (prosperity):- justice, moderately, right (-eous) (act, -ly, -ness).
>
> (6663) pronounced tsaw-dak'; prim. root; to be (causat., make) right (in a moral or forensic sense):- cleanse, clear self (be, do) just (-ice, -ify, -ify self), (be, turn to) righteous (-ness).

Can horses gallop on a rock? Can it be plowed with oxen? Yet you have turned justice into poison weed and the fruit of righteousness to wormwood. 'AMOS 6:12 (AMOS 6:12)

> Can it be plowed with oxen?: Meaning of Heb. uncertain; emendation yields "Can one plow the sea with oxen?" (TANAKH footnote)

Shall horses run upon the rock? Will *one plow there* with oxen? for *ye* have turned judgment into gall, and the fruit of righteousness (6666) into hemlock: AMOS 6:12

righteousness (6666) pronounced tsed-aw-kaw'; from 6663; rightness (abstr.), subj. (rectitude); obj. (justice) , mor. (virtue) or fig. (prosperity):- justice, moderately, right (-eous) (act, -ly, -ness).

(6663) pronounced tsaw-dak'; prim. root; to be (causat., make) right (in a moral or forensic sense):- cleanse, clear self (be, do) just (-ice, -ify, -ify self), (be, turn to) righteous (-ness).

"My people, remember what Balak king of Moab plotted against you, and how Balaam son of Beor responded to him. [Recall your passage] from Shittim to Gilgal- and you will recognize the gracious acts of the LORD." MIKHAH 6:5 (MICAH 6:5)

Gilgal: i.e. the crossing of the Jordan; see Josh. 3.1, 14---4.19. (TANAKH footnote)

Early next morning, Joshua and all the Israelites set out from Shittim and marched to the Jordan. They did not cross immediately, but spent the night there. Y'HOSHUA 3:1 (JOSHUA 3:1)

And Joshua rose early in the morning; and they removed from Shittim; and came to Jordan, he and all the children of Israel, and lodged there before they passed over. JOSHUA 3:1

When the people set out from their encampment to cross the Jordan, the priests bearing the Ark of the Covenant were at the head of the people. Y'HOSHUA 3:14 (JOSHUA 3:14)

And it came to pass, when the people removed from their tents, to pass over Jordan, and the priests bearing the ark of the covenant before the people; JOSHUA 3:14

The people came up from the Jordan on the tenth day of the first month, and encamped at Gilgal on the eastern border of Jericho. Y'HOSHUA 4:19 (JOSHUA 4:19)

And the people came up out of Jordan on the tenth day of the first month, and encamped in Gilgal, in the east border of Jericho. JOSHUA 4:19

O my people, remember now what Balak king of Moab consulted, and what Balaam the son of Beor answered him from Shittim unto Gilgal; that ye may know the righteousness (6666) of the LORD. MICAH 6:5

righteousness (6666) pronounced tsed-aw-kaw'; from 6663; rightness (abstr.), subj. (rectitude); obj. (justice) , mor. (virtue) or fig. (prosperity):- justice, moderately, right (-eous) (act, -ly, -ness).

(6663) pronounced tsaw-dak'; prim. root; to be (causat., make) right (in a moral or forensic sense):- cleanse, clear self (be, do) just (-ice, -ify, -ify self), (be, turn to) righteous (-ness).

I must bear the anger of the LORD, since I have sinned against Him, until He champions my cause and upholds my claim. He will let me out into the light; I will enjoy vindication by Him. MIKHAH 7:9 (MICAH 7:9)

I will bear the indignation of the LORD, because I have sinned against him, until he plead my cause and execute judgment for me; he will bring me forth to the light, *and* I shall behold his righteousness (6666). MICAH 7:9

> righteousness (6666) pronounced tsed-aw-kaw'; from 6663; rightness (abstr.), subj. (rectitude); obj. (justice) , mor. (virtue) or fig. (prosperity):- justice, moderately, right (-eous) (act, -ly, -ness).
>
> (6663) pronounced tsaw-dak'; prim. root; to be (causat., make) right (in a moral or forensic sense):- cleanse, clear self (be, do) just (-ice, -ify, -ify self), (be, turn to) righteous (-ness).

Seek the LORD, all you humble of the land who have fulfilled His law; seek righteousness, seek humility. Perhaps you will find shelter on the day of the LORD's anger. TZ'FANYAH 2;3 (ZEPHANIAH 2:3)

Seek ye the LORD, all ye meek of the earth, which have wrought his judgment: seek righteousness (6664), seek meekness: it may be ye shall be hid in the day of the LORD'S anger. ZEPHANIAH 2:3

> righteousness (6664) pronounced tseh'-dek; from 6663; the right (nat., mor., or legal); also (abstr.) equity or (fig.) prosperity:- x even, (x that which is altogether) just (-ice), ([un-]) right (-eous) (cause, -ly, -ness).
>
> (6663) pronounced tsaw-dak'; prim. root; to be (causat., make) right (in a moral or forensic sense):- cleanse, clear self (be, do) just (-ice, -ify, -ify self), (be, turn to) righteous (-ness).

And I will bring them home to dwell in Jerusalem. They shall be my people, and I will be their God- in truth and sincerity. Z'KHARYAH 8:8 (ZECHARIAH 8:8)

And I will bring them, and they shall dwell in the midst of Jerusalem: and they shall be my people, and I will be their God in truth and in righteousness (6666). ZECHARIAH 8:8

> righteousness (6666) pronounced tsed-aw-kaw'; from 6663; rightness (abstr.), subj. (rectitude); obj. (justice) , mor. (virtue) or fig. (prosperity):- justice, moderately, right (-eous) (act, -ly, -ness).
>
> (6663) pronounced tsaw-dak'; prim. root; to be (causat., make) right (in a moral or forensic sense):- cleanse, clear self (be, do) just (-ice, -ify, -ify self), (be, turn to) righteous (-ness).

He shall act like a smelter and purger of silver; and he shall purify the descendants of Levi and refine them like gold and silver, so that they shall present offerings in righteousness. MAL'AKHI 3:3 (MALACHI 3:3)

And he shall sit as a refiner and purifier of silver: and he shall purify the sons of Levi, and purge them as gold and silver, that they may offer unto the LORD an offering in righteousness (6666). MALACHI 3:3

righteousness (6666) pronounced tsed-aw-kaw'; from 6663; rightness (abstr.), subj. (rectitude); obj. (justice) , mor. (virtue) or fig. (prosperity):- justice, moderately, right (-eous) (act, -ly, -ness).

(6663) pronounced tsaw-dak'; prim. root; to be (causat., make) right (in a moral or forensic sense):- cleanse, clear self (be, do) just (-ice, -ify, -ify self), (be, turn to) righteous (-ness).

But for you who revere My name a sun of victory shall rise to bring healing. You shall go forth and stamp like stall-fed calves. MAL'AKHI 3:20* (MALACHI 4:2)

to bring healing: Lit. "with healing in the folds of its garments"; others, "with healing in its wings." (TANAKH footnote)

But unto you that fear my name shall the Sun of righteousness (6666) arise with healing in his wings: and ye shall go forth, and grow up as calves of the stall. MALACHI 4:2*

*TANAKH includes all of chapter 4 within chapter 3.

righteousness (6666) pronounced tsed-aw-kaw'; from 6663; rightness (abstr.), subj. (rectitude); obj. (justice) , mor. (virtue) or fig. (prosperity):- justice, moderately, right (-eous) (act, -ly, -ness).

(6663) pronounced tsaw-dak'; prim. root; to be (causat., make) right (in a moral or forensic sense):- cleanse, clear self (be, do) just (-ice, -ify, -ify self), (be, turn to) righteous (-ness).

Book Three

Walking the Same Sure Foundation of Grace

Introduction

This is the third of five books in a mini-series with a unique purpose. Each book provides a verse to verse comparison of *TANAKH THE HOLY SCRIPTURES* (hereafter referred to as *Tanakh)* and the *AUTHORIZED KING JAMES VERSION* (Old Testament only, hereafter referred to as *KJV)* on a particular subject. The subject of Book One is *SALVATION*; Book Two's subject is *RIGHTEOUSNESS*. Book Three, *GRACE*, is the shortest, most repetitious of the books but has an interesting surprise in one verse. Readers will discover that all spiritual concepts presented on the following pages have physical actions that can be observed and experienced. This series is about relationship, not religion.

Each of the five books are in the same order and format for ease of use. Format, as well as use of *TANAKH* footnotes and *STRONG'S CONCORDANCE* will be discussed in the section *How This Book is Organized*. Yeshua (Jesus) spoke about each of these subjects often before the New Testament was written. Modern-day readers who grasp these truths will be able to understand the teachings of the New Testament in the same way as people of Yeshua's (Jesus's) generation.

How This Book is Organized

TANAKH verse followed by TANAKH reference (each letter capitalized) with corresponding KJV reference (also capitalized) in parenthesis. Sometimes numbers will not match exactly but will be close. TANAKH reference will be highlighted in gray.

Example:

My heart is astir with gracious words; I speak my poem to a king; my tongue is the pen of an expert scribe. You are fairer than all men; your speech is endowed with grace; rightly has God given you an eternal blessing. TEHILLIM 45:2-3 (PSALMS 45:1-2)

Spelling of highlighted *TANAKH* references is the same as the *COMPLETE JEWISH BIBLE* throughout the book to maintain its sense of Jewishness. Refer to *Works Cited* for additional information.

KJV will include the word grace followed by a highlighted number in parenthesis within the verse. The highlighted number will be a reference number to *STRONG'S CONCORDANCE* (original Hebrew or Chaldee). The verse will be followed by the highlighted KJV reference only. Words in italic in the original text will be in italics. Archaic spelling of words will also be presented as the original authors intended.

Example:

My heart is inditing a good matter: I speak of the things which I have made touching the King: my tongue *is* the pen of a ready writer. Thou art fairer than the children of men: grace (2580) is poured into thy lips: therefore God hath blessed thee forever. PSALMS 45:1-2

> grace (2580) pronounced khane; from 2603; graciousness, i.e. subj. (kindness, favor) or objective (beauty):- favour, grace (-ious), pleasant, precious, [well-] favoured.
>
> (2603) pronounced khaw-nan'; a prim. root [comp. 2583]; prop. to bend or stoop in kindness to an inferior; to favor, bestow, causat. to implore (i.e. to move to favor by petition):- beseech, x fair, (be, find, shew) favour (-able), be (deal, give, grant) gracious (-ly), entreat, (be) merciful, have (shew) mercy (on, upon), have pity upon, pray, make supplication, x very.
>
> (2583) pronounced khaw-naw'; a prim. root [comp. 2603]; prop. to incline; by impl. to decline (of the slanting rays of evening); spec. to pitch a tent; gen. to encamp (for abode or siege):- abide (in tents), camp, dwell, encamp, grow to an end, lie, pitch (tent), rest in tent.

Pronunciation is provided with the complete definition by *STRONG'S CONCORDANCE*. The second highlighted number is the primitive root and normally will be listed last unless it is the only reference or the first of several references. In this case, however, it has a second highlighted number which is also a primitive root and is there for comparison.

Abbreviations such as subj. and impl. will be identified in *Abbreviations Employed*, the next section of the book.

Occasionally, footnotes will be provided in TANAKH. When this occurs, the footnote will be noted exactly as referenced. If scripture references are available, they will also be included in the same format as above so that readers may be able to have immediate access to as much information as possible without turning pages.

The first of two examples below supplies a literal explanation as to how the original context would have been understood by its listeners.

The beginning of wisdom is acquire wisdom; with all your acquisitions, acquire discernment. Hug her to you and she will exalt you; she will bring you honor if you embrace her. She will adorn your head with a graceful wreath; crown you with a glorious diadem. MISHLEI 4:7-9 (PROVERBS 4:7-9)

> beginning: Or "best part". (TANAKH footnote)

The second example directs the reader's attention to an additional scripture for more information.

In that day I will all but annihilate all the nations that came up against Jerusalem. But I will fill the House of David and the inhabitants of Jerusalem with a spirit of pity and compassion: and they shall lament to Me about those who are slain, wailing over them as over a favorite son and showing bitter grief as over a first-born. Z'KHARYAH 12:9-10 (ZECHARIAH 12:9-10)

all but annihilate: For the idiom cf. Gen.43.30; it is also attested in post biblical Hebrew. (TANAKH footnote)

> With that, Joseph hurried out, for he was overcome with feeling toward his brother and was on the verge of tears; he went into a room and wept there.
> B'RESHEET 43:30 (GENESIS 43:30)

> And Joseph made haste; for his bowels did yearn upon his brother; and he sought *where to weep*; and he entered into *his* chamber, and wept there.
> GENESIS 43:30

KJV reference will always be added for comparison and continuity of the TANAKH footnote before continuing on to the corresponding KJV. In this example, ZECHARIAH 12:9-10 will be the next entry.

Abbreviations Employed

Caus., causat.: causative, causatively

Comp.: compare, comparative, comparatively, comparison

Gen.: general, generally, generical, generically

i.e.: id est, that is

impl.: implication, implied

prim.: primitive, primary

prop.: proper, properly

spec.: specific, specifically

subj.: subject, subjective, subjectively

But Noah found favor with the LORD. B'RESHEET 6:8 (GENESIS 6:8)

But Noah found grace (2580) in the eyes of the Lord. GENESIS 6:8

> grace (2580) pronounced khane; from 2603; graciousness, i.e. subj. (kindness, favor) or objective (beauty):- favour, grace (-ious), pleasant, precious, [well-] favoured.
>
> (2603) pronounced khaw-nan'; a prim. root {comp. 2583]; prop. to bend or stoop in kindness to an inferior; to favor, bestow; causat. to implore (i.e. to move to favor by petition):- beseech, x fair, (be, find, shew) favour (-able), be (deal, give, grant) gracious (-ly), entreat, (be) merciful, have (shew) mercy (on, upon), have pity upon, pray, make supplication, x very.
>
> (2583) pronounced khaw-naw'; a prim. root [comp. 2603]; prop. to incline; by impl. to decline (of the slanting rays of evening); spec. to pitch a tent; gen. to encamp (for abode or siege):- abide (in tents), camp, dwell, encamp, grow to an end, lie, pitch (tent), rest in tent.

You have been so gracious to your servant, and have already shown me so much kindness in order to save my life; but I cannot flee to the hills lest the disaster overtake me and I die. B'RESHEET 19:19 (GENESIS 19:19)

Behold now, thy servant hath found grace (2580) in thy sight, and thou hast magnified thy mercy, which thou hast shown unto me in saving my life; and I cannot escape to the mountain, lest some evil take me, and I die. GENESIS 19:19

> grace (2580) pronounced khane; from 2603; graciousness, i.e. subj. (kindness, favor) or objective (beauty):- favour, grace (-ious), pleasant, precious, [well-] favoured.
>
> (2603) pronounced khaw-nan'; a prim. root {comp. 2583]; prop. to bend or stoop in kindness to an inferior; to favor, bestow; causat. to implore (i.e. to move to favor by petition):- beseech, x fair, (be, find, shew) favour (-able), be (deal, give, grant) gracious (-ly), entreat, (be) merciful, have (shew) mercy (on, upon), have pity upon, pray, make supplication, x very.
>
> (2583) pronounced khaw-naw'; a prim. root [comp. 2603]; prop. to incline; by impl. to decline (of the slanting rays of evening); spec. to pitch a tent; gen. to encamp (for abode or siege):- abide (in tents), camp, dwell, encamp, grow to an end, lie, pitch (tent), rest in tent.

Jacob sent messengers ahead to his brother Esau in the land of Seir, the country of Edom, and instructed them as follows: "Thus shall you say, 'To my lord Esau, thus says your servant Jacob: I stayed with Laban and remained until now; I have acquired cattle, asses, sheep, and male and female slaves; and I send this message to my lord in the hope of gaining your favor.' " B'RESHEET 32:4-6 (GENESIS 32:4-5)

And he commanded them, saying, Thus shall you speak unto my lord Esau: Thy servant Jacob saith thus, I have sojourned with Laban, and stayed there until now; and I have oxen, and asses, flocks, and menservants, and women servants; and I have sent to tell my lord, that I may find grace (2580) in thy sight. GENESIS 32:4-5

> grace (2580) pronounced khane; from 2603; graciousness, i.e. subj. (kindness, favor) or objective (beauty):- favour, grace (-ious), pleasant, precious, [well-] favoured.
>
> (2603) pronounced khaw-nan'; a prim. root {comp. 2583]; prop. to bend or stoop in kindness to an inferior; to favor, bestow; causat. to implore (i.e. to move to favor by petition):- beseech, x fair, (be, find, shew) favour (-able), be (deal, give, grant) gracious (-ly), entreat, (be) merciful, have (shew) mercy (on, upon), have pity upon, pray, make supplication, x very.
>
> (2583) pronounced khaw-naw'; a prim. root [comp. 2603]; prop. to incline; by impl. to decline (of the slanting rays of evening); spec. to pitch a tent; gen. to encamp (for abode or siege):- abide (in tents), camp, dwell, encamp, grow to an end, lie, pitch (tent), rest in tent.

And he asked, "What do you mean by all this company which I have met?" He answered, "To gain my lord's favor." Esau said, "I have enough, my brother; let what you have remain yours." But Jacob said, "No, I pray you; if you would do me this favor, accept from me this gift; for to see your face is like seeing the face of God, and you have received me favorably. B'RESHEET 33:8-10 (GENESIS 33:8-10)

And he said, What *meanest* thou by all this drove which I met? And he said, *These are* to find grace (2580) in the sight of my lord. And Esau said, I have enough, my brother; keep that thou hast unto thyself. And Jacob said, Nay, I pray thee, if now I have found grace (2580) in thy sight, then receive my present at my hand: for therefore I have seen thy face, as though I had seen the face of God, and thou wast pleased with me. GENESIS 33:8-10

> grace (2580) pronounced khane; from 2603; graciousness, i.e. subj. (kindness, favor) or objective (beauty):- favour, grace (-ious), pleasant, precious, [well-] favoured.
>
> (2603) pronounced khaw-nan'; a prim. root {comp. 2583]; prop. to bend or stoop in kindness to an inferior; to favor, bestow; causat. to implore (i.e. to move to favor by petition):- beseech, x fair, (be, find, shew) favour (-able), be (deal, give, grant) gracious (-ly), entreat, (be) merciful, have (shew) mercy (on, upon), have pity upon, pray, make supplication, x very.
>
> (2583) pronounced khaw-naw'; a prim. root [comp. 2603]; prop. to incline; by impl. to decline (of the slanting rays of evening); spec. to pitch a tent; gen. to encamp (for abode or siege):- abide (in tents), camp, dwell, encamp, grow to an end, lie, pitch (tent), rest in tent.

Then Esau said, "Let me assign to you some of the men who are with me." But he said, "Oh, no, my lord is too kind to me!" B'RESHEET 33:15 (GENESIS 33:15)

And Esau said, Let me now leave with thee *some* of the folk that *are* with me. And he said, What needeth it? Let me find grace (2580) in the sight of my lord. GENESIS 33:15

> grace (2580) pronounced khane; from 2603; graciousness, i.e. subj. (kindness, favor) or objective (beauty):- favour, grace (-ious), pleasant, precious, [well-] favoured.

(2603) pronounced khaw-nan'; a prim. root {comp. 2583]; prop. to bend or stoop in kindness to an inferior; to favor, bestow; causat. to implore (i.e. to move to favor by petition):- beseech, x fair, (be, find, shew) favour (-able), be (deal, give, grant) gracious (-ly), entreat, (be) merciful, have (shew) mercy (on, upon), have pity upon, pray, make supplication, x very.

(2583) pronounced khaw-naw'; a prim. root [comp. 2603]; prop. to incline; by impl. to decline (of the slanting rays of evening); spec. to pitch a tent; gen. to encamp (for abode or siege):- abide (in tents), camp, dwell, encamp, grow to an end, lie, pitch (tent), rest in tent.

Then Shechem said to her father and brothers, "Do me this favor, and I will pay whatever you tell me. " B'RESHEET 34:11 (GENESIS 34:11)

And Shechem said unto her father and unto her brethren, Let me find grace (2580) in your eyes, and what ye shall say unto me I will give. GENESIS 34:11

grace (2580) pronounced khane; from 2603; graciousness, i.e. subj. (kindness, favor) or objective (beauty):- favour, grace (-ious), pleasant, precious, [well-] favoured.

(2603) pronounced khaw-nan'; a prim. root {comp. 2583]; prop. to bend or stoop in kindness to an inferior; to favor, bestow; causat. to implore (i.e. to move to favor by petition):- beseech, x fair, (be, find, shew) favour (-able), be (deal, give, grant) gracious (-ly), entreat, (be) merciful, have (shew) mercy (on, upon), have pity upon, pray, make supplication, x very.

(2583) pronounced khaw-naw'; a prim. root [comp. 2603]; prop. to incline; by impl. to decline (of the slanting rays of evening); spec. to pitch a tent; gen. to encamp (for abode or siege):- abide (in tents), camp, dwell, encamp, grow to an end, lie, pitch (tent), rest in tent.

And when his master saw that the LORD was with him and that the LORD lent success to everything that he undertook, he took a liking to Joseph. B'RESHEET 39:3-4 (GENESIS 39:3-4)

And his master saw that the LORD *was* with him, and that the LORD made all that he did to prosper in his hand, and Joseph found grace (2580) in his sight, and he served him: and he made him overseer over his house, and all *that* he had he put into his hand. GENESIS 39:3-4

grace (2580) pronounced khane; from 2603; graciousness, i.e. subj. (kindness, favor) or objective (beauty):- favour, grace (-ious), pleasant, precious, [well-] favoured.

(2603) pronounced khaw-nan'; a prim. root {comp. 2583]; prop. to bend or stoop in kindness to an inferior; to favor, bestow; causat. to implore (i.e. to move to favor by petition):- beseech, x fair, (be, find, shew) favour (-able), be (deal, give, grant) gracious (-ly), entreat, (be) merciful, have (shew) mercy (on, upon), have pity upon, pray, make supplication, x very.

(2583) pronounced khaw-naw'; a prim. root [comp. 2603]; prop. to incline; by impl. to decline (of the slanting rays of evening); spec. to pitch a tent; gen. to encamp (for abode or siege):- abide (in tents), camp, dwell, encamp, grow to an end, lie, pitch (tent), rest in tent.

And they said, "You have saved our lives! We are grateful to my lord, and we shall be serfs to Pharaoh." B'RESHEET 47:25 (GENESIS 47:25)

And they said, Thou hast saved our lives: let us find grace (2580) in the sight of my lord, and we will be Pharaoh's servants. GENESIS 47:25

> grace (2580) pronounced khane; from 2603; graciousness, i.e. subj. (kindness, favor) or objective (beauty):- favour, grace (-ious), pleasant, precious, [well-] favoured.
>
> (2603) pronounced khaw-nan'; a prim. root {comp. 2583]; prop. to bend or stoop in kindness to an inferior; to favor, bestow; causat. to implore (i.e. to move to favor by petition):- beseech, x fair, (be, find, shew) favour (-able), be (deal, give, grant) gracious (-ly), entreat, (be) merciful, have (shew) mercy (on, upon), have pity upon, pray, make supplication, x very.
>
> (2583) pronounced khaw-naw'; a prim. root [comp. 2603]; prop. to incline; by impl. to decline (of the slanting rays of evening); spec. to pitch a tent; gen. to encamp (for abode or siege):- abide (in tents), camp, dwell, encamp, grow to an end, lie, pitch (tent), rest in tent.

And when the time approached for Israel to die, he summoned his son Joseph and said to him, "Do me this favor, place your hand under my thigh as a pledge of your steadfast loyalty: please do not bury me in Egypt. B'RESHEET 47:29 (GENESIS 47:29)

And the time drew nigh that Israel must die: and he called his son Joseph, and said unto him, If now I have found grace (2580) in thy sight, put, I pray thee, thy hand under my thigh, and deal kindly and truly with me; bury me not, I pray thee, in Egypt: GENESIS 47:29

> grace (2580) pronounced khane; from 2603; graciousness, i.e. subj. (kindness, favor) or objective (beauty):- favour, grace (-ious), pleasant, precious, [well-] favoured.
>
> (2603) pronounced khaw-nan'; a prim. root {comp. 2583]; prop. to bend or stoop in kindness to an inferior; to favor, bestow; causat. to implore (i.e. to move to favor by petition):- beseech, x fair, (be, find, shew) favour (-able), be (deal, give, grant) gracious (-ly), entreat, (be) merciful, have (shew) mercy (on, upon), have pity upon, pray, make supplication, x very.
>
> (2583) pronounced khaw-naw'; a prim. root [comp. 2603]; prop. to incline; by impl. to decline (of the slanting rays of evening); spec. to pitch a tent; gen. to encamp (for abode or siege):- abide (in tents), camp, dwell, encamp, grow to an end, lie, pitch (tent), rest in tent.

It required forty days, for such is the full period of embalming. The Egyptians bewailed him seventy days; and when the wailing period was over, Joseph spoke to Pharaoh's court, saying, "Do me this favor, and lay this appeal before Pharaoh: My father made me swear, saying, "I am about to die. Be sure to bury me in the grave which I made ready for myself in the land of Canaan." B'RESHEET 50:3-5 (GENESIS 50:3-5)

And forty days were fulfilled for him; for so are fulfilled the days of those which are embalmed; and the Egyptians mourned for him threescore and ten days. And when the days of his mourning were past, Joseph spake unto the house of Pharaoh, saying, If now I have found grace (2580) in your eyes, speak, I pray you in the ears of Pharaoh saying, My father made me swear saying, Lo, I die: in my grave which I have digged for me in the land of Canaan, there shalt thou bury me. Now therefore let me go up, I pray thee, and bury my father, and I will come again. GENESIS 50:3-5

> grace (2580) pronounced khane; from 2603; graciousness, i.e. subj. (kindness, favor) or objective (beauty):- favour, grace (-ious), pleasant, precious, [well-] favoured.
>
> (2603) pronounced khaw-nan'; a prim. root {comp. 2583]; prop. to bend or stoop in kindness to an inferior; to favor, bestow; causat. to implore (i.e. to move to favor by petition):- beseech, x fair, (be, find, shew) favour (-able), be (deal, give, grant) gracious (-ly), entreat, (be) merciful, have (shew) mercy (on, upon), have pity upon, pray, make supplication, x very.
>
> (2583) pronounced khaw-naw'; a prim. root [comp. 2603]; prop. to incline; by impl. to decline (of the slanting rays of evening); spec. to pitch a tent; gen. to encamp (for abode or siege):- abide (in tents), camp, dwell, encamp, grow to an end, lie, pitch (tent), rest in tent.

Moses said to the LORD, "See, You say to me, 'Lead this people forward', but You have not made known to me whom You will send with me. Further, You have said, I have singled you out by name, and you have, indeed, gained My favor.' Now, if I have truly gained Your favor, pray let me know Your ways, that I may know You and continue in Your favor. Consider too, that this nation is Your people."
SH'MOT 33:12-13 (EXODUS 33:12-13)

And Moses said unto the LORD, See, thou sayest unto me, Bring up this people: and thou hast not let me know whom thou wilt send with me. Yet thou hast said, I know thee by name, and thou hast also found grace (2580) in my sight. Now therefore, I pray thee, if I have found grace (2580) in thy sight, show me now thy way, that I may know thee, that I may find grace (2580) in thy sight: and consider that this nation *is* thy people. EXODUS 33:12-13

> grace (2580) pronounced khane; from 2603; graciousness, i.e. subj. (kindness, favor) or objective (beauty):- favour, grace (-ious), pleasant, precious, [well-] favoured.
>
> (2603) pronounced khaw-nan'; a prim. root {comp. 2583]; prop. to bend or stoop in kindness to an inferior; to favor, bestow; causat. to implore (i.e. to move to favor by petition):- beseech, x fair, (be, find, shew) favour (-able), be (deal, give, grant) gracious (-ly), entreat, (be) merciful, have (shew) mercy (on, upon), have pity upon, pray, make supplication, x very.
>
> (2583) pronounced khaw-naw'; a prim. root [comp. 2603]; prop. to incline; by impl. to decline (of the slanting rays of evening); spec. to pitch a tent; gen. to encamp (for abode or siege):- abide (in tents), camp, dwell, encamp, grow to an end, lie, pitch (tent), rest in tent.

"For how shall it be known that Your people have gained Your favor unless You go with us, so that we may be distinguished, Your people and I, from every people on the face of the earth?" And the LORD said to Moses, "I will also do this thing that you have asked; for you have truly gained My favor and I have singled you out by name": SH'MOT 33:16-17 (EXODUS 33:16-17)

For wherein shall it be known here that I and thy people have found grace (2580) in thy sight? *Is it* not in that thou goest with us? So shall we be separated, I and thy people, from all the people that *are* upon the face of the earth. And the LORD said unto Moses, I will do this thing also that thou hast spoken: for thou hast found grace (2580) in my sight, and I know thee by name. EXODUS 33:16-17

> grace (2580) pronounced khane; from 2603; graciousness, i.e. subj. (kindness, favor) or objective (beauty):- favour, grace (-ious), pleasant, precious, [well-] favoured.
>
> (2603) pronounced khaw-nan'; a prim. root {comp. 2583]; prop. to bend or stoop in kindness to an inferior; to favor, bestow; causat. to implore (i.e. to move to favor by petition):- beseech, x fair, (be, find, shew) favour (-able), be (deal, give, grant) gracious (-ly), entreat, (be) merciful, have (shew) mercy (on, upon), have pity upon, pray, make supplication, x very.
>
> (2583) pronounced khaw-naw'; a prim. root [comp. 2603]; prop. to incline; by impl. to decline (of the slanting rays of evening); spec. to pitch a tent; gen. to encamp (for abode or siege):- abide (in tents), camp, dwell, encamp, grow to an end, lie, pitch (tent), rest in tent.

Moses hastened to bow low to the ground in homage, and said, "If I have gained Your favor, O LORD, pray, let the LORD go in our midst, even though this is a stiffnecked people. Pardon our iniquity and our sin, and take us for Your own!" SH'MOT 34:8-9 (EXODUS 34:8-9)

And Moses made haste, and bowed his head toward the earth, and worshipped. And he said, If now I have found grace (2580) in thy sight, O LORD, let my LORD, I pray thee, go among us; for it *is* a stiffnecked people; and pardon our iniquity and our sin, and take us for thine inheritance.
EXODUS 34:8-9

> grace (2580) pronounced khane; from 2603; graciousness, i.e. subj. (kindness, favor) or objective (beauty):- favour, grace (-ious), pleasant, precious, [well-] favoured.
>
> (2603) pronounced khaw-nan'; a prim. root {comp. 2583]; prop. to bend or stoop in kindness to an inferior; to favor, bestow; causat. to implore (i.e. to move to favor by petition):- beseech, x fair, (be, find, shew) favour (-able), be (deal, give, grant) gracious (-ly), entreat, (be) merciful, have (shew) mercy (on, upon), have pity upon, pray, make supplication, x very.
>
> (2583) pronounced khaw-naw'; a prim. root [comp. 2603]; prop. to incline; by impl. to decline (of the slanting rays of evening); spec. to pitch a tent; gen. to encamp (for abode or siege):- abide (in tents), camp, dwell, encamp, grow to an end, lie, pitch (tent), rest in tent.

"It would be a favor to us," they continued, "if this land were given to your servants as a holding: do not move us across the Jordan." B'MIDBAR 32:5 (NUMBERS 32:5)

Wherefore said they, if we have found grace (2580) in thy sight, let this land be given unto thy servants for a possession, *and* bring us not over Jordan. NUMBERS 32:5

grace (2580) pronounced khane; from 2603; graciousness, i.e. subj. (kindness, favor) or objective (beauty):- favour, grace (-ious), pleasant, precious, [well-] favoured.

(2603) pronounced khaw-nan'; a prim. root {comp. 2583]; prop. to bend or stoop in kindness to an inferior; to favor, bestow; causat. to implore (i.e. to move to favor by petition):- beseech, x fair, (be, find, shew) favour (-able), be (deal, give, grant) gracious (-ly), entreat, (be) merciful, have (shew) mercy (on, upon), have pity upon, pray, make supplication, x very.

(2583) pronounced khaw-naw'; a prim. root [comp. 2603]; prop. to incline; by impl. to decline (of the slanting rays of evening); spec. to pitch a tent; gen. to encamp (for abode or siege):- abide (in tents), camp, dwell, encamp, grow to an end, lie, pitch (tent), rest in tent.

And he said to Him, "If I have gained Your favor, give me a sign that it is You who are speaking to me: SHOF'TIM 6:17 (JUDGES 6:17)

And he said unto him, If now I have found grace (2580) in thy sight, then show me a sign that thou talkest with me. JUDGES 6:17

grace (2580) pronounced khane; from 2603; graciousness, i.e. subj. (kindness, favor) or objective (beauty):- favour, grace (-ious), pleasant, precious, [well-] favoured.

(2603) pronounced khaw-nan'; a prim. root {comp. 2583]; prop. to bend or stoop in kindness to an inferior; to favor, bestow; causat. to implore (i.e. to move to favor by petition):- beseech, x fair, (be, find, shew) favour (-able), be (deal, give, grant) gracious (-ly), entreat, (be) merciful, have (shew) mercy (on, upon), have pity upon, pray, make supplication, x very.

(2583) pronounced khaw-naw'; a prim. root [comp. 2603]; prop. to incline; by impl. to decline (of the slanting rays of evening); spec. to pitch a tent; gen. to encamp (for abode or siege):- abide (in tents), camp, dwell, encamp, grow to an end, lie, pitch (tent), rest in tent.

Ruth the Moabite said to Naomi, "I would like to go to the fields and glean among the ears of grain, behind someone who may show me kindness." "Yes, daughter, go", she replied. RUT 2:2 RUTH 2:2

And Ruth the Moabitess said unto Naomi, Let me now go to the field, and glean ears of corn after *him* in whose sight I shall find grace (2580). And she said unto her, Go, my daughter. RUTH 2:2

grace (2580) pronounced khane; from 2603; graciousness, i.e. subj. (kindness, favor) or objective (beauty):- favour, grace (-ious), pleasant, precious, [well-] favoured.

(2603) pronounced khaw-nan'; a prim. root {comp. 2583]; prop. to bend or stoop in kindness to an inferior; to favor, bestow; causat. to implore (i.e. to move to favor by petition):- beseech, x fair, (be, find, shew) favour (-able), be (deal, give, grant) gracious (-ly), entreat, (be) merciful, have (shew) mercy (on, upon), have pity upon, pray, make supplication, x very.

> (2583) pronounced khaw-naw'; a prim. root [comp. 2603]; prop. to incline; by impl. to decline (of the slanting rays of evening); spec. to pitch a tent; gen. to encamp (for abode or siege):- abide (in tents), camp, dwell, encamp, grow to an end, lie, pitch (tent), rest in tent.

She prostrated herself with her face to the ground, and said to him, "Why are you so kind as to single me out, when I am a foreigner?" RUT 2:10 (RUTH 2:10)

Then she fell on her face, and bowed herself to the ground, and said unto him, Why have I *found* grace (2580) in thine eyes, that thou shouldest take knowledge of me, seeing I *am* a stranger? RUTH 2:10

> grace (2580) pronounced khane; from 2603; graciousness, i.e. subj. (kindness, favor) or objective (beauty):- favour, grace (-ious), pleasant, precious, [well-] favoured.

> (2603) pronounced khaw-nan'; a prim. root {comp. 2583]; prop. to bend or stoop in kindness to an inferior; to favor, bestow; causat. to implore (i.e. to move to favor by petition):- beseech, x fair, (be, find, shew) favour (-able), be (deal, give, grant) gracious (-ly), entreat, (be) merciful, have (shew) mercy (on, upon), have pity upon, pray, make supplication, x very.

> (2583) pronounced khaw-naw'; a prim. root [comp. 2603]; prop. to incline; by impl. to decline (of the slanting rays of evening); spec. to pitch a tent; gen. to encamp (for abode or siege):- abide (in tents), camp, dwell, encamp, grow to an end, lie, pitch (tent), rest in tent.

"Then go in peace," said Eli, "and may the God of Israel grant you what you have asked of Him." She answered, "You are most kind to your handmaid." So the woman left, and she ate, and was no longer downcast. SH'MU'EL ALEF 1:17-18 (I SAMUEL 1:17-18)

Then Eli answered and said, Go in peace: and the God of Israel grant *thee* thy petition that thou hast asked of him. And she said, Let thine handmaid find grace (2580) in thy sight. So the woman went her way, and did eat, and her countenance was no more *sad*. I SAMUEL 1:17-18

> grace (2580) pronounced khane; from 2603; graciousness, i.e. subj. (kindness, favor) or objective (beauty):- favour, grace (-ious), pleasant, precious, [well-] favoured.

> (2603) pronounced khaw-nan'; a prim. root {comp. 2583]; prop. to bend or stoop in kindness to an inferior; to favor, bestow; causat. to implore (i.e. to move to favor by petition):- beseech, x fair, (be, find, shew) favour (-able), be (deal, give, grant) gracious (-ly), entreat, (be) merciful, have (shew) mercy (on, upon), have pity upon, pray, make supplication, x very.

> (2583) pronounced khaw-naw'; a prim. root [comp. 2603]; prop. to incline; by impl. to decline (of the slanting rays of evening); spec. to pitch a tent; gen. to encamp (for abode or siege):- abide (in tents), camp, dwell, encamp, grow to an end, lie, pitch (tent), rest in tent.

David swore further, "Your father knows well that you are fond of me and has decided: Jonathan must not learn of this or he will be grieved. But, as the LORD lives and as you live, there is only a step between me and death." SH'MU'EL ALEF 20:3 (I SAMUEL 20:3)

And David sware moreover, and said, Thy father certainly knoweth that I have found grace (2580) in thine eyes; and he saith, Let not Jonathan know this, lest he be grieved: but truly, as the LORD liveth, and *as* thy soul liveth, *there is but* a step between me and death. I SAMUEL 20:3

> grace (2580) pronounced khane; from 2603; graciousness, i.e. subj. (kindness, favor) or objective (beauty):- favour, grace (-ious), pleasant, precious, [well-] favoured.
>
> (2603) pronounced khaw-nan'; a prim. root {comp. 2583]; prop. to bend or stoop in kindness to an inferior; to favor, bestow; causat. to implore (i.e. to move to favor by petition):- beseech, x fair, (be, find, shew) favour (-able), be (deal, give, grant) gracious (-ly), entreat, (be) merciful, have (shew) mercy (on, upon), have pity upon, pray, make supplication, x very.
>
> (2583) pronounced khaw-naw'; a prim. root [comp. 2603]; prop. to incline; by impl. to decline (of the slanting rays of evening); spec. to pitch a tent; gen. to encamp (for abode or siege):- abide (in tents), camp, dwell, encamp, grow to an end, lie, pitch (tent), rest in tent.

David said to Achish, "If you please, let a place be granted me in one of the country towns where I can live; why should your servant remain with you in the royal city?" SH'MU'EL ALEF 27:5 (I SAMUEL 27:5)

And David said unto Achish, If I have now found grace (2580) in thine eyes, let them give me a place in some town in the country, that I may dwell there: for why should thy servant dwell in the royal city with thee? I SAMUEL 27:5

> grace (2580) pronounced khane; from 2603; graciousness, i.e. subj. (kindness, favor) or objective (beauty):- favour, grace (-ious), pleasant, precious, [well-] favoured.
>
> (2603) pronounced khaw-nan'; a prim. root {comp. 2583]; prop. to bend or stoop in kindness to an inferior; to favor, bestow; causat. to implore (i.e. to move to favor by petition):- beseech, x fair, (be, find, shew) favour (-able), be (deal, give, grant) gracious (-ly), entreat, (be) merciful, have (shew) mercy (on, upon), have pity upon, pray, make supplication, x very.
>
> (2583) pronounced khaw-naw'; a prim. root [comp. 2603]; prop. to incline; by impl. to decline (of the slanting rays of evening); spec. to pitch a tent; gen. to encamp (for abode or siege):- abide (in tents), camp, dwell, encamp, grow to an end, lie, pitch (tent), rest in tent.

Joab flung himself face down on the ground and prostrated himself. Joab blessed the king and said, "Today your servant knows that he has found favor with you, my lord king, for Your Majesty has granted his servant's request." SH'MU'EL BET 14:22 (II SAMUEL 14:22)

And Joab fell to the ground on his face, and bowed himself, and thanked the king: and Joab said, Today thy servant knoweth that I have found grace (2580) in thy sight, my lord, O king, in that the king hath fulfilled the request of his servant. II SAMUEL 14:22

> grace (2580) pronounced khane; from 2603; graciousness, i.e. subj. (kindness, favor) or objective (beauty):- favour, grace (-ious), pleasant, precious, [well-] favoured.

(2603) pronounced khaw-nan'; a prim. root {comp. 2583]; prop. to bend or stoop in kindness to an inferior; to favor, bestow; causat. to implore (i.e. to move to favor by petition):- beseech, x fair, (be, find, shew) favour (-able), be (deal, give, grant) gracious (-ly), entreat, (be) merciful, have (shew) mercy (on, upon), have pity upon, pray, make supplication, x very.

(2583) pronounced khaw-naw'; a prim. root [comp. 2603]; prop. to incline; by impl. to decline (of the slanting rays of evening); spec. to pitch a tent; gen. to encamp (for abode or siege):- abide (in tents), camp, dwell, encamp, grow to an end, lie, pitch (tent), rest in tent.

The king said to Ziba, "Then all that belongs to Mephibosheth is now yours!" And Ziba replied, "I bow low. Your Majesty is most gracious to me." SH'MU'EL BET 16:4 (IISAMUEL 16:4)

Then said the king to Ziba, Behold, thine *are* all that *pertained* unto Mephibosheth, And Ziba said, I humbly beseech thee *that* I may find grace (2580) in thy sight, my lord, O king. II SAMUEL 16:4

grace (2580) pronounced khane; from 2603; graciousness, i.e. subj. (kindness, favor) or objective (beauty):- favour, grace (-ious), pleasant, precious, [well-] favoured.

(2603) pronounced khaw-nan'; a prim. root {comp. 2583]; prop. to bend or stoop in kindness to an inferior; to favor, bestow; causat. to implore (i.e. to move to favor by petition):- beseech, x fair, (be, find, shew) favour (-able), be (deal, give, grant) gracious (-ly), entreat, (be) merciful, have (shew) mercy (on, upon), have pity upon, pray, make supplication, x very.

(2583) pronounced khaw-naw'; a prim. root [comp. 2603]; prop. to incline; by impl. to decline (of the slanting rays of evening); spec. to pitch a tent; gen. to encamp (for abode or siege):- abide (in tents), camp, dwell, encamp, grow to an end, lie, pitch (tent), rest in tent.

But now, for a short while, there has been a reprieve from the LORD our God, who has granted us a surviving remnant and given us a stake in His holy place; our God has restored the luster to our eyes and furnished us with a little sustenance in our bondage. 'EZRA 9:8 (EZRA 9:8)

And now for a little space grace (8467) hath been *shown* from the LORD our God, to leave us a remnant to escape, and to give us a nail in his holy place, that our God may lighten *our* eyes, and give us a little reviving in our bondage. EZRA 9:8

grace (8467) pronounced tekh-in-naw'; from 2603; graciousness; caus. entreaty:- favour, grace, supplication.

(2603) pronounced khaw-nan'; a prim. root {comp. 2583]; prop. to bend or stoop in kindness to an inferior; to favor, bestow; causat. to implore (i.e. to move to favor by petition):- beseech, x fair, (be, find, shew) favour (-able), be (deal, give, grant) gracious (-ly), entreat, (be) merciful, have (shew) mercy (on, upon), have pity upon, pray, make supplication, x very.

(2583) pronounced khaw-naw'; a prim. root [comp. 2603]; prop. to incline; by impl. to decline (of the slanting rays of evening); spec. to pitch a tent; gen. to encamp (for abode or siege):- abide (in tents), camp, dwell, encamp, grow to an end, lie, pitch (tent), rest in tent.

The king loved Esther more than all the other women, and she won his grace and favor more than all the virgins. So he set a royal diadem on her head, and made her queen instead of Vashti. ESTER 2:17 (ESTHER 2:17)

And the king loved Esther above all the women, and she obtained grace (2580) and favour in his sight more than all the virgins; so that he set the royal crown upon her head, and made her queen instead of Vashti. ESTHER 2:17

grace (2580) pronounced khane; from 2603; graciousness, i.e. subj. (kindness, favor) or objective (beauty):- favour, grace (-ious), pleasant, precious, [well-] favoured.

(2603) pronounced khaw-nan'; a prim. root {comp. 2583]; prop. to bend or stoop in kindness to an inferior; to favor, bestow; causat. to implore (i.e. to move to favor by petition):- beseech, x fair, (be, find, shew) favour (-able), be (deal, give, grant) gracious (-ly), entreat, (be) merciful, have (shew) mercy (on, upon), have pity upon, pray, make supplication, x very.

(2583) pronounced khaw-naw'; a prim. root [comp. 2603]; prop. to incline; by impl. to decline (of the slanting rays of evening); spec. to pitch a tent; gen. to encamp (for abode or siege):- abide (in tents), camp, dwell, encamp, grow to an end, lie, pitch (tent), rest in tent.

My heart is astir with gracious words; I speak my poem to a king; my tongue is the pen of an expert scribe. You are fairer than all men; your speech is endowed with grace; rightly has God given you an eternal blessing. TEHILLIM 45:2-3 (PSALMS 45:1-2)

My heart is inditing a good matter: I speak of the things which I have made touching the King: my tongue *is* the pen of a ready writer. Thou art fairer than the children of men: grace (2580) is poured into thy lips: therefore God hath blessed thee forever. PSALMS 45:1-2

grace (2580) pronounced khane; from 2603; graciousness, i.e. subj. (kindness, favor) or objective (beauty):- favour, grace (-ious), pleasant, precious, [well-] favoured.

(2603) pronounced khaw-nan'; a prim. root {comp. 2583]; prop. to bend or stoop in kindness to an inferior; to favor, bestow; causat. to implore (i.e. to move to favor by petition):- beseech, x fair, (be, find, shew) favour (-able), be (deal, give, grant) gracious (-ly), entreat, (be) merciful, have (shew) mercy (on, upon), have pity upon, pray, make supplication, x very.

(2583) pronounced khaw-naw'; a prim. root [comp. 2603]; prop. to incline; by impl. to decline (of the slanting rays of evening); spec. to pitch a tent; gen. to encamp (for abode or siege):- abide (in tents), camp, dwell, encamp, grow to an end, lie, pitch (tent), rest in tent.

GRACE

For the LORD God is sun and shield; the LORD bestows grace and glory; He does not withhold His bounty from those who live without blame. TEHILLIM 84:12 (PSALMS 84:11)

sun: Or "have forgiven." (TANAKH footnote)

For the LORD God *is* a sun and shield: the LORD will give grace (2580) and glory: no good *thing* will he withhold from them that walk uprightly. PSALMS 84:11

grace (2580) pronounced khane; from 2603; graciousness, i.e. subj. (kindness, favor) or objective (beauty):- favour, grace (-ious), pleasant, precious, [well-] favoured.

(2603) pronounced khaw-nan'; a prim. root {comp. 2583]; prop. to bend or stoop in kindness to an inferior; to favor, bestow; causat. to implore (i.e. to move to favor by petition):- beseech, x fair, (be, find, shew) favour (-able), be (deal, give, grant) gracious (-ly), entreat, (be) merciful, have (shew) mercy (on, upon), have pity upon, pray, make supplication, x very.

(2583) pronounced khaw-naw'; a prim. root [comp. 2603]; prop. to incline; by impl. to decline (of the slanting rays of evening); spec. to pitch a tent; gen. to encamp (for abode or siege):- abide (in tents), camp, dwell, encamp, grow to an end, lie, pitch (tent), rest in tent.

My son, heed the discipline of your father, and do not forsake the instruction of your mother; for they are a graceful wreath upon your head, a necklace about your throat. MISHLEI 1:8-9 (PROVERBS 1:8-9)

My son, hear the instruction of thy father, and forsake not the law of thy mother: for they *shall be* an ornament of grace (2580) unto thy head, and chains about thy neck. PROVERBS 1:8-9

grace (2580) pronounced khane; from 2603; graciousness, i.e. subj. (kindness, favor) or objective (beauty):- favour, grace (-ious), pleasant, precious, [well-] favoured.

(2603) pronounced khaw-nan'; a prim. root {comp. 2583]; prop. to bend or stoop in kindness to an inferior; to favor, bestow; causat. to implore (i.e. to move to favor by petition):- beseech, x fair, (be, find, shew) favour (-able), be (deal, give, grant) gracious (-ly), entreat, (be) merciful, have (shew) mercy (on, upon), have pity upon, pray, make supplication, x very.

(2583) pronounced khaw-naw'; a prim. root [comp. 2603]; prop. to incline; by impl. to decline (of the slanting rays of evening); spec. to pitch a tent; gen. to encamp (for abode or siege):- abide (in tents), camp, dwell, encamp, grow to an end, lie, pitch (tent), rest in tent.

My son, do not lose sight of them; hold on to resourcefulness and foresight. They will give life to your spirit and grace to your throat. MISHLEI 3:21-22 (PROVERBS 3:21-22)

My son, let not them depart from thine eyes: keep sound wisdom and discretion: so shall they be life unto thy soul, and grace (2580) to thy neck. PROVERBS 3:21-22

grace (2580) pronounced khane; from 2603; graciousness, i.e. subj. (kindness, favor) or objective (beauty):- favour, grace (-ious), pleasant, precious, [well-] favoured.

(2603) pronounced khaw-nan'; a prim. root {comp. 2583]; prop. to bend or stoop in kindness to an inferior; to favor, bestow; causat. to implore (i.e. to move to favor by petition):- beseech, x fair, (be, find, shew) favour (-able), be (deal, give, grant) gracious (-ly), entreat, (be) merciful, have (shew) mercy (on, upon), have pity upon, pray, make supplication, x very.

(2583) pronounced khaw-naw'; a prim. root [comp. 2603]; prop. to incline; by impl. to decline (of the slanting rays of evening); spec. to pitch a tent; gen. to encamp (for abode or siege):- abide (in tents), camp, dwell, encamp, grow to an end, lie, pitch (tent), rest in tent.

At scoffers He scoffs, but to the lowly He shows grace. MISHLEI 3:34 (PROVERBS 3:34)

Surely He scorneth the scorners: but He giveth grace (2580) unto the lowly. PROVERBS 3:34

grace (2580) pronounced khane; from 2603; graciousness, i.e. subj. (kindness, favor) or objective (beauty):- favour, grace (-ious), pleasant, precious, [well-] favoured.

(2603) pronounced khaw-nan'; a prim. root {comp. 2583]; prop. to bend or stoop in kindness to an inferior; to favor, bestow; causat. to implore (i.e. to move to favor by petition):- beseech, x fair, (be, find, shew) favour (-able), be (deal, give, grant) gracious (-ly), entreat, (be) merciful, have (shew) mercy (on, upon), have pity upon, pray, make supplication, x very.

(2583) pronounced khaw-naw'; a prim. root [comp. 2603]; prop. to incline; by impl. to decline (of the slanting rays of evening); spec. to pitch a tent; gen. to encamp (for abode or siege):- abide (in tents), camp, dwell, encamp, grow to an end, lie, pitch (tent), rest in tent.

The beginning of wisdom is acquire wisdom; with all your acquisitions, acquire discernment. Hug her to you and she will exalt you; she will bring you honor if you embrace her. She will adorn your head with a graceful wreath; crown you with a glorious diadem. MISHLEI 4:7-9 (PROVERBS 4:7-9)

beginning: Or "best part." (TANAKH footnote)

Wisdom is the principal thing; *therefore* get wisdom: and with all thy getting get understanding. Exalt her, and she shall promote thee: she shall bring thee to honour when thou dost embrace her. She shall give to thine head an ornament of grace (2580); a crown of glory shall she deliver to thee.
PROVERBS 4:7-9

grace (2580) pronounced khane; from 2603; graciousness, i.e. subj. (kindness, favor) or objective (beauty):- favour, grace (-ious), pleasant, precious, [well-] favoured.

(2603) pronounced khaw-nan'; a prim. root {comp. 2583]; prop. to bend or stoop in kindness to an inferior; to favor, bestow; causat. to implore (i.e. to move to favor by petition):- beseech, x fair, (be, find, shew) favour (-able), be (deal, give, grant) gracious (-ly), entreat, (be) merciful, have (shew) mercy (on, upon), have pity upon, pray, make supplication, x very.

(2583) pronounced khaw-naw'; a prim. root [comp. 2603]; prop. to incline; by impl. to decline (of the slanting rays of evening); spec. to pitch a tent; gen. to encamp (for abode or siege):- abide (in tents), camp, dwell, encamp, grow to an end, lie, pitch (tent), rest in tent.

A pure-hearted friend, his speech is gracious; he has the king for his companion. MISHLEI 22:11 (PROVERBS 22:11)

He that loveth pureness of heart, for the grace (2580) of his lips the king *shall be* his friend. PROVERBS 22:11

grace (2580) pronounced khane; from 2603; graciousness, i.e. subj. (kindness, favor) or objective (beauty):- favour, grace (-ious), pleasant, precious, [well-] favoured.

(2603) pronounced khaw-nan'; a prim. root {comp. 2583]; prop. to bend or stoop in kindness to an inferior; to favor, bestow; causat. to implore (i.e. to move to favor by petition):- beseech, x fair, (be, find, shew) favour (-able), be (deal, give, grant) gracious (-ly), entreat, (be) merciful, have (shew) mercy (on, upon), have pity upon, pray, make supplication, x very.

(2583) pronounced khaw-naw'; a prim. root [comp. 2603]; prop. to incline; by impl. to decline (of the slanting rays of evening); spec. to pitch a tent; gen. to encamp (for abode or siege):- abide (in tents), camp, dwell, encamp, grow to an end, lie, pitch (tent), rest in tent.

Thus said the LORD: The people escaped from the sword, found favor in the wilderness; when Israel was marching homeward. YIRMEYAHU 31:2 (JEREMIAH 31:2)

Thus saith the LORD, The people *which were* left of the sword found grace (2580) in the wilderness; *even* Israel, when I went to cause him to rest. JEREMIAH 31:2

grace (2580) pronounced khane; from 2603; graciousness, i.e. subj. (kindness, favor) or objective (beauty):- favour, grace (-ious), pleasant, precious, [well-] favoured.

(2603) pronounced khaw-nan'; a prim. root {comp. 2583]; prop. to bend or stoop in kindness to an inferior; to favor, bestow; causat. to implore (i.e. to move to favor by petition):- beseech, x fair, (be, find, shew) favour (-able), be (deal, give, grant) gracious (-ly), entreat, (be) merciful, have (shew) mercy (on, upon), have pity upon, pray, make supplication, x very.

(2583) pronounced khaw-naw'; a prim. root [comp. 2603]; prop. to incline; by impl. to decline (of the slanting rays of evening); spec. to pitch a tent; gen. to encamp (for abode or siege):- abide (in tents), camp, dwell, encamp, grow to an end, lie, pitch (tent), rest in tent.

Whoever you are, O great mountain in the path of Zerubbabel, turn into level ground! For he shall produce that excellent stone; it shall be greeted with shouts of "Beautiful! Beautiful!" Z'KHARYAH 4:7 (ZECHARIAH 4:7)

Who *art* thou, O great mountain? before Zerubbabel *thou shalt become* a plain: and he shall bring forth the headstone *thereof* with shoutings, *crying* Grace (2580), grace unto it. ZECHARIAH 4:7

> grace (2580) pronounced khane; from 2603; graciousness, i.e. subj. (kindness, favor) or objective (beauty):- favour, grace (-ious), pleasant, precious, [well-] favoured.
>
> (2603) pronounced khaw-nan'; a prim. root {comp. 2583]; prop. to bend or stoop in kindness to an inferior; to favor, bestow; causat. to implore (i.e. to move to favor by petition):- beseech, x fair, (be, find, shew) favour (-able), be (deal, give, grant) gracious (-ly), entreat, (be) merciful, have (shew) mercy (on, upon), have pity upon, pray, make supplication, x very.
>
> (2583) pronounced khaw-naw'; a prim. root [comp. 2603]; prop. to incline; by impl. to decline (of the slanting rays of evening); spec. to pitch a tent; gen. to encamp (for abode or siege):- abide (in tents), camp, dwell, encamp, grow to an end, lie, pitch (tent), rest in tent.

In that day I will all but annihilate all the nations that came up against Jerusalem. But I will fill the House of David and the inhabitants of Jerusalem with a spirit of pity and compassion: and they shall lament to Me about those who are slain, wailing over them as over a favorite son and showing bitter grief as over a first-born. Z'KHARYAH 12:9-10 (ZECHARIAH 12:9-10)

> All but annihilate: For the idiom cf. Gen. 43.30; it is also attested in post biblical Hebrew (TANAKH footnote)
>
> > With that, Joseph hurried out, for he was overcome with feeling toward his brother and was on the verge of tears; he went into a room and wept there. B'RESHEET 43:30 (GENESIS 43:30)
> >
> > And Joseph made haste; for his bowels did yearn upon his brother: and he sought *where to weep*; and he entered into *his* chamber, and wept there. GENESIS 43:30

And it shall come to pass in that day, *that* I will seek to destroy all the nations that come against Jerusalem. And I will pour upon the house of David, and upon the inhabitants of Jerusalem, the spirit of grace (2580) and of supplications; and they shall look upon me whom they have pierced, and they shall mourn for him, as one mourneth for *his* only *son,* and shall be in bitterness for him, as one that is in bitterness for *his* firstborn. ZECHARIAH 12:9-10

> grace (2580) pronounced khane; from 2603; graciousness, i.e. subj. (kindness, favor) or objective (beauty):- favour, grace (-ious), pleasant, precious, [well-] favoured.
>
> (2603) pronounced khaw-nan'; a prim. root {comp. 2583]; prop. to bend or stoop in kindness to an inferior; to favor, bestow; causat. to implore (i.e. to move to favor by petition):- beseech, x fair, (be, find, shew) favour (-able), be (deal, give, grant) gracious (-ly), entreat, (be) merciful, have (shew) mercy (on, upon), have pity upon, pray, make supplication, x very.
>
> (2583) pronounced khaw-naw'; a prim. root [comp. 2603]; prop. to incline; by impl. to decline (of the slanting rays of evening); spec. to pitch a tent; gen. to encamp (for abode or siege):- abide (in tents), camp, dwell, encamp, grow to an end, lie, pitch (tent), rest in tent.

Book Four

Walking the Same Sure Foundation of Mercy

Introduction

This is the fourth of five books in a mini-series with a unique purpose. Each book provides a verse to verse comparison of *TANAKH THE HOLY SCRIPTURES (hereafter referred to as Tanakh), and the AUTHORIZED KING JAMES VERSION (Old Testament only, hereafter referred to as KJV)* on a particular subject. The subject of Book One is *SALVATION;* Book Two is *RIGHTEOUSNESS;* Book Three is *GRACE.* Book Four, *MERCY,* provides references from *TANAKH* footnotes and *STRONG'S CONCORDANCE.* Readers will quickly discover that all spiritual concepts presented on the following pages have physical actions that can be observed and experienced. This series is about relationship, not religion.

Each of the five books are in the same order and format for ease of use. Format, as well as use of *TANAKH* footnotes and *STRONG'S CONCORDANCE* will be discussed in the section *How This Book is Organized.* Yeshua (Jesus) spoke about each of these subjects often before the New Testament was written. Modern-day readers who grasp these truths will be able to understand the teachings of the New Testament in the same way as people of Yeshua's (Jesus's) generation.

How This Book is Organized

TANAKH verse followed by TANAKH reference (each letter capitalized) with corresponding KJV reference (also capitalized) in parenthesis. Sometimes numbers will not match exactly but will be close. TANAKH reference will be highlighted in gray.

Example:

Therefore, O king, may my advice be acceptable to you. Redeem your sins by beneficence and your iniquities by generosity to the poor; then your serenity may be extended." DANI'EL 4:24 (DANIEL 4:27)

Spelling of highlighted *TANAKH* references is the same as the *COMPLETE JEWISH BIBLE* throughout the book to maintain its sense of Jewishness. Refer to *Works Cited* for additional information.

KJV will include the word mercy followed by a highlighted number in parenthesis within the verse. The highlighted number will be a reference number to *STRONG'S CONCORDANCE* (original Hebrew or Chaldee). The verse will be followed by the highlighted KJV reference only. Words in italic in the original text will be in italics. Archaic spelling of words will also be presented as the original authors intended.

Example:

Wherefore, O king, let my counsel be acceptable unto thee, and break off thy sins by righteousness, and thine iniquities by showing mercy (2604) to the poor; if it may be a lengthening of thy tranquility. DANIEL 4:27

> mercy (2604) (Chald.) pronounced khan-an'; corresp. to 2603; to favor or (causat.) entreat:- shew mercy; make supplication.

Pronunciation is provided with the complete definition shown in STRONG'S CONCORDANCE. Readers will notice a second highlighted number in the above example. This is the primitive root word. It will be shown with pronunciation and complete definition by STRONG'S CONCORDANCE also.

The primitive root will generally be listed last unless it is the only reference or the first of several references. The number of the root will be indented, under the verse, lining up with the first reference.

Example:

> mercy (2604) ...
>
> (2603) pronounced khaw-nan'; a prim. root [comp. 2583]; prop. to bend or stoop in kindness to an inferior, to favor, bestow; causat. to implore (i.e. to move to favor by petition):- beseech, x fair, (be, find, shew) favour (-able), be (deal, give, grant) gracious (-ly), entreat (be) merciful, have (shew) mercy (on, upon), have pity upon, pray, make supplication, x very.
>
> (2583) pronounced khaw-naw'; a prim. root [comp. 2603]; prop. to incline; by impl. to decline (of the slanting rays of evening); spec. to pitch a tent; gen. to encamp (for abode or siege): abide (in tents), camp, dwell, encamp, grow to an end, lie, pitch (tent), rest in tent.

In this instance, the root word has a second highlighted number which is also a primitive root and is there for comparison.

Abbreviations such as prop. and causat. will be identified in *Abbreviations Employed,* the next section of the book.

Occasionally, footnotes will be provided in TANAKH. When this occurs, the footnote will be noted exactly as referenced. If scripture references are available, they will also be included in the same format as above so that readers may be able to have immediate access to as much information as possible without turning pages.

The first of two examples below supplies a literal explanation as to how the original context would have been understood by its listeners.

He said, "Oh, let me behold Your Presence!" And he answered, "I will make all My goodness pass before you, and I will proclaim before you the name LORD, and the grace that I grant and the compassion that I show." SH'MOT 33:18-19 (EXODUS 33:18-19)

and the grace that I grant and the compassion that I show: Lit. "and I will grant the grace that I will grant and show the compassion that I will show." (TANAKH footnote).

The second example directs the reader's attention to additional scripture for more information.

You came only yesterday; should I make you wander about with us today, when I myself must go wherever I can? Go back, and take your kinsmen with you, [in] true faithfulness." SH'MU'EL BET 15:20 (II SAMUEL 15:20)

[in] true faithfulness: Meaning of Heb. uncertain. Septuagint reads "and may the LORD show you" (c.f., e.g., 2.6). (TANAKH footnote)

May the LORD in turn show you true faithfulness and I too will reward you generously because you performed this act. SH'MU'EL BET 2:6 (II SAMUEL 2:6)

And now the LORD show kindness and truth unto you, and I also will requite you this kindness, because ye have done this thing. II SAMUEL 2:6

KJV reference will always be added for comparison and continuity of the TANAKH footnote before continuing on to the corresponding KJV. In this example, II SAMUEL 15:20 will be the next entry.

Abbreviations Employed

Caus., causat.: causative, causatively

Cf.: confer, compare

Chald.: Chaldee, Chaldaism

Comp.: compare, comparative, comparatively, comparison

Corr., corresp.: corresponding, correspondingly

e.g.: exempli gratia, for example

esp., espec.: especial, especially

euph., euphem.: euphemism, euphemistic, euphemistically

ext., extens.: extension

fig.: figurative, figuratively

gen.: general, generally, generical, generically

Heb.: Hebrew, Hebraism

i.e.: id est, that is

impl.: implication, implied

lit.: literal, literally

opp.: opposed, opposite

perh.: perhaps

pl., plur.: plural

prim.: primitive, primary

prop.: proper, properly

spec.: specific, specifically

subj.: subject, subjective, subjectively

You have been so gracious to your servant, and have already shown me so much kindness in order to save my life; but I cannot flee to the hills, lest the disaster overtake me and I die. B'RESHEET 19:19 (GENESIS 19:19)

Behold now, thy servant hath found grace in thy sight, and thou hast magnified thy mercy (2617), which thou hast shown unto me in saving my life: and I cannot escape to the mountain, lest some evil take me, and I die. GENESIS 19:19

> mercy (2617) pronounced kheh'-sed; from 2616; kindness: by impl. (toward God) piety; rarely (by opp.) reproof, or (subject.) beauty:- favour, good deed (-liness, -ness), kindly. (loving-) kindness, merciful (kindness), mercy, pity, reproach, wicked thing.
>
> (2616) pronounced khaw-sad'; a prim. root; prop. perh. to bow (the neck only [comp. 2603] in courteousy to an equal); i.e. to be kind, also (by euphem. [comp. 1288] but rarely); to reprove:- shew self merciful, put to shame.
>
> (2603) pronounced khaw-nan'; a prim. root [comp. 2583]; prop. to bend or stoop in kindness to an inferior; to favor, bestow; causat. to implore (i.e. to move to favor by petition):- beseech, x fair, (be, find, shew) favour (-able), be (deal, give, grant) gracious (-ly), entreat (be)merciful, have (shew) mercy (on, upon), have pity upon, pray, make supplication, x very.
>
> (2583) pronounced khaw-naw'; a prim. root [comp. 2603]; prop. to incline; by impl. to decline (of the slanting rays of evening); spec. to pitch a tent; gen. to encamp (for abode or siege): abide (in tents), camp, dwell, encamp, grow to an end, lie, pitch (tent), rest in tent.
>
> (1288) pronounced baw-rak'; a prim. root; to kneel: by impl. to bless God (as an act of adoration), and (vice versa) man (as a benefit); also (by euphemism) to curse (God or the king, as treason):- x abundantly, x altogether, x at all, blaspheme, bless, congratulate, curse, x greatly, x indeed, kneel (down), praise, salute, x still, thank.

The man bowed low in homage to the LORD and said "Blessed be the LORD, the God of my master Abraham, who has not withheld His steadfast faithfulness from my master. For I have been guided on my errand by the LORD, to the house of my master's kinsmen." B'RESHEET 24:26-27 (GENESIS 24:26-27)

And the man bowed down his head, and worshipped the LORD. And he said, Blessed *be* the LORD God of my master Abraham, who hath not left destitute my master of his mercy (2617), and his truth: I *being* in the way, the LORD led me to the house of my master's brethren. GENESIS 24:26-27

> mercy (2617) pronounced kheh'-sed; from 2616; kindness: by impl. (toward God) piety; rarely (by opp.) reproof, or (subject.) beauty:- favour, good deed (-liness, -ness), kindly. (loving-) kindness, merciful (kindness), mercy, pity, reproach, wicked thing.

(2616) pronounced khaw-sad'; a prim. root; prop. perh. to bow (the neck only [comp. 2603] in courteousy to an equal); i.e. to be kind, also (by euphem. [comp. 1288] but rarely); to reprove:- shew self merciful, put to shame.

(2603) pronounced khaw-nan'; a prim. root [comp. 2583]; prop. to bend or stoop in kindness to an inferior; to favor, bestow; causat. to implore (i.e. to move to favor by petition):- beseech, x fair, (be, find, shew) favour (-able), be (deal, give, grant) gracious (-ly), entreat (be)merciful, have (shew) mercy (on, upon), have pity upon, pray, make supplication, x very.

(2583) pronounced khaw-naw'; a prim. root [comp. 2603]; prop. to incline; by impl. to decline (of the slanting rays of evening); spec. to pitch a tent; gen. to encamp (for abode or siege): abide (in tents), camp, dwell, encamp, grow to an end, lie, pitch (tent), rest in tent.

(1288) pronounced baw-rak'; a prim. root; to kneel: by impl. to bless God (as an act of adoration), and (vice versa) man (as a benefit); also (by euphemism) to curse (God or the king, as treason):- x abundantly, x altogether, x at all, blaspheme, bless, congratulate, curse, x greatly, x indeed, kneel (down), praise, salute, x still, thank.

The LORD was with Joseph: He extended kindness to him and disposed the chief jailer favorably toward him. B'RESHEET 39:21 (GENESIS 39:21)

But the LORD was with Joseph, and showed him mercy (2617), and gave him favour in the sight of the keeper of the prison. GENESIS 39:21

mercy (2617) pronounced kheh'-sed; from 2616; kindness: by impl. (toward God) piety; rarely (by opp.) reproof, or (subject.) beauty:- favour, good deed (-liness, -ness), kindly. (loving-) kindness, merciful (kindness), mercy, pity, reproach, wicked thing.

(2616) pronounced khaw-sad'; a prim. root; prop. perh. to bow (the neck only [comp. 2603] in courteousy to an equal); i.e. to be kind, also (by euphem. [comp. 1288] but rarely); to reprove:- shew self merciful, put to shame.

(2603) pronounced khaw-nan'; a prim. root [comp. 2583]; prop. to bend or stoop in kindness to an inferior; to favor, bestow; causat. to implore (i.e. to move to favor by petition):- beseech, x fair, (be, find, shew) favour (-able), be (deal, give, grant) gracious (-ly), entreat (be)merciful, have (shew) mercy (on, upon), have pity upon, pray, make supplication, x very.

(2583) pronounced khaw-naw'; a prim. root [comp. 2603]; prop. to incline; by impl. to decline (of the slanting rays of evening); spec. to pitch a tent; gen. to encamp (for abode or siege): abide (in tents), camp, dwell, encamp, grow to an end, lie, pitch (tent), rest in tent.

(1288) pronounced baw-rak'; a prim. root; to kneel: by impl. to bless God (as an act of adoration), and (vice versa) man (as a benefit); also (by euphemism) to curse (God or the king, as treason):- x abundantly, x altogether, x at all, blaspheme, bless, congratulate, curse, x greatly, x indeed, kneel (down), praise, salute, x still, thank.

And may El Shaddai dispose the man to mercy toward you, that he may release to you your other brother, as well as Benjamin. As for me, if I am to be bereaved, I shall be bereaved. B'RESHEET 43:14 (GENESIS 43:14)

And God Almighty give you mercy (7356) before the man, that he may send away your other brother, and Benjamin. If I be bereaved *of my children*, I am bereaved. GENESIS 43:14

> mercy (7356) pronounced rakh'-am' from 7355; compassion (in the plur.); by extens. the womb (as cherishing the fetus); by impl. a maiden:- bowels, compassion, damsel, tender love, (great, tender) mercy, pity, womb.
>
> (7355) pronounced raw-kham'; a prim. root; to fondle; by impl. to love, espec. to compassionate:- have compassion (on, upon), love, (find, have, obtain, shew) mercy (-iful, on, upon), (have) pity, Ruhamah, x surely.

In Your love You lead the people You redeemed: in Your strength You guide them to Your holy abode. SH'MOT 15:13 (EXODUS 15:13)

Thou in thy mercy (2617) hast led forth the people *which* thou hast redeemed: thou hast guided *them* in thy strength unto thy holy habitation. EXODUS 15:13

> mercy (2617) pronounced kheh'-sed; from 2616; kindness: by impl. (toward God) piety; rarely (by opp.) reproof, or (subject.) beauty:- favour, good deed (-liness, -ness), kindly. (loving-) kindness, merciful (kindness), mercy, pity, reproach, wicked thing.
>
> (2616) pronounced khaw-sad'; a prim. root; prop. perh. to bow (the neck only [comp. 2603] in courteousy to an equal); i.e. to be kind, also (by euphem. [comp. 1288] but rarely); to reprove:- shew self merciful, put to shame.
>
> (2603) pronounced khaw-nan'; a prim. root [comp. 2583]; prop. to bend or stoop in kindness to an inferior; to favor, bestow; causat. to implore (i.e. to move to favor by petition):- beseech, x fair, (be, find, shew) favour (-able), be (deal, give, grant) gracious (-ly), entreat (be)merciful, have (shew) mercy (on, upon), have pity upon, pray, make supplication, x very.
>
> (2583) pronounced khaw-naw'; a prim. root [comp. 2603]; prop. to incline; by impl. to decline (of the slanting rays of evening); spec. to pitch a tent; gen. to encamp (for abode or siege): abide (in tents), camp, dwell, encamp, grow to an end, lie, pitch (tent), rest in tent.
>
> (1288) pronounced baw-rak'; a prim. root; to kneel: by impl. to bless God (as an act of adoration), and (vice versa) man (as a benefit); also (by euphemism) to curse (God or the king, as treason):- x abundantly, x altogether, x at all, blaspheme, bless, congratulate, curse, x greatly, x indeed, kneel (down), praise, salute, x still, thank.

You shall not bow down to them or serve them. For I the LORD your God am an impassioned God, visiting the guilt of the parents upon the children, upon the third and upon the fourth generations of those who reject Me, but showing kindness to the thousandth generation of those who love Me and keep My commandments. SH'MOT 20:5-6 (EXODUS 20:5-6)

Thou shalt not bow down thyself to them, nor serve them: for I the LORD thy God *am* a jealous God, visiting the iniquity of the fathers upon the children unto the third and fourth *generation* of them that hate me; and showing mercy (2617) unto thousands of them that love me, and keep my commandments. EXODUS 20:5-6

> mercy (2617) pronounced kheh'-sed; from 2616; kindness: by impl. (toward God) piety; rarely (by opp.) reproof, or (subject.) beauty:- favour, good deed (-liness, -ness), kindly. (loving-) kindness, merciful (kindness), mercy, pity, reproach, wicked thing.
>
> (2616) pronounced khaw-sad'; a prim. root; prop. perh. to bow (the neck only [comp. 2603] in courteousy to an equal); i.e. to be kind, also (by euphem. [comp. 1288] but rarely); to reprove:- shew self merciful, put to shame.
>
> (2603) pronounced khaw-nan'; a prim. root [comp. 2583]; prop. to bend or stoop in kindness to an inferior; to favor, bestow; causat. to implore (i.e. to move to favor by petition):- beseech, x fair, (be, find, shew) favour (-able), be (deal, give, grant) gracious (-ly), entreat (be)merciful, have (shew) mercy (on, upon), have pity upon, pray, make supplication, x very.
>
> (2583) pronounced khaw-naw'; a prim. root [comp. 2603]; prop. to incline; by impl. to decline (of the slanting rays of evening); spec. to pitch a tent; gen. to encamp (for abode or siege): abide (in tents), camp, dwell, encamp, grow to an end, lie, pitch (tent), rest in tent.
>
> (1288) pronounced baw-rak'; a prim. root; to kneel: by impl. to bless God (as an act of adoration), and (vice versa) man (as a benefit); also (by euphemism) to curse (God or the king, as treason):- x abundantly, x altogether, x at all, blaspheme, bless, congratulate, curse, x greatly, x indeed, kneel (down), praise, salute, x still, thank.

You shall make a cover of pure gold, two and a half cubits long and a cubit and a half wide. Make two cherubim of gold- make them of hammered work- at the two ends of the cover. Make one cherub at one end and the other cherub at the other end; of one piece with the cover shall you make the cherubim at its two ends. The cherubim shall have their wings spread out above, shielding the cover with their wings. They shall confront each other, the faces of the cherubim being turned toward the cover. Place the cover on top of the Ark, after depositing inside the Ark the Pact that I will give you. There I will meet with you, and I will impart to you, from above the cover, from between the two cherubim that are on top of the Ark of the Pact I will give you. There I will meet with you, and I will impart to you, from above the cover, from between the two cherubim that are on top of the Ark of the Pact- all that I will command you concerning the Israelite people. SH'MOT 25:17-22 (EXODUS 25:17-22)

And thou shalt make a mercy seat (3727) of pure gold; two cubits and a half *shall be* the length thereof, and a cubit and a half the breadth thereof. And thou shalt make two cherubim of gold, of beaten work shalt thou make them, in the two ends of the mercy seat (3727). And make one cherub on the one end,

and the other cherub on the other end: *even* of the mercy seat (3727) shall you make the cherubim on the two ends thereof. And the cherubim shall stretch forth *their* wings on high, covering the mercy seat (3727) with their wings, and their faces *shall look* one to another; toward the mercy seat (3727) shall the faces of the cherubim be. And thou shall put the mercy seat (3727) above the ark; and in the ark thou shalt put the testimony that I shall give thee. And there I will meet with thee, and I will commune with thee from above the mercy seat (3727), from between the two cherubim which *are* upon the ark of the testimony, of all *things* which I will give thee in commandment unto the children of Israel.
EXODUS 25:17-22

> mercy seat (3727) pronounced kap-po'-reth; from 3722; a lid (used only of the cover of the sacred Ark):- mercy seat.
>
> (3722) pronounced kaw-far; a prim. root; to cover (spec. with bitumen); fig. to expiate or condone; to placate or cancel:- appease, make (an) atonement, cleanse, disannul, forgive, be merciful, pacify, pardon, to pitch, purge (away), put off, (make) reconcile (-iation).

Place the cover upon the Ark of the Pact in the Holy of Holies. SH'MOT 26:34 (EXODUS26:34)

And thou shalt put the mercy seat (3727) upon the ark of the testimony in the most holy *place*.
EXODUS 26:34

> mercy seat (3727) pronounced kap-po'-reth; from 3722; a lid (used only of the cover of the sacred Ark):- mercy seat.
>
> (3722) pronounced kaw-far; a prim. root; to cover (spec. with bitumen); fig. to expiate or condone; to placate or cancel:- appease, make (an) atonement, cleanse, disannul, forgive, be merciful, pacify, pardon, to pitch, purge (away), put off, (make) reconcile (-iation).

Place it in front of the curtain that is over the Ark of the Pact- in front of the cover that is over the Pact- where I will meet with you. SH'MOT 30:6 (EXODUS 30;6)

And thou shalt put it before the veil that *is* by the ark of the testimony, before the mercy seat (3727), that *is* over the testimony, where I will meet with thee. EXODUS 30:6

> mercy seat (3727) pronounced kap-po'-reth; from 3722; a lid (used only of the cover of the sacred Ark):- mercy seat.
>
> (3722) pronounced kaw-far; a prim. root; to cover (spec. with bitumen); fig. to expiate or condone; to placate or cancel:- appease, make (an) atonement, cleanse, disannul, forgive, be merciful, pacify, pardon, to pitch, purge (away), put off, (make) reconcile (-iation).

the Tent of Meeting, the Ark for the Pact, and the cover upon it, and all the furnishings of the Tent: SH'MOT 31:7 (EXODUS 31:7)

The tabernacle of the congregation, and of the ark of the testimony, and the mercy seat (3727) that is thereupon, and all the furniture of the tabernacle, EXODUS 31:7

mercy seat (3727) pronounced kap-po'-reth; from 3722; a lid (used only of the cover of the sacred Ark):- mercy seat.

(3722) pronounced kaw-far; a prim. root; to cover (spec. with bitumen); fig. to expiate or condone; to placate or cancel:- appease, make (an) atonement, cleanse, disannul, forgive, be merciful, pacify, pardon, to pitch, purge (away), put off, (make) reconcile (-iation).

He said, "Oh, let me behold Your Presence!" And he answered, "I will make all My goodness pass before you, and I will proclaim before you the name LORD, and the grace that I grant and the compassion that I show. " SH'MOT 33:18-19 (EXODUS 33:18-19)

And the grace that I grant and the compassion that I show: Lit: "and I will grant the grace that I will grant and show the compassion that I will show." (TANAKH footnote)

And he said, I beseech thee, show me thy glory. And he said, I will make all my goodness pass before thee, and I will proclaim the name of the LORD before thee; and will be gracious to whom I will be gracious, and will show mercy (7355) on whom I will show mercy (7355). EXODUS 33:18-19

(7355) pronounced raw-kham'; a prim. root; to fondle; by impl. to love, espec. to compassionate:- have compassion (on, upon), love, (find, have, obtain, shew) mercy (-iful, on, upon), (have) pity, Ruhamah, x surely.

The LORD passed before him and proclaimed: "The LORD! The LORD! A God compassionate and gracious, slow to anger, abounding in kindness and faithfulness, extending kindness to the thousandth generation forgiving iniquity, transgression, and sin; yet He does not remit all punishment, but visits the iniquity of parents upon children and children's children, upon the third and fourth generations." SH'MOT 34:6-7 (EXODUS 34:6-7)

The LORD! The LORD! : Or "and the LORD proclaimed: The LORD! A God, compassionate," etc.: cf. Num. 14.17-18. (TANAKH footnote)

Therefore, I pray, let my LORD's forbearance be great, as You have declared, saying, The LORD! slow to anger and abounding in kindness; forgiving iniquity and transgression; yet not remitting all punishment, but visiting the iniquity of fathers upon children, upon the third and fourth generations.
B'MIDBAR 14:17-18 (NUMBERS 14:17-18)

And now, I beseech thee, let the power of my LORD be great, according as thou hast spoken, saying, the LORD is long-suffering, and of great mercy, forgiving iniquity and transgression, and by no means clearing *the guilty*, visiting the iniquity of the fathers upon the children unto the third and fourth *generation.*
NUMBERS 14:17-18

And the LORD passed by before him, and proclaimed, The LORD, The LORD God, merciful (7349) and gracious, long-suffering and abundant in goodness and truth, keeping mercy (2617) for thousands, forgiving iniquity and transgression and sin, and that will by no means clear *the guilty*; visiting the iniquity of the fathers upon the children and upon the children's children unto the third and to the fourth *generation*. EXODUS 34:6-7

merciful (7349) pronounced rakh-oom'; from 7355; compassionate:- full of compassion, merciful.

(7355) pronounced raw-kham'; a prim. root; to fondle; by impl. to love, espec. to compassionate:- have compassion (on, upon), love, (find, have, obtain, shew) mercy (-iful, on, upon), (have) pity, Ruhamah, x surely.

mercy (2617) pronounced kheh'-sed; from 2616; kindness: by impl. (toward God) piety; rarely (by opp.) reproof, or (subject.) beauty:- favour, good deed (-liness, -ness), kindly. (loving-) kindness, merciful (kindness), mercy, pity, reproach, wicked thing.

(2616) pronounced khaw-sad'; a prim. root; prop. perh. to bow (the neck only [comp. 2603] in courteousy to an equal); i.e. to be kind, also (by euphem. [comp. 1288] but rarely); to reprove:- shew self merciful, put to shame.

(2603) pronounced khaw-nan'; a prim. root [comp. 2583]; prop. to bend or stoop in kindness to an inferior; to favor, bestow; causat. to implore (i.e. to move to favor by petition):- beseech, x fair, (be, find, shew) favour (-able), be (deal, give, grant) gracious (-ly), entreat (be)merciful, have (shew) mercy (on, upon), have pity upon, pray, make supplication, x very.

(2583) pronounced khaw-naw'; a prim. root [comp. 2603]; prop. to incline; by impl. to decline (of the slanting rays of evening); spec. to pitch a tent; gen. to encamp (for abode or siege): abide (in tents), camp, dwell, encamp, grow to an end, lie, pitch (tent), rest in tent.

(1288) pronounced baw-rak'; a prim. root; to kneel: by impl. to bless God (as an act of adoration), and (vice versa) man (as a benefit); also (by euphemism) to curse (God or the king, as treason):- x abundantly, x altogether, x at all, blaspheme, bless, congratulate, curse, x greatly, x indeed, kneel (down), praise, salute, x still, thank.

the ark and its poles, the cover, and the curtain for the screen; SH'MOT 35:12 (EXODUS 35:12)

the ark, and the staves thereof, *with* the mercy seat (3727), and the veil of the covering, EXODUS 35:12

mercy seat (3727) pronounced kap-po'-reth; from 3722; a lid (used only of the cover of the sacred Ark):- mercy seat.

(3722) pronounced kaw-far; a prim. root; to cover (spec. with bitumen); fig. to expiate or condone; to placate or cancel:- appease, make (an) atonement, cleanse, disannul, forgive, be merciful, pacify, pardon, to pitch, purge (away), put off, (make) reconcile (-iation).

He made a cover of pure gold, two and a half cubits long and a cubit and a half wide. He made two cherubim of gold; he made them of hammered work, at the two ends of the cover; one cherub at one end and the other cherub at the other end; he made the cherubim of one piece with the cover, at its two ends. The cherubim had their wings spread out above; shielding the cover with their wings. They faced each other; the faces of the cherubim were turned toward the cover. SH'MOT 37:6-9 (EXODUS 37:6-9)

And he made the mercy seat (3727) *of* pure gold: two cubits and a half *was* the length thereof, and one cubit and a half the breadth thereof. And he made two cherubim *of* gold, beaten out of one piece made he them, on the two ends of the mercy seat (3727): one cherub on the end on this side, and another cherub on the *other* end on that side: out of the mercy seat (3727) made he the cherubim on the two ends thereof. And the cherubim spread out *their* wings on high, *and* covered with their wings over the mercy seat (3727), with their faces one to another; *even* to the mercy seatward (3727) were the faces of the cherubim. EXODUS 37:6-9

> mercy seat (3727) pronounced kap-po'-reth; from 3722; a lid (used only of the cover of the sacred Ark):- mercy seat.
>
> (3722) pronounced kaw-far; a prim. root; to cover (spec. with bitumen); fig. to expiate or condone; to placate or cancel:- appease, make (an) atonement, cleanse, disannul, forgive, be merciful, pacify, pardon, to pitch, purge (away), put off, (make) reconcile (-iation).

the Ark of the Pact and its poles, and the cover; SH'MOT 39:35 (EXODUS 39:35)

the ark of the testimony, and the staves thereof, and the mercy seat (3727); EXODUS 39:35

> mercy seat (3727) pronounced kap-po'-reth; from 3722; a lid (used only of the cover of the sacred Ark):- mercy seat.
>
> (3722) pronounced kaw-far; a prim. root; to cover (spec. with bitumen); fig. to expiate or condone; to placate or cancel:- appease, make (an) atonement, cleanse, disannul, forgive, be merciful, pacify, pardon, to pitch, purge (away), put off, (make) reconcile (-iation).

He took the Pact and placed it in the Ark; he fixed the poles to the Ark, placed the cover on top of the Ark, SH'MOT 40:20 (EXODUS 40:20)

And he took and put the testimony into the ark, and set the staves on the ark, and put the mercy seat (3727) above upon the ark: EXODUS 40:20

> mercy seat (3727) pronounced kap-po'-reth; from 3722; a lid (used only of the cover of the sacred Ark):- mercy seat.
>
> (3722) pronounced kaw-far; a prim. root; to cover (spec. with bitumen); fig. to expiate or condone; to placate or cancel:- appease, make (an) atonement, cleanse, disannul, forgive, be merciful, pacify, pardon, to pitch, purge (away), put off, (make) reconcile (-iation).

The LORD said to Moses: "Tell your brother Aaron that he is not to come at will into the Shrine behind the curtain, in front of the cover that is upon the ark, lest he die; for I appear in the cloud over the cover." VAYIKRA 16:2 (LEVITICUS 16:2)

> at will: Lit. "at any time." (TANAKH footnote)

And the LORD said unto Moses, Speak unto Aaron thy brother, that he come not at all times into the holy *place* within the veil before the mercy seat (3727) which is upon the ark; that he die not: for I will appear in the cloud upon the mercy seat (3727). LEVITICUS 16:2

> mercy seat (3727) pronounced kap-po'-reth; from 3722; a lid (used only of the cover of the sacred Ark):- mercy seat.
>
> (3722) pronounced kaw-far; a prim. root; to cover (spec. with bitumen); fig. to expiate or condone; to placate or cancel:- appease, make (an) atonement, cleanse, disannul, forgive, be merciful, pacify, pardon, to pitch, purge (away), put off, (make) reconcile (-iation).

He shall put the incense on the fire before the LORD, so that the cloud from the incense screens the cover that is over [the Ark of] the Pact, lest he die. He shall take some of the blood of the bull and sprinkle it with his finger over the cover on the east side; and in front of the cover he shall sprinkle some of the blood with his finger seven times. He shall then slaughter the people's goat of sin offering, bring its blood behind the curtain, and do with its blood as he has done with the blood of the bull: he shall sprinkle it over the cover and in front of the cover. VAYIKRA 16:13-15 (LEVITICUS 16:13-15)

And he shall put the incense upon the fire before the LORD, that the cloud of the incense may cover the mercy seat (3727) that is upon the testimony, that he die not: and he shall take of the blood of the bullock, and sprinkle it with his finger upon the mercy seat (3727) eastward; and before the mercy seat (3727) shall he sprinkle of the blood with his finger seven times. Then shall he kill the goat of the sin offering, that is for the people, and bring his blood within the veil, and do with that blood as he did with the blood of the bullock, and sprinkle it upon the mercy seat (3727), and before the mercy seat (3727): LEVITICUS 16: 13-15

> mercy seat (3727) pronounced kap-po'-reth; from 3722; a lid (used only of the cover of the sacred Ark):- mercy seat.
>
> (3722) pronounced kaw-far; a prim. root; to cover (spec. with bitumen); fig. to expiate or condone; to placate or cancel:- appease, make (an) atonement, cleanse, disannul, forgive, be merciful, pacify, pardon, to pitch, purge (away), put off, (make) reconcile (-iation).

When Moses went into the Tent of Meeting to speak with Him, he would hear the Voice addressing him from above the cover that was on top of the Ark of the Pact between the two cherubim; thus He spoke to him. B'MIDBAR 7:89 (NUMBERS 7:89)

And when Moses was gone into the tabernacle of the congregation to speak with him, then he heard the voice of one speaking unto him from off the mercy seat (3727) that was upon the ark of testimony from between the two cherubim; and he spake unto him. NUMBERS 7:89

> mercy seat (3727) pronounced kap-po'-reth; from 3722; a lid (used only of the cover of the sacred Ark):- mercy seat.
>
> (3722) pronounced kaw-far; a prim. root; to cover (spec. with bitumen); fig. to expiate or condone; to placate or cancel:- appease, make (an) atonement, cleanse, disannul, forgive, be merciful, pacify, pardon, to pitch, purge (away), put off, (make) reconcile (-iation).

You shall not bow down to them or serve them. For I the LORD your God am an impassioned God, visiting the guilt of the parents upon the children, upon the third and upon the fourth generations of those who reject Me, but showing kindness to the thousandth generation of those who love Me and keep My commandments. D'VARIM 5:9-10 (DEUTERONOMY 5:9-10)

Thou shalt not bow down thyself unto them, nor serve them: for I the LORD thy God *am* a jealous God, visiting the iniquity of the fathers upon the children unto the third and fourth *generation* of them that hate me, and showing mercy (2617) unto thousands of them that love me and keep my commandments. DEUTERONOMY 5:9-10

> mercy (2617) pronounced kheh'-sed; from 2616; kindness: by impl. (toward God) piety; rarely (by opp.) reproof, or (subject.) beauty:- favour, good deed (-liness, -ness), kindly. (loving-) kindness, merciful (kindness), mercy, pity, reproach, wicked thing.
>
> (2616) pronounced khaw-sad'; a prim. root; prop. perh. to bow (the neck only [comp. 2603] in courteousy to an equal); i.e. to be kind, also (by euphem. [comp. 1288] but rarely); to reprove:- shew self merciful, put to shame.
>
> (2603) pronounced khaw-nan'; a prim. root [comp. 2583]; prop. to bend or stoop in kindness to an inferior; to favor, bestow; causat. to implore (i.e. to move to favor by petition):- beseech, x fair, (be, find, shew) favour (-able), be (deal, give, grant) gracious (-ly), entreat (be)merciful, have (shew) mercy (on, upon), have pity upon, pray, make supplication, x very.
>
> (2583) pronounced khaw-naw'; a prim. root [comp. 2603]; prop. to incline; by impl. to decline (of the slanting rays of evening); spec. to pitch a tent; gen. to encamp (for abode or siege): abide (in tents), camp, dwell, encamp, grow to an end, lie, pitch (tent), rest in tent.
>
> (1288) pronounced baw-rak'; a prim. root; to kneel: by impl. to bless God (as an act of adoration), and (vice versa) man (as a benefit); also (by euphemism) to curse (God or the king, as treason):- x abundantly, x altogether, x at all, blaspheme, bless, congratulate, curse, x greatly, x indeed, kneel (down), praise, salute, x still, thank.

When the LORD your God brings you to the land that you are about to enter and possess, and He dislodges many nations before you- the Hittites, Girgashites, Amorites, Canaanites, Perizzites, Hivites, and Jebusites, seven nations much larger than you- and the LORD your God delivers them to you and you defeat them, you must doom them to destruction; grant them no terms and give them no quarter. D'VARIM 7:1-2 (DEUTERONOMY 7:1-2)

When the LORD thy God shall bring thee into the land whither thou goest to possess it, and hath cast out many nations before thee, the Hittites, and the Girgashites, and the Amorites, and the Canaanites, and the Perizzites, and the Hivites, and the Jebusites, seven nations greater and mightier than thou; and when the LORD thy God shall deliver them before thee; thou shalt smite them, and utterly destroy them; thou shalt make no covenant with them, nor show mercy (2603) unto them:
DEUTERONOMY 7:1-2

> mercy (2603) pronounced khaw-nan'; a prim. root [comp. 2583]; prop. to bend or stoop in kindness to an inferior; to favor, bestow; causat. to implore (i.e. to move to favor by petition):- beseech, x fair, (be, find, shew) favour (-able), be (deal, give, grant) gracious (-ly), entreat (be)merciful, have (shew) mercy (on, upon), have pity upon, pray, make supplication, x very.
>
> (2583) pronounced khaw-naw'; a prim. root [comp. 2603]; prop. to incline; by impl. to decline (of the slanting rays of evening); spec. to pitch a tent; gen. to encamp (for abode or siege): abide (in tents), camp, dwell, encamp, grow to an end, lie, pitch (tent), rest in tent.

Know, therefore, that only the LORD your God is God, the steadfast God who keeps His covenant faithfully to the thousandth generation of those who love Him and keep His commandments, but who instantly requites with destruction those who reject Him- never slow with those who reject Him, but requiting them instantly. Therefore, observe faithfully the Instruction- the laws and the rules- with which I charge you today. And if you do obey these rules and observe them carefully, the LORD your God will maintain faithfully for you the covenant that He made on oath with your fathers:
D'VARIM 7:9-12 (DEUTERONOMY 7:9-12)

Know therefore that the LORD thy God, he *is* God, the faithful God, which keepeth covenant and mercy (2617) with them that love him and keep his commandments to a thousand generations; and repayeth them that hate him to their face, to destroy them: he will not be slack to him that hateth him, he will repay him to his face. Thou shalt therefore keep the commandments, and the statutes, and the judgments, which I command thee this day, to do them. Wherefore it shall come to pass, if ye hearken to these judgments, and keep and do them, that the LORD thy God shall keep unto thee the covenant and the mercy (2617) which he sware unto thy fathers: DEUTERONOMY 7:9-12

> mercy (2617) pronounced kheh'-sed; from 2616; kindness: by impl. (toward God) piety; rarely (by opp.) reproof, or (subject.) beauty:- favour, good deed (-liness, -ness), kindly. (loving-) kindness, merciful (kindness), mercy, pity, reproach, wicked thing.
>
> (2616) pronounced khaw-sad'; a prim. root; prop. perh. to bow (the neck only [comp. 2603] in courteousy to an equal); i.e. to be kind, also (by euphem. [comp. 1288] but rarely); to reprove:- shew self merciful, put to shame.

(2603) pronounced khaw-nan'; a prim. root [comp. 2583]; prop. to bend or stoop in kindness to an inferior; to favor, bestow; causat. to implore (i.e. to move to favor by petition):- beseech, x fair, (be, find, shew) favour (-able), be (deal, give, grant) gracious (-ly), entreat (be)merciful, have (shew) mercy (on, upon), have pity upon, pray, make supplication, x very.

(2583) pronounced khaw-naw'; a prim. root [comp. 2603]; prop. to incline; by impl. to decline (of the slanting rays of evening); spec. to pitch a tent; gen. to encamp (for abode or siege): abide (in tents), camp, dwell, encamp, grow to an end, lie, pitch (tent), rest in tent.

(1288) pronounced baw-rak'; a prim. root; to kneel: by impl. to bless God (as an act of adoration), and (vice versa) man (as a benefit); also (by euphemism) to curse (God or the king, as treason):- x abundantly, x altogether, x at all, blaspheme, bless, congratulate, curse, x greatly, x indeed, kneel (down), praise, salute, x still, thank.

---put the inhabitants of that town to the sword and put its cattle to the sword. Doom it and all that is in it to destruction: gather all its spoil into the open square, and burn the town and all its spoil as a holocaust to the LORD your God. And it shall remain an everlasting ruin, never to be rebuilt. Let nothing that has been doomed stick to your hand, in order that the LORD may turn from His blazing anger and show you compassion, and in His compassion increase you as He promised your fathers on oath. D'VARIM 13:16-18 (DEUTERONOMY 13:16-17)

And thou shalt gather all the spoil of it into the midst of the street thereof, and shalt burn with fire the city, and all the spoil thereof every whit, for the LORD thy God: and it shall be a heap forever; it shall not be built again. And there shall cleave nought of the cursed thing to thine hand: that the LORD may turn from the fierceness of his anger, and show thee mercy (7356), and have compassion upon thee, and multiply thee, as he hath sworn unto thy fathers: DEUTERONOMY 13:16-17

mercy (7356) pronounced rakh'-am' from 7355; compassion (in the plur.); by extens. the womb (as cherishing the fetus); by impl. a maiden:- bowels, compassion, damsel, tender love, (great, tender) mercy, pity, womb.

(7355) pronounced raw-kham'; a prim. root; to fondle; by impl. to love, espec. to compassionate:- have compassion (on, upon), love, (find, have, obtain, shew) mercy (-iful, on, upon), (have) pity, Ruhamah, x surely.

While the House of Joseph were scouting at Bethel (the name of the town was formerly Luz.) their patrols saw a man leaving the town. They said to him, "Just show us how to get into the town, and we will treat you kindly." SHOF'TIM 1:23-24 (JUDGES 1:23-24)

And the house of Joseph sent to descry Beth-el. (Now the name of the city before *was* Luz.) And the spies saw a man come forth out of the city, and they said unto him, Show us, we pray thee, the entrance into the city, and we will show thee mercy (2617). JUDGES 1:23-24

mercy (2617) pronounced kheh'-sed; from 2616; kindness: by impl. (toward God) piety; rarely (by opp.) reproof, or (subject.) beauty:- favour, good deed (-liness, -ness), kindly. (loving-) kindness, merciful (kindness), mercy, pity, reproach, wicked thing.

(2616) pronounced khaw-sad'; a prim. root; prop. perh. to bow (the neck only [comp. 2603] in courteousy to an equal); i.e. to be kind, also (by euphem. [comp. 1288] but rarely); to reprove:- shew self merciful, put to shame.

(2603) pronounced khaw-nan'; a prim. root [comp. 2583]; prop. to bend or stoop in kindness to an inferior; to favor, bestow; causat. to implore (i.e. to move to favor by petition):- beseech, x fair, (be, find, shew) favour (-able), be (deal, give, grant) gracious (-ly), entreat (be)merciful, have (shew) mercy (on, upon), have pity upon, pray, make supplication, x very.

(2583) pronounced khaw-naw'; a prim. root [comp. 2603]; prop. to incline; by impl. to decline (of the slanting rays of evening); spec. to pitch a tent; gen. to encamp (for abode or siege): abide (in tents), camp, dwell, encamp, grow to an end, lie, pitch (tent), rest in tent.

(1288) pronounced baw-rak'; a prim. root; to kneel: by impl. to bless God (as an act of adoration), and (vice versa) man (as a benefit); also (by euphemism) to curse (God or the king, as treason):- x abundantly, x altogether, x at all, blaspheme, bless, congratulate, curse, x greatly, x indeed, kneel (down), praise, salute, x still, thank.

I will be a father to him, and he shall be a son to Me. When he does wrong, I will chastise him with the rod of men and the affliction of mortals; but I will never withdraw my favor from him as I withdrew it from Saul whom I removed to make room for you. SH'MU'EL BET 7:14-15 (II SAMUEL 7:14-15)

rod of men and the affliction of mortals: i.e., only as a human father would. (TANAKH footnote)

make room for you: Lit. "from before you." (TANAKH footnote)

I will be his father, and he shall be my son. If he commit iniquity, I will chasten him with the rod of men, and with the stripes of the children of men: but my mercy (2617) shall not depart away from him, as I took *it* from Saul, whom I put away before thee. II SAMUEL 7:14-15

mercy (2617) pronounced kheh'-sed; from 2616; kindness: by impl. (toward God) piety; rarely (by opp.) reproof, or (subject.) beauty:- favour, good deed (-liness, -ness), kindly. (loving-) kindness, merciful (kindness), mercy, pity, reproach, wicked thing.

(2616) pronounced khaw-sad'; a prim. root; prop. perh. to bow (the neck only [comp. 2603] in courteousy to an equal); i.e. to be kind, also (by euphem. [comp. 1288] but rarely); to reprove:- shew self merciful, put to shame.

(2603) pronounced khaw-nan'; a prim. root [comp. 2583]; prop. to bend or stoop in kindness to an inferior; to favor, bestow; causat. to implore (i.e. to move to favor by petition):- beseech,

x fair, (be, find, shew) favour (-able), be (deal, give, grant) gracious (-ly), entreat (be)merciful, have (shew) mercy (on, upon), have pity upon, pray, make supplication, x very.

(2583) pronounced khaw-naw'; a prim. root [comp. 2603]; prop. to incline; by impl. to decline (of the slanting rays of evening); spec. to pitch a tent; gen. to encamp (for abode or siege): abide (in tents), camp, dwell, encamp, grow to an end, lie, pitch (tent), rest in tent.

(1288) pronounced baw-rak'; a prim. root; to kneel: by impl. to bless God (as an act of adoration), and (vice versa) man (as a benefit); also (by euphemism) to curse (God or the king, as treason):- x abundantly, x altogether, x at all, blaspheme, bless, congratulate, curse, x greatly, x indeed, kneel (down), praise, salute, x still, thank.

You came only yesterday; should I make you wander about with us today, when I myself must go wherever I can? Go back, and take your kinsmen with you, [in] true faithfulness." SH'MU'EL BET 15:20 (ii SAMUEL 15:20)

[in] true faithfulness: Meaning of Heb. uncertain. Septuagint reads "and may the LORD show you" (c.f., e.g., 2.6). (TANAKH footnote)

May the LORD in turn show you true faithfulness; and I too will reward you generously because you performed this act. SH'MU'EL BET 2:6 (II SAMUEL 2:6)

And now the LORD show kindness and truth unto you, and I also will requite you this kindness, because ye have done this thing. II SAMUEL 2:6

Whereas thou camest *but* yesterday, should I this day make thee go up and down with us? seeing I go whither I may, return thou, and take back thy brethren: mercy (2617) and truth *be* with thee.
II SAMUEL 15:20

mercy (2617) pronounced kheh'-sed; from 2616; kindness: by impl. (toward God) piety; rarely (by opp.) reproof, or (subject.) beauty:- favour, good deed (-liness, -ness), kindly. (loving-) kindness, merciful (kindness), mercy, pity, reproach, wicked thing.

(2616) pronounced khaw-sad'; a prim. root; prop. perh. to bow (the neck only [comp. 2603] in courteousy to an equal); i.e. to be kind, also (by euphem. [comp. 1288] but rarely); to reprove:- shew self merciful, put to shame.

(2603) pronounced khaw-nan'; a prim. root [comp. 2583]; prop. to bend or stoop in kindness to an inferior; to favor, bestow; causat. to implore (i.e. to move to favor by petition):- beseech, x fair, (be, find, shew) favour (-able), be (deal, give, grant) gracious (-ly), entreat (be)merciful, have (shew) mercy (on, upon), have pity upon, pray, make supplication, x very.

(2583) pronounced khaw-naw'; a prim. root [comp. 2603]; prop. to incline; by impl. to decline (of the slanting rays of evening); spec. to pitch a tent; gen. to encamp (for abode or siege): abide (in tents), camp, dwell, encamp, grow to an end, lie, pitch (tent), rest in tent.

(1288) pronounced baw-rak'; a prim. root; to kneel: by impl. to bless God (as an act of adoration), and (vice versa) man (as a benefit); also (by euphemism) to curse (God or the king, as treason):- x abundantly, x altogether, x at all, blaspheme, bless, congratulate, curse, x greatly, x indeed, kneel (down), praise, salute, x still, thank.

For this I sing Your praise among the nations and hymn Your name: Tower of victory to His king, who deals graciously with His anointed, with David and his offspring evermore. SH'MU'EL BET 22:50-51 (II SAMUEL 22:50-51)

Therefore I will give thanks unto thee, O LORD, among the heathen, and I will sing praises unto thy name. *He is* the tower of salvation for his king: and showeth mercy (2617) to his anointed, unto David, and to his seed for evermore. II SAMUEL 22:50-51

mercy (2617) pronounced kheh'-sed; from 2616; kindness: by impl. (toward God) piety; rarely (by opp.) reproof, or (subject.) beauty:- favour, good deed (-liness, -ness), kindly. (loving-) kindness, merciful (kindness), mercy, pity, reproach, wicked thing.

(2616) pronounced khaw-sad'; a prim. root; prop. perh. to bow (the neck only [comp. 2603] in courteousy to an equal); i.e. to be kind, also (by euphem. [comp. 1288] but rarely); to reprove:- shew self merciful, put to shame.

(2603) pronounced khaw-nan'; a prim. root [comp. 2583]; prop. to bend or stoop in kindness to an inferior; to favor, bestow; causat. to implore (i.e. to move to favor by petition):- beseech, x fair, (be, find, shew) favour (-able), be (deal, give, grant) gracious (-ly), entreat (be)merciful, have (shew) mercy (on, upon), have pity upon, pray, make supplication, x very.

(2583) pronounced khaw-naw'; a prim. root [comp. 2603]; prop. to incline; by impl. to decline (of the slanting rays of evening); spec. to pitch a tent; gen. to encamp (for abode or siege): abide (in tents), camp, dwell, encamp, grow to an end, lie, pitch (tent), rest in tent.

(1288) pronounced baw-rak'; a prim. root; to kneel: by impl. to bless God (as an act of adoration), and (vice versa) man (as a benefit); also (by euphemism) to curse (God or the king, as treason):- x abundantly, x altogether, x at all, blaspheme, bless, congratulate, curse, x greatly, x indeed, kneel (down), praise, salute, x still, thank.

Solomon said, "You dealt most graciously with Your servant my father David, because he walked before You in faithfulness and righteousness and in integrity of heart. You have continued this great kindness to him by giving him a son to occupy his throne, as is now the case. M'LAKHIM ALEF 3:6 (I KINGS 3:6)

And Solomon said, Thou hast shown unto thy servant David my father great mercy (2617), according as he walked before thee in truth, and in righteousness, and in uprightness of heart with thee; and thou hast kept for him this great kindness, that thou hast given him a son to sit on his throne, as *it is* this day. I KINGS 3:6

mercy (2617) pronounced kheh'-sed; from 2616; kindness: by impl. (toward God) piety; rarely (by opp.) reproof, or (subject.) beauty:- favour, good deed (-liness, -ness), kindly. (loving-) kindness, merciful (kindness), mercy, pity, reproach, wicked thing.

(2616) pronounced khaw-sad'; a prim. root; prop. perh. to bow (the neck only [comp. 2603] in courteousy to an equal); i.e. to be kind, also (by euphem. [comp. 1288] but rarely); to reprove:- shew self merciful, put to shame.

(2603) pronounced khaw-nan'; a prim. root [comp. 2583]; prop. to bend or stoop in kindness to an inferior; to favor, bestow; causat. to implore (i.e. to move to favor by petition):- beseech, x fair, (be, find, shew) favour (-able), be (deal, give, grant) gracious (-ly), entreat (be)merciful, have (shew) mercy (on, upon), have pity upon, pray, make supplication, x very.

(2583) pronounced khaw-naw'; a prim. root [comp. 2603]; prop. to incline; by impl. to decline (of the slanting rays of evening); spec. to pitch a tent; gen. to encamp (for abode or siege): abide (in tents), camp, dwell, encamp, grow to an end, lie, pitch (tent), rest in tent.

(1288) pronounced baw-rak'; a prim. root; to kneel: by impl. to bless God (as an act of adoration), and (vice versa) man (as a benefit); also (by euphemism) to curse (God or the king, as treason):- x abundantly, x altogether, x at all, blaspheme, bless, congratulate, curse, x greatly, x indeed, kneel (down), praise, salute, x still, thank.

Then Solomon stood before the altar of the LORD in the presence of the whole community of Israel; he spread the palms of his hands toward heaven and said, "O LORD God of Israel, in the heavens above and on the earth below there is no god like You, who keep Your gracious covenant with Your servants when they walk before You in wholehearted devotion: M'LAKHIM ALEF 8:22-23 (I KINGS 8:22-23)

And Solomon stood before the altar of the LORD in the presence of all the congregation of Israel, and spread forth his hands toward heaven: and he said, LORD God of Israel, *there is* no God like thee, in heaven above, or on earth beneath, who keepest covenant and mercy (2617) with thy servants that walk before thee with all their heart: I KINGS 8:22-23

mercy (2617) pronounced kheh'-sed; from 2616; kindness: by impl. (toward God) piety; rarely (by opp.) reproof, or (subject.) beauty:- favour, good deed (-liness, -ness), kindly. (loving-) kindness, merciful (kindness), mercy, pity, reproach, wicked thing.

(2616) pronounced khaw-sad'; a prim. root; prop. perh. to bow (the neck only [comp. 2603] in courteousy to an equal); i.e. to be kind, also (by euphem. [comp. 1288] but rarely); to reprove:- shew self merciful, put to shame.

(2603) pronounced khaw-nan'; a prim. root [comp. 2583]; prop. to bend or stoop in kindness to an inferior; to favor, bestow; causat. to implore (i.e. to move to favor by petition):- beseech, x fair, (be, find, shew) favour (-able), be (deal, give, grant) gracious (-ly), entreat (be)merciful, have (shew) mercy (on, upon), have pity upon, pray, make supplication, x very.

(2583) pronounced khaw-naw'; a prim. root [comp. 2603]; prop. to incline; by impl. to decline (of the slanting rays of evening); spec. to pitch a tent; gen. to encamp (for abode or siege): abide (in tents), camp, dwell, encamp, grow to an end, lie, pitch (tent), rest in tent.

(1288) pronounced baw-rak'; a prim. root; to kneel: by impl. to bless God (as an act of adoration), and (vice versa) man (as a benefit); also (by euphemism) to curse (God or the king, as treason):- x abundantly, x altogether, x at all, blaspheme, bless, congratulate, curse, x greatly, x indeed, kneel (down), praise, salute, x still, thank.

Praise the LORD for He is good; His steadfast love is eternal. DIVREI-HAYAMIM ALEF 16:34
(I CHRONICLES 16:34)

O give thanks unto the LORD; for *he is* good; for his mercy (2617) *endureth* forever.
I CHRONICLES 16:34)

mercy (2617) pronounced kheh'-sed; from 2616; kindness: by impl. (toward God) piety; rarely (by opp.) reproof, or (subject.) beauty:- favour, good deed (-liness, -ness), kindly. (loving-) kindness, merciful (kindness), mercy, pity, reproach, wicked thing.

(2616) pronounced khaw-sad'; a prim. root; prop. perh. to bow (the neck only [comp. 2603] in courteousy to an equal); i.e. to be kind, also (by euphem. [comp. 1288] but rarely); to reprove:- shew self merciful, put to shame.

(2603) pronounced khaw-nan'; a prim. root [comp. 2583]; prop. to bend or stoop in kindness to an inferior; to favor, bestow; causat. to implore (i.e. to move to favor by petition):- beseech, x fair, (be, find, shew) favour (-able), be (deal, give, grant) gracious (-ly), entreat (be)merciful, have (shew) mercy (on, upon), have pity upon, pray, make supplication, x very.

(2583) pronounced khaw-naw'; a prim. root [comp. 2603]; prop. to incline; by impl. to decline (of the slanting rays of evening); spec. to pitch a tent; gen. to encamp (for abode or siege): abide (in tents), camp, dwell, encamp, grow to an end, lie, pitch (tent), rest in tent.

(1288) pronounced baw-rak'; a prim. root; to kneel: by impl. to bless God (as an act of adoration), and (vice versa) man (as a benefit); also (by euphemism) to curse (God or the king, as treason):- x abundantly, x altogether, x at all, blaspheme, bless, congratulate, curse, x greatly, x indeed, kneel (down), praise, salute, x still, thank.

With them were Heman and Jeduthun and the other selected men designated by name to give praise to the LORD, "For His steadfast love is eternal." DIVREI-HAYAMIM ALEF 16:41 (I CHRONICLES 16:41)

And with them Heman and Jeduthun, and the rest that were chosen, who were expressed by name, to give thanks to the LORD, because his mercy (2617) *endureth* for ever; I CHRONICLES 16:41

mercy (2617) pronounced kheh'-sed; from 2616; kindness: by impl. (toward God) piety; rarely (by opp.) reproof, or (subject.) beauty:- favour, good deed (-liness, -ness), kindly. (loving-) kindness, merciful (kindness), mercy, pity, reproach, wicked thing.

(2616) pronounced khaw-sad'; a prim. root; prop. perh. to bow (the neck only [comp. 2603] in courteousy to an equal); i.e. to be kind, also (by euphem. [comp. 1288] but rarely); to reprove:- shew self merciful, put to shame.

(2603) pronounced khaw-nan'; a prim. root [comp. 2583]; prop. to bend or stoop in kindness to an inferior; to favor, bestow; causat. to implore (i.e. to move to favor by petition):- beseech, x fair, (be, find, shew) favour (-able), be (deal, give, grant) gracious (-ly), entreat (be)merciful, have (shew) mercy (on, upon), have pity upon, pray, make supplication, x very.

(2583) pronounced khaw-naw'; a prim. root [comp. 2603]; prop. to incline; by impl. to decline (of the slanting rays of evening); spec. to pitch a tent; gen. to encamp (for abode or siege): abide (in tents), camp, dwell, encamp, grow to an end, lie, pitch (tent), rest in tent.

(1288) pronounced baw-rak'; a prim. root; to kneel: by impl. to bless God (as an act of adoration), and (vice versa) man (as a benefit); also (by euphemism) to curse (God or the king, as treason):- x abundantly, x altogether, x at all, blaspheme, bless, congratulate, curse, x greatly, x indeed, kneel (down), praise, salute, x still, thank.

I will be a father to him, and he shall be a son to Me, but I will never withdraw My favor from him as I withdrew it from your predecessor. DIVREI-HAYAMIM ALEF 17:13 (I CHRONICLES 17:13)

I will be his father, and he shall be my son; and I will not take my mercy (2617) away from him, as I took *it* from *him* that was before thee: I CHRONICLES 17:13

mercy (2617) pronounced kheh'-sed; from 2616; kindness: by impl. (toward God) piety; rarely (by opp.) reproof, or (subject.) beauty:- favour, good deed (-liness, -ness), kindly. (loving-) kindness, merciful (kindness), mercy, pity, reproach, wicked thing.

(2616) pronounced khaw-sad'; a prim. root; prop. perh. to bow (the neck only [comp. 2603] in courteousy to an equal); i.e. to be kind, also (by euphem. [comp. 1288] but rarely); to reprove:- shew self merciful, put to shame.

(2603) pronounced khaw-nan'; a prim. root [comp. 2583]; prop. to bend or stoop in kindness to an inferior; to favor, bestow; causat. to implore (i.e. to move to favor by petition):- beseech, x fair, (be, find, shew) favour (-able), be (deal, give, grant) gracious (-ly), entreat (be)merciful, have (shew) mercy (on, upon), have pity upon, pray, make supplication, x very.

(2583) pronounced khaw-naw'; a prim. root [comp. 2603]; prop. to incline; by impl. to decline (of the slanting rays of evening); spec. to pitch a tent; gen. to encamp (for abode or siege): abide (in tents), camp, dwell, encamp, grow to an end, lie, pitch (tent), rest in tent.

(1288) pronounced baw-rak'; a prim. root; to kneel: by impl. to bless God (as an act of adoration), and (vice versa) man (as a benefit); also (by euphemism) to curse (God or the king, as treason):- x abundantly, x altogether, x at all, blaspheme, bless, congratulate, curse, x greatly, x indeed, kneel (down), praise, salute, x still, thank.

David gave his son Solomon the plan of the porch and its houses, its storerooms and its upper chambers and inner chambers; and of the place of the Ark-cover; DIVREI-HAYAMIM ALEF 28:11
(I CHRONICLES 28:11)

Then David gave to Solomon his son the pattern of the porch, and of the houses thereof, and of the treasuries thereof, and of the upper chambers thereof, and of the inner parlours thereof, and of the place of the mercy seat (3727). I CHRONICLES 28:11

mercy seat (3727) pronounced kap-po'-reth; from 3722; a lid (used only of the cover of the sacred Ark):- mercy seat.

(3722) pronounced kaw-far; a prim. root; to cover (spec. with bitumen); fig. to expiate or condone; to placate or cancel:- appease, make (an) atonement, cleanse, disannul, forgive, be merciful, pacify, pardon, to pitch, purge (away), put off, (make) reconcile (-iation).

Solomon said to God, "You dealt most graciously with my father David, and now You have made me king in his stead." DIVREI-HAYAMIM BET 1:8 (II CHRONICLES 1:8)

And Solomon said unto God, Thou hast shown great mercy (2617) unto David my father, and hast made me to reign in his stead. II CHRONICLES 1:8

mercy (2617) pronounced kheh'-sed; from 2616; kindness: by impl. (toward God) piety; rarely (by opp.) reproof, or (subject.) beauty:- favour, good deed (-liness, -ness), kindly. (loving-) kindness, merciful (kindness), mercy, pity, reproach, wicked thing.

(2616) pronounced khaw-sad'; a prim. root; prop. perh. to bow (the neck only [comp. 2603] in courteousy to an equal); i.e. to be kind, also (by euphem. [comp. 1288] but rarely); to reprove:- shew self merciful, put to shame.

(2603) pronounced khaw-nan'; a prim. root [comp. 2583]; prop. to bend or stoop in kindness to an inferior; to favor, bestow; causat. to implore (i.e. to move to favor by petition):- beseech, x fair, (be, find, shew) favour (-able), be (deal, give, grant) gracious (-ly), entreat (be)merciful, have (shew) mercy (on, upon), have pity upon, pray, make supplication, x very.

(2583) pronounced khaw-naw'; a prim. root [comp. 2603]; prop. to incline; by impl. to decline (of the slanting rays of evening); spec. to pitch a tent; gen. to encamp (for abode or siege): abide (in tents), camp, dwell, encamp, grow to an end, lie, pitch (tent), rest in tent.

(1288) pronounced baw-rak'; a prim. root; to kneel: by impl. to bless God (as an act of adoration), and (vice versa) man (as a benefit); also (by euphemism) to curse (God or the king,

as treason):- x abundantly, x altogether, x at all, blaspheme, bless, congratulate, curse, x greatly, x indeed, kneel (down), praise, salute, x still, thank.

The trumpeters and the singers joined in unison to praise and extol the LORD; and as the sound of the trumpets, cymbals, and other musical instruments, and the praise of the LORD, "For He is good, for His steadfast love is eternal," grew louder, the House, the House of the LORD, was filled with a cloud. DIVREI-HAYAMIM BET 5:13 (II CHRONICLES 5:13)

It came *even* to pass, as the trumpeters and singers *were* as one, to make one sound to be heard in praising and thanking the LORD; and when they lifted up *their* voice with the trumpets and cymbals and instruments of music, and praised the LORD, *saying,* For *he is* good; for his mercy (2617) *endureth* for ever: that *then* the house was filled with a cloud, *even* the house of the LORD; II CHRONICLES 5:13

mercy (2617) pronounced kheh'-sed; from 2616; kindness: by impl. (toward God) piety; rarely (by opp.) reproof, or (subject.) beauty:- favour, good deed (-liness, -ness), kindly. (loving-) kindness, merciful (kindness), mercy, pity, reproach, wicked thing.

(2616) pronounced khaw-sad'; a prim. root; prop. perh. to bow (the neck only [comp. 2603] in courteousy to an equal); i.e. to be kind, also (by euphem. [comp. 1288] but rarely); to reprove:- shew self merciful, put to shame.

(2603) pronounced khaw-nan'; a prim. root [comp. 2583]; prop. to bend or stoop in kindness to an inferior; to favor, bestow; causat. to implore (i.e. to move to favor by petition):- beseech, x fair, (be, find, shew) favour (-able), be (deal, give, grant) gracious (-ly), entreat (be)merciful, have (shew) mercy (on, upon), have pity upon, pray, make supplication, x very.

(2583) pronounced khaw-naw'; a prim. root [comp. 2603]; prop. to incline; by impl. to decline (of the slanting rays of evening); spec. to pitch a tent; gen. to encamp (for abode or siege): abide (in tents), camp, dwell, encamp, grow to an end, lie, pitch (tent), rest in tent.

(1288) pronounced baw-rak'; a prim. root; to kneel: by impl. to bless God (as an act of adoration), and (vice versa) man (as a benefit); also (by euphemism) to curse (God or the king, as treason):- x abundantly, x altogether, x at all, blaspheme, bless, congratulate, curse, x greatly, x indeed, kneel (down), praise, salute, x still, thank.

Solomon had made a bronze platform and placed it in the midst of the Great Court; it was 5 cubits long and 5 cubits wide and 3 cubits high. He stood on it; then, kneeling in front of the whole congregation of Israel, he spread forth his hands to heaven and said, "O LORD God of Israel, there is no god like You in the heavens and on the earth, You who steadfastly maintain the Covenant with Your servants who walk before You with all their heart; DIVREI-HAYAMIM BET 6:13-14 (II CHRONICLES 6:13-14)

For Solomon had made a brazen scaffold, of five cubits long, and five cubits broad, and three cubits high, and had set it in the midst of the court: and upon it he stood, and kneeled down *upon* his knees before all the congregation of Israel, and spread forth his hands toward heaven. And said, O LORD God of

Israel, *there is* no God like thee in the heaven, nor in the earth; which keepest covenant, and *showest* mercy (2617) unto thy servants, that walk before thee with all their hearts: II CHRONICLES 6:13-14

> mercy (2617) pronounced kheh'-sed; from 2616; kindness: by impl. (toward God) piety; rarely (by opp.) reproof, or (subject.) beauty:- favour, good deed (-liness, -ness), kindly. (loving-) kindness, merciful (kindness), mercy, pity, reproach, wicked thing.
>
> (2616) pronounced khaw-sad'; a prim. root; prop. perh. to bow (the neck only [comp. 2603] in courteousy to an equal); i.e. to be kind, also (by euphem. [comp. 1288] but rarely); to reprove:- shew self merciful, put to shame.
>
> (2603) pronounced khaw-nan'; a prim. root [comp. 2583]; prop. to bend or stoop in kindness to an inferior; to favor, bestow; causat. to implore (i.e. to move to favor by petition):- beseech, x fair, (be, find, shew) favour (-able), be (deal, give, grant) gracious (-ly), entreat (be)merciful, have (shew) mercy (on, upon), have pity upon, pray, make supplication, x very.
>
> (2583) pronounced khaw-naw'; a prim. root [comp. 2603]; prop. to incline; by impl. to decline (of the slanting rays of evening); spec. to pitch a tent; gen. to encamp (for abode or siege): abide (in tents), camp, dwell, encamp, grow to an end, lie, pitch (tent), rest in tent.
>
> (1288) pronounced baw-rak'; a prim. root; to kneel: by impl. to bless God (as an act of adoration), and (vice versa) man (as a benefit); also (by euphemism) to curse (God or the king, as treason):- x abundantly, x altogether, x at all, blaspheme, bless, congratulate, curse, x greatly, x indeed, kneel (down), praise, salute, x still, thank.

All the Israelites witnessed the descent of the fire and the glory of the LORD on the House; they knelt with their faces to the ground and prostrated themselves, praising the LORD. DIVREI-HAYAMIM BET 7:3 (II CHRONICLES 7:3)

And when all the children of Israel saw how the fire came down, and the glory of the LORD upon the house, they bowed themselves with their faces to the ground upon the pavement, and worshipped, and praised the LORD, *saying*, For he *is* good; for his mercy (2617) *endureth* for ever. II CHRONICLES 7:3

> mercy (2617) pronounced kheh'-sed; from 2616; kindness: by impl. (toward God) piety; rarely (by opp.) reproof, or (subject.) beauty:- favour, good deed (-liness, -ness), kindly. (loving-) kindness, merciful (kindness), mercy, pity, reproach, wicked thing.
>
> (2616) pronounced khaw-sad'; a prim. root; prop. perh. to bow (the neck only [comp. 2603] in courteousy to an equal); i.e. to be kind, also (by euphem. [comp. 1288] but rarely); to reprove:- shew self merciful, put to shame.
>
> (2603) pronounced khaw-nan'; a prim. root [comp. 2583]; prop. to bend or stoop in kindness to an inferior; to favor, bestow; causat. to implore (i.e. to move to favor by petition):- beseech, x fair, (be, find, shew) favour (-able), be (deal, give, grant) gracious (-ly), entreat (be)merciful, have (shew) mercy (on, upon), have pity upon, pray, make supplication, x very.

(2583) pronounced khaw-naw'; a prim. root [comp. 2603]; prop. to incline; by impl. to decline (of the slanting rays of evening); spec. to pitch a tent; gen. to encamp (for abode or siege): abide (in tents), camp, dwell, encamp, grow to an end, lie, pitch (tent), rest in tent.

(1288) pronounced baw-rak'; a prim. root; to kneel: by impl. to bless God (as an act of adoration), and (vice versa) man (as a benefit); also (by euphemism) to curse (God or the king, as treason):- x abundantly, x altogether, x at all, blaspheme, bless, congratulate, curse, x greatly, x indeed, kneel (down), praise, salute, x still, thank.

The priests stood at their watches; the Levites with the instruments for the LORD's music that King David had made to praise the LORD, "For His steadfast love is eternal," by means of the psalms of David that they knew. The priests opposite them blew trumpets while all Israel were standing.
DIVREI-HAYAMIM BET 7:6 (II CHRONICLES 7:6)

And the priests waited on their offices: the Levites also with instruments of music of the LORD, which David the king had made to praise the LORD, because his mercy (2617) *endureth* for ever, when David praised by their ministry; and the priests sounded trumpets before them, and all Israel stood.
II CHRONICLES 7:6

mercy (2617) pronounced kheh'-sed; from 2616; kindness: by impl. (toward God) piety; rarely (by opp.) reproof, or (subject.) beauty:- favour, good deed (-liness, -ness), kindly. (loving-) kindness, merciful (kindness), mercy, pity, reproach, wicked thing.

(2616) pronounced khaw-sad'; a prim. root; prop. perh. to bow (the neck only [comp. 2603] in courteousy to an equal); i.e. to be kind, also (by euphem. [comp. 1288] but rarely); to reprove:- shew self merciful, put to shame.

(2603) pronounced khaw-nan'; a prim. root [comp. 2583]; prop. to bend or stoop in kindness to an inferior; to favor, bestow; causat. to implore (i.e. to move to favor by petition):- beseech, x fair, (be, find, shew) favour (-able), be (deal, give, grant) gracious (-ly), entreat (be)merciful, have (shew) mercy (on, upon), have pity upon, pray, make supplication, x very.

(2583) pronounced khaw-naw'; a prim. root [comp. 2603]; prop. to incline; by impl. to decline (of the slanting rays of evening); spec. to pitch a tent; gen. to encamp (for abode or siege): abide (in tents), camp, dwell, encamp, grow to an end, lie, pitch (tent), rest in tent.

(1288) pronounced baw-rak'; a prim. root; to kneel: by impl. to bless God (as an act of adoration), and (vice versa) man (as a benefit); also (by euphemism) to curse (God or the king, as treason):- x abundantly, x altogether, x at all, blaspheme, bless, congratulate, curse, x greatly, x indeed, kneel (down), praise, salute, x still, thank.

After taking counsel with the people, he stationed singers to the LORD extolling the One majestic in holiness as they went forth ahead of the vanguard, saying, "Praise the LORD, for His steadfast love is eternal." DIVREI-HAYAMIM BET 20:21 (II CHRONICLES 20:21)

And when he had consulted with the people, he appointed singers unto the LORD, and that should praise the beauty of holiness, as they went out before the army, and to say, Praise the LORD; *for* his mercy (2617) *endureth* for ever. II CHRONICLES 20:21

> mercy (2617) pronounced kheh'-sed; from 2616; kindness: by impl. (toward God) piety; rarely (by opp.) reproof, or (subject.) beauty:- favour, good deed (-liness, -ness), kindly. (loving-) kindness, merciful (kindness), mercy, pity, reproach, wicked thing.
>
> (2616) pronounced khaw-sad'; a prim. root; prop. perh. to bow (the neck only [comp. 2603] in courteousy to an equal); i.e. to be kind, also (by euphem. [comp. 1288] but rarely); to reprove:- shew self merciful, put to shame.
>
> (2603) pronounced khaw-nan'; a prim. root [comp. 2583]; prop. to bend or stoop in kindness to an inferior; to favor, bestow; causat. to implore (i.e. to move to favor by petition):- beseech, x fair, (be, find, shew) favour (-able), be (deal, give, grant) gracious (-ly), entreat (be)merciful, have (shew) mercy (on, upon), have pity upon, pray, make supplication, x very.
>
> (2583) pronounced khaw-naw'; a prim. root [comp. 2603]; prop. to incline; by impl. to decline (of the slanting rays of evening); spec. to pitch a tent; gen. to encamp (for abode or siege): abide (in tents), camp, dwell, encamp, grow to an end, lie, pitch (tent), rest in tent.
>
> (1288) pronounced baw-rak'; a prim. root; to kneel: by impl. to bless God (as an act of adoration), and (vice versa) man (as a benefit); also (by euphemism) to curse (God or the king, as treason):- x abundantly, x altogether, x at all, blaspheme, bless, congratulate, curse, x greatly, x indeed, kneel (down), praise, salute, x still, thank.

They sang songs extolling and praising the LORD, "For He is good, His steadfast love for Israel is eternal." All the people raised a great shout extolling the LORD because the foundation of the House of the LORD had been laid. 'EZRA 3:11 (EZRA 3:11)

And they sang together by course in praising and giving thanks unto the LORD; because *he is* good, for his mercy (2617) *endureth* for ever toward Israel. And *all* the people shouted with a great shout, when they praised the LORD, because the foundation of the house of the LORD was laid. EZRA 3:11

> mercy (2617) pronounced kheh'-sed; from 2616; kindness: by impl. (toward God) piety; rarely (by opp.) reproof, or (subject.) beauty:- favour, good deed (-liness, -ness), kindly. (loving-) kindness, merciful (kindness), mercy, pity, reproach, wicked thing.
>
> (2616) pronounced khaw-sad'; a prim. root; prop. perh. to bow (the neck only [comp. 2603] in courteousy to an equal); i.e. to be kind, also (by euphem. [comp. 1288] but rarely); to reprove:- shew self merciful, put to shame.
>
> (2603) pronounced khaw-nan'; a prim. root [comp. 2583]; prop. to bend or stoop in kindness to an inferior; to favor, bestow; causat. to implore (i.e. to move to favor by petition):- beseech,

x fair, (be, find, shew) favour (-able), be (deal, give, grant) gracious (-ly), entreat (be) merciful, have (shew) mercy (on, upon), have pity upon, pray, make supplication, x very.

(2583) pronounced khaw-naw'; a prim. root [comp. 2603]; prop. to incline; by impl. to decline (of the slanting rays of evening); spec. to pitch a tent; gen. to encamp (for abode or siege): abide (in tents), camp, dwell, encamp, grow to an end, lie, pitch (tent), rest in tent.

(1288) pronounced baw-rak'; a prim. root; to kneel: by impl. to bless God (as an act of adoration), and (vice versa) man (as a benefit); also (by euphemism) to curse (God or the king, as treason):- x abundantly, x altogether, x at all, blaspheme, bless, congratulate, curse, x greatly, x indeed, kneel (down), praise, salute, x still, thank.

Blessed is the LORD God of our fathers, who put it into the mind of the king to glorify the House of the LORD in Jerusalem, and who inclined the king and his counselors and the king's military officers to be favorably disposed toward me. For my part, thanks to the care of the LORD for me, I summoned up courage and assembled leading men in Israel to go with me. 'EZRA 7:27-28 (EZRA 7:27-28)

Blessed *be* the LORD God of our fathers which hath put *such a thing* as this in the king's heart, to beautify the house of the LORD which *is* in Jerusalem: and hath extended mercy (2617) unto me before the king, and his counselors, and before all the king's mighty princes. And I was strengthened as the hand of the LORD my God was upon me, and I gathered together out of Israel chief men to go up with me. EZRA 7:27-28

mercy (2617) pronounced kheh'-sed; from 2616; kindness: by impl. (toward God) piety; rarely (by opp.) reproof, or (subject.) beauty:- favour, good deed (-liness, -ness), kindly. (loving-) kindness, merciful (kindness), mercy, pity, reproach, wicked thing.

(2616) pronounced khaw-sad'; a prim. root; prop. perh. to bow (the neck only [comp. 2603] in courteousy to an equal); i.e. to be kind, also (by euphem. [comp. 1288] but rarely); to reprove:- shew self merciful, put to shame.

(2603) pronounced khaw-nan'; a prim. root [comp. 2583]; prop. to bend or stoop in kindness to an inferior; to favor, bestow; causat. to implore (i.e. to move to favor by petition):- beseech, x fair, (be, find, shew) favour (-able), be (deal, give, grant) gracious (-ly), entreat (be)merciful, have (shew) mercy (on, upon), have pity upon, pray, make supplication, x very.

(2583) pronounced khaw-naw'; a prim. root [comp. 2603]; prop. to incline; by impl. to decline (of the slanting rays of evening); spec. to pitch a tent; gen. to encamp (for abode or siege): abide (in tents), camp, dwell, encamp, grow to an end, lie, pitch (tent), rest in tent.

(1288) pronounced baw-rak'; a prim. root; to kneel: by impl. to bless God (as an act of adoration), and (vice versa) man (as a benefit); also (by euphemism) to curse (God or the king, as treason):- x abundantly, x altogether, x at all, blaspheme, bless, congratulate, curse, x greatly, x indeed, kneel (down), praise, salute, x still, thank.

For bondsmen we are, though even in our bondage God has not forsaken us, but has disposed the king of Persia favorably toward us, to furnish us with sustenance and to raise again the House of our God, repairing its ruins and giving us a hold in Judah and Jerusalem. 'EZRA 9:9 (EZRA 9:9)

hold: Lit. "fence." (TANAKH footnote)

For we *were* bondsmen; yet our God hath not forsaken us in our bondage, but hath extended mercy (2617) unto us in the sight of the kings of Persia, to give us a reviving, to set up the house of our God, and to repair the desolations thereof, and to give us a wall in Judah and in Jerusalem. EZRA 9:9

mercy (2617) pronounced kheh'-sed; from 2616; kindness: by impl. (toward God) piety; rarely (by opp.) reproof, or (subject.) beauty:- favour, good deed (-liness, -ness), kindly. (loving-) kindness, merciful (kindness), mercy, pity, reproach, wicked thing.

(2616) pronounced khaw-sad'; a prim. root; prop. perh. to bow (the neck only [comp. 2603] in courteousy to an equal); i.e. to be kind, also (by euphem. [comp. 1288] but rarely); to reprove:- shew self merciful, put to shame.

(2603) pronounced khaw-nan'; a prim. root [comp. 2583]; prop. to bend or stoop in kindness to an inferior; to favor, bestow; causat. to implore (i.e. to move to favor by petition):- beseech, x fair, (be, find, shew) favour (-able), be (deal, give, grant) gracious (-ly), entreat (be)merciful, have (shew) mercy (on, upon), have pity upon, pray, make supplication, x very.

(2583) pronounced khaw-naw'; a prim. root [comp. 2603]; prop. to incline; by impl. to decline (of the slanting rays of evening); spec. to pitch a tent; gen. to encamp (for abode or siege): abide (in tents), camp, dwell, encamp, grow to an end, lie, pitch (tent), rest in tent.

(1288) pronounced baw-rak'; a prim. root; to kneel: by impl. to bless God (as an act of adoration), and (vice versa) man (as a benefit); also (by euphemism) to curse (God or the king, as treason):- x abundantly, x altogether, x at all, blaspheme, bless, congratulate, curse, x greatly, x indeed, kneel (down), praise, salute, x still, thank.

When I heard that, I sat and wept, and was in mourning for days, fasting and praying to the God of Heaven. I said, "O LORD, God of Heaven, great and awesome God, who stays faithful to His covenant with those who love Him and keep His commandments!" NECHEMYAH 1:4-5 (NEHEMIAH 1:4-5)

And it came to pass, when I heard these words, that I sat down and wept, and mourned *certain* days, and fasted, and prayed before the God of heaven, and said, I beseech thee, O LORD God of heaven, the great and terrible God, that keepeth covenant and mercy (2617) for them that love him and observe his commandments: NEHEMIAH 1:4-5

mercy (2617) pronounced kheh'-sed; from 2616; kindness: by impl. (toward God) piety; rarely (by opp.) reproof, or (subject.) beauty:- favour, good deed (-liness, -ness), kindly. (loving-) kindness, merciful (kindness), mercy, pity, reproach, wicked thing.

(2616) pronounced khaw-sad'; a prim. root; prop. perh. to bow (the neck only [comp. 2603] in courteousy to an equal); i.e. to be kind, also (by euphem. [comp. 1288] but rarely); to reprove:- shew self merciful, put to shame.

(2603) pronounced khaw-nan'; a prim. root [comp. 2583]; prop. to bend or stoop in kindness to an inferior; to favor, bestow; causat. to implore (i.e. to move to favor by petition):- beseech, x fair, (be, find, shew) favour (-able), be (deal, give, grant) gracious (-ly), entreat (be)merciful, have (shew) mercy (on, upon), have pity upon, pray, make supplication, x very.

(2583) pronounced khaw-naw'; a prim. root [comp. 2603]; prop. to incline; by impl. to decline (of the slanting rays of evening); spec. to pitch a tent; gen. to encamp (for abode or siege): abide (in tents), camp, dwell, encamp, grow to an end, lie, pitch (tent), rest in tent.

(1288) pronounced baw-rak'; a prim. root; to kneel: by impl. to bless God (as an act of adoration), and (vice versa) man (as a benefit); also (by euphemism) to curse (God or the king, as treason):- x abundantly, x altogether, x at all, blaspheme, bless, congratulate, curse, x greatly, x indeed, kneel (down), praise, salute, x still, thank.

O LORD! Let Your ear be attentive to the prayer of Your servant, and to the prayer of Your servants who desire to hold Your name in awe. Grant Your servant success today, and dispose that man to be compassionate toward him! I was the king's cupbearer at the time. NECHEMYAH 1:11 (NEHEMIAH 1:11)

O LORD, I beseech thee, let now thine ear be attentive to the prayer of thy servant, and to the prayer of thy servants, who desire to fear thy name: and prosper, I pray thee, thy servant this day and grant him mercy (7356) in the sight of this man. For I was the king's cupbearer. NEHEMIAH 1:11

mercy (7356) pronounced rakh'-am' from 7355; compassion (in the plur.); by extens. the womb (as cherishing the fetus); by impl. a maiden:- bowels, compassion, damsel, tender love, (great, tender) mercy, pity, womb.

(7355) pronounced raw-kham'; a prim. root; to fondle; by impl. to love, espec. to compassionate:- have compassion (on, upon), love, (find, have, obtain, shew) mercy (-iful, on, upon), (have) pity, Ruhamah, x surely.

And now, our God, great, mighty, and awesome God, who stays faithful to His covenant, do not treat lightly all the suffering that has overtaken us- our kings, our officers, our priests, our prophets, our fathers, and all Your people- from the time of the Assyrian kings to this day. NECHEMYAH 9:32 (NEHEMIAH 9:32)

Now therefore, our God, the great, the mighty, and the terrible God, who keepest covenant and mercy (2617), let not all the trouble seem little before thee, that hath come upon us, on our kings, on our princes, and on our priests, and on our prophets, and on our fathers, and on all thy people, since the time of the kings of Assyria unto this day. NEHEMIAH 9:32

mercy (2617) pronounced kheh'-sed; from 2616; kindness: by impl. (toward God) piety; rarely (by opp.) reproof, or (subject.) beauty:- favour, good deed (-liness, -ness), kindly. (loving-) kindness, merciful (kindness), mercy, pity, reproach, wicked thing.

(2616) pronounced khaw-sad'; a prim. root; prop. perh. to bow (the neck only [comp. 2603] in courteousy to an equal); i.e. to be kind, also (by euphem. [comp. 1288] but rarely); to reprove:- shew self merciful, put to shame.

(2603) pronounced khaw-nan'; a prim. root [comp. 2583]; prop. to bend or stoop in kindness to an inferior; to favor, bestow; causat. to implore (i.e. to move to favor by petition):- beseech, x fair, (be, find, shew) favour (-able), be (deal, give, grant) gracious (-ly), entreat (be)merciful, have (shew) mercy (on, upon), have pity upon, pray, make supplication, x very.

(2583) pronounced khaw-naw'; a prim. root [comp. 2603]; prop. to incline; by impl. to decline (of the slanting rays of evening); spec. to pitch a tent; gen. to encamp (for abode or siege): abide (in tents), camp, dwell, encamp, grow to an end, lie, pitch (tent), rest in tent.

(1288) pronounced baw-rak'; a prim. root; to kneel: by impl. to bless God (as an act of adoration), and (vice versa) man (as a benefit); also (by euphemism) to curse (God or the king, as treason):- x abundantly, x altogether, x at all, blaspheme, bless, congratulate, curse, x greatly, x indeed, kneel (down), praise, salute, x still, thank.

I gave orders to the Levites to purify themselves and come and guard the gates, to preserve the sanctity of the Sabbath. This too, O my God, remember to my credit, and spare me in accord with Your abundant faithfulness. NECHEMYAH 13:22 (NEHEMIAH 13:22)

And I commanded the Levites, that they should cleanse themselves, and *that* they should come *and* keep the gates, to sanctify the Sabbath day. Remember me, O my God, *concerning* this also, and spare me according to the greatness of thy mercy (2617). NEHEMIAH 13:22

mercy (2617) pronounced kheh'-sed; from 2616; kindness: by impl. (toward God) piety; rarely (by opp.) reproof, or (subject.) beauty:- favour, good deed (-liness, -ness), kindly. (loving-) kindness, merciful (kindness), mercy, pity, reproach, wicked thing.

(2616) pronounced khaw-sad'; a prim. root; prop. perh. to bow (the neck only [comp. 2603] in courteousy to an equal); i.e. to be kind, also (by euphem. [comp. 1288] but rarely); to reprove:- shew self merciful, put to shame.

(2603) pronounced khaw-nan'; a prim. root [comp. 2583]; prop. to bend or stoop in kindness to an inferior; to favor, bestow; causat. to implore (i.e. to move to favor by petition):- beseech, x fair, (be, find, shew) favour (-able), be (deal, give, grant) gracious (-ly), entreat (be)merciful, have (shew) mercy (on, upon), have pity upon, pray, make supplication, x very.

(2583) pronounced khaw-naw'; a prim. root [comp. 2603]; prop. to incline; by impl. to decline (of the slanting rays of evening); spec. to pitch a tent; gen. to encamp (for abode or siege): abide (in tents), camp, dwell, encamp, grow to an end, lie, pitch (tent), rest in tent.

(1288) pronounced baw-rak'; a prim. root; to kneel: by impl. to bless God (as an act of adoration), and (vice versa) man (as a benefit); also (by euphemism) to curse (God or the king, as treason):- x abundantly, x altogether, x at all, blaspheme, bless, congratulate, curse, x greatly, x indeed, kneel (down), praise, salute, x still, thank.

He keeps turning events by His stratagems, that they might accomplish all that He commands them throughout the inhabited earth, causing each of them to happen to His land, whether as a scourge or as a blessing. IYOV 37:12-13 (JOB 37:12-13)

And it is turned round about by his counsels: that they may do whatsoever he commandeth them upon the face of the world in the earth. He causeth it to come, whether for correction, or for his land, or for mercy (2617). JOB 37:12-13

mercy (2617) pronounced kheh'-sed; from 2616; kindness: by impl. (toward God) piety; rarely (by opp.) reproof, or (subject.) beauty:- favour, good deed (-liness, -ness), kindly. (loving-) kindness, merciful (kindness), mercy, pity, reproach, wicked thing.

(2616) pronounced khaw-sad'; a prim. root; prop. perh. to bow (the neck only [comp. 2603] in courteousy to an equal); i.e. to be kind, also (by euphem. [comp. 1288] but rarely); to reprove:- shew self merciful, put to shame.

(2603) pronounced khaw-nan'; a prim. root [comp. 2583]; prop. to bend or stoop in kindness to an inferior; to favor, bestow; causat. to implore (i.e. to move to favor by petition):- beseech, x fair, (be, find, shew) favour (-able), be (deal, give, grant) gracious (-ly), entreat (be)merciful, have (shew) mercy (on, upon), have pity upon, pray, make supplication, x very.

(2583) pronounced khaw-naw'; a prim. root [comp. 2603]; prop. to incline; by impl. to decline (of the slanting rays of evening); spec. to pitch a tent; gen. to encamp (for abode or siege): abide (in tents), camp, dwell, encamp, grow to an end, lie, pitch (tent), rest in tent.

(1288) pronounced baw-rak'; a prim. root; to kneel: by impl. to bless God (as an act of adoration), and (vice versa) man (as a benefit); also (by euphemism) to curse (God or the king, as treason):- x abundantly, x altogether, x at all, blaspheme, bless, congratulate, curse, x greatly, x indeed, kneel (down), praise, salute, x still, thank.

Answer me when I call, O God, my vindicator! You freed me from distress; have mercy on me and hear my prayer. TEHILLIM 4:2 (PSALMS 4:1)

Hear me when I call, O God of my righteousness: thou hast enlarged me *when I was* in distress; have mercy (2603) upon me, and hear my prayer. PSALMS 4:1

mercy (2603) pronounced khaw-nan'; a prim. root [comp. 2583]; prop. to bend or stoop in kindness to an inferior; to favor, bestow; causat. to implore (i.e. to move to favor by petition):- beseech, x fair, (be, find, shew) favour (-able), be (deal, give, grant) gracious (-ly), entreat (be) merciful, have (shew) mercy (on, upon), have pity upon, pray, make supplication, x very.

(2583) pronounced khaw-naw'; a prim. root [comp. 2603]; prop. to incline; by impl. to decline (of the slanting rays of evening); spec. to pitch a tent; gen. to encamp (for abode or siege): abide (in tents), camp, dwell, encamp, grow to an end, lie, pitch (tent), rest in tent.

But I, through Your abundant love, enter Your house; I bow down in awe at Your holy temple.
TEHILLIM 5:8 (PSALMS 5:7)

But as for me, I will come *into* thy house in the multitude of thy mercy (2617); *and* in thy fear will I worship toward thy holy temple. PSALMS 5:7

mercy (2617) pronounced kheh'-sed; from 2616; kindness: by impl. (toward God) piety; rarely (by opp.) reproof, or (subject.) beauty:- favour, good deed (-liness, -ness), kindly. (loving-) kindness, merciful (kindness), mercy, pity, reproach, wicked thing.

(2616) pronounced khaw-sad'; a prim. root; prop. perh. to bow (the neck only [comp. 2603] in courteousy to an equal); i.e. to be kind, also (by euphem. [comp. 1288] but rarely); to reprove:- shew self merciful, put to shame.

(2603) pronounced khaw-nan'; a prim. root [comp. 2583]; prop. to bend or stoop in kindness to an inferior; to favor, bestow; causat. to implore (i.e. to move to favor by petition):- beseech, x fair, (be, find, shew) favour (-able), be (deal, give, grant) gracious (-ly), entreat (be) merciful, have (shew) mercy (on, upon), have pity upon, pray, make supplication, x very.

(2583) pronounced khaw-naw'; a prim. root [comp. 2603]; prop. to incline; by impl. to decline (of the slanting rays of evening); spec. to pitch a tent; gen. to encamp (for abode or siege): abide (in tents), camp, dwell, encamp, grow to an end, lie, pitch (tent), rest in tent.

(1288) pronounced baw-rak'; a prim. root; to kneel: by impl. to bless God (as an act of adoration), and (vice versa) man (as a benefit); also (by euphemism) to curse (God or the king, as treason):- x abundantly, x altogether, x at all, blaspheme, bless, congratulate, curse, x greatly, x indeed, kneel (down), praise, salute, x still, thank.

Have mercy on me, O LORD, for I languish; heal me, O LORD, for my bones shake with terror.
TEHILLIM 6:3 (PSALMS 6:2)

Have mercy (2603) upon me, O LORD; for I *am* weak; O LORD, heal me; for my bones are vexed.
PSALMS 6:2

mercy (2603) pronounced khaw-nan'; a prim. root [comp. 2583]; prop. to bend or stoop in kindness to an inferior; to favor, bestow; causat. to implore (i.e. to move to favor by petition):-

beseech, x fair, (be, find, shew) favour (-able), be (deal, give, grant) gracious (-ly), entreat (be) merciful, have (shew) mercy (on, upon), have pity upon, pray, make supplication, x very.

(2583) pronounced khaw-naw'; a prim. root [comp. 2603]; prop. to incline; by impl. to decline (of the slanting rays of evening); spec. to pitch a tent; gen. to encamp (for abode or siege): abide (in tents), camp, dwell, encamp, grow to an end, lie, pitch (tent), rest in tent.

Have mercy on me, O LORD; see my affliction at the hands of my foes, You who lift me from the gates of death, TEHILLIM 9:14 (PSALMS 9:13)

Have mercy (2603) upon me, O LORD; consider my trouble *which I suffer* of them that hate me, thou that liftest me up from the gates of death: PSALMS 9:13

mercy (2603) pronounced khaw-nan'; a prim. root [comp. 2583]; prop. to bend or stoop in kindness to an inferior; to favor, bestow; causat. to implore (i.e. to move to favor by petition):- beseech, x fair, (be, find, shew) favour (-able), be (deal, give, grant) gracious (-ly), entreat (be) merciful, have (shew) mercy (on, upon), have pity upon, pray, make supplication, x very.

(2583) pronounced khaw-naw'; a prim. root [comp. 2603]; prop. to incline; by impl. to decline (of the slanting rays of evening); spec. to pitch a tent; gen. to encamp (for abode or siege): abide (in tents), camp, dwell, encamp, grow to an end, lie, pitch (tent), rest in tent.

But I trust in Your faithfulness, my heart will exult in Your deliverance. I will sing to the LORD, for He has been good to me. TEHILLIM 13:6 (PSALMS 13:5-6)

But I have trusted in thy mercy (2617); my heart shall rejoice in thy salvation. I will sing unto the LORD, because he hath dealt bountifully with me. PSALMS 13:5-6

mercy (2617) pronounced kheh'-sed; from 2616; kindness: by impl. (toward God) piety; rarely (by opp.) reproof, or (subject.) beauty:- favour, good deed (-liness, -ness), kindly. (loving-) kindness, merciful (kindness), mercy, pity, reproach, wicked thing.

(2616) pronounced khaw-sad'; a prim. root; prop. perh. to bow (the neck only [comp. 2603] in courteousy to an equal); i.e. to be kind, also (by euphem. [comp. 1288] but rarely); to reprove:- shew self merciful, put to shame.

(2603) pronounced khaw-nan'; a prim. root [comp. 2583]; prop. to bend or stoop in kindness to an inferior; to favor, bestow; causat. to implore (i.e. to move to favor by petition):- beseech, x fair, (be, find, shew) favour (-able), be (deal, give, grant) gracious (-ly), entreat (be)merciful, have (shew) mercy (on, upon), have pity upon, pray, make supplication, x very.

(2583) pronounced khaw-naw'; a prim. root [comp. 2603]; prop. to incline; by impl. to decline (of the slanting rays of evening); spec. to pitch a tent; gen. to encamp (for abode or siege): abide (in tents), camp, dwell, encamp, grow to an end, lie, pitch (tent), rest in tent.

(1288) pronounced baw-rak'; a prim. root; to kneel: by impl. to bless God (as an act of adoration), and (vice versa) man (as a benefit); also (by euphemism) to curse (God or the king, as treason):- x abundantly, x altogether, x at all, blaspheme, bless, congratulate, curse, x greatly, x indeed, kneel (down), praise, salute, x still, thank.

He accords great victories to His king, keeps faith with His anointed, with David and his offspring forever. TEHILLIM 18:51 (PSALMS 18:50)

He accords great victories: 2 Sam. 22.51, "Tower of victory." (TANAKH footnote)

For this I sing Your praise among the nations and hymn Your name: Tower of victory to His king, who deals graciously with His anointed, with David and his offspring evermore. SH'MU'EL BET 22:50-51 (II SAMUEL 22:51)

He *is* the tower of salvation for his king; and showeth mercy to his anointed, unto David, and to his seed for evermore. II SAMUEL 22:51

Great deliverance giveth he to his king; and showeth mercy (2617) to his anointed, to David, and to his seed for evermore. PSALMS 18:50

mercy (2617) pronounced kheh'-sed; from 2616; kindness: by impl. (toward God) piety; rarely (by opp.) reproof, or (subject.) beauty:- favour, good deed (-liness, -ness), kindly. (loving-) kindness, merciful (kindness), mercy, pity, reproach, wicked thing.

(2616) pronounced khaw-sad'; a prim. root; prop. perh. to bow (the neck only [comp. 2603] in courteousy to an equal); i.e. to be kind, also (by euphem. [comp. 1288] but rarely); to reprove:- shew self merciful, put to shame.

(2603) pronounced khaw-nan'; a prim. root [comp. 2583]; prop. to bend or stoop in kindness to an inferior; to favor, bestow; causat. to implore (i.e. to move to favor by petition):- beseech, x fair, (be, find, shew) favour (-able), be (deal, give, grant) gracious (-ly), entreat (be) merciful, have (shew) mercy (on, upon), have pity upon, pray, make supplication, x very.

(2583) pronounced khaw-naw'; a prim. root [comp. 2603]; prop. to incline; by impl. to decline (of the slanting rays of evening); spec. to pitch a tent; gen. to encamp (for abode or siege): abide (in tents), camp, dwell, encamp, grow to an end, lie, pitch (tent), rest in tent.

(1288) pronounced baw-rak'; a prim. root; to kneel: by impl. to bless God (as an act of adoration), and (vice versa) man (as a benefit); also (by euphemism) to curse (God or the king, as treason):- x abundantly, x altogether, x at all, blaspheme, bless, congratulate, curse, x greatly, x indeed, kneel (down), praise, salute, x still, thank.

For the king trusts in the LORD; through the faithfulness of the Most High he will not be shaken. TEHILLIM 21:8 (PSALMS 21:7)

For the king trusteth in the LORD, and through the mercy (2617) of the Most High he shall not be moved. PSALMS 21:7

> mercy (2617) pronounced kheh'-sed; from 2616; kindness: by impl. (toward God) piety; rarely (by opp.) reproof, or (subject.) beauty:- favour, good deed (-liness, -ness), kindly. (loving-) kindness, merciful (kindness), mercy, pity, reproach, wicked thing.
>
> (2616) pronounced khaw-sad'; a prim. root; prop. perh. to bow (the neck only [comp. 2603] in courteousy to an equal); i.e. to be kind, also (by euphem. [comp. 1288] but rarely); to reprove:- shew self merciful, put to shame.
>
> (2603) pronounced khaw-nan'; a prim. root [comp. 2583]; prop. to bend or stoop in kindness to an inferior; to favor, bestow; causat. to implore (i.e. to move to favor by petition):- beseech, x fair, (be, find, shew) favour (-able), be (deal, give, grant) gracious (-ly), entreat (be) merciful, have (shew) mercy (on, upon), have pity upon, pray, make supplication, x very.
>
> (2583) pronounced khaw-naw'; a prim. root [comp. 2603]; prop. to incline; by impl. to decline (of the slanting rays of evening); spec. to pitch a tent; gen. to encamp (for abode or siege): abide (in tents), camp, dwell, encamp, grow to an end, lie, pitch (tent), rest in tent.
>
> (1288) pronounced baw-rak'; a prim. root; to kneel: by impl. to bless God (as an act of adoration), and (vice versa) man (as a benefit); also (by euphemism) to curse (God or the king, as treason):- x abundantly, x altogether, x at all, blaspheme, bless, congratulate, curse, x greatly, x indeed, kneel (down), praise, salute, x still, thank.

Only goodness and steadfast love shall pursue me all the days of my life, and I shall dwell in the house of the LORD for many long years. TEHILLIM 23:6 (PSALMS 23:6)

Surely goodness and mercy (2617) shall follow me all the days of my life: and I will dwell in the house of the LORD for ever. PSALMS 23:6

> mercy (2617) pronounced kheh'-sed; from 2616; kindness: by impl. (toward God) piety; rarely (by opp.) reproof, or (subject.) beauty:- favour, good deed (-liness, -ness), kindly. (loving-) kindness, merciful (kindness), mercy, pity, reproach, wicked thing.
>
> (2616) pronounced khaw-sad'; a prim. root; prop. perh. to bow (the neck only [comp. 2603] in courteousy to an equal); i.e. to be kind, also (by euphem. [comp. 1288] but rarely); to reprove:- shew self merciful, put to shame.
>
> (2603) pronounced khaw-nan'; a prim. root [comp. 2583]; prop. to bend or stoop in kindness to an inferior; to favor, bestow; causat. to implore (i.e. to move to favor by petition):- beseech, x fair, (be, find, shew) favour (-able), be (deal, give, grant) gracious (-ly), entreat (be) merciful, have (shew) mercy (on, upon), have pity upon, pray, make supplication, x very.

(2583) pronounced khaw-naw'; a prim. root [comp. 2603]; prop. to incline; by impl. to decline (of the slanting rays of evening); spec. to pitch a tent; gen. to encamp (for abode or siege): abide (in tents), camp, dwell, encamp, grow to an end, lie, pitch (tent), rest in tent.

(1288) pronounced baw-rak'; a prim. root; to kneel: by impl. to bless God (as an act of adoration), and (vice versa) man (as a benefit); also (by euphemism) to curse (God or the king, as treason):- x abundantly, x altogether, x at all, blaspheme, bless, congratulate, curse, x greatly, x indeed, kneel (down), praise, salute, x still, thank.

Be not mindful of my youthful sins and transgressions; in keeping with Your faithfulness consider what is in my favor, as befits Your goodness, O LORD. TEHILLIM 25:7 (PSALMS 25:7)

Remember not the sins of my youth, nor my transgressions: according to thy mercy (2617) remember thou me for thy goodness' sake, O LORD. PSALMS 25:7

mercy (2617) pronounced kheh'-sed; from 2616; kindness: by impl. (toward God) piety; rarely (by opp.) reproof, or (subject.) beauty:- favour, good deed (-liness, -ness), kindly. (loving-) kindness, merciful (kindness), mercy, pity, reproach, wicked thing.

(2616) pronounced khaw-sad'; a prim. root; prop. perh. to bow (the neck only [comp. 2603] in courteousy to an equal); i.e. to be kind, also (by euphem. [comp. 1288] but rarely); to reprove:- shew self merciful, put to shame.

(2603) pronounced khaw-nan'; a prim. root [comp. 2583]; prop. to bend or stoop in kindness to an inferior; to favor, bestow; causat. to implore (i.e. to move to favor by petition):- beseech, x fair, (be, find, shew) favour (-able), be (deal, give, grant) gracious (-ly), entreat (be) merciful, have (shew) mercy (on, upon), have pity upon, pray, make supplication, x very.

(2583) pronounced khaw-naw'; a prim. root [comp. 2603]; prop. to incline; by impl. to decline (of the slanting rays of evening); spec. to pitch a tent; gen. to encamp (for abode or siege): abide (in tents), camp, dwell, encamp, grow to an end, lie, pitch (tent), rest in tent.

(1288) pronounced baw-rak'; a prim. root; to kneel: by impl. to bless God (as an act of adoration), and (vice versa) man (as a benefit); also (by euphemism) to curse (God or the king, as treason):- x abundantly, x altogether, x at all, blaspheme, bless, congratulate, curse, x greatly, x indeed, kneel (down), praise, salute, x still, thank.

All the LORD's paths are steadfast love for those who keep the decrees of His covenant. TEHILLIM 25:10 (PSALMS 25:10)

All the paths of the LORD *are* mercy (2617) and truth unto such as keep his covenant and his testimonies. PSALMS 25:10

mercy (2617) pronounced kheh'-sed; from 2616; kindness: by impl. (toward God) piety; rarely (by opp.) reproof, or (subject.) beauty:- favour, good deed (-liness, -ness), kindly. (loving-) kindness, merciful (kindness), mercy, pity, reproach, wicked thing.

(2616) pronounced khaw-sad'; a prim. root; prop. perh. to bow (the neck only [comp. 2603] in courteousy to an equal); i.e. to be kind, also (by euphem. [comp. 1288] but rarely); to reprove:- shew self merciful, put to shame.

(2603) pronounced khaw-nan'; a prim. root [comp. 2583]; prop. to bend or stoop in kindness to an inferior; to favor, bestow; causat. to implore (i.e. to move to favor by petition):- beseech, x fair, (be, find, shew) favour (-able), be (deal, give, grant) gracious (-ly), entreat (be) merciful, have (shew) mercy (on, upon), have pity upon, pray, make supplication, x very.

(2583) pronounced khaw-naw'; a prim. root [comp. 2603]; prop. to incline; by impl. to decline (of the slanting rays of evening); spec. to pitch a tent; gen. to encamp (for abode or siege): abide (in tents), camp, dwell, encamp, grow to an end, lie, pitch (tent), rest in tent.

(1288) pronounced baw-rak'; a prim. root; to kneel: by impl. to bless God (as an act of adoration), and (vice versa) man (as a benefit); also (by euphemism) to curse (God or the king, as treason):- x abundantly, x altogether, x at all, blaspheme, bless, congratulate, curse, x greatly, x indeed, kneel (down), praise, salute, x still, thank.

Turn to me, have mercy on me, for I am alone and afflicted. TEHILLIM 25:16 (PSALMS 25:16)

Turn thee unto me, and have mercy (2603) upon me; for I *am* desolate and afflicted. PSALMS 25:16

mercy (2603) pronounced khaw-nan'; a prim. root [comp. 2583]; prop. to bend or stoop in kindness to an inferior; to favor, bestow; causat. to implore (i.e. to move to favor by petition):- beseech, x fair, (be, find, shew) favour (-able), be (deal, give, grant) gracious (-ly), entreat (be) merciful, have (shew) mercy (on, upon), have pity upon, pray, make supplication, x very.

(2583) pronounced khaw-naw'; a prim. root [comp. 2603]; prop. to incline; by impl. to decline (of the slanting rays of evening); spec. to pitch a tent; gen. to encamp (for abode or siege): abide (in tents), camp, dwell, encamp, grow to an end, lie, pitch (tent), rest in tent.

Hear, O LORD, when I cry aloud; have mercy on me, answer me. TEHILLIM 27:7 (PSALMS 27:7)

Hear, O LORD, *when* I cry with my voice: have mercy (2603) also upon me, and answer me. PSALMS 27:7

mercy (2603) pronounced khaw-nan'; a prim. root [comp. 2583]; prop. to bend or stoop in kindness to an inferior; to favor, bestow; causat. to implore (i.e. to move to favor by petition):- beseech, x fair, (be, find, shew) favour (-able), be (deal, give, grant) gracious (-ly), entreat (be) merciful, have (shew) mercy (on, upon), have pity upon, pray, make supplication, x very.

(2583) pronounced khaw-naw'; a prim. root [comp. 2603]; prop. to incline; by impl. to decline (of the slanting rays of evening); spec. to pitch a tent; gen. to encamp (for abode or siege): abide (in tents), camp, dwell, encamp, grow to an end, lie, pitch (tent), rest in tent.

Hear, O LORD, and have mercy on me: "O LORD, be my help!" TEHILLIM 30:11 (PSALMS 30:10)

Hear, O LORD, and have mercy (2603) upon me: LORD, be thou my helper. PSALMS 30:10

mercy (2603) pronounced khaw-nan'; a prim. root [comp. 2583]; prop. to bend or stoop in kindness to an inferior; to favor, bestow; causat. to implore (i.e. to move to favor by petition):- beseech, x fair, (be, find, shew) favour (-able), be (deal, give, grant) gracious (-ly), entreat (be) merciful, have (shew) mercy (on, upon), have pity upon, pray, make supplication, x very.

(2583) pronounced khaw-naw'; a prim. root [comp. 2603]; prop. to incline; by impl. to decline (of the slanting rays of evening); spec. to pitch a tent; gen. to encamp (for abode or siege): abide (in tents), camp, dwell, encamp, grow to an end, lie, pitch (tent), rest in tent.

Let me exult and rejoice in Your faithfulness when You notice my affliction, are mindful of my deep distress, and do not hand me over to my enemy, but grant me relief. Have mercy on me, O LORD, for I am in distress; my eyes are wasted by vexation, my substance and body too. TEHILLIM 31:8-10 (PSALMS 31:7-9)

I will be glad and rejoice in thy mercy (2617): for thou hast considered my trouble; thou hast known my soul in adversities; and hast not shut me up into the hand of the enemy: thou hast set my feet in a large room. Have mercy (2603) upon me, O LORD, for I am in trouble: mine eye is consumed with grief, *yea*, my soul and my belly. PSALMS 31:7-9

mercy (2617) pronounced kheh'-sed; from 2616; kindness: by impl. (toward God) piety; rarely (by opp.) reproof, or (subject.) beauty:- favour, good deed (-liness, -ness), kindly. (loving-) kindness, merciful (kindness), mercy, pity, reproach, wicked thing.

(2616) pronounced khaw-sad'; a prim. root; prop. perh. to bow (the neck only [comp. 2603] in courteousy to an equal); i.e. to be kind, also (by euphem. [comp. 1288] but rarely); to reprove:- shew self merciful, put to shame.

(2603) pronounced khaw-nan'; a prim. root [comp. 2583]; prop. to bend or stoop in kindness to an inferior; to favor, bestow; causat. to implore (i.e. to move to favor by petition):- beseech, x fair, (be, find, shew) favour (-able), be (deal, give, grant) gracious (-ly), entreat (be) merciful, have (shew) mercy (on, upon), have pity upon, pray, make supplication, x very.

(2583) pronounced khaw-naw'; a prim. root [comp. 2603]; prop. to incline; by impl. to decline (of the slanting rays of evening); spec. to pitch a tent; gen. to encamp (for abode or siege): abide (in tents), camp, dwell, encamp, grow to an end, lie, pitch (tent), rest in tent.

(1288) pronounced baw-rak'; a prim. root; to kneel: by impl. to bless God (as an act of adoration), and (vice versa) man (as a benefit); also (by euphemism) to curse (God or the king, as treason):- x abundantly, x altogether, x at all, blaspheme, bless, congratulate, curse, x greatly, x indeed, kneel (down), praise, salute, x still, thank.

Many are the torments of the wicked, but he who trusts in the LORD shall be surrounded with favor. TEHILLIM 32:10 (PSALMS 32:10)

Many sorrows *shall be* to the wicked: but he that trusteth in the LORD, mercy (2617) shall compass him about. PSALMS 32:10

mercy (2617) pronounced kheh'-sed; from 2616; kindness: by impl. (toward God) piety; rarely (by opp.) reproof, or (subject.) beauty:- favour, good deed (-liness, -ness), kindly. (loving-) kindness, merciful (kindness), mercy, pity, reproach, wicked thing.

(2616) pronounced khaw-sad'; a prim. root; prop. perh. to bow (the neck only [comp. 2603] in courteousy to an equal); i.e. to be kind, also (by euphem. [comp. 1288] but rarely); to reprove:- shew self merciful, put to shame.

(2603) pronounced khaw-nan'; a prim. root [comp. 2583]; prop. to bend or stoop in kindness to an inferior; to favor, bestow; causat. to implore (i.e. to move to favor by petition):- beseech, x fair, (be, find, shew) favour (-able), be (deal, give, grant) gracious (-ly), entreat (be) merciful, have (shew) mercy (on, upon), have pity upon, pray, make supplication, x very.

(2583) pronounced khaw-naw'; a prim. root [comp. 2603]; prop. to incline; by impl. to decline (of the slanting rays of evening); spec. to pitch a tent; gen. to encamp (for abode or siege): abide (in tents), camp, dwell, encamp, grow to an end, lie, pitch (tent), rest in tent.

(1288) pronounced baw-rak'; a prim. root; to kneel: by impl. to bless God (as an act of adoration), and (vice versa) man (as a benefit); also (by euphemism) to curse (God or the king, as treason):- x abundantly, x altogether, x at all, blaspheme, bless, congratulate, curse, x greatly, x indeed, kneel (down), praise, salute, x still, thank.

Truly the eye of the LORD is on those who fear Him, who wait for His faithful care. TEHILLIM 33:18 (PSALMS 33:18)

Behold, the eye of the LORD is upon them that fear him, upon them that hope in his mercy (2617); PSALMS 33:18

mercy (2617) pronounced kheh'-sed; from 2616; kindness: by impl. (toward God) piety; rarely (by opp.) reproof, or (subject.) beauty:- favour, good deed (-liness, -ness), kindly. (loving-) kindness, merciful (kindness), mercy, pity, reproach, wicked thing.

(2616) pronounced khaw-sad'; a prim. root; prop. perh. to bow (the neck only [comp. 2603] in courteousy to an equal); i.e. to be kind, also (by euphem. [comp. 1288] but rarely); to reprove:- shew self merciful, put to shame.

(2603) pronounced khaw-nan'; a prim. root [comp. 2583]; prop. to bend or stoop in kindness to an inferior; to favor, bestow; causat. to implore (i.e. to move to favor by petition):- beseech, x fair, (be, find, shew) favour (-able), be (deal, give, grant) gracious (-ly), entreat (be) merciful, have (shew) mercy (on, upon), have pity upon, pray, make supplication, x very.

(2583) pronounced khaw-naw'; a prim. root [comp. 2603]; prop. to incline; by impl. to decline (of the slanting rays of evening); spec. to pitch a tent; gen. to encamp (for abode or siege): abide (in tents), camp, dwell, encamp, grow to an end, lie, pitch (tent), rest in tent.

(1288) pronounced baw-rak'; a prim. root; to kneel: by impl. to bless God (as an act of adoration), and (vice versa) man (as a benefit); also (by euphemism) to curse (God or the king, as treason):- x abundantly, x altogether, x at all, blaspheme, bless, congratulate, curse, x greatly, x indeed, kneel (down), praise, salute, x still, thank.

May we enjoy, O LORD, Your faithful care, as we have put our hope in You. TEHILLIM 33:22 (PSALMS 33:22)

Let thy mercy (2617), O LORD, be upon us, according as we hope in thee. PSALMS 33:22

mercy (2617) pronounced kheh'-sed; from 2616; kindness: by impl. (toward God) piety; rarely (by opp.) reproof, or (subject.) beauty:- favour, good deed (-liness, -ness), kindly. (loving-) kindness, merciful (kindness), mercy, pity, reproach, wicked thing.

(2616) pronounced khaw-sad'; a prim. root; prop. perh. to bow (the neck only [comp. 2603] in courteousy to an equal); i.e. to be kind, also (by euphem. [comp. 1288] but rarely); to reprove:- shew self merciful, put to shame.

(2603) pronounced khaw-nan'; a prim. root [comp. 2583]; prop. to bend or stoop in kindness to an inferior; to favor, bestow; causat. to implore (i.e. to move to favor by petition):- beseech, x fair, (be, find, shew) favour (-able), be (deal, give, grant) gracious (-ly), entreat (be) merciful, have (shew) mercy (on, upon), have pity upon, pray, make supplication, x very.

(2583) pronounced khaw-naw'; a prim. root [comp. 2603]; prop. to incline; by impl. to decline (of the slanting rays of evening); spec. to pitch a tent; gen. to encamp (for abode or siege): abide (in tents), camp, dwell, encamp, grow to an end, lie, pitch (tent), rest in tent.

(1288) pronounced baw-rak'; a prim. root; to kneel: by impl. to bless God (as an act of adoration), and (vice versa) man (as a benefit); also (by euphemism) to curse (God or the king, as treason):- x abundantly, x altogether, x at all, blaspheme, bless, congratulate, curse, x greatly, x indeed, kneel (down), praise, salute, x still, thank.

O LORD, Your faithfulness reaches to heaven; Your steadfastness to the sky: TEHILLIM 36:6 (PSALMS 36:5)

Thy mercy (2617), O LORD, *is* in the heavens *and* thy faithfulness *reacheth* unto the clouds. PSALMS 36:5

> mercy (2617) pronounced kheh'-sed; from 2616; kindness: by impl. (toward God) piety; rarely (by opp.) reproof, or (subject.) beauty:- favour, good deed (-liness, -ness), kindly. (loving-) kindness, merciful (kindness), mercy, pity, reproach, wicked thing.
>
> (2616) pronounced khaw-sad'; a prim. root; prop. perh. to bow (the neck only [comp. 2603] in courteousy to an equal); i.e. to be kind, also (by euphem. [comp. 1288] but rarely); to reprove:- shew self merciful, put to shame.
>
> (2603) pronounced khaw-nan'; a prim. root [comp. 2583]; prop. to bend or stoop in kindness to an inferior; to favor, bestow; causat. to implore (i.e. to move to favor by petition):- beseech, x fair, (be, find, shew) favour (-able), be (deal, give, grant) gracious (-ly), entreat (be) merciful, have (shew) mercy (on, upon), have pity upon, pray, make supplication, x very.
>
> (2583) pronounced khaw-naw'; a prim. root [comp. 2603]; prop. to incline; by impl. to decline (of the slanting rays of evening); spec. to pitch a tent; gen. to encamp (for abode or siege): abide (in tents), camp, dwell, encamp, grow to an end, lie, pitch (tent), rest in tent.
>
> (1288) pronounced baw-rak'; a prim. root; to kneel: by impl. to bless God (as an act of adoration), and (vice versa) man (as a benefit); also (by euphemism) to curse (God or the king, as treason):- x abundantly, x altogether, x at all, blaspheme, bless, congratulate, curse, x greatly, x indeed, kneel (down), praise, salute, x still, thank.

The wicked man borrows and does not repay; the righteous is generous and keeps giving. TEHILLIM 37:21 (PSALMS 37:21)

The wicked borroweth, and payeth not again: but the righteous showeth mercy (2603), and giveth. PSALMS 37:21

> mercy (2603) pronounced khaw-nan'; a prim. root [comp. 2583]; prop. to bend or stoop in kindness to an inferior; to favor, bestow; causat. to implore (i.e. to move to favor by petition):- beseech, x fair, (be, find, shew) favour (-able), be (deal, give, grant) gracious (-ly), entreat (be) merciful, have (shew) mercy (on, upon), have pity upon, pray, make supplication, x very.
>
> (2583) pronounced khaw-naw'; a prim. root [comp. 2603]; prop. to incline; by impl. to decline (of the slanting rays of evening); spec. to pitch a tent; gen. to encamp (for abode or siege): abide (in tents), camp, dwell, encamp, grow to an end, lie, pitch (tent), rest in tent.

Have mercy upon me, O God, as befits Your faithfulness; in keeping with Your abundant compassion, blot out my transgressions. TEHILLIM 51:3 (PSALMS 51:1)

Have mercy (2603) upon me, O God, according to thy lovingkindness: according unto the multitude of thy tender mercies (7356) blot out my transgressions. PSALMS 51:1

> mercy (2603) pronounced khaw-nan'; a prim. root [comp. 2583]; prop. to bend or stoop in kindness to an inferior; to favor, bestow; causat. to implore (i.e. to move to favor by petition):- beseech, x fair, (be, find, shew) favour (-able), be (deal, give, grant) gracious (-ly), entreat (be) merciful, have (shew) mercy (on, upon), have pity upon, pray, make supplication, x very.
>
> (2583) pronounced khaw-naw'; a prim. root [comp. 2603]; prop. to incline; by impl. to decline (of the slanting rays of evening); spec. to pitch a tent; gen. to encamp (for abode or siege): abide (in tents), camp, dwell, encamp, grow to an end, lie, pitch (tent), rest in tent.
>
> mercies (7356) pronounced rakh'-am' from 7355; compassion (in the plur.); by extens. the womb (as cherishing the fetus); by impl. a maiden:- bowels, compassion, damsel, tender love, (great, tender) mercy, pity, womb.
>
> (7355) pronounced raw-kham'; a prim. root; to fondle; by impl. to love, espec. to compassionate:- have compassion (on, upon), love, (find, have, obtain, shew) mercy (-iful, on, upon), (have) pity, Ruhamah, x surely.

But I am like a thriving olive tree in God's house; I trust in the faithfulness of God forever and ever. TEHILLIM 52:10 (PSALMS 52:8)

But I *am* like a green olive tree in the house of God: I trust in the mercy (2617) of God for ever and ever. PSALMS 52:8

> mercy (2617) pronounced kheh'-sed; from 2616; kindness: by impl. (toward God) piety; rarely (by opp.) reproof, or (subject.) beauty:- favour, good deed (-liness, -ness), kindly. (loving-) kindness, merciful (kindness), mercy, pity, reproach, wicked thing.
>
> (2616) pronounced khaw-sad'; a prim. root; prop. perh. to bow (the neck only [comp. 2603] in courteousy to an equal); i.e. to be kind, also (by euphem. [comp. 1288] but rarely); to reprove:- shew self merciful, put to shame.
>
> (2603) pronounced khaw-nan'; a prim. root [comp. 2583]; prop. to bend or stoop in kindness to an inferior; to favor, bestow; causat. to implore (i.e. to move to favor by petition):- beseech, x fair, (be, find, shew) favour (-able), be (deal, give, grant) gracious (-ly), entreat (be) merciful, have (shew) mercy (on, upon), have pity upon, pray, make supplication, x very.
>
> (2583) pronounced khaw-naw'; a prim. root [comp. 2603]; prop. to incline; by impl. to decline (of the slanting rays of evening); spec. to pitch a tent; gen. to encamp (for abode or siege): abide (in tents), camp, dwell, encamp, grow to an end, lie, pitch (tent), rest in tent.
>
> (1288) pronounced baw-rak'; a prim. root; to kneel: by impl. to bless God (as an act of adoration), and (vice versa) man (as a benefit); also (by euphemism) to curse (God or the king,

as treason):- x abundantly, x altogether, x at all, blaspheme, bless, congratulate, curse, x greatly, x indeed, kneel (down), praise, salute, x still, thank.

He will reach down from heaven and deliver me: God will send down His steadfast love; my persecutor reviles. TEHILLIM 57:4 (PSALMS 57:3)

He shall send from heaven and save me *from* the reproach of him that would swallow me up. Selah. God shall send forth his mercy (2617) and his truth. PSALMS 57:3

mercy (2617) pronounced kheh'-sed; from 2616; kindness: by impl. (toward God) piety; rarely (by opp.) reproof, or (subject.) beauty:- favour, good deed (-liness, -ness), kindly. (loving-) kindness, merciful (kindness), mercy, pity, reproach, wicked thing.

(2616) pronounced khaw-sad'; a prim. root; prop. perh. to bow (the neck only [comp. 2603] in courteousy to an equal); i.e. to be kind, also (by euphem. [comp. 1288] but rarely); to reprove:- shew self merciful, put to shame.

(2603) pronounced khaw-nan'; a prim. root [comp. 2583]; prop. to bend or stoop in kindness to an inferior; to favor, bestow; causat. to implore (i.e. to move to favor by petition):- beseech, x fair, (be, find, shew) favour (-able), be (deal, give, grant) gracious (-ly), entreat (be) merciful, have (shew) mercy (on, upon), have pity upon, pray, make supplication, x very.

(2583) pronounced khaw-naw'; a prim. root [comp. 2603]; prop. to incline; by impl. to decline (of the slanting rays of evening); spec. to pitch a tent; gen. to encamp (for abode or siege): abide (in tents), camp, dwell, encamp, grow to an end, lie, pitch (tent), rest in tent.

(1288) pronounced baw-rak'; a prim. root; to kneel: by impl. to bless God (as an act of adoration), and (vice versa) man (as a benefit); also (by euphemism) to curse (God or the king, as treason):- x abundantly, x altogether, x at all, blaspheme, bless, congratulate, curse, x greatly, x indeed, kneel (down), praise, salute, x still, thank.

For Your faithfulness is as high as heaven; Your steadfastness reaches to the sky. TEHILLIM 57:11 (PSALMS 57:10)

For thy mercy (2617) is great unto the heavens, and thy truth unto the clouds. PSALMS 57:10

mercy (2617) pronounced kheh'-sed; from 2616; kindness: by impl. (toward God) piety; rarely (by opp.) reproof, or (subject.) beauty:- favour, good deed (-liness, -ness), kindly. (loving-) kindness, merciful (kindness), mercy, pity, reproach, wicked thing.

(2616) pronounced khaw-sad'; a prim. root; prop. perh. to bow (the neck only [comp. 2603] in courteousy to an equal); i.e. to be kind, also (by euphem. [comp. 1288] but rarely); to reprove:- shew self merciful, put to shame.

(2603) pronounced khaw-nan'; a prim. root [comp. 2583]; prop. to bend or stoop in kindness to an inferior; to favor, bestow; causat. to implore (i.e. to move to favor by petition):- beseech,

x fair, (be, find, shew) favour (-able), be (deal, give, grant) gracious (-ly), entreat (be) merciful, have (shew) mercy (on, upon), have pity upon, pray, make supplication, x very.

(2583) pronounced khaw-naw'; a prim. root [comp. 2603]; prop. to incline; by impl. to decline (of the slanting rays of evening); spec. to pitch a tent; gen. to encamp (for abode or siege): abide (in tents), camp, dwell, encamp, grow to an end, lie, pitch (tent), rest in tent.

(1288) pronounced baw-rak'; a prim. root; to kneel: by impl. to bless God (as an act of adoration), and (vice versa) man (as a benefit); also (by euphemism) to curse (God or the king, as treason):- x abundantly, x altogether, x at all, blaspheme, bless, congratulate, curse, x greatly, x indeed, kneel (down), praise, salute, x still, thank.

My faithful God will come to aid me; God will let me gloat over my watchful foes. TEHILLIM 59:11 (PSALMS 59:10)

The God of my mercy (2617) shall prevent me: God shall let me see *my desire* upon mine enemies. PSALMS 59:10

mercy (2617) pronounced kheh'-sed; from 2616; kindness: by impl. (toward God) piety; rarely (by opp.) reproof, or (subject.) beauty:- favour, good deed (-liness, -ness), kindly. (loving-) kindness, merciful (kindness), mercy, pity, reproach, wicked thing.

(2616) pronounced khaw-sad'; a prim. root; prop. perh. to bow (the neck only [comp. 2603] in courteousy to an equal); i.e. to be kind, also (by euphem. [comp. 1288] but rarely); to reprove:- shew self merciful, put to shame.

(2603) pronounced khaw-nan'; a prim. root [comp. 2583]; prop. to bend or stoop in kindness to an inferior; to favor, bestow; causat. to implore (i.e. to move to favor by petition):- beseech, x fair, (be, find, shew) favour (-able), be (deal, give, grant) gracious (-ly), entreat (be) merciful, have (shew) mercy (on, upon), have pity upon, pray, make supplication, x very.

(2583) pronounced khaw-naw'; a prim. root [comp. 2603]; prop. to incline; by impl. to decline (of the slanting rays of evening); spec. to pitch a tent; gen. to encamp (for abode or siege): abide (in tents), camp, dwell, encamp, grow to an end, lie, pitch (tent), rest in tent.

(1288) pronounced baw-rak'; a prim. root; to kneel: by impl. to bless God (as an act of adoration), and (vice versa) man (as a benefit); also (by euphemism) to curse (God or the king, as treason):- x abundantly, x altogether, x at all, blaspheme, bless, congratulate, curse, x greatly, x indeed, kneel (down), praise, salute, x still, thank.

But I will sing of Your strength, extol each morning Your faithfulness; for You have been my haven, a refuge in time of trouble. O my strength, to You I sing hymns; for God is my haven, my faithful God. TEHILLIM 59:17-18 (PSALMS 59:16-17)

But I will sing of thy power; yea, I will sing aloud of thy mercy (2617) in the morning: for thou hast been my defense and refuge in the day of my trouble. Unto thee, O my strength, will I sing: for God is my defense, *and* the God of my mercy (2617). PSALMS 59:16-17

> mercy (2617) pronounced kheh'-sed; from 2616; kindness: by impl. (toward God) piety; rarely (by opp.) reproof, or (subject.) beauty:- favour, good deed (-liness, -ness), kindly. (loving-) kindness, merciful (kindness), mercy, pity, reproach, wicked thing.
>
> (2616) pronounced khaw-sad'; a prim. root; prop. perh. to bow (the neck only [comp. 2603] in courteousy to an equal); i.e. to be kind, also (by euphem. [comp. 1288] but rarely); to reprove:- shew self merciful, put to shame.
>
> (2603) pronounced khaw-nan'; a prim. root [comp. 2583]; prop. to bend or stoop in kindness to an inferior; to favor, bestow; causat. to implore (i.e. to move to favor by petition):- beseech, x fair, (be, find, shew) favour (-able), be (deal, give, grant) gracious (-ly), entreat (be) merciful, have (shew) mercy (on, upon), have pity upon, pray, make supplication, x very.
>
> (2583) pronounced khaw-naw'; a prim. root [comp. 2603]; prop. to incline; by impl. to decline (of the slanting rays of evening); spec. to pitch a tent; gen. to encamp (for abode or siege): abide (in tents), camp, dwell, encamp, grow to an end, lie, pitch (tent), rest in tent.
>
> (1288) pronounced baw-rak'; a prim. root; to kneel: by impl. to bless God (as an act of adoration), and (vice versa) man (as a benefit); also (by euphemism) to curse (God or the king, as treason):- x abundantly, x altogether, x at all, blaspheme, bless, congratulate, curse, x greatly, x indeed, kneel (down), praise, salute, x still, thank.

Add days to the days of the king: may his years extend through generations; may he dwell in God's presence forever: appoint steadfast love to guard him. TEHILLIM 61:7-8 (PSALMS 61:6-7)

Thou wilt prolong the king's life: *and* his years as many generations. He shall abide before God for ever: O prepare mercy (2617) and truth, *which* may preserve him. PSALMS 61:6-7

> mercy (2617) pronounced kheh'-sed; from 2616; kindness: by impl. (toward God) piety; rarely (by opp.) reproof, or (subject.) beauty:- favour, good deed (-liness, -ness), kindly. (loving-) kindness, merciful (kindness), mercy, pity, reproach, wicked thing.
>
> (2616) pronounced khaw-sad'; a prim. root; prop. perh. to bow (the neck only [comp. 2603] in courteousy to an equal); i.e. to be kind, also (by euphem. [comp. 1288] but rarely); to reprove:- shew self merciful, put to shame.
>
> (2603) pronounced khaw-nan'; a prim. root [comp. 2583]; prop. to bend or stoop in kindness to an inferior; to favor, bestow; causat. to implore (i.e. to move to favor by petition):- beseech, x fair, (be, find, shew) favour (-able), be (deal, give, grant) gracious (-ly), entreat (be) merciful, have (shew) mercy (on, upon), have pity upon, pray, make supplication, x very.

(2583) pronounced khaw-naw'; a prim. root [comp. 2603]; prop. to incline; by impl. to decline (of the slanting rays of evening); spec. to pitch a tent; gen. to encamp (for abode or siege): abide (in tents), camp, dwell, encamp, grow to an end, lie, pitch (tent), rest in tent.

(1288) pronounced baw-rak'; a prim. root; to kneel: by impl. to bless God (as an act of adoration), and (vice versa) man (as a benefit); also (by euphemism) to curse (God or the king, as treason):- x abundantly, x altogether, x at all, blaspheme, bless, congratulate, curse, x greatly, x indeed, kneel (down), praise, salute, x still, thank.

One thing God has spoken: two things have I heard: that might belongs to God, and faithfulness is Yours, O LORD, to reward each man according to his deeds. TEHILLIM 62:12-13 (PSALMS 62:11-12)

God hath spoken once; twice have I heard this; that power *belongeth* unto God. Also unto thee, O LORD, *belongeth* mercy (2617): for thou renderest to every man according to his work.
PSALMS 62:11-12

mercy (2617) pronounced kheh'-sed; from 2616; kindness: by impl. (toward God) piety; rarely (by opp.) reproof, or (subject.) beauty:- favour, good deed (-liness, -ness), kindly. (loving-) kindness, merciful (kindness), mercy, pity, reproach, wicked thing.

(2616) pronounced khaw-sad'; a prim. root; prop. perh. to bow (the neck only [comp. 2603] in courteousy to an equal); i.e. to be kind, also (by euphem. [comp. 1288] but rarely); to reprove:- shew self merciful, put to shame.

(2603) pronounced khaw-nan'; a prim. root [comp. 2583]; prop. to bend or stoop in kindness to an inferior; to favor, bestow; causat. to implore (i.e. to move to favor by petition):- beseech, x fair, (be, find, shew) favour (-able), be (deal, give, grant) gracious (-ly), entreat (be) merciful, have (shew) mercy (on, upon), have pity upon, pray, make supplication, x very.

(2583) pronounced khaw-naw'; a prim. root [comp. 2603]; prop. to incline; by impl. to decline (of the slanting rays of evening); spec. to pitch a tent; gen. to encamp (for abode or siege): abide (in tents), camp, dwell, encamp, grow to an end, lie, pitch (tent), rest in tent.

(1288) pronounced baw-rak'; a prim. root; to kneel: by impl. to bless God (as an act of adoration), and (vice versa) man (as a benefit); also (by euphemism) to curse (God or the king, as treason):- x abundantly, x altogether, x at all, blaspheme, bless, congratulate, curse, x greatly, x indeed, kneel (down), praise, salute, x still, thank.

Blessed is God who has not turned away my prayer, or His faithful care from me. TEHILLIM 66:20 (PSALMS 66:20)

Blessed *be* God, which hath not turned away my prayer, nor his mercy (2617) from me. PSALMS 66:20

mercy (2617) pronounced kheh'-sed; from 2616; kindness: by impl. (toward God) piety; rarely (by opp.) reproof, or (subject.) beauty:- favour, good deed (-liness, -ness), kindly. (loving-) kindness, merciful (kindness), mercy, pity, reproach, wicked thing.

(2616) pronounced khaw-sad'; a prim. root; prop. perh. to bow (the neck only [comp. 2603] in courteousy to an equal); i.e. to be kind, also (by euphem. [comp. 1288] but rarely); to reprove:- shew self merciful, put to shame.

(2603) pronounced khaw-nan'; a prim. root [comp. 2583]; prop. to bend or stoop in kindness to an inferior; to favor, bestow; causat. to implore (i.e. to move to favor by petition):- beseech, x fair, (be, find, shew) favour (-able), be (deal, give, grant) gracious (-ly), entreat (be) merciful, have (shew) mercy (on, upon), have pity upon, pray, make supplication, x very.

(2583) pronounced khaw-naw'; a prim. root [comp. 2603]; prop. to incline; by impl. to decline (of the slanting rays of evening); spec. to pitch a tent; gen. to encamp (for abode or siege): abide (in tents), camp, dwell, encamp, grow to an end, lie, pitch (tent), rest in tent.

(1288) pronounced baw-rak'; a prim. root; to kneel: by impl. to bless God (as an act of adoration), and (vice versa) man (as a benefit); also (by euphemism) to curse (God or the king, as treason):- x abundantly, x altogether, x at all, blaspheme, bless, congratulate, curse, x greatly, x indeed, kneel (down), praise, salute, x still, thank.

As for me, may my prayer come to You, O LORD, at a favorable moment; O God, in Your abundant faithfulness, answer me with Your sure deliverance. TEHILLIM 69:14 (PSALMS 69:13)

But as for me, my prayer *is* unto thee, O LORD, *in* an acceptable time: O God, in the multitude of thy mercy (2617) hear me, in the truth of thy salvation. PSALMS 69:13

mercy (2617) pronounced kheh'-sed; from 2616; kindness: by impl. (toward God) piety; rarely (by opp.) reproof, or (subject.) beauty:- favour, good deed (-liness, -ness), kindly. (loving-) kindness, merciful (kindness), mercy, pity, reproach, wicked thing.

(2616) pronounced khaw-sad'; a prim. root; prop. perh. to bow (the neck only [comp. 2603] in courteousy to an equal); i.e. to be kind, also (by euphem. [comp. 1288] but rarely); to reprove:- shew self merciful, put to shame.

(2603) pronounced khaw-nan'; a prim. root [comp. 2583]; prop. to bend or stoop in kindness to an inferior; to favor, bestow; causat. to implore (i.e. to move to favor by petition):- beseech, x fair, (be, find, shew) favour (-able), be (deal, give, grant) gracious (-ly), entreat (be) merciful, have (shew) mercy (on, upon), have pity upon, pray, make supplication, x very.

(2583) pronounced khaw-naw'; a prim. root [comp. 2603]; prop. to incline; by impl. to decline (of the slanting rays of evening); spec. to pitch a tent; gen. to encamp (for abode or siege): abide (in tents), camp, dwell, encamp, grow to an end, lie, pitch (tent), rest in tent.

(1288) pronounced baw-rak'; a prim. root; to kneel: by impl. to bless God (as an act of adoration), and (vice versa) man (as a benefit); also (by euphemism) to curse (God or the king, as treason):- x abundantly, x altogether, x at all, blaspheme, bless, congratulate, curse, x greatly, x indeed, kneel (down), praise, salute, x still, thank.

Has His faithfulness disappeared forever? Will His promise be unfulfilled for all time? TEHILLIM 77:9 (PSALMS 77:8)

Is his mercy (2617) clean gone for ever? Doth *his* promise fail for evermore? PSALMS 77:8

mercy (2617) pronounced kheh'-sed; from 2616; kindness: by impl. (toward God) piety; rarely (by opp.) reproof, or (subject.) beauty:- favour, good deed (-liness, -ness), kindly. (loving-) kindness, merciful (kindness), mercy, pity, reproach, wicked thing.

(2616) pronounced khaw-sad'; a prim. root; prop. perh. to bow (the neck only [comp. 2603] in courteousy to an equal); i.e. to be kind, also (by euphem. [comp. 1288] but rarely); to reprove:- shew self merciful, put to shame.

(2603) pronounced khaw-nan'; a prim. root [comp. 2583]; prop. to bend or stoop in kindness to an inferior; to favor, bestow; causat. to implore (i.e. to move to favor by petition):- beseech, x fair, (be, find, shew) favour (-able), be (deal, give, grant) gracious (-ly), entreat (be) merciful, have (shew) mercy (on, upon), have pity upon, pray, make supplication, x very.

(2583) pronounced khaw-naw'; a prim. root [comp. 2603]; prop. to incline; by impl. to decline (of the slanting rays of evening); spec. to pitch a tent; gen. to encamp (for abode or siege): abide (in tents), camp, dwell, encamp, grow to an end, lie, pitch (tent), rest in tent.

(1288) pronounced baw-rak'; a prim. root; to kneel: by impl. to bless God (as an act of adoration), and (vice versa) man (as a benefit); also (by euphemism) to curse (God or the king, as treason):- x abundantly, x altogether, x at all, blaspheme, bless, congratulate, curse, x greatly, x indeed, kneel (down), praise, salute, x still, thank.

Show us, O LORD, Your faithfulness: grant us Your deliverance. TEHILLIM 85:8 (PSALMS 85:7)

Show us thy mercy (2617), O LORD, and grant us thy salvation. PSALMS 85:7

mercy (2617) pronounced kheh'-sed; from 2616; kindness: by impl. (toward God) piety; rarely (by opp.) reproof, or (subject.) beauty:- favour, good deed (-liness, -ness), kindly. (loving-) kindness, merciful (kindness), mercy, pity, reproach, wicked thing.

(2616) pronounced khaw-sad'; a prim. root; prop. perh. to bow (the neck only [comp. 2603] in courteousy to an equal); i.e. to be kind, also (by euphem. [comp. 1288] but rarely); to reprove:- shew self merciful, put to shame.

(2603) pronounced khaw-nan'; a prim. root [comp. 2583]; prop. to bend or stoop in kindness to an inferior; to favor, bestow; causat. to implore (i.e. to move to favor by petition):- beseech,

x fair, (be, find, shew) favour (-able), be (deal, give, grant) gracious (-ly), entreat (be) merciful, have (shew) mercy (on, upon), have pity upon, pray, make supplication, x very.

(2583) pronounced khaw-naw'; a prim. root [comp. 2603]; prop. to incline; by impl. to decline (of the slanting rays of evening); spec. to pitch a tent; gen. to encamp (for abode or siege): abide (in tents), camp, dwell, encamp, grow to an end, lie, pitch (tent), rest in tent.

(1288) pronounced baw-rak'; a prim. root; to kneel: by impl. to bless God (as an act of adoration), and (vice versa) man (as a benefit); also (by euphemism) to curse (God or the king, as treason):- x abundantly, x altogether, x at all, blaspheme, bless, congratulate, curse, x greatly, x indeed, kneel (down), praise, salute, x still, thank.

Faithfulness and truth meet; justice and well-being kiss. TEHILLIM 85:11 (PSALMS 85:10)

Mercy (2617) and truth are met together; righteousness and peace have kissed *each other*.
PSALMS 85:10

mercy (2617) pronounced kheh'-sed; from 2616; kindness: by impl. (toward God) piety; rarely (by opp.) reproof, or (subject.) beauty:- favour, good deed (-liness, -ness), kindly. (loving-) kindness, merciful (kindness), mercy, pity, reproach, wicked thing.

(2616) pronounced khaw-sad'; a prim. root; prop. perh. to bow (the neck only [comp. 2603] in courteousy to an equal); i.e. to be kind, also (by euphem. [comp. 1288] but rarely); to reprove:- shew self merciful, put to shame.

(2603) pronounced khaw-nan'; a prim. root [comp. 2583]; prop. to bend or stoop in kindness to an inferior; to favor, bestow; causat. to implore (i.e. to move to favor by petition):- beseech, x fair, (be, find, shew) favour (-able), be (deal, give, grant) gracious (-ly), entreat (be) merciful, have (shew) mercy (on, upon), have pity upon, pray, make supplication, x very.

(2583) pronounced khaw-naw'; a prim. root [comp. 2603]; prop. to incline; by impl. to decline (of the slanting rays of evening); spec. to pitch a tent; gen. to encamp (for abode or siege): abide (in tents), camp, dwell, encamp, grow to an end, lie, pitch (tent), rest in tent.

(1288) pronounced baw-rak'; a prim. root; to kneel: by impl. to bless God (as an act of adoration), and (vice versa) man (as a benefit); also (by euphemism) to curse (God or the king, as treason):- x abundantly, x altogether, x at all, blaspheme, bless, congratulate, curse, x greatly, x indeed, kneel (down), praise, salute, x still, thank.

For You, LORD, are good and forgiving, abounding in steadfast love to all who call on You. Give ear, O LORD, to my prayer: heed my plea for mercy. TEHILLIM 86:5-6 (PSALMS 86:5-6)

For thou, LORD, *art* good, and ready to forgive; and plenteous in mercy (2617) unto all them that call upon thee. Give ear, O LORD, unto my prayer: and attend to the voice of my supplications.
PSALMS 86:5-6

mercy (2617) pronounced kheh'-sed; from 2616; kindness: by impl. (toward God) piety; rarely (by opp.) reproof, or (subject.) beauty:- favour, good deed (-liness, -ness), kindly. (loving-) kindness, merciful (kindness), mercy, pity, reproach, wicked thing.

(2616) pronounced khaw-sad'; a prim. root; prop. perh. to bow (the neck only [comp. 2603] in courteousy to an equal); i.e. to be kind, also (by euphem. [comp. 1288] but rarely); to reprove:- shew self merciful, put to shame.

(2603) pronounced khaw-nan'; a prim. root [comp. 2583]; prop. to bend or stoop in kindness to an inferior; to favor, bestow; causat. to implore (i.e. to move to favor by petition):- beseech, x fair, (be, find, shew) favour (-able), be (deal, give, grant) gracious (-ly), entreat (be) merciful, have (shew) mercy (on, upon), have pity upon, pray, make supplication, x very.

(2583) pronounced khaw-naw'; a prim. root [comp. 2603]; prop. to incline; by impl. to decline (of the slanting rays of evening); spec. to pitch a tent; gen. to encamp (for abode or siege): abide (in tents), camp, dwell, encamp, grow to an end, lie, pitch (tent), rest in tent.

(1288) pronounced baw-rak'; a prim. root; to kneel: by impl. to bless God (as an act of adoration), and (vice versa) man (as a benefit); also (by euphemism) to curse (God or the king, as treason):- x abundantly, x altogether, x at all, blaspheme, bless, congratulate, curse, x greatly, x indeed, kneel (down), praise, salute, x still, thank.

For Your steadfast love toward me is great: You have saved me from the depths of Sheol.
TEHILLIM 86:13 (PSALMS 86:13)

For great is thy mercy (2617) toward me: and thou hast delivered my soul from the lowest hell.
PSALMS 86:13

mercy (2617) pronounced kheh'-sed; from 2616; kindness: by impl. (toward God) piety; rarely (by opp.) reproof, or (subject.) beauty:- favour, good deed (-liness, -ness), kindly. (loving-) kindness, merciful (kindness), mercy, pity, reproach, wicked thing.

(2616) pronounced khaw-sad'; a prim. root; prop. perh. to bow (the neck only [comp. 2603] in courteousy to an equal); i.e. to be kind, also (by euphem. [comp. 1288] but rarely); to reprove:- shew self merciful, put to shame.

(2603) pronounced khaw-nan'; a prim. root [comp. 2583]; prop. to bend or stoop in kindness to an inferior; to favor, bestow; causat. to implore (i.e. to move to favor by petition):- beseech, x fair, (be, find, shew) favour (-able), be (deal, give, grant) gracious (-ly), entreat (be) merciful, have (shew) mercy (on, upon), have pity upon, pray, make supplication, x very.

(2583) pronounced khaw-naw'; a prim. root [comp. 2603]; prop. to incline; by impl. to decline (of the slanting rays of evening); spec. to pitch a tent; gen. to encamp (for abode or siege): abide (in tents), camp, dwell, encamp, grow to an end, lie, pitch (tent), rest in tent.

(1288) pronounced baw-rak'; a prim. root; to kneel: by impl. to bless God (as an act of adoration), and (vice versa) man (as a benefit); also (by euphemism) to curse (God or the king, as treason):- x abundantly, x altogether, x at all, blaspheme, bless, congratulate, curse, x greatly, x indeed, kneel (down), praise, salute, x still, thank.

But You, O LORD, are a God compassionate and merciful, slow to anger, abounding in steadfast love and faithfulness. Turn to me and have mercy on me; grant Your strength to Your servant and deliver the son of Your maidservant. TEHILLIM 86:15-16 (PSALMS 86:15-16)

But thou, O LORD, *art* a God full of compassion, and gracious, long-suffering, and plenteous in mercy (2617) and truth. O turn unto me, and have mercy (2603) upon me; give thy strength unto thy servant, and save the son of thine handmaid. PSALMS 86:15-16

mercy (2617) pronounced kheh'-sed; from 2616; kindness: by impl. (toward God) piety; rarely (by opp.) reproof, or (subject.) beauty:- favour, good deed (-liness, -ness), kindly. (loving-) kindness, merciful (kindness), mercy, pity, reproach, wicked thing.

(2616) pronounced khaw-sad'; a prim. root; prop. perh. to bow (the neck only [comp. 2603] in courteousy to an equal); i.e. to be kind, also (by euphem. [comp. 1288] but rarely); to reprove:- shew self merciful, put to shame.

(2603) pronounced khaw-nan'; a prim. root [comp. 2583]; prop. to bend or stoop in kindness to an inferior; to favor, bestow; causat. to implore (i.e. to move to favor by petition):- beseech, x fair, (be, find, shew) favour (-able), be (deal, give, grant) gracious (-ly), entreat (be) merciful, have (shew) mercy (on, upon), have pity upon, pray, make supplication, x very.

(2583) pronounced khaw-naw'; a prim. root [comp. 2603]; prop. to incline; by impl. to decline (of the slanting rays of evening); spec. to pitch a tent; gen. to encamp (for abode or siege): abide (in tents), camp, dwell, encamp, grow to an end, lie, pitch (tent), rest in tent.

(1288) pronounced baw-rak'; a prim. root; to kneel: by impl. to bless God (as an act of adoration), and (vice versa) man (as a benefit); also (by euphemism) to curse (God or the king, as treason):- x abundantly, x altogether, x at all, blaspheme, bless, congratulate, curse, x greatly, x indeed, kneel (down), praise, salute, x still, thank.

I will sing of the LORD's steadfast love forever; to all generations I will proclaim Your faithfulness with my mouth. I declare, "Your steadfast love is confirmed forever; there in the heavens You establish Your faithfulness." TEHILLIM 89:2-3 (PSALMS 89:1-2)

I will sing of the mercies (2617) of the LORD for ever: with my mouth will I make known thy faithfulness to all generations. For I have said, Mercy (2617) shall be built up for ever; thy faithfulness shalt thou establish in the very heavens. PSALMS 89:1-2

mercy (2617) pronounced kheh'-sed; from 2616; kindness: by impl. (toward God) piety; rarely (by opp.) reproof, or (subject.) beauty:- favour, good deed (-liness, -ness), kindly. (loving-) kindness, merciful (kindness), mercy, pity, reproach, wicked thing.

(2616) pronounced khaw-sad'; a prim. root; prop. perh. to bow (the neck only [comp. 2603] in courteousy to an equal); i.e. to be kind, also (by euphem. [comp. 1288] but rarely); to reprove:- shew self merciful, put to shame.

(2603) pronounced khaw-nan'; a prim. root [comp. 2583]; prop. to bend or stoop in kindness to an inferior; to favor, bestow; causat. to implore (i.e. to move to favor by petition):- beseech, x fair, (be, find, shew) favour (-able), be (deal, give, grant) gracious (-ly), entreat (be) merciful, have (shew) mercy (on, upon), have pity upon, pray, make supplication, x very.

(2583) pronounced khaw-naw'; a prim. root [comp. 2603]; prop. to incline; by impl. to decline (of the slanting rays of evening); spec. to pitch a tent; gen. to encamp (for abode or siege): abide (in tents), camp, dwell, encamp, grow to an end, lie, pitch (tent), rest in tent.

(1288) pronounced baw-rak'; a prim. root; to kneel: by impl. to bless God (as an act of adoration), and (vice versa) man (as a benefit); also (by euphemism) to curse (God or the king, as treason):- x abundantly, x altogether, x at all, blaspheme, bless, congratulate, curse, x greatly, x indeed, kneel (down), praise, salute, x still, thank.

Righteousness and justice are the base of Your throne; steadfast love and faithfulness stand before You. TEHILLIM 89:15 (PSALMS 89:14)

Justice and judgment *are* the habitation of thy throne: mercy (2617) and truth shall go before thy face. PSALMS 89:14

mercy (2617) pronounced kheh'-sed; from 2616; kindness: by impl. (toward God) piety; rarely (by opp.) reproof, or (subject.) beauty:- favour, good deed (-liness, -ness), kindly. (loving-) kindness, merciful (kindness), mercy, pity, reproach, wicked thing.

(2616) pronounced khaw-sad'; a prim. root; prop. perh. to bow (the neck only [comp. 2603] in courteousy to an equal); i.e. to be kind, also (by euphem. [comp. 1288] but rarely); to reprove:- shew self merciful, put to shame.

(2603) pronounced khaw-nan'; a prim. root [comp. 2583]; prop. to bend or stoop in kindness to an inferior; to favor, bestow; causat. to implore (i.e. to move to favor by petition):- beseech, x fair, (be, find, shew) favour (-able), be (deal, give, grant) gracious (-ly), entreat (be) merciful, have (shew) mercy (on, upon), have pity upon, pray, make supplication, x very.

(2583) pronounced khaw-naw'; a prim. root [comp. 2603]; prop. to incline; by impl. to decline (of the slanting rays of evening); spec. to pitch a tent; gen. to encamp (for abode or siege): abide (in tents), camp, dwell, encamp, grow to an end, lie, pitch (tent), rest in tent.

(1288) pronounced baw-rak'; a prim. root; to kneel: by impl. to bless God (as an act of adoration), and (vice versa) man (as a benefit); also (by euphemism) to curse (God or the king, as treason):- x abundantly, x altogether, x at all, blaspheme, bless, congratulate, curse, x greatly, x indeed, kneel (down), praise, salute, x still, thank.

My faithfulness and steadfast love shall be with him; his horn shall be exalted through My name. TEHILLIM 89:25 (PSALMS 89:24)

But my faithfulness and my mercy (2617) *shall be* with him: and in my name shall his horn be exalted. PSALMS 89:24

mercy (2617) pronounced kheh'-sed; from 2616; kindness: by impl. (toward God) piety; rarely (by opp.) reproof, or (subject.) beauty:- favour, good deed (-liness, -ness), kindly. (loving-) kindness, merciful (kindness), mercy, pity, reproach, wicked thing.

(2616) pronounced khaw-sad'; a prim. root; prop. perh. to bow (the neck only [comp. 2603] in courteousy to an equal); i.e. to be kind, also (by euphem. [comp. 1288] but rarely); to reprove:- shew self merciful, put to shame.

(2603) pronounced khaw-nan'; a prim. root [comp. 2583]; prop. to bend or stoop in kindness to an inferior; to favor, bestow; causat. to implore (i.e. to move to favor by petition):- beseech, x fair, (be, find, shew) favour (-able), be (deal, give, grant) gracious (-ly), entreat (be) merciful, have (shew) mercy (on, upon), have pity upon, pray, make supplication, x very.

(2583) pronounced khaw-naw'; a prim. root [comp. 2603]; prop. to incline; by impl. to decline (of the slanting rays of evening); spec. to pitch a tent; gen. to encamp (for abode or siege): abide (in tents), camp, dwell, encamp, grow to an end, lie, pitch (tent), rest in tent.

(1288) pronounced baw-rak'; a prim. root; to kneel: by impl. to bless God (as an act of adoration), and (vice versa) man (as a benefit); also (by euphemism) to curse (God or the king, as treason):- x abundantly, x altogether, x at all, blaspheme, bless, congratulate, curse, x greatly, x indeed, kneel (down), praise, salute, x still, thank.

I will maintain My steadfast love for him always; My covenant with him shall endure. TEHILLIM 89:29 (PSALMS 89:28)

My mercy (2617) will I keep for him for evermore, and my covenant shall stand fast with him. PSALMS 89:28

mercy (2617) pronounced kheh'-sed; from 2616; kindness: by impl. (toward God) piety; rarely (by opp.) reproof, or (subject.) beauty:- favour, good deed (-liness, -ness), kindly. (loving-) kindness, merciful (kindness), mercy, pity, reproach, wicked thing.

(2616) pronounced khaw-sad'; a prim. root; prop. perh. to bow (the neck only [comp. 2603] in courteousy to an equal); i.e. to be kind, also (by euphem. [comp. 1288] but rarely); to reprove:- shew self merciful, put to shame.

(2603) pronounced khaw-nan'; a prim. root [comp. 2583]; prop. to bend or stoop in kindness to an inferior; to favor, bestow; causat. to implore (i.e. to move to favor by petition):- beseech, x fair, (be, find, shew) favour (-able), be (deal, give, grant) gracious (-ly), entreat (be) merciful, have (shew) mercy (on, upon), have pity upon, pray, make supplication, x very.

(2583) pronounced khaw-naw'; a prim. root [comp. 2603]; prop. to incline; by impl. to decline (of the slanting rays of evening); spec. to pitch a tent; gen. to encamp (for abode or siege): abide (in tents), camp, dwell, encamp, grow to an end, lie, pitch (tent), rest in tent.

(1288) pronounced baw-rak'; a prim. root; to kneel: by impl. to bless God (as an act of adoration), and (vice versa) man (as a benefit); also (by euphemism) to curse (God or the king, as treason):- x abundantly, x altogether, x at all, blaspheme, bless, congratulate, curse, x greatly, x indeed, kneel (down), praise, salute, x still, thank.

Satisfy us at daybreak with Your steadfast love that we may sing for joy all our days. TEHILLIM 90:14 (PSALMS 90:14)

O satisfy us early with thy mercy (2617); that we may rejoice and be glad all our days. PSALMS 90:14

mercy (2617) pronounced kheh'-sed; from 2616; kindness: by impl. (toward God) piety; rarely (by opp.) reproof, or (subject.) beauty:- favour, good deed (-liness, -ness), kindly. (loving-) kindness, merciful (kindness), mercy, pity, reproach, wicked thing.

(2616) pronounced khaw-sad'; a prim. root; prop. perh. to bow (the neck only [comp. 2603] in courteousy to an equal); i.e. to be kind, also (by euphem. [comp. 1288] but rarely); to reprove:- shew self merciful, put to shame.

(2603) pronounced khaw-nan'; a prim. root [comp. 2583]; prop. to bend or stoop in kindness to an inferior; to favor, bestow; causat. to implore (i.e. to move to favor by petition):- beseech, x fair, (be, find, shew) favour (-able), be (deal, give, grant) gracious (-ly), entreat (be) merciful, have (shew) mercy (on, upon), have pity upon, pray, make supplication, x very.

(2583) pronounced khaw-naw'; a prim. root [comp. 2603]; prop. to incline; by impl. to decline (of the slanting rays of evening); spec. to pitch a tent; gen. to encamp (for abode or siege): abide (in tents), camp, dwell, encamp, grow to an end, lie, pitch (tent), rest in tent.

(1288) pronounced baw-rak'; a prim. root; to kneel: by impl. to bless God (as an act of adoration), and (vice versa) man (as a benefit); also (by euphemism) to curse (God or the king, as treason):- x abundantly, x altogether, x at all, blaspheme, bless, congratulate, curse, x greatly, x indeed, kneel (down), praise, salute, x still, thank.

When I think my foot has given way, Your faithfulness, O LORD, supports me. TEHILLIM 94:18 (PSALMS 94:18)

When I said, My foot slippeth; thy mercy (2617), O LORD, held me up. PSALMS 94:18

> mercy (2617) pronounced kheh'-sed; from 2616; kindness: by impl. (toward God) piety; rarely (by opp.) reproof, or (subject.) beauty:- favour, good deed (-liness, -ness), kindly. (loving-) kindness, merciful (kindness), mercy, pity, reproach, wicked thing.
>
> (2616) pronounced khaw-sad'; a prim. root; prop. perh. to bow (the neck only [comp. 2603] in courteousy to an equal); i.e. to be kind, also (by euphem. [comp. 1288] but rarely); to reprove:- shew self merciful, put to shame.
>
> (2603) pronounced khaw-nan'; a prim. root [comp. 2583]; prop. to bend or stoop in kindness to an inferior; to favor, bestow; causat. to implore (i.e. to move to favor by petition):- beseech, x fair, (be, find, shew) favour (-able), be (deal, give, grant) gracious (-ly), entreat (be) merciful, have (shew) mercy (on, upon), have pity upon, pray, make supplication, x very.
>
> (2583) pronounced khaw-naw'; a prim. root [comp. 2603]; prop. to incline; by impl. to decline (of the slanting rays of evening); spec. to pitch a tent; gen. to encamp (for abode or siege): abide (in tents), camp, dwell, encamp, grow to an end, lie, pitch (tent), rest in tent.
>
> (1288) pronounced baw-rak'; a prim. root; to kneel: by impl. to bless God (as an act of adoration), and (vice versa) man (as a benefit); also (by euphemism) to curse (God or the king, as treason):- x abundantly, x altogether, x at all, blaspheme, bless, congratulate, curse, x greatly, x indeed, kneel (down), praise, salute, x still, thank.

He was mindful of His steadfast love and faithfulness toward the house of Israel; all the ends of the earth beheld the victory of our God. TEHILLIM 98:3 (PSALMS 98:3)

He hath remembered his mercy (2617) and his truth toward the house of Israel: all the ends of the earth have seen the salvation of our God. PSALMS 98:3

> mercy (2617) pronounced kheh'-sed; from 2616; kindness: by impl. (toward God) piety; rarely (by opp.) reproof, or (subject.) beauty:- favour, good deed (-liness, -ness), kindly. (loving-) kindness, merciful (kindness), mercy, pity, reproach, wicked thing.
>
> (2616) pronounced khaw-sad'; a prim. root; prop. perh. to bow (the neck only [comp. 2603] in courteousy to an equal); i.e. to be kind, also (by euphem. [comp. 1288] but rarely); to reprove:- shew self merciful, put to shame.
>
> (2603) pronounced khaw-nan'; a prim. root [comp. 2583]; prop. to bend or stoop in kindness to an inferior; to favor, bestow; causat. to implore (i.e. to move to favor by petition):- beseech, x fair, (be, find, shew) favour (-able), be (deal, give, grant) gracious (-ly), entreat (be) merciful, have (shew) mercy (on, upon), have pity upon, pray, make supplication, x very.

(2583) pronounced khaw-naw'; a prim. root [comp. 2603]; prop. to incline; by impl. to decline (of the slanting rays of evening); spec. to pitch a tent; gen. to encamp (for abode or siege): abide (in tents), camp, dwell, encamp, grow to an end, lie, pitch (tent), rest in tent.

(1288) pronounced baw-rak'; a prim. root; to kneel: by impl. to bless God (as an act of adoration), and (vice versa) man (as a benefit); also (by euphemism) to curse (God or the king, as treason):- x abundantly, x altogether, x at all, blaspheme, bless, congratulate, curse, x greatly, x indeed, kneel (down), praise, salute, x still, thank.

For the LORD is good: His steadfast love is eternal; His faithfulness is for all generations.
TEHILLIM 100:5 (PSALMS 100:5)

For the LORD *is good*; his mercy (2617) is everlasting; and his truth *endureth* to all generations.
PSALMS 100:5

mercy (2617) pronounced kheh'-sed; from 2616; kindness: by impl. (toward God) piety; rarely (by opp.) reproof, or (subject.) beauty:- favour, good deed (-liness, -ness), kindly. (loving-) kindness, merciful (kindness), mercy, pity, reproach, wicked thing.

(2616) pronounced khaw-sad'; a prim. root; prop. perh. to bow (the neck only [comp. 2603] in courteousy to an equal); i.e. to be kind, also (by euphem. [comp. 1288] but rarely); to reprove:- shew self merciful, put to shame.

(2603) pronounced khaw-nan'; a prim. root [comp. 2583]; prop. to bend or stoop in kindness to an inferior; to favor, bestow; causat. to implore (i.e. to move to favor by petition):- beseech, x fair, (be, find, shew) favour (-able), be (deal, give, grant) gracious (-ly), entreat (be) merciful, have (shew) mercy (on, upon), have pity upon, pray, make supplication, x very.

(2583) pronounced khaw-naw'; a prim. root [comp. 2603]; prop. to incline; by impl. to decline (of the slanting rays of evening); spec. to pitch a tent; gen. to encamp (for abode or siege): abide (in tents), camp, dwell, encamp, grow to an end, lie, pitch (tent), rest in tent.

(1288) pronounced baw-rak'; a prim. root; to kneel: by impl. to bless God (as an act of adoration), and (vice versa) man (as a benefit); also (by euphemism) to curse (God or the king, as treason):- x abundantly, x altogether, x at all, blaspheme, bless, congratulate, curse, x greatly, x indeed, kneel (down), praise, salute, x still, thank.

I will sing of faithfulness and justice; I will chant a hymn to You, O LORD. TEHILLIM 101:1
(PSALMS 101:1)

I will sing of mercy (2617) and judgment: unto thee, O LORD, will I sing. PSALMS 101:1

mercy (2617) pronounced kheh'-sed; from 2616; kindness: by impl. (toward God) piety; rarely (by opp.) reproof, or (subject.) beauty:- favour, good deed (-liness, -ness), kindly. (loving-) kindness, merciful (kindness), mercy, pity, reproach, wicked thing.

(2616) pronounced khaw-sad'; a prim. root; prop. perh. to bow (the neck only [comp. 2603] in courteousy to an equal); i.e. to be kind, also (by euphem. [comp. 1288] but rarely); to reprove:- shew self merciful, put to shame.

(2603) pronounced khaw-nan'; a prim. root [comp. 2583]; prop. to bend or stoop in kindness to an inferior; to favor, bestow; causat. to implore (i.e. to move to favor by petition):- beseech, x fair, (be, find, shew) favour (-able), be (deal, give, grant) gracious (-ly), entreat (be) merciful, have (shew) mercy (on, upon), have pity upon, pray, make supplication, x very.

(2583) pronounced khaw-naw'; a prim. root [comp. 2603]; prop. to incline; by impl. to decline (of the slanting rays of evening); spec. to pitch a tent; gen. to encamp (for abode or siege): abide (in tents), camp, dwell, encamp, grow to an end, lie, pitch (tent), rest in tent.

(1288) pronounced baw-rak'; a prim. root; to kneel: by impl. to bless God (as an act of adoration), and (vice versa) man (as a benefit); also (by euphemism) to curse (God or the king, as treason):- x abundantly, x altogether, x at all, blaspheme, bless, congratulate, curse, x greatly, x indeed, kneel (down), praise, salute, x still, thank.

You will surely arise and take pity on Zion, for it is time to be gracious to her; the appointed time has come. TEHILLIM 102:14 (PSALMS 102:13)

Thou shalt arise, *and* have mercy (7355) upon Zion: for the time to favour her, yea, the set time, is come. PSALMS 102:13

mercy (7355) pronounced raw-kham'; a prim. root; to fondle; by impl. to love, espec. to compassionate:- have compassion (on, upon), love, (find, have, obtain, shew) mercy (-iful, on, upon), (have) pity, Ruhamah, x surely.

The LORD is compassionate and gracious, slow to anger, abounding in steadfast love. TEHILLIM 103:8 (PSALMS 103:8)

The LORD is merciful (7349) and gracious, slow to anger, and plenteous in mercy (2617). PSALMS 103:8

merciful (7349) pronounced rakh-oom'; from 7355; compassionate:- full of compassion, merciful.

(7355) pronounced raw-kham'; a prim. root; to fondle; by impl. to love, espec. to compassionate:- have compassion (on, upon), love, (find, have, obtain, shew) mercy (-iful, on, upon), (have) pity, Ruhamah, x surely.

mercy (2617) pronounced kheh'-sed; from 2616; kindness: by impl. (toward God) piety; rarely (by opp.) reproof, or (subject.) beauty:- favour, good deed (-liness, -ness), kindly. (loving-) kindness, merciful (kindness), mercy, pity, reproach, wicked thing.

(2616) pronounced khaw-sad'; a prim. root; prop. perh. to bow (the neck only [comp. 2603] in courteousy to an equal); i.e. to be kind, also (by euphem. [comp. 1288] but rarely); to reprove:- shew self merciful, put to shame.

(2603) pronounced khaw-nan'; a prim. root [comp. 2583]; prop. to bend or stoop in kindness to an inferior; to favor, bestow; causat. to implore (i.e. to move to favor by petition):- beseech, x fair, (be, find, shew) favour (-able), be (deal, give, grant) gracious (-ly), entreat (be) merciful, have (shew) mercy (on, upon), have pity upon, pray, make supplication, x very.

(2583) pronounced khaw-naw'; a prim. root [comp. 2603]; prop. to incline; by impl. to decline (of the slanting rays of evening); spec. to pitch a tent; gen. to encamp (for abode or siege): abide (in tents), camp, dwell, encamp, grow to an end, lie, pitch (tent), rest in tent.

(1288) pronounced baw-rak'; a prim. root; to kneel: by impl. to bless God (as an act of adoration), and (vice versa) man (as a benefit); also (by euphemism) to curse (God or the king, as treason):- x abundantly, x altogether, x at all, blaspheme, bless, congratulate, curse, x greatly, x indeed, kneel (down), praise, salute, x still, thank.

For as the heavens are high above the earth, so great is His steadfast love toward those who fear Him. TEHILLIM 103:11 (PSALMS 103:11)

For as the heaven is high above the earth, *so* great in his mercy (2617) toward them that fear him. PSALMS 103:11

mercy (2617) pronounced kheh'-sed; from 2616; kindness: by impl. (toward God) piety; rarely (by opp.) reproof, or (subject.) beauty:- favour, good deed (-liness, -ness), kindly. (loving-) kindness, merciful (kindness), mercy, pity, reproach, wicked thing.

(2616) pronounced khaw-sad'; a prim. root; prop. perh. to bow (the neck only [comp. 2603] in courteousy to an equal); i.e. to be kind, also (by euphem. [comp. 1288] but rarely); to reprove:- shew self merciful, put to shame.

(2603) pronounced khaw-nan'; a prim. root [comp. 2583]; prop. to bend or stoop in kindness to an inferior; to favor, bestow; causat. to implore (i.e. to move to favor by petition):- beseech, x fair, (be, find, shew) favour (-able), be (deal, give, grant) gracious (-ly), entreat (be) merciful, have (shew) mercy (on, upon), have pity upon, pray, make supplication, x very.

(2583) pronounced khaw-naw'; a prim. root [comp. 2603]; prop. to incline; by impl. to decline (of the slanting rays of evening); spec. to pitch a tent; gen. to encamp (for abode or siege): abide (in tents), camp, dwell, encamp, grow to an end, lie, pitch (tent), rest in tent.

(1288) pronounced baw-rak'; a prim. root; to kneel: by impl. to bless God (as an act of adoration), and (vice versa) man (as a benefit); also (by euphemism) to curse (God or the king, as treason):- x abundantly, x altogether, x at all, blaspheme, bless, congratulate, curse, x greatly, x indeed, kneel (down), praise, salute, x still, thank.

But the LORD's steadfast love is for all eternity toward those who fear Him, and His beneficence is for the children's children of those who keep His covenant and remember to observe His precepts. TEHILLIM 103:17-18 (PSALMS 103:17-18)

But the mercy (2617) of the LORD *is* from everlasting to everlasting upon them that fear him, and his righteousness unto children's children; to such as keep his covenant, and to those that remember His commandments to do them. PSALMS 103:17-18

> mercy (2617) pronounced kheh'-sed; from 2616; kindness: by impl. (toward God) piety; rarely (by opp.) reproof, or (subject.) beauty:- favour, good deed (-liness, -ness), kindly. (loving-) kindness, merciful (kindness), mercy, pity, reproach, wicked thing.
>
> (2616) pronounced khaw-sad'; a prim. root; prop. perh. to bow (the neck only [comp. 2603] in courteousy to an equal); i.e. to be kind, also (by euphem. [comp. 1288] but rarely); to reprove:- shew self merciful, put to shame.
>
> (2603) pronounced khaw-nan'; a prim. root [comp. 2583]; prop. to bend or stoop in kindness to an inferior; to favor, bestow; causat. to implore (i.e. to move to favor by petition):- beseech, x fair, (be, find, shew) favour (-able), be (deal, give, grant) gracious (-ly), entreat (be) merciful, have (shew) mercy (on, upon), have pity upon, pray, make supplication, x very.
>
> (2583) pronounced khaw-naw'; a prim. root [comp. 2603]; prop. to incline; by impl. to decline (of the slanting rays of evening); spec. to pitch a tent; gen. to encamp (for abode or siege): abide (in tents), camp, dwell, encamp, grow to an end, lie, pitch (tent), rest in tent.
>
> (1288) pronounced baw-rak'; a prim. root; to kneel: by impl. to bless God (as an act of adoration), and (vice versa) man (as a benefit); also (by euphemism) to curse (God or the king, as treason):- x abundantly, x altogether, x at all, blaspheme, bless, congratulate, curse, x greatly, x indeed, kneel (down), praise, salute, x still, thank.

Hallelujah. Praise the LORD for He is good; His steadfast love is eternal. TEHILLIM 106:1 (PSALMS 106:1)

Praise ye the LORD. O give thanks unto the LORD; for *he is* good: for his mercy (2617) *endureth* for ever. PSALMS 106:1

> mercy (2617) pronounced kheh'-sed; from 2616; kindness: by impl. (toward God) piety; rarely (by opp.) reproof, or (subject.) beauty:- favour, good deed (-liness, -ness), kindly. (loving-) kindness, merciful (kindness), mercy, pity, reproach, wicked thing.
>
> (2616) pronounced khaw-sad'; a prim. root; prop. perh. to bow (the neck only [comp. 2603] in courteousy to an equal); i.e. to be kind, also (by euphem. [comp. 1288] but rarely); to reprove:- shew self merciful, put to shame.

(2603) pronounced khaw-nan'; a prim. root [comp. 2583]; prop. to bend or stoop in kindness to an inferior; to favor, bestow; causat. to implore (i.e. to move to favor by petition):- beseech, x fair, (be, find, shew) favour (-able), be (deal, give, grant) gracious (-ly), entreat (be) merciful, have (shew) mercy (on, upon), have pity upon, pray, make supplication, x very.

(2583) pronounced khaw-naw'; a prim. root [comp. 2603]; prop. to incline; by impl. to decline (of the slanting rays of evening); spec. to pitch a tent; gen. to encamp (for abode or siege): abide (in tents), camp, dwell, encamp, grow to an end, lie, pitch (tent), rest in tent.

(1288) pronounced baw-rak'; a prim. root; to kneel: by impl. to bless God (as an act of adoration), and (vice versa) man (as a benefit); also (by euphemism) to curse (God or the king, as treason):- x abundantly, x altogether, x at all, blaspheme, bless, congratulate, curse, x greatly, x indeed, kneel (down), praise, salute, x still, thank.

"Praise the LORD, for He is good; His steadfast love is eternal!" TEHILLIM 107:1 (PSALMS 107:1)

O give thanks unto the LORD, for *he is* good: for his mercy (2617) *endureth* for ever. PSALMS 107:1

mercy (2617) pronounced kheh'-sed; from 2616; kindness: by impl. (toward God) piety; rarely (by opp.) reproof, or (subject.) beauty:- favour, good deed (-liness, -ness), kindly. (loving-) kindness, merciful (kindness), mercy, pity, reproach, wicked thing.

(2616) pronounced khaw-sad'; a prim. root; prop. perh. to bow (the neck only [comp. 2603] in courteousy to an equal); i.e. to be kind, also (by euphem. [comp. 1288] but rarely); to reprove:- shew self merciful, put to shame.

(2603) pronounced khaw-nan'; a prim. root [comp. 2583]; prop. to bend or stoop in kindness to an inferior; to favor, bestow; causat. to implore (i.e. to move to favor by petition):- beseech, x fair, (be, find, shew) favour (-able), be (deal, give, grant) gracious (-ly), entreat (be) merciful, have (shew) mercy (on, upon), have pity upon, pray, make supplication, x very.

(2583) pronounced khaw-naw'; a prim. root [comp. 2603]; prop. to incline; by impl. to decline (of the slanting rays of evening); spec. to pitch a tent; gen. to encamp (for abode or siege): abide (in tents), camp, dwell, encamp, grow to an end, lie, pitch (tent), rest in tent.

(1288) pronounced baw-rak'; a prim. root; to kneel: by impl. to bless God (as an act of adoration), and (vice versa) man (as a benefit); also (by euphemism) to curse (God or the king, as treason):- x abundantly, x altogether, x at all, blaspheme, bless, congratulate, curse, x greatly, x indeed, kneel (down), praise, salute, x still, thank.

I will praise You among the peoples, O LORD, sing a hymn to You among the nations; for Your faithfulness is higher than the heavens; Your steadfastness reaches to the sky. TEHILLIM 108:4-5 (PSALMS 108:3-4)

I will praise thee, O LORD, among the people: and I will sing praises unto thee among the nations. For thy mercy (2617) *is* great above the heavens: and thy truth *reacheth* unto the clouds. PSALMS 108:3-4

mercy (2617) pronounced kheh'-sed; from 2616; kindness: by impl. (toward God) piety; rarely (by opp.) reproof, or (subject.) beauty:- favour, good deed (-liness, -ness), kindly. (loving-) kindness, merciful (kindness), mercy, pity, reproach, wicked thing.

(2616) pronounced khaw-sad'; a prim. root; prop. perh. to bow (the neck only [comp. 2603] in courteousy to an equal); i.e. to be kind, also (by euphem. [comp. 1288] but rarely); to reprove:- shew self merciful, put to shame.

(2603) pronounced khaw-nan'; a prim. root [comp. 2583]; prop. to bend or stoop in kindness to an inferior; to favor, bestow; causat. to implore (i.e. to move to favor by petition):- beseech, x fair, (be, find, shew) favour (-able), be (deal, give, grant) gracious (-ly), entreat (be) merciful, have (shew) mercy (on, upon), have pity upon, pray, make supplication, x very.

(2583) pronounced khaw-naw'; a prim. root [comp. 2603]; prop. to incline; by impl. to decline (of the slanting rays of evening); spec. to pitch a tent; gen. to encamp (for abode or siege): abide (in tents), camp, dwell, encamp, grow to an end, lie, pitch (tent), rest in tent.

(1288) pronounced baw-rak'; a prim. root; to kneel: by impl. to bless God (as an act of adoration), and (vice versa) man (as a benefit); also (by euphemism) to curse (God or the king, as treason):- x abundantly, x altogether, x at all, blaspheme, bless, congratulate, curse, x greatly, x indeed, kneel (down), praise, salute, x still, thank.

May no one show him mercy; may none pity his orphans; TEHILLIM 109:12 (PSALMS 109:12)

Let there be none to extend mercy (2617) unto him: neither let there be any to favour his fatherless children. PSALMS 109:12

mercy (2617) pronounced kheh'-sed; from 2616; kindness: by impl. (toward God) piety; rarely (by opp.) reproof, or (subject.) beauty:- favour, good deed (-liness, -ness), kindly. (loving-) kindness, merciful (kindness), mercy, pity, reproach, wicked thing.

(2616) pronounced khaw-sad'; a prim. root; prop. perh. to bow (the neck only [comp. 2603] in courteousy to an equal); i.e. to be kind, also (by euphem. [comp. 1288] but rarely); to reprove:- shew self merciful, put to shame.

(2603) pronounced khaw-nan'; a prim. root [comp. 2583]; prop. to bend or stoop in kindness to an inferior; to favor, bestow; causat. to implore (i.e. to move to favor by petition):- beseech, x fair, (be, find, shew) favour (-able), be (deal, give, grant) gracious (-ly), entreat (be) merciful, have (shew) mercy (on, upon), have pity upon, pray, make supplication, x very.

(2583) pronounced khaw-naw'; a prim. root [comp. 2603]; prop. to incline; by impl. to decline (of the slanting rays of evening); spec. to pitch a tent; gen. to encamp (for abode or siege): abide (in tents), camp, dwell, encamp, grow to an end, lie, pitch (tent), rest in tent.

(1288) pronounced baw-rak'; a prim. root; to kneel: by impl. to bless God (as an act of adoration), and (vice versa) man (as a benefit); also (by euphemism) to curse (God or the king, as treason):- x abundantly, x altogether, x at all, blaspheme, bless, congratulate, curse, x greatly, x indeed, kneel (down), praise, salute, x still, thank.

May the LORD be aware of them always and cause their names to be cut off from the earth, because he was not minded to act kindly, and hounded to death the poor and needy man, one crushed in spirit. TEHILLIM 109:15-16 (PSALMS 109:15-16)

Let them be before the LORD continually, that he may cut off the memory of them from the earth. Because that he remembered not to show mercy (2617), but persecuted the poor and needy man, that he might even slay the broken in heart. PSALMS 109:15-16

mercy (2617) pronounced kheh'-sed; from 2616; kindness: by impl. (toward God) piety; rarely (by opp.) reproof, or (subject.) beauty:- favour, good deed (-liness, -ness), kindly. (loving-) kindness, merciful (kindness), mercy, pity, reproach, wicked thing.

(2616) pronounced khaw-sad'; a prim. root; prop. perh. to bow (the neck only [comp. 2603] in courteousy to an equal); i.e. to be kind, also (by euphem. [comp. 1288] but rarely); to reprove:- shew self merciful, put to shame.

(2603) pronounced khaw-nan'; a prim. root [comp. 2583]; prop. to bend or stoop in kindness to an inferior; to favor, bestow; causat. to implore (i.e. to move to favor by petition):- beseech, x fair, (be, find, shew) favour (-able), be (deal, give, grant) gracious (-ly), entreat (be) merciful, have (shew) mercy (on, upon), have pity upon, pray, make supplication, x very.

(2583) pronounced khaw-naw'; a prim. root [comp. 2603]; prop. to incline; by impl. to decline (of the slanting rays of evening); spec. to pitch a tent; gen. to encamp (for abode or siege): abide (in tents), camp, dwell, encamp, grow to an end, lie, pitch (tent), rest in tent.

(1288) pronounced baw-rak'; a prim. root; to kneel: by impl. to bless God (as an act of adoration), and (vice versa) man (as a benefit); also (by euphemism) to curse (God or the king, as treason):- x abundantly, x altogether, x at all, blaspheme, bless, congratulate, curse, x greatly, x indeed, kneel (down), praise, salute, x still, thank.

Now You, O God, my LORD, act on my behalf as befits Your name. Good and faithful as You are, save me. TEHILLIM 109:21 (PSALMS 109:21)

But do thou for me, O God the LORD, for thy name's sake: Because thy mercy (2617) *is good*, deliver thou me. PSALMS 109:21

mercy (2617) pronounced kheh'-sed; from 2616; kindness: by impl. (toward God) piety; rarely (by opp.) reproof, or (subject.) beauty:- favour, good deed (-liness, -ness), kindly. (loving-) kindness, merciful (kindness), mercy, pity, reproach, wicked thing.

(2616) pronounced khaw-sad'; a prim. root; prop. perh. to bow (the neck only [comp. 2603] in courteousy to an equal); i.e. to be kind, also (by euphem. [comp. 1288] but rarely); to reprove:- shew self merciful, put to shame.

(2603) pronounced khaw-nan'; a prim. root [comp. 2583]; prop. to bend or stoop in kindness to an inferior; to favor, bestow; causat. to implore (i.e. to move to favor by petition):- beseech, x fair, (be, find, shew) favour (-able), be (deal, give, grant) gracious (-ly), entreat (be) merciful, have (shew) mercy (on, upon), have pity upon, pray, make supplication, x very.

(2583) pronounced khaw-naw'; a prim. root [comp. 2603]; prop. to incline; by impl. to decline (of the slanting rays of evening); spec. to pitch a tent; gen. to encamp (for abode or siege): abide (in tents), camp, dwell, encamp, grow to an end, lie, pitch (tent), rest in tent.

(1288) pronounced baw-rak'; a prim. root; to kneel: by impl. to bless God (as an act of adoration), and (vice versa) man (as a benefit); also (by euphemism) to curse (God or the king, as treason):- x abundantly, x altogether, x at all, blaspheme, bless, congratulate, curse, x greatly, x indeed, kneel (down), praise, salute, x still, thank.

Help me, O LORD, my God; save me in accord with Your faithfulness that men may know that it is Your hand, that You, O LORD, have done it. TEHILLIM 109:26-27 (PSALMS 109:26-27)

Help me, O LORD, my God: O save me according to thy mercy (2617): that they may know that this is thy hand; *that* thou, LORD, hast done it. PSALMS 109:26-27

mercy (2617) pronounced kheh'-sed; from 2616; kindness: by impl. (toward God) piety; rarely (by opp.) reproof, or (subject.) beauty:- favour, good deed (-liness, -ness), kindly. (loving-) kindness, merciful (kindness), mercy, pity, reproach, wicked thing.

(2616) pronounced khaw-sad'; a prim. root; prop. perh. to bow (the neck only [comp. 2603] in courteousy to an equal); i.e. to be kind, also (by euphem. [comp. 1288] but rarely); to reprove:- shew self merciful, put to shame.

(2603) pronounced khaw-nan'; a prim. root [comp. 2583]; prop. to bend or stoop in kindness to an inferior; to favor, bestow; causat. to implore (i.e. to move to favor by petition):- beseech, x fair, (be, find, shew) favour (-able), be (deal, give, grant) gracious (-ly), entreat (be) merciful, have (shew) mercy (on, upon), have pity upon, pray, make supplication, x very.

(2583) pronounced khaw-naw'; a prim. root [comp. 2603]; prop. to incline; by impl. to decline (of the slanting rays of evening); spec. to pitch a tent; gen. to encamp (for abode or siege): abide (in tents), camp, dwell, encamp, grow to an end, lie, pitch (tent), rest in tent.

(1288) pronounced baw-rak'; a prim. root; to kneel: by impl. to bless God (as an act of adoration), and (vice versa) man (as a benefit); also (by euphemism) to curse (God or the king, as treason):- x abundantly, x altogether, x at all, blaspheme, bless, congratulate, curse, x greatly, x indeed, kneel (down), praise, salute, x still, thank.

Not to us, O LORD, not to us but to Your name bring glory for the sake of Your love and Your faithfulness. TEHILLIM 115:1 (PSALMS 115:1)

Not unto us, O LORD, not unto us, but unto thy name give glory, for thy mercy (2617), *and* for thy truth's sake. PSALMS 115:1

mercy (2617) pronounced kheh'-sed; from 2616; kindness: by impl. (toward God) piety; rarely (by opp.) reproof, or (subject.) beauty:- favour, good deed (-liness, -ness), kindly. (loving-) kindness, merciful (kindness), mercy, pity, reproach, wicked thing.

(2616) pronounced khaw-sad'; a prim. root; prop. perh. to bow (the neck only [comp. 2603] in courteousy to an equal); i.e. to be kind, also (by euphem. [comp. 1288] but rarely); to reprove:- shew self merciful, put to shame.

(2603) pronounced khaw-nan'; a prim. root [comp. 2583]; prop. to bend or stoop in kindness to an inferior; to favor, bestow; causat. to implore (i.e. to move to favor by petition):- beseech, x fair, (be, find, shew) favour (-able), be (deal, give, grant) gracious (-ly), entreat (be) merciful, have (shew) mercy (on, upon), have pity upon, pray, make supplication, x very.

(2583) pronounced khaw-naw'; a prim. root [comp. 2603]; prop. to incline; by impl. to decline (of the slanting rays of evening); spec. to pitch a tent; gen. to encamp (for abode or siege): abide (in tents), camp, dwell, encamp, grow to an end, lie, pitch (tent), rest in tent.

(1288) pronounced baw-rak'; a prim. root; to kneel: by impl. to bless God (as an act of adoration), and (vice versa) man (as a benefit); also (by euphemism) to curse (God or the king, as treason):- x abundantly, x altogether, x at all, blaspheme, bless, congratulate, curse, x greatly, x indeed, kneel (down), praise, salute, x still, thank.

Praise the LORD, for He is good, His steadfast love is eternal. Let Israel declare, "His steadfast love is eternal." Let the house of Aaron declare, "His steadfast love is eternal." Let those who fear the LORD declare, "His steadfast love is eternal." TEHILLIM 118:1-4 (PSALMS 118:1-4)

O give thanks unto the LORD; for *he is* good: because his mercy (2617) *endureth* for ever. Let Israel now say, that his mercy (2617) *endureth* for ever. Let the house of Aaron now say, that his mercy (2617) *endureth* for ever. Let them *now* that fear the LORD say, that his mercy (2617) *endureth* for ever. PSALMS 118:1-4

mercy (2617) pronounced kheh'-sed; from 2616; kindness: by impl. (toward God) piety; rarely (by opp.) reproof, or (subject.) beauty:- favour, good deed (-liness, -ness), kindly. (loving-) kindness, merciful (kindness), mercy, pity, reproach, wicked thing.

(2616) pronounced khaw-sad'; a prim. root; prop. perh. to bow (the neck only [comp. 2603] in courteousy to an equal); i.e. to be kind, also (by euphem. [comp. 1288] but rarely); to reprove:- shew self merciful, put to shame.

(2603) pronounced khaw-nan'; a prim. root [comp. 2583]; prop. to bend or stoop in kindness to an inferior; to favor, bestow; causat. to implore (i.e. to move to favor by petition):- beseech, x fair, (be, find, shew) favour (-able), be (deal, give, grant) gracious (-ly), entreat (be) merciful, have (shew) mercy (on, upon), have pity upon, pray, make supplication, x very.

(2583) pronounced khaw-naw'; a prim. root [comp. 2603]; prop. to incline; by impl. to decline (of the slanting rays of evening); spec. to pitch a tent; gen. to encamp (for abode or siege): abide (in tents), camp, dwell, encamp, grow to an end, lie, pitch (tent), rest in tent.

(1288) pronounced baw-rak'; a prim. root; to kneel: by impl. to bless God (as an act of adoration), and (vice versa) man (as a benefit); also (by euphemism) to curse (God or the king, as treason):- x abundantly, x altogether, x at all, blaspheme, bless, congratulate, curse, x greatly, x indeed, kneel (down), praise, salute, x still, thank.

Praise the LORD for He is good, His steadfast love is eternal. TEHILLIM 118:29 (PSALMS 118:29)

O give thanks unto the LORD; for *he is* good: *for* his mercy (2617) *endureth* for ever. PSALMS 118:29

mercy (2617) pronounced kheh'-sed; from 2616; kindness: by impl. (toward God) piety; rarely (by opp.) reproof, or (subject.) beauty:- favour, good deed (-liness, -ness), kindly. (loving-) kindness, merciful (kindness), mercy, pity, reproach, wicked thing.

(2616) pronounced khaw-sad'; a prim. root; prop. perh. to bow (the neck only [comp. 2603] in courteousy to an equal); i.e. to be kind, also (by euphem. [comp. 1288] but rarely); to reprove:- shew self merciful, put to shame.

(2603) pronounced khaw-nan'; a prim. root [comp. 2583]; prop. to bend or stoop in kindness to an inferior; to favor, bestow; causat. to implore (i.e. to move to favor by petition):- beseech, x fair, (be, find, shew) favour (-able), be (deal, give, grant) gracious (-ly), entreat (be) merciful, have (shew) mercy (on, upon), have pity upon, pray, make supplication, x very.

(2583) pronounced khaw-naw'; a prim. root [comp. 2603]; prop. to incline; by impl. to decline (of the slanting rays of evening); spec. to pitch a tent; gen. to encamp (for abode or siege): abide (in tents), camp, dwell, encamp, grow to an end, lie, pitch (tent), rest in tent.

(1288) pronounced baw-rak'; a prim. root; to kneel: by impl. to bless God (as an act of adoration), and (vice versa) man (as a benefit); also (by euphemism) to curse (God or the king, as treason):- x abundantly, x altogether, x at all, blaspheme, bless, congratulate, curse, x greatly, x indeed, kneel (down), praise, salute, x still, thank.

Your steadfast love, O LORD, fills the earth: teach me Your laws. TEHILLIM 119:64 (PSALMS 119:64)

The earth, O LORD, is full of thy mercy (2617): teach me thy statutes. PSALMS 119:64

> mercy (2617) pronounced kheh'-sed; from 2616; kindness: by impl. (toward God) piety; rarely (by opp.) reproof, or (subject.) beauty:- favour, good deed (-liness, -ness), kindly. (loving-) kindness, merciful (kindness), mercy, pity, reproach, wicked thing.
>
> (2616) pronounced khaw-sad'; a prim. root; prop. perh. to bow (the neck only [comp. 2603] in courteousy to an equal); i.e. to be kind, also (by euphem. [comp. 1288] but rarely); to reprove:- shew self merciful, put to shame.
>
> (2603) pronounced khaw-nan'; a prim. root [comp. 2583]; prop. to bend or stoop in kindness to an inferior; to favor, bestow; causat. to implore (i.e. to move to favor by petition):- beseech, x fair, (be, find, shew) favour (-able), be (deal, give, grant) gracious (-ly), entreat (be) merciful, have (shew) mercy (on, upon), have pity upon, pray, make supplication, x very.
>
> (2583) pronounced khaw-naw'; a prim. root [comp. 2603]; prop. to incline; by impl. to decline (of the slanting rays of evening); spec. to pitch a tent; gen. to encamp (for abode or siege): abide (in tents), camp, dwell, encamp, grow to an end, lie, pitch (tent), rest in tent.
>
> (1288) pronounced baw-rak'; a prim. root; to kneel: by impl. to bless God (as an act of adoration), and (vice versa) man (as a benefit); also (by euphemism) to curse (God or the king, as treason):- x abundantly, x altogether, x at all, blaspheme, bless, congratulate, curse, x greatly, x indeed, kneel (down), praise, salute, x still, thank.

Deal with Your servant as befits Your steadfast love; teach me Your laws. TEHILLIM 119:124 (PSALMS 119:124)

Deal with thy servant according unto thy mercy (2617), and teach me thy statutes. PSALMS 119:124

> mercy (2617) pronounced kheh'-sed; from 2616; kindness: by impl. (toward God) piety; rarely (by opp.) reproof, or (subject.) beauty:- favour, good deed (-liness, -ness), kindly. (loving-) kindness, merciful (kindness), mercy, pity, reproach, wicked thing.
>
> (2616) pronounced khaw-sad'; a prim. root; prop. perh. to bow (the neck only [comp. 2603] in courteousy to an equal); i.e. to be kind, also (by euphem. [comp. 1288] but rarely); to reprove:- shew self merciful, put to shame.
>
> (2603) pronounced khaw-nan'; a prim. root [comp. 2583]; prop. to bend or stoop in kindness to an inferior; to favor, bestow; causat. to implore (i.e. to move to favor by petition):- beseech, x fair, (be, find, shew) favour (-able), be (deal, give, grant) gracious (-ly), entreat (be) merciful, have (shew) mercy (on, upon), have pity upon, pray, make supplication, x very.
>
> (2583) pronounced khaw-naw'; a prim. root [comp. 2603]; prop. to incline; by impl. to decline (of the slanting rays of evening); spec. to pitch a tent; gen. to encamp (for abode or siege): abide (in tents), camp, dwell, encamp, grow to an end, lie, pitch (tent), rest in tent.

> (1288) pronounced baw-rak'; a prim. root; to kneel: by impl. to bless God (as an act of adoration), and (vice versa) man (as a benefit); also (by euphemism) to curse (God or the king, as treason):- x abundantly, x altogether, x at all, blaspheme, bless, congratulate, curse, x greatly, x indeed, kneel (down), praise, salute, x still, thank.

As the eyes of slaves follow their master's hand, as the eyes of a slave-girl follow the hand of her mistress, so our eyes are toward the LORD our God, awaiting His favor. Show us favor, O LORD, show us favor! We have had more than enough of contempt. TEHILLIM 123:2-3 (PSALMS 123:2-3)

Behold, as the eyes of servants *look* unto the hand of their masters, *and* as the eyes of a maiden unto the hand of her mistress; so our eyes *wait* upon the LORD *our God*, until that he have mercy (2603) upon us. Have mercy (2603) upon us, O LORD, have mercy (2603) upon us: for we are exceedingly filled with contempt. PSALMS 123:2-3

> mercy (2603) pronounced khaw-nan'; a prim. root [comp. 2583]; prop. to bend or stoop in kindness to an inferior; to favor, bestow; causat. to implore (i.e. to move to favor by petition):- beseech, x fair, (be, find, shew) favour (-able), be (deal, give, grant) gracious (-ly), entreat (be) merciful, have (shew) mercy (on, upon), have pity upon, pray, make supplication, x very.

> (2583) pronounced khaw-naw'; a prim. root [comp. 2603]; prop. to incline; by impl. to decline (of the slanting rays of evening); spec. to pitch a tent; gen. to encamp (for abode or siege): abide (in tents), camp, dwell, encamp, grow to an end, lie, pitch (tent), rest in tent.

O Israel, wait for the LORD; for with the LORD is steadfast love and great power to redeem.
TEHILLIM 130:7 (PSALMS 130:7)

Let Israel hope in the LORD: *for* with the LORD *there is* mercy (2617), and with him *is* plenteous redemption. PSALMS 130:7

> mercy (2617) pronounced kheh'-sed; from 2616; kindness: by impl. (toward God) piety; rarely (by opp.) reproof, or (subject.) beauty:- favour, good deed (-liness, -ness), kindly. (loving-) kindness, merciful (kindness), mercy, pity, reproach, wicked thing.

> (2616) pronounced khaw-sad'; a prim. root; prop. perh. to bow (the neck only [comp. 2603] in courteousy to an equal); i.e. to be kind, also (by euphem. [comp. 1288] but rarely); to reprove:- shew self merciful, put to shame.

> (2603) pronounced khaw-nan'; a prim. root [comp. 2583]; prop. to bend or stoop in kindness to an inferior; to favor, bestow; causat. to implore (i.e. to move to favor by petition):- beseech, x fair, (be, find, shew) favour (-able), be (deal, give, grant) gracious (-ly), entreat (be) merciful, have (shew) mercy (on, upon), have pity upon, pray, make supplication, x very.

> (2583) pronounced khaw-naw'; a prim. root [comp. 2603]; prop. to incline; by impl. to decline (of the slanting rays of evening); spec. to pitch a tent; gen. to encamp (for abode or siege): abide (in tents), camp, dwell, encamp, grow to an end, lie, pitch (tent), rest in tent.

(1288) pronounced baw-rak'; a prim. root; to kneel: by impl. to bless God (as an act of adoration), and (vice versa) man (as a benefit); also (by euphemism) to curse (God or the king, as treason):- x abundantly, x altogether, x at all, blaspheme, bless, congratulate, curse, x greatly, x indeed, kneel (down), praise, salute, x still, thank.

Praise the LORD; for He is good, His steadfast love is eternal. TEHILLIM 136:1 (PSALMS 136:1)

O give thanks unto the LORD; for *he is* good: for his mercy (2617) *endureth* for ever. PSALMS 136:1

mercy (2617) pronounced kheh'-sed; from 2616; kindness: by impl. (toward God) piety; rarely (by opp.) reproof, or (subject.) beauty:- favour, good deed (-liness, -ness), kindly. (loving-) kindness, merciful (kindness), mercy, pity, reproach, wicked thing.

(2616) pronounced khaw-sad'; a prim. root; prop. perh. to bow (the neck only [comp. 2603] in courteousy to an equal); i.e. to be kind, also (by euphem. [comp. 1288] but rarely); to reprove:- shew self merciful, put to shame.

(2603) pronounced khaw-nan'; a prim. root [comp. 2583]; prop. to bend or stoop in kindness to an inferior; to favor, bestow; causat. to implore (i.e. to move to favor by petition):- beseech, x fair, (be, find, shew) favour (-able), be (deal, give, grant) gracious (-ly), entreat (be) merciful, have (shew) mercy (on, upon), have pity upon, pray, make supplication, x very.

(2583) pronounced khaw-naw'; a prim. root [comp. 2603]; prop. to incline; by impl. to decline (of the slanting rays of evening); spec. to pitch a tent; gen. to encamp (for abode or siege): abide (in tents), camp, dwell, encamp, grow to an end, lie, pitch (tent), rest in tent.

(1288) pronounced baw-rak'; a prim. root; to kneel: by impl. to bless God (as an act of adoration), and (vice versa) man (as a benefit); also (by euphemism) to curse (God or the king, as treason):- x abundantly, x altogether, x at all, blaspheme, bless, congratulate, curse, x greatly, x indeed, kneel (down), praise, salute, x still, thank.

Praise the God of gods, His steadfast love is eternal. TEHILLIM 136:2 (PSALMS 136:2)

O give thanks unto the God of gods: for his mercy (2617) *endureth* for ever. PSALMS 136:2

mercy (2617) pronounced kheh'-sed; from 2616; kindness: by impl. (toward God) piety; rarely (by opp.) reproof, or (subject.) beauty:- favour, good deed (-liness, -ness), kindly. (loving-) kindness, merciful (kindness), mercy, pity, reproach, wicked thing.

(2616) pronounced khaw-sad'; a prim. root; prop. perh. to bow (the neck only [comp. 2603] in courteousy to an equal); i.e. to be kind, also (by euphem. [comp. 1288] but rarely); to reprove:- shew self merciful, put to shame.

(2603) pronounced khaw-nan'; a prim. root [comp. 2583]; prop. to bend or stoop in kindness to an inferior; to favor, bestow; causat. to implore (i.e. to move to favor by petition):- beseech,

x fair, (be, find, shew) favour (-able), be (deal, give, grant) gracious (-ly), entreat (be) merciful, have (shew) mercy (on, upon), have pity upon, pray, make supplication, x very.

(2583) pronounced khaw-naw'; a prim. root [comp. 2603]; prop. to incline; by impl. to decline (of the slanting rays of evening); spec. to pitch a tent; gen. to encamp (for abode or siege): abide (in tents), camp, dwell, encamp, grow to an end, lie, pitch (tent), rest in tent.

(1288) pronounced baw-rak'; a prim. root; to kneel: by impl. to bless God (as an act of adoration), and (vice versa) man (as a benefit); also (by euphemism) to curse (God or the king, as treason):- x abundantly, x altogether, x at all, blaspheme, bless, congratulate, curse, x greatly, x indeed, kneel (down), praise, salute, x still, thank.

Praise the LORD of lords, His steadfast love is eternal. TEHILLIM 136:3 (PSALMS 136:3)

O give thanks to the LORD of lords: for his mercy (2617) *endureth* for ever. PSALMS 136:3

mercy (2617) pronounced kheh'-sed; from 2616; kindness: by impl. (toward God) piety; rarely (by opp.) reproof, or (subject.) beauty:- favour, good deed (-liness, -ness), kindly. (loving-) kindness, merciful (kindness), mercy, pity, reproach, wicked thing.

(2616) pronounced khaw-sad'; a prim. root; prop. perh. to bow (the neck only [comp. 2603] in courteousy to an equal); i.e. to be kind, also (by euphem. [comp. 1288] but rarely); to reprove:- shew self merciful, put to shame.

(2603) pronounced khaw-nan'; a prim. root [comp. 2583]; prop. to bend or stoop in kindness to an inferior; to favor, bestow; causat. to implore (i.e. to move to favor by petition):- beseech, x fair, (be, find, shew) favour (-able), be (deal, give, grant) gracious (-ly), entreat (be) merciful, have (shew) mercy (on, upon), have pity upon, pray, make supplication, x very.

(2583) pronounced khaw-naw'; a prim. root [comp. 2603]; prop. to incline; by impl. to decline (of the slanting rays of evening); spec. to pitch a tent; gen. to encamp (for abode or siege): abide (in tents), camp, dwell, encamp, grow to an end, lie, pitch (tent), rest in tent.

(1288) pronounced baw-rak'; a prim. root; to kneel: by impl. to bless God (as an act of adoration), and (vice versa) man (as a benefit); also (by euphemism) to curse (God or the king, as treason):- x abundantly, x altogether, x at all, blaspheme, bless, congratulate, curse, x greatly, x indeed, kneel (down), praise, salute, x still, thank.

Who alone works great marvels, His steadfast love is eternal; TEHILLIM 136:4 (PSALMS 136:4)

To him who alone doeth great wonders: for his mercy (2617) *endureth* for ever. PSALMS 136:4

mercy (2617) pronounced kheh'-sed; from 2616; kindness: by impl. (toward God) piety; rarely (by opp.) reproof, or (subject.) beauty:- favour, good deed (-liness, -ness), kindly. (loving-) kindness, merciful (kindness), mercy, pity, reproach, wicked thing.

(2616) pronounced khaw-sad'; a prim. root; prop. perh. to bow (the neck only [comp. 2603] in courteousy to an equal); i.e. to be kind, also (by euphem. [comp. 1288] but rarely); to reprove:- shew self merciful, put to shame.

(2603) pronounced khaw-nan'; a prim. root [comp. 2583]; prop. to bend or stoop in kindness to an inferior; to favor, bestow; causat. to implore (i.e. to move to favor by petition):- beseech, x fair, (be, find, shew) favour (-able), be (deal, give, grant) gracious (-ly), entreat (be) merciful, have (shew) mercy (on, upon), have pity upon, pray, make supplication, x very.

(2583) pronounced khaw-naw'; a prim. root [comp. 2603]; prop. to incline; by impl. to decline (of the slanting rays of evening); spec. to pitch a tent; gen. to encamp (for abode or siege): abide (in tents), camp, dwell, encamp, grow to an end, lie, pitch (tent), rest in tent.

(1288) pronounced baw-rak'; a prim. root; to kneel: by impl. to bless God (as an act of adoration), and (vice versa) man (as a benefit); also (by euphemism) to curse (God or the king, as treason):- x abundantly, x altogether, x at all, blaspheme, bless, congratulate, curse, x greatly, x indeed, kneel (down), praise, salute, x still, thank.

Who made the heavens with wisdom, His steadfast love is eternal; TEHILLIM 136:5 (PSALMS 136:5)

To him that by wisdom made the heavens: for his mercy (2617) *endureth* for ever. PSALMS 136:5

mercy (2617) pronounced kheh'-sed; from 2616; kindness: by impl. (toward God) piety; rarely (by opp.) reproof, or (subject.) beauty:- favour, good deed (-liness, -ness), kindly. (loving-) kindness, merciful (kindness), mercy, pity, reproach, wicked thing.

(2616) pronounced khaw-sad'; a prim. root; prop. perh. to bow (the neck only [comp. 2603] in courteousy to an equal); i.e. to be kind, also (by euphem. [comp. 1288] but rarely); to reprove:- shew self merciful, put to shame.

(2603) pronounced khaw-nan'; a prim. root [comp. 2583]; prop. to bend or stoop in kindness to an inferior; to favor, bestow; causat. to implore (i.e. to move to favor by petition):- beseech, x fair, (be, find, shew) favour (-able), be (deal, give, grant) gracious (-ly), entreat (be) merciful, have (shew) mercy (on, upon), have pity upon, pray, make supplication, x very.

(2583) pronounced khaw-naw'; a prim. root [comp. 2603]; prop. to incline; by impl. to decline (of the slanting rays of evening); spec. to pitch a tent; gen. to encamp (for abode or siege): abide (in tents), camp, dwell, encamp, grow to an end, lie, pitch (tent), rest in tent.

(1288) pronounced baw-rak'; a prim. root; to kneel: by impl. to bless God (as an act of adoration), and (vice versa) man (as a benefit); also (by euphemism) to curse (God or the king, as treason):- x abundantly, x altogether, x at all, blaspheme, bless, congratulate, curse, x greatly, x indeed, kneel (down), praise, salute, x still, thank.

Who spread the earth over the water, His steadfast love is eternal; TEHILLIM 136:6 (PSALMS 136:6)

To him that stretched out the earth above the waters: for his mercy (2617) *endureth* for ever. PSALMS 136:6

mercy (2617) pronounced kheh'-sed; from 2616; kindness: by impl. (toward God) piety; rarely (by opp.) reproof, or (subject.) beauty:- favour, good deed (-liness, -ness), kindly. (loving-) kindness, merciful (kindness), mercy, pity, reproach, wicked thing.

(2616) pronounced khaw-sad'; a prim. root; prop. perh. to bow (the neck only [comp. 2603] in courteousy to an equal); i.e. to be kind, also (by euphem. [comp. 1288] but rarely); to reprove:- shew self merciful, put to shame.

(2603) pronounced khaw-nan'; a prim. root [comp. 2583]; prop. to bend or stoop in kindness to an inferior; to favor, bestow; causat. to implore (i.e. to move to favor by petition):- beseech, x fair, (be, find, shew) favour (-able), be (deal, give, grant) gracious (-ly), entreat (be) merciful, have (shew) mercy (on, upon), have pity upon, pray, make supplication, x very.

(2583) pronounced khaw-naw'; a prim. root [comp. 2603]; prop. to incline; by impl. to decline (of the slanting rays of evening); spec. to pitch a tent; gen. to encamp (for abode or siege): abide (in tents), camp, dwell, encamp, grow to an end, lie, pitch (tent), rest in tent.

(1288) pronounced baw-rak'; a prim. root; to kneel: by impl. to bless God (as an act of adoration), and (vice versa) man (as a benefit); also (by euphemism) to curse (God or the king, as treason):- x abundantly, x altogether, x at all, blaspheme, bless, congratulate, curse, x greatly, x indeed, kneel (down), praise, salute, x still, thank.

Who made the great lights, His steadfast love is eternal; TEHILLIM 136:7 (PSALMS 136:7)

To him that made great lights: for his mercy (2617) *endureth* for ever. PSALMS 136:7

mercy (2617) pronounced kheh'-sed; from 2616; kindness: by impl. (toward God) piety; rarely (by opp.) reproof, or (subject.) beauty:- favour, good deed (-liness, -ness), kindly. (loving-) kindness, merciful (kindness), mercy, pity, reproach, wicked thing.

(2616) pronounced khaw-sad'; a prim. root; prop. perh. to bow (the neck only [comp. 2603] in courteousy to an equal); i.e. to be kind, also (by euphem. [comp. 1288] but rarely); to reprove:- shew self merciful, put to shame.

(2603) pronounced khaw-nan'; a prim. root [comp. 2583]; prop. to bend or stoop in kindness to an inferior; to favor, bestow; causat. to implore (i.e. to move to favor by petition):- beseech, x fair, (be, find, shew) favour (-able), be (deal, give, grant) gracious (-ly), entreat (be) merciful, have (shew) mercy (on, upon), have pity upon, pray, make supplication, x very.

(2583) pronounced khaw-naw'; a prim. root [comp. 2603]; prop. to incline; by impl. to decline (of the slanting rays of evening); spec. to pitch a tent; gen. to encamp (for abode or siege): abide (in tents), camp, dwell, encamp, grow to an end, lie, pitch (tent), rest in tent.

(1288) pronounced baw-rak'; a prim. root; to kneel: by impl. to bless God (as an act of adoration), and (vice versa) man (as a benefit); also (by euphemism) to curse (God or the king, as treason):- x abundantly, x altogether, x at all, blaspheme, bless, congratulate, curse, x greatly, x indeed, kneel (down), praise, salute, x still, thank.

the sun to dominate the day, His steadfast love is eternal; the moon and the stars to dominate the night, His steadfast love is eternal; TEHILLIM 136:8-9 (PSALMS 136:8-9)

the sun to rule by day: for his mercy (2617) *endureth* for ever; the moon and stars to rule by night: for his mercy (2617*) endureth* for ever. PSALMS 136:8-9

mercy (2617) pronounced kheh'-sed; from 2616; kindness: by impl. (toward God) piety; rarely (by opp.) reproof, or (subject.) beauty:- favour, good deed (-liness, -ness), kindly. (loving-) kindness, merciful (kindness), mercy, pity, reproach, wicked thing.

(2616) pronounced khaw-sad'; a prim. root; prop. perh. to bow (the neck only [comp. 2603] in courteousy to an equal); i.e. to be kind, also (by euphem. [comp. 1288] but rarely); to reprove:- shew self merciful, put to shame.

(2603) pronounced khaw-nan'; a prim. root [comp. 2583]; prop. to bend or stoop in kindness to an inferior; to favor, bestow; causat. to implore (i.e. to move to favor by petition):- beseech, x fair, (be, find, shew) favour (-able), be (deal, give, grant) gracious (-ly), entreat (be) merciful, have (shew) mercy (on, upon), have pity upon, pray, make supplication, x very.

(2583) pronounced khaw-naw'; a prim. root [comp. 2603]; prop. to incline; by impl. to decline (of the slanting rays of evening); spec. to pitch a tent; gen. to encamp (for abode or siege): abide (in tents), camp, dwell, encamp, grow to an end, lie, pitch (tent), rest in tent.

(1288) pronounced baw-rak'; a prim. root; to kneel: by impl. to bless God (as an act of adoration), and (vice versa) man (as a benefit); also (by euphemism) to curse (God or the king, as treason):- x abundantly, x altogether, x at all, blaspheme, bless, congratulate, curse, x greatly, x indeed, kneel (down), praise, salute, x still, thank.

Who struck Egypt through their first-born, His steadfast love is eternal; and brought Israel out of their midst, His steadfast love is eternal: with a strong hand and outstretched arm, His steadfast love is eternal; TEHILLIM 136:10-12 (PSALMS 136:10-12)

To him that smote Egypt in their firstborn: for his mercy (2617) *endureth* for ever: and brought out Israel from among them: for his mercy (2617*) endureth* for ever: with a strong hand, and with a stretched out arm: for his mercy (2617) *endureth* for ever. PSALMS 136:10-12

mercy (2617) pronounced kheh'-sed; from 2616; kindness: by impl. (toward God) piety; rarely (by opp.) reproof, or (subject.) beauty:- favour, good deed (-liness, -ness), kindly. (loving-) kindness, merciful (kindness), mercy, pity, reproach, wicked thing.

(2616) pronounced khaw-sad'; a prim. root; prop. perh. to bow (the neck only [comp. 2603] in courteousy to an equal); i.e. to be kind, also (by euphem. [comp. 1288] but rarely); to reprove:- shew self merciful, put to shame.

(2603) pronounced khaw-nan'; a prim. root [comp. 2583]; prop. to bend or stoop in kindness to an inferior; to favor, bestow; causat. to implore (i.e. to move to favor by petition):- beseech, x fair, (be, find, shew) favour (-able), be (deal, give, grant) gracious (-ly), entreat (be) merciful, have (shew) mercy (on, upon), have pity upon, pray, make supplication, x very.

(2583) pronounced khaw-naw'; a prim. root [comp. 2603]; prop. to incline; by impl. to decline (of the slanting rays of evening); spec. to pitch a tent; gen. to encamp (for abode or siege): abide (in tents), camp, dwell, encamp, grow to an end, lie, pitch (tent), rest in tent.

(1288) pronounced baw-rak'; a prim. root; to kneel: by impl. to bless God (as an act of adoration), and (vice versa) man (as a benefit); also (by euphemism) to curse (God or the king, as treason):- x abundantly, x altogether, x at all, blaspheme, bless, congratulate, curse, x greatly, x indeed, kneel (down), praise, salute, x still, thank.

Who split apart the Sea of Reeds, His steadfast love is eternal; TEHILLIM 136:13 (PSALMS 136:13)

To him which divided the Red sea into parts: for his mercy (2617) *endureth* for ever. PSALMS 136:13

mercy (2617) pronounced kheh'-sed; from 2616; kindness: by impl. (toward God) piety; rarely (by opp.) reproof, or (subject.) beauty:- favour, good deed (-liness, -ness), kindly. (loving-) kindness, merciful (kindness), mercy, pity, reproach, wicked thing.

(2616) pronounced khaw-sad'; a prim. root; prop. perh. to bow (the neck only [comp. 2603] in courteousy to an equal); i.e. to be kind, also (by euphem. [comp. 1288] but rarely); to reprove:- shew self merciful, put to shame.

(2603) pronounced khaw-nan'; a prim. root [comp. 2583]; prop. to bend or stoop in kindness to an inferior; to favor, bestow; causat. to implore (i.e. to move to favor by petition):- beseech, x fair, (be, find, shew) favour (-able), be (deal, give, grant) gracious (-ly), entreat (be) merciful, have (shew) mercy (on, upon), have pity upon, pray, make supplication, x very.

(2583) pronounced khaw-naw'; a prim. root [comp. 2603]; prop. to incline; by impl. to decline (of the slanting rays of evening); spec. to pitch a tent; gen. to encamp (for abode or siege): abide (in tents), camp, dwell, encamp, grow to an end, lie, pitch (tent), rest in tent.

(1288) pronounced baw-rak'; a prim. root; to kneel: by impl. to bless God (as an act of adoration), and (vice versa) man (as a benefit); also (by euphemism) to curse (God or the king, as treason):- x abundantly, x altogether, x at all, blaspheme, bless, congratulate, curse, x greatly, x indeed, kneel (down), praise, salute, x still, thank.

and made Israel pass through it, His steadfast love is eternal: Who hurled Pharaoh and his army into the Sea of Reeds, His steadfast love is eternal; TEHILLIM 136:14-15 (PSALMS 136:14-15)

and made Israel to pass through the midst of it: for his mercy (2617) *endureth* for ever: but overthrew Pharaoh and his host in the Red sea: for his mercy (2617) *endureth* for ever. PSALMS 136:14-15

> mercy (2617) pronounced kheh'-sed; from 2616; kindness: by impl. (toward God) piety; rarely (by opp.) reproof, or (subject.) beauty:- favour, good deed (-liness, -ness), kindly. (loving-) kindness, merciful (kindness), mercy, pity, reproach, wicked thing.
>
> (2616) pronounced khaw-sad'; a prim. root; prop. perh. to bow (the neck only [comp. 2603] in courteousy to an equal); i.e. to be kind, also (by euphem. [comp. 1288] but rarely); to reprove:- shew self merciful, put to shame.
>
> (2603) pronounced khaw-nan'; a prim. root [comp. 2583]; prop. to bend or stoop in kindness to an inferior; to favor, bestow; causat. to implore (i.e. to move to favor by petition):- beseech, x fair, (be, find, shew) favour (-able), be (deal, give, grant) gracious (-ly), entreat (be) merciful, have (shew) mercy (on, upon), have pity upon, pray, make supplication, x very.
>
> (2583) pronounced khaw-naw'; a prim. root [comp. 2603]; prop. to incline; by impl. to decline (of the slanting rays of evening); spec. to pitch a tent; gen. to encamp (for abode or siege): abide (in tents), camp, dwell, encamp, grow to an end, lie, pitch (tent), rest in tent.
>
> (1288) pronounced baw-rak'; a prim. root; to kneel: by impl. to bless God (as an act of adoration), and (vice versa) man (as a benefit); also (by euphemism) to curse (God or the king, as treason):- x abundantly, x altogether, x at all, blaspheme, bless, congratulate, curse, x greatly, x indeed, kneel (down), praise, salute, x still, thank.

Who led His people through the wilderness, His steadfast love is eternal; TEHILLIM 136:16 (PSALMS 136:16)

To him which led his people through the wilderness: for his mercy (2617) *endureth* for ever. PSALMS 136:16

> mercy (2617) pronounced kheh'-sed; from 2616; kindness: by impl. (toward God) piety; rarely (by opp.) reproof, or (subject.) beauty:- favour, good deed (-liness, -ness), kindly. (loving-) kindness, merciful (kindness), mercy, pity, reproach, wicked thing.
>
> (2616) pronounced khaw-sad'; a prim. root; prop. perh. to bow (the neck only [comp. 2603] in courteousy to an equal); i.e. to be kind, also (by euphem. [comp. 1288] but rarely); to reprove:- shew self merciful, put to shame.
>
> (2603) pronounced khaw-nan'; a prim. root [comp. 2583]; prop. to bend or stoop in kindness to an inferior; to favor, bestow; causat. to implore (i.e. to move to favor by petition):- beseech,

x fair, (be, find, shew) favour (-able), be (deal, give, grant) gracious (-ly), entreat (be) merciful, have (shew) mercy (on, upon), have pity upon, pray, make supplication, x very.

(2583) pronounced khaw-naw'; a prim. root [comp. 2603]; prop. to incline; by impl. to decline (of the slanting rays of evening); spec. to pitch a tent; gen. to encamp (for abode or siege): abide (in tents), camp, dwell, encamp, grow to an end, lie, pitch (tent), rest in tent.

(1288) pronounced baw-rak'; a prim. root; to kneel: by impl. to bless God (as an act of adoration), and (vice versa) man (as a benefit); also (by euphemism) to curse (God or the king, as treason):- x abundantly, x altogether, x at all, blaspheme, bless, congratulate, curse, x greatly, x indeed, kneel (down), praise, salute, x still, thank.

Who struck down great kings, His steadfast love is eternal; and slew mighty kings- His steadfast love is eternal; Sihon, king of the Amorites, His steadfast love is eternal; Og, king of Bashan- His steadfast love is eternal; TEHILLIM 136:17-20 (PSALMS 136:17-20)

To him which smote great kings: for his mercy (2617) *endureth* for ever; and slew famous kings: for his mercy (2617) *endureth* for ever: Sihon king of the Amorites: for his mercy (2617) *endureth* for ever: and Og the king of Bashan: for his mercy (2617) *endureth* for ever: PSALMS 136:17-20

mercy (2617) pronounced kheh'-sed; from 2616; kindness: by impl. (toward God) piety; rarely (by opp.) reproof, or (subject.) beauty:- favour, good deed (-liness, -ness), kindly. (loving-) kindness, merciful (kindness), mercy, pity, reproach, wicked thing.

(2616) pronounced khaw-sad'; a prim. root; prop. perh. to bow (the neck only [comp. 2603] in courteousy to an equal); i.e. to be kind, also (by euphem. [comp. 1288] but rarely); to reprove:- shew self merciful, put to shame.

(2603) pronounced khaw-nan'; a prim. root [comp. 2583]; prop. to bend or stoop in kindness to an inferior; to favor, bestow; causat. to implore (i.e. to move to favor by petition):- beseech, x fair, (be, find, shew) favour (-able), be (deal, give, grant) gracious (-ly), entreat (be) merciful, have (shew) mercy (on, upon), have pity upon, pray, make supplication, x very.

(2583) pronounced khaw-naw'; a prim. root [comp. 2603]; prop. to incline; by impl. to decline (of the slanting rays of evening); spec. to pitch a tent; gen. to encamp (for abode or siege): abide (in tents), camp, dwell, encamp, grow to an end, lie, pitch (tent), rest in tent.

(1288) pronounced baw-rak'; a prim. root; to kneel: by impl. to bless God (as an act of adoration), and (vice versa) man (as a benefit); also (by euphemism) to curse (God or the king, as treason):- x abundantly, x altogether, x at all, blaspheme, bless, congratulate, curse, x greatly, x indeed, kneel (down), praise, salute, x still, thank.

and gave their land as a heritage, His steadfast love is eternal: a heritage to His servant Israel, His steadfast love is eternal; TEHILLIM 136:21-22 (PSALMS 136:21-22) and gave their land for a heritage: for his mercy (2617) *endureth* for ever: even a heritage unto Israel his servant: for his mercy (2617) *endureth* for ever. PSALMS 136:21-22

> mercy (2617) pronounced kheh'-sed; from 2616; kindness: by impl. (toward God) piety; rarely (by opp.) reproof, or (subject.) beauty:- favour, good deed (-liness, -ness), kindly. (loving-) kindness, merciful (kindness), mercy, pity, reproach, wicked thing.
>
> (2616) pronounced khaw-sad'; a prim. root; prop. perh. to bow (the neck only [comp. 2603] in courteousy to an equal); i.e. to be kind, also (by euphem. [comp. 1288] but rarely); to reprove:- shew self merciful, put to shame.
>
> (2603) pronounced khaw-nan'; a prim. root [comp. 2583]; prop. to bend or stoop in kindness to an inferior; to favor, bestow; causat. to implore (i.e. to move to favor by petition):- beseech, x fair, (be, find, shew) favour (-able), be (deal, give, grant) gracious (-ly), entreat (be) merciful, have (shew) mercy (on, upon), have pity upon, pray, make supplication, x very.
>
> (2583) pronounced khaw-naw'; a prim. root [comp. 2603]; prop. to incline; by impl. to decline (of the slanting rays of evening); spec. to pitch a tent; gen. to encamp (for abode or siege): abide (in tents), camp, dwell, encamp, grow to an end, lie, pitch (tent), rest in tent.
>
> (1288) pronounced baw-rak'; a prim. root; to kneel: by impl. to bless God (as an act of adoration), and (vice versa) man (as a benefit); also (by euphemism) to curse (God or the king, as treason):- x abundantly, x altogether, x at all, blaspheme, bless, congratulate, curse, x greatly, x indeed, kneel (down), praise, salute, x still, thank.

Who took note of us in our degradation, His steadfast love is eternal; and rescued us from our enemies, His steadfast love is eternal; Who gives food to all flesh, His steadfast love is eternal. Praise the God of heaven, His steadfast love is eternal. TEHILLIM 136:23-26 (PSALMS 136:23-26)

Who remembered us in our low estate: for his mercy (2617) *endureth* for ever; and hath redeemed us from our enemies: for his mercy (2617) *endureth* for ever. Who giveth food to all flesh: for his mercy (2617) *endureth* for ever. O give thanks unto the God of heaven: for his mercy (2617) *endureth* for ever. PSALMS 136:23-26

> mercy (2617) pronounced kheh'-sed; from 2616; kindness: by impl. (toward God) piety; rarely (by opp.) reproof, or (subject.) beauty:- favour, good deed (-liness, -ness), kindly. (loving-) kindness, merciful (kindness), mercy, pity, reproach, wicked thing.
>
> (2616) pronounced khaw-sad'; a prim. root; prop. perh. to bow (the neck only [comp. 2603] in courteousy to an equal); i.e. to be kind, also (by euphem. [comp. 1288] but rarely); to reprove:- shew self merciful, put to shame.
>
> (2603) pronounced khaw-nan'; a prim. root [comp. 2583]; prop. to bend or stoop in kindness to an inferior; to favor, bestow; causat. to implore (i.e. to move to favor by petition):- beseech,

x fair, (be, find, shew) favour (-able), be (deal, give, grant) gracious (-ly), entreat (be) merciful, have (shew) mercy (on, upon), have pity upon, pray, make supplication, x very.

(2583) pronounced khaw-naw'; a prim. root [comp. 2603]; prop. to incline; by impl. to decline (of the slanting rays of evening); spec. to pitch a tent; gen. to encamp (for abode or siege): abide (in tents), camp, dwell, encamp, grow to an end, lie, pitch (tent), rest in tent.

(1288) pronounced baw-rak'; a prim. root; to kneel: by impl. to bless God (as an act of adoration), and (vice versa) man (as a benefit); also (by euphemism) to curse (God or the king, as treason):- x abundantly, x altogether, x at all, blaspheme, bless, congratulate, curse, x greatly, x indeed, kneel (down), praise, salute, x still, thank.

The LORD will settle accounts for me. O LORD, Your steadfast love is eternal; do not forsake the work of Your hands. TEHILLIM 138:8 (PSALMS 138:8)

The LORD will perfect *that which* concerneth me: thy mercy (2617), O LORD, *endureth* for ever: forsake not the works of thine own hands. PSALMS 138:8

mercy (2617) pronounced kheh'-sed; from 2616; kindness: by impl. (toward God) piety; rarely (by opp.) reproof, or (subject.) beauty:- favour, good deed (-liness, -ness), kindly. (loving-) kindness, merciful (kindness), mercy, pity, reproach, wicked thing.

(2616) pronounced khaw-sad'; a prim. root; prop. perh. to bow (the neck only [comp. 2603] in courteousy to an equal); i.e. to be kind, also (by euphem. [comp. 1288] but rarely); to reprove:- shew self merciful, put to shame.

(2603) pronounced khaw-nan'; a prim. root [comp. 2583]; prop. to bend or stoop in kindness to an inferior; to favor, bestow; causat. to implore (i.e. to move to favor by petition):- beseech, x fair, (be, find, shew) favour (-able), be (deal, give, grant) gracious (-ly), entreat (be) merciful, have (shew) mercy (on, upon), have pity upon, pray, make supplication, x very.

(2583) pronounced khaw-naw'; a prim. root [comp. 2603]; prop. to incline; by impl. to decline (of the slanting rays of evening); spec. to pitch a tent; gen. to encamp (for abode or siege): abide (in tents), camp, dwell, encamp, grow to an end, lie, pitch (tent), rest in tent.

(1288) pronounced baw-rak'; a prim. root; to kneel: by impl. to bless God (as an act of adoration), and (vice versa) man (as a benefit); also (by euphemism) to curse (God or the king, as treason):- x abundantly, x altogether, x at all, blaspheme, bless, congratulate, curse, x greatly, x indeed, kneel (down), praise, salute, x still, thank.

As You are faithful, put an end to my foes; destroy all my mortal enemies, for I am Your servant. TEHILLIM 143:12 (PSALMS 143:12)

And of thy mercy (2617) cut off mine enemies, and destroy all them that afflict my soul: for I *am* thy servant. PSALMS 143:12

mercy (2617) pronounced kheh'-sed; from 2616; kindness: by impl. (toward God) piety; rarely (by opp.) reproof, or (subject.) beauty:- favour, good deed (-liness, -ness), kindly. (loving-) kindness, merciful (kindness), mercy, pity, reproach, wicked thing.

(2616) pronounced khaw-sad'; a prim. root; prop. perh. to bow (the neck only [comp. 2603] in courteousy to an equal); i.e. to be kind, also (by euphem. [comp. 1288] but rarely); to reprove:- shew self merciful, put to shame.

(2603) pronounced khaw-nan'; a prim. root [comp. 2583]; prop. to bend or stoop in kindness to an inferior; to favor, bestow; causat. to implore (i.e. to move to favor by petition):- beseech, x fair, (be, find, shew) favour (-able), be (deal, give, grant) gracious (-ly), entreat (be) merciful, have (shew) mercy (on, upon), have pity upon, pray, make supplication, x very.

(2583) pronounced khaw-naw'; a prim. root [comp. 2603]; prop. to incline; by impl. to decline (of the slanting rays of evening); spec. to pitch a tent; gen. to encamp (for abode or siege): abide (in tents), camp, dwell, encamp, grow to an end, lie, pitch (tent), rest in tent.

(1288) pronounced baw-rak'; a prim. root; to kneel: by impl. to bless God (as an act of adoration), and (vice versa) man (as a benefit); also (by euphemism) to curse (God or the king, as treason):- x abundantly, x altogether, x at all, blaspheme, bless, congratulate, curse, x greatly, x indeed, kneel (down), praise, salute, x still, thank.

The LORD is gracious and compassionate, slow to anger and abounding in kindness. TEHILLIM 145:8 (PSALMS 145:8)

The LORD *is* gracious, and full of compassion; slow to anger, and of great mercy (2617). PSALMS 145:8

mercy (2617) pronounced kheh'-sed; from 2616; kindness: by impl. (toward God) piety; rarely (by opp.) reproof, or (subject.) beauty:- favour, good deed (-liness, -ness), kindly. (loving-) kindness, merciful (kindness), mercy, pity, reproach, wicked thing.

(2616) pronounced khaw-sad'; a prim. root; prop. perh. to bow (the neck only [comp. 2603] in courteousy to an equal); i.e. to be kind, also (by euphem. [comp. 1288] but rarely); to reprove:- shew self merciful, put to shame.

(2603) pronounced khaw-nan'; a prim. root [comp. 2583]; prop. to bend or stoop in kindness to an inferior; to favor, bestow; causat. to implore (i.e. to move to favor by petition):- beseech, x fair, (be, find, shew) favour (-able), be (deal, give, grant) gracious (-ly), entreat (be) merciful, have (shew) mercy (on, upon), have pity upon, pray, make supplication, x very.

(2583) pronounced khaw-naw'; a prim. root [comp. 2603]; prop. to incline; by impl. to decline (of the slanting rays of evening); spec. to pitch a tent; gen. to encamp (for abode or siege): abide (in tents), camp, dwell, encamp, grow to an end, lie, pitch (tent), rest in tent.

(1288) pronounced baw-rak'; a prim. root; to kneel: by impl. to bless God (as an act of adoration), and (vice versa) man (as a benefit); also (by euphemism) to curse (God or the king, as treason):- x abundantly, x altogether, x at all, blaspheme, bless, congratulate, curse, x greatly, x indeed, kneel (down), praise, salute, x still, thank.

He does not prize the strength of horses, nor value the fleetness of men; but the LORD values those who fear Him, those who depend on His faithful care. TEHILLIM 147:10-11 (PSALMS 147:10-11)

fleetness: Lit. "thighs." (TANAKH footnote)

He delighteth not in the strength of the horse: he taketh not pleasure in the legs of a man. The LORD taketh pleasure in them that fear him, in those that hope in his mercy (2617). PSALMS 147:10-11

mercy (2617) pronounced kheh'-sed; from 2616; kindness: by impl. (toward God) piety; rarely (by opp.) reproof, or (subject.) beauty:- favour, good deed (-liness, -ness), kindly. (loving-) kindness, merciful (kindness), mercy, pity, reproach, wicked thing.

(2616) pronounced khaw-sad'; a prim. root; prop. perh. to bow (the neck only [comp. 2603] in courteousy to an equal); i.e. to be kind, also (by euphem. [comp. 1288] but rarely); to reprove:- shew self merciful, put to shame.

(2603) pronounced khaw-nan'; a prim. root [comp. 2583]; prop. to bend or stoop in kindness to an inferior; to favor, bestow; causat. to implore (i.e. to move to favor by petition):- beseech, x fair, (be, find, shew) favour (-able), be (deal, give, grant) gracious (-ly), entreat (be) merciful, have (shew) mercy (on, upon), have pity upon, pray, make supplication, x very.

(2583) pronounced khaw-naw'; a prim. root [comp. 2603]; prop. to incline; by impl. to decline (of the slanting rays of evening); spec. to pitch a tent; gen. to encamp (for abode or siege): abide (in tents), camp, dwell, encamp, grow to an end, lie, pitch (tent), rest in tent.

(1288) pronounced baw-rak'; a prim. root; to kneel: by impl. to bless God (as an act of adoration), and (vice versa) man (as a benefit); also (by euphemism) to curse (God or the king, as treason):- x abundantly, x altogether, x at all, blaspheme, bless, congratulate, curse, x greatly, x indeed, kneel (down), praise, salute, x still, thank.

Let fidelity and steadfastness not leave you; bind them about your throat, write them on the tablet of your mind. MISHLEI 3:3 (PROVERBS 3:3)

Let not mercy (2617) and truth forsake thee: bind them about thy neck; write them upon the table of thine heart: PROVERBS 3:3

mercy (2617) pronounced kheh'-sed; from 2616; kindness: by impl. (toward God) piety; rarely (by opp.) reproof, or (subject.) beauty:- favour, good deed (-liness, -ness), kindly. (loving-) kindness, merciful (kindness), mercy, pity, reproach, wicked thing.

(2616) pronounced khaw-sad'; a prim. root; prop. perh. to bow (the neck only [comp. 2603] in courteousy to an equal); i.e. to be kind, also (by euphem. [comp. 1288] but rarely); to reprove:- shew self merciful, put to shame.

(2603) pronounced khaw-nan'; a prim. root [comp. 2583]; prop. to bend or stoop in kindness to an inferior; to favor, bestow; causat. to implore (i.e. to move to favor by petition):- beseech, x fair, (be, find, shew) favour (-able), be (deal, give, grant) gracious (-ly), entreat (be) merciful, have (shew) mercy (on, upon), have pity upon, pray, make supplication, x very.

(2583) pronounced khaw-naw'; a prim. root [comp. 2603]; prop. to incline; by impl. to decline (of the slanting rays of evening); spec. to pitch a tent; gen. to encamp (for abode or siege): abide (in tents), camp, dwell, encamp, grow to an end, lie, pitch (tent), rest in tent.

(1288) pronounced baw-rak'; a prim. root; to kneel: by impl. to bless God (as an act of adoration), and (vice versa) man (as a benefit); also (by euphemism) to curse (God or the king, as treason):- x abundantly, x altogether, x at all, blaspheme, bless, congratulate, curse, x greatly, x indeed, kneel (down), praise, salute, x still, thank.

He who despises his fellow is wrong; He who shows pity for the lowly is happy. Surely those who plan evil go astray, while those who plan good earn steadfast love. MISHLEI 14:21-22 (PROVERBS 14:21-22)

He that despiseth his neighbour sinneth: but he that hath mercy (2603) on the poor, happy is he. Do they not err that devise evil? But mercy (2617) and truth *shall be* to them that devise good. PROVERBS 14 :21-22

mercy (2603) pronounced khaw-nan'; a prim. root [comp. 2583]; prop. to bend or stoop in kindness to an inferior; to favor, bestow; causat. to implore (i.e. to move to favor by petition):- beseech, x fair, (be, find, shew) favour (-able), be (deal, give, grant) gracious (-ly), entreat (be) merciful, have (shew) mercy (on, upon), have pity upon, pray, make supplication, x very.

(2583) pronounced khaw-naw'; a prim. root [comp. 2603]; prop. to incline; by impl. to decline (of the slanting rays of evening); spec. to pitch a tent; gen. to encamp (for abode or siege): abide (in tents), camp, dwell, encamp, grow to an end, lie, pitch (tent), rest in tent.

mercy (2617) pronounced kheh'-sed; from 2616; kindness: by impl. (toward God) piety; rarely (by opp.) reproof, or (subject.) beauty:- favour, good deed (-liness, -ness), kindly. (loving-) kindness, merciful (kindness), mercy, pity, reproach, wicked thing.

(2616) pronounced khaw-sad'; a prim. root; prop. perh. to bow (the neck only [comp. 2603] in courteousy to an equal); i.e. to be kind, also (by euphem. [comp. 1288] but rarely); to reprove:- shew self merciful, put to shame.

(1288) pronounced baw-rak'; a prim. root; to kneel: by impl. to bless God (as an act of adoration), and (vice versa) man (as a benefit); also (by euphemism) to curse (God or the king,

as treason):- x abundantly, x altogether, x at all, blaspheme, bless, congratulate, curse, x greatly, x indeed, kneel (down), praise, salute, x still, thank.

He that withholds what is due to the poor affronts his Maker; he who shows pity for the needy honors him. MISHLEI 14:31 (PROVERBS 14:31)

He that oppresseth the poor reproacheth his Maker: but he that honoureth him hath mercy (2603) on the poor. PROVERBS 14:31

mercy (2603) pronounced khaw-nan'; a prim. root [comp. 2583]; prop. to bend or stoop in kindness to an inferior; to favor, bestow; causat. to implore (i.e. to move to favor by petition):- beseech, x fair, (be, find, shew) favour (-able), be (deal, give, grant) gracious (-ly), entreat (be) merciful, have (shew) mercy (on, upon), have pity upon, pray, make supplication, x very.

(2583) pronounced khaw-naw'; a prim. root [comp. 2603]; prop. to incline; by impl. to decline (of the slanting rays of evening); spec. to pitch a tent; gen. to encamp (for abode or siege): abide (in tents), camp, dwell, encamp, grow to an end, lie, pitch (tent), rest in tent.

Iniquity is expiated by loyalty and faithfulness, and evil is avoided through fear of the LORD. MISHLEI 16:6 (PROVERBS 16:6)

By mercy (2617) and truth iniquity is purged: and by the fear of the LORD *men* depart from evil. PROVERBS 16:6

mercy (2617) pronounced kheh'-sed; from 2616; kindness: by impl. (toward God) piety; rarely (by opp.) reproof, or (subject.) beauty:- favour, good deed (-liness, -ness), kindly. (loving-) kindness, merciful (kindness), mercy, pity, reproach, wicked thing.

(2616) pronounced khaw-sad'; a prim. root; prop. perh. to bow (the neck only [comp. 2603] in courteousy to an equal); i.e. to be kind, also (by euphem. [comp. 1288] but rarely); to reprove:- shew self merciful, put to shame.

(2603) pronounced khaw-nan'; a prim. root [comp. 2583]; prop. to bend or stoop in kindness to an inferior; to favor, bestow; causat. to implore (i.e. to move to favor by petition):- beseech, x fair, (be, find, shew) favour (-able), be (deal, give, grant) gracious (-ly), entreat (be) merciful, have (shew) mercy (on, upon), have pity upon, pray, make supplication, x very.

(2583) pronounced khaw-naw'; a prim. root [comp. 2603]; prop. to incline; by impl. to decline (of the slanting rays of evening); spec. to pitch a tent; gen. to encamp (for abode or siege): abide (in tents), camp, dwell, encamp, grow to an end, lie, pitch (tent), rest in tent.

(1288) pronounced baw-rak'; a prim. root; to kneel: by impl. to bless God (as an act of adoration), and (vice versa) man (as a benefit); also (by euphemism) to curse (God or the king, as treason):- x abundantly, x altogether, x at all, blaspheme, bless, congratulate, curse, x greatly, x indeed, kneel (down), praise, salute, x still, thank.

Faithfulness and loyalty protect the king; He maintains his throne by faithfulness. MISHLEI 20:28 (PROVERBS 20:28)

Mercy (2617) and truth preserve the king: and his throne is upholden by mercy (2617). PROVERBS 20:28

mercy (2617) pronounced kheh'-sed; from 2616; kindness: by impl. (toward God) piety; rarely (by opp.) reproof, or (subject.) beauty:- favour, good deed (-liness, -ness), kindly. (loving-) kindness, merciful (kindness), mercy, pity, reproach, wicked thing.

(2616) pronounced khaw-sad'; a prim. root; prop. perh. to bow (the neck only [comp. 2603] in courteousy to an equal); i.e. to be kind, also (by euphem. [comp. 1288] but rarely); to reprove:- shew self merciful, put to shame.

(2603) pronounced khaw-nan'; a prim. root [comp. 2583]; prop. to bend or stoop in kindness to an inferior; to favor, bestow; causat. to implore (i.e. to move to favor by petition):- beseech, x fair, (be, find, shew) favour (-able), be (deal, give, grant) gracious (-ly), entreat (be) merciful, have (shew) mercy (on, upon), have pity upon, pray, make supplication, x very.

(2583) pronounced khaw-naw'; a prim. root [comp. 2603]; prop. to incline; by impl. to decline (of the slanting rays of evening); spec. to pitch a tent; gen. to encamp (for abode or siege): abide (in tents), camp, dwell, encamp, grow to an end, lie, pitch (tent), rest in tent.

(1288) pronounced baw-rak'; a prim. root; to kneel: by impl. to bless God (as an act of adoration), and (vice versa) man (as a benefit); also (by euphemism) to curse (God or the king, as treason):- x abundantly, x altogether, x at all, blaspheme, bless, congratulate, curse, x greatly, x indeed, kneel (down), praise, salute, x still, thank.

He who strives to do good and kind deeds attains life, success, and honor. MISHLEI 21:21 (PROVERBS 21:21)

He that followeth after righteousness and mercy (2617) findeth life, righteousness, and honour. PROVERBS 21:21

mercy (2617) pronounced kheh'-sed; from 2616; kindness: by impl. (toward God) piety; rarely (by opp.) reproof, or (subject.) beauty:- favour, good deed (-liness, -ness), kindly. (loving-) kindness, merciful (kindness), mercy, pity, reproach, wicked thing.

(2616) pronounced khaw-sad'; a prim. root; prop. perh. to bow (the neck only [comp. 2603] in courteousy to an equal); i.e. to be kind, also (by euphem. [comp. 1288] but rarely); to reprove:- shew self merciful, put to shame.

(2603) pronounced khaw-nan'; a prim. root [comp. 2583]; prop. to bend or stoop in kindness to an inferior; to favor, bestow; causat. to implore (i.e. to move to favor by petition):- beseech,

x fair, (be, find, shew) favour (-able), be (deal, give, grant) gracious (-ly), entreat (be) merciful, have (shew) mercy (on, upon), have pity upon, pray, make supplication, x very.

(2583) pronounced khaw-naw'; a prim. root [comp. 2603]; prop. to incline; by impl. to decline (of the slanting rays of evening); spec. to pitch a tent; gen. to encamp (for abode or siege): abide (in tents), camp, dwell, encamp, grow to an end, lie, pitch (tent), rest in tent.

(1288) pronounced baw-rak'; a prim. root; to kneel: by impl. to bless God (as an act of adoration), and (vice versa) man (as a benefit); also (by euphemism) to curse (God or the king, as treason):- x abundantly, x altogether, x at all, blaspheme, bless, congratulate, curse, x greatly, x indeed, kneel (down), praise, salute, x still, thank.

He who covers up his faults will not succeed; he who confesses and gives them up will find mercy. MISHLEI 28:13 (PROVERBS 28:13)

He that covereth his sins shall not prosper: but whoso confesseth and forsaketh *them* shall have mercy (7355). PROVERBS 28:13

mercy (7355) pronounced raw-kham'; a prim. root; to fondle; by impl. to love, espec. to compassionate:- have compassion (on, upon), love, (find, have, obtain, shew) mercy (-iful, on, upon), (have) pity, Ruhamah, x surely.

Elders and magnates- such are the heads; prophets who give false instruction, such are the tails that people's leaders have been misleaders, so they that are led have been confused. That is why my LORD will not spare their youths, nor show compassion to their orphans and widows; for all are ungodly and wicked, and every mouth speaks impiety. YESHA'YAHU 9:14-16 (ISAIAH 9:15-17)

magnates: Emendation yields "who practice partiality." (TANAKH footnote)

tails: Emendation yields "palm branches"; the elders and the prophets are the leaders; the people are the led; cf. 3.1-2.12 (TANAKH footnote)

For lo! The Sovereign LORD of Hosts will remove from Jerusalem and from Judah prop and stay, every prop of food and every prop of water; soldier and warrior, magistrate and prophet, augur and elder; YESHA'YAHU 3:1-2 (ISAIAH 3:1-2)

For, behold, the LORD, the LORD of hosts, doth take away from Jerusalem and from Judah the stay and the staff, the whole stay of bread, and the whole stay of water, the mighty man, and the man of war, the judge, and the prophet, and the prudent, and the ancient. ISAIAH 3:1-2

My people's rulers are babes, it is governed by women. O my people! Your leaders are misleaders: they have confused the course of your paths. YESHA'YAHU 3:12 (ISAIAH 3:12)

> As for my people, children *are* their oppressors, and women rule over them. O my people, they which lead thee cause *thee* to err, and destroy the way of thy paths. ISAIAH 3:12

The ancient and honourable, he *is* the head; and the prophet that teacheth lies, he *is* the tail. For the leaders of this people cause *them* to err; and *they that are* led of them *are* destroyed. Therefore the LORD shall have no joy in their young men, neither shall have mercy (7355) on their fatherless and widows: for everyone is a hypocrite and an evildoer, and every mouth speaketh folly. For all this his anger is not turned away, but his hand *is* stretched out still. ISAIAH 9:15-17

> mercy (7355) pronounced raw-kham'; a prim. root; to fondle; by impl. to love, espec. to compassionate:- have compassion (on, upon), love, (find, have, obtain, shew) mercy (-iful, on, upon), (have) pity, Ruhamah, x surely.

But the LORD will pardon Jacob, and will again choose Israel, and will settle them on their own soil. And strangers shall join them and shall cleave to the House of Jacob. YESHA'YAHU 14:1 (ISAIAH 14:1)

For the LORD will have mercy (7355) on Jacob, and will yet choose Israel, and set them in their own land: and the strangers shall be joined with them, and they shall cleave to the house of Jacob. ISAIAH 14:1

> mercy (7355) pronounced raw-kham'; a prim. root; to fondle; by impl. to love, espec. to compassionate:- have compassion (on, upon), love, (find, have, obtain, shew) mercy (-iful, on, upon), (have) pity, Ruhamah, x surely.

And a throne shall be established in goodness in the tent of David, and on it shall sit in faithfulness a ruler devoted to justice and zealous for equity. YESHA'YAHU 16:5 (ISAIAH 16:5)

> 14.32 above, would read well here. (TANAKH footnote)
>
> > And what will he answer the messengers of any nation? That Zion has been established by the LORD: in it, the needy of His people shall find shelter. YESHA'YAHU 14:32 (ISAIAH 14:32)
> >
> > What shall *one* then answer the messengers of any nation? That the LORD hath founded Zion, and the poor of his people shall trust in it. ISAIAH 14:32

And in mercy (2617) shall the throne be established: and he shall sit upon it in truth in the tabernacle of David, judging, and seeking judgment, and hasting righteousness. ISAIAH 16:5

> mercy (2617) pronounced kheh'-sed; from 2616; kindness: by impl. (toward God) piety; rarely (by opp.) reproof, or (subject.) beauty:- favour, good deed (-liness, -ness), kindly. (loving-) kindness, merciful (kindness), mercy, pity, reproach, wicked thing.
>
> (2616) pronounced khaw-sad'; a prim. root; prop. perh. to bow (the neck only [comp. 2603] in courteousy to an equal); i.e. to be kind, also (by euphem. [comp. 1288] but rarely); to reprove:- shew self merciful, put to shame.

(2603) pronounced khaw-nan'; a prim. root [comp. 2583]; prop. to bend or stoop in kindness to an inferior; to favor, bestow; causat. to implore (i.e. to move to favor by petition):- beseech, x fair, (be, find, shew) favour (-able), be (deal, give, grant) gracious (-ly), entreat (be) merciful, have (shew) mercy (on, upon), have pity upon, pray, make supplication, x very.

(2583) pronounced khaw-naw'; a prim. root [comp. 2603]; prop. to incline; by impl. to decline (of the slanting rays of evening); spec. to pitch a tent; gen. to encamp (for abode or siege): abide (in tents), camp, dwell, encamp, grow to an end, lie, pitch (tent), rest in tent.

(1288) pronounced baw-rak'; a prim. root; to kneel: by impl. to bless God (as an act of adoration), and (vice versa) man (as a benefit); also (by euphemism) to curse (God or the king, as treason):- x abundantly, x altogether, x at all, blaspheme, bless, congratulate, curse, x greatly, x indeed, kneel (down), praise, salute, x still, thank.

Thus fortified cities lie desolate, homesteads deserted, forsaken like a wilderness; there calves graze, there they lie down and consume its boughs. When its crown is withered, they break; women come and make fires with them. For they are a people without understanding; that is why their Maker will show them no mercy, their Creator will deny them grace. YESHA'YAHU 27:10-11 (ISAIAH 27:10-11)

when its crown is withered, they break: Meaning of Heb. uncertain. Emendation yields: "Or like a terebinth whose boughs/Break when its crown is withered."
(TANAKH footnote)

Yet the defensed city *shall be* desolate, *and* the habitation forsaken, and left like a wilderness; there shall the calf feed, and there shall he lie down, and consume the branches thereof. When the boughs thereof are withered, they shall be broken off; the women come, *and* set them on fire; for it *is* a people of no understanding: therefore he that made them will not have mercy (7355) on them, and he that formed them will show them no favour. ISAIAH 27:10-11

mercy (7355) pronounced raw-kham'; a prim. root; to fondle; by impl. to love, espec. to compassionate:- have compassion (on, upon), love, (find, have, obtain, shew) mercy (-iful, on, upon), (have) pity, Ruhamah, x surely.

Truly, the LORD is waiting to show you grace. Truly, He will arise to pardon you. For the LORD is a God of justice: Happy are all who wait for Him. YESHA'YAHU 30:18 (ISAIAH 30:18)

And therefore will the LORD wait, that he may be gracious unto you, and therefore will he be exalted, that he may have mercy (7355) upon you: for the LORD *is* a God of judgment: blessed *are* all they that wait for him. ISAIAH 30:18

mercy (7355) pronounced raw-kham'; a prim. root; to fondle; by impl. to love, espec. to compassionate:- have compassion (on, upon), love, (find, have, obtain, shew) mercy (-iful, on, upon), (have) pity, Ruhamah, x surely.

I was angry at My people, I defiled My heritage: I put them into your hands, but you showed them no mercy. Even upon the aged you made your yoke exceedingly heavy. YESHA'YAHU 47:6 (ISAIAH 47:6)

I was wroth with my people. I have polluted mine inheritance, and given them into thine hand: thou didst show them no mercy (7356); upon the ancient hast thou very heavily laid thy yoke. ISAIAH 47:6

> mercy (7356) pronounced rakh'-am' from 7355; compassion (in the plur.); by extens. the womb (as cherishing the fetus); by impl. a maiden:- bowels, compassion, damsel, tender love, (great, tender) mercy, pity, womb.
>
> (7355) pronounced raw-kham'; a prim. root; to fondle; by impl. to love, espec. to compassionate:- have compassion (on, upon), love, (find, have, obtain, shew) mercy (-iful, on, upon), (have) pity, Ruhamah, x surely.

They shall not hunger or thirst, hot wind and sun shall not strike them; for He who loves them will lead them, He will guide them to springs of water. YESHA'YAHU 49:10 (ISAIAH 49:10)

They shall not hunger nor thirst: neither shall the heat nor sun smite them: for he that hath mercy (7355) on them shall lead them, even by the springs of water shall he guide them. ISAIAH 49:10

> mercy (7355) pronounced raw-kham'; a prim. root; to fondle; by impl. to love, espec. to compassionate:- have compassion (on, upon), love, (find, have, obtain, shew) mercy (-iful, on, upon), (have) pity, Ruhamah, x surely.

Shout, O heavens, and rejoice, O earth! Break into shouting, O hills! For the LORD has comforted His people, and has taken back His afflicted ones in love. YESHA'YAHU 49:13 (ISAIAH 49:13)

Sing, O heavens; and be joyful, O earth; and break forth into singing, O mountains: for the LORD hath comforted his people, and will have mercy (7355) upon his afflicted. ISAIAH 49:13

> mercy (7355) pronounced raw-kham'; a prim. root; to fondle; by impl. to love, espec. to compassionate:- have compassion (on, upon), love, (find, have, obtain, shew) mercy (-iful, on, upon), (have) pity, Ruhamah, x surely.

In slight anger, for a moment, I hid My face from you; but with kindness everlasting I will take you back in love- said the LORD your Redeemer. YESHA'YAHU 54:8 (ISAIAH 54:8)

In a little wrath I hid my face from thee for a moment; but with everlasting kindness will I have mercy (7355) on thee; saith the LORD thy Redeemer. ISAIAH 54:8

> mercy (7355) pronounced raw-kham'; a prim. root; to fondle; by impl. to love, espec. to compassionate:- have compassion (on, upon), love, (find, have, obtain, shew) mercy (-iful, on, upon), (have) pity, Ruhamah, x surely.

For the mountains may move and the hills be shaken, but My loyalty shall never move from you, nor My covenant of friendship be shaken- said the LORD, who takes you back in love. YESHA'YAHU 54:10 (ISAIAH 54:10)

For the mountains shall depart, and the hills be removed; but my kindness shall not depart from thee, neither shall the covenant of my peace be removed, saith the LORD that hath mercy (7355) on thee. ISAIAH 54:10

> mercy (7355) pronounced raw-kham'; a prim. root; to fondle; by impl. to love, espec. to compassionate:- have compassion (on, upon), love, (find, have, obtain, shew) mercy (-iful, on, upon), (have) pity, Ruhamah, x surely.

Let the wicked give up his ways, the sinful man his plans; let him turn back to the LORD, and He will pardon him; to our God, for He freely forgives. YESHA'YAHU 55:7 (ISAIAH 55:7)

Let the wicked forsake his way, and the unrighteous man his thoughts: and let him return unto the LORD, and he will have mercy (7355) upon him; and to our God, for he will abundantly pardon. ISAIAH 55:7

> mercy (7355) pronounced raw-kham'; a prim. root; to fondle; by impl. to love, espec. to compassionate:- have compassion (on, upon), love, (find, have, obtain, shew) mercy (-iful, on, upon), (have) pity, Ruhamah, x surely.

Aliens shall rebuild your walls, their kings shall wait upon you- for in anger I struck you down, but in favor I take you back. YESHA'YAHU 60:10 (ISAIAH 60:10)

And the sons of strangers shall build up thy walls, and their kings shall minister unto thee: for in my wrath I smote thee, but in my favour have I had mercy (7355) on thee. ISAIAH 60:10

> mercy (7355) pronounced raw-kham'; a prim. root; to fondle; by impl. to love, espec. to compassionate:- have compassion (on, upon), love, (find, have, obtain, shew) mercy (-iful, on, upon), (have) pity, Ruhamah, x surely.

They grasp the bow and javelin; they are cruel, they show no mercy; the sound of them is like the roaring sea. They ride upon horses, accoutered like a man for battle; against you, O Fair Zion! YIRMEYAHU 6:23 (JEREMIAH 6:23)

They shall lay hold on bow and spear; they *are* cruel, and have no mercy (7355); their voice roareth like the sea; and they ride upon horses, set in array as men for war against thee, O daughter of Zion. JEREMIAH 6:23

> mercy (7355) pronounced raw-kham'; a prim. root; to fondle; by impl. to love, espec. to compassionate:- have compassion (on, upon), love, (find, have, obtain, shew) mercy (-iful, on, upon), (have) pity, Ruhamah, x surely.

And I will smash them one against the other, parents and children alike- declares the LORD; no pity, compassion, or mercy will stop Me from destroying them." YIRMEYAHU 13:14 (JEREMIAH 13:14)

And I will dash them one against another, even the fathers and the sons together, saith the LORD: I will not pity, nor spare, nor have mercy (7355), but destroy them. JEREMIAH 13:14

> mercy (7355) pronounced raw-kham'; a prim. root; to fondle; by impl. to love, espec. to compassionate:- have compassion (on, upon), love, (find, have, obtain, shew) mercy (-iful, on, upon), (have) pity, Ruhamah, x surely.

And then-declares the LORD- I will deliver King Zedekiah of Judah and his courtiers and the people-those in this city who survive the pestilence, the sword, and the famine- into the hands of King Nebuchadrezzar of Babylon, into the hands of their enemies, into the hands of those who seek their lives. He will put them to the sword without pity, without compassion, without mercy. YIRMEYAHU 21:7 (JEREMIAH 21:7)

And afterward, saith the LORD, I will deliver Zedekiah king of Judah, and his servants, and the people, and such as are left in this city from the pestilence, from the sword, and from the famine, into the hand of Nebuchadnezzar king of Babylon, and into the hand of their enemies, and into the hand of those that seek their life: and he shall smite them with the edge of the sword; he shall not spare them, neither have pity, nor have mercy (7355). JEREMIAH 21:7

> mercy (7355) pronounced raw-kham'; a prim. root; to fondle; by impl. to love, espec. to compassionate:- have compassion (on, upon), love, (find, have, obtain, shew) mercy (-iful, on, upon), (have) pity, Ruhamah, x surely.

Thus said the LORD: I will restore the fortunes of Jacob's tents and have compassion upon his dwellings. The city shall be rebuilt on its mound, and the fortress in its proper place. YIRMEYAHU 30:18 (JEREMIAH 30:18)

Thus saith the LORD: Behold, I will bring again the captivity of Jacob's tents, and have mercy (7355) on his dwelling places; and the city shall be builded upon her own heap, and the palace shall remain after the manner thereof. JEREMIAH 30:18

> mercy (7355) pronounced raw-kham'; a prim. root; to fondle; by impl. to love, espec. to compassionate:- have compassion (on, upon), love, (find, have, obtain, shew) mercy (-iful, on, upon), (have) pity, Ruhamah, x surely.

Truly, Ephraim is a dear son to Me, a child that is dandled! Whenever I have turned against him, My thoughts would dwell on him still. That is why My heart yearns for him; I will receive him back in love- declares the LORD. YIRMEYAHU 31:20 (JEREMIAH 31:20)

> turned: Lit. "spoken" (TANAKH footnote)

Is Ephraim my dear son? *Is he* a pleasant child? for since I spake against him, I do earnestly remember him still: therefore my bowels are troubled for him; I will surely have mercy (7355) upon him, saith the LORD. JEREMIAH 31:20

> mercy (7355) pronounced raw-kham'; a prim. root; to fondle; by impl. to love, espec. to compassionate:- have compassion (on, upon), love, (find, have, obtain, shew) mercy (-iful, on, upon), (have) pity, Ruhamah, x surely.

Thus said the LORD: again there shall be heard in this place, which you say is ruined, without man or beast-in the towns of Judah and the streets of Jerusalem that are desolate, without man, without inhabitants, without beast-the sound of mirth and gladness, the voice of bridegroom and bride, the voice of those who cry, "Give thanks to the LORD of Hosts, for the LORD is good, for His kindness is everlasting!" as they bring thanksgiving offerings to the House of the LORD. For I will restore the fortunes of the land as of old-said the LORD. YIRMEYAHU 33:10-11 (JEREMIAH 33:10-11)

Thus saith the LORD: Again there shall be heard in this place, which ye say *shall be* desolate without man and without beast, *even* in the cities of Judah, and in the streets of Jerusalem, that are desolate, without man, and without inhabitant, and without beast. The voice of joy, and the voice of gladness, the voice of the bridegroom, and the voice of the bride, the voice of them that shall say, Praise the LORD of hosts: for the LORD is good; for his mercy (2617) *endureth* for ever: *and* of them that shall bring the sacrifice of praise into the house of the LORD. For I will cause to return the captivity of the land, as at first, saith the LORD. JEREMIAH 33:10-11

> mercy (2617) pronounced kheh'-sed; from 2616; kindness: by impl. (toward God) piety; rarely (by opp.) reproof, or (subject.) beauty:- favour, good deed (-liness, -ness), kindly. (loving-) kindness, merciful (kindness), mercy, pity, reproach, wicked thing.
>
> (2616) pronounced khaw-sad'; a prim. root; prop. perh. to bow (the neck only [comp. 2603] in courteousy to an equal); i.e. to be kind, also (by euphem. [comp. 1288] but rarely); to reprove:- shew self merciful, put to shame.
>
> (2603) pronounced khaw-nan'; a prim. root [comp. 2583]; prop. to bend or stoop in kindness to an inferior; to favor, bestow; causat. to implore (i.e. to move to favor by petition):- beseech, x fair, (be, find, shew) favour (-able), be (deal, give, grant) gracious (-ly), entreat (be) merciful, have (shew) mercy (on, upon), have pity upon, pray, make supplication, x very.
>
> (2583) pronounced khaw-naw'; a prim. root [comp. 2603]; prop. to incline; by impl. to decline (of the slanting rays of evening); spec. to pitch a tent; gen. to encamp (for abode or siege): abide (in tents), camp, dwell, encamp, grow to an end, lie, pitch (tent), rest in tent.
>
> (1288) pronounced baw-rak'; a prim. root; to kneel: by impl. to bless God (as an act of adoration), and (vice versa) man (as a benefit); also (by euphemism) to curse (God or the king, as treason):- x abundantly, x altogether, x at all, blaspheme, bless, congratulate, curse, x greatly, x indeed, kneel (down), praise, salute, x still, thank.

Thus said the LORD: As surely as I have established My covenant with day and night-the laws of heaven and earth- so I will never reject the offspring of Jacob and My servant David: I will never fail to take from his offspring rulers for the descendants of Abraham, Isaac, and Jacob. Indeed, I will restore their fortunes and take them back in love. YIRMEYAHU 33:25-26 (JEREMIAH 33:25-26)

Thus saith the LORD: If my covenant *be* not with day and night, *and if* I have not appointed the ordinances of heaven and earth; then will I cast away the seed of Jacob and David my servant, so that I will not take *any* of his seed *to be* rulers over the seed of Abraham, Isaac, and Jacob: for I will cause their captivity to return, and have mercy (7355) on them. JEREMIAH 33:25-26

> mercy (7355) pronounced raw-kham'; a prim. root; to fondle; by impl. to love, espec. to compassionate:- have compassion (on, upon), love, (find, have, obtain, shew) mercy (-iful, on, upon), (have) pity, Ruhamah, x surely.

Do not be afraid of the king of Babylon, whom you fear; do not be afraid of him-declares the LORD- for I am with you to save you and to rescue you from his hands. I will dispose him to be merciful to you; he shall show you mercy and bring you back to your own land. YIRMEYAHU 42:11-12 (JEREMIAH 42:11-12)

Be not afraid of the king of Babylon, of whom ye are afraid; be not afraid of him, saith the LORD: for I *am* with you to save you, and to deliver you from his hand. And I will show mercies (7356) unto you that he may have mercy (7355) upon you, and cause you to return to your own land. JEREMIAH 42:11-12

> mercies (7356) pronounced rakh'-am' from 7355; compassion (in the plur.); by extens. the womb (as cherishing the fetus); by impl. a maiden:- bowels, compassion, damsel, tender love, (great, tender) mercy, pity, womb.

> mercy (7355) pronounced raw-kham'; a prim. root; to fondle; by impl. to love, espec. to compassionate:- have compassion (on, upon), love, (find, have, obtain, shew) mercy (-iful, on, upon), (have) pity, Ruhamah, x surely.

They grasp the bow and javelin; they are cruel, they show no mercy; the sound of them is like the roaring sea. They ride upon horses, accoutered like a man for battle, against you, O Fair Babylon! YIRMEYAHU 50:42 (JEREMIAH 50:42)

They shall hold the bow and the lance; they *are* cruel and will not show mercy (7355): their voice shall roar like the sea, and they shall ride upon horses, *every one* put in array, like a man to the battle, against thee, O daughter of Babylon. JEREMIAH 50:42

> mercy (7355) pronounced raw-kham'; a prim. root; to fondle; by impl. to love, espec. to compassionate:- have compassion (on, upon), love, (find, have, obtain, shew) mercy (-iful, on, upon), (have) pity, Ruhamah, x surely.

Assuredly, thus said the LORD God: I will now restore the fortunes of Jacob and take the whole House of Israel back in love; and I will be zealous for My holy name. YECHEZK'EL 39:25 (EZEKIEL 39:25)

Therefore thus saith the LORD God: Now will I bring again the captivity of Jacob, and have mercy (7355) upon the whole house of Israel, and will be jealous for my holy name. EZEKIEL 39:25

> mercy (7355) pronounced raw-kham'; a prim. root; to fondle; by impl. to love, espec. to compassionate:- have compassion (on, upon), love, (find, have, obtain, shew) mercy (-iful, on, upon), (have) pity, Ruhamah, x surely.

Therefore, O king, may my advice be acceptable to you. Redeem your sins by beneficence and your iniquities by generosity to the poor; then your serenity may be extended." DANI'EL 4:24 (DANIEL 4:27)

Wherefore, O king, let my counsel be acceptable unto thee, and break off thy sins by righteousness, and thine iniquities by showing mercy (2604) to the poor; if it may be a lengthening of thy tranquility. DANIEL 4:27

> mercy (2604) (Chald.) pronounced khan-an'; corresp. to 2603; to favor or (causat.) entreat:- shew mercy; make supplication.

> (2603) pronounced khaw-nan'; a prim. root [comp. 2583]; prop. to bend or stoop in kindness to an inferior; to favor, bestow; causat. to implore (i.e. to move to favor by petition):- beseech, x fair, (be, find, shew) favour (-able), be (deal, give, grant) gracious (-ly), entreat (be) merciful, have (shew) mercy (on, upon), have pity upon, pray, make supplication, x very.

> (2583) pronounced khaw-naw'; a prim. root [comp. 2603]; prop. to incline; by impl. to decline (of the slanting rays of evening); spec. to pitch a tent; gen. to encamp (for abode or siege): abide (in tents), camp, dwell, encamp, grow to an end, lie, pitch (tent), rest in tent.

I prayed to the LORD my God, making confession thus: O LORD, great and awesome God, who stays faithful to His covenant with those who love Him and keep His commandments! DANI'EL 9:4 (DANIEL 9:4)

And I prayed unto the LORD my God, and made my confession, and said, O LORD, the great and dreadful God keeping the covenant and mercy (2617) to them that love him, and to them that keep his commandments. DANIEL 9:4

> mercy (2617) pronounced kheh'-sed; from 2616; kindness: by impl. (toward God) piety; rarely (by opp.) reproof, or (subject.) beauty:- favour, good deed (-liness, -ness), kindly. (loving-) kindness, merciful (kindness), mercy, pity, reproach, wicked thing.

> (2616) pronounced khaw-sad'; a prim. root; prop. perh. to bow (the neck only [comp. 2603] in courteousy to an equal); i.e. to be kind, also (by euphem. [comp. 1288] but rarely); to reprove:- shew self merciful, put to shame.

> (2603) pronounced khaw-nan'; a prim. root [comp. 2583]; prop. to bend or stoop in kindness to an inferior; to favor, bestow; causat. to implore (i.e. to move to favor by petition):- beseech,

x fair, (be, find, shew) favour (-able), be (deal, give, grant) gracious (-ly), entreat (be) merciful, have (shew) mercy (on, upon), have pity upon, pray, make supplication, x very.

(2583) pronounced khaw-naw'; a prim. root [comp. 2603]; prop. to incline; by impl. to decline (of the slanting rays of evening); spec. to pitch a tent; gen. to encamp (for abode or siege): abide (in tents), camp, dwell, encamp, grow to an end, lie, pitch (tent), rest in tent.

(1288) pronounced baw-rak'; a prim. root; to kneel: by impl. to bless God (as an act of adoration), and (vice versa) man (as a benefit); also (by euphemism) to curse (God or the king, as treason):- x abundantly, x altogether, x at all, blaspheme, bless, congratulate, curse, x greatly, x indeed, kneel (down), praise, salute, x still, thank.

She conceived again and bore a daughter; and He said to him, "Name her Lo-ruhamah; for I will no longer accept the House of Israel or pardon them. (But I will accept the House of Judah. And I will give them victory through the LORD their God: I will not give them victory with bow and sword and battle, by horses and riders.)" HOSHEA 1:6-7 (HOSEA 1:6-7)

Lo-ruhamah: i.e., "not accepted"; cf.2.3, 6 and 25. (TANAKH footnote)

Oh, call your brothers "My People" and your sisters "Lovingly Accepted!" HOSHEA 2:3 (HOSEA 2:1)

Say ye unto your brethren, Ammi; and to your sisters, Ruhamah. HOSEA 2:1

I will also disown her children; for they are now a harlot's brood. HOSHEA 2:6 (HOSEA 2:4)

And I will not have mercy upon her children, for they be the children of whoredoms. HOSEA 2:4

I will sow her in the land as My own; and take Lo-ruhamah back in favor; and I will say to Lo-ammi, "You are My People," and he will respond "[You are] my God." HOSHEA 2:25 (HOSEA 2:23)

And I will sow her unto me in the earth; and I will have mercy upon her that had not obtained mercy; and I will say to *them which were not* my people, *Thou art* my people; and they shall say, *Thou art* my God. HOSEA 2:23

And she conceived again and bare a daughter. And God said unto him, Call her name Lo-ruhamah: for I will no more have mercy (7355) upon the house of Israel; but I will utterly take them away. But I will have mercy (7355) upon the house of Judah, and will save them by the LORD their God, and will not save them by bow, nor be sword, nor by battle, by horses, nor by horsemen. HOSEA 1:6-7

mercy (7355) pronounced raw-kham'; a prim. root; to fondle; by impl. to love, espec. to compassionate:- have compassion (on, upon), love, (find, have, obtain, shew) mercy (-iful, on, upon), (have) pity, Ruhamah, x surely.

I will also disown her children; for they are now a harlot's brood, in that their mother has played the harlot, she that conceived them has acted shamelessly-because she thought "I will go after my lovers, who supply my bread and my water, my wool and my linen, my oil and my drink." HOSHEA 2:6-7 (HOSEA 2:4-5)

And I will not have mercy (7355) upon her children; for they *be* the children of whoredoms. For their mother hath played the harlot; she that conceived them hath done shamefully; for she said, I will go after my lovers that give *me my* bread and my water, my wool and my flax, mine oil and my drink. HOSEA 2:4-5

> mercy (7355) pronounced raw-kham'; a prim. root; to fondle; by impl. to love, espec. to compassionate:- have compassion (on, upon), love, (find, have, obtain, shew) mercy (-iful, on, upon), (have) pity, Ruhamah, x surely.

I will sow her in the land as My own; and take Lo-ruhamah back in favor; and I will say to Lo-ammi, "You are my people." And he will respond "[You are] my God." HOSHEA 2:25 (HOSEA 2:23)

And I will sow her unto me in the earth; and I will have mercy (7355) upon her that had not obtained mercy (7355); and I will say to *them which were not* my people, *Thou art* my people; and they shall say, *Thou art* my God. HOSEA 2:23

> mercy (7355) pronounced raw-kham'; a prim. root; to fondle; by impl. to love, espec. to compassionate:- have compassion (on, upon), love, (find, have, obtain, shew) mercy (-iful, on, upon), (have) pity, Ruhamah, x surely.

Hear the word of the LORD, O people of Israel! For the LORD has a case against the inhabitants of this land, because there is no honesty and no goodness and no obedience to God in the land. HOSHEA 4:1 (HOSEA 4:1)

Hear the word of the LORD, ye children of Israel: for the LORD hath a controversy with the inhabitants of the land, because *there is* no truth, *nor* mercy (2617), *nor* knowledge of God in the land. HOSEA 4:1

> mercy (2617) pronounced kheh'-sed; from 2616; kindness: by impl. (toward God) piety; rarely (by opp.) reproof, or (subject.) beauty:- favour, good deed (-liness, -ness), kindly. (loving-) kindness, merciful (kindness), mercy, pity, reproach, wicked thing.
>
> (2616) pronounced khaw-sad'; a prim. root; prop. perh. to bow (the neck only [comp. 2603] in courteousy to an equal); i.e. to be kind, also (by euphem. [comp. 1288] but rarely); to reprove:- shew self merciful, put to shame.
>
> (2603) pronounced khaw-nan'; a prim. root [comp. 2583]; prop. to bend or stoop in kindness to an inferior; to favor, bestow; causat. to implore (i.e. to move to favor by petition):- beseech, x fair, (be, find, shew) favour (-able), be (deal, give, grant) gracious (-ly), entreat (be) merciful, have (shew) mercy (on, upon), have pity upon, pray, make supplication, x very.

(2583) pronounced khaw-naw'; a prim. root [comp. 2603]; prop. to incline; by impl. to decline (of the slanting rays of evening); spec. to pitch a tent; gen. to encamp (for abode or siege): abide (in tents), camp, dwell, encamp, grow to an end, lie, pitch (tent), rest in tent.

(1288) pronounced baw-rak'; a prim. root; to kneel: by impl. to bless God (as an act of adoration), and (vice versa) man (as a benefit); also (by euphemism) to curse (God or the king, as treason):- x abundantly, x altogether, x at all, blaspheme, bless, congratulate, curse, x greatly, x indeed, kneel (down), praise, salute, x still, thank.

For I desire goodness, not sacrifice; obedience to God, rather than burnt offerings. HOSHEA 6:6 (HOSEA 6:6)

For I desired mercy (2617), and not sacrifice; and the knowledge of God more than burnt offerings. HOSEA 6:6

mercy (2617) pronounced kheh'-sed; from 2616; kindness: by impl. (toward God) piety; rarely (by opp.) reproof, or (subject.) beauty:- favour, good deed (-liness, -ness), kindly. (loving-) kindness, merciful (kindness), mercy, pity, reproach, wicked thing.

(2616) pronounced khaw-sad'; a prim. root; prop. perh. to bow (the neck only [comp. 2603] in courteousy to an equal); i.e. to be kind, also (by euphem. [comp. 1288] but rarely); to reprove:- shew self merciful, put to shame.

(2603) pronounced khaw-nan'; a prim. root [comp. 2583]; prop. to bend or stoop in kindness to an inferior; to favor, bestow; causat. to implore (i.e. to move to favor by petition):- beseech, x fair, (be, find, shew) favour (-able), be (deal, give, grant) gracious (-ly), entreat (be) merciful, have (shew) mercy (on, upon), have pity upon, pray, make supplication, x very.

(2583) pronounced khaw-naw'; a prim. root [comp. 2603]; prop. to incline; by impl. to decline (of the slanting rays of evening); spec. to pitch a tent; gen. to encamp (for abode or siege): abide (in tents), camp, dwell, encamp, grow to an end, lie, pitch (tent), rest in tent.

(1288) pronounced baw-rak'; a prim. root; to kneel: by impl. to bless God (as an act of adoration), and (vice versa) man (as a benefit); also (by euphemism) to curse (God or the king, as treason):- x abundantly, x altogether, x at all, blaspheme, bless, congratulate, curse, x greatly, x indeed, kneel (down), praise, salute, x still, thank.

Sow righteousness for yourselves; reap the fruits of goodness; break for yourselves betimes fresh ground of seeking the LORD, so that you may obtain a teacher of righteousness. HOSHEA 10:12 (HOSEA 10:12)

the fruits of: Lit. "according to" (TANAKH footnote)

a teacher: meaning of Heb. uncertain; Septuagint reads "the fruits". (TANAKH footnote)

Sow to yourselves in righteousness, reap in mercy (2617); break up your fallow ground; for *it is* time to seek the LORD, till he come and rain righteousness upon you. HOSEA 10:12

> mercy (2617) pronounced kheh'-sed; from 2616; kindness: by impl. (toward God) piety; rarely (by opp.) reproof, or (subject.) beauty:- favour, good deed (-liness, -ness), kindly. (loving-) kindness, merciful (kindness), mercy, pity, reproach, wicked thing.
>
> (2616) pronounced khaw-sad'; a prim. root; prop. perh. to bow (the neck only [comp. 2603] in courteousy to an equal); i.e. to be kind, also (by euphem. [comp. 1288] but rarely); to reprove:- shew self merciful, put to shame.
>
> (2603) pronounced khaw-nan'; a prim. root [comp. 2583]; prop. to bend or stoop in kindness to an inferior; to favor, bestow; causat. to implore (i.e. to move to favor by petition):- beseech, x fair, (be, find, shew) favour (-able), be (deal, give, grant) gracious (-ly), entreat (be) merciful, have (shew) mercy (on, upon), have pity upon, pray, make supplication, x very.
>
> (2583) pronounced khaw-naw'; a prim. root [comp. 2603]; prop. to incline; by impl. to decline (of the slanting rays of evening); spec. to pitch a tent; gen. to encamp (for abode or siege): abide (in tents), camp, dwell, encamp, grow to an end, lie, pitch (tent), rest in tent.
>
> (1288) pronounced baw-rak'; a prim. root; to kneel: by impl. to bless God (as an act of adoration), and (vice versa) man (as a benefit); also (by euphemism) to curse (God or the king, as treason):- x abundantly, x altogether, x at all, blaspheme, bless, congratulate, curse, x greatly, x indeed, kneel (down), praise, salute, x still, thank.

You must return to your God! Practice goodness and justice, and constantly trust in your God. HOSHEA 12:7 (HOSEA 12:6)

Therefore turn thou to thy God: keep mercy (2617) and judgment, and wait on thy God continually. HOSEA 12:6

> mercy (2617) pronounced kheh'-sed; from 2616; kindness: by impl. (toward God) piety; rarely (by opp.) reproof, or (subject.) beauty:- favour, good deed (-liness, -ness), kindly. (loving-) kindness, merciful (kindness), mercy, pity, reproach, wicked thing.
>
> (2616) pronounced khaw-sad'; a prim. root; prop. perh. to bow (the neck only [comp. 2603] in courteousy to an equal); i.e. to be kind, also (by euphem. [comp. 1288] but rarely); to reprove:- shew self merciful, put to shame.
>
> (2603) pronounced khaw-nan'; a prim. root [comp. 2583]; prop. to bend or stoop in kindness to an inferior; to favor, bestow; causat. to implore (i.e. to move to favor by petition):- beseech, x fair, (be, find, shew) favour (-able), be (deal, give, grant) gracious (-ly), entreat (be) merciful, have (shew) mercy (on, upon), have pity upon, pray, make supplication, x very.

(2583) pronounced khaw-naw'; a prim. root [comp. 2603]; prop. to incline; by impl. to decline (of the slanting rays of evening); spec. to pitch a tent; gen. to encamp (for abode or siege): abide (in tents), camp, dwell, encamp, grow to an end, lie, pitch (tent), rest in tent.

(1288) pronounced baw-rak'; a prim. root; to kneel: by impl. to bless God (as an act of adoration), and (vice versa) man (as a benefit); also (by euphemism) to curse (God or the king, as treason):- x abundantly, x altogether, x at all, blaspheme, bless, congratulate, curse, x greatly, x indeed, kneel (down), praise, salute, x still, thank.

Assyria shall not save us, no more will we ride on steeds; nor ever again will we call our handiwork our god, since in You alone orphans find pity!" HOSHEA 14:4 (HOSEA 14:3)

Asshur shall not save us; we will not ride upon horses; neither will we say any more to the work of our hands, Ye *are* our gods: for in thee the fatherless findeth mercy (7355). HOSEA 14:3

mercy (7355) pronounced raw-kham'; a prim. root; to fondle; by impl. to love, espec. to compassionate:- have compassion (on, upon), love, (find, have, obtain, shew) mercy (-iful, on, upon), (have) pity, Ruhamah, x surely.

They who cling to empty folly forsake their own welfare. YONAH 2:9 (JONAH 2:8)

They that observe lying vanities forsake their own mercy (2617). JONAH 2:8

mercy (2617) pronounced kheh'-sed; from 2616; kindness: by impl. (toward God) piety; rarely (by opp.) reproof, or (subject.) beauty:- favour, good deed (-liness, -ness), kindly. (loving-) kindness, merciful (kindness), mercy, pity, reproach, wicked thing.

(2616) pronounced khaw-sad'; a prim. root; prop. perh. to bow (the neck only [comp. 2603] in courteousy to an equal); i.e. to be kind, also (by euphem. [comp. 1288] but rarely); to reprove:- shew self merciful, put to shame.

(2603) pronounced khaw-nan'; a prim. root [comp. 2583]; prop. to bend or stoop in kindness to an inferior; to favor, bestow; causat. to implore (i.e. to move to favor by petition):- beseech, x fair, (be, find, shew) favour (-able), be (deal, give, grant) gracious (-ly), entreat (be) merciful, have (shew) mercy (on, upon), have pity upon, pray, make supplication, x very.

(2583) pronounced khaw-naw'; a prim. root [comp. 2603]; prop. to incline; by impl. to decline (of the slanting rays of evening); spec. to pitch a tent; gen. to encamp (for abode or siege): abide (in tents), camp, dwell, encamp, grow to an end, lie, pitch (tent), rest in tent.

(1288) pronounced baw-rak'; a prim. root; to kneel: by impl. to bless God (as an act of adoration), and (vice versa) man (as a benefit); also (by euphemism) to curse (God or the king, as treason):- x abundantly, x altogether, x at all, blaspheme, bless, congratulate, curse, x greatly, x indeed, kneel (down), praise, salute, x still, thank.

He has told you, O man, what is good, and what the LORD requires of you: only to do justice and to love goodness, and to walk modestly with your God: MIKHAH 6:8 (MICAH 6:8)

walk modestly with your God: Or "It is prudent to serve your God." (TANAKH footnote)

He hath shown thee, O man, what is good; and what doth the LORD require of thee, but to do justly, and to love mercy (2617), and to walk humbly with thy God? MICAH 6:8

mercy (2617) pronounced kheh'-sed; from 2616; kindness: by impl. (toward God) piety; rarely (by opp.) reproof, or (subject.) beauty:- favour, good deed (-liness, -ness), kindly. (loving-) kindness, merciful (kindness), mercy, pity, reproach, wicked thing.

(2616) pronounced khaw-sad'; a prim. root; prop. perh. to bow (the neck only [comp. 2603] in courteousy to an equal); i.e. to be kind, also (by euphem. [comp. 1288] but rarely); to reprove:- shew self merciful, put to shame.

(2603) pronounced khaw-nan'; a prim. root [comp. 2583]; prop. to bend or stoop in kindness to an inferior; to favor, bestow; causat. to implore (i.e. to move to favor by petition):- beseech, x fair, (be, find, shew) favour (-able), be (deal, give, grant) gracious (-ly), entreat (be) merciful, have (shew) mercy (on, upon), have pity upon, pray, make supplication, x very.

(2583) pronounced khaw-naw'; a prim. root [comp. 2603]; prop. to incline; by impl. to decline (of the slanting rays of evening); spec. to pitch a tent; gen. to encamp (for abode or siege): abide (in tents), camp, dwell, encamp, grow to an end, lie, pitch (tent), rest in tent.

(1288) pronounced baw-rak'; a prim. root; to kneel: by impl. to bless God (as an act of adoration), and (vice versa) man (as a benefit); also (by euphemism) to curse (God or the king, as treason):- x abundantly, x altogether, x at all, blaspheme, bless, congratulate, curse, x greatly, x indeed, kneel (down), praise, salute, x still, thank.

Who is a God like You, forgiving iniquity and remitting transgression; who has not maintained His wrath forever against the remnant of His own people, because He loves graciousness! MIKHAH 7:18 (MICAH 7:18)

Who *is* a God like unto thee, that pardoneth iniquity, and passeth by the transgression of the remnant of his heritage? He retaineth not his anger for ever because he delighteth in mercy (2617). MICAH 7:18

mercy (2617) pronounced kheh'-sed; from 2616; kindness: by impl. (toward God) piety; rarely (by opp.) reproof, or (subject.) beauty:- favour, good deed (-liness, -ness), kindly. (loving-) kindness, merciful (kindness), mercy, pity, reproach, wicked thing.

(2616) pronounced khaw-sad'; a prim. root; prop. perh. to bow (the neck only [comp. 2603] in courteousy to an equal); i.e. to be kind, also (by euphem. [comp. 1288] but rarely); to reprove:- shew self merciful, put to shame.

(2603) pronounced khaw-nan'; a prim. root [comp. 2583]; prop. to bend or stoop in kindness to an inferior; to favor, bestow; causat. to implore (i.e. to move to favor by petition):- beseech, x fair, (be, find, shew) favour (-able), be (deal, give, grant) gracious (-ly), entreat (be) merciful, have (shew) mercy (on, upon), have pity upon, pray, make supplication, x very.

(2583) pronounced khaw-naw'; a prim. root [comp. 2603]; prop. to incline; by impl. to decline (of the slanting rays of evening); spec. to pitch a tent; gen. to encamp (for abode or siege): abide (in tents), camp, dwell, encamp, grow to an end, lie, pitch (tent), rest in tent.

(1288) pronounced baw-rak'; a prim. root; to kneel: by impl. to bless God (as an act of adoration), and (vice versa) man (as a benefit); also (by euphemism) to curse (God or the king, as treason):- x abundantly, x altogether, x at all, blaspheme, bless, congratulate, curse, x greatly, x indeed, kneel (down), praise, salute, x still, thank.

You will keep faith with Jacob, loyalty to Abraham, as You promised on oath to our fathers in days gone by. MIKHAH 7:20 (MICAH 7:20)

Thou wilt perform the truth to Jacob, *and* the mercy (2617) to Abraham, which thou hast sworn unto our fathers from the days of old. MICAH 7:20

mercy (2617) pronounced kheh'-sed; from 2616; kindness: by impl. (toward God) piety; rarely (by opp.) reproof, or (subject.) beauty:- favour, good deed (-liness, -ness), kindly. (loving-) kindness, merciful (kindness), mercy, pity, reproach, wicked thing.

(2616) pronounced khaw-sad'; a prim. root; prop. perh. to bow (the neck only [comp. 2603] in courteousy to an equal); i.e. to be kind, also (by euphem. [comp. 1288] but rarely); to reprove:- shew self merciful, put to shame.

(2603) pronounced khaw-nan'; a prim. root [comp. 2583]; prop. to bend or stoop in kindness to an inferior; to favor, bestow; causat. to implore (i.e. to move to favor by petition):- beseech, x fair, (be, find, shew) favour (-able), be (deal, give, grant) gracious (-ly), entreat (be) merciful, have (shew) mercy (on, upon), have pity upon, pray, make supplication, x very.

(2583) pronounced khaw-naw'; a prim. root [comp. 2603]; prop. to incline; by impl. to decline (of the slanting rays of evening); spec. to pitch a tent; gen. to encamp (for abode or siege): abide (in tents), camp, dwell, encamp, grow to an end, lie, pitch (tent), rest in tent.

(1288) pronounced baw-rak'; a prim. root; to kneel: by impl. to bless God (as an act of adoration), and (vice versa) man (as a benefit); also (by euphemism) to curse (God or the king, as treason):- x abundantly, x altogether, x at all, blaspheme, bless, congratulate, curse, x greatly, x indeed, kneel (down), praise, salute, x still, thank.

O LORD! I have learned of Your renown; I am awed, O LORD, by Your deeds. Renew them in these years, oh, make them known in these years! Though angry, may You remember compassion. HAVAKUK 3:2 (HABAKKUK 3:2)

O LORD, I have heard thy speech, *and* was afraid: O LORD, revive thy work in the midst of the years, in the midst of the years make known; in wrath remember mercy (7355). HABAKKUK 3:2

> mercy (7355) pronounced raw-kham'; a prim. root; to fondle; by impl. to love, espec. to compassionate:- have compassion (on, upon), love, (find, have, obtain, shew) mercy (-iful, on, upon), (have) pity, Ruhamah, x surely.

And in fact, they reported to the angel of the LORD who was standing among the myrtles, "We have roamed the earth, and have found all the earth dwelling in tranquility." Thereupon the angel of the LORD exclaimed, "O LORD of Hosts! How long will You withhold pardon from Jerusalem and the towns of Judah, which You placed under a curse seventy years ago?" Z'KHARYAH 1:11-12
(ZECHARIAH 1:11-12)

> Among the myrtles: Septuagint reads "between the mountains", c.f. 6.1. In 6.1 ff. four teams of horses leave the LORD's abode to roam the four quarters of the earth; in 1.8 ff. they are about to reenter His abode after such a reconnaissance. (TANAKH footnote)
>
> > I looked up again, and I saw: Four chariots were coming out from between the two mountains; the mountains were of copper. Z'KHARYAH 6:1
> > (ZECHARIAH 6:1)
> >
> > And I turned, and lifted up mine eyes, and looked, and, behold, there came four chariots out from between two mountains; and the mountains were mountains of brass. ZECHARIAH 6:1
> >
> > In the night, I had a vision. I saw a man, mounted on a bay horse, standing among the myrtles in the Deep, and behind him were bay, sorrel, and white horses. Z'KHARYAH 1:8 (ZECHARIAH 1:8)
> >
> > I saw by night, and behold a man riding upon a red horse, and he stood among the myrtle trees that *were* in the bottom; and behind him *were there* red horses, speckled, and white. ZECHARIAH 1:8
>
> tranquility: upheavals at the start of Darius' reign had encouraged hopes of an early restoration of the Davidic dynasty (cf. Hag. 2.21 ff). Now these hopes were dashed. (TANAKH footnote)
>
> > Speak to Zerubbabel the governor of Judah: I am going to shake the heavens and the earth. HAGAI 2:21 (HAGGAI 2:21)
> >
> > Speak to Zerubbabel, governor of Judah, saying, I will shake the heavens and the earth: HAGGAI 2:21

And they answered the angel of the LORD that stood among the myrtle trees, and said, We have walked to and fro through the earth, and behold, all the earth sitteth still, and is at rest. Then the angel of the

LORD answered and said, O LORD of hosts, how long wilt thou not have mercy (7355) on Jerusalem and on the cities of Judah, against which thou hast had indignation these threescore and ten years? ZECHARIAH 1:11-12

> mercy (7355) pronounced raw-kham'; a prim. root; to fondle; by impl. to love, espec. to compassionate:- have compassion (on, upon), love, (find, have, obtain, shew) mercy (-iful, on, upon), (have) pity, Ruhamah, x surely.

Thus said the LORD of Hosts: Execute true justice; deal loyally and compassionately with one another. Z'KHARYAH 7:9 (ZECHARIAH 7:9)

Thus speaketh the LORD of hosts, saying, Execute true judgment, and show mercy (2617) and compassions every man to his brother: ZECHARIAH 7:9

> mercy (2617) pronounced kheh'-sed; from 2616; kindness: by impl. (toward God) piety; rarely (by opp.) reproof, or (subject.) beauty:- favour, good deed (-liness, -ness), kindly. (loving-) kindness, merciful (kindness), mercy, pity, reproach, wicked thing.

> (2616) pronounced khaw-sad'; a prim. root; prop. perh. to bow (the neck only [comp. 2603] in courteousy to an equal); i.e. to be kind, also (by euphem. [comp. 1288] but rarely); to reprove:- shew self merciful, put to shame.

> (2603) pronounced khaw-nan'; a prim. root [comp. 2583]; prop. to bend or stoop in kindness to an inferior; to favor, bestow; causat. to implore (i.e. to move to favor by petition):- beseech, x fair, (be, find, shew) favour (-able), be (deal, give, grant) gracious (-ly), entreat (be) merciful, have (shew) mercy (on, upon), have pity upon, pray, make supplication, x very.

> (2583) pronounced khaw-naw'; a prim. root [comp. 2603]; prop. to incline; by impl. to decline (of the slanting rays of evening); spec. to pitch a tent; gen. to encamp (for abode or siege): abide (in tents), camp, dwell, encamp, grow to an end, lie, pitch (tent), rest in tent.

> (1288) pronounced baw-rak'; a prim. root; to kneel: by impl. to bless God (as an act of adoration), and (vice versa) man (as a benefit); also (by euphemism) to curse (God or the king, as treason):- x abundantly, x altogether, x at all, blaspheme, bless, congratulate, curse, x greatly, x indeed, kneel (down), praise, salute, x still, thank.

I will give victory to the House of Judah, and triumph to the House of Joseph. I will restore them, for I have pardoned them, and they shall be as though I had never disowned them; for I the LORD am their God. Z'KHARYAH 10:6 (ZECHARIAH 10:6)

And I will strengthen the house of Judah, and I will save the house of Joseph, and I will bring them again to place them; for I have mercy (7355) upon them: and they shall be as though I had not cast them off: for I am the LORD their God, and will hear them. ZECHARIAH 10:6

mercy (7355) pronounced raw-kham'; a prim. root; to fondle; by impl. to love, espec. to compassionate:- have compassion (on, upon), love, (find, have, obtain, shew) mercy (-iful, on, upon), (have) pity, Ruhamah, x surely.

Book Five

Walking the Same Sure Foundation of Truth

Introduction

This is the fifth of five books in a mini-series with a unique purpose. Each book provides a verse to verse comparison of *TANAKH THE HOLY SCRIPTURES* (hereafter referred to as Tanakh)and the *AUTHORIZED KING JAMES VERSION* (Old Testament only, hereafter referred to as KJV) on a particular subject. Subjects of the four prior books are: salvation, righteousness, grace, and mercy. Book Five, *TRUTH*, provides references from *TANAKH* footnotes and *STRONG'S CONCORDANCE.* Readers will quickly discover that spiritual concepts presented on the following pages have physical actions that can be observed and experienced. This series is about relationship, not religion.

Each of the five books are in the same order and format for ease of use. Format, as well as use of *TANAKH* footnotes and *STRONG'S CONCORDANCE* will be discussed in the section *How This Book is Organized*. Yeshua (Jesus) spoke about each of these subjects often before the New Testament was written. Modern-day readers who grasp these truths will be able to understand the teachings of the New Testament in the same way as people of Yeshua's (Jesus's) generation.

How This Book is Organized

TANAKH verse followed by TANAKH reference (each letter capitalized) with corresponding KJV references also capitalized in parenthesis. Sometimes numbers will not match exactly but will be close. TANAKH reference will be highlighted in gray.

Example:

He will repay the evil of my watchful foes; by Your faithfulness, destroy them! TEHILLIM 54:7 (PSALMS 54:5)

Spelling of highlighted *TANAKH* references is the same as the *COMPLETE JEWISH BIBLE* throughout the book to maintain its sense of Jewishness. Refer to *Works Cited* for additional information.

KJV will include the word truth followed by a highlighted number in parenthesis within the verse. The highlighted number will be a reference number to *STRONG'S CONCORDANCE* (original Hebrew or Chaldee). The verse will be followed by the highlighted KJV reference only. Words in italic in the original text will be in italics. Archaic spelling of words will also be presented as the original authors intended.

Example:

He shall reward evil unto mine enemies: cut them off in thy truth (571). PSALMS 54:5

truth (571) pronounced eh'meth; contr. From 539; stability; fig. certainty, truth, trustworthiness:- assured (-ly), establishment, faithful, right, sure, true (-ly, -th), verity.

Pronunciation is provided with the complete definition shown in STRONG'S CONCORDANCE. Readers will notice a second highlighted number in the above example. This is the primitive root word. It will be shown with pronunciation and complete definition as in STRONG'S CONCORDANCE also.

The primitive root will generally be listed last unless it is the only reference or the first of several references. The number of the root will be indented, under the verse, lining up with the first reference.

Example:

truth (571)...

(539) pronounced aw-man'; a prim. root; to build up or support; to foster as a parent or nurse; fig. to render (or be) firm or faithful, to trust or believe, to be permanent or quiet; mor. to be true or certain; once (Isa. 30:21; by interch. for 541) to go to the right hand:- hence assurance, believe, bring up, establish, + fail, be faithful, (of long continuance, steadfast, sure, surely, trusty, verified) nurse (-ing father), (put) trust, turn to the right.

In this instance, the root word has two additional highlights. They will be be addressed in order of appearance. The scripture will be indented under (539). The (541) reference will line up under the first reference since it also is a root word and is there for comparison.

Example:

truth (571)...

(539)...

And whenever you deviate to the right or to the left, your ears will heed the command from behind you: "This is the road; follow it!" YESHA'YAHU 30:21 (ISAIAH 30:21)

And thine ears shall hear a word behind thee, saying, This is the way, walk ye in it, when ye turn to the right hand, and when ye turn to the left. ISAIAH 30:21

(541) pronounced aw'man'; denom. from 3225; to take the right-hand road:- turn to the right. See 539.

(3225) pronounced yaw-meen'; from 3231; the right hand or side (leg, eye) of a person or other object (as the stronger and most dexterous): locally, the south:- + left handed, right (hand, side), south.

(3231) pronounced yaw-man'; a prim. root; to be (phys.) right (i.e. firm); but used only as denom. from 3225 and transit., to be right-handed or take the right-hand side:- go turn) to (on, use) the right hand.

In the above example, a third root word is also presented. Highlights are especially helpful in these instances.

Abbreviations such as denom. and transit. will be identified in *Abbreviations Employed*, the next section of the book.

Occasionally, footnotes will be provided in TANAKH. When this occurs, the footnote will be noted exactly as referenced. If scripture references are available, they will also be included in the same format as above so that readers may be able to have immediate access to as much information as possible without turning pages.

The first of two examples below supplies a literal explanation as to how the original context would have been understood by its listeners.

For my eyes are on Your steadfast love; I have set my course by it. TEHILLIM 26:3 (PSALMS 26:3)

> Lit. the distress of my heart. (TANAKH footnote)

The second example directs the reader's attention to additional scripture for more information.

Dispatches were sent to all the Jews in the hundred and twenty-seven provinces of the realm of Ahasuerus with an ordinance of "equity and honesty." ESTER 9:30 (ESTHER 9:30)

> "equity and honesty": i.e., of new holidays, the instituting of which is linked to love of equity and honesty in Zech. 8:19 (TANAKH footnote)
>
>> And the word of the LORD of Hosts came to me, saying, Thus said the LORD of Hosts: the fast of the fourth month, and the fast of the tenth month shall become occasions for joy and gladness, happy festivals for the House of Judah: but you must love honesty and integrity. Z'KHARYAH 8:19 (ZECHARIAH 8:19)
>>
>> Thus saith the LORD of hosts: the fast of the fourth month, and the fast of the fifth, and the fast of the seventh, and the fast of the tenth, shall be to the house of Judah joy and gladness, and cheerful feasts; therefore love the truth (571) and peace. ZECHARIAH 8:19
>>
>>> truth (571)...
>>>
>>> (539)...
>>>
>>>> Etc. (same as shown previously)

KJV reference will always be added for comparison and continuity of the TANAKH footnote before continuing on to the corresponding KJV. In this example, ESTHER 9:30 will be the next entry.

Abbreviations Employed

Abstr.: abstract, abstractly

Adv.: adverb, adverbial, adverbially

Cf.: confer, compare

Chald.: Chaldee, Chaldaism

Concr..: concrete, concretely

Contr.: contracted, contraction

Corr., corresp.: corresponding, correspondingly

Demonstr.: demonstrate, demonstrable, demonstration

Denom.: denominative, denominatively

e.g.: exempli gratia, for example

etc.: et cetera, and others, and so forth, and so on

fem.: feminine

fig.: figurative, figuratively

Heb.: Hebrew, Hebraism

i.e.: id est, that is

interch.: interchange

interrog.: interrogative, interrogate, interrogatory

lit.: literal, literally

lol: act of lolling; recline or lean in a relaxed or indolent manner; hang loosely or droopingly

mean.: meaning

mor.: moral, morally

mss.: message, messages

neg.: negative, negatively

phys.: physical, physically

prim.: primitive, primary

prop.: proper, properly

refl., reflex.: reflexive, reflexively

transit.: transitive, transitively

The man bowed low in homage to the LORD and said, Blessed be the LORD, the God of my master Abraham, who has not withheld His steadfast faithfulness from my master. For I have been guided on my errand by the LORD, to the house of my master's kinsmen." B'RESHEET 24:26-27 (GENESIS 24:26-27)

And the man bowed down his head, and worshipped the LORD. And he said, Blessed *be* the LORD God of my master Abraham, who hath not left destitute my master of his mercy and his truth (571): I *being* in the way, the LORD led me to the house of my master's brethren. GENESIS 24:26-27

> truth (571) pronounced eh'meth; contr. From 539; stability; fig. certainty, truth, trustworthiness:-assured (-ly), establishment, faithful, right, sure, true (-ly, -th), verity.
>
> (539) pronounced aw-man'; a prim. root; prop. to build up or support; to foster as a parent or nurse; fig. to render (or be) firm or faithful, to trust or believe, to be permanent or quiet; mor. to be true or certain; once (Isa. 30:21; by interch. for 541) to go to the right hand:- hence assurance, believe, bring up, establish, + fail, be faithful (of long continuance, steadfast, sure, surely, trusty, verified) nurse (-ing father), (put) trust, turn to the right.
>
>> And whenever you deviate to the right or to the left, your ears will heed the command from behind you: "This is the road; follow it!" YESHA'YAHU 30:21 (ISAIAH 30:21)
>>
>> And thine ears shall hear a word behind thee, saying, This is the way, walk ye in it, when ye turn to the right hand, and when ye turn to the left. ISAIAH 30:21
>
> (541) pronounced aw-man'; denom. from 3225; to take the right-hand road:- turn to the right. See 539.
>
> (3225) pronounced yaw-meen'; from 3231; the right hand or side (leg, eye) of a person or other object (as the stronger and most dexterous): locally, the south:- + left handed, right (hand, side), south.
>
> (3231) pronounced yaw-man'; a prim. root; to be (phys.) right (i.e. firm); but used only as denom. from 3225 and transit., to be right-handed or take the right-hand side:- go turn) to (on, use) the right hand.

Then Jacob said, "O God of my father Abraham and God of my father Isaac, O LORD, who said to me, 'Return to your native land and I will deal bountifully with you!' I am unworthy of all the kindness that You have so steadfastly shown Your servant: with my staff alone I crossed this Jordan, and now I have become two camps. B'RESHEET 32:10-11 (GENESIS 32:9-10)

And Jacob said, O God of my father Abraham, and God of my father Isaac, the LORD which saidst unto me, Return unto thy country, and to thy kindred, and I will deal well with thee: I am not worthy of the least of all the mercies, and of all the truth (571), which thou hast shown unto thy servant; for with my staff I passed over this Jordan; and now I am become two bands. GENESIS 32:9-10

truth (571) pronounced eh'meth; contr. From 539; stability; fig. certainty, truth, trustworthiness:-assured (-ly), establishment, faithful, right, sure, true (-ly, -th), verity.

(539) pronounced aw-man'; a prim. root; prop. to build up or support; to foster as a parent or nurse; fig. to render (or be) firm or faithful, to trust or believe, to be permanent or quiet; mor. to be true or certain; once (Isa. 30:21; by interch. for 541) to go to the right hand:- hence assurance, believe, bring up, establish, + fail, be faithful (of long continuance, steadfast, sure, surely, trusty, verified) nurse (-ing father), (put) trust, turn to the right.

> and whenever you deviate to the right or to the left, your ears will heed the command from behind you: "This is the road; follow it!" YESHA'YAHU 30:21 (ISAIAH 30:21)
>
> And thine ears shall hear a word behind thee, saying, This is the way, walk ye in it, when ye turn to the right hand, and when ye turn to the left. ISAIAH 30:21

(541) pronounced aw-man'; denom. from 3225; to take the right-hand road:- turn to the right. See 539.

(3225) pronounced yaw-meen'; from 3231; the right hand or side (leg, eye) of a person or other object (as the stronger and most dexterous): locally, the south:- + left handed, right (hand, side), south.

(3231) pronounced yaw-man'; a prim. root; to be (phys.) right (i.e. firm); but used only as denom. from 3225 and transit., to be right-handed or take the right-hand side:- go turn) to (on, use) the right hand.

Let one of you go and bring your brother, while the rest of you remain confined, that your words may be put to the test whether there is truth in you. B'RESHEET 42:16 (GENESIS 42:16)

Send one of you, and let him fetch your brother, and ye shall be kept in prison, that your words may be proved, whether *there be any* truth (571) in you: or else by the life of Pharaoh surely ye are spies. GENESIS 42:16

truth (571) pronounced eh'meth; contr. From 539; stability; fig. certainty, truth, trustworthiness:-assured (-ly), establishment, faithful, right, sure, true (-ly, -th), verity.

(539) pronounced aw-man'; a prim. root; prop. to build up or support; to foster as a parent or nurse; fig. to render (or be) firm or faithful, to trust or believe, to be permanent or quiet; mor. to be true or certain; once (Isa. 30:21; by interch. for 541) to go to the right hand:- hence assurance, believe, bring up, establish, + fail, be faithful (of long continuance, steadfast, sure, surely, trusty, verified) nurse (-ing father), (put) trust, turn to the right.

> And whenever you deviate to the right or to the left, your ears will heed the command from behind you: "This is the road; follow it!" YESHA'YAHU 30:21 (ISAIAH 30:21)
>
> And thine ears shall hear a word behind thee, saying, This is the way, walk ye in it, when ye turn to the right hand, and when ye turn to the left. ISAIAH 30:21

(541) pronounced aw-man'; denom. from 3225; to take the right-hand road:- turn to the right. See 539.

(3225) pronounced yaw-meen'; from 3231; the right hand or side (leg, eye) of a person or other object (as the stronger and most dexterous): locally, the south:- + left handed, right (hand, side), south.

(3231) pronounced yaw-man'; a prim. root; to be (phys.) right (i.e. firm); but used only as denom. from 3225 and transit., to be right-handed or take the right-hand side:- go turn) to (on, use) the right hand.

You shall also seek out from among all the people capable men who fear God, trustworthy men who spurn ill-gotten gain. Set these over them as chiefs of thousands, hundreds, fifties, and tens. SH'MOT 18:21 (EXODUS 18:21)

Moreover thou shalt provide out of all the people able men, such as fear God, men of truth (571), hating covetousness; and place *such* over them, *to be* rulers of thousands, *and* rulers of hundreds, rulers of fifties, *and* rulers of tens: EXODUS 18:21

truth (571) pronounced eh'meth; contr. From 539; stability; fig. certainty, truth, trustworthiness:-assured (-ly), establishment, faithful, right, sure, true (-ly, -th), verity.

(539) pronounced aw-man'; a prim. root; prop. to build up or support; to foster as a parent or nurse; fig. to render (or be) firm or faithful, to trust or believe, to be permanent or quiet; mor. to be true or certain; once (Isa. 30:21; by interch. for 541) to go to the right hand:- hence assurance, believe, bring up, establish, + fail, be faithful (of long continuance, steadfast, sure, surely, trusty, verified) nurse (-ing father), (put) trust, turn to the right.

> And whenever you deviate to the right or to the left, your ears will heed the command from behind you: "This is the road; follow it!" YESHA'YAHU 30:21 (ISAIAH 30:21)
>
> And thine ears shall hear a word behind thee, saying, This is the way, walk ye in it, when ye turn to the right hand, and when ye turn to the left. ISAIAH 30:21

(541) pronounced aw-man'; denom. from 3225; to take the right-hand road:- turn to the right. See 539.

(3225) pronounced yaw-meen'; from 3231; the right hand or side (leg, eye) of a person or other object (as the stronger and most dexterous): locally, the south:- + left handed, right (hand, side), south.

(3231) pronounced yaw-man'; a prim. root; to be (phys.) right (i.e. firm); but used only as denom. from 3225 and transit., to be right-handed or take the right-hand side:- go turn) to (on, use) the right hand.

The LORD passed before him and proclaimed: "The LORD! the LORD! a God compassionate and gracious, slow to anger, abounding in kindness and faithfulness, SH'MOT 34:6 (EXODUS 34:6)

Or "and the LORD proclaimed: The LORD! a God compassionate," etc.; cf. Num. 14:17-18. (TANAKH footnote)

Therefore, I pray, let my Lord's forbearance be great, as You have declared, saying, 'The LORD! slow to anger and abounding in kindness; forgiving iniquity and transgression; yet not remitting all punishment, but visiting iniquity of fathers upon children, upon the third and fourth generations.'
B'MIDBAR 14:17-18 (NUMBERS 14:17-18)

And now, I beseech thee, let the power of my LORD be great, according as thou hast spoken, saying, The LORD is long-suffering, and of great mercy, forgiving iniquity and transgression, and by no means clearing *the guilty*, visiting the iniquity of the fathers upon the children unto the third and fourth *generation*.
NUMBERS 14:17-18

And the LORD passed by before him, and proclaimed, The LORD, The LORD God, is merciful and gracious, long-suffering and abundant in goodness and truth (571). EXODUS 34:6

truth (571) pronounced eh'meth; contr. From 539; stability; fig. certainty, truth, trustworthiness:-assured (-ly), establishment, faithful, right, sure, true (-ly, -th), verity.

(539) pronounced aw-man'; a prim. root; prop. to build up or support; to foster as a parent or nurse; fig. to render (or be) firm or faithful, to trust or believe, to be permanent or quiet; mor. to be true or certain; once (Isa. 30:21; by interch. for 541) to go to the right hand:- hence assurance, believe, bring up, establish, + fail, be faithful (of long continuance, steadfast, sure, surely, trusty, verified) nurse (-ing father), (put) trust, turn to the right.

And whenever you deviate to the right or to the left, your ears will heed the command from behind you: "This is the road; follow it!" YESHA'YAHU 30:21 (ISAIAH 30:21)

And thine ears shall hear a word behind thee, saying, This is the way, walk ye in it, when ye turn to the right hand, and when ye turn to the left. ISAIAH 30:21

(541) pronounced aw-man'; denom. from 3225; to take the right-hand road:- turn to the right. See 539.

(3225) pronounced yaw-meen'; from 3231; the right hand or side (leg, eye) of a person or other object (as the stronger and most dexterous): locally, the south:- + left handed, right (hand, side), south.

(3231) pronounced yaw-man'; a prim. root; to be (phys.) right (i.e. firm); but used only as denom. from 3225 and transit., to be right-handed or take the right-hand side:- go turn) to (on, use) the right hand.

If you hear it said, of one of the towns that the LORD your God is giving you to dwell in, that some scoundrels from among you have gone and subverted the inhabitants of their town, saying, "Come let us worship other gods"--- whom you have not experienced---you shall investigate and inquire and interrogate thoroughly. If it is true, the fact is established---that abhorrent thing was perpetrated in your midst---put the inhabitants of that town to the sword and put its cattle to the sword. Doom it and all that is in it to destruction: D'VARIM 13:13-16 (DEUTERONOMY 13:13-15)

Certain men, the children of Belial, are gone out from among you, and have withdrawn the inhabitants of their city, saying, Let us go and serve other gods, which ye have not known; then shalt thou inquire, and make search, and ask diligently; and, behold, *if it be* truth (571), *and* the thing certain, *that* such abomination is wrought among you; thou shalt surely smite the inhabitants of that city with the edge of the sword, destroying it utterly, and all that is therein, and the cattle thereof, with the edge of the sword. DEUTERONOMY 13:13-15

truth (571) pronounced eh'meth; contr. From 539; stability; fig. certainty, truth, trustworthiness:-assured (-ly), establishment, faithful, right, sure, true (-ly, -th), verity.

(539) pronounced aw-man'; a prim. root; prop. to build up or support; to foster as a parent or nurse; fig. to render (or be) firm or faithful, to trust or believe, to be permanent or quiet; mor. to be true or certain; once (Isa. 30:21; by interch. for 541) to go to the right hand:- hence assurance, believe, bring up, establish, + fail, be faithful (of long continuance, steadfast, sure, surely, trusty, verified) nurse (-ing father), (put) trust, turn to the right.

> And whenever you deviate to the right or to the left, your ears will heed the command from behind you: "This is the road; follow it!" YESHA'YAHU 30:21 (ISAIAH 30:21)
>
> And thine ears shall hear a word behind thee, saying, This is the way, walk ye in it, when ye turn to the right hand, and when ye turn to the left. ISAIAH 30:21

(541) pronounced aw-man'; denom. from 3225; to take the right-hand road:- turn to the right. See 539.

(3225) pronounced yaw-meen'; from 3231; the right hand or side (leg, eye) of a person or other object (as the stronger and most dexterous): locally, the south:- + left handed, right (hand, side), south.

(3231) pronounced yaw-man'; a prim. root; to be (phys.) right (i.e. firm); but used only as denom. from 3225 and transit., to be right-handed or take the right-hand side:- go turn) to (on, use) the right hand.

The Rock!---His deeds are perfect, yea, all His ways are just; a faithful God, never false, true and upright is He. D'VARIM 32:4 (DEUTERONOMY 32:4)

He *is* the Rock, his work *is* perfect: for all his ways *are* judgment: a God of truth (530) and without iniquity, just and right *is* he. DEUTERONOMY 32:4

truth (530) pronounced em-oo-naw'; fem. of 529; lit. firmness; fig. security; mor. fidelity:- faith (-ful, -ly, -ness, [man]), set office, stability, steady, truly, truth, verity.

(529) pronounced ay-moon'; from 539; established, i.e. (fig.) trusty; also (abstr.) trustworthiness:-faith (-ful), truth.

(539) pronounced aw-man'; a prim. root; prop. to build up or support; to foster as a parent or nurse; fig. to render (or be) firm or faithful, to trust or believe, to be permanent or quiet; mor. to be true or certain; once (Isa. 30:21; by interch. for 541) to go to the right hand:- hence assurance, believe, bring up, establish, + fail, be faithful (of long continuance, steadfast, sure, surely, trusty, verified) nurse (-ing father), (put) trust, turn to the right.

And whenever you deviate to the right or to the left, your ears will heed the command from behind you: "This is the road; follow it!" YESHA'YAHU 30:21 (ISAIAH 30:21)

And thine ears shall hear a word behind thee, saying, This is the way, walk ye in it, when ye turn to the right hand, and when ye turn to the left. ISAIAH 30:21

(541) pronounced aw-man'; denom. from 3225; to take the right-hand road:- turn to the right. See 539.

(3225) pronounced yaw-meen'; from 3231; the right hand or side (leg, eye) of a person or other object (as the stronger and most dexterous): locally, the south:- + left handed, right (hand, side), south.

(3231) pronounced yaw-man'; a prim. root; to be (phys.) right (i.e. firm); but used only as denom. from 3225 and transit., to be right-handed or take the right-hand side:- go turn) to (on, use) the right hand.

Now, therefore, revere the LORD and serve Him with undivided loyalty; put away the gods that your forefathers served beyond the Euphrates and in Egypt, and serve the LORD. Y'HOSHUA 24:14 (JOSHUA 24:14)

Now therefore fear the LORD, and serve him in sincerity and in truth (571): and put away the gods which your fathers served on the other side of the flood, and in Egypt; and serve ye the LORD. JOSHUA 24:14

> truth (571) pronounced eh'meth; contr. From 539; stability; fig. certainty, truth, trustworthiness:-assured (-ly), establishment, faithful, right, sure, true (-ly, -th), verity.
>
> (539) pronounced aw-man'; a prim. root; prop. to build up or support; to foster as a parent or nurse; fig. to render (or be) firm or faithful, to trust or believe, to be permanent or quiet; mor. to be true or certain; once (Isa. 30:21; by interch. for 541) to go to the right hand:- hence assurance, believe, bring up, establish, + fail, be faithful (of long continuance, steadfast, sure, surely, trusty, verified) nurse (-ing father), (put) trust, turn to the right.
>
>> And whenever you deviate to the right or to the left, your ears will heed the command from behind you: "This is the road; follow it!" YESHA'YAHU 30:21 (ISAIAH 30:21)
>>
>> And thine ears shall hear a word behind thee, saying, This is the way, walk ye in it, when ye turn to the right hand, and when ye turn to the left. ISAIAH 30:21
>
> (541) pronounced aw-man'; denom. from 3225; to take the right-hand road:- turn to the right. See 539.
>
> (3225) pronounced yaw-meen'; from 3231; the right hand or side (leg, eye) of a person or other object (as the stronger and most dexterous): locally, the south:- + left handed, right (hand, side), south.
>
> (3231) pronounced yaw-man'; a prim. root; to be (phys.) right (i.e. firm); but used only as denom. from 3225 and transit., to be right-handed or take the right-hand side:- go turn) to (on, use) the right hand.

And the thornbush said to the trees, 'If you are acting honorably in anointing me king over you, come and take shelter in my shade; but if not, may fire issue from the thornbush and consume the cedars of Lebanon! SHOF'TIM 9:15 (JUDGES 9:15)

And the bramble said unto the trees, If in truth (571) ye anoint me king over you, *then* come *and* put your trust in my shadow; and if not, let fire come out of the bramble, and devour the cedars of Lebanon. JUDGES 9:15

> truth (571) pronounced eh'meth; contr. From 539; stability; fig. certainty, truth, trustworthiness:-assured (-ly), establishment, faithful, right, sure, true (-ly, -th), verity.

(539) pronounced aw-man'; a prim. root; prop. to build up or support; to foster as a parent or nurse; fig. to render (or be) firm or faithful, to trust or believe, to be permanent or quiet; mor. to be true or certain; once (Isa. 30:21; by interch. for 541) to go to the right hand:- hence assurance, believe, bring up, establish, + fail, be faithful (of long continuance, steadfast, sure, surely, trusty, verified) nurse (-ing father), (put) trust, turn to the right.

> And whenever you deviate to the right or to the left, your ears will heed the command from behind you: "This is the road; follow it!" YESHA'YAHU 30:21 (ISAIAH 30:21)
>
> And thine ears shall hear a word behind thee, saying, This is the way, walk ye in it, when ye turn to the right hand, and when ye turn to the left. ISAIAH 30:21

(541) pronounced aw-man'; denom. from 3225; to take the right-hand road:- turn to the right. See 539.

(3225) pronounced yaw-meen'; from 3231; the right hand or side (leg, eye) of a person or other object (as the stronger and most dexterous): locally, the south:- + left handed, right (hand, side), south.

(3231) pronounced yaw-man'; a prim. root; to be (phys.) right (i.e. firm); but used only as denom. from 3225 and transit., to be right-handed or take the right-hand side:- go turn) to (on, use) the right hand.

Above all, you must revere the LORD and serve Him faithfully with all your heart; and consider how grandly He has dealt with you. SH'MU'EL ALEF 12:24 (I SAMUEL 12:24)

Only fear the LORD and serve him in truth (571) with all your heart: for consider how great *things* he hath done for you. I SAMUEL 12:24

truth (571) pronounced eh'meth; contr. From 539; stability; fig. certainty, truth, trustworthiness:-assured (-ly), establishment, faithful, right, sure, true (-ly, -th), verity.

(539) pronounced aw-man'; a prim. root; prop. to build up or support; to foster as a parent or nurse; fig. to render (or be) firm or faithful, to trust or believe, to be permanent or quiet; mor. to be true or certain; once (Isa. 30:21; by interch. for 541) to go to the right hand:- hence assurance, believe, bring up, establish, + fail, be faithful (of long continuance, steadfast, sure, surely, trusty, verified) nurse (-ing father), (put) trust, turn to the right.

> And whenever you deviate to the right or to the left, your ears will heed the command from behind you: "This is the road; follow it!" YESHA'YAHU 30:21 (ISAIAH 30:21)
>
> And thine ears shall hear a word behind thee, saying, This is the way, walk ye in it, when ye turn to the right hand, and when ye turn to the left. ISAIAH 30:21

(541) pronounced aw-man'; denom. from 3225; to take the right-hand road:- turn to the right. See 539.

(3225) pronounced yaw-meen'; from 3231; the right hand or side (leg, eye) of a person or other object (as the stronger and most dexterous): locally, the south:- + left handed, right (hand, side), south.

(3231) pronounced yaw-man'; a prim. root; to be (phys.) right (i.e. firm); but used only as denom. from 3225 and transit., to be right-handed or take the right-hand side:- go turn) to (on, use) the right hand.

The priest answered David, "I have no ordinary bread on hand; there is only consecrated bread---provided the young men have kept away from women." In reply to the priest, David said, "I assure you that women have been kept from us, as always. Whenever I went on a mission, even if the journey was a common one, the vessels of the young men were consecrated; all the more then may consecrated food be put into their vessels today." SH'MU'EL ALEF 21:5-6 (I SAMUEL 21:4-5)

Then the priest answered David, and said, *There is* no common bread under mine hand, but there is hallowed bread; if the young men have kept themselves at least from women. And David answered the priest, and said unto him, Of a truth (518) women *have been* kept from us about these three days, since I came out, and the vessels of the young men are holy, and *the bread is* in a manner common, yea, though it were sanctified this day in the vessel. I SAMUEL 21:4-5

truth (518) pronounced eem; a prim. particle; used very widely as a demonstr., lol; interrog. whether ?; or conditional, if, although; also oh that!, when; hence as a neg., not:- (and, can-, doubtless, if, that) (not), + but, either, + except, + more (-over if, than), neither, nevertheless, nor, oh that, or, + save (only, -ing), seeing, since, sith, + surely (no more, none, not), though, + of a truth, + unless, + verily, when, whereas, whether, while, + yet.

May the LORD in turn show you true faithfulness; and I too will reward you generously because you performed this act. SH'MU'EL BET 2:6 (II SAMUEL 2:6)

And now the LORD show kindness and truth (571) unto you: and I also will requite you this kindness, because ye have done this thing. II SAMUEL 2:6

truth (571) pronounced eh'meth; contr. From 539; stability; fig. certainty, truth, trustworthiness:-assured (-ly), establishment, faithful, right, sure, true (-ly, -th), verity.

(539) pronounced aw-man'; a prim. root; prop. to build up or support; to foster as a parent or nurse; fig. to render (or be) firm or faithful, to trust or believe, to be permanent or quiet; mor. to be true or certain; once (Isa. 30:21; by interch. for 541) to go to the right hand:- hence assurance, believe, bring up, establish, + fail, be faithful (of long continuance, steadfast, sure, surely, trusty, verified) nurse (-ing father), (put) trust, turn to the right.

> And whenever you deviate to the right or to the left, your ears will heed the command from behind you: "This is the road; follow it!" YESHA'YAHU 30:21 (ISAIAH 30:21)
>
> And thine ears shall hear a word behind thee, saying, This is the way, walk ye in it, when ye turn to the right hand, and when ye turn to the left. ISAIAH 30:21

(541) pronounced aw-man'; denom. from 3225; to take the right-hand road:- turn to the right. See 539.

(3225) pronounced yaw-meen'; from 3231; the right hand or side (leg, eye) of a person or other object (as the stronger and most dexterous): locally, the south:- + left handed, right (hand, side), south.

(3231) pronounced yaw-man'; a prim. root; to be (phys.) right (i.e. firm); but used only as denom. from 3225 and transit., to be right-handed or take the right-hand side:- go turn) to (on, use) the right hand.

You came only yesterday; should I make you wander about with us today, when I myself must go wherever I can? Go back, and take your kinsmen with you, [in] true faithfulness. SH'MU'EL BET 15:20 (II SAMUEL 15:20)

> [in]: meaning of Heb. uncertain. Septuagint reads "and may the LORD show you" cf., e.g., 2.6). (TANAKH footnote)
>
> > May the LORD in turn show you true faithfulness; and I too will reward you generously because you performed this act. SH'MU'EL BET 2:6 (II SAMUEL 2:6)
> >
> > And now the LORD show kindness and truth (571) unto you: and I also will requite you this kindness, because ye have done this thing. II SAMUEL 2:6
> >
> > > truth (571) pronounced eh'meth; contr. From 539; stability; fig. certainty, truth, trustworthiness:-assured (-ly), establishment, faithful, right, sure, true (-ly, -th), verity.
> > >
> > > (539) pronounced aw-man'; a prim. root; prop. to build up or support; to foster as a parent or nurse; fig. to render (or be) firm or faithful, to trust or believe, to be permanent or quiet; mor. to be true or certain; once (Isa. 30:21; by interch. for 541) to go to the right hand:- hence assurance, believe, bring up, establish, + fail, be faithful (of long continuance, steadfast, sure, surely, trusty, verified) nurse (-ing father), (put) trust, turn to the right.

> And whenever you deviate to the right or to the left, your ears will heed the command from behind you: "This is the road; follow it!" YESHA'YAHU 30:21 (ISAIAH 30:21)
>
> And thine ears shall hear a word behind thee, saying, This is the way, walk ye in it, when ye turn to the right hand, and when ye turn to the left. ISAIAH 30:21

(541) pronounced aw-man'; denom. from 3225; to take the right-hand road:- turn to the right. See 539.

(3225) pronounced yaw-meen'; from 3231; the right hand or side (leg, eye) of a person or other object (as the stronger and most dexterous): locally, the south:- + left handed, right (hand, side), south.

(3231) pronounced yaw-man'; a prim. root; to be (phys.) right (i.e. firm); but used only as denom. from 3225 and transit., to be right-handed or take the right-hand side:- go turn) to (on, use) the right hand.

Whereas thou camest *but* yesterday, should I this day make thee go up and down with us? Seeing I go whither I may, return thou, and take back thy brethren: mercy and truth (571) *be* with thee.
II SAMUEL 15:20

truth (571) pronounced eh'meth; contr. From 539; stability; fig. certainty, truth, trustworthiness:-assured (-ly), establishment, faithful, right, sure, true (-ly, -th), verity.

(539) pronounced aw-man'; a prim. root; prop. to build up or support; to foster as a parent or nurse; fig. to render (or be) firm or faithful, to trust or believe, to be permanent or quiet; mor. to be true or certain; once (Isa. 30:21; by interch. for 541) to go to the right hand:- hence assurance, believe, bring up, establish, + fail, be faithful (of long continuance, steadfast, sure, surely, trusty, verified) nurse (-ing father), (put) trust, turn to the right.

> And whenever you deviate to the right or to the left, your ears will heed the command from behind you: "This is the road; follow it!" YESHA'YAHU 30:21 (ISAIAH 30:21)
>
> And thine ears shall hear a word behind thee, saying, This is the way, walk ye in it, when ye turn to the right hand, and when ye turn to the left. ISAIAH 30:21

(541) pronounced aw-man'; denom. from 3225; to take the right-hand road:- turn to the right. See 539.

(3225) pronounced yaw-meen'; from 3231; the right hand or side (leg, eye) of a person or other object (as the stronger and most dexterous): locally, the south:- + left handed, right (hand, side), south.

(3231) pronounced yaw-man'; a prim. root; to be (phys.) right (i.e. firm); but used only as denom. from 3225 and transit., to be right-handed or take the right-hand side:- go turn) to (on, use) the right hand.

Then the LORD will fulfill the promise that He made concerning me: 'If your descendants are scrupulous in their conduct and walk before Me faithfully, with all their heart and soul, your line on the throne of Israel shall never end!" M'LAKHIM ALEF 2:4 (I KINGS 2:4)

Your line on the throne of Israel shall never end: Lit. "there shall never cease to be a man of yours on the throne of Israel." Cf. 2 Sam.7.12-16. (TANAKH footnote)

"When your days are done and you lie with your fathers, I will raise up your offspring after you, one of your own issue, and I will establish his kingship. He shall build a house for My name, and I will establish his royal throne forever. I will be a father to him, and he shall be a son to Me. When he does wrong, I will chastise him with the rod of men and the affliction of mortals; but I will never withdraw My favor from him as I withdrew it from Saul whom I removed to make room for you. Your house and your kingship shall ever be secure before you; your throne shall be established forever." SH'MU'EL BET 7:12-16 (II SAMUEL 7:12-16)

house: i.e. a dynasty; play on "house" (i.e. Temple) in v.5. (TANAKH footnote)

with the rod of men and the affliction of mortals: i.e., only as a human father would. (TANAKH footnote)

Go and say to my servant David: Thus said the LORD: Are you the one to build a house for Me to dwell in?
SH'MU'EL BET 7:5 (II SAMUEL 7:5)

Go and tell my servant David, Thus saith the LORD, Shalt thou build me a house for me to dwell in? II SAMUEL 7:5

And when thy days be fulfilled, and thou shalt sleep with thy fathers, I will set up thy seed after thee, which shall proceed out of thy bowels, and I will establish his kingdom. He shall build a house for my name, and I will stablish the throne of his kingdom for ever. I will be his father, and he shall be my son. If he commit iniquity, I will chasten him with the rod of men, and with the stripes of the children of men: but my mercy shall not depart away from him, as I took it from Saul, whom I put away before thee. And thine house and thy kingdom shall be established for ever before thee: thy throne shall be established for ever. II SAMUEL 7:12-16

That the LORD may continue his word which he spake concerning me, saying, If thy children take heed to their way, to walk before me in truth (571) with all their heart and with all their soul, there shall not fail thee (said he) a man on the throne of Israel. I KINGS 2:4

> truth (571) pronounced eh'meth; contr. From 539; stability; fig. certainty, truth, trustworthiness:-assured (-ly), establishment, faithful, right, sure, true (-ly, -th), verity.
>
> (539) pronounced aw-man'; a prim. root; prop. to build up or support; to foster as a parent or nurse; fig. to render (or be) firm or faithful, to trust or believe, to be permanent or quiet; mor. to be true or certain; once (Isa. 30:21; by interch. for 541) to go to the right hand:- hence assurance, believe, bring up, establish, + fail, be faithful (of long continuance, steadfast, sure, surely, trusty, verified) nurse (-ing father), (put) trust, turn to the right.
>
> > And whenever you deviate to the right or to the left, your ears will heed the command from behind you: "This is the road; follow it!" YESHA'YAHU 30:21 (ISAIAH 30:21)
> >
> > And thine ears shall hear a word behind thee, saying, This is the way, walk ye in it, when ye turn to the right hand, and when ye turn to the left. ISAIAH 30:21
>
> (541) pronounced aw-man'; denom. from 3225; to take the right-hand road:- turn to the right. See 539.
>
> (3225) pronounced yaw-meen'; from 3231; the right hand or side (leg, eye) of a person or other object (as the stronger and most dexterous): locally, the south:- + left handed, right (hand, side), south.
>
> (3231) pronounced yaw-man'; a prim. root; to be (phys.) right (i.e. firm); but used only as denom. from 3225 and transit., to be right-handed or take the right-hand side:- go turn) to (on, use) the right hand.

Solomon said, "You dealt most graciously with Your servant my father David, because he walked before you in faithfulness and righteousness and in integrity of heart. You have continued this great kindness to him by giving him a son to occupy his throne, as is now the case. M'LAKHIM ALEF 3:6 (I KINGS 3:6)

And Solomon said, Thou hast shown unto thy servant David my father great mercy, according as he walked before thee in truth (571), and in righteousness, and in uprightness of heart with thee; and thou hast kept for him this great kindness, that thou hast given him a son to sit on his throne, as *it is* this day. I KINGS 3:6

> truth (571) pronounced eh'meth; contr. From 539; stability; fig. certainty, truth, trustworthiness:-assured (-ly), establishment, faithful, right, sure, true (-ly, -th), verity.
>
> (539) pronounced aw-man'; a prim. root; prop. to build up or support; to foster as a parent or nurse; fig. to render (or be) firm or faithful, to trust or believe, to be permanent or quiet; mor.

to be true or certain; once (Isa. 30:21; by interch. for 541) to go to the right hand:- hence assurance, believe, bring up, establish, + fail, be faithful (of long continuance, steadfast, sure, surely, trusty, verified) nurse (-ing father), (put) trust, turn to the right.

> And whenever you deviate to the right or to the left, your ears will heed the command from behind you: "This is the road; follow it!" YESHA'YAHU 30:21 (ISAIAH 30:21)
>
> And thine ears shall hear a word behind thee, saying, This is the way, walk ye in it, when ye turn to the right hand, and when ye turn to the left. ISAIAH 30:21

(541) pronounced aw-man'; denom. from 3225; to take the right-hand road:- turn to the right. See 539.

(3225) pronounced yaw-meen'; from 3231; the right hand or side (leg, eye) of a person or other object (as the stronger and most dexterous): locally, the south:- + left handed, right (hand, side), south.

(3231) pronounced yaw-man'; a prim. root; to be (phys.) right (i.e. firm); but used only as denom. from 3225 and transit., to be right-handed or take the right-hand side:- go turn) to (on, use) the right hand.

And the woman answered Elijah, "Now I know that you are a man of God and that the word of the LORD is truly in your mouth." M'LAKHIM ALEF 17:24 (I KINGS 17:24)

And the woman said to Elijah, *Now* by this I know that thou *art* a man of God *and* that the word of the LORD in thy mouth *is* truth (571). I KINGS 17:24

truth (571) pronounced eh'meth; contr. From 539; stability; fig. certainty, truth, trustworthiness:-assured (-ly), establishment, faithful, right, sure, true (-ly, -th), verity.

(539) pronounced aw-man'; a prim. root; prop. to build up or support; to foster as a parent or nurse; fig. to render (or be) firm or faithful, to trust or believe, to be permanent or quiet; mor. to be true or certain; once (Isa. 30:21; by interch. for 541) to go to the right hand:- hence assurance, believe, bring up, establish, + fail, be faithful (of long continuance, steadfast, sure, surely, trusty, verified) nurse (-ing father), (put) trust, turn to the right.

> And whenever you deviate to the right or to the left, your ears will heed the command from behind you: "This is the road; follow it!" YESHA'YAHU 30:21 (ISAIAH 30:21)
>
> And thine ears shall hear a word behind thee, saying, This is the way, walk ye in it, when ye turn to the right hand, and when ye turn to the left. ISAIAH 30:21

(541) pronounced aw-man'; denom. from 3225; to take the right-hand road:- turn to the right. See 539.

(3225) pronounced yaw-meen'; from 3231; the right hand or side (leg, eye) of a person or other object (as the stronger and most dexterous): locally, the south:- + left handed, right (hand, side), south.

(3231) pronounced yaw-man'; a prim. root; to be (phys.) right (i.e. firm); but used only as denom. from 3225 and transit., to be right-handed or take the right-hand side:- go turn) to (on, use) the right hand.

True, O LORD, the kings of Assyria have annihilated the nations and their lands. M'LAKHIM BET 19:17 (II KINGS 19:17)

Of a truth (551), LORD, the kings of Assyria have destroyed the nations and their lands. II KINGS 19:17

truth (551) pronounced om-nawm'; adv. From 544; verily:-indeed, no doubt, surely, (it is, of a) true (-ly, -th).

(544) pronounced oh-men'; from 539; verity:-truth.

(539) pronounced aw-man'; a prim. root; prop. to build up or support; to foster as a parent or nurse; fig. to render (or be) firm or faithful, to trust or believe, to be permanent or quiet; mor. to be true or certain; once (Isa. 30:21; by interch. for 541) to go to the right hand:- hence assurance, believe, bring up, establish, + fail, be faithful (of long continuance, steadfast, sure, surely, trusty, verified) nurse (-ing father), (put) trust, turn to the right.

And whenever you deviate to the right or to the left, your ears will heed the command from behind you: "This is the road; follow it!" YESHA'YAHU 30:21 (ISAIAH 30:21)

And thine ears shall hear a word behind thee, saying, This is the way, walk ye in it, when ye turn to the right hand, and when ye turn to the left. ISAIAH 30:21

(541) pronounced aw-man'; denom. from 3225; to take the right-hand road:- turn to the right. See 539.

(3225) pronounced yaw-meen'; from 3231; the right hand or side (leg, eye) of a person or other object (as the stronger and most dexterous): locally, the south:- + left handed, right (hand, side), south.

(3231) pronounced yaw-man'; a prim. root; to be (phys.) right (i.e. firm); but used only as denom. from 3225 and transit., to be right-handed or take the right-hand side:- go turn) to (on, use) the right hand.

"Please, O LORD, remember how I have walked before You sincerely and whole-heartedly, and have done what is pleasing to You." And Hezekiah wept profusely. M'LAKHIM BET 20:3 (II KINGS 20:3)

I beseech thee, O LORD, remember now how I have walked before thee in truth (571) and with a perfect heart, and have done *that which is* good in thy sight. And Hezekiah wept sore. II KINGS 20:3

truth (571) pronounced eh'meth; contr. From 539; stability; fig. certainty, truth, trustworthiness:-assured (-ly), establishment, faithful, right, sure, true (-ly, -th), verity.

(539) pronounced aw-man'; a prim. root; prop. to build up or support; to foster as a parent or nurse; fig. to render (or be) firm or faithful, to trust or believe, to be permanent or quiet; mor. to be true or certain; once (Isa. 30:21; by interch. for 541) to go to the right hand:- hence assurance, believe, bring up, establish, + fail, be faithful (of long continuance, steadfast, sure, surely, trusty, verified) nurse (-ing father), (put) trust, turn to the right.

And whenever you deviate to the right or to the left, your ears will heed the command from behind you: "This is the road; follow it!" YESHA'YAHU 30:21 (ISAIAH 30:21)

And thine ears shall hear a word behind thee, saying, This is the way, walk ye in it, when ye turn to the right hand, and when ye turn to the left. ISAIAH 30:21

(541) pronounced aw-man'; denom. from 3225; to take the right-hand road:- turn to the right. See 539.

(3225) pronounced yaw-meen'; from 3231; the right hand or side (leg, eye) of a person or other object (as the stronger and most dexterous): locally, the south:- + left handed, right (hand, side), south.

(3231) pronounced yaw-man'; a prim. root; to be (phys.) right (i.e. firm); but used only as denom. from 3225 and transit., to be right-handed or take the right-hand side:- go turn) to (on, use) the right hand.

Hezekiah declared to Isaiah, "The word of the LORD that you have spoken is good." For he thought, It means that safety is assured for my time." M'LAKHIM BET 20:19 (II KINGS 20:19)

safety is assured: Several mss. and the parallel Isa. 39.1 read "Merodach." (TANAKH footnote)

At that time, Merodach-baladan, son of Baladan, the king of Babylon, sent [envoys with] a letter and a gift to Hezekiah, for he had heard about his illness and recovery. YESHA'YAHU 39:1 (ISAIAH 39:1)

At that time Merodach-baladan, the son of Baladan , king of Babylon, sent letters and a present to Hezekiah; for he had heard that he had been sick, and was recovered. ISAIAH 39:1

Then said Hezekiah to Isaiah, Good *is* the word of the LORD which thou hast spoken. And he said, *Is* it not *good*, if peace and truth (571) be in my days? II KINGS 20:19

> truth (571) pronounced eh'meth; contr. From 539; stability; fig. certainty, truth, trustworthiness:-assured (-ly), establishment, faithful, right, sure, true (-ly, -th), verity.
>
> (539) pronounced aw-man'; a prim. root; prop. to build up or support; to foster as a parent or nurse; fig. to render (or be) firm or faithful, to trust or believe, to be permanent or quiet; mor. to be true or certain; once (Isa. 30:21; by interch. for 541) to go to the right hand:- hence assurance, believe, bring up, establish, + fail, be faithful (of long continuance, steadfast, sure, surely, trusty, verified) nurse (-ing father), (put) trust, turn to the right.
>
>> And whenever you deviate to the right or to the left, your ears will heed the command from behind you: "This is the road; follow it!" YESHA'YAHU 30:21 (ISAIAH 30:21)
>>
>> And thine ears shall hear a word behind thee, saying, This is the way, walk ye in it, when ye turn to the right hand, and when ye turn to the left. ISAIAH 30:21
>
> (541) pronounced aw-man'; denom. from 3225; to take the right-hand road:- turn to the right. See 539.
>
> (3225) pronounced yaw-meen'; from 3231; the right hand or side (leg, eye) of a person or other object (as the stronger and most dexterous): locally, the south:- + left handed, right (hand, side), south.
>
> (3231) pronounced yaw-man'; a prim. root; to be (phys.) right (i.e. firm); but used only as denom. from 3225 and transit., to be right-handed or take the right-hand side:- go turn) to (on, use) the right hand.

The king said to him, "How many times must I adjure you to tell me nothing but the truth in the name of the LORD?" DIVREI-HAYAMIM BET 18:15 (II CHRONICLES 18:15)

And the king said to him, How many times shall I adjure thee that thou say nothing but the truth (571) to me in the name of the LORD? II CHRONICLES 18:15

> truth (571) pronounced eh'meth; contr. From 539; stability; fig. certainty, truth, trustworthiness:-assured (-ly), establishment, faithful, right, sure, true (-ly, -th), verity.
>
> (539) pronounced aw-man'; a prim. root; prop. to build up or support; to foster as a parent or nurse; fig. to render (or be) firm or faithful, to trust or believe, to be permanent or quiet; mor. to be true or certain; once (Isa. 30:21; by interch. for 541) to go to the right hand:- hence assurance, believe, bring up, establish, + fail, be faithful (of long continuance, steadfast, sure, surely, trusty, verified) nurse (-ing father), (put) trust, turn to the right.
>
>> And whenever you deviate to the right or to the left, your ears will heed the command from behind you: "This is the road; follow it!" YESHA'YAHU 30:21 (ISAIAH 30:21)

> And thine ears shall hear a word behind thee, saying, This is the way, walk ye in it, when ye turn to the right hand, and when ye turn to the left. ISAIAH 30:21

(541) pronounced aw-man'; denom. from 3225; to take the right-hand road:- turn to the right. See 539.

(3225) pronounced yaw-meen'; from 3231; the right hand or side (leg, eye) of a person or other object (as the stronger and most dexterous): locally, the south:- + left handed, right (hand, side), south.

(3231) pronounced yaw-man'; a prim. root; to be (phys.) right (i.e. firm); but used only as denom. from 3225 and transit., to be right-handed or take the right-hand side:- go turn) to (on, use) the right hand.

Hezekiah did this throughout Judah. He acted in a way that was good, upright, and faithful before the LORD his God. DIVREI-HAYAMIM BET 31:20 (II CHRONICLES 31:20)

And thus did Hezekiah throughout all Judah, and wrought *that which was* good and right and truth (571) before the LORD his God. II CHRONICLES 31:20

truth (571) pronounced eh'meth; contr. From 539; stability; fig. certainty, truth, trustworthiness:-assured (-ly), establishment, faithful, right, sure, true (-ly, -th), verity.

(539) pronounced aw-man'; a prim. root; prop. to build up or support; to foster as a parent or nurse; fig. to render (or be) firm or faithful, to trust or believe, to be permanent or quiet; mor. to be true or certain; once (Isa. 30:21; by interch. for 541) to go to the right hand:- hence assurance, believe, bring up, establish, + fail, be faithful (of long continuance, steadfast, sure, surely, trusty, verified) nurse (-ing father), (put) trust, turn to the right.

> And whenever you deviate to the right or to the left, your ears will heed the command from behind you: "This is the road; follow it!" YESHA'YAHU 30:21 (ISAIAH 30:21)
>
> And thine ears shall hear a word behind thee, saying, This is the way, walk ye in it, when ye turn to the right hand, and when ye turn to the left. ISAIAH 30:21

(541) pronounced aw-man'; denom. from 3225; to take the right-hand road:- turn to the right. See 539.

(3225) pronounced yaw-meen'; from 3231; the right hand or side (leg, eye) of a person or other object (as the stronger and most dexterous): locally, the south:- + left handed, right (hand, side), south.

(3231) pronounced yaw-man'; a prim. root; to be (phys.) right (i.e. firm); but used only as denom. from 3225 and transit., to be right-handed or take the right-hand side:- go turn) to (on, use) the right hand.

Dispatches were sent to all the Jews in the hundred and twenty-seven provinces of the realm of Ahasuerus with an ordinance of "equity and honesty:" ESTER 9:30 (ESTHER 9:30)

> "equity and honesty": i.e., of new holidays, the instituting of which is linked to love of equity and honesty in Zech. 8:19 (TANAKH footnote)
>
> > And the word of the LORD of Hosts came to me, saying, Thus said the LORD of Hosts: the fast of the fourth month, and the fast of the tenth month shall become occasions for joy and gladness, happy festivals for the House of Judah: but you must love honesty and integrity. Z'KHARYAH 8:19 (ZECHARIAH 8:19)
> >
> > Thus saith the LORD of hosts: the fast of the fourth month, and the fast of the fifth, and the fast of the seventh, and the fast of the tenth, shall be to the house of Judah joy and gladness, and cheerful feasts; therefore love the truth (571) and peace. ZECHARIAH 8:19
> >
> > > truth (571) pronounced eh'meth; contr. From 539; stability; fig. certainty, truth, trustworthiness:-assured (-ly), establishment, faithful, right, sure, true (-ly, -th), verity.
> > >
> > > (539) pronounced aw-man'; a prim. root; prop. to build up or support; to foster as a parent or nurse; fig. to render (or be) firm or faithful, to trust or believe, to be permanent or quiet; mor. to be true or certain; once (Isa. 30:21; by interch. for 541) to go to the right hand:- hence assurance, believe, bring up, establish, + fail, be faithful (of long continuance, steadfast, sure, surely, trusty, verified) nurse (-ing father), (put) trust, turn to the right.
> > >
> > > > And whenever you deviate to the right or to the left, your ears will heed the command from behind you: "This is the road; follow it!" YESHA'YAHU 30:21 (ISAIAH 30:21)
> > > >
> > > > And thine ears shall hear a word behind thee, saying, This is the way, walk ye in it, when ye turn to the right hand, and when ye turn to the left. ISAIAH 30:21
> > >
> > > (541) pronounced aw-man'; denom. from 3225; to take the right-hand road:- turn to the right. See 539.
> > >
> > > (3225) pronounced yaw-meen'; from 3231; the right hand or side (leg, eye) of a person or other object (as the stronger and most dexterous): locally, the south:- + left handed, right (hand, side), south.

(3231) pronounced yaw-man'; a prim. root; to be (phys.) right (i.e. firm); but used only as denom. from 3225 and transit., to be right-handed or take the right-hand side:- go turn) to (on, use) the right hand.

And he sent the letters unto all the Jews, to the hundred twenty and seven provinces of the kingdom of Ahasuerus, *with* words of peace and truth (571). ESTHER 9:30

truth (571) pronounced eh'meth; contr. From 539; stability; fig. certainty, truth, trustworthiness:-assured (-ly), establishment, faithful, right, sure, true (-ly, -th), verity.

(539) pronounced aw-man'; a prim. root; prop. to build up or support; to foster as a parent or nurse; fig. to render (or be) firm or faithful, to trust or believe, to be permanent or quiet; mor. to be true or certain; once (Isa. 30:21; by interch. for 541) to go to the right hand:- hence assurance, believe, bring up, establish, + fail, be faithful (of long continuance, steadfast, sure, surely, trusty, verified) nurse (-ing father), (put) trust, turn to the right.

And whenever you deviate to the right or to the left, your ears will heed the command from behind you: "This is the road; follow it!" YESHA'YAHU 30:21 (ISAIAH 30:21)

And thine ears shall hear a word behind thee, saying, This is the way, walk ye in it, when ye turn to the right hand, and when ye turn to the left. ISAIAH 30:21

(541) pronounced aw-man'; denom. from 3225; to take the right-hand road:- turn to the right. See 539.

(3225) pronounced yaw-meen'; from 3231; the right hand or side (leg, eye) of a person or other object (as the stronger and most dexterous): locally, the south:- + left handed, right (hand, side), south.

(3231) pronounced yaw-man'; a prim. root; to be (phys.) right (i.e. firm); but used only as denom. from 3225 and transit., to be right-handed or take the right-hand side:- go turn) to (on, use) the right hand.

Indeed I know that it is so: Man cannot win a suit against God. IYOV 9:2 (JOB 9:2)

I know it is so of a truth (551): but how should man be just with God? JOB 9:2

truth (551) pronounced om-nawm'; adv. From 544; verily:-indeed, no doubt, surely, (it is, of a) true (-ly, -th).

(544) pronounced oh-men'; from 539; verity:-truth.

(539) pronounced aw-man'; a prim. root; prop. to build up or support; to foster as a parent or nurse; fig. to render (or be) firm or faithful, to trust or believe, to be permanent or quiet; mor. to be true or certain; once (Isa. 30:21; by interch. for 541) to go to the right hand:- hence

assurance, believe, bring up, establish, + fail, be faithful (of long continuance, steadfast, sure, surely, trusty, verified) nurse (-ing father), (put) trust, turn to the right.

> And whenever you deviate to the right or to the left, your ears will heed the command from behind you: "This is the road; follow it!" YESHA'YAHU 30:21 (ISAIAH 30:21)
>
> And thine ears shall hear a word behind thee, saying, This is the way, walk ye in it, when ye turn to the right hand, and when ye turn to the left. ISAIAH 30:21

(541) pronounced aw-man'; denom. from 3225; to take the right-hand road:- turn to the right. See 539.

(3225) pronounced yaw-meen'; from 3231; the right hand or side (leg, eye) of a person or other object (as the stronger and most dexterous): locally, the south:- + left handed, right (hand, side), south.

(3231) pronounced yaw-man'; a prim. root; to be (phys.) right (i.e. firm); but used only as denom. from 3225 and transit., to be right-handed or take the right-hand side:- go turn) to (on, use) the right hand.

LORD, who may sojourn in Your tent, who may dwell on Your holy mountain? He who lives without blame, who does what is right, and in his heart acknowledges the truth: TEHILLIM 15:1-2 (PSALMS 15:1-2)

LORD, who shall abide in thy tabernacle? Who shall dwell in thy holy hill? He that walketh uprightly, and worketh righteousness, and speaketh the truth (571) in his heart. PSALMS 15:1-2

truth (571) pronounced eh'meth; contr. From 539; stability; fig. certainty, truth, trustworthiness:-assured (-ly), establishment, faithful, right, sure, true (-ly, -th), verity.

(539) pronounced aw-man'; a prim. root; prop. to build up or support; to foster as a parent or nurse; fig. to render (or be) firm or faithful, to trust or believe, to be permanent or quiet; mor. to be true or certain; once (Isa. 30:21; by interch. for 541) to go to the right hand:- hence assurance, believe, bring up, establish, + fail, be faithful (of long continuance, steadfast, sure, surely, trusty, verified) nurse (-ing father), (put) trust, turn to the right.

> And whenever you deviate to the right or to the left, your ears will heed the command from behind you: "This is the road; follow it!" YESHA'YAHU 30:21 (ISAIAH 30:21)
>
> And thine ears shall hear a word behind thee, saying, This is the way, walk ye in it, when ye turn to the right hand, and when ye turn to the left. ISAIAH 30:21

(541) pronounced aw-man'; denom. from 3225; to take the right-hand road:- turn to the right. See 539.

(3225) pronounced yaw-meen'; from 3231; the right hand or side (leg, eye) of a person or other object (as the stronger and most dexterous): locally, the south:- + left handed, right (hand, side), south.

(3231) pronounced yaw-man'; a prim. root; to be (phys.) right (i.e. firm); but used only as denom. from 3225 and transit., to be right-handed or take the right-hand side:- go turn) to (on, use) the right hand.

Guide me in Your true way and teach me, for You are God, my deliverer; it is You I look to at all times. TEHILLIM 25:5 (PSALMS 25:5)

Lead me in thy truth (571) and teach me: for thou *art* the God of my salvation; on thee do I wait all the day. PSALMS 25:5

truth (571) pronounced eh'meth; contr. From 539; stability; fig. certainty, truth, trustworthiness:-assured (-ly), establishment, faithful, right, sure, true (-ly, -th), verity.

(539) pronounced aw-man'; a prim. root; prop. to build up or support; to foster as a parent or nurse; fig. to render (or be) firm or faithful, to trust or believe, to be permanent or quiet; mor. to be true or certain; once (Isa. 30:21; by interch. for 541) to go to the right hand:- hence assurance, believe, bring up, establish, + fail, be faithful (of long continuance, steadfast, sure, surely, trusty, verified) nurse (-ing father), (put) trust, turn to the right.

And whenever you deviate to the right or to the left, your ears will heed the command from behind you: "This is the road; follow it!" YESHA'YAHU 30:21 (ISAIAH 30:21)

And thine ears shall hear a word behind thee, saying, This is the way, walk ye in it, when ye turn to the right hand, and when ye turn to the left. ISAIAH 30:21

(541) pronounced aw-man'; denom. from 3225; to take the right-hand road:- turn to the right. See 539.

(3225) pronounced yaw-meen'; from 3231; the right hand or side (leg, eye) of a person or other object (as the stronger and most dexterous): locally, the south:- + left handed, right (hand, side), south.

(3231) pronounced yaw-man'; a prim. root; to be (phys.) right (i.e. firm); but used only as denom. from 3225 and transit., to be right-handed or take the right-hand side:- go turn) to (on, use) the right hand.

All the LORD's paths are steadfast love for those who keep the decrees of His covenant. TEHILLIM 25:10 (PSALMS 25:10)

All the paths of the LORD are mercy and truth (571) unto such as keep his covenant and his testimonies. PSALMS 25:10

truth (571) pronounced eh'meth; contr. From 539; stability; fig. certainty, truth, trustworthiness:-assured (-ly), establishment, faithful, right, sure, true (-ly, -th), verity.

(539) pronounced aw-man'; a prim. root; prop. to build up or support; to foster as a parent or nurse; fig. to render (or be) firm or faithful, to trust or believe, to be permanent or quiet; mor. to be true or certain; once (Isa. 30:21; by interch. for 541) to go to the right hand:- hence assurance, believe, bring up, establish, + fail, be faithful (of long continuance, steadfast, sure, surely, trusty, verified) nurse (-ing father), (put) trust, turn to the right.

> And whenever you deviate to the right or to the left, your ears will heed the command from behind you: "This is the road; follow it!" YESHA'YAHU 30:21 (ISAIAH 30:21)
>
> And thine ears shall hear a word behind thee, saying, This is the way, walk ye in it, when ye turn to the right hand, and when ye turn to the left. ISAIAH 30:21

(541) pronounced aw-man'; denom. from 3225; to take the right-hand road:- turn to the right. See 539.

(3225) pronounced yaw-meen'; from 3231; the right hand or side (leg, eye) of a person or other object (as the stronger and most dexterous): locally, the south:- + left handed, right (hand, side), south.

(3231) pronounced yaw-man'; a prim. root; to be (phys.) right (i.e. firm); but used only as denom. from 3225 and transit., to be right-handed or take the right-hand side:- go turn) to (on, use) the right hand.

For my eyes are on Your steadfast love; I have set my course by it. TEHILLIM 26:3 (PSALMS 26:3)

> Lit. the distress of my heart. (TANAKH footnote)

For thy lovingkindness is before mine eyes: and I have walked in thy truth (571). PSALMS 26:3

truth (571) pronounced eh'meth; contr. From 539; stability; fig. certainty, truth, trustworthiness:-assured (-ly), establishment, faithful, right, sure, true (-ly, -th), verity.

(539) pronounced aw-man'; a prim. root; prop. to build up or support; to foster as a parent or nurse; fig. to render (or be) firm or faithful, to trust or believe, to be permanent or quiet; mor. to be true or certain; once (Isa. 30:21; by interch. for 541) to go to the right hand:- hence assurance, believe, bring up, establish, + fail, be faithful (of long continuance, steadfast, sure, surely, trusty, verified) nurse (-ing father), (put) trust, turn to the right.

> And whenever you deviate to the right or to the left, your ears will heed the command from behind you: "This is the road; follow it!" YESHA'YAHU 30:21 (ISAIAH 30:21)

> And thine ears shall hear a word behind thee, saying, This is the way, walk ye in it, when ye turn to the right hand, and when ye turn to the left. ISAIAH 30:21

(541) pronounced aw-man'; denom. from 3225; to take the right-hand road:- turn to the right. See 539.

(3225) pronounced yaw-meen'; from 3231; the right hand or side (leg, eye) of a person or other object (as the stronger and most dexterous): locally, the south:- + left handed, right (hand, side), south.

(3231) pronounced yaw-man'; a prim. root; to be (phys.) right (i.e. firm); but used only as denom. from 3225 and transit., to be right-handed or take the right-hand side:- go turn) to (on, use) the right hand.

I called to You, O LORD; to my LORD I made appeal, "What is to be gained from my death, from my descent into the Pit?" TEHILLIM 30:9-10 (PSALMS 30:9)

"What is to be gained from my death…: Lit. "blood". (TANAKH footnote).

What profit is there in my blood when I go down to the pit? Shall the dust praise thee? Shall it declare thy truth (571)? PSALMS 30:9

truth (571) pronounced eh'meth; contr. From 539; stability; fig. certainty, truth, trustworthiness:-assured (-ly), establishment, faithful, right, sure, true (-ly, -th), verity.

(539) pronounced aw-man'; a prim. root; prop. to build up or support; to foster as a parent or nurse; fig. to render (or be) firm or faithful, to trust or believe, to be permanent or quiet; mor. to be true or certain; once (Isa. 30:21; by interch. for 541) to go to the right hand:- hence assurance, believe, bring up, establish, + fail, be faithful (of long continuance, steadfast, sure, surely, trusty, verified) nurse (-ing father), (put) trust, turn to the right.

> And whenever you deviate to the right or to the left, your ears will heed the command from behind you: "This is the road; follow it!" YESHA'YAHU 30:21 (ISAIAH 30:21)

> And thine ears shall hear a word behind thee, saying, This is the way, walk ye in it, when ye turn to the right hand, and when ye turn to the left. ISAIAH 30:21

(541) pronounced aw-man'; denom. from 3225; to take the right-hand road:- turn to the right. See 539.

(3225) pronounced yaw-meen'; from 3231; the right hand or side (leg, eye) of a person or other object (as the stronger and most dexterous): locally, the south:- + left handed, right (hand, side), south.

(3231) pronounced yaw-man'; a prim. root; to be (phys.) right (i.e. firm); but used only as denom. from 3225 and transit., to be right-handed or take the right-hand side:- go turn) to (on, use) the right hand.

Into Your hand I entrust my spirit; You redeem me, O LORD, faithful God. TEHILLIM 31:6 (PSALMS 31:5)

Into thine hand I commit my spirit: thou hast redeemed me, O LORD God of truth (571). PSALMS 31:5

truth (571) pronounced eh'meth; contr. From 539; stability; fig. certainty, truth, trustworthiness:-assured (-ly), establishment, faithful, right, sure, true (-ly, -th), verity.

(539) pronounced aw-man'; a prim. root; prop. to build up or support; to foster as a parent or nurse; fig. to render (or be) firm or faithful, to trust or believe, to be permanent or quiet; mor. to be true or certain; once (Isa. 30:21; by interch. for 541) to go to the right hand:- hence assurance, believe, bring up, establish, + fail, be faithful (of long continuance, steadfast, sure, surely, trusty, verified) nurse (-ing father), (put) trust, turn to the right.

> And whenever you deviate to the right or to the left, your ears will heed the command from behind you: "This is the road; follow it!" YESHA'YAHU 30:21 (ISAIAH 30:21)
>
> And thine ears shall hear a word behind thee, saying, This is the way, walk ye in it, when ye turn to the right hand, and when ye turn to the left. ISAIAH 30:21

(541) pronounced aw-man'; denom. from 3225; to take the right-hand road:- turn to the right. See 539.

(3225) pronounced yaw-meen'; from 3231; the right hand or side (leg, eye) of a person or other object (as the stronger and most dexterous): locally, the south:- + left handed, right (hand, side), south.

(3231) pronounced yaw-man'; a prim. root; to be (phys.) right (i.e. firm); but used only as denom. from 3225 and transit., to be right-handed or take the right-hand side:- go turn) to (on, use) the right hand.

For the word of the LORD is right; His every deed is faithful. TEHILLIM 33:4 (PSALMS 33:4)

For the word of the LORD is right: and all his works *are done* in truth (530). PSALMS 33:4

truth (530) pronounced em-oo-naw'; fem. of 529; lit. firmness; fig. security; mor. fidelity:- faith (-ful, -ly, -ness, [man]), set office, stability, steady, truly, truth, verity.

(529) pronounced ay-moon'; from 539; established, i.e. (fig.) trusty; also (abstr.) trustworthiness:-faith (-ful), truth.

(539) pronounced aw-man'; a prim. root; prop. to build up or support; to foster as a parent or nurse; fig. to render (or be) firm or faithful, to trust or believe, to be permanent or quiet; mor.

to be true or certain; once (Isa. 30:21; by interch. for 541) to go to the right hand:- hence assurance, believe, bring up, establish, + fail, be faithful (of long continuance, steadfast, sure, surely, trusty, verified) nurse (-ing father), (put) trust, turn to the right.

> And whenever you deviate to the right or to the left, your ears will heed the command from behind you: "This is the road; follow it!" YESHA'YAHU 30:21 (ISAIAH 30:21)
>
> And thine ears shall hear a word behind thee, saying, This is the way, walk ye in it, when ye turn to the right hand, and when ye turn to the left. ISAIAH 30:21

(541) pronounced aw-man'; denom. from 3225; to take the right-hand road:- turn to the right. See 539.

(3225) pronounced yaw-meen'; from 3231; the right hand or side (leg, eye) of a person or other object (as the stronger and most dexterous): locally, the south:- + left handed, right (hand, side), south.

(3231) pronounced yaw-man'; a prim. root; to be (phys.) right (i.e. firm); but used only as denom. from 3225 and transit., to be right-handed or take the right-hand side:- go turn) to (on, use) the right hand.

I proclaimed [Your] righteousness in a great congregation; see, I did not withhold my words; O LORD, You must know it. I did not keep Your beneficence to myself; I declared Your faithful deliverance: I did not fail to speak of Your steadfast love in a great congregation. TEHILLIM 40:10-11 (PSALMS 40:10-11)

I have not hid thy righteousness within my heart: I have declared thy faithfulness and thy salvation: I have not concealed thy lovingkindness and thy truth (571) from the great congregation. Withhold not thou thy tender mercies from me, O LORD: let thy lovingkindness and thy truth (571) continually preserve me. PSALMS 40:10-11

truth (571) pronounced eh'meth; contr. From 539; stability; fig. certainty, truth, trustworthiness:-assured (-ly), establishment, faithful, right, sure, true (-ly, -th), verity.

(539) pronounced aw-man'; a prim. root; prop. to build up or support; to foster as a parent or nurse; fig. to render (or be) firm or faithful, to trust or believe, to be permanent or quiet; mor. to be true or certain; once (Isa. 30:21; by interch. for 541) to go to the right hand:- hence assurance, believe, bring up, establish, + fail, be faithful (of long continuance, steadfast, sure, surely, trusty, verified) nurse (-ing father), (put) trust, turn to the right.

> And whenever you deviate to the right or to the left, your ears will heed the command from behind you: "This is the road; follow it!" YESHA'YAHU 30:21 (ISAIAH 30:21)

> And thine ears shall hear a word behind thee, saying, This is the way, walk ye in it, when ye turn to the right hand, and when ye turn to the left. ISAIAH 30:21

(541) pronounced aw-man'; denom. from 3225; to take the right-hand road:- turn to the right. See 539.

(3225) pronounced yaw-meen'; from 3231; the right hand or side (leg, eye) of a person or other object (as the stronger and most dexterous): locally, the south:- + left handed, right (hand, side), south.

(3231) pronounced yaw-man'; a prim. root; to be (phys.) right (i.e. firm); but used only as denom. from 3225 and transit., to be right-handed or take the right-hand side:- go turn) to (on, use) the right hand.

Send forth Your light and Your truth; they will lead me; they will bring me to Your holy mountain, to Your dwelling place. TEHILLIM 43:3 (PSALMS 43:3)

O send out thy light and thy truth (571): let them lead me; let them bring me unto thy holy hill, and to thy tabernacles. PSALMS 43:3

truth (571) pronounced eh'meth; contr. From 539; stability; fig. certainty, truth, trustworthiness:-assured (-ly), establishment, faithful, right, sure, true (-ly, -th), verity.

(539) pronounced aw-man'; a prim. root; prop. to build up or support; to foster as a parent or nurse; fig. to render (or be) firm or faithful, to trust or believe, to be permanent or quiet; mor. to be true or certain; once (Isa. 30:21; by interch. for 541) to go to the right hand:- hence assurance, believe, bring up, establish, + fail, be faithful (of long continuance, steadfast, sure, surely, trusty, verified) nurse (-ing father), (put) trust, turn to the right.

> And whenever you deviate to the right or to the left, your ears will heed the command from behind you: "This is the road; follow it!" YESHA'YAHU 30:21 (ISAIAH 30:21)

> And thine ears shall hear a word behind thee, saying, This is the way, walk ye in it, when ye turn to the right hand, and when ye turn to the left. ISAIAH 30:21

(541) pronounced aw-man'; denom. from 3225; to take the right-hand road:- turn to the right. See 539.

(3225) pronounced yaw-meen'; from 3231; the right hand or side (leg, eye) of a person or other object (as the stronger and most dexterous): locally, the south:- + left handed, right (hand, side), south.

(3231) pronounced yaw-man'; a prim. root; to be (phys.) right (i.e. firm); but used only as denom. from 3225 and transit., to be right-handed or take the right-hand side:- go turn) to (on, use) the right hand.

In Your glory, win success; ride on in the cause of truth and meekness and right; and let Your right hand lead You to awesome deeds. TEHILLIM 45:5 (PSALMS 45:4)

meaning of Heb. uncertain. (TANAKH footnote).

And in thy majesty ride prosperously because of truth (571) and meekness and righteousness; and thy right hand shall teach thee terrible things. PSALMS 45:4

truth (571) pronounced eh'meth; contr. From 539; stability; fig. certainty, truth, trustworthiness:-assured (-ly), establishment, faithful, right, sure, true (-ly, -th), verity.

(539) pronounced aw-man'; a prim. root; prop. to build up or support; to foster as a parent or nurse; fig. to render (or be) firm or faithful, to trust or believe, to be permanent or quiet; mor. to be true or certain; once (Isa. 30:21; by interch. for 541) to go to the right hand:- hence assurance, believe, bring up, establish, + fail, be faithful (of long continuance, steadfast, sure, surely, trusty, verified) nurse (-ing father), (put) trust, turn to the right.

And whenever you deviate to the right or to the left, your ears will heed the command from behind you: "This is the road; follow it!" YESHA'YAHU 30:21 (ISAIAH 30:21)

And thine ears shall hear a word behind thee, saying, This is the way, walk ye in it, when ye turn to the right hand, and when ye turn to the left. ISAIAH 30:21

(541) pronounced aw-man'; denom. from 3225; to take the right-hand road:- turn to the right. See 539.

(3225) pronounced yaw-meen'; from 3231; the right hand or side (leg, eye) of a person or other object (as the stronger and most dexterous): locally, the south:- + left handed, right (hand, side), south.

(3231) pronounced yaw-man'; a prim. root; to be (phys.) right (i.e. firm); but used only as denom. from 3225 and transit., to be right-handed or take the right-hand side:- go turn) to (on, use) the right hand.

Indeed You desire truth about that which is hidden; teach me wisdom about secret things. TEHILLIM 51:8 (PSALMS 51:6)

meaning of Heb. uncertain. (TANAKH footnote).

Behold, thou desirest truth (571) in the inward parts: and in the hidden *part* thou shalt make me to know wisdom. PSALMS 51:6

truth (571) pronounced eh'meth; contr. From 539; stability; fig. certainty, truth, trustworthiness:-assured (-ly), establishment, faithful, right, sure, true (-ly, -th), verity.

(539) pronounced aw-man'; a prim. root; prop. to build up or support; to foster as a parent or nurse; fig. to render (or be) firm or faithful, to trust or believe, to be permanent or quiet; mor. to be true or certain; once (Isa. 30:21; by interch. for 541) to go to the right hand:- hence assurance, believe, bring up, establish, + fail, be faithful (of long continuance, steadfast, sure, surely, trusty, verified) nurse (-ing father), (put) trust, turn to the right.

> And whenever you deviate to the right or to the left, your ears will heed the command from behind you: "This is the road; follow it!" YESHA'YAHU 30:21 (ISAIAH 30:21)
>
> And thine ears shall hear a word behind thee, saying, This is the way, walk ye in it, when ye turn to the right hand, and when ye turn to the left. ISAIAH 30:21

(541) pronounced aw-man'; denom. from 3225; to take the right-hand road:- turn to the right. See 539.

(3225) pronounced yaw-meen'; from 3231; the right hand or side (leg, eye) of a person or other object (as the stronger and most dexterous): locally, the south:- + left handed, right (hand, side), south.

(3231) pronounced yaw-man'; a prim. root; to be (phys.) right (i.e. firm); but used only as denom. from 3225 and transit., to be right-handed or take the right-hand side:- go turn) to (on, use) the right hand.

He will repay the evil of my watchful foes; by Your faithfulness, destroy them! TEHILLIM 54:7 (PSALMS 54:5)

He shall reward evil unto mine enemies: cut them off in thy truth (571). PSALMS 54:5

truth (571) pronounced eh'meth; contr. From 539; stability; fig. certainty, truth, trustworthiness:-assured (-ly), establishment, faithful, right, sure, true (-ly, -th), verity.

(539) pronounced aw-man'; a prim. root; prop. to build up or support; to foster as a parent or nurse; fig. to render (or be) firm or faithful, to trust or believe, to be permanent or quiet; mor. to be true or certain; once (Isa. 30:21; by interch. for 541) to go to the right hand:- hence assurance, believe, bring up, establish, + fail, be faithful (of long continuance, steadfast, sure, surely, trusty, verified) nurse (-ing father), (put) trust, turn to the right.

> And whenever you deviate to the right or to the left, your ears will heed the command from behind you: "This is the road; follow it!" YESHA'YAHU 30:21 (ISAIAH 30:21)
>
> And thine ears shall hear a word behind thee, saying, This is the way, walk ye in it, when ye turn to the right hand, and when ye turn to the left. ISAIAH 30:21

(541) pronounced aw-man'; denom. from 3225; to take the right-hand road:- turn to the right. See 539.

(3225) pronounced yaw-meen'; from 3231; the right hand or side (leg, eye) of a person or other object (as the stronger and most dexterous): locally, the south:- + left handed, right (hand, side), south.

(3231) pronounced yaw-man'; a prim. root; to be (phys.) right (i.e. firm); but used only as denom. from 3225 and transit., to be right-handed or take the right-hand side:- go turn) to (on, use) the right hand.

He will reach down from Heaven and deliver me: God will send down His steadfast love; my persecutor reviles. TEHILLIM 57:4 (PSALMS 57:3)

He shall send from heaven, and save me from the reproach of him that would swallow me up. Selah. God shall send forth his mercy and his truth (571). PSALMS 57:3

truth (571) pronounced eh'meth; contr. From 539; stability; fig. certainty, truth, trustworthiness:-assured (-ly), establishment, faithful, right, sure, true (-ly, -th), verity.

(539) pronounced aw-man'; a prim. root; prop. to build up or support; to foster as a parent or nurse; fig. to render (or be) firm or faithful, to trust or believe, to be permanent or quiet; mor. to be true or certain; once (Isa. 30:21; by interch. for 541) to go to the right hand:- hence assurance, believe, bring up, establish, + fail, be faithful (of long continuance, steadfast, sure, surely, trusty, verified) nurse (-ing father), (put) trust, turn to the right.

> And whenever you deviate to the right or to the left, your ears will heed the command from behind you: "This is the road; follow it!" YESHA'YAHU 30:21 (ISAIAH 30:21)
>
> And thine ears shall hear a word behind thee, saying, This is the way, walk ye in it, when ye turn to the right hand, and when ye turn to the left. ISAIAH 30:21

(541) pronounced aw-man'; denom. from 3225; to take the right-hand road:- turn to the right. See 539.

(3225) pronounced yaw-meen'; from 3231; the right hand or side (leg, eye) of a person or other object (as the stronger and most dexterous): locally, the south:- + left handed, right (hand, side), south.

(3231) pronounced yaw-man'; a prim. root; to be (phys.) right (i.e. firm); but used only as denom. from 3225 and transit., to be right-handed or take the right-hand side:- go turn) to (on, use) the right hand.

For Your faithfulness is as high as heaven; Your steadfastness reaches to the sky. TEHILLIM 57:11 (PSALMS 57:10)

For thy mercy is great unto the heavens, and thy truth (571) unto the clouds. PSALMS 57:10

> truth (571) pronounced eh'meth; contr. From 539; stability; fig. certainty, truth, trustworthiness:-assured (-ly), establishment, faithful, right, sure, true (-ly, -th), verity.
>
> (539) pronounced aw-man'; a prim. root; prop. to build up or support; to foster as a parent or nurse; fig. to render (or be) firm or faithful, to trust or believe, to be permanent or quiet; mor. to be true or certain; once (Isa. 30:21; by interch. for 541) to go to the right hand:- hence assurance, believe, bring up, establish, + fail, be faithful (of long continuance, steadfast, sure, surely, trusty, verified) nurse (-ing father), (put) trust, turn to the right.
>
>> And whenever you deviate to the right or to the left, your ears will heed the command from behind you: "This is the road; follow it!" YESHA'YAHU 30:21 (ISAIAH 30:21)
>>
>> And thine ears shall hear a word behind thee, saying, This is the way, walk ye in it, when ye turn to the right hand, and when ye turn to the left. ISAIAH 30:21
>
> (541) pronounced aw-man'; denom. from 3225; to take the right-hand road:- turn to the right. See 539.
>
> (3225) pronounced yaw-meen'; from 3231; the right hand or side (leg, eye) of a person or other object (as the stronger and most dexterous): locally, the south:- + left handed, right (hand, side), south.
>
> (3231) pronounced yaw-man'; a prim. root; to be (phys.) right (i.e. firm); but used only as denom. from 3225 and transit., to be right-handed or take the right-hand side:- go turn) to (on, use) the right hand.

Give those who fear You because of Your truth a banner for rallying. TEHILLIM 60:6 (PSALMS 60:4)

> Meaning of Heb. uncertain. (TANAKH footnote).

Thou hast given a banner to them that fear thee, that it may be displayed because of the truth (7189). Selah. PSALMS 60:4

> truth (7189) pronounced ko'-shet or kosht; from an unused root mean. to balance; equity (as evenly weighed); i.e. reality:-certainty, truth.

May he dwell in God's presence forever; appoint steadfast love to guard him. TEHILLIM 61:8 (PSALMS 61:7)

> appoint steadfast love to guard him: meaning of Heb. uncertain. (TANAKH footnote).

He shall abide before God for ever: O prepare mercy and truth (571), *which* may preserve him. PSALMS 61:7

truth (571) pronounced eh'meth; contr. From 539; stability; fig. certainty, truth, trustworthiness:-assured (-ly), establishment, faithful, right, sure, true (-ly, -th), verity.

(539) pronounced aw-man'; a prim. root; prop. to build up or support; to foster as a parent or nurse; fig. to render (or be) firm or faithful, to trust or believe, to be permanent or quiet; mor. to be true or certain; once (Isa. 30:21; by interch. for 541) to go to the right hand:- hence assurance, believe, bring up, establish, + fail, be faithful (of long continuance, steadfast, sure, surely, trusty, verified) nurse (-ing father), (put) trust, turn to the right.

> And whenever you deviate to the right or to the left, your ears will heed the command from behind you: "This is the road; follow it!" YESHA'YAHU 30:21 (ISAIAH 30:21)
>
> And thine ears shall hear a word behind thee, saying, This is the way, walk ye in it, when ye turn to the right hand, and when ye turn to the left. ISAIAH 30:21

(541) pronounced aw-man'; denom. from 3225; to take the right-hand road:- turn to the right. See 539.

(3225) pronounced yaw-meen'; from 3231; the right hand or side (leg, eye) of a person or other object (as the stronger and most dexterous): locally, the south:- + left handed, right (hand, side), south.

(3231) pronounced yaw-man'; a prim. root; to be (phys.) right (i.e. firm); but used only as denom. from 3225 and transit., to be right-handed or take the right-hand side:- go turn) to (on, use) the right hand.

As for me, may my prayer come to You, O LORD, at a favorable moment; O God, in Your abundant faithfulness, answer me with Your sure deliverance. TEHILLIM 69:14 (PSALMS 69:13)

But as for me, my prayer is unto thee, O LORD, in an acceptable time: O God, in the multitude of thy mercy hear me, in the truth (571) of thy salvation. PSALMS 69:13

truth (571) pronounced eh'meth; contr. From 539; stability; fig. certainty, truth, trustworthiness:-assured (-ly), establishment, faithful, right, sure, true (-ly, -th), verity.

(539) pronounced aw-man'; a prim. root; prop. to build up or support; to foster as a parent or nurse; fig. to render (or be) firm or faithful, to trust or believe, to be permanent or quiet; mor. to be true or certain; once (Isa. 30:21; by interch. for 541) to go to the right hand:- hence assurance, believe, bring up, establish, + fail, be faithful (of long continuance, steadfast, sure, surely, trusty, verified) nurse (-ing father), (put) trust, turn to the right.

> And whenever you deviate to the right or to the left, your ears will heed the command from behind you: "This is the road; follow it!" YESHA'YAHU 30:21 (ISAIAH 30:21)

> And thine ears shall hear a word behind thee, saying, This is the way, walk ye in it, when ye turn to the right hand, and when ye turn to the left. ISAIAH 30:21

(541) pronounced aw-man'; denom. from 3225; to take the right-hand road:- turn to the right. See 539.

(3225) pronounced yaw-meen'; from 3231; the right hand or side (leg, eye) of a person or other object (as the stronger and most dexterous): locally, the south:- + left handed, right (hand, side), south.

(3231) pronounced yaw-man'; a prim. root; to be (phys.) right (i.e. firm); but used only as denom. from 3225 and transit., to be right-handed or take the right-hand side:- go turn) to (on, use) the right hand.

Then I will acclaim You to the music of the lyre for Your faithfulness, O my God; I will sing a hymn to You with a harp, O Holy One of Israel. TEHILLIM 71:22 (PSALMS 71:22)

I will also praise thee with the psaltery, *even* thy truth (571), O my God: unto thee will I sing with the harp, O thou Holy One of Israel. PSALMS 71:22

truth (571) pronounced eh'meth; contr. From 539; stability; fig. certainty, truth, trustworthiness:-assured (-ly), establishment, faithful, right, sure, true (-ly, -th), verity.

(539) pronounced aw-man'; a prim. root; prop. to build up or support; to foster as a parent or nurse; fig. to render (or be) firm or faithful, to trust or believe, to be permanent or quiet; mor. to be true or certain; once (Isa. 30:21; by interch. for 541) to go to the right hand:- hence assurance, believe, bring up, establish, + fail, be faithful (of long continuance, steadfast, sure, surely, trusty, verified) nurse (-ing father), (put) trust, turn to the right.

> And whenever you deviate to the right or to the left, your ears will heed the command from behind you: "This is the road; follow it!" YESHA'YAHU 30:21 (ISAIAH 30:21)

> And thine ears shall hear a word behind thee, saying, This is the way, walk ye in it, when ye turn to the right hand, and when ye turn to the left. ISAIAH 30:21

(541) pronounced aw-man'; denom. from 3225; to take the right-hand road:- turn to the right. See 539.

(3225) pronounced yaw-meen'; from 3231; the right hand or side (leg, eye) of a person or other object (as the stronger and most dexterous): locally, the south:- + left handed, right (hand, side), south.

(3231) pronounced yaw-man'; a prim. root; to be (phys.) right (i.e. firm); but used only as denom. from 3225 and transit., to be right-handed or take the right-hand side:- go turn) to (on, use) the right hand.

Faithfulness and truth meet; justice and well-being kiss. Truth springs up from the earth; justice looks down from heaven. The LORD also bestows His bounty; our land yields its produce. TEHILLIM 85:11-13 (PSALMS 85:10-12)

Mercy and truth (571) are met together; righteousness and peace have kissed each other. Truth shall spring out of the earth; and righteousness shall look down from heaven. Yea, the LORD shall give that which is good; and our land shall yield her increase. PSALMS 85:10-12

> truth (571) pronounced eh'meth; contr. From 539; stability; fig. certainty, truth, trustworthiness:-assured (-ly), establishment, faithful, right, sure, true (-ly, -th), verity.
>
> (539) pronounced aw-man'; a prim. root; prop. to build up or support; to foster as a parent or nurse; fig. to render (or be) firm or faithful, to trust or believe, to be permanent or quiet; mor. to be true or certain; once (Isa. 30:21; by interch. for 541) to go to the right hand:- hence assurance, believe, bring up, establish, + fail, be faithful (of long continuance, steadfast, sure, surely, trusty, verified) nurse (-ing father), (put) trust, turn to the right.
>
>> And whenever you deviate to the right or to the left, your ears will heed the command from behind you: "This is the road; follow it!" YESHA'YAHU 30:21 (ISAIAH 30:21)
>>
>> And thine ears shall hear a word behind thee, saying, This is the way, walk ye in it, when ye turn to the right hand, and when ye turn to the left. ISAIAH 30:21
>
> (541) pronounced aw-man'; denom. from 3225; to take the right-hand road:- turn to the right. See 539.
>
> (3225) pronounced yaw-meen'; from 3231; the right hand or side (leg, eye) of a person or other object (as the stronger and most dexterous): locally, the south:- + left handed, right (hand, side), south.
>
> (3231) pronounced yaw-man'; a prim. root; to be (phys.) right (i.e. firm); but used only as denom. from 3225 and transit., to be right-handed or take the right-hand side:- go turn) to (on, use) the right hand.

Teach me Your way, O LORD; I will walk in Your truth; let my heart be undivided in reverence for Your name. TEHILLIM 86:11 (PSALMS 86:11)

Teach me thy way, O LORD; I will walk in thy truth (571): smite my heart to fear thy name. PSALMS 86:11

> truth (571) pronounced eh'meth; contr. From 539; stability; fig. certainty, truth, trustworthiness:-assured (-ly), establishment, faithful, right, sure, true (-ly, -th), verity.
>
> (539) pronounced aw-man'; a prim. root; prop. to build up or support; to foster as a parent or nurse; fig. to render (or be) firm or faithful, to trust or believe, to be permanent or quiet; mor.

to be true or certain; once (Isa. 30:21; by interch. for 541) to go to the right hand:- hence assurance, believe, bring up, establish, + fail, be faithful (of long continuance, steadfast, sure, surely, trusty, verified) nurse (-ing father), (put) trust, turn to the right.

> And whenever you deviate to the right or to the left, your ears will heed the command from behind you: "This is the road; follow it!" YESHA'YAHU 30:21 (ISAIAH 30:21)
>
> And thine ears shall hear a word behind thee, saying, This is the way, walk ye in it, when ye turn to the right hand, and when ye turn to the left. ISAIAH 30:21

(541) pronounced aw-man'; denom. from 3225; to take the right-hand road:- turn to the right. See 539.

(3225) pronounced yaw-meen'; from 3231; the right hand or side (leg, eye) of a person or other object (as the stronger and most dexterous): locally, the south:- + left handed, right (hand, side), south.

(3231) pronounced yaw-man'; a prim. root; to be (phys.) right (i.e. firm); but used only as denom. from 3225 and transit., to be right-handed or take the right-hand side:- go turn) to (on, use) the right hand.

But You, O LORD, are a God compassionate and merciful, slow to anger, abounding in steadfast love and faithfulness. TEHILLIM 86:15 (PSALMS 86:15)

But thou, O LORD, *art* a God full of compassion, and gracious long-suffering, and plenteous in mercy and truth (571). PSALMS 86:15

truth (571) pronounced eh'meth; contr. From 539; stability; fig. certainty, truth, trustworthiness:-assured (-ly), establishment, faithful, right, sure, true (-ly, -th), verity.

(539) pronounced aw-man'; a prim. root; prop. to build up or support; to foster as a parent or nurse; fig. to render (or be) firm or faithful, to trust or believe, to be permanent or quiet; mor. to be true or certain; once (Isa. 30:21; by interch. for 541) to go to the right hand:- hence assurance, believe, bring up, establish, + fail, be faithful (of long continuance, steadfast, sure, surely, trusty, verified) nurse (-ing father), (put) trust, turn to the right.

> And whenever you deviate to the right or to the left, your ears will heed the command from behind you: "This is the road; follow it!" YESHA'YAHU 30:21 (ISAIAH 30:21)
>
> And thine ears shall hear a word behind thee, saying, This is the way, walk ye in it, when ye turn to the right hand, and when ye turn to the left. ISAIAH 30:21

(541) pronounced aw-man'; denom. from 3225; to take the right-hand road:- turn to the right. See 539.

(3225) pronounced yaw-meen'; from 3231; the right hand or side (leg, eye) of a person or other object (as the stronger and most dexterous): locally, the south:- + left handed, right (hand, side), south.

(3231) pronounced yaw-man'; a prim. root; to be (phys.) right (i.e. firm); but used only as denom. from 3225 and transit., to be right-handed or take the right-hand side:- go turn) to (on, use) the right hand.

Righteousness and justice are the base of Your throne; steadfast love and faithfulness stand before You. TEHILLIM 89:15 (PSALMS 89:14)

Justice and judgment are the habitation of thy throne: mercy and truth (571) shall go before thy face. PSALMS 89:14

truth (571) pronounced eh'meth; contr. From 539; stability; fig. certainty, truth, trustworthiness:-assured (-ly), establishment, faithful, right, sure, true (-ly, -th), verity.

(539) pronounced aw-man'; a prim. root; prop. to build up or support; to foster as a parent or nurse; fig. to render (or be) firm or faithful, to trust or believe, to be permanent or quiet; mor. to be true or certain; once (Isa. 30:21; by interch. for 541) to go to the right hand:- hence assurance, believe, bring up, establish, + fail, be faithful (of long continuance, steadfast, sure, surely, trusty, verified) nurse (-ing father), (put) trust, turn to the right.

And whenever you deviate to the right or to the left, your ears will heed the command from behind you: "This is the road; follow it!" YESHA'YAHU 30:21 (ISAIAH 30:21)

And thine ears shall hear a word behind thee, saying, This is the way, walk ye in it, when ye turn to the right hand, and when ye turn to the left. ISAIAH 30:21

(541) pronounced aw-man'; denom. from 3225; to take the right-hand road:- turn to the right. See 539.

(3225) pronounced yaw-meen'; from 3231; the right hand or side (leg, eye) of a person or other object (as the stronger and most dexterous): locally, the south:- + left handed, right (hand, side), south.

(3231) pronounced yaw-man'; a prim. root; to be (phys.) right (i.e. firm); but used only as denom. from 3225 and transit., to be right-handed or take the right-hand side:- go turn) to (on, use) the right hand.

O LORD, where is Your steadfast love of old which You swore to David in Your faithfulness? TEHILLIM 89:50 (PSALMS 89:49)

LORD, where *are* thy former lovingkindnesses, *which* thou swarest unto David in thy truth (530)? PSALMS 89:49

truth (530) pronounced em-oo-naw'; fem. of 529; lit. firmness; fig. security; mor. fidelity:- faith (-ful, -ly, -ness, [man]), set office, stability, steady, truly, truth, verity.

(529) pronounced ay-moon'; from 539; established, i.e. (fig.) trusty; also (abstr.) trustworthiness:-faith (-ful), truth.

(539) pronounced aw-man'; a prim. root; prop. to build up or support; to foster as a parent or nurse; fig. to render (or be) firm or faithful, to trust or believe, to be permanent or quiet; mor. to be true or certain; once (Isa. 30:21; by interch. for 541) to go to the right hand:- hence assurance, believe, bring up, establish, + fail, be faithful (of long continuance, steadfast, sure, surely, trusty, verified) nurse (-ing father), (put) trust, turn to the right.

> And whenever you deviate to the right or to the left, your ears will heed the command from behind you: "This is the road; follow it!" YESHA'YAHU 30:21 (ISAIAH 30:21)
>
> And thine ears shall hear a word behind thee, saying, This is the way, walk ye in it, when ye turn to the right hand, and when ye turn to the left. ISAIAH 30:21

(541) pronounced aw-man'; denom. from 3225; to take the right-hand road:- turn to the right. See 539.

(3225) pronounced yaw-meen'; from 3231; the right hand or side (leg, eye) of a person or other object (as the stronger and most dexterous): locally, the south:- + left handed, right (hand, side), south.

(3231) pronounced yaw-man'; a prim. root; to be (phys.) right (i.e. firm); but used only as denom. from 3225 and transit., to be right-handed or take the right-hand side:- go turn) to (on, use) the right hand.

He will cover you with His pinions; you will find refuge under His wings; His fidelity is an encircling shield. TEHILLIM 91:4 (PSALMS 91:4)

He shall cover thee with his feathers, and under his wings shalt thou trust: his truth (571) shall be thy shield and buckler. PSALMS 91:4

truth (571) pronounced eh'meth; contr. From 539; stability; fig. certainty, truth, trustworthiness:-assured (-ly), establishment, faithful, right, sure, true (-ly, -th), verity.

(539) pronounced aw-man'; a prim. root; prop. to build up or support; to foster as a parent or nurse; fig. to render (or be) firm or faithful, to trust or believe, to be permanent or quiet; mor. to be true or certain; once (Isa. 30:21; by interch. for 541) to go to the right hand:- hence assurance, believe, bring up, establish, + fail, be faithful (of long continuance, steadfast, sure, surely, trusty, verified) nurse (-ing father), (put) trust, turn to the right.

And whenever you deviate to the right or to the left, your ears will heed the command from behind you: "This is the road; follow it!" YESHA'YAHU 30:21 (ISAIAH 30:21)

And thine ears shall hear a word behind thee, saying, This is the way, walk ye in it, when ye turn to the right hand, and when ye turn to the left. ISAIAH 30:21

(541) pronounced aw-man'; denom. from 3225; to take the right-hand road:- turn to the right. See 539.

(3225) pronounced yaw-meen'; from 3231; the right hand or side (leg, eye) of a person or other object (as the stronger and most dexterous): locally, the south:- + left handed, right (hand, side), south.

(3231) pronounced yaw-man'; a prim. root; to be (phys.) right (i.e. firm); but used only as denom. from 3225 and transit., to be right-handed or take the right-hand side:- go turn) to (on, use) the right hand.

The fields and everything in them exult; then shall all the trees of the forest shout for joy at the presence of the LORD, for He is coming, for He is coming to rule the earth: He will rule the world justly, and its people in faithfulness. TEHILLIM 96:12-13 (PSALMS 96:12-13)

Let the field be joyful, and all that is therein: then shall all the trees of the wood rejoice before the LORD: for he cometh, for he cometh to judge the earth: he shall judge the world with righteousness, and the people with his truth (530). PSALMS 96:12-13

truth (530) pronounced em-oo-naw'; fem. of 529; lit. firmness; fig. security; mor. fidelity:- faith (-ful, -ly, -ness, [man]), set office, stability, steady, truly, truth, verity.

(529) pronounced ay-moon'; from 539; established, i.e. (fig.) trusty; also (abstr.) trustworthiness:-faith (-ful), truth.

(539) pronounced aw-man'; a prim. root; prop. to build up or support; to foster as a parent or nurse; fig. to render (or be) firm or faithful, to trust or believe, to be permanent or quiet; mor. to be true or certain; once (Isa. 30:21; by interch. for 541) to go to the right hand:- hence assurance, believe, bring up, establish, + fail, be faithful (of long continuance, steadfast, sure, surely, trusty, verified) nurse (-ing father), (put) trust, turn to the right.

And whenever you deviate to the right or to the left, your ears will heed the command from behind you: "This is the road; follow it!" YESHA'YAHU 30:21 (ISAIAH 30:21)

And thine ears shall hear a word behind thee, saying, This is the way, walk ye in it, when ye turn to the right hand, and when ye turn to the left. ISAIAH 30:21

(541) pronounced aw-man'; denom. from 3225; to take the right-hand road:- turn to the right. See 539.

(3225) pronounced yaw-meen'; from 3231; the right hand or side (leg, eye) of a person or other object (as the stronger and most dexterous): locally, the south:- + left handed, right (hand, side), south.

(3231) pronounced yaw-man'; a prim. root; to be (phys.) right (i.e. firm); but used only as denom. from 3225 and transit., to be right-handed or take the right-hand side:- go turn) to (on, use) the right hand.

He was mindful of His steadfast love and faithfulness toward the house of Israel; all the ends of the earth beheld the victory of our God. TEHILLIM 98:3 (PSALMS 98:3)

He hath remembered his mercy and his truth (530) toward the house of Israel: all the ends of the earth have seen the salvation of our God. PSALMS 98:3

truth (530) pronounced em-oo-naw'; fem. of 529; lit. firmness; fig. security; mor. fidelity:- faith (-ful, -ly, -ness, [man]), set office, stability, steady, truly, truth, verity.

(529) pronounced ay-moon'; from 539; established, i.e. (fig.) trusty; also (abstr.) trustworthiness:-faith (-ful), truth.

(539) pronounced aw-man'; a prim. root; prop. to build up or support; to foster as a parent or nurse; fig. to render (or be) firm or faithful, to trust or believe, to be permanent or quiet; mor. to be true or certain; once (Isa. 30:21; by interch. for 541) to go to the right hand:- hence assurance, believe, bring up, establish, + fail, be faithful (of long continuance, steadfast, sure, surely, trusty, verified) nurse (-ing father), (put) trust, turn to the right.

> And whenever you deviate to the right or to the left, your ears will heed the command from behind you: "This is the road; follow it!" YESHA'YAHU 30:21 (ISAIAH 30:21)
>
> And thine ears shall hear a word behind thee, saying, This is the way, walk ye in it, when ye turn to the right hand, and when ye turn to the left. ISAIAH 30:21

(541) pronounced aw-man'; denom. from 3225; to take the right-hand road:- turn to the right. See 539.

(3225) pronounced yaw-meen'; from 3231; the right hand or side (leg, eye) of a person or other object (as the stronger and most dexterous): locally, the south:- + left handed, right (hand, side), south.

(3231) pronounced yaw-man'; a prim. root; to be (phys.) right (i.e. firm); but used only as denom. from 3225 and transit., to be right-handed or take the right-hand side:- go turn) to (on, use) the right hand.

For the LORD is good; His steadfast love is eternal; His faithfulness is for all generations. TEHILLIM 100:5 (PSALMS 100:5)

For the LORD is good; his mercy is everlasting; and his truth (530) *endureth* to all generations. PSALMS 100:5

> truth (530) pronounced em-oo-naw'; fem. of 529; lit. firmness; fig. security; mor. fidelity:- faith (-ful, -ly, -ness, [man]), set office, stability, steady, truly, truth, verity.
>
> (529) pronounced ay-moon'; from 539; established, i.e. (fig.) trusty; also (abstr.) trustworthiness:-faith (-ful), truth.
>
> (539) pronounced aw-man'; a prim. root; prop. to build up or support; to foster as a parent or nurse; fig. to render (or be) firm or faithful, to trust or believe, to be permanent or quiet; mor. to be true or certain; once (Isa. 30:21; by interch. for 541) to go to the right hand:- hence assurance, believe, bring up, establish, + fail, be faithful (of long continuance, steadfast, sure, surely, trusty, verified) nurse (-ing father), (put) trust, turn to the right.
>
>> And whenever you deviate to the right or to the left, your ears will heed the command from behind you: "This is the road; follow it!" YESHA'YAHU 30:21 (ISAIAH 30:21)
>>
>> And thine ears shall hear a word behind thee, saying, This is the way, walk ye in it, when ye turn to the right hand, and when ye turn to the left. ISAIAH 30:21
>
> (541) pronounced aw-man'; denom. from 3225; to take the right-hand road:- turn to the right. See 539.
>
> (3225) pronounced yaw-meen'; from 3231; the right hand or side (leg, eye) of a person or other object (as the stronger and most dexterous): locally, the south:- + left handed, right (hand, side), south.
>
> (3231) pronounced yaw-man'; a prim. root; to be (phys.) right (i.e. firm); but used only as denom. from 3225 and transit., to be right-handed or take the right-hand side:- go turn) to (on, use) the right hand.

I will praise You among the peoples, O LORD, sing a hymn to You among the nations; for Your faithfulness is higher than the heavens; Your steadfastness reaches to the sky. TEHILLIM 108:4-5 (PSALMS 108:4)

For thy mercy is great above the heavens: and thy truth (571) reacheth unto the clouds. PSALMS 108:4

> truth (571) pronounced eh'meth; contr. From 539; stability; fig. certainty, truth, trustworthiness:-assured (-ly), establishment, faithful, right, sure, true (-ly, -th), verity.

(539) pronounced aw-man'; a prim. root; prop. to build up or support; to foster as a parent or nurse; fig. to render (or be) firm or faithful, to trust or believe, to be permanent or quiet; mor. to be true or certain; once (Isa. 30:21; by interch. for 541) to go to the right hand:- hence assurance, believe, bring up, establish, + fail, be faithful (of long continuance, steadfast, sure, surely, trusty, verified) nurse (-ing father), (put) trust, turn to the right.

> And whenever you deviate to the right or to the left, your ears will heed the command from behind you: "This is the road; follow it!" YESHA'YAHU 30:21 (ISAIAH 30:21)
>
> And thine ears shall hear a word behind thee, saying, This is the way, walk ye in it, when ye turn to the right hand, and when ye turn to the left. ISAIAH 30:21

(541) pronounced aw-man'; denom. from 3225; to take the right-hand road:- turn to the right. See 539.

(3225) pronounced yaw-meen'; from 3231; the right hand or side (leg, eye) of a person or other object (as the stronger and most dexterous): locally, the south:- + left handed, right (hand, side), south.

(3231) pronounced yaw-man'; a prim. root; to be (phys.) right (i.e. firm); but used only as denom. from 3225 and transit., to be right-handed or take the right-hand side:- go turn) to (on, use) the right hand.

His handiwork is truth and justice; all His precepts are enduring, well-founded for all eternity, wrought of truth and equity. TEHILLIM 111:7-8 (PSALMS 111:7-8)

The works of his hands *are* verity (571) and judgment; all his commandments *are* sure. They stand fast for ever and ever, *and are* done in truth (571) and uprightness. PSALMS 111:7-8

truth (571) pronounced eh'meth; contr. From 539; stability; fig. certainty, truth, trustworthiness:-assured (-ly), establishment, faithful, right, sure, true (-ly, -th), verity.

(539) pronounced aw-man'; a prim. root; prop. to build up or support; to foster as a parent or nurse; fig. to render (or be) firm or faithful, to trust or believe, to be permanent or quiet; mor. to be true or certain; once (Isa. 30:21; by interch. for 541) to go to the right hand:- hence assurance, believe, bring up, establish, + fail, be faithful (of long continuance, steadfast, sure, surely, trusty, verified) nurse (-ing father), (put) trust, turn to the right.

> And whenever you deviate to the right or to the left, your ears will heed the command from behind you: "This is the road; follow it!" YESHA'YAHU 30:21 (ISAIAH 30:21)
>
> And thine ears shall hear a word behind thee, saying, This is the way, walk ye in it, when ye turn to the right hand, and when ye turn to the left. ISAIAH 30:21

(541) pronounced aw-man'; denom. from 3225; to take the right-hand road:- turn to the right. See 539.

(3225) pronounced yaw-meen'; from 3231; the right hand or side (leg, eye) of a person or other object (as the stronger and most dexterous): locally, the south:- + left handed, right (hand, side), south.

(3231) pronounced yaw-man'; a prim. root; to be (phys.) right (i.e. firm); but used only as denom. from 3225 and transit., to be right-handed or take the right-hand side:- go turn) to (on, use) the right hand.

Not to us, O LORD, not to us but to Your name bring glory for the sake of Your love and Your faithfulness. TEHILLIM 115:1 (PSALMS 115:1)

Not unto us, O LORD, not unto us, but unto thy name give glory, for thy mercy, *and* for thy truth's (571) sake. PSALMS 115:1

truth (571) pronounced eh'meth; contr. From 539; stability; fig. certainty, truth, trustworthiness:-assured (-ly), establishment, faithful, right, sure, true (-ly, -th), verity.

(539) pronounced aw-man'; a prim. root; prop. to build up or support; to foster as a parent or nurse; fig. to render (or be) firm or faithful, to trust or believe, to be permanent or quiet; mor. to be true or certain; once (Isa. 30:21; by interch. for 541) to go to the right hand:- hence assurance, believe, bring up, establish, + fail, be faithful (of long continuance, steadfast, sure, surely, trusty, verified) nurse (-ing father), (put) trust, turn to the right.

And whenever you deviate to the right or to the left, your ears will heed the command from behind you: "This is the road; follow it!" YESHA'YAHU 30:21 (ISAIAH 30:21)

And thine ears shall hear a word behind thee, saying, This is the way, walk ye in it, when ye turn to the right hand, and when ye turn to the left. ISAIAH 30:21

(541) pronounced aw-man'; denom. from 3225; to take the right-hand road:- turn to the right. See 539.

(3225) pronounced yaw-meen'; from 3231; the right hand or side (leg, eye) of a person or other object (as the stronger and most dexterous): locally, the south:- + left handed, right (hand, side), south.

(3231) pronounced yaw-man'; a prim. root; to be (phys.) right (i.e. firm); but used only as denom. from 3225 and transit., to be right-handed or take the right-hand side:- go turn) to (on, use) the right hand.

For great is His steadfast love toward us; the faithfulness of the LORD endures forever. Hallelujah. TEHILLIM 117:2 (PSALMS 117:2)

For his merciful kindness is great toward us: and the truth (571) of the LORD endureth for ever. Praise ye the LORD. PSALMS 117:2

> truth (571) pronounced eh'meth; contr. From 539; stability; fig. certainty, truth, trustworthiness:-assured (-ly), establishment, faithful, right, sure, true (-ly, -th), verity.
>
> (539) pronounced aw-man'; a prim. root; prop. to build up or support; to foster as a parent or nurse; fig. to render (or be) firm or faithful, to trust or believe, to be permanent or quiet; mor. to be true or certain; once (Isa. 30:21; by interch. for 541) to go to the right hand:- hence assurance, believe, bring up, establish, + fail, be faithful (of long continuance, steadfast, sure, surely, trusty, verified) nurse (-ing father), (put) trust, turn to the right.
>
>> And whenever you deviate to the right or to the left, your ears will heed the command from behind you: "This is the road; follow it!" YESHA'YAHU 30:21 (ISAIAH 30:21)
>>
>> And thine ears shall hear a word behind thee, saying, This is the way, walk ye in it, when ye turn to the right hand, and when ye turn to the left. ISAIAH 30:21
>
> (541) pronounced aw-man'; denom. from 3225; to take the right-hand road:- turn to the right. See 539.
>
> (3225) pronounced yaw-meen'; from 3231; the right hand or side (leg, eye) of a person or other object (as the stronger and most dexterous): locally, the south:- + left handed, right (hand, side), south.
>
> (3231) pronounced yaw-man'; a prim. root; to be (phys.) right (i.e. firm); but used only as denom. from 3225 and transit., to be right-handed or take the right-hand side:- go turn) to (on, use) the right hand.

I have chosen the way of faithfulness; I have set Your rules before me. TEHILLIM 119:30 (PSALMS 119:30)

I have chosen the way of truth (530): thy judgments have I laid *before me*. PSALMS 119:30

> truth (530) pronounced em-oo-naw'; fem. of 529; lit. firmness; fig. security; mor. fidelity:- faith (-ful, -ly, -ness, [man]), set office, stability, steady, truly, truth, verity.
>
> (529) pronounced ay-moon'; from 539; established, i.e. (fig.) trusty; also (abstr.) trustworthiness:-faith (-ful), truth.
>
> (539) pronounced aw-man'; a prim. root; prop. to build up or support; to foster as a parent or nurse; fig. to render (or be) firm or faithful, to trust or believe, to be permanent or quiet; mor. to be true or certain; once (Isa. 30:21; by interch. for 541) to go to the right hand:- hence assurance, believe, bring up, establish, + fail, be faithful (of long continuance, steadfast, sure, surely, trusty, verified) nurse (-ing father), (put) trust, turn to the right.

> And whenever you deviate to the right or to the left, your ears will heed the command from behind you: "This is the road; follow it!" YESHA'YAHU 30:21 (ISAIAH 30:21)
>
> And thine ears shall hear a word behind thee, saying, This is the way, walk ye in it, when ye turn to the right hand, and when ye turn to the left. ISAIAH 30:21

(541) pronounced aw-man'; denom. from 3225; to take the right-hand road:- turn to the right. See 539.

(3225) pronounced yaw-meen'; from 3231; the right hand or side (leg, eye) of a person or other object (as the stronger and most dexterous): locally, the south:- + left handed, right (hand, side), south.

(3231) pronounced yaw-man'; a prim. root; to be (phys.) right (i.e. firm); but used only as denom. from 3225 and transit., to be right-handed or take the right-hand side:- go turn) to (on, use) the right hand.

Do not utterly take the truth away from my mouth, for I have put my hope in Your rules. TEHILLIM 119:43 (PSALMS 119:43)

And take not the word of truth (571) utterly out of my mouth; for I have hoped in thy judgments. PSALMS 119:43

truth (571) pronounced eh'meth; contr. From 539; stability; fig. certainty, truth, trustworthiness:-assured (-ly), establishment, faithful, right, sure, true (-ly, -th), verity.

(539) pronounced aw-man'; a prim. root; prop. to build up or support; to foster as a parent or nurse; fig. to render (or be) firm or faithful, to trust or believe, to be permanent or quiet; mor. to be true or certain; once (Isa. 30:21; by interch. for 541) to go to the right hand:- hence assurance, believe, bring up, establish, + fail, be faithful (of long continuance, steadfast, sure, surely, trusty, verified) nurse (-ing father), (put) trust, turn to the right.

> And whenever you deviate to the right or to the left, your ears will heed the command from behind you: "This is the road; follow it!" YESHA'YAHU 30:21 (ISAIAH 30:21)
>
> And thine ears shall hear a word behind thee, saying, This is the way, walk ye in it, when ye turn to the right hand, and when ye turn to the left. ISAIAH 30:21

(541) pronounced aw-man'; denom. from 3225; to take the right-hand road:- turn to the right. See 539.

(3225) pronounced yaw-meen'; from 3231; the right hand or side (leg, eye) of a person or other object (as the stronger and most dexterous): locally, the south:- + left handed, right (hand, side), south.

(3231) pronounced yaw-man'; a prim. root; to be (phys.) right (i.e. firm); but used only as denom. from 3225 and transit., to be right-handed or take the right-hand side:- go turn) to (on, use) the right hand.

Your righteousness is eternal; Your teaching is true. TEHILLIM 119:142 (PSALMS 119:142)

Thy righteousness is an everlasting righteousness, and thy law is the truth (571). PSALMS 119:142

truth (571) pronounced eh'meth; contr. From 539; stability; fig. certainty, truth, trustworthiness:-assured (-ly), establishment, faithful, right, sure, true (-ly, -th), verity.

(539) pronounced aw-man'; a prim. root; prop. to build up or support; to foster as a parent or nurse; fig. to render (or be) firm or faithful, to trust or believe, to be permanent or quiet; mor. to be true or certain; once (Isa. 30:21; by interch. for 541) to go to the right hand:- hence assurance, believe, bring up, establish, + fail, be faithful (of long continuance, steadfast, sure, surely, trusty, verified) nurse (-ing father), (put) trust, turn to the right.

And whenever you deviate to the right or to the left, your ears will heed the command from behind you: "This is the road; follow it!" YESHA'YAHU 30:21 (ISAIAH 30:21)

And thine ears shall hear a word behind thee, saying, This is the way, walk ye in it, when ye turn to the right hand, and when ye turn to the left. ISAIAH 30:21

(541) pronounced aw-man'; denom. from 3225; to take the right-hand road:- turn to the right. See 539.

(3225) pronounced yaw-meen'; from 3231; the right hand or side (leg, eye) of a person or other object (as the stronger and most dexterous): locally, the south:- + left handed, right (hand, side), south.

(3231) pronounced yaw-man'; a prim. root; to be (phys.) right (i.e. firm); but used only as denom. from 3225 and transit., to be right-handed or take the right-hand side:- go turn) to (on, use) the right hand.

You, O LORD, are near, and all Your commandments are true. TEHILLIM 119:151 (PSALMS 119:151)

Thou *art* near, O LORD; and all thy commandments *are* truth (571). PSALMS 119:151

truth (571) pronounced eh'meth; contr. From 539; stability; fig. certainty, truth, trustworthiness:-assured (-ly), establishment, faithful, right, sure, true (-ly, -th), verity.

(539) pronounced aw-man'; a prim. root; prop. to build up or support; to foster as a parent or nurse; fig. to render (or be) firm or faithful, to trust or believe, to be permanent or quiet; mor. to be true or certain; once (Isa. 30:21; by interch. for 541) to go to the right hand:- hence

assurance, believe, bring up, establish, + fail, be faithful (of long continuance, steadfast, sure, surely, trusty, verified) nurse (-ing father), (put) trust, turn to the right.

> And whenever you deviate to the right or to the left, your ears will heed the command from behind you: "This is the road; follow it!" YESHA'YAHU 30:21 (ISAIAH 30:21)
>
> And thine ears shall hear a word behind thee, saying, This is the way, walk ye in it, when ye turn to the right hand, and when ye turn to the left. ISAIAH 30:21

(541) pronounced aw-man'; denom. from 3225; to take the right-hand road:- turn to the right. See 539.

(3225) pronounced yaw-meen'; from 3231; the right hand or side (leg, eye) of a person or other object (as the stronger and most dexterous): locally, the south:- + left handed, right (hand, side), south.

(3231) pronounced yaw-man'; a prim. root; to be (phys.) right (i.e. firm); but used only as denom. from 3225 and transit., to be right-handed or take the right-hand side:- go turn) to (on, use) the right hand.

The LORD swore to David a firm oath that He will not renounce, "One of your own issue I will set upon your throne." TEHILLIM 132:11 (PSALMS 132:11)

The LORD hath sworn in truth (571) unto David; he will not turn from it; Of the fruit of thy body will I set upon thy throne. PSALMS 132:11

truth (571) pronounced eh'meth; contr. From 539; stability; fig. certainty, truth, trustworthiness:-assured (-ly), establishment, faithful, right, sure, true (-ly, -th), verity.

(539) pronounced aw-man'; a prim. root; prop. to build up or support; to foster as a parent or nurse; fig. to render (or be) firm or faithful, to trust or believe, to be permanent or quiet; mor. to be true or certain; once (Isa. 30:21; by interch. for 541) to go to the right hand:- hence assurance, believe, bring up, establish, + fail, be faithful (of long continuance, steadfast, sure, surely, trusty, verified) nurse (-ing father), (put) trust, turn to the right.

> And whenever you deviate to the right or to the left, your ears will heed the command from behind you: "This is the road; follow it!" YESHA'YAHU 30:21 (ISAIAH 30:21)
>
> And thine ears shall hear a word behind thee, saying, This is the way, walk ye in it, when ye turn to the right hand, and when ye turn to the left. ISAIAH 30:21

(541) pronounced aw-man'; denom. from 3225; to take the right-hand road:- turn to the right. See 539.

(3225) pronounced yaw-meen'; from 3231; the right hand or side (leg, eye) of a person or other object (as the stronger and most dexterous): locally, the south:- + left handed, right (hand, side), south.

(3231) pronounced yaw-man'; a prim. root; to be (phys.) right (i.e. firm); but used only as denom. from 3225 and transit., to be right-handed or take the right-hand side:- go turn) to (on, use) the right hand.

I bow toward Your holy temple and praise Your name for Your steadfast love and faithfulness, because You have exalted Your name, Your word, above all. TEHILLIM 138:2 (PSALMS 138:2)

Your name, Your word, above all: meaning of Heb. uncertain. (TANAKH footnote)

I will worship toward thy holy temple, and praise thy name for thy lovingkindness and for thy truth (571): for thou hast magnified thy word above all thy name. PSALMS 138:2

truth (571) pronounced eh'meth; contr. From 539; stability; fig. certainty, truth, trustworthiness:-assured (-ly), establishment, faithful, right, sure, true (-ly, -th), verity.

(539) pronounced aw-man'; a prim. root; prop. to build up or support; to foster as a parent or nurse; fig. to render (or be) firm or faithful, to trust or believe, to be permanent or quiet; mor. to be true or certain; once (Isa. 30:21; by interch. for 541) to go to the right hand:- hence assurance, believe, bring up, establish, + fail, be faithful (of long continuance, steadfast, sure, surely, trusty, verified) nurse (-ing father), (put) trust, turn to the right.

And whenever you deviate to the right or to the left, your ears will heed the command from behind you: "This is the road; follow it!" YESHA'YAHU 30:21 (ISAIAH 30:21)

And thine ears shall hear a word behind thee, saying, This is the way, walk ye in it, when ye turn to the right hand, and when ye turn to the left. ISAIAH 30:21

(541) pronounced aw-man'; denom. from 3225; to take the right-hand road:- turn to the right. See 539.

(3225) pronounced yaw-meen'; from 3231; the right hand or side (leg, eye) of a person or other object (as the stronger and most dexterous): locally, the south:- + left handed, right (hand, side), south.

(3231) pronounced yaw-man'; a prim. root; to be (phys.) right (i.e. firm); but used only as denom. from 3225 and transit., to be right-handed or take the right-hand side:- go turn) to (on, use) the right hand.

The LORD is near to all who call Him, to all who call Him with sincerity. TEHILLIM 145:18 (PSALMS 145:18)

The LORD is nigh unto all them that call upon him, to all that call upon him in truth (571).
PSALMS 145:18

> truth (571) pronounced eh'meth; contr. From 539; stability; fig. certainty, truth, trustworthiness:-assured (-ly), establishment, faithful, right, sure, true (-ly, -th), verity.
>
> (539) pronounced aw-man'; a prim. root; prop. to build up or support; to foster as a parent or nurse; fig. to render (or be) firm or faithful, to trust or believe, to be permanent or quiet; mor. to be true or certain; once (Isa. 30:21; by interch. for 541) to go to the right hand:- hence assurance, believe, bring up, establish, + fail, be faithful (of long continuance, steadfast, sure, surely, trusty, verified) nurse (-ing father), (put) trust, turn to the right.
>
>> And whenever you deviate to the right or to the left, your ears will heed the command from behind you: "This is the road; follow it!" YESHA'YAHU 30:21 (ISAIAH 30:21)
>>
>> And thine ears shall hear a word behind thee, saying, This is the way, walk ye in it, when ye turn to the right hand, and when ye turn to the left. ISAIAH 30:21
>
> (541) pronounced aw-man'; denom. from 3225; to take the right-hand road:- turn to the right. See 539.
>
> (3225) pronounced yaw-meen'; from 3231; the right hand or side (leg, eye) of a person or other object (as the stronger and most dexterous): locally, the south:- + left handed, right (hand, side), south.
>
> (3231) pronounced yaw-man'; a prim. root; to be (phys.) right (i.e. firm); but used only as denom. from 3225 and transit., to be right-handed or take the right-hand side:- go turn) to (on, use) the right hand.

Happy is he who has the God of Jacob for his help, whose hope is in the LORD his God, maker of heaven and earth, the sea and all that is in them; who keeps faith forever; TEHILLIM 146:5-6 (PSALMS 146:5-6)

Happy *is he* that *hath* the God of Jacob for his help, whose hope is in the LORD his God: which made heaven, and earth, the sea, and all that therein is: which keepeth truth (571) for ever: PSALMS 146:5-6

> truth (571) pronounced eh'meth; contr. From 539; stability; fig. certainty, truth, trustworthiness:-assured (-ly), establishment, faithful, right, sure, true (-ly, -th), verity.
>
> (539) pronounced aw-man'; a prim. root; prop. to build up or support; to foster as a parent or nurse; fig. to render (or be) firm or faithful, to trust or believe, to be permanent or quiet; mor. to be true or certain; once (Isa. 30:21; by interch. for 541) to go to the right hand:- hence assurance, believe, bring up, establish, + fail, be faithful (of long continuance, steadfast, sure, surely, trusty, verified) nurse (-ing father), (put) trust, turn to the right.

> And whenever you deviate to the right or to the left, your ears will heed the command from behind you: "This is the road; follow it!" YESHA'YAHU 30:21 (ISAIAH 30:21)
>
> And thine ears shall hear a word behind thee, saying, This is the way, walk ye in it, when ye turn to the right hand, and when ye turn to the left. ISAIAH 30:21

(541) pronounced aw-man'; denom. from 3225; to take the right-hand road:- turn to the right. See 539.

(3225) pronounced yaw-meen'; from 3231; the right hand or side (leg, eye) of a person or other object (as the stronger and most dexterous): locally, the south:- + left handed, right (hand, side), south.

(3231) pronounced yaw-man'; a prim. root; to be (phys.) right (i.e. firm); but used only as denom. from 3225 and transit., to be right-handed or take the right-hand side:- go turn) to (on, use) the right hand.

Let fidelity and steadfastness not leave you; bind them about your throat, write them on the tablet of your mind. MISHLEI 3:3 (PROVERBS 3:3)

Let not mercy and truth (571) forsake thee; bind them about thy neck; write them upon the table of thine heart: PROVERBS 3:3

truth (571) pronounced eh'meth; contr. From 539; stability; fig. certainty, truth, trustworthiness:-assured (-ly), establishment, faithful, right, sure, true (-ly, -th), verity.

(539) pronounced aw-man'; a prim. root; prop. to build up or support; to foster as a parent or nurse; fig. to render (or be) firm or faithful, to trust or believe, to be permanent or quiet; mor. to be true or certain; once (Isa. 30:21; by interch. for 541) to go to the right hand:- hence assurance, believe, bring up, establish, + fail, be faithful (of long continuance, steadfast, sure, surely, trusty, verified) nurse (-ing father), (put) trust, turn to the right.

> And whenever you deviate to the right or to the left, your ears will heed the command from behind you: "This is the road; follow it!" YESHA'YAHU 30:21 (ISAIAH 30:21)
>
> And thine ears shall hear a word behind thee, saying, This is the way, walk ye in it, when ye turn to the right hand, and when ye turn to the left. ISAIAH 30:21

(541) pronounced aw-man'; denom. from 3225; to take the right-hand road:- turn to the right. See 539.

(3225) pronounced yaw-meen'; from 3231; the right hand or side (leg, eye) of a person or other object (as the stronger and most dexterous): locally, the south:- + left handed, right (hand, side), south.

(3231) pronounced yaw-man'; a prim. root; to be (phys.) right (i.e. firm); but used only as denom. from 3225 and transit., to be right-handed or take the right-hand side:- go turn) to (on, use) the right hand.

My mouth utters truth; wickedness is abhorrent to my lips. MISHLEI 8:7 (PROVERBS 8:7)

For my mouth shall speak truth (571); and wickedness is an abomination to my lips. PROVERBS 8:7

truth (571) pronounced eh'meth; contr. From 539; stability; fig. certainty, truth, trustworthiness:-assured (-ly), establishment, faithful, right, sure, true (-ly, -th), verity.

(539) pronounced aw-man'; a prim. root; prop. to build up or support; to foster as a parent or nurse; fig. to render (or be) firm or faithful, to trust or believe, to be permanent or quiet; mor. to be true or certain; once (Isa. 30:21; by interch. for 541) to go to the right hand:- hence assurance, believe, bring up, establish, + fail, be faithful (of long continuance, steadfast, sure, surely, trusty, verified) nurse (-ing father), (put) trust, turn to the right.

And whenever you deviate to the right or to the left, your ears will heed the command from behind you: "This is the road; follow it!" YESHA'YAHU 30:21 (ISAIAH 30:21)

And thine ears shall hear a word behind thee, saying, This is the way, walk ye in it, when ye turn to the right hand, and when ye turn to the left. ISAIAH 30:21

(541) pronounced aw-man'; denom. from 3225; to take the right-hand road:- turn to the right. See 539.

(3225) pronounced yaw-meen'; from 3231; the right hand or side (leg, eye) of a person or other object (as the stronger and most dexterous): locally, the south:- + left handed, right (hand, side), south.

(3231) pronounced yaw-man'; a prim. root; to be (phys.) right (i.e. firm); but used only as denom. from 3225 and transit., to be right-handed or take the right-hand side:- go turn) to (on, use) the right hand.

He who testifies faithfully tells the truth, but a false witness, deceit. MISHLEI 12:17 (PROVERBS 12:17)

He that speaketh truth (530) showeth forth righteousness: but a false witness deceit. PROVERBS 12:17

truth (530) pronounced em-oo-naw'; fem. of 529; lit. firmness; fig. security; mor. fidelity:- faith (-ful, -ly, -ness, [man]), set office, stability, steady, truly, truth, verity.

(529) pronounced ay-moon'; from 539; established, i.e. (fig.) trusty; also (abstr.) trustworthiness:-faith (-ful), truth.

(539) pronounced aw-man'; a prim. root; prop. to build up or support; to foster as a parent or nurse; fig. to render (or be) firm or faithful, to trust or believe, to be permanent or quiet; mor.

to be true or certain; once (Isa. 30:21; by interch. for 541) to go to the right hand:- hence assurance, believe, bring up, establish, + fail, be faithful (of long continuance, steadfast, sure, surely, trusty, verified) nurse (-ing father), (put) trust, turn to the right.

> And whenever you deviate to the right or to the left, your ears will heed the command from behind you: "This is the road; follow it!" YESHA'YAHU 30:21 (ISAIAH 30:21)
>
> And thine ears shall hear a word behind thee, saying, This is the way, walk ye in it, when ye turn to the right hand, and when ye turn to the left. ISAIAH 30:21

(541) pronounced aw-man'; denom. from 3225; to take the right-hand road:- turn to the right. See 539.

(3225) pronounced yaw-meen'; from 3231; the right hand or side (leg, eye) of a person or other object (as the stronger and most dexterous): locally, the south:- + left handed, right (hand, side), south.

(3231) pronounced yaw-man'; a prim. root; to be (phys.) right (i.e. firm); but used only as denom. from 3225 and transit., to be right-handed or take the right-hand side:- go turn) to (on, use) the right hand.

Truthful speech abides forever, a lying tongue for but a moment. MISHLEI 12:19 (PROVERBS 12:19)

The lip of truth (571) shall be established forever; but a lying tongue is but for a moment. PROVERBS 12:19

truth (571) pronounced eh'meth; contr. From 539; stability; fig. certainty, truth, trustworthiness:-assured (-ly), establishment, faithful, right, sure, true (-ly, -th), verity.

(539) pronounced aw-man'; a prim. root; prop. to build up or support; to foster as a parent or nurse; fig. to render (or be) firm or faithful, to trust or believe, to be permanent or quiet; mor. to be true or certain; once (Isa. 30:21; by interch. for 541) to go to the right hand:- hence assurance, believe, bring up, establish, + fail, be faithful (of long continuance, steadfast, sure, surely, trusty, verified) nurse (-ing father), (put) trust, turn to the right.

> And whenever you deviate to the right or to the left, your ears will heed the command from behind you: "This is the road; follow it!" YESHA'YAHU 30:21 (ISAIAH 30:21)
>
> And thine ears shall hear a word behind thee, saying, This is the way, walk ye in it, when ye turn to the right hand, and when ye turn to the left. ISAIAH 30:21

(541) pronounced aw-man'; denom. from 3225; to take the right-hand road:- turn to the right. See 539.

(3225) pronounced yaw-meen'; from 3231; the right hand or side (leg, eye) of a person or other object (as the stronger and most dexterous): locally, the south:- + left handed, right (hand, side), south.

(3231) pronounced yaw-man'; a prim. root; to be (phys.) right (i.e. firm); but used only as denom. from 3225 and transit., to be right-handed or take the right-hand side:- go turn) to (on, use) the right hand.

Surely those who plan evil go astray, while those who plan good earn steadfast love. MISHLEI 14:22 (PROVERBS 14:22)

Do they not err that devise evil? But mercy and truth (571) shall be to them that devise good. PROVERBS 14:22

truth (571) pronounced eh'meth; contr. From 539; stability; fig. certainty, truth, trustworthiness:-assured (-ly), establishment, faithful, right, sure, true (-ly, -th), verity.

(539) pronounced aw-man'; a prim. root; prop. to build up or support; to foster as a parent or nurse; fig. to render (or be) firm or faithful, to trust or believe, to be permanent or quiet; mor. to be true or certain; once (Isa. 30:21; by interch. for 541) to go to the right hand:- hence assurance, believe, bring up, establish, + fail, be faithful (of long continuance, steadfast, sure, surely, trusty, verified) nurse (-ing father), (put) trust, turn to the right.

And whenever you deviate to the right or to the left, your ears will heed the command from behind you: "This is the road; follow it!" YESHA'YAHU 30:21 (ISAIAH 30:21)

And thine ears shall hear a word behind thee, saying, This is the way, walk ye in it, when ye turn to the right hand, and when ye turn to the left. ISAIAH 30:21

(541) pronounced aw-man'; denom. from 3225; to take the right-hand road:- turn to the right. See 539.

(3225) pronounced yaw-meen'; from 3231; the right hand or side (leg, eye) of a person or other object (as the stronger and most dexterous): locally, the south:- + left handed, right (hand, side), south.

(3231) pronounced yaw-man'; a prim. root; to be (phys.) right (i.e. firm); but used only as denom. from 3225 and transit., to be right-handed or take the right-hand side:- go turn) to (on, use) the right hand.

Iniquity is expiated by loyalty and faithfulness, and evil is avoided through fear of the LORD. MISHLEI 16:6 (PROVERBS 16:6)

By mercy and truth (571) iniquity is purged: and by the fear of the LORD *men* depart from evil. PROVERBS 16:6

truth (571) pronounced eh'meth; contr. From 539; stability; fig. certainty, truth, trustworthiness:-assured (-ly), establishment, faithful, right, sure, true (-ly, -th), verity.

(539) pronounced aw-man'; a prim. root; prop. to build up or support; to foster as a parent or nurse; fig. to render (or be) firm or faithful, to trust or believe, to be permanent or quiet; mor. to be true or certain; once (Isa. 30:21; by interch. for 541) to go to the right hand:- hence assurance, believe, bring up, establish, + fail, be faithful (of long continuance, steadfast, sure, surely, trusty, verified) nurse (-ing father), (put) trust, turn to the right.

> And whenever you deviate to the right or to the left, your ears will heed the command from behind you: "This is the road; follow it!" YESHA'YAHU 30:21 (ISAIAH 30:21)
>
> And thine ears shall hear a word behind thee, saying, This is the way, walk ye in it, when ye turn to the right hand, and when ye turn to the left. ISAIAH 30:21

(541) pronounced aw-man'; denom. from 3225; to take the right-hand road:- turn to the right. See 539.

(3225) pronounced yaw-meen'; from 3231; the right hand or side (leg, eye) of a person or other object (as the stronger and most dexterous): locally, the south:- + left handed, right (hand, side), south.

(3231) pronounced yaw-man'; a prim. root; to be (phys.) right (i.e. firm); but used only as denom. from 3225 and transit., to be right-handed or take the right-hand side:- go turn) to (on, use) the right hand.

Faithfulness and loyalty protect the king; he maintains his throne by faithfulness. MISHLEI 20:28 (PROVERBS 20:28)

Mercy and truth (571) preserve the king: and his throne is upholden by mercy. PROVERBS 20:28

truth (571) pronounced eh'meth; contr. From 539; stability; fig. certainty, truth, trustworthiness:-assured (-ly), establishment, faithful, right, sure, true (-ly, -th), verity.

(539) pronounced aw-man'; a prim. root; prop. to build up or support; to foster as a parent or nurse; fig. to render (or be) firm or faithful, to trust or believe, to be permanent or quiet; mor. to be true or certain; once (Isa. 30:21; by interch. for 541) to go to the right hand:- hence assurance, believe, bring up, establish, + fail, be faithful (of long continuance, steadfast, sure, surely, trusty, verified) nurse (-ing father), (put) trust, turn to the right.

> And whenever you deviate to the right or to the left, your ears will heed the command from behind you: "This is the road; follow it!" YESHA'YAHU 30:21 (ISAIAH 30:21)

> And thine ears shall hear a word behind thee, saying, This is the way, walk ye in it, when ye turn to the right hand, and when ye turn to the left. ISAIAH 30:21

(541) pronounced aw-man'; denom. from 3225; to take the right-hand road:- turn to the right. See 539.

(3225) pronounced yaw-meen'; from 3231; the right hand or side (leg, eye) of a person or other object (as the stronger and most dexterous): locally, the south:- + left handed, right (hand, side), south.

(3231) pronounced yaw-man'; a prim. root; to be (phys.) right (i.e. firm); but used only as denom. from 3225 and transit., to be right-handed or take the right-hand side:- go turn) to (on, use) the right hand.

Indeed, I wrote down for you a threefold lore, wise counsel to let you know truly, reliable words, that you may give a faithful reply to him who sent you. MISHLEI 22:20-21 (PROVERBS 22:20-21)

a threefold lore: meaning of Heb. uncertain. (TANAKH footnote)

Have not I written to thee excellent things in counsels and knowledge that I might make thee know the certainty of the words of truth (7189); that thou mightest answer the words of truth (571) to them that send unto thee? PROVERBS 22:20-21

truth (7189) pronounced ko'-shet or kosht; from an unused root mean. to balance; equity (as evenly weighed), i.e. reality:-certainty, truth.

truth (571) pronounced eh'meth; contr. From 539; stability; fig. certainty, truth, trustworthiness:-assured (-ly), establishment, faithful, right, sure, true (-ly, -th), verity.

(539) pronounced aw-man'; a prim. root; prop. to build up or support; to foster as a parent or nurse; fig. to render (or be) firm or faithful, to trust or believe, to be permanent or quiet; mor. to be true or certain; once (Isa. 30:21; by interch. for 541) to go to the right hand:- hence assurance, believe, bring up, establish, + fail, be faithful (of long continuance, steadfast, sure, surely, trusty, verified) nurse (-ing father), (put) trust, turn to the right.

> And whenever you deviate to the right or to the left, your ears will heed the command from behind you: "This is the road; follow it!" YESHA'YAHU 30:21 (ISAIAH 30:21)

> And thine ears shall hear a word behind thee, saying, This is the way, walk ye in it, when ye turn to the right hand, and when ye turn to the left. ISAIAH 30:21

(541) pronounced aw-man'; denom. from 3225; to take the right-hand road:- turn to the right. See 539.

(3225) pronounced yaw-meen'; from 3231; the right hand or side (leg, eye) of a person or other object (as the stronger and most dexterous): locally, the south:- + left handed, right (hand, side), south.

(3231) pronounced yaw-man'; a prim. root; to be (phys.) right (i.e. firm); but used only as denom. from 3225 and transit., to be right-handed or take the right-hand side:- go turn) to (on, use) the right hand.

Buy truth and never sell it, and wisdom, discipline, and understanding. MISHLEI 23:23 (PROVERBS 23:23)

Buy the truth (571), and sell it not; *also* wisdom, and instruction, and understanding. PROVERBS 23:23

truth (571) pronounced eh'meth; contr. From 539; stability; fig. certainty, truth, trustworthiness:-assured (-ly), establishment, faithful, right, sure, true (-ly, -th), verity.

(539) pronounced aw-man'; a prim. root; prop. to build up or support; to foster as a parent or nurse; fig. to render (or be) firm or faithful, to trust or believe, to be permanent or quiet; mor. to be true or certain; once (Isa. 30:21; by interch. for 541) to go to the right hand:- hence assurance, believe, bring up, establish, + fail, be faithful (of long continuance, steadfast, sure, surely, trusty, verified) nurse (-ing father), (put) trust, turn to the right.

And whenever you deviate to the right or to the left, your ears will heed the command from behind you: "This is the road; follow it!" YESHA'YAHU 30:21 (ISAIAH 30:21)

And thine ears shall hear a word behind thee, saying, This is the way, walk ye in it, when ye turn to the right hand, and when ye turn to the left. ISAIAH 30:21

(541) pronounced aw-man'; denom. from 3225; to take the right-hand road:- turn to the right. See 539.

(3225) pronounced yaw-meen'; from 3231; the right hand or side (leg, eye) of a person or other object (as the stronger and most dexterous): locally, the south:- + left handed, right (hand, side), south.

(3231) pronounced yaw-man'; a prim. root; to be (phys.) right (i.e. firm); but used only as denom. from 3225 and transit., to be right-handed or take the right-hand side:- go turn) to (on, use) the right hand.

Koheleth sought to discover useful sayings and recorded genuinely truthful sayings. KOHELET 12:10 (ECCLESIASTES 12:10)

Recorded: Wekhathub is equivalent to wekhathob, an infinitive employed as in Esth.9.16 and elsewhere. (TANAKH footnote)

> The rest of the Jews, those in the king's provinces, likewise mustered and fought for their lives. They disposed of their enemies, killing seventy-five thousand of their foes; but they did not lay hands on the spoil. ESTER 9:16 (ESTHER 9:16)
>
> But the other Jews that *were* in the king's provinces gathered themselves together, and stood for their lives, and had rest from their enemies, and slew of their foes seventy and five thousand, but they laid not their hands on the prey. ESTHER 9:16

The Preacher sought to find out acceptable words: and that which was written was upright, even words of truth (571). ECCLESIASTES 12:10

truth (571) pronounced eh'meth; contr. From 539; stability; fig. certainty, truth, trustworthiness:-assured (-ly), establishment, faithful, right, sure, true (-ly, -th), verity.

(539) pronounced aw-man'; a prim. root; prop. to build up or support; to foster as a parent or nurse; fig. to render (or be) firm or faithful, to trust or believe, to be permanent or quiet; mor. to be true or certain; once (Isa. 30:21; by interch. for 541) to go to the right hand:- hence assurance, believe, bring up, establish, + fail, be faithful (of long continuance, steadfast, sure, surely, trusty, verified) nurse (-ing father), (put) trust, turn to the right.

> And whenever you deviate to the right or to the left, your ears will heed the command from behind you: "This is the road; follow it!" YESHA'YAHU 30:21 (ISAIAH 30:21)
>
> And thine ears shall hear a word behind thee, saying, This is the way, walk ye in it, when ye turn to the right hand, and when ye turn to the left. ISAIAH 30:21

(541) pronounced aw-man'; denom. from 3225; to take the right-hand road:- turn to the right. See 539.

(3225) pronounced yaw-meen'; from 3231; the right hand or side (leg, eye) of a person or other object (as the stronger and most dexterous): locally, the south:- + left handed, right (hand, side), south.

(3231) pronounced yaw-man'; a prim. root; to be (phys.) right (i.e. firm); but used only as denom. from 3225 and transit., to be right-handed or take the right-hand side:- go turn) to (on, use) the right hand.

In my hearing, [said] the LORD of Hosts: Surely, great houses shall lie forlorn, spacious and splendid ones without occupants. YESHA'YAHU 5:9 (ISAIAH 5:9)

In mine ears *said* the LORD of hosts, Of a truth (518) many houses shall be desolate, *even* great and fair, without inhabitant. ISAIAH 5:9

truth (518) pronounced eem; a prim. particle; used very widely as a demonstr., lol; interrog. whether ?; or conditional, if, although; also oh that!, when; hence as a neg., not:- (and, can-, doubtless, if, that) (not), + but, either, + except, + more (-over if, than), neither, nevertheless, nor, oh that, or, + save (only, -ing), seeing, since, sith, + surely (no more, none, not), though, + of a truth, + unless, + verily, when, whereas, whether, while, + yet.

And in that day, the remnant of Israel and the escaped of the House of Jacob shall lean no more upon him that beats it, but shall lean sincerely on the LORD, the Holy One of Israel. YESHA'YAHU 10:20 (ISAIAH 10:20)

shall lean no more upon him that beats it: i.e., upon Assyria (see v.24). Ahaz's reliance on Assyria was interpreted by Isaiah as lack of faith in the LORD; see 7.13 with note. (TANAKH footnote)

Assuredly, thus said my LORD God of Hosts: "O my people that dwells in Zion, have no fear of Assyria, who beats you with a rod and yields his staff over you as did the Egyptians. YESHA'YAHU 10:24 (ISAIAH 10:24)

Therefore thus saith the LORD God of hosts, O my people that dwellest in Zion, be not afraid of the Assyrian: he small smite thee with a rod, and shall lift up his staff against thee, after the manner of Egypt. ISAIAH 10:24

"Listen, House of David," [Isaiah] retorted, is it not enough for you to treat men as helpless that you also treat my God as helpless? YESHA'YAHU 7:13 (ISAIAH 7:13)

By insisting on soliciting the aid of Assyria (see 2 Kings 16.7 ff: cf. below v.20). "Treat as helpless" follows the translation of Saadia; cf. Gen. 19.11. (TANAKH footnote)

Ahaz sent messengers to King Tiglath-pileser of Assyria to say "I am your servant and your son; come and deliver me from the hands of the king of Aram and from the hands of the king of Israel, who are attacking me. M'LAKHIM BET 16:7 (II KINGS 16:7)

So Ahaz sent messengers to Tiglath-pileser king of Assyria, saying, I *am* thy servant and thy son: come up, and save me out of the hand of the king of Syria, and out of the hand of the king of Israel, which rise up against me. II KINGS 16:7

And the people who were at the entrance of the house, young and old, were struck with blinding light, so that they were helpless to find the entrance. B'RESHEET 19:11 (GENESIS 19:11)

And they smote the men that *were* at the door of the house with blindness, both small and great; so that they wearied themselves to find the door. GENESIS 19:11

And he said, Hear ye now, O house of David: *Is it* a small thing for you to weary men, but will ye weary my God also? ISAIAH 7:13

And it shall come to pass in that day, *that* the remnant of Israel, and such as are escaped of the house of Jacob, shall no more again stay upon him that smote them; but shall stay upon the LORD, the Holy One of Israel, in truth (571). ISAIAH 10:20

truth (571) pronounced eh'meth; contr. From 539; stability; fig. certainty, truth, trustworthiness:-assured (-ly), establishment, faithful, right, sure, true (-ly, -th), verity.

(539) pronounced aw-man'; a prim. root; prop. to build up or support; to foster as a parent or nurse; fig. to render (or be) firm or faithful, to trust or believe, to be permanent or quiet; mor. to be true or certain; once (Isa. 30:21; by interch. for 541) to go to the right hand:- hence assurance, believe, bring up, establish, + fail, be faithful (of long continuance, steadfast, sure, surely, trusty, verified) nurse (-ing father), (put) trust, turn to the right.

And whenever you deviate to the right or to the left, your ears will heed the command from behind you: "This is the road; follow it!" YESHA'YAHU 30:21 (ISAIAH 30:21)

And thine ears shall hear a word behind thee, saying, This is the way, walk ye in it, when ye turn to the right hand, and when ye turn to the left. ISAIAH 30:21

(541) pronounced aw-man'; denom. from 3225; to take the right-hand road:- turn to the right. See 539.

(3225) pronounced yaw-meen'; from 3231; the right hand or side (leg, eye) of a person or other object (as the stronger and most dexterous): locally, the south:- + left handed, right (hand, side), south.

(3231) pronounced yaw-man'; a prim. root; to be (phys.) right (i.e. firm); but used only as denom. from 3225 and transit., to be right-handed or take the right-hand side:- go turn) to (on, use) the right hand.

And a throne shall be established in goodness in the tent of David, and on it shall sit in faithfulness a ruler devoted to justice and zealous for equity. YESHA'YAHU 16:5 (ISAIAH 16:5)

14.32 above, would read well here. (TANAKH footnote)

And what will he answer the messengers of any nation? That Zion has been established by the LORD: In it, the needy of His people shall find shelter. YESHA'YAHU 14:32 (ISAIAH 14:32)

What shall *one* then answer the messengers of the nation? That the LORD hath founded Zion, and the poor of his people shall trust in it. ISAIAH 14:32

And in mercy shall the throne be established: and he shall sit upon it in truth (571) in the tabernacle of David, judging, and seeking judgment, and hasting righteousness. ISAIAH 16:5

truth (571) pronounced eh'meth; contr. From 539; stability; fig. certainty, truth, trustworthiness:-assured (-ly), establishment, faithful, right, sure, true (-ly, -th), verity.

(539) pronounced aw-man'; a prim. root; prop. to build up or support; to foster as a parent or nurse; fig. to render (or be) firm or faithful, to trust or believe, to be permanent or quiet; mor. to be true or certain; once (Isa. 30:21; by interch. for 541) to go to the right hand:- hence assurance, believe, bring up, establish, + fail, be faithful (of long continuance, steadfast, sure, surely, trusty, verified) nurse (-ing father), (put) trust, turn to the right.

And whenever you deviate to the right or to the left, your ears will heed the command from behind you: "This is the road; follow it!" YESHA'YAHU 30:21 (ISAIAH 30:21)

And thine ears shall hear a word behind thee, saying, This is the way, walk ye in it, when ye turn to the right hand, and when ye turn to the left. ISAIAH 30:21

(541) pronounced aw-man'; denom. from 3225; to take the right-hand road:- turn to the right. See 539.

(3225) pronounced yaw-meen'; from 3231; the right hand or side (leg, eye) of a person or other object (as the stronger and most dexterous): locally, the south:- + left handed, right (hand, side), south.

(3231) pronounced yaw-man'; a prim. root; to be (phys.) right (i.e. firm); but used only as denom. from 3225 and transit., to be right-handed or take the right-hand side:- go turn) to (on, use) the right hand.

O LORD, You are my God; I will extol You, I will praise Your name. For You planned graciousness of old, counsels of steadfast faithfulness. YESHA'YAHU 25:1 (ISAIAH 25:1)

See 9.5. (TANAKH footnote)

For a child has been born to us, a son has been given us. And authority has settled on his shoulders. He has been named, "The Mighty God is planning grace; The Eternal Father, a peaceable ruler"--- YESHA'YAHU 9:5 (ISAIAH 9:6)

planning grace: as in 25.1 (TANAKH footnote)

> For unto us a child is born, unto us a son is given; and the government shall be upon his shoulder: and his name shall be called Wonderful, Counsellor, The mighty God, The everlasting Father, The Prince of Peace. ISAIAH 9:6

O LORD, *thou art* my God: I will exalt thee, I will praise thy name; for thou hast done wonderful things; thy counsels of old *are* faithfulness *and* truth (544). ISAIAH 25:1

truth (544) pronounced oh-men'; from 539; verity:-truth.

(539) pronounced aw-man'; a prim. root; prop. to build up or support; to foster as a parent or nurse; fig. to render (or be) firm or faithful, to trust or believe, to be permanent or quiet; mor. to be true or certain; once (Isa. 30:21; by interch. for 541) to go to the right hand:- hence assurance, believe, bring up, establish, + fail, be faithful (of long continuance, steadfast, sure, surely, trusty, verified) nurse (-ing father), (put) trust, turn to the right.

> And whenever you deviate to the right or to the left, your ears will heed the command from behind you: "This is the road; follow it!" YESHA'YAHU 30:21 (ISAIAH 30:21)

> And thine ears shall hear a word behind thee, saying, This is the way, walk ye in it, when ye turn to the right hand, and when ye turn to the left. ISAIAH 30:21

(541) pronounced aw-man'; denom. from 3225; to take the right-hand road:- turn to the right. See 539.

(3225) pronounced yaw-meen'; from 3231; the right hand or side (leg, eye) of a person or other object (as the stronger and most dexterous): locally, the south:- + left handed, right (hand, side), south.

(3231) pronounced yaw-man'; a prim. root; to be (phys.) right (i.e. firm); but used only as denom. from 3225 and transit., to be right-handed or take the right-hand side:- go turn) to (on, use) the right hand.

Open the gates and let a righteous nation enter, [a nation] that keeps faith. YESHA'YAHU 26:2 (ISAIAH 26:2)

Open ye the gates, that the righteous nation which keepeth the truth (529) may enter in ISAIAH 26:2

(529) pronounced ay-moon'; from 539; established, i.e. (fig.) trusty; also (abstr.) trustworthiness:-faith (-ful), truth.

(539) pronounced aw-man'; a prim. root; prop. to build up or support; to foster as a parent or nurse; fig. to render (or be) firm or faithful, to trust or believe, to be permanent or quiet; mor. to be true or certain; once (Isa. 30:21; by interch. for 541) to go to the right hand:- hence assurance, believe, bring up, establish, + fail, be faithful (of long continuance, steadfast, sure, surely, trusty, verified) nurse (-ing father), (put) trust, turn to the right.

> And whenever you deviate to the right or to the left, your ears will heed the command from behind you: "This is the road; follow it!" YESHA'YAHU 30:21 (ISAIAH 30:21)
>
> And thine ears shall hear a word behind thee, saying, This is the way, walk ye in it, when ye turn to the right hand, and when ye turn to the left. ISAIAH 30:21

(541) pronounced aw-man'; denom. from 3225; to take the right-hand road:- turn to the right. See 539.

(3225) pronounced yaw-meen'; from 3231; the right hand or side (leg, eye) of a person or other object (as the stronger and most dexterous): locally, the south:- + left handed, right (hand, side), south.

(3231) pronounced yaw-man'; a prim. root; to be (phys.) right (i.e. firm); but used only as denom. from 3225 and transit., to be right-handed or take the right-hand side:- go turn) to (on, use) the right hand.

True, O LORD, the kings of Assyria have annihilated all the nations and their lands. YESHA'YAHU 37:18 (ISAIAH 37:18)

> So 2 Kings 19.17, and 13 mss. here; most mss. and editions read "lands".
> (TANAKH footnote)
>
> True, O LORD, the kings of Assyria have annihilated the nations and their lands. M'LAKHIM BET 19:17 (II KINGS 19:17)
>
> Of a truth, LORD, the kings of Assyria have destroyed the nations and their lands. II KINGS 19:17

Of a truth (551), LORD, the kings of Assyria have laid waste all the nations, and their countries. ISAIAH 37:18

truth (551) pronounced om-nawm'; adv. From 544; verily:-indeed, no doubt, surely, (it is, of a) true (-ly, -th).

(544) pronounced oh-men'; from 539; verity:-truth.

(539) pronounced aw-man'; a prim. root; prop. to build up or support; to foster as a parent or nurse; fig. to render (or be) firm or faithful, to trust or believe, to be permanent or quiet; mor. to be true or certain; once (Isa. 30:21; by interch. for 541) to go to the right hand:- hence assurance, believe, bring up, establish, + fail, be faithful (of long continuance, steadfast, sure, surely, trusty, verified) nurse (-ing father), (put) trust, turn to the right.

> And whenever you deviate to the right or to the left, your ears will heed the command from behind you: "This is the road; follow it!" YESHA'YAHU 30:21 (ISAIAH 30:21)
>
> And thine ears shall hear a word behind thee, saying, This is the way, walk ye in it, when ye turn to the right hand, and when ye turn to the left. ISAIAH 30:21

(541) pronounced aw-man'; denom. from 3225; to take the right-hand road:- turn to the right. See 539.

(3225) pronounced yaw-meen'; from 3231; the right hand or side (leg, eye) of a person or other object (as the stronger and most dexterous): locally, the south:- + left handed, right (hand, side), south.

(3231) pronounced yaw-man'; a prim. root; to be (phys.) right (i.e. firm); but used only as denom. from 3225 and transit., to be right-handed or take the right-hand side:- go turn) to (on, use) the right hand.

"Please, O LORD," he said, "remember how I have walked before You sincerely and wholeheartedly, and have done what is pleasing to You." And Hezekiah wept profusely. YESHA'YAHU 38:3 (ISAIAH 38:3)

And said, Remember now, O LORD, I beseech thee, how I have walked before thee in truth (571), and with a perfect heart, and have done *that which is* good in thy sight. And Hezekiah wept sore. ISAIAH 38:3

truth (571) pronounced eh'meth; contr. From 539; stability; fig. certainty, truth, trustworthiness:-assured (-ly), establishment, faithful, right, sure, true (-ly, -th), verity.

(539) pronounced aw-man'; a prim. root; prop. to build up or support; to foster as a parent or nurse; fig. to render (or be) firm or faithful, to trust or believe, to be permanent or quiet; mor. to be true or certain; once (Isa. 30:21; by interch. for 541) to go to the right hand:- hence assurance, believe, bring up, establish, + fail, be faithful (of long continuance, steadfast, sure, surely, trusty, verified) nurse (-ing father), (put) trust, turn to the right.

> And whenever you deviate to the right or to the left, your ears will heed the command from behind you: "This is the road; follow it!" YESHA'YAHU 30:21 (ISAIAH 30:21)
>
> And thine ears shall hear a word behind thee, saying, This is the way, walk ye in it, when ye turn to the right hand, and when ye turn to the left. ISAIAH 30:21

(541) pronounced aw-man'; denom. from 3225; to take the right-hand road:- turn to the right. See 539.

(3225) pronounced yaw-meen'; from 3231; the right hand or side (leg, eye) of a person or other object (as the stronger and most dexterous): locally, the south:- + left handed, right (hand, side), south.

(3231) pronounced yaw-man'; a prim. root; to be (phys.) right (i.e. firm); but used only as denom. from 3225 and transit., to be right-handed or take the right-hand side:- go turn) to (on, use) the right hand.

For it is not Sheol that praises You, not [the land of] Death that extols You; nor do they who descend into the Pit hope for Your grace. The living, only the living can give thanks to You as I do this day; Fathers relate to children Your acts of grace: YESHA'YAHU 38:18-19 (ISAIAH 38:18-19)

For the grave cannot praise thee, death cannot celebrate thee: they that go down into the pit cannot hope for thy truth (571). The living, the living, he shall praise thee, as I do this day: the father to the children shall make known thy truth (571). ISAIAH 38:18-19

truth (571) pronounced eh'meth; contr. From 539; stability; fig. certainty, truth, trustworthiness:-assured (-ly), establishment, faithful, right, sure, true (-ly, -th), verity.

(539) pronounced aw-man'; a prim. root; prop. to build up or support; to foster as a parent or nurse; fig. to render (or be) firm or faithful, to trust or believe, to be permanent or quiet; mor. to be true or certain; once (Isa. 30:21; by interch. for 541) to go to the right hand:- hence assurance, believe, bring up, establish, + fail, be faithful (of long continuance, steadfast, sure, surely, trusty, verified) nurse (-ing father), (put) trust, turn to the right.

And whenever you deviate to the right or to the left, your ears will heed the command from behind you: "This is the road; follow it!" YESHA'YAHU 30:21 (ISAIAH 30:21)

And thine ears shall hear a word behind thee, saying, This is the way, walk ye in it, when ye turn to the right hand, and when ye turn to the left. ISAIAH 30:21

(541) pronounced aw-man'; denom. from 3225; to take the right-hand road:- turn to the right. See 539.

(3225) pronounced yaw-meen'; from 3231; the right hand or side (leg, eye) of a person or other object (as the stronger and most dexterous): locally, the south:- + left handed, right (hand, side), south.

(3231) pronounced yaw-man'; a prim. root; to be (phys.) right (i.e. firm); but used only as denom. from 3225 and transit., to be right-handed or take the right-hand side:- go turn) to (on, use) the right hand.

Hezekiah declared to Isaiah, "The word of the LORD that you have spoken is good." For he thought, "It means that safety is assured for my time." YESHA'YAHU 39:8 (ISAIAH 39:8) safety is assured for my time: Lit. "there shall be safety and faithfulness in." (TANAKH footnote)

Then said Hezekiah to Isaiah, Good is the word of the LORD which thou hast spoken. He said moreover, for there shall be peace and truth (571) in my days. ISAIAH 39:8

truth (571) pronounced eh'meth; contr. From 539; stability; fig. certainty, truth, trustworthiness:-assured (-ly), establishment, faithful, right, sure, true (-ly, -th), verity.

(539) pronounced aw-man'; a prim. root; prop. to build up or support; to foster as a parent or nurse; fig. to render (or be) firm or faithful, to trust or believe, to be permanent or quiet; mor. to be true or certain; once (Isa. 30:21; by interch. for 541) to go to the right hand:- hence assurance, believe, bring up, establish, + fail, be faithful (of long continuance, steadfast, sure, surely, trusty, verified) nurse (-ing father), (put) trust, turn to the right.

And whenever you deviate to the right or to the left, your ears will heed the command from behind you: "This is the road; follow it!" YESHA'YAHU 30:21 (ISAIAH 30:21)

And thine ears shall hear a word behind thee, saying, This is the way, walk ye in it, when ye turn to the right hand, and when ye turn to the left. ISAIAH 30:21

(541) pronounced aw-man'; denom. from 3225; to take the right-hand road:- turn to the right. See 539.

(3225) pronounced yaw-meen'; from 3231; the right hand or side (leg, eye) of a person or other object (as the stronger and most dexterous): locally, the south:- + left handed, right (hand, side), south.

(3231) pronounced yaw-man'; a prim. root; to be (phys.) right (i.e. firm); but used only as denom. from 3225 and transit., to be right-handed or take the right-hand side:- go turn) to (on, use) the right hand.

He shall not break even a bruised reed, or snuff out even a dim wick. He shall bring forth the true way. YESHA'YAHU 42:3 (ISAIAH 42:3)

Or "A bruised reed, he shall not be broken;/A dim wick, he shall not be snuffed out." (TANAKH footnote)

A bruised reed shall he not break, and the smoking flax shall he not quench: he shall bring forth judgment unto truth (571). ISAIAH 42:3

truth (571) pronounced eh'meth; contr. From 539; stability; fig. certainty, truth, trustworthiness:-assured (-ly), establishment, faithful, right, sure, true (-ly, -th), verity.

(539) pronounced aw-man'; a prim. root; prop. to build up or support; to foster as a parent or nurse; fig. to render (or be) firm or faithful, to trust or believe, to be permanent or quiet; mor. to be true or certain; once (Isa. 30:21; by interch. for 541) to go to the right hand:- hence assurance, believe, bring up, establish, + fail, be faithful (of long continuance, steadfast, sure, surely, trusty, verified) nurse (-ing father), (put) trust, turn to the right.

> And whenever you deviate to the right or to the left, your ears will heed the command from behind you: "This is the road; follow it!" YESHA'YAHU 30:21 (ISAIAH 30:21)
>
> And thine ears shall hear a word behind thee, saying, This is the way, walk ye in it, when ye turn to the right hand, and when ye turn to the left. ISAIAH 30:21

(541) pronounced aw-man'; denom. from 3225; to take the right-hand road:- turn to the right. See 539.

(3225) pronounced yaw-meen'; from 3231; the right hand or side (leg, eye) of a person or other object (as the stronger and most dexterous): locally, the south:- + left handed, right (hand, side), south.

(3231) pronounced yaw-man'; a prim. root; to be (phys.) right (i.e. firm); but used only as denom. from 3225 and transit., to be right-handed or take the right-hand side:- go turn) to (on, use) the right hand.

All the nations assemble as one, the peoples gather. Who among them declared this, foretold to us the things that happened? Let them produce their witnesses and be vindicated, that men, hearing them, may say, "It is true!" YESHA'YAHU 43:9 (ISAIAH 43:9)

> "It is true!" i.e. that the other nations' gods are real. (TANAKH footnote)

Let all the nations be gathered together, and let the people be assembled: who among them can declare this, and show us *former* things? Let them bring forth their witnesses, that they may be justified; or let them hear, and say, *It is* truth (571). ISAIAH 43:9

truth (571) pronounced eh'meth; contr. From 539; stability; fig. certainty, truth, trustworthiness:-assured (-ly), establishment, faithful, right, sure, true (-ly, -th), verity.

(539) pronounced aw-man'; a prim. root; prop. to build up or support; to foster as a parent or nurse; fig. to render (or be) firm or faithful, to trust or believe, to be permanent or quiet; mor. to be true or certain; once (Isa. 30:21; by interch. for 541) to go to the right hand:- hence assurance, believe, bring up, establish, + fail, be faithful (of long continuance, steadfast, sure, surely, trusty, verified) nurse (-ing father), (put) trust, turn to the right.

> And whenever you deviate to the right or to the left, your ears will heed the command from behind you: "This is the road; follow it!" YESHA'YAHU 30:21 (ISAIAH 30:21)
>
> And thine ears shall hear a word behind thee, saying, This is the way, walk ye in it, when ye turn to the right hand, and when ye turn to the left. ISAIAH 30:21

(541) pronounced aw-man'; denom. from 3225; to take the right-hand road:- turn to the right. See 539.

(3225) pronounced yaw-meen'; from 3231; the right hand or side (leg, eye) of a person or other object (as the stronger and most dexterous): locally, the south:- + left handed, right (hand, side), south.

(3231) pronounced yaw-man'; a prim. root; to be (phys.) right (i.e. firm); but used only as denom. from 3225 and transit., to be right-handed or take the right-hand side:- go turn) to (on, use) the right hand.

Listen to this, O House of Jacob, who bear the name Israel and have issued from the waters of Judah, who swear by the name of the LORD and invoke the God of Israel---though not in truth and sincerity--- YESHA'YAHU 48:1 (ISAIAH 48:1)

waters: emendation yields "loins". (TANAKH footnote)

Hear ye this, O house of Jacob, which are called by the name of Israel, and are come forth out of the waters of Judah, which swear by the name of the LORD, and make mention of the God of Israel, *but* not in truth (571), nor in righteousness. ISAIAH 48:1

truth (571) pronounced eh'meth; contr. From 539; stability; fig. certainty, truth, trustworthiness:-assured (-ly), establishment, faithful, right, sure, true (-ly, -th), verity.

(539) pronounced aw-man'; a prim. root; prop. to build up or support; to foster as a parent or nurse; fig. to render (or be) firm or faithful, to trust or believe, to be permanent or quiet; mor. to be true or certain; once (Isa. 30:21; by interch. for 541) to go to the right hand:- hence assurance, believe, bring up, establish, + fail, be faithful (of long continuance, steadfast, sure, surely, trusty, verified) nurse (-ing father), (put) trust, turn to the right.

> And whenever you deviate to the right or to the left, your ears will heed the command from behind you: "This is the road; follow it!" YESHA'YAHU 30:21 (ISAIAH 30:21)
>
> And thine ears shall hear a word behind thee, saying, This is the way, walk ye in it, when ye turn to the right hand, and when ye turn to the left. ISAIAH 30:21

(541) pronounced aw-man'; denom. from 3225; to take the right-hand road:- turn to the right. See 539.

(3225) pronounced yaw-meen'; from 3231; the right hand or side (leg, eye) of a person or other object (as the stronger and most dexterous): locally, the south:- + left handed, right (hand, side), south.

(3231) pronounced yaw-man'; a prim. root; to be (phys.) right (i.e. firm); but used only as denom. from 3225 and transit., to be right-handed or take the right-hand side:- go turn) to (on, use) the right hand.

No one sues justly or pleads honestly; they rely on emptiness and speak falsehood, conceiving wrong and begetting evil. YESHA'YAHU 59:4 (ISAIAH 59:4)

None calleth for justice, nor *any* pleadeth for truth (530): they trust in vanity, and speak lies; they conceive mischief, and bring forth iniquity. ISAIAH 59:4

truth (530) pronounced em-oo-naw'; fem. of 529; lit. firmness; fig. security; mor. fidelity:- faith (-ful, -ly, -ness, [man]), set office, stability, steady, truly, truth, verity.

(529) pronounced ay-moon'; from 539; established, i.e. (fig.) trusty; also (abstr.) trustworthiness:-faith (-ful), truth.

(539) pronounced aw-man'; a prim. root; prop. to build up or support; to foster as a parent or nurse; fig. to render (or be) firm or faithful, to trust or believe, to be permanent or quiet; mor. to be true or certain; once (Isa. 30:21; by interch. for 541) to go to the right hand:- hence assurance, believe, bring up, establish, + fail, be faithful (of long continuance, steadfast, sure, surely, trusty, verified) nurse (-ing father), (put) trust, turn to the right.

> And whenever you deviate to the right or to the left, your ears will heed the command from behind you: "This is the road; follow it!" YESHA'YAHU 30:21 (ISAIAH 30:21)
>
> And thine ears shall hear a word behind thee, saying, This is the way, walk ye in it, when ye turn to the right hand, and when ye turn to the left. ISAIAH 30:21

(541) pronounced aw-man'; denom. from 3225; to take the right-hand road:- turn to the right. See 539.

(3225) pronounced yaw-meen'; from 3231; the right hand or side (leg, eye) of a person or other object (as the stronger and most dexterous): locally, the south:- + left handed, right (hand, side), south.

(3231) pronounced yaw-man'; a prim. root; to be (phys.) right (i.e. firm); but used only as denom. from 3225 and transit., to be right-handed or take the right-hand side:- go turn) to (on, use) the right hand.

And so redress is turned back and vindication stays afar, because honesty stumbles in the public square and uprightness cannot enter. Honesty has been lacking, he who turns away from evil is despoiled. The LORD saw and was displeased that there was no redress. YESHA'YAHU 59:14-15 (ISAIAH 59:14-15)

And judgment is turned away backward, and justice standeth afar off: for truth (571) is fallen in the street, and equity cannot enter. Yea, truth (571) faileth; and he *that* departeth from evil maketh himself a prey. And the LORD saw *it,* and it displeased him that *there was* no judgment. ISAIAH 59:14-15

> truth (571) pronounced eh'meth; contr. From 539; stability; fig. certainty, truth, trustworthiness:-assured (-ly), establishment, faithful, right, sure, true (-ly, -th), verity.
>
> (539) pronounced aw-man'; a prim. root; prop. to build up or support; to foster as a parent or nurse; fig. to render (or be) firm or faithful, to trust or believe, to be permanent or quiet; mor. to be true or certain; once (Isa. 30:21; by interch. for 541) to go to the right hand:- hence assurance, believe, bring up, establish, + fail, be faithful (of long continuance, steadfast, sure, surely, trusty, verified) nurse (-ing father), (put) trust, turn to the right.
>
>> And whenever you deviate to the right or to the left, your ears will heed the command from behind you: "This is the road; follow it!" YESHA'YAHU 30:21 (ISAIAH 30:21)
>>
>> And thine ears shall hear a word behind thee, saying, This is the way, walk ye in it, when ye turn to the right hand, and when ye turn to the left. ISAIAH 30:21
>
> (541) pronounced aw-man'; denom. from 3225; to take the right-hand road:- turn to the right. See 539.
>
> (3225) pronounced yaw-meen'; from 3231; the right hand or side (leg, eye) of a person or other object (as the stronger and most dexterous): locally, the south:- + left handed, right (hand, side), south.
>
> (3231) pronounced yaw-man'; a prim. root; to be (phys.) right (i.e. firm); but used only as denom. from 3225 and transit., to be right-handed or take the right-hand side:- go turn) to (on, use) the right hand.

For I the LORD love justice. I hate robbery with a burnt offering. I will pay them their wages faithfully, and make a covenant with them for all time. YESHA'YAHU 61:8 (ISAIAH 61:8)

> robbery with a burnt offering: emendation yields, "the robbing of wages". (TANAKH footnote)

For I the LORD love judgment. I hate robbery for burnt offering; and I will direct their work in truth (571), and I will make an everlasting covenant with them. ISAIAH 61:8

> truth (571) pronounced eh'meth; contr. From 539; stability; fig. certainty, truth, trustworthiness:-assured (-ly), establishment, faithful, right, sure, true (-ly, -th), verity.

(539) pronounced aw-man'; a prim. root; prop. to build up or support; to foster as a parent or nurse; fig. to render (or be) firm or faithful, to trust or believe, to be permanent or quiet; mor. to be true or certain; once (Isa. 30:21; by interch. for 541) to go to the right hand:- hence assurance, believe, bring up, establish, + fail, be faithful (of long continuance, steadfast, sure, surely, trusty, verified) nurse (-ing father), (put) trust, turn to the right.

> And whenever you deviate to the right or to the left, your ears will heed the command from behind you: "This is the road; follow it!" YESHA'YAHU 30:21 (ISAIAH 30:21)
>
> And thine ears shall hear a word behind thee, saying, This is the way, walk ye in it, when ye turn to the right hand, and when ye turn to the left. ISAIAH 30:21

(541) pronounced aw-man'; denom. from 3225; to take the right-hand road:- turn to the right. See 539.

(3225) pronounced yaw-meen'; from 3231; the right hand or side (leg, eye) of a person or other object (as the stronger and most dexterous): locally, the south:- + left handed, right (hand, side), south.

(3231) pronounced yaw-man'; a prim. root; to be (phys.) right (i.e. firm); but used only as denom. from 3225 and transit., to be right-handed or take the right-hand side:- go turn) to (on, use) the right hand.

For whoever blesses himself in the land shall bless himself by the true God; and whoever swears in the land shall swear by the true God. The former troubles shall be forgotten, shall be hidden from My eyes. YESHA'YAHU 65:16 (ISAIAH 65:16)

That he who blesseth himself in the earth shall bless himself in the God of truth (543); and he that sweareth in the earth shall swear by the God of truth (543); because the former troubles are forgotten, and because they are hid from mine eyes. ISAIAH 65:16

truth (543) pronounced aw-mane'; from 539; sure; abstr. faithfulness; adv. truly:-Amen, so be it, truth.

(539) pronounced aw-man'; a prim. root; prop. to build up or support; to foster as a parent or nurse; fig. to render (or be) firm or faithful, to trust or believe, to be permanent or quiet; mor. to be true or certain; once (Isa. 30:21; by interch. for 541) to go to the right hand:- hence assurance, believe, bring up, establish, + fail, be faithful (of long continuance, steadfast, sure, surely, trusty, verified) nurse (-ing father), (put) trust, turn to the right.

> And whenever you deviate to the right or to the left, your ears will heed the command from behind you: "This is the road; follow it!" YESHA'YAHU 30:21 (ISAIAH 30:21)

> And thine ears shall hear a word behind thee, saying, This is the way, walk ye in it, when ye turn to the right hand, and when ye turn to the left. ISAIAH 30:21

(541) pronounced aw-man'; denom. from 3225; to take the right-hand road:- turn to the right. See 539.

(3225) pronounced yaw-meen'; from 3231; the right hand or side (leg, eye) of a person or other object (as the stronger and most dexterous): locally, the south:- + left handed, right (hand, side), south.

(3231) pronounced yaw-man'; a prim. root; to be (phys.) right (i.e. firm); but used only as denom. from 3225 and transit., to be right-handed or take the right-hand side:- go turn) to (on, use) the right hand.

And swear, "As the LORD lives," in sincerity, justice, and righteousness---nations shall bless themselves by you and praise themselves by you. YIRMEYAHU 4:2 (JEREMIAH 4:2)

> swear "As the LORD lives"; profess the worship of the LORD. (TANAKH footnote)
>
> nations shall bless themselves by you and praise themselves by you: Heb. "him". (TANAKH footnote)

And thou shalt swear, The LORD liveth, in truth (571), in judgment, and in righteousness; and the nations shall bless themselves in him, and in him shall they glory. JEREMIAH 4:2

truth (571) pronounced eh'meth; contr. From 539; stability; fig. certainty, truth, trustworthiness:-assured (-ly), establishment, faithful, right, sure, true (-ly, -th), verity.

(539) pronounced aw-man'; a prim. root; prop. to build up or support; to foster as a parent or nurse; fig. to render (or be) firm or faithful, to trust or believe, to be permanent or quiet; mor. to be true or certain; once (Isa. 30:21; by interch. for 541) to go to the right hand:- hence assurance, believe, bring up, establish, + fail, be faithful (of long continuance, steadfast, sure, surely, trusty, verified) nurse (-ing father), (put) trust, turn to the right.

> And whenever you deviate to the right or to the left, your ears will heed the command from behind you: "This is the road; follow it!" YESHA'YAHU 30:21 (ISAIAH 30:21)

> And thine ears shall hear a word behind thee, saying, This is the way, walk ye in it, when ye turn to the right hand, and when ye turn to the left. ISAIAH 30:21

(541) pronounced aw-man'; denom. from 3225; to take the right-hand road:- turn to the right. See 539.

(3225) pronounced yaw-meen'; from 3231; the right hand or side (leg, eye) of a person or other object (as the stronger and most dexterous): locally, the south:- + left handed, right (hand, side), south.

(3231) pronounced yaw-man'; a prim. root; to be (phys.) right (i.e. firm); but used only as denom. from 3225 and transit., to be right-handed or take the right-hand side:- go turn) to (on, use) the right hand.

Roam the streets of Jerusalem, search its squares, look about and take note: you will not find a man, there is none who acts justly, who seeks integrity---that I should pardon her. Even when they say, "As the LORD lives," they are sure to be swearing falsely. O LORD, Your eyes look for integrity. You have struck them, but they sensed no pain: You have consumed them, but they would accept no discipline. They made their faces harder than rock, they refused to turn back. YIRMEYAHU 5:1-3 (JEREMIAH 5:1-3)

Run ye to and fro through the streets of Jerusalem, and see now, and know, and seek in the broad places, thereof, if ye can find a man, if there be *any* that executeth judgment, that seeketh the truth (530); and I will pardon it. And though they say, The LORD liveth, surely they swear falsely. O LORD, are *not* thine eyes upon the truth (530)? Thou hast stricken them, but they have not grieved; thou hast consumed them, *but* they have refused to receive correction: they have made their faces harder than a rock; they have refused to return. JEREMIAH 5:1-3

truth (530) pronounced em-oo-naw'; fem. of 529; lit. firmness; fig. security; mor. fidelity:- faith (-ful, -ly, -ness, [man]), set office, stability, steady, truly, truth, verity.

(529) pronounced ay-moon'; from 539; established, i.e. (fig.) trusty; also (abstr.) trustworthiness:-faith (-ful), truth.

(539) pronounced aw-man'; a prim. root; prop. to build up or support; to foster as a parent or nurse; fig. to render (or be) firm or faithful, to trust or believe, to be permanent or quiet; mor. to be true or certain; once (Isa. 30:21; by interch. for 541) to go to the right hand:- hence assurance, believe, bring up, establish, + fail, be faithful (of long continuance, steadfast, sure, surely, trusty, verified) nurse (-ing father), (put) trust, turn to the right.

And whenever you deviate to the right or to the left, your ears will heed the command from behind you: "This is the road; follow it!" YESHA'YAHU 30:21 (ISAIAH 30:21)

And thine ears shall hear a word behind thee, saying, This is the way, walk ye in it, when ye turn to the right hand, and when ye turn to the left. ISAIAH 30:21

(541) pronounced aw-man'; denom. from 3225; to take the right-hand road:- turn to the right. See 539.

(3225) pronounced yaw-meen'; from 3231; the right hand or side (leg, eye) of a person or other object (as the stronger and most dexterous): locally, the south:- + left handed, right (hand, side), south.

(3231) pronounced yaw-man'; a prim. root; to be (phys.) right (i.e. firm); but used only as denom. from 3225 and transit., to be right-handed or take the right-hand side:- go turn) to (on, use) the right hand.

Then say to them: This is the nation that would not obey the LORD their God, that would not accept rebuke. Faithfulness has perished, vanished from their mouths. YIRMEYAHU 7:28 JEREMIAH 7:28

But thou shalt say unto them, This is a nation that obeyeth not the voice of the LORD their God, nor receiveth correction: truth (530) is perished, and is cut off from their mouth. JEREMIAH 7:28

truth (530) pronounced em-oo-naw'; fem. of 529; lit. firmness; fig. security; mor. fidelity:- faith (-ful, -ly, -ness, [man]), set office, stability, steady, truly, truth, verity.

(529) pronounced ay-moon'; from 539; established, i.e. (fig.) trusty; also (abstr.) trustworthiness:-faith (-ful), truth.

(539) pronounced aw-man'; a prim. root; prop. to build up or support; to foster as a parent or nurse; fig. to render (or be) firm or faithful, to trust or believe, to be permanent or quiet; mor. to be true or certain; once (Isa. 30:21; by interch. for 541) to go to the right hand:- hence assurance, believe, bring up, establish, + fail, be faithful (of long continuance, steadfast, sure, surely, trusty, verified) nurse (-ing father), (put) trust, turn to the right.

> And whenever you deviate to the right or to the left, your ears will heed the command from behind you: "This is the road; follow it!" YESHA'YAHU 30:21 (ISAIAH 30:21)
>
> And thine ears shall hear a word behind thee, saying, This is the way, walk ye in it, when ye turn to the right hand, and when ye turn to the left. ISAIAH 30:21

(541) pronounced aw-man'; denom. from 3225; to take the right-hand road:- turn to the right. See 539.

(3225) pronounced yaw-meen'; from 3231; the right hand or side (leg, eye) of a person or other object (as the stronger and most dexterous): locally, the south:- + left handed, right (hand, side), south.

(3231) pronounced yaw-man'; a prim. root; to be (phys.) right (i.e. firm); but used only as denom. from 3225 and transit., to be right-handed or take the right-hand side:- go turn) to (on, use) the right hand.

They bend their tongues like bows; they are valorous in the land for treachery, not for honesty; they advance from evil to evil. And they do not heed Me---declares the LORD. YIRMEYAHU 9:2 (JEREMIAH 9:3)

And they bend their tongues *like* their bow *for* lies: but they are not valiant for the truth (530) upon the earth; for they proceed from evil to evil, and they know not me, saith the LORD. JEREMIAH 9:3

> truth (530) pronounced em-oo-naw'; fem. of 529; lit. firmness; fig. security; mor. fidelity:- faith (-ful, -ly, -ness, [man]), set office, stability, steady, truly, truth, verity.
>
> (529) pronounced ay-moon'; from 539; established, i.e. (fig.) trusty; also (abstr.) trustworthiness:-faith (-ful), truth.
>
> (539) pronounced aw-man'; a prim. root; prop. to build up or support; to foster as a parent or nurse; fig. to render (or be) firm or faithful, to trust or believe, to be permanent or quiet; mor. to be true or certain; once (Isa. 30:21; by interch. for 541) to go to the right hand:- hence assurance, believe, bring up, establish, + fail, be faithful (of long continuance, steadfast, sure, surely, trusty, verified) nurse (-ing father), (put) trust, turn to the right.
>
>> And whenever you deviate to the right or to the left, your ears will heed the command from behind you: "This is the road; follow it!" YESHA'YAHU 30:21 (ISAIAH 30:21)
>>
>> And thine ears shall hear a word behind thee, saying, This is the way, walk ye in it, when ye turn to the right hand, and when ye turn to the left. ISAIAH 30:21
>
> (541) pronounced aw-man'; denom. from 3225; to take the right-hand road:- turn to the right. See 539.
>
> (3225) pronounced yaw-meen'; from 3231; the right hand or side (leg, eye) of a person or other object (as the stronger and most dexterous): locally, the south:- + left handed, right (hand, side), south.
>
> (3231) pronounced yaw-man'; a prim. root; to be (phys.) right (i.e. firm); but used only as denom. from 3225 and transit., to be right-handed or take the right-hand side:- go turn) to (on, use) the right hand.

One man cheats the other, they will not speak truth; they have trained their tongues to speak falsely; they wear themselves out working iniquity. YIRMEYAHU 9:4 (JEREMIAH 9:5)

> they wear themselves out working iniquity: meaning of Heb. uncertain. (TANAKH footnote)

And they will deceive every one his neighbour, and will not speak the truth (571): they have taught their tongue to speak lies*, and* weary themselves to commit iniquity. JEREMIAH 9:5

truth (571) pronounced eh'meth; contr. From 539; stability; fig. certainty, truth, trustworthiness:-assured (-ly), establishment, faithful, right, sure, true (-ly, -th), verity.

(539) pronounced aw-man'; a prim. root; prop. to build up or support; to foster as a parent or nurse; fig. to render (or be) firm or faithful, to trust or believe, to be permanent or quiet; mor. to be true or certain; once (Isa. 30:21; by interch. for 541) to go to the right hand:- hence assurance, believe, bring up, establish, + fail, be faithful (of long continuance, steadfast, sure, surely, trusty, verified) nurse (-ing father), (put) trust, turn to the right.

> And whenever you deviate to the right or to the left, your ears will heed the command from behind you: "This is the road; follow it!" YESHA'YAHU 30:21 (ISAIAH 30:21)
>
> And thine ears shall hear a word behind thee, saying, This is the way, walk ye in it, when ye turn to the right hand, and when ye turn to the left. ISAIAH 30:21

(541) pronounced aw-man'; denom. from 3225; to take the right-hand road:- turn to the right. See 539.

(3225) pronounced yaw-meen'; from 3231; the right hand or side (leg, eye) of a person or other object (as the stronger and most dexterous): locally, the south:- + left handed, right (hand, side), south.

(3231) pronounced yaw-man'; a prim. root; to be (phys.) right (i.e. firm); but used only as denom. from 3225 and transit., to be right-handed or take the right-hand side:- go turn) to (on, use) the right hand.

But know that if you put me to death, you and this city and its inhabitants will be guilty of shedding the blood of an innocent man. For in truth the LORD has sent me to you, to speak all these words to you. YIRMEYAHU 26:15 (JEREMIAH 26:15)

But know ye for certain, that if ye put me to death, ye shall surely bring innocent blood upon yourselves, and upon this city, and upon the inhabitants thereof: for of a truth (571), the LORD hath sent me unto you to speak all these words in your ears. JEREMIAH 26:15

truth (571) pronounced eh'meth; contr. From 539; stability; fig. certainty, truth, trustworthiness:-assured (-ly), establishment, faithful, right, sure, true (-ly, -th), verity.

(539) pronounced aw-man'; a prim. root; prop. to build up or support; to foster as a parent or nurse; fig. to render (or be) firm or faithful, to trust or believe, to be permanent or quiet; mor. to be true or certain; once (Isa. 30:21; by interch. for 541) to go to the right hand:- hence assurance, believe, bring up, establish, + fail, be faithful (of long continuance, steadfast, sure, surely, trusty, verified) nurse (-ing father), (put) trust, turn to the right.

> And whenever you deviate to the right or to the left, your ears will heed the command from behind you: "This is the road; follow it!" YESHA'YAHU 30:21 (ISAIAH 30:21)
>
> And thine ears shall hear a word behind thee, saying, This is the way, walk ye in it, when ye turn to the right hand, and when ye turn to the left. ISAIAH 30:21

(541) pronounced aw-man'; denom. from 3225; to take the right-hand road:- turn to the right. See 539.

(3225) pronounced yaw-meen'; from 3231; the right hand or side (leg, eye) of a person or other object (as the stronger and most dexterous): locally, the south:- + left handed, right (hand, side), south.

(3231) pronounced yaw-man'; a prim. root; to be (phys.) right (i.e. firm); but used only as denom. from 3225 and transit., to be right-handed or take the right-hand side:- go turn) to (on, use) the right hand.

I am going to bring her relief and healing. I will heal them and reveal to them abundance of true favor. YIRMEYAHU 33:6 (JEREMIAH 33:6)

abundance of true favor: meaning of Heb. uncertain. (TANAKH footnote)

Behold, I will bring it health and cure, and I will cure them, and will reveal unto them the abundance of peace and truth (571). JEREMIAH 33:6

truth (571) pronounced eh'meth; contr. From 539; stability; fig. certainty, truth, trustworthiness:-assured (-ly), establishment, faithful, right, sure, true (-ly, -th), verity.

(539) pronounced aw-man'; a prim. root; prop. to build up or support; to foster as a parent or nurse; fig. to render (or be) firm or faithful, to trust or believe, to be permanent or quiet; mor. to be true or certain; once (Isa. 30:21; by interch. for 541) to go to the right hand:- hence assurance, believe, bring up, establish, + fail, be faithful (of long continuance, steadfast, sure, surely, trusty, verified) nurse (-ing father), (put) trust, turn to the right.

> And whenever you deviate to the right or to the left, your ears will heed the command from behind you: "This is the road; follow it!" YESHA'YAHU 30:21 (ISAIAH 30:21)
>
> And thine ears shall hear a word behind thee, saying, This is the way, walk ye in it, when ye turn to the right hand, and when ye turn to the left. ISAIAH 30:21

(541) pronounced aw-man'; denom. from 3225; to take the right-hand road:- turn to the right. See 539.

(3225) pronounced yaw-meen'; from 3231; the right hand or side (leg, eye) of a person or other object (as the stronger and most dexterous): locally, the south:- + left handed, right (hand, side), south.

(3231) pronounced yaw-man'; a prim. root; to be (phys.) right (i.e. firm); but used only as denom. from 3225 and transit., to be right-handed or take the right-hand side:- go turn) to (on, use) the right hand.

The king said in reply to Daniel, "Truly your God must be the God of gods and LORD of kings and the revealer of mysteries to have enabled you to reveal this mystery." DANI'EL 2:47 (DANIEL 2:47)

The king answered unto Daniel, and said, Of a truth (7187), *it is*, that your God is a God of gods, and a LORD of kings, and a revealer of secrets, seeing thou couldest reveal this secret. DANIEL 2:47

truth (7187) (Chald.) pronounced kesh-ote'; corresp. to 7189; fidelity:-truth.

truth (7189) pronounced ko'-shet or kosht; from an unused root mean. to balance; equity (as evenly weighed), i.e. reality:-certainty, truth.

So now I, Nebuchadnezzar, praise, exalt, and glorify the King of Heaven, all of whose works are just and whose ways are right, and who is able to humble those who behave arrogantly. DANI'EL 4:34 (DANIEL 4:37)

Now I Nebuchadnezzar praise and extol and honour the King of heaven, all whose works *are* truth (7187), and his ways judgment; and those that walk in pride he is able to abase. DANIEL 4:37

truth (7187) (Chald.) pronounced kesh-ote'; corresp. to 7189; fidelity:-truth.

truth (7189) pronounced ko'-shet or kosht; from an unused root mean. to balance; equity (as evenly weighed), i.e. reality:-certainty, truth.

I approached one of the attendants and asked him the true meaning of all this. He gave me this interpretation of the matter. DANI'EL 7:16 (DANIEL 7:16)

I came near unto one of them that stood by, and asked him the truth (3330) of all this. So he told me, and made me know the interpretation of the things. DANIEL 7:16

truth (3330) (Chald.) pronounced yats-tseeb'; from 3321; fixed; sure; concr. certainty:- certain (-ty), true, truth.

(3321) (Chald.) pronounced yets-abe'; corresp. to 3320; to be firm; hence to speak surely:-truth.

(3320) pronounced yaw-tsab; a prim. root; to place (any thing, so as to stay); reflex. to station, offer, continue:- present selves, remaining, resort, set (selves), (be able to, can, with-) stand (fast, forth, -ing, still, up).

Then I wanted to ascertain the true meaning of the fourth beast, which was different from them all, very fearsome, with teeth of iron, claws of bronze, that devoured and crushed, and stamped the remains; DANI'EL 7:19 (DANIEL 7:19)

Then I would know the truth (3321) of the fourth beast, which was diverse from all the others, exceeding dreadful, whose teeth *were of* iron, and his nails *of* brass; *which* devoured, brake in pieces, and stamped the residue with his feet; DANIEL 7:19

> (3321) (Chald.) pronounced yets-abe'; corresp. to 3320; to be firm; hence to speak surely:-truth.
>
> (3320) pronounced yaw-tsab; a prim. root; to place (any thing, so as to stay); reflex. to station, offer, continue:- present selves, remaining, resort, set (selves), (be able to, can, with-) stand (fast, forth, -ing, still, up).

An army was arrayed iniquitously against the regular offering; it hurled truth to the ground and prospered in what it did. DANI'EL 8:12 (DANIEL 8:12)

> > An army was arrayed iniquitously against the regular offering: meaning of Heb. uncertain. (TANAKH footnote)

And a host was given *him* against the daily *sacrifice* by reason of transgression, and it cast down the truth (571) to the ground; and it practised and prospered. DANIEL 8:12

> truth (571) pronounced eh'meth; contr. From 539; stability; fig. certainty, truth, trustworthiness:-assured (-ly), establishment, faithful, right, sure, true (-ly, -th), verity.
>
> (539) pronounced aw-man'; a prim. root; prop. to build up or support; to foster as a parent or nurse; fig. to render (or be) firm or faithful, to trust or believe, to be permanent or quiet; mor. to be true or certain; once (Isa. 30:21; by interch. for 541) to go to the right hand:- hence assurance, believe, bring up, establish, + fail, be faithful (of long continuance, steadfast, sure, surely, trusty, verified) nurse (-ing father), (put) trust, turn to the right.
>
> > And whenever you deviate to the right or to the left, your ears will heed the command from behind you: "This is the road; follow it!" YESHA'YAHU 30:21 (ISAIAH 30:21)
> >
> > And thine ears shall hear a word behind thee, saying, This is the way, walk ye in it, when ye turn to the right hand, and when ye turn to the left. ISAIAH 30:21
>
> (541) pronounced aw-man'; denom. from 3225; to take the right-hand road:- turn to the right. See 539.
>
> (3225) pronounced yaw-meen'; from 3231; the right hand or side (leg, eye) of a person or other object (as the stronger and most dexterous): locally, the south:- + left handed, right (hand, side), south.

(3231) pronounced yaw-man'; a prim. root; to be (phys.) right (i.e. firm); but used only as denom. from 3225 and transit., to be right-handed or take the right-hand side:- go turn) to (on, use) the right hand.

All that calamity, just as it is written in the Teaching of Moses, came upon us, yet we did not supplicate the LORD our God, did not repent of our iniquity or become wise through Your truth. DANI'EL 9:13 (DANIEL 9:13)

As *it is* written in the law of Moses, all this evil is come upon us: yet made we not our prayer before the LORD our God, that we might turn from our iniquities, and understand thy truth (571). DANIEL 9:13

truth (571) pronounced eh'meth; contr. From 539; stability; fig. certainty, truth, trustworthiness:-assured (-ly), establishment, faithful, right, sure, true (-ly, -th), verity.

(539) pronounced aw-man'; a prim. root; prop. to build up or support; to foster as a parent or nurse; fig. to render (or be) firm or faithful, to trust or believe, to be permanent or quiet; mor. to be true or certain; once (Isa. 30:21; by interch. for 541) to go to the right hand:- hence assurance, believe, bring up, establish, + fail, be faithful (of long continuance, steadfast, sure, surely, trusty, verified) nurse (-ing father), (put) trust, turn to the right.

And whenever you deviate to the right or to the left, your ears will heed the command from behind you: "This is the road; follow it!" YESHA'YAHU 30:21 (ISAIAH 30:21)

And thine ears shall hear a word behind thee, saying, This is the way, walk ye in it, when ye turn to the right hand, and when ye turn to the left. ISAIAH 30:21

(541) pronounced aw-man'; denom. from 3225; to take the right-hand road:- turn to the right. See 539.

(3225) pronounced yaw-meen'; from 3231; the right hand or side (leg, eye) of a person or other object (as the stronger and most dexterous): locally, the south:- + left handed, right (hand, side), south.

(3231) pronounced yaw-man'; a prim. root; to be (phys.) right (i.e. firm); but used only as denom. from 3225 and transit., to be right-handed or take the right-hand side:- go turn) to (on, use) the right hand.

No one is helping me against them except Your prince, Michael. However, I will tell you what is recorded in the book of truth. DANI'EL 10:21 (DANIEL 10:21)

order of clauses inverted for clarity. (TANAKH footnote)

But I will show thee that which is noted in the Scripture of truth (571): and *there is* none that holdeth with me in these things, but Michael your prince. DANIEL 10:21

truth (571) pronounced eh'meth; contr. From 539; stability; fig. certainty, truth, trustworthiness:-assured (-ly), establishment, faithful, right, sure, true (-ly, -th), verity.

(539) pronounced aw-man'; a prim. root; prop. to build up or support; to foster as a parent or nurse; fig. to render (or be) firm or faithful, to trust or believe, to be permanent or quiet; mor. to be true or certain; once (Isa. 30:21; by interch. for 541) to go to the right hand:- hence assurance, believe, bring up, establish, + fail, be faithful (of long continuance, steadfast, sure, surely, trusty, verified) nurse (-ing father), (put) trust, turn to the right.

> And whenever you deviate to the right or to the left, your ears will heed the command from behind you: "This is the road; follow it!" YESHA'YAHU 30:21 (ISAIAH 30:21)
>
> And thine ears shall hear a word behind thee, saying, This is the way, walk ye in it, when ye turn to the right hand, and when ye turn to the left. ISAIAH 30:21

(541) pronounced aw-man'; denom. from 3225; to take the right-hand road:- turn to the right. See 539.

(3225) pronounced yaw-meen'; from 3231; the right hand or side (leg, eye) of a person or other object (as the stronger and most dexterous): locally, the south:- + left handed, right (hand, side), south.

(3231) pronounced yaw-man'; a prim. root; to be (phys.) right (i.e. firm); but used only as denom. from 3225 and transit., to be right-handed or take the right-hand side:- go turn) to (on, use) the right hand.

And now I will tell you the truth: Persia will have three more kings, and the fourth will be wealthier than them all; by the power he obtains through his wealth, he will stir everyone up against the kingdom of Greece. DANI'EL 11:2 (DANIEL 11:2)

And now will I show thee the truth (571). Behold, there shall stand up yet three kings in Persia; and the fourth shall be far richer than *they* all: and by his strength through his riches he shall stir up all against the realm of Grecia. DANIEL 11:2

truth (571) pronounced eh'meth; contr. From 539; stability; fig. certainty, truth, trustworthiness:-assured (-ly), establishment, faithful, right, sure, true (-ly, -th), verity.

(539) pronounced aw-man'; a prim. root; prop. to build up or support; to foster as a parent or nurse; fig. to render (or be) firm or faithful, to trust or believe, to be permanent or quiet; mor. to be true or certain; once (Isa. 30:21; by interch. for 541) to go to the right hand:- hence assurance, believe, bring up, establish, + fail, be faithful (of long continuance, steadfast, sure, surely, trusty, verified) nurse (-ing father), (put) trust, turn to the right.

> And whenever you deviate to the right or to the left, your ears will heed the command from behind you: "This is the road; follow it!" YESHA'YAHU 30:21 (ISAIAH 30:21)
>
> And thine ears shall hear a word behind thee, saying, This is the way, walk ye in it, when ye turn to the right hand, and when ye turn to the left. ISAIAH 30:21

(541) pronounced aw-man'; denom. from 3225; to take the right-hand road:- turn to the right. See 539.

(3225) pronounced yaw-meen'; from 3231; the right hand or side (leg, eye) of a person or other object (as the stronger and most dexterous): locally, the south:- + left handed, right (hand, side), south.

(3231) pronounced yaw-man'; a prim. root; to be (phys.) right (i.e. firm); but used only as denom. from 3225 and transit., to be right-handed or take the right-hand side:- go turn) to (on, use) the right hand.

Hear the word of the LORD, O people of Israel! For the LORD has a case against the inhabitants of this land, because there is no honesty and no goodness and no obedience to God in the land. HOSHEA 4:1 (HOSEA 4:1)

Hear the word of the LORD, ye children of Israel: for the LORD hath a controversy with the inhabitants of the land, because *there is* no truth (571), nor mercy, nor knowledge of God in the land. HOSEA 4:1

truth (571) pronounced eh'meth; contr. From 539; stability; fig. certainty, truth, trustworthiness:-assured (-ly), establishment, faithful, right, sure, true (-ly, -th), verity.

(539) pronounced aw-man'; a prim. root; prop. to build up or support; to foster as a parent or nurse; fig. to render (or be) firm or faithful, to trust or believe, to be permanent or quiet; mor. to be true or certain; once (Isa. 30:21; by interch. for 541) to go to the right hand:- hence assurance, believe, bring up, establish, + fail, be faithful (of long continuance, steadfast, sure, surely, trusty, verified) nurse (-ing father), (put) trust, turn to the right.

> And whenever you deviate to the right or to the left, your ears will heed the command from behind you: "This is the road; follow it!" YESHA'YAHU 30:21 (ISAIAH 30:21)
>
> And thine ears shall hear a word behind thee, saying, This is the way, walk ye in it, when ye turn to the right hand, and when ye turn to the left. ISAIAH 30:21

(541) pronounced aw-man'; denom. from 3225; to take the right-hand road:- turn to the right. See 539.

(3225) pronounced yaw-meen'; from 3231; the right hand or side (leg, eye) of a person or other object (as the stronger and most dexterous): locally, the south:- + left handed, right (hand, side), south.

(3231) pronounced yaw-man'; a prim. root; to be (phys.) right (i.e. firm); but used only as denom. from 3225 and transit., to be right-handed or take the right-hand side:- go turn) to (on, use) the right hand.

You will keep faith with Jacob, loyalty to Abraham, as You promised on oath to our fathers in days gone by. MIKHAH 7:20 (MICAH 7:20)

Thou wilt perform the truth (571) to Jacob, *and* the mercy to Abraham, which thou hast sworn unto our fathers from the days of old. MICAH 7:20

truth (571) pronounced eh'meth; contr. From 539; stability; fig. certainty, truth, trustworthiness:-assured (-ly), establishment, faithful, right, sure, true (-ly, -th), verity.

(539) pronounced aw-man'; a prim. root; prop. to build up or support; to foster as a parent or nurse; fig. to render (or be) firm or faithful, to trust or believe, to be permanent or quiet; mor. to be true or certain; once (Isa. 30:21; by interch. for 541) to go to the right hand:- hence assurance, believe, bring up, establish, + fail, be faithful (of long continuance, steadfast, sure, surely, trusty, verified) nurse (-ing father), (put) trust, turn to the right.

And whenever you deviate to the right or to the left, your ears will heed the command from behind you: "This is the road; follow it!" YESHA'YAHU 30:21 (ISAIAH 30:21)

And thine ears shall hear a word behind thee, saying, This is the way, walk ye in it, when ye turn to the right hand, and when ye turn to the left. ISAIAH 30:21

(541) pronounced aw-man'; denom. from 3225; to take the right-hand road:- turn to the right. See 539.

(3225) pronounced yaw-meen'; from 3231; the right hand or side (leg, eye) of a person or other object (as the stronger and most dexterous): locally, the south:- + left handed, right (hand, side), south.

(3231) pronounced yaw-man'; a prim. root; to be (phys.) right (i.e. firm); but used only as denom. from 3225 and transit., to be right-handed or take the right-hand side:- go turn) to (on, use) the right hand.

Thus said the LORD: I have returned to Zion, and I will dwell in Jerusalem. Jerusalem will be called the City of Faithfulness, and the mount of the Lord of Hosts the Holy Mount. Z'KHARYAH 8:3 (ZECHARIAH 8:3)

Thus saith the LORD: I am returned unto Zion, and will dwell in the midst of Jerusalem: and Jerusalem shall be called a city of truth (571); and the mountain of the LORD of hosts, the holy mountain. ZECHARIAH 8:3

> truth (571) pronounced eh'meth; contr. From 539; stability; fig. certainty, truth, trustworthiness:-assured (-ly), establishment, faithful, right, sure, true (-ly, -th), verity.
>
> (539) pronounced aw-man'; a prim. root; prop. to build up or support; to foster as a parent or nurse; fig. to render (or be) firm or faithful, to trust or believe, to be permanent or quiet; mor. to be true or certain; once (Isa. 30:21; by interch. for 541) to go to the right hand:- hence assurance, believe, bring up, establish, + fail, be faithful (of long continuance, steadfast, sure, surely, trusty, verified) nurse (-ing father), (put) trust, turn to the right.
>
>> And whenever you deviate to the right or to the left, your ears will heed the command from behind you: "This is the road; follow it!" YESHA'YAHU 30:21 (ISAIAH 30:21)
>>
>> And thine ears shall hear a word behind thee, saying, This is the way, walk ye in it, when ye turn to the right hand, and when ye turn to the left. ISAIAH 30:21
>
> (541) pronounced aw-man'; denom. from 3225; to take the right-hand road:- turn to the right. See 539.
>
> (3225) pronounced yaw-meen'; from 3231; the right hand or side (leg, eye) of a person or other object (as the stronger and most dexterous): locally, the south:- + left handed, right (hand, side), south.
>
> (3231) pronounced yaw-man'; a prim. root; to be (phys.) right (i.e. firm); but used only as denom. from 3225 and transit., to be right-handed or take the right-hand side:- go turn) to (on, use) the right hand.

And I will bring them home to dwell in Jerusalem. They shall be My people, and I will be their God---in truth and sincerity. Z'KHARYAH 8:8 (ZECHARIAH 8:8)

And I will bring them, and they shall dwell in the midst of Jerusalem: and they shall be my people, and I will be their God, in truth (571) and in righteousness. ZECHARIAH 8:8

> truth (571) pronounced eh'meth; contr. From 539; stability; fig. certainty, truth, trustworthiness:-assured (-ly), establishment, faithful, right, sure, true (-ly, -th), verity.
>
> (539) pronounced aw-man'; a prim. root; prop. to build up or support; to foster as a parent or nurse; fig. to render (or be) firm or faithful, to trust or believe, to be permanent or quiet; mor. to be true or certain; once (Isa. 30:21; by interch. for 541) to go to the right hand:- hence assurance, believe, bring up, establish, + fail, be faithful (of long continuance, steadfast, sure, surely, trusty, verified) nurse (-ing father), (put) trust, turn to the right.

> And whenever you deviate to the right or to the left, your ears will heed the command from behind you: "This is the road; follow it!" YESHA'YAHU 30:21 (ISAIAH 30:21)
>
> And thine ears shall hear a word behind thee, saying, This is the way, walk ye in it, when ye turn to the right hand, and when ye turn to the left. ISAIAH 30:21

(541) pronounced aw-man'; denom. from 3225; to take the right-hand road:- turn to the right. See 539.

(3225) pronounced yaw-meen'; from 3231; the right hand or side (leg, eye) of a person or other object (as the stronger and most dexterous): locally, the south:- + left handed, right (hand, side), south.

(3231) pronounced yaw-man'; a prim. root; to be (phys.) right (i.e. firm); but used only as denom. from 3225 and transit., to be right-handed or take the right-hand side:- go turn) to (on, use) the right hand.

These are the things you are to do: Speak the truth to one another, render true and perfect justice in your gates. Z'KHARYAH 8:16 (ZECHARIAH 8:16)

These *are* the things that ye shall do: Speak ye every man the truth (571) to his neighbour; execute the judgment of truth (571) and peace in your gates. ZECHARIAH 8:16

truth (571) pronounced eh'meth; contr. From 539; stability; fig. certainty, truth, trustworthiness:-assured (-ly), establishment, faithful, right, sure, true (-ly, -th), verity.

(539) pronounced aw-man'; a prim. root; prop. to build up or support; to foster as a parent or nurse; fig. to render (or be) firm or faithful, to trust or believe, to be permanent or quiet; mor. to be true or certain; once (Isa. 30:21; by interch. for 541) to go to the right hand:- hence assurance, believe, bring up, establish, + fail, be faithful (of long continuance, steadfast, sure, surely, trusty, verified) nurse (-ing father), (put) trust, turn to the right.

> And whenever you deviate to the right or to the left, your ears will heed the command from behind you: "This is the road; follow it!" YESHA'YAHU 30:21 (ISAIAH 30:21)
>
> And thine ears shall hear a word behind thee, saying, This is the way, walk ye in it, when ye turn to the right hand, and when ye turn to the left. ISAIAH 30:21

(541) pronounced aw-man'; denom. from 3225; to take the right-hand road:- turn to the right. See 539.

(3225) pronounced yaw-meen'; from 3231; the right hand or side (leg, eye) of a person or other object (as the stronger and most dexterous): locally, the south:- + left handed, right (hand, side), south.

(3231) pronounced yaw-man'; a prim. root; to be (phys.) right (i.e. firm); but used only as denom. from 3225 and transit., to be right-handed or take the right-hand side:- go turn) to (on, use) the right hand.

Thus said the LORD of Hosts: The fast of the fourth month, the fast of the fifth month, the fast of the seventh month, and the fast of the tenth month shall become occasions for joy and gladness, happy festivals for the House of Judah; but you must love honesty and integrity. Z'KHARYAH 8:19 (ZECHARIAH 8:19)

Thus saith the LORD of hosts: the fast of the fourth *month*, and the fast of the fifth, and the fast of the seventh, and the fast of the tenth, shall be to the house of Judah joy and gladness, and cheerful feasts; therefore love the truth (571) and peace. ZECHARIAH 8:19

truth (571) pronounced eh'meth; contr. From 539; stability; fig. certainty, truth, trustworthiness:-assured (-ly), establishment, faithful, right, sure, true (-ly, -th), verity.

(539) pronounced aw-man'; a prim. root; prop. to build up or support; to foster as a parent or nurse; fig. to render (or be) firm or faithful, to trust or believe, to be permanent or quiet; mor. to be true or certain; once (Isa. 30:21; by interch. for 541) to go to the right hand:- hence assurance, believe, bring up, establish, + fail, be faithful (of long continuance, steadfast, sure, surely, trusty, verified) nurse (-ing father), (put) trust, turn to the right.

And whenever you deviate to the right or to the left, your ears will heed the command from behind you: "This is the road; follow it!" YESHA'YAHU 30:21 (ISAIAH 30:21)

And thine ears shall hear a word behind thee, saying, This is the way, walk ye in it, when ye turn to the right hand, and when ye turn to the left. ISAIAH 30:21

(541) pronounced aw-man'; denom. from 3225; to take the right-hand road:- turn to the right. See 539.

(3225) pronounced yaw-meen'; from 3231; the right hand or side (leg, eye) of a person or other object (as the stronger and most dexterous): locally, the south:- + left handed, right (hand, side), south.

(3231) pronounced yaw-man'; a prim. root; to be (phys.) right (i.e. firm); but used only as denom. from 3225 and transit., to be right-handed or take the right-hand side:- go turn) to (on, use) the right hand.

Proper rulings were in his mouth, and nothing perverse was on his lips; he served Me with complete loyalty and held the many back from iniquity. MAL'AKHI 2:6 (MALACHI 2:6)

The law of truth (571) was in his mouth, and iniquity was not found in his lips: he walked with me in peace and equity, and did turn many away from iniquity. MALACHI 2:6

truth (571) pronounced eh'meth; contr. From 539; stability; fig. certainty, truth, trustworthiness:-assured (-ly), establishment, faithful, right, sure, true (-ly, -th), verity.

(539) pronounced aw-man'; a prim. root; prop. to build up or support; to foster as a parent or nurse; fig. to render (or be) firm or faithful, to trust or believe, to be permanent or quiet; mor. to be true or certain; once (Isa. 30:21; by interch. for 541) to go to the right hand:- hence assurance, believe, bring up, establish, + fail, be faithful (of long continuance, steadfast, sure, surely, trusty, verified) nurse (-ing father), (put) trust, turn to the right.

> And whenever you deviate to the right or to the left, your ears will heed the command from behind you: "This is the road; follow it!" YESHA'YAHU 30:21 (ISAIAH 30:21)
>
> And thine ears shall hear a word behind thee, saying, This is the way, walk ye in it, when ye turn to the right hand, and when ye turn to the left. ISAIAH 30:21

(541) pronounced aw-man'; denom. from 3225; to take the right-hand road:- turn to the right. See 539.

(3225) pronounced yaw-meen'; from 3231; the right hand or side (leg, eye) of a person or other object (as the stronger and most dexterous): locally, the south:- + left handed, right (hand, side), south.

(3231) pronounced yaw-man'; a prim. root; to be (phys.) right (i.e. firm); but used only as denom. from 3225 and transit., to be right-handed or take the right-hand side:- go turn) to (on, use) the right hand.

www.ingramcontent.com/pod-product-compliance
Lightning Source LLC
Chambersburg PA
CBHW081356270326
41930CB00015B/3318

* 9 7 8 1 9 5 1 7 7 4 1 8 9 *